Reader's Digest

You and Your Rights

Reader's Digest

You and Your Rights

The Reader's Digest Association, Inc.
Pleasantville, New York · Montreal

You and Your Rights

Edited and designed by Maxwell Associates
with the editors of The Reader's Digest Association, Inc.

Editor: James A. Maxwell
Art Director: Walter Brooks
Senior Editors: William K. Goolrick, Peter M. Chaitin
Associate Editor: Lynne Rogers
Research Editors: Rosanne M. Morey, Martha Goolrick, Harriet Heck
Copy Editor: Elaine Andrews

The credits and acknowledgments that appear on page 448
are hereby made a part of this copyright page.

Library of Congress Catalog Card Number 81-84665
ISBN 0-89577-137-3

Printed in the United States of America

About This Book

This book appears at a time when government benefits and services and the role of the government itself are being debated, reevaluated and revised. But even after recent cuts and the possibility of further changes in surviving programs, the range of government benefits and services remains formidable. It extends from prenatal care through most people's working lives to include sums for burial services and payments to the survivors and dependents.

The organization of this book derives from that simple fact. It is designed to take you through your life in terms of the rights to government benefits that you enjoy. The volume starts with programs that are aimed at helping with the education of children—from pre-school care through early education and the college years. Then the book deals with government help for those who are seeking employment and with programs to protect people on the job. It also discusses aid to individuals who want to establish their own business.

In the chapter that follows, government housing aid—in obtaining mortgages, improving, repairing and protecting residences—is explored. Government health services—including the two major government health programs, Medicare and Medicaid—come next. Then the book takes up services and benefits that are designed to help the handicapped of all ages in overcoming their special problems, finding jobs that are suited to their talents and leading more normal lives.

A chapter on veterans' benefits follows. It describes the programs that are designed to help the millions of men and women who have served in their country's armed forces in time of war and peace. The book then moves to Social Security and retirement, setting forth the many benefits and services that are available to older Americans. From there, it turns to two matters that affect people of all ages. The first of these is recreation. Chapter 9 is devoted to that subject, and it explains how you and your family can enjoy relatively inexpensive vacations in the hundreds of national, state and local parks, refuges, preserves and forest areas. The second topic of general application is taxes, which are discussed in Chapter 10. Compiled with the assistance of the Internal Revenue Service, that chapter offers practical advice that may help you save money when faced with the annual ordeal of filing your income tax return.

Finally, the book contains a section on the wealth of practical and helpful information compiled by government agencies and tells you how to obtain some of these highly useful publications from the Government Printing Office in Washington or through its local offices across the country.

You may be surprised by the variety and scope of the benefits and services that are available to you. Some of the programs that are included in this book are "discretionary," which means that it is up to the officials at one level of government or another to decide whether money from block grants or other sources will be spent on a given project. Many others are "entitlements," meaning that anyone who meets the eligibility requirements is entitled to the money or can claim the benefits and services as a matter of right.

You can locate the benefits and services that especially interest you by consulting the contents page at the beginning of each chapter or the index at the back of the book. Once you have read the description of a particular benefit or service, you can find out more about it, and make sure the requirements and benefit amounts have not been changed, by getting in touch with the appropriate office listed in the directory at the end of most chapters.

—The Editors

CAUTION: The information in this book was accurate at the time of publication. But laws and regulations may be changed, and programs may be discontinued or expanded. Before acting in reliance on this information, therefore, be sure to check its currency with the offices or agencies named in the various chapters.

Contents

Education: From Kindergarten Through College—Programs and Benefits to Help Students

In 1637 the Puritans of the Massachusetts Bay Colony passed a law requiring each community of 100 or more families to set up a grammar school. Attendance by the young was mandatory. Ever since that time, the concept of mass education has been deeply rooted in America. Today, both federal and state governments offer a broad variety of programs aimed at guaranteeing equal educational opportunity for all Americans and enhancing the quality of education at the elementary and high school levels.
In addition, students attending colleges and community colleges, as well as graduate, professional and technical schools, are eligible for various forms of state and federal financial aid. In this chapter the major programs in these fields are described, together with information on how you, as a parent or student, can take advantage of these benefits.

Contents

Securing Federal Funds

The federal government provides billions of dollars for educational programs across the country. The money is generally distributed to state departments of education which, in turn, disburse the funds to local school districts.

Federal education grants to the states come in two major forms: categorical and block. A categorical grant may be used by the states for a specific program only. For example, Chapter I of the Educational Act of 1981 (pages 11–17) establishes guidelines for projects to help the educationally disadvantaged. Money appropriated by Congress for Chapter I purposes may be used only for projects that fall within those guidelines.

Some programs, however, may be financed by block grants, money that the federal government distributes to the states on the basis of state population for general education purposes. State departments of education then disburse the block grant money to local school districts. The money may then be used to finance a variety of programs at the discretion of local education officials. A state education department may retain about 20 percent of the block grant funds to finance programs that it deems to be educationally worthy. Certain projects, such as Ethnic Heritage Studies (page 20) and the Gifted and Talented Program (page 20) that formerly were funded by categorical grants will now be financed at the local level by money from block grants—if local school officials wish to maintain those programs. Otherwise, the money may be used to finance other projects that the local school board believes to be more urgent.

There are, however, certain programs, such as the Alcohol and Drug Abuse Program (page 19) that Congress has voted to extend, but not on a categorical grant basis. These programs fall under the block grant grouping, but to encourage school districts to maintain these projects, part of the financing will come from the educational discretionary funds.

In order to make sure that your school district takes advantage of the full range of categorical and block grant financing possibilities, you, as a parent, should become involved in the workings of your local school system through such organizations as the Parent-Teacher Association and other citizens' groups. Now that a great deal of discretionary power in the spending of federal funds has been placed in the hands of local school boards, parents must be willing to apply pressure on local school officials, not only to make certain that they employ all the resources at their command to get their full share of federal money, but also to make certain that this money is used for programs that parents want. Participation by the community is vital.

The best way to set in motion a request for funds for a particular project is to approach the local board of education or the superintendent of schools. If the project is one that falls within the categorical grant grouping, the local education agency can help plan it, write the application in the proper manner to gain the attention of the state education officials and, if necessary, lobby for the project at the state capital. However, if the project is one that falls within the block grant group, then the matter can be attended to entirely on the local level. But remember that your project will have to compete with numerous other programs for block grant financing.

Should your local education agency fail to pursue a categorical grant project, write to your state legislator—often the most effective method of getting action—or to the state department of education (see pages 46–48 for addresses). For block grant programs, lobbying on the local level will probably achieve better results.

But whether dealing with the state or with local education officials, make the most of your group affiliation. It cannot be emphasized too strongly that you are more likely to get a positive response if you are writing as a member of an organized citizens' group rather than as an individual.

Head Start—Education

This is the primary federal program to aid pre-school children from educationally and economically deprived backgrounds. Because Head Start includes nutritional and social services, it is administered by the Department of Health and Human Services.

Hundreds of millions of dollars are spent each year on the Head Start program through grants awarded to non-profit organizations that establish and maintain the program on the local level.

About 12 percent of all Head Start students are handicapped. Children are eligible for Head Start aid from the age of 3 until they enter school. The overwhelming majority are from families whose incomes are at or below the poverty line. These children receive the benefits of the program free of charge. If, however, the youngsters are from families with higher incomes, the parents are sometimes required to pay a small fee.

All told, nearly 400,000 youngsters are now enrolled in Head Start programs throughout the nation. Athough the programs vary in nature, most operate for half a day, five days a week during the school year. Some, however, offer full-day care, 12 months a year. Teachers with degrees in early childhood education, together with trained aides and community volunteers, employ a wide range of learning games to build students' vocabularies and teach them number and letter recognition. Frequent field trips to local libraries, stores, dairies and similar establishments help broaden the children's intellectual horizons. Under federal law, each Head Start program must include parents of children in the program on its governing board. These parents play a major role in determining policy and hiring personnel.

If you as a parent are interested in obtaining more information about Head Start, call or write your nearest regional office of the Department of Health and Human Services which appears at the end of Chapter 4.

Chapter I: Education, Consolidation and Improvement Act of 1981

This multibillion-dollar, federally funded project, administered by state departments of education, is far and away the most important program for enhancing the educational effectiveness of local school systems. Each year, billions of taxpayers' dollars are disbursed through the Chapter I (formerly Title I) program to state departments of education. Funds are then made available to local school districts to establish supplementary educational projects for children who are deemed "educationally disadvantaged." However, a school district, in order to qualify for Chapter I aid, must include students from economically deprived families.

The Meaning of "Educationally Disadvantaged"

A child is considered educationally disadvantaged if he or she is performing below grade level in any basic subject. For example, a fourth grader reading at a third-grade level is considered educationally disadvantaged even if that child's work in all other academic subjects is at or above grade level. Similarly, a child having significant trouble with arithmetic may be classified as educationally disadvantaged, even though he or she has reading scores that are well above average.

Defining a Supplementary Educational Project

If a project is to qualify for Chapter I aid, it must *supplement,* rather than pay for, a standard academic activity already available in a school. For instance, all elementary schools teach reading. Therefore, Chapter I funds may not be used to pay for a school's standard reading program. However, if a school wishes to establish an *additional* special program in reading for children who are below grade level in that subject, such a program may qualify for Chapter I support.

How a School District Qualifies for Chapter I Aid

A school district qualifies for Chapter I aid if it has at least 10 children between the ages of 5 and 17 who are officially classified as financially deprived. In fact, more than 14,000 (over 90 percent) of the nation's school districts receive some degree of Chapter I aid. The amount of aid a district receives depends largely on the number of financially deprived children living within its borders. A district with the minimum number is likely to receive far less Chapter I aid than a district with a heavy concentration of children from poor families.

A school that participates in a Chapter I pro-gram may not be denied its fair share of local funding on the assumption that federal money will make up the difference. Similarly, a state may not reduce its financial aid to a school district because that district is receiving Chapter I funds. Nor may such funds be used to finance programs that are required by state law.

How Individuals Qualify for Chapter I Aid

If a Chapter I program is in operation in your child's school, any student who is functioning below grade level in one or more basic subjects qualifies for this supplementary program.

Chapter I Aid to Private and Parochial School Children

Neither private nor parochial schools may receive Chapter I aid directly. However, chil-

Suspension and Expulsion

Among the most drastic actions public school officials can take against a child are suspension and expulsion—particularly the latter, which cuts a boy or girl off from the educational process. Suspension, usually for periods of up to 10 days, is a fairly common procedure. In some school systems, it has been employed as a punishment for relatively minor infractions. In others, it has long been considered a penalty of last resort.

In the past, suspensions could be enforced in most jurisdictions without reference to hearings, evidence or any of the procedures associated with due process of law. In the mid-1970s, however, the U. S. Supreme Court ruled on the matter, deciding that students have a property interest in a public school system, and that suspension without due process violates their property rights. The court further decided that suspension without due process is an arbitrary use of a government agency's power, one that denies a child his or her "good name, reputation, honor or integrity."

The Supreme Court did not establish hard and fast rules for hearings. It merely stated that a child should be informed of the reasons for the contemplated penalty, and offered an opportunity to deny the charges and present evidence pertinent to the charge.

But in situations where a child's continued presence in school presents, in the authorities' view, an immediate threat to other students, teachers or property, the child may be removed without a hearing. As soon as practical, however, fair procedures must be instituted to protect the rights of the child and his or her parents.

Similarly, in cases of long-term suspensions or expulsions, the courts have not laid down detailed procedures.

As a rule, however, the courts require a formal hearing in which the child of the parents may answer the charges, employ competent legal assistance and cross-examine witnesses for the other side. If the suspension or expulsion is upheld, the child will still have the right of appeal.

dren attending such schools who live within a Chapter I area *are* eligible. The youngsters may be taken to a local public school where Chapter I programs operate, or mobile classrooms may make regular visits to the private or parochial school to make Chapter I services available to the students.

Major Categories of Programs

Chapter I programs include the following general categories:

(A) Projects that reinforce general classroom work in such subjects as reading, mathematics, composition, grammar, language usage and comprehension. The object is to bring students who are having difficulties in these subjects up to grade level.

(B) The employment of additional teachers and teachers' aides to give children in Chapter I programs intensive instruction.

(C) Summertime instruction to help students upgrade their skills during vacation periods, and reinforce understanding of subjects taught during the regular school year.

(D) On-the-job training for teachers, teachers' aides and parents who participate in Chapter I projects.

The Role of Parents in Chapter I

A primary goal of Chapter I is to involve parents directly in the education of their children.

Conduct and Grades

May a teacher mark down a student in an academic subject because the child is obstreperous in class? In recent years, the courts have held with increasing frequency that academic grades must be based *only* on academic achievement. A teacher may, of course, send home a note to the parents complaining of the child's conduct, or institute various forms of disciplinary action. But one thing the teacher may *not* do is to give the child a lower mark than he or she has actually earned. Similarly, a school may not deny a child a diploma on behavioral grounds. If the student has fulfilled the academic requirements for the diploma, it must be awarded regardless of non-academic factors.

Participating school districts must therefore establish parent advisory councils on both district and individual school levels. The functions of a parent advisory council include helping to plan the contents of the Chapter I programs, assisting in their implementation once they are approved by the staff of the state coordinating agency and working with school officials and teachers to assure the success of the various programs.

Searches and Seizures

The widespread use of alcohol and other drugs by children, and the increasing violence in the nation's schools, have stirred serious discussion as to whether students or their possessions may be searched for contraband believed to be on their persons or hidden in their lockers. The key question is: Should school officials be required to obtain a warrant before searching a student or his or her locker? The courts have taken a middle-of-the-road position. School officials may not routinely search students' lockers or subject the children themselves to bodily searches. Nor may a school official demand, solely on the basis of a vague suspicion, that a student open the locker or submit to a search. But if there is evidence that a child is carrying or hiding weapons or illegal substances, the school officials are well within their authority to order and conduct a search.

Some Successful Chapter I Projects

Chapter I projects vary greatly from one part of the country to another and from one school to the next, but all of them are designed to help school children who are "educationally disadvantaged." A sampling of some of the more successful programs follows:

Helping One Student To Succeed (HOSTS), Vancouver, Washington: Elementary through High School. When Bill Gibbons was a high-school football coach in the Vancouver school system, he discovered to his dismay that many of his players were unable to follow written instructions. A lack of reading ability, he believed, was the basic problem, and it seemed to him that intensive, individual instruction would help. Gibbons quit coaching, went into classroom teaching and evolved the HOSTS program. The project begins with tests to determine each student's reading problems. Daily lessons are then developed to deal with these deficiencies, and volunteers from the community are recruited to help each student complete the lesson plan.

Every student has a folder listing the skills on which he or she needs to work, such as vocabulary, phonetics and grammar. Some 200 such skills have been identified and appropriate lessons developed. The teacher puts a new lesson plan in each student's folder every day, and he or she, with the help of a volunteer, completes the assignment. All student work is then reviewed by a specialist.

In the fall, the community organizes a campaign to recruit volunteers. Houses are canvassed, food store check-out clerks stuff bags with flyers, and newspapers and radio and TV stations carry recruiting announcements. Just about everyone who can read is welcome as a volunteer. The program's success if measured by the way it has spread. All told, some 1,700 students in 27 Vancouver public schools and two parochial schools are involved, together with 2,000 volunteers.

The Upstairs School, Portland, Oregon: Grades 9 through 12. The top floor of Portland, Oregon's, Roosevelt High School has become the Upstairs School, a place where teen-agers who are at least two years behind in their reading or math—some of the youngsters can barely read first-grade texts when they begin the program—receive remedial instruction in a no-nonsense environment. Structure, discipline and personalized attention are the keys to the program's success. When the student begins work with the Upstairs School, he or she is given only short, simple assignments so that day-by-day improvement can be easily discerned. Later the assignments become longer and more complex. Careful records are kept so that teachers and students can chart each day's progress and be informed about areas in which extra remedial work is needed. About 250 pupils are involved in the Upstairs School. Most remain for about a year before returning to the regular high school.

Baptist Hill Kindergarten Project, Greenville, Alabama: Early Childhood. Baptist Hill, which opened its doors in 1970, was the first public kindergarten in Alabama. Many of the children are from poverty-stricken families and have never owned a book, been read to or worked with pencils, crayons and paper. The program is designed to help them through individual instruction. Teachers and aides work closely with a child or a small group of children and explain such basic tasks as how to use a telephone. Staff members draw the children into personal conversations, providing many of the youngsters with their first experience of adults who have time to listen to them and take an interest in what they have to say. Through it all, the children develop basic skills and an understanding of the world around them as well as a new appreciation of their own worth.

A major success of the program has been its ability to involve parents. Typically, 100 or more parents attend each of the parents advisory council meetings, and many volunteer their time as aides on the project. Public kindergartens are now in operation throughout Alabama, many of them modeled on the Baptist Hill Program.

Catch Up—Keep Up, Tucson, Arizona: Grades 5 through 8. Middle school students in Tucson's Flowing Wells School District who are reading below grade level are assigned to the Catch Up—Keep Up program. The project consists of laboratory work and special instruction for teachers. In the lab phase, groups of up to six students meet with reading specialists, each of whom has an advanced degree. Students with particularly severe reading problems may be tutored individually. The amount of time for each lab session is based primarily on the boy's or girl's attention span. Specialists also work with regular classroom teachers, demonstrating the most effective methods of reading instruction.

The remedial reading program provides an excellent example of parent-school co-operation. When Catch Up—Keep Up began a decade ago, it was an elementary school program with classes in all three of the Flowing Wells' primary schools. There were not, however, enough federal funds to keep the project in operation in three places at once. The program was therefore consolidated at Flowing Wells' middle school. Parents who were concerned about their elementary school childrens' poor reading skills formed a committee to press for a larger local school budget. The campaign proved successful; the program continues at the middle school, supported by federal funds, while instruction at the primary level is funded by local tax dollars.

High Intensity Tutoring (HIT), Highland Park, Michigan: Grades 6 through 8. This project makes use of youngsters as tutors. So successful is the program that it has been copied in school districts all across the nation. Every day of the school week, tutors and their students get together for 30 minutes. The tutors, many of whom were first involved in the program as learners, are drawn from the seventh and eighth grades, and the learners are sixth and seventh graders who test below grade level in reading and math. The first 10 minutes of each session is devoted to quick drill, in which the pupils read word lists aloud and use drill sheets and flash cards in math. The final 10 minutes is then spent on reading and math workbooks, with the young instructor and the student working closely together.

Teachers and aides discreetly monitor the tutoring and keep detailed records of the percentage of errors made by each pupil. As the student advances in skills, he or she is given progressively harder material to master. The results of Project HIT have been encouraging. Test results at Highland Park indicate that 70 percent of the children enrolled in the project have upgraded their reading levels by a year and a half for each year of tutoring, and 54 percent have substantially improved their math scores.

Examining School Records

One of the most important rights you can exercise as a parent is the right to examine your child's school records and object to the inclusion of any information that appears to be erroneous, damaging or irrelevant. Until fairly recently, school records not only were open to a child's teachers and local school officials, but were often made accessible to such outsiders as prospective employers, the local police, credit-rating services and others. Parents, however, were generally barred from examining these documents, and were thereby denied vital information about their children's progress and problems within the school system. Lacking this information, parents frequently could not participate effectively in their children's education.

In 1974, the U.S. Congress changed this situation with the passage of the Family Educational Rights and Privacy Act. The measure denies federal funds to school districts that fail to give parents complete access to their children's school records. At the same time, the measure severely restricts access to these records by non-school personnel. Under the terms of the act, each school must inform parents in writing that they have access to the records. The school must also facilitate meetings between parents and school officials to explain anything in the records that may be unclear.

After examining your child's records, you may request that material that appears to be incorrect, damaging or irrelevant be removed or modified. The school may refuse that request, but it must then arrange for a hearing before a local education official "who does not have a direct interest in the outcome" of the dispute.

Should the hearing officer decide in favor of the school, the records must nonetheless be amended to show that you have objected to specific items, and the nature of your objections must be recorded.

Other Aspects of Parent Participation

Aside from working on advisory councils, parents are also encouraged to act as volunteers in the programs themselves. If you, for example, are the parent of a child in a Chapter I project, you may be asked to provide tutoring in reading, writing or math for one child or a small group of children. You will be working under the direction of the Chapter I teacher.

If your regular job relates in any way to a subject being taught in the Chapter I program, you may be asked to give a talk on your job. Suppose, for example, that you work in a library. The Chapter I teacher at your child's school might ask you to talk about the function of the library's card catalogue, so that the children will know how to find the books they need. If you are the owner of a small shop, you might be asked to talk about the importance of arithmetic in running your business.

Whether you are a member of an advisory council or not, you will be encouraged to observe the Chapter I program at work. If you feel that the program is not achieving its goals, you are free to complain to local school officials or Chapter I program directors. If such complaints fail to change the situation, you may request a hearing before the school board or the district Chapter I parent advisory council.

How a Chapter I Proposal Is Processed

A proposal for a Chapter I project usually is initiated at the local school district level. The initiating group may be made up of parents who share a concern about their children's lack of progress in an academic subject. Or a school principal, a teacher, members of the local school board or a school administrator may take the first step.

When the idea for a project has taken shape,

a formal grant request is submitted to the state co-ordinator of Chapter I programs. In many school systems, particularly the larger ones, there may be an official whose primary job is writing grant requests. This is a highly specialized field. School systems that do not have the services of such professionals may obtain help in writing up grant applications from experts at their state department of education.

Once a grant request has been submitted, the state department of education, through its Chapter I co-ordinator, decides whether or not to approve the project. The decision will be based only in part on the worthiness of the proposed project. Other considerations that will be taken into account include the amount of Chapter I money available to the state; the percentage or number of children from economically deprived backgrounds in the district or school in which the money will be spent; the number of educationally disadvantaged children who are likely to benefit from the program; and the comparative needs of other schools or districts applying for Chapter I aid. Thus a perfectly sound project may be turned down because state education officials feel that some other school in another district is in greater need of the available funds.

Obtaining More Information on Chapter I

Because Chapter I is the primary source of federal funds for local school systems, every board of education should be fully informed about the nature of the program. Up-to-date information may also be obtained from the responsible state agencies. (See pages 48–50 for the addresses of these agencies.)

Chapter II: Education, Consolidation and Improvement Act of 1981

This portion of the education act provides federal block grants to the states. Each state sets up its own criteria for distributing the money to local school districts. These, in turn, may continue financing programs that formerly were funded by categorical grants or use the money to establish new programs in conformity with state guidelines. This means that the responsibility for continuing many valuable programs now rests with the states and local school boards. Among the most important programs that are affected are those dealing with educational experiments, alcohol and drug abuse, student internships in Washington, education for gifted and talented children, educational TV and radio courses and education in the metric system. Detailed discussions of these programs follow.

Experimental Education

Almost any education program that is innovative and shows definite promise of improving the academic performance of a significant body of elementary or high school students fits into this category. One school may bring in professionals in various fields to lecture on their specialties. Another may provide extensive nature studies for students with special interest in that field. A third may experiment with a new type of remedial reading program. A description of several such experimental programs appears below.

Projects that fall into this category and have been particularly successful become part of the "educational bank." School officials from all over the nation are invited to view these models in action and adapt them to the needs of their own school districts. In some instances, grants are made to teachers or administrators to travel from city to city and lecture to representatives of local school districts on the workings of their demonstration programs. This process is supported by a special federal office known as the National Diffusion Program which is financed by the federal government's educational discretionary fund.

For more information on National Diffusion, write to:

A Sampling of Experimental Programs

High School in the Community, New Haven, Connecticut. Volunteers from a variety of fields act as part-time teachers on this project. On any given day a visitor to the school might find an attorney discussing law, an actress lecturing on the theater, or a professor of architecture from nearby Yale University explaining the design of a great building to the students. Another part of this special training involves students directly in the life of the city. They may spend part of their time working in such areas as drug therapy, advertising, engineering, data processing and photography. High school credits are given for the work experience. Because applications to attend the school are far more numerous than the places available, a lottery is held each year to select students for the High School in the Community program.

Environmental Study Center, Martin County, Florida: Kindergarten and Elementary Grades. The world outside the classroom is a laboratory for the elementary school children of Martin County, Florida. Separate programs have been established for each grade level, and children may spend from two hours to two full days each week in the field studying local flora and fauna.

The Environmental Study Center itself is located in an old, rebuilt schoolhouse which now serves as a combination classroom and museum. Children from all over Martin County go there to hear lectures, view the exhibits and engage in nature projects. Kindergarten children, for example, are given environmental coloring books to stimulate an interest in nature. From time to time, they are also taken on treasure hunts on which they search for particular plants, flowers and rocks. Sixth graders learn about the local Indian River, boat handling and water safety, then go on a two-day field trip along the river they have studied. About 90 percent of Martin County's elementary school children take part in the Environmental Study Center's activities, as do many adults who volunteer their services and act as aides during field trips. The Center has served as a model for similar programs in several Florida counties and in North Carolina as well.

Institute for Political and Legal Education (IPLE), New Jersey: Grades 9 through 12.

Director
Division of Educational Replication
Office of Evaluation and Dissemination
Trans Point Building
Washington, DC 20202

Alcohol and Drug Abuse Program

This program is designed not only to discourage the abuse of alcohol and other drugs among students, but also to deal with such problems as truancy and vandalism. It is financed through a combination of block grant funds and money from the educational discretionary fund. Discretionary fund money is used to train selected teachers and administrators at one of the five training and resource centers established in various parts of the country. These teachers return to their own school districts and then train local personnel. Block grant funds support whatever local program is established to deal with such problems as alcohol and drug abuse.

Additional information may be obtained

A social studies course designed to help students become informed citizens and voters, IPLE takes teen-agers outside the classroom to involve them in the world of mayors, senators and lobbyists. The program, which is now operating in 27 New Jersey high schools, consists of three basic units: voter education, government decision-making and individual rights. Voter education includes a project in which students help register voters, organize babysitting pools, arrange for transportation services on election day and conduct simulated elections within their schools. In the government unit, a Student Lobbyist Training Center in the state capital at Trenton advises students on how to draft bills and monitor their progress through the state legislature.

The individual rights unit deals mostly with consumer legislation and the juvenile court system. IPLE has served as a model for similar programs that are now in operation in 30 states.

Computer Achievement Monitoring (CAM), Hopkins, Minnesota: Grades 2 through 12. Aside from standing for Computer Achievement Monitoring, CAM is the name of a computer that some 16,000 students in the town of Hopkins, Minnesota, consider a friend.

So attached are many of them to CAM that some actually write letters to the computer, and others regale it with accounts of vacation-time adventures.

Although CAM "answers" all of the letters it receives, its real role is to keep track of each student's progress in a variety of subjects and pinpoint, for both students and teachers, not only areas where remedial instruction may be warranted, but also areas where a student may proceed at a faster pace than usual. Throughout the Hopkins school system, students take frequent tests in their academic courses, and their answers are fed into CAM for grading and analysis of each child's strengths and weaknesses. In this manner, teachers are provided with information that permits them to tailor their assignments to the specific needs and abilities of each student. So successful has CAM been that several school districts in areas around Hopkins have purchased computers and adopted the CAM system for their own use.

from:

Division of Alcohol and Drug Education Programs
Bureau of Elementary and Secondary Education
400 Maryland Ave., SW
Washington, DC 20202

Close Up

This program is designed to provide a week in Washington for high school students who are interested in the inner workings of the federal government. Students attend workshops and seminars with congressmen, department heads and media representatives. The project is funded through contributions from a combination of private and corporate foundations and the federal government. Federal funding comes through a special fellowship established by Congress and a grant from the Justice Department that enables former juvenile offenders to participate. Particular emphasis is placed on involving handicapped students in Close Up. Expenses are held as low as possible and students are expected to pay part of the cost. A number of full-expense fellowships are available, however, for students from economically deprived families. Close Up personnel travel to high schools throughout the country each year to describe the program to teachers and principals and conduct follow-up surveys among students who made the trip the year before.

Additional information may be obtained from:

The Close Up Foundation
1235 Jefferson Davis Hwy.
Arlington, VA 22202

Ethnic Heritage Studies Program

The federal government maintains resource help—general information, teaching aids, books and pamphlets—for states and school districts that wish to devote a portion of their block grants to ethnic studies. Such studies emphasize the contributions of America's diverse ethnic groups to the development of the nation. Projects usually include training of selected teachers in materials that will help their students develop a sense of pride in their own ethnic groups. For example, in a district with a large Hispanic population, an ethnic studies program would undoubtedly emphasize the important role of Spanish-Americans and Latin-Americans in business, labor, government and the professions.

For additional information, write to:
Ethnic Heritage Studies Staff
Bureau of School Improvement
400 Maryland Ave., SW
Washington, DC 20202

Educational Programs for the Handicapped
The federal and state goverments operate a vast array of educational programs aimed at helping handicapped students achieve their educational goals. Information on the major programs for the handicapped will be found in Chapter 5.

Education for Gifted and Talented Children

This block grant program is designed to meet the special needs of children with high academic potential. Funds are awarded, through state departments of education, to statewide and local projects catering to the academic needs of gifted children from the pre-school level through high school.

The money may be used for special courses, for the training of teachers who will be working with these students or for the dissemination of information about the specialized education of gifted and talented youngsters. Awards may also be made for the development of special instructional materials.

Additional information may be obtained from state departments of education (pages 46-48) or from:
Office for Gifted and Talented Children
400 Maryland Ave., SW
Washington, DC 20202

Arts in Education Program

The dissemination of knowledge and appreciation of the arts among elementary and high school students is the purpose of the Arts in Education Program. Those school districts that use part of their block grant funds to support this program usually distribute money to local school boards, museums and performing arts groups offering projects that qualify. These programs are made available to students at various grade levels and are keyed to classroom activities. For example, children who are studying the history of the American Revolution might also learn about dance, drama, art and music of that period. Funds used in this program help pay for the services of members of the artistic community who work with students. Projects are often planned by an advisory panel made up of artists as well as business people, professionals, parents and representatives of youth groups.

Additional information may be obtained from:

Humanities Staff
400 Maryland Ave. SW
Washington, DC 20202

Educational Television and Radio

Federal education officials maintain a resource office for state and local school districts that employ part of their block grant funds for teaching via television and radio. Local and state projects in this field may avail themselves of television tapes, films and audio cassettes of instructional programs on various subjects and at different grade levels for transmission on educational or cable stations. In addition, a variety of teaching and learning aids relating to these and other programs are available. Federal education authorities publish a catalogue listing the materials that states and local school districts may order on a rental basis.

For additional information, write to:
Division of Educational Technology
Office of Libraries and Learning
    Technologies
400 Maryland Ave., SW
Washington, D.C. 20202

Metric System Education

Federal education officials maintain a resource center—books, pamphlets, teaching aids and the like—for local school districts that use a portion of their block grant funds for instruction in the fundamentals of the metric system of weights and measures. This system may eventually become standard in the United States. Projects in metric education that prove to be particularly successful may become part of the education bank and serve as models for school districts around the nation. In such instances, dissemination of information on

these projects will be financed by the National Diffusion Network (page 17).

For more information, write to:
Metric Education Program
400 6th St., SW
Washington, DC 20202

Financing Higher Education

Parents and students considering the cost of college or graduate school might be forgiven for succumbing, at least momentarily, to despair. Typical costs—tuition, books, food, lodging etc.—at the best private universities and colleges can be about $10,000 a year for undergraduates. Expenses are considerably higher at professional graduate institutions like medical and law schools. Fortunately, financial help is often available. With some imaginative planning—for example, a combination of government grants, government-backed loans, state and federally financed scholarships, private scholarships, campus jobs and some help from parents—high educational expenses can frequently be handled even by families with limited incomes. As the following pages show, the degree to which you, as a student, or your parents can take advantage of the many financial aid opportunities depends, to some extent, on where you live, where you are going to school, your career goals and the amount of money your parents can contribute. But whether your family is middle income or poor, there are programs available to help meet the cost of a college education.

The Private Sector

This book deals primarily with government programs, but where higher education is concerned, mention must be made of the many private scholarships and aid packages available to college students. These two sources of financial help are closely related. The aid you can get from private sources may determine the size of the government-secured loans you will need.

College Scholarships and Aid Packages

Just about every accredited private and public institution of higher education in the United States offers a variety of financial aid plans to students who need money to pay their expenses. College scholarships, which once were granted largely on the basis of academic achievement and potential, now tend to be awarded more often on the basis of need.

Once a college accepts you, it probably will also help you pay for the education it offers. To some degree, this aid may come in the form of scholarships, but it may also come in the form of a work program. Your college may offer you such jobs as waiting on tables or running a dormitory switchboard. Or it may offer you employment that is partly subsidized by federal or state work-study programs (see pages 28–29). In any case, the number of hours you are expected to work will be carefully limited so that the job does not interfere with your academic obligations.

A college may also help you find summer employment, but it will expect that a portion of your earnings be used to defray the following year's tuition and expenses. One factor you should be aware of is that sources of income from outside the college—such as gifts from relatives, or the GI Bill—will, in most instances, lead the school administration to revise its aid package downward.

Before enrolling in any college, you should talk with its financial aid officer and compare the aid package he or she is willing to provide with that offered by other colleges that have accepted you.

Scholarships From Private Organizations

Hundreds of millions of dollars in scholarship aid are offered each year by private and religious organizations in the United States. In a recent year, more than $100 million in such funds went unclaimed merely because those qualified for the aid did not know it was available. Organizations as diverse as the American Legion, the Methodist Church, the Association of the Sons of Poland, the 4-H and Rotary clubs—to mention just several out of hundreds—have put aside considerable amounts of money for scholarship aid. In some instances the applicant must be a member of a particular church, the child or grandchild of a veteran or a member of an ethnic group to qualify. In other cases, anyone may apply. Often the scholarships are awarded on the basis of competition among the qualified applicants. The cash amounts of the awards vary greatly: some scholarships may be for as little as $100; others may be for several thousand dollars.

One of the most efficient ways for you to avail yourself of this frequently overlooked source of financial aid is to write to:

The Scholarship Search Company
1775 Broadway
New York, NY 10019

This organization maintains a file of a quarter of a million scholarships. It will send you a questionnaire to fill out. For a modest fee, it will then match your qualifications with the requirements listed for each one of the scholarships it has on file. Finally, Scholarship Search will advise you about which grants to apply for, and provide information on how to go about making applications.

National Merit Scholarships

Sponsored by corporations and a number of colleges, the National Merit Scholarships are awarded in three categories: the Merit Scholarships themselves; corporate scholarships; and college-endowed scholarships. The scholarships range in value from a single payment of $250 to as much as $4,000 per year. If you are interested in competing, you must take the Preliminary Scholastic Aptitude Test before the end of your junior year in high school. Top scorers on this test are listed as semi-finalists. Should you be among them, you must then take the Scholastic Aptitude Test, preferably early in your senior year. Your score on this test will help determine your eligibility for a Merit Scholarship and the amount you will be awarded. Other factors include your high school academic record, a written essay on your

Comparative Costs at Public and Private Institutions

Public colleges and universities cost considerably less than private institutions. When John H., a top student from Cleveland, Ohio enrolled at Yale University, it cost a total of $11,300 to put him through his freshman year. Of this, $7,150 was spent on tuition. $3,190 on room and board, and the rest on books and personal expenses.

When Mary R. of Staunton, Virginia, attended the University of Virginia in Charlottesville, the total costs of her freshman year were $4,181, barely more than a third of John H.'s at Yale.

Even out-of-state students do much better at state-supported schools. The freshman year at the University of Virginia cost James D., of Terre Haute, Indiana, $5,681, less than half John H.'s expenses at Yale.

Tuition is, of course, the biggest item. The comparison of tuition costs below, indicates the basic savings that may be achieved by attending a state-supported school.

PRIVATE INSTITUTIONS

	$1,500	$3,000	$4,500	$6,000	$7,500
Oberlin					
Waynesburg					
Georgetown					
Brown Univ.					
Scripps					
Harvard					
Amherst					
Carleton					

STATE INSTITUTIONS

	$1,500	$3,000	$4,500	$6,000	$7,500
Univ. of Mass. (Amherst)					
Resident					
Out of State					
Univ. of Texas (El Paso)					
Resident					
Out of State					
Bowling Green (Ohio)					
Resident					
Out of State					
Univ. of Kansas (Lawrence)					
Resident					
Out of State					
Louisiana Tech (Rustin)					
Resident					
Out of State					
Univ. of Cincinnati					
Resident					
Out of State					
Univ. of Calif. (Santa Cruz)					
Resident					
Out of State					
Univ. of Wisconsin (Madison)					
Resident					
Out of State					

academic and life goals, your record of community and school activities and your high school's recommendation. Some 1,200 scholarships are awarded without consideration of financial need. These awards are for $1,000 per year.

Additionally, there are about 1,400 corporate-sponsored scholarships and about 2,000 college-sponsored awards. The amounts given to those who qualify, according to the requirements above, are based on financial need.

Your high school guidance counselor should have complete details on this program. But act as early as possible. Remember that if you are to be considered, you must indicate your interest no later than the fall of your junior year. In addition, much information is available on this program from:

National Merit Scholarship Corporation
One American Plaza
Evanston, IL 60201

State Universities

The biggest financial break you as a student can arrange for yourself is to attend a branch of the publicly supported university in your home state rather than attending a privately endowed college. By making such a choice, you insure that your education is already partially subsidized. A portion of the tax money paid by the citizens in each state goes to the state university to help defray the cost of tuition for its resident students.

Most state universities are academically comparable to the best private colleges. In addition, many states, particularly the larger and wealthier ones, maintain several university campuses, each with its own character, strengths and academic requirements. A few states have reciprocity agreements with their nearest neighbors. For example, citizens of Minnesota may attend the state universities of Wisconsin for the same tuition rates that Wisconsinites pay. Students from Wisconsin are accorded the same privilege at Minnesota state universities. Students considering attendance at a public university outside their home state, even where no reciprocity agreement exists, will probably find that the tuition fees are still far lower than those at a private college or university.

Achieving Independent Status

Students enrolled at institutions outside their home states may find it advantageous to establish themselves as legal residents of the state in which they are attending school. This is especially true if a student's home state offers little in the way of financial aid while the host state has a generous program for needy residents.

The process of establishing legal residence in a host state may be long and arduous. Usually it requires that a student receive no significant financial aid from his or her parents for one or two years while studying in the host state. Once such independent status is achieved, however, the student becomes eligible to receive financial aid from the state in which he or she is now a resident.

Even if you are a student attending school in your home state, you may benefit greatly from achieving independent status. Once the family income is no longer a factor in determining your eligibility for financial aid from the state, you have a good chance of falling within an income bracket that will make you eligible for maximum state subsidies. To determine the exact requirements for achieving independent status in the state where you are enrolled in college, consult your school's financial aid officer or the state agencies listed on pages 46–48.

Basic Education Opportunity Grants

In 1978, President Jimmy Carter signed legislation extending federal grants to college students from middle-income families. These Basic Educational Opportunity Grants (BEOG)—often called "Pell Grants" after Senator Claiborne Pell of Rhode Island, who sponsored the enabling legislation—help hundreds of thousands of students from families with moderate incomes to pay for their higher education. Because the financial qualifications for such grants may be modified each year by Congress, it is impossible to state with certainty how much money a given applicant might get for a particular year.

However in 1980–1981 the grants ranged from a low of $200 to a high of $1,670, depending on such variables as the cost at the school the applicant was planning to attend, and the income, the number of dependents and the expenses of the applicant's family.

The BEOG is not intended to meet all of a student's school expenses, but to form a base to which other forms of financial aid can be added and thereby ease the burden for eligible students. Unlike scholarships, of which there are only a specified number, the BEOG is an "entitlement" program. This means that *any* student who is financially and academically qualified for the grant will receive one as a matter of right.

Qualifying for a BEOG

If you are enrolling in an accredited college, university, community (two-year) college or post high-school technical institution, you may be eligible for a BEOG.

In order to qualify for a grant, you must be a citizen or permanent resident of the United States and must be planning to attend the institution on at least a half-time basis.

Yearly Awards

You may receive a BEOG once a year for as many years as you remain in an undergraduate program, provided that your progress is determined to be satisfactory by educational authorities.

How to Apply

Your school guidance counselors probably will have one of the forms used in applying for a BEOG.

Any one of the following will do: the Financial Aid Form (FAF); the Family Financial Statement (FFS); or the Basic Educational Opportunity Grant (program) application. The last of these is good only for the BEOG, however. But because you will probably be applying for other types of financial aid, it's usually a good idea to have your parents fill out the FAF or the FFS. Either one of these is essential for obtaining college or state-supported grants and scholarships and will be useful when you apply for government-guaranteed education loans.

Filling Out the Forms

Both the FFS and FAF are complex documents. A single mistake in filling them out—even so minor an error as leaving out a home-address zip code—may result in a long delay in the processing.

If you are a high school senior, you may want to ask your guidance counselor for help in completing the form. At the very least, let the counselor review the form before it is submitted. If you are already in college, you may obtain the same type of help from your financial aid officer.

When to Submit a Financial Aid Form

The form should be submitted no later than early March for aid that is to begin the following September. To be on the safe side, however, complete the form in January or February. High school seniors probably will not yet have been accepted by a college when they complete the form. But they will have applied to various colleges and universities, and can indicate which schools should receive the required financial information.

Two Vital Questionnaires for Determining Financial Aid

Students needing extensive financial aid to begin, continue or complete their college educations must resubmit the Financial Aid Form (FAF) or the Family Financial Statement (FFS) each year. Colleges and state scholarship agencies use one or the other of these forms to determine the amount of aid to be provided. Both forms come with pre-addressed envelopes that route the questionnaires to the private agencies that process them. The agencies then recommend the amount of aid they feel a student should have. The FAF is processed by the College Scholarship Service; the FFS goes to the American College Testing Service.

The information given by the student and his or her family in these forms will probably be the primary factor in determining how much financial aid will be forthcoming from the school or the state scholarship agency. The most important elements in these forms concern the family's financial position. Both forms require parents to list their gross incomes for the preceding year and their estimated gross incomes for the current and following year.

In addition, other assets, such as stocks and bonds, trust funds and the market value of all real estate—minus unpaid mortgage liability—must be listed, as well as assets in the student's name. Liabilities such as medical expenses, debts and losses due to theft or fire must also be listed. The forms must be filled out exactly as the directions indicate, and a false statement concerning assets or liabilities may result in criminal prosecution. Verification requested by the processing agency may include the previous year's income tax statements and a copy of the current year's income tax form when completed.

As soon as the processing agency receives a completed form, it feeds the information into a computer, which then prints out an estimate of how much financial aid the applicant

National Direct Student Loans

This is one of the major avenues available to needy students for securing education funds. In this program, the federal government makes funds available directly to participating colleges, universities and other institutions of higher education. These institutions, through their financial aid officers, then lend the money at low interest rates to qualified students.

How Much Money May Be Borrowed

As an undergraduate, you may borrow as much as $6,000 over your entire four-year course of study.

However, you may borrow no more than $3,000 during your first two years. If you bor-row less, the surplus may be credited to your account for your use during the last two years of study. For example, if you borrow only $500 during your freshman year and another $500 during your sophomore year, you may have $5,000 available to you during your junior and senior years.

Graduate students who have not taken a Direct Student Loan during their undergraduate years may borrow up to $12,000 to finance graduate or professional education. A graduate student who has borrowed $5,000 while an undergraduate may borrow an additional $7,000 to complete the requirements for an advanced degree.

The Role of the Financial Aid Officer

The figures just given are maximum amounts. The college financial aid officer is the final will need. A copy of this estimate goes to the Basic Education Opportunity Grant (BEOG) program, and in some instances another copy automatically goes to the applicant's home-state scholarship agency. Additional copies will go to the applicant on the form. A fee, indicated on the form, is required for this service. For an additional small fee, the processing agency will provide the applicant with a copy of its financial aid recommendations.

About six weeks after completing either the FAF or the FFS, the applicant should receive from the BEOG program a Student Eligibility Report. This will *not* include information of the cash award. Instead, it will contain an index number to be interpreted by the financial aid officer of the college at which the student is enrolled or has been accepted. Therefore, the student should immediately send the Eligibility Report to that financial aid officer. If the student has been accepted by several schools, but has not yet decided among them, a photocopy of the report should be sent to each college's financial aid officer. The actual amount of money an applicant will receive as a BEOG will be determined in part by the costs at the college he or she eventually decides to attend. The same index number will bring a student a higher award at Harvard—an expensive school—than at a home state university or community college, where the costs are much lower.

Using a BEOG as a base, the financial officers at each of the colleges in question will then be able to compute a financial aid package. They will take into account the recommendations of the processing agency and figure in any awards the student may have won from a state or private organization. But it is they who will make the final decision on the amount of aid to be forthcoming from the college they represent. They may recommend a college scholarship and a student loan, and they may offer part-time employment.

arbiter of loans under the Direct Student Loan program.

That official surveys each student's financial situation and decides whether the applicant may borrow the maximum amount, a smaller amount or will be awarded any funds at all. In part, the decision will depend on how much money is available to the college or university under the program.

Qualifying for a Direct Student Loan

Citizens or permanent residents of the United States who are enrolled in participating institutions and carrying at least half a full course load may apply for Direct Student Loans. Students who are in this country on a visa, or who are in default on their payments for other federally subsidized or college loans, are barred from participating in the program.

How the Loans Are Disbursed

The college may give you a check to use for any educational purpose, including room and board. Or the college may credit your student account and draw on the loan to pay for your expenses. Usually the institution will provide you directly with a portion of the loan and retain the rest in an account established in your name. Withdrawals are made as needed.

Repayment of the Direct Student Loan

Interest on the loan does not begin accumulating until after you have completed your education, and you do not have to begin repaying the loan until six months after you have finished your studies. Payments may be made, at the lender's discretion, on a monthly, bimonthly or quarterly basis, but the minimum payment is $90 per quarter or $30 per month, and the entire loan may come due if you default on any payment.

The entire loan must be repaid over a ten-year period. In emergencies, however, you can usually work out new schedules of repayment through consultation with your school's financial aid officer.

Cancellation of Repayment Obligations

The repayment of the loan will be canceled in case of the borrower's death, complete and permanent disability or legal bankruptcy. The government also provides for complete or partial forgiveness of the loan under the following circumstances:

* if the borrower becomes a teacher of the handicapped in a public or non-profit elementary or high school;
* if the borrower becomes a teacher in a public or non-profit elementary or high school in which a large proportion of the student body comes from low-income families;
* if the borrower becomes a staff member of a federal teaching program for educationally disadvantaged pre-school children;
* if the borrower is serving as a volunteer in the Peace Corps, or is a member of certain designated occupations within the Public Health Service or an employee of certain designated non-profit voluntary organizations.

Your college financial aid officer will be able to give you exact information on which occupations offer forgiveness of Direct Student Loan repayment obligations. That official will also be able to tell you how long you must remain in a designated occupation to secure complete or partial forgiveness.

For example, a teacher of the handicapped or the poor may secure complete forgiveness of Direct Student Loan obligations after five years on the job, while a staff member of a federally financed preschool program such as Head Start will have to be employed seven years in that program before the loan repayments are completely canceled.

Federal Work-Study Program

The federal government provides funds to colleges and universities to defray the cost of hiring students for campus jobs. Financially needy students are offered these jobs as part of their aid packages. As 80 percent of the funding for these jobs comes from the federal government, and only 20 percent from the school itself, the program has the advantage of releasing some college funds for other student employment opportunities that are paid for wholly by the institution.

Eligibility for the Work-Study Program

Candidates for the program must prove financial need and be enrolled at least half time in order to qualify. They must not be in default on payments of government or college loans, and their academic records must indicate that they can successfully pursue academic work while holding employment.

Types of Jobs Available

Almost any useful job for which a student is qualified—such as library assistant, nurse's aide or undergraduate teaching assistant—is available under this program. If you qualify for the Work-Study Program, your financial aid officer will try to place you in an area suited to your interests and background, but the needs of the college are paramount in the selection of jobs.

The Workweek and Rate of Pay

Under the program a student may be employed no more than 20 hours per week, but in most instances the workweek is considerably shorter. Colleges are required to pay at least the federal minimum wage; some jobs pay more. There is no hard and fast rule about the frequency of payment, but students are usually paid on a bi-weekly basis and receive their wages directly rather than in the form of credits against their college account.

Although wages earned through this program are theoretically taxable, few students earn enough income in the work-study program alone to make them liable for federal and state income taxes.

Guaranteed Student Loans

A joint venture of the states and the federal government, the Guaranteed Student Loan Program is one of the primary sources of funds

Television and the Home Classroom

Back in the early days of television, many educators believed that the new medium would turn the living rooms of Americans into classrooms, where adults could view high school and college lectures and complete their educations. Though there were some experiments in this field, by and large, the optimism was premature. There were just too few television stations in any one area and television time on the commercial outlets was too expensive to allow for high schools or universities of the air.

Today, however, courses for credit via television are a reality in some areas and a lively possibility in others. The proliferation of television stations on the ultra-high frequency band and through cable TV as well as the technology of beaming programs off earth-orbiting satellites has opened up television time for both high school and college courses. Recently, for example, Columbus, Ohio's, experimental two-way cable system, known as QUBE, began offering both high school and college courses to subscribers. A highly complex computerized video system, QUBE is unique in that it allows subscribers to participate directly by pressing buttons on their cable boxes. Thus a viewer of a course can answer questions posed by the teacher in the studio.

Less technologically advanced, perhaps, but more far-reaching, is a new network that beams college courses from a studio at the University of Maryland to various parts of the country where subscribing colleges are located. The network is known as the National University Consortium and currently includes The University of Maryland and six other schools: Southern Vermont University; Pennsylvania State University; the University of Tennessee at Chattanooga; California State University at Dominguez Hills; Iona College in New York State; and Linfield College in Oregon. Lectures are beamed to 10 public television stations and two cable systems, and viewers living near these schools may take courses in their homes. Anyone, of course, may watch, but to gain credit, the viewer must register with the local participating college, buy the required text books and pay whatever credit fee the school requires. Matriculating students are expected to submit home work and complete exams.

Currently, the National University Consortium offers only a few courses—each one for nine credits. But as additional schools and students sign up, a much enlarged curriculum will be offered.

For more information on this program, write to:

National University Consortium
Box 430
Owings Mills, MD 21117

In addition to the programs described above, many local cable systems co-operate with nearby high schools and colleges to offer course work via television. To find out what educational opportunities exist via TV in your area, get in touch with your local board of education, the college or community college located nearest you or with the cable company that services your town.

for students attending or about to attend a college, university, community college, graduate school or post high-school technical institution. Though the state and federal governments guarantee repayment, the loans themselves are made through private commercial banks, savings banks and savings and loan companies.

Qualifications for Taking Out a Guaranteed Student Loan

Any student enrolled or about to be enrolled in an accredited institution of higher education is eligible for a guaranteed loan provided that his or her family's gross adjusted income—the amount that appears on line 31 of the 1040 income tax form or line 11 of the 1040A tax form—is no more than $30,000 per year. But in the current budget-cutting climate, it is to be expected that high-income families will experience increasing difficulty in securing these loans. The degree of eligibility will be determined by a complex formula which takes into account such factors as the amount of financial aid the college is providing through scholarships and campus jobs as well as the total family income.

Students may take out one loan per academic year. Those who have completed their undergraduate education and are studying for higher degrees may also participate in the program, even if they have already borrowed the full amount permitted undergraduates.

Amounts Available Under the Program

A student participating in the guaranteed loan program may borrow as much as $12,500 to finance up to five years of undergraduate education. In some instances, however, the available amount may be less, as in situations where family income is relatively high and need can be demonstrated only for a lesser amount. However, there is a minimum amount ($1,000) that may be borrowed in any one year and, for undergraduates, a maximum amount of $2,500.

Until recently, students taking less than half a full course load were barred from the Guaranteed Loan Program. Now, however, funds in lesser amounts are also available for these part-time students.

A graduate student who has already borrowed the maximum $12,500 as an undergraduate may incur an additional $12,500 indebtedness to help defray expenses in graduate or professional school.

If you, as an undergraduate, had borrowed less than the maximum $12,500, the unborrowed funds may be credited toward paying for an advanced degree. For example, if you borrowed only $2,000 during your four years as an undergraduate in college, you may be able to borrow as much as $23,000 under the Guaranteed Loan Program to finance your graduate studies. In no case, however, may your personal indebtedness total more than $25,000 under the program, nor may you borrow more than $2,500 in any one academic year. If you are planning a program of graduate study requiring many years of schooling, the fact that you may be able to borrow as much as $25,000 under the program should improve your chances of completing the course.

Origination Fee

A 5 percent fee is now charged for making each year's loan. Suppose, for example, you are qualified to receive a loan of $2,500 for the current academic year. The charge would be $125. The actual amount you will receive, therefore, will be $2,375, but you will be responsible for repaying the entire $2,500.

Repayment Schedules

In most instances the Guaranteed Loan Program carries a 9 percent interest charge. Borrowers need not begin repayment until six months after they have completed their education. Once repayment begins—and if the student does not return to school—the entire loan must be paid off within 10 years, with a minimum repayment schedule of $30 per month. A student may, however, complete his or her undergraduate education, take a job, begin repayment and later return to school to take an advanced degree. In such circumstances, repayment may be postponed until six months after completion of the requirements for the advanced degree.

How to Apply for a Guaranteed Loan

The first step is to find a bank that makes these loans. Though the loans are guaranteed by the government, some banks prefer not to make them because of the paperwork involved, particularly when a borrower defaults. Other banks will make the loans only on a limited basis, usually to long-term customers or their sons and daughters. It is therefore best for you, as a student, to seek a loan from a bank with which your family has dealt for a number of years.

If that bank is not making guaranteed loans at the time you apply, an officer of the institution will probably be able to tell you where such loans are currently available.

When a student applies for a loan, the bank furnishes a Guaranteed Student Loan application. A section of this is to be filled out by you, a section by your parents and a section by the college you are attending or plan to attend. The form should be filled out at least three months before the beginning of the academic year. When you and your parents have completed your respective portions of the application, send it immediately to the college financial aid officer. Ask him or her to fill out the remaining section of the form and then return it to you with the college's recommendation on the loan. With this information on hand, you will know exactly how large a loan you are likely to get.

After you submit the completed form to the bank, it usually takes about six weeks for the loan to be approved. You must then pay a small fee for life insurance in order to guarantee repayment of the loan in case of your death. Once you have completed this step, a check should be promptly issued to you for the amount of the loan.

Guaranteed Loans to Parents and Independent Students

Informally known as the Parent Loan Program, these government guaranteed loans help parents finance their childrens' higher education and assist independent students (those who are totally independent of financial support from their families) on both the graduate and undergraduate level. This program differs from Guaranteed Student Loans in several important respects.

* The borrower may take out loans amounting to a maximum of $3,000 per year to finance higher education.
* There is no income limitation. A parent or independent student may borrow up to the maximum amount regardless of income.
* The interest rate for repayment is 14 percent a year, but subject to change.
* Repayment must begin within two months of the time the money is made available.
* As with student loans, lending institutions, such as savings banks and commercial banks, are the primary sources of funds. Several colleges and universities, however, are now directly participating in this program, making their own funds available. In the future, more colleges and universities are likely to follow suit.

In the Parent Loan Program, the legal responsibility for repayment rests with the person in whose name the loan is granted rather than the beneficiary. Thus, a parent taking out a loan in his or her own name to finance a child's education is the responsible party.

It is possible to combine Guaranteed Student Loans with guaranteed loans to parents. For example, if you are attending college and meet the qualifications, you may borrow $2,500 to finance your own education during the academic year. Your parents may borrow an additional $3,000 to help pay your fees. You will be responsible for repaying the first loan, and your parents will be charged with the responsibility for repaying the second.

What To Do if the Bank Won't Help

You may discover that the demand for guaranteed loans is so great that local banks have exhausted the funds they have committed to the program. If that happens, write to your college's financial aid officer for help in securing a loan through a bank near the school. Failing that, write to your home state's guaranteed loan agency, listed on pages 50–52, which will help you find a bank willing to make the loan. Be sure to write to the agency in the state where you live, *not* the state where you are planning to attend college.

Combining Government-Secured Loans

College financial aid officers often recommend that a student not take out both a Guaranteed Loan and a Direct Student Loan (see pages 26–28). One reason is that funds under the Direct Student Loan Program are limited. Another is that the officers do not wish to saddle a student with an onerous repayment schedule. But, as the cost of a higher education continues to rise, it is no longer unusual to combine the Guaranteed and Direct Student loans. Anyone who is considering a career in a field that offers forgiveness of Direct Student Loans (see page 28) may well be a particularly suitable candidate for combining the two loans. Approval by the college financial aid officer is needed, however, and this may be difficult to obtain. If you should find yourself choosing between the Direct Student Loan and the Guaranteed Loan, by all means take the former. Even if you are not going to be working in a field where forgiveness may be obtained, the interest rate on the Direct Sudent Loan is much lower than that on the Guaranteed Loan.

Supplemental Educational Opportunity Grants

In addition to the Basic Educational Opportu-

nity Grants made by the federal government, additional funds are available to colleges through the Supplemental Educational Opportunity Grant (SEOG) program. Awarded at the discretion of college financial aid officers, these grants run between $200 and $2,000 per academic year, and are intended only for students who would not be able to attend school without such help.

Qualifying for an SEOG

Any undergraduate who is a citizen or permanent resident of the United States is eligible for the program provided that:
* in the opinion of the college's financial aid officer, the grant is necessary for the student to continue his or her education;
* the student is carrying at least 50 percent of a full academic course load;
* the student is not in default on any education loans made by the college or guaranteed by the government;
* the student gives evidence that he or she is able to maintain an acceptable academic standing.

As is the case with most monetary awards, the information contained in the student's Financial Aid Form or Family Financial Statement plays a major role in determining whether or not a grant will be awarded.

ROTC Scholarships

The Army, Navy, Marine Corps and Air Force all offer a limited number of scholarships (those offered by the Army, from one to four years; by other services, from two to four years) to both male and female undergraduates who meet the program's physical and academic standards. Because these awards may be worth more than $30,000 over a four-year period, competition for them is intense. To receive one of these scholarships, you must be attending or planning to attend a college that offers an ROTC program. In some instances, however, if you are attending a college that has no ROTC program but is near a school that does, you may be able to receive your service training at the latter and apply your scholarship money to fees charged by the other institution.

The programs offered by the services are similar, but differ in some details. For example, the Navy, Marine Corps and Air Force programs require scholarship recipients to concentrate on courses that will be useful to those services. The Army program makes fewer demands in that respect. But all of the programs require a graduate who has received scholarship aid to serve on active duty for at least four years. (Those who have service specialties in great demand, such as airplane pilots or navigators, are required to serve longer.) You will also be obligated to serve additional periods in the reserve.

For medical students, the services also operate a special ROTC program called the Armed Forces Health Professions Program. Applications are restricted to medical students who have already received ROTC commissions. Those who are awarded scholarships in this highly competitive program will have all of their medical tuition paid by the government and, in addition, will receive a monthly living allowance of approximately $500. Recipients must agree to serve a minimum of eight years in the Medical Corps of the services in which they hold commissions. High school guidance counselors, local recruiting personnel and college ROTC commands can provide complete information on these programs. You may also write to one of the following.

Army ROTC Scholarships
P.O. Box 9000
Clifton, NJ 07015

NROTC Navy Marine Corps Scholarship
    Program
P.O. Box 30
Iowa City, IA 52240

Air Force ROTC Advisory Service,
    Registrar
Maxwell AFB, AL 36112

Nursing Loans

Administered by participating colleges and schools of nursing, this program offers federally funded, low-interest loans of up to $10,000 for a four-year course, with a maximum of $2,500 per academic year. The amount actually lent is determined by the school's financial aid officer. Repayment of the loan need not begin until 9 months after the borrower has completed his or her education. Payments are quarterly at the rate of 6 percent interest; minimum payments are based on the amount of the loan, with the nursing school determining how much must be repaid each quarter. The loans may be used to obtain either an undergraduate or a graduate degree in nursing.

College financial aid officers usually have full information on these programs. If, for some reason, the information is not available to you, write to:

U.S. Public Health Service
Division of Student Services
3700 East-West Hwy.
Hyattsville, MD 20782

State Aid to College Students

Apart from their participation in the Guaranteed Loan program, all states offer their own forms of financial aid to needy students in colleges, community colleges, graduate schools and certain post-secondary technical schools. The amounts and types of aid vary greatly from state to state. A rundown of the states follows, together with the kinds of aid that are available and the addresses where complete information may be obtained. The amounts shown here are approximate; appropriations differ from year to year. Qualifying requirements also vary from state to state, but it is safe to assume that you must be a native or permanent resident of the state *to* which you are applying for funds. In some instances the money you receive must be spent at an institution within the state; in others, your grant or loan may be applied against expenses at any accredited institution within the United States. Be sure to write to the appropriate agency of your state—shown below—for the most up-to-date information.

Alabama

Student Assistance Program. Offers grants of up to $236 per semester or quarter to needy students studying at institutions within the state.

Teaching Grants. Offers up to $100 per semester to Alabama residents attending any of the following schools: University of Alabama, Auburn, University of Montevallo, Florence State College, Livingston University, Jacksonville State University and Troy State University. Recipients are required to teach within the state for at least three years.

Responsible Agency:
Alabama Student Assistance Program
Suite 221, One Court St.
Montgomery, AL 36104

Alaska

Student Loan Program. Provides loans of up to $5,000 per year at 5 percent interest to students who have been residents of Alaska for at least two years. Funds may be used at any accredited U.S. institution. Repayment begins a year after termination of studies.

Incentive Grant Program. Provides awards of up to $1,500 per year to needy students for study at approved institutions within the state.

Responsible Agency:
Alaska Department of Education
Pouch F, State Office Building
Juneau, AK 99811

Arizona

State Student Incentive Grant Program.
Administered by the three campuses of the state university. Grants are awarded at the discretion of state university administrators.

For Information:
Arizona Commission for Post-secondary Education
1650 Alameda Dr.
Tempe, AZ 85028

Arkansas

State Scholarship Program. To be eligible, students must attend institutions in the state and file for a federal Basic Educational Opportunity Grant (BEOG). The amount granted by the BEOG program helps determine the amount of the state award. Eligible students receive between $100 and $300 each year.

Responsible Agency:
Coordinator of Student Aid
Arkansas Department of Higher Education
1301 West Seventh St.
Little Rock, AR 72201

California

To be eligible for state financial aid, applicants must be residents of California. They must also submit a Financial Aid Form and apply for a federal Basic Educational Opportunity Grant (BEOG).

State Scholarships. For students attending colleges within the state. Depending on need, the award may be between $180 and $2,500 per year. Demonstrated academic ability enhances chances for an award. Applicants must submit Scholastic Aptitude Test scores.

College Opportunity Grants. Successful applicants usually but not always come from minority and low-income families. Grants vary between $500 and $900 annually, and are made on the basis of need, grades and school recommendation.

Occupational Educational and Training Grants. Annual awards of between $500 and

$2,000 are made to needy students in post-secondary vocational schools or community colleges in California who are training in areas where there is a shortage of qualified labor. Students pursuing a four-year academic program leading to a baccalaureate degree are not eligible.

Responsible Agency:
California Student Aid Commission
1410 Fifth St.
Sacramento, CA 95814

Colorado
Junior College Grant Program. Applicants enrolled in junior colleges in the state who can demonstrate need may be awarded, on a one-time basis, a grant of up to $1,000. Participating junior colleges administer the program.

Student Grant Program. Part-time or full-time students at public or private colleges in the state may apply for an award of up to $1,000 per academic year.

Colorado Work-Study Program. Provides Colorado residents with part-time jobs while they attend college within the state.

Responsible Agency:
Colorado Commission on Higher
    Education
1550 Lincoln St.
Denver, CO 80203

Connecticut
State Scholarships. Residents of Connecticut may be awarded grants of $100 to $1,000 per year to attend any accredited institution of higher education in the United States. Awards are made on the basis of class rank, Scholastic Aptitude Test scores and demonstrated financial need.

Independent College Awards. Grants in varying amounts, depending on financial need, are awarded to state residents attending private post-secondary schools within Connecticut.

State Supplemental Grant Program. Awards of up to $1,000 per academic year are given to state residents attending any Connecticut college and enrolled in at least a half-time program. Academic record and financial need determine the amount.

Connecticut Work-Study Program. Supplements the federal program to provide jobs for Connecticut residents studying at institutions within the state, and carrying at least a half-time academic load.

Responsible Agency:
Board of Higher Education for the
    State Student
Financial Assistance Commission
P.O. Box 1320
Hartford, CT 06101

Delaware
Incentive Grants and Scholarships. Awards are made on the basis of demonstrated financial need to Delaware residents in the following three categories: (1) Full-time students at in-state colleges, universities, community colleges and post-secondary technical schools may be eligible for grants of up to $900 per year. (2) Full-time students at degree-granting institutions in New Jersey and Pennsylvania may be eligible for awards of up to $500 per year in New Jersey and $600 per year in Pennsylvania under reciprocal arrangements between those states. (3) Undergraduate and graduate students at public or private institutions outside Delaware may be awarded up to $900 per year provided their particular courses of study are not available at publicly supported colleges within the state.

Responsible Agency:
Delaware Post-Secondary Education
    Commission
1228 Scott St.
Wilmington, DE 19806

Florida
Student Assistance Grants. Applicants must

have been permanent residents of Florida for two consecutive years. Grants are made only to those who are attending or planning to attend accredited institutions within the state. Amount of aid may vary from year to year depending upon available funds and the applicant's financial need.

Responsible Agency:
Florida Student Financial Assistance
    Commission
Knott Building, Room 563
Tallahassee, FL 32304

Georgia
Incentive Scholarship Program. Students who are state residents may apply for grants of $150 to $450 per academic year for study at in-state institutions. Applicants must be full-time students.

Responsible Agency:
Georgia Higher Education Assistance
    Authority
9 LaVista Perimeter Park
2187 Northlake Parkway
Tucker, GA 30084

Hawaii
Incentive Grants. Grants are made in cash or in the form of waivers of tuition at institutions within the state to needy students who have been residents of Hawaii for five years before applying. Only full-time students are qualified for this program. Students taking a half-time program at Hawaii institutions may qualify for annual $500 Merit Scholarships.

Higher Education Loans. Loans covering tuition, books and room and board may be made to full-time graduate and undergraduate students who have been residents of Hawaii for at least a year and can prove financial need. The amount of the loan depends on need. Loans carry 3 percent interest, and quarterly repayments begin nine months after the borrower ceases to be a full-time student.

Responsible Agency:
State Post-Secondary Education
    Commission
210 Bachman Hall
2444 Dole St.
Honolulu, HI 96822

Idaho
Incentive Grant Program. State residents who are full-time undergraduates and can demonstrate financial need may receive up to $2,000 per academic year for study within the state.

Scholarship Program. Students who are state residents and have demonstrated exceptional academic ability may be eligible for scholarships of up to $1,500 each year for study in Idaho.

Responsible Agency:
Office of the State Board of Higher
    Education
Jordon Building
650 West State St.
Boise, ID 83720

Illinois
Monetary Award Program. Awards of up to $1,900 per academic year are made to residents of Illinois who are United States citizens and are enrolled for a minimum of six credit hours at approved institutions within the state. Applicants must demonstrate financial need to be considered.

State Scholar Program. Awards, usually of $1,000 per academic year, are granted to those who have demonstrated superior academic ability through high scores on an exam taken during the junior year in high school. Applicants must use the scholarships at Illinois institutions, and the amount is based partly on financial need.

Responsible Agency:
Illinois State Scholarship Commission
102 Wilmot Rd.
Deerfield, IL 60015

Indiana

State Scholarship Program. Awards are made on a competitive basis to state residents about to enroll in institutions of higher education in Indiana. Applications must be filed by December 1 of the student's senior year in high school. Scholarships may be for as little as $100 or as much as $1,400 annually, and may be renewed for three years. Successful applicants must have demonstrated high academic ability on the Scholastic Aptitude Test, and financial need on the Financial Aid Form.

Freedom of Choice Grants. Awards are given to Indiana residents attending privately endowed colleges or universities within the state. Grants supplement state scholarships and educational grants to help defray higher tuition expenses at private institutions.

Educational Grants. Annual grants of $100 to $400 are awarded to students at Indiana institutions on the basis of financial need.

Responsible Agency:
State Student Assistance Commission
EDP Building
219 North Senate Ave.
Indianapolis, IN 46204

Iowa

State Scholarship Program. Offers grants to Iowa residents who are, or are about to become, freshmen or sophomores at accredited institutions of higher learning within the state. The maximum award is $600 and may be renewed for the sophomore year only. Grants are made on the basis of academic achievement and need.

Tuition Grant Program. Offers awards of up to $1,700 per year to Iowa residents attending privately endowed institutions of higher learning within the state. Awards are made solely on the basis of financial need, as demonstrated on the Financial Aid Form.

Vocational-Technical Grant Program. Awards of up to $400 per year are given to Iowa residents enrolled as full-time students in technical or vocational courses within the state.

Responsible Agency:
Iowa Higher Education Facilities
  Commission
201 Jewett Building
9th and Grant
Des Moines, IA 50309

Kansas

Tuition Grant Program. Awards of up to $1,000 per year are made to needy Kansas residents who are, or are about to be, full-time students at privately endowed institutions of higher learning within the state. Application should be made by April of the student's senior year in high school.

State Scholarships. Awards of up to $500 per year are granted to outstanding Kansas high school seniors. The amount is determined by financial need.

Responsible Agency:
Board of Regents—State of Kansas
1100 Merchants National Bank Tower
Topeka, KS 66612

Kentucky

Higher Education Grants. Awards are made to needy Kentucky residents enrolled or about to enroll in state institutions on a full-time basis. Annual grants range from $200 to $750 depending on need.

Higher Education Loans. Low-interest loans are made to needy Kentucky residents enrolled as undergraduates in institutions within the state. Loans range from $400 to $1,000 each year, and repayments need not begin until nine months after the borrower graduates.

Responsible Agency:
Kentucky Higher Education Assistance
  Authority
691 Teton Trail
Frankfort, KY 40601

Louisiana

Student Incentive Grants. Awards of $200 to $500 are made each year to Louisiana residents who are full-time students at state institutions. The amount is based on financial need.

Responsible Agency:
Louisiana Higher Education Assistance
  Commission
P.O. Box 44127, Capitol Station
Baton Rouge, LA 70804

Maine

Tuition Equalization Program. Awards of up to $900 per year are made to students who are residents of Maine and attending non-state-supported institutions of higher learning. Eligible students come from low-income families and must demonstrate financial need.

Responsible Agency:
Division of Higher Education Services
State Department of Educational and
  Cultural Services
State Education Building
Augusta, ME 04333

Maryland

General State Scholarships. Awards of $200 to $1,500 per academic year are made to Maryland residents with demonstrated academic potential and financial need. Students must submit scores on the Scholastic Aptitude Test or the American College Test, and proof of financial need. Awards are limited to those enrolled or about to be enrolled in degree-granting institutions in Maryland.

Senatorial and House of Delegates Scholarships. Requirements and awards for a Senatorial Scholarship are the same as for a General Scholarship, but application must be made to a student's state senator. For a House of Delegates Scholarship, a recommendation must come from the applicant's representative in the House of Delegates. Recipients are permitted to attend the University of Maryland or a community college within the state without paying tuition or fees. Benefits are not restricted to students attending public institutions. Recipients enrolled at private colleges in Maryland may receive up to $7,500 per academic year to defray expenses. Each member of the House of Delegates may select two students from his or her district to receive these awards.

Responsible Agency:
Maryland State Scholarship Board
2100 Guilford Ave.,
Baltimore, MD 21218

Massachusetts

General Scholarships. Awards are made to Massachusetts residents who are full-time students at in-state or out-of-state public or private institutions of higher education. Applicants who demonstrate financial need may receive annual payments equal to tuition costs at public institutions within the state, up to $600 at out-of-state public institutions or up to $900 at private institutions within or outside the state.

Honor Scholarships. Awards in varying amounts are given to four students from each Massachusetts state senatorial district. Based on scores on the Scholastic Aptitude Test, these awards can be used at any of 14 state-supported institutions of higher learning.

Responsible Agency:
Board of Higher Education
Park Square Building
31 St. James Ave.
Boston, MA 02116

Michigan

State Scholarships. Awards range from $100 to $1,200 per academic year for Michigan residents who are full-time undergraduates at colleges in the state. Successful applicants must have extremely high scores on the American College Test. The amount of the award is based on both academic potential and financial need.

Differential Grant Program. Every Michigan resident enrolled at a private college within the state is automatically granted a $500 award each year to help defray his or her academic expenses.

Tuition Grants. Michigan residents who are full-time undergraduates at private institutions within the state are eligible for these grants, which range from $100 to $1,200 per academic year. The amount of each grant is based on financial need.

Responsible Agency:
Michigan Department of Education
P.O. Box 30008
Lansing, MI 48909

Minnesota

Grant Programs. Financially needy undergraduates enrolled in institutions in the state may receive grants of up to $1,000 per year. All applicants must, however, be Minnesota residents.

Scholarship Program. Maximum scholarships of $1,000 per year are available for residents enrolled in Minnesota institutions. Applicants must have graduated in the top quarter of their high school class.

Responsible Agency:
Minnesota Higher Education Coordinating
  Board
Capitol Square Building
555 Cedar St.
St. Paul, MN 55101

Mississippi

Incentive Grant Program. Awards are made to Mississippi residents enrolled at in-state institutions who demonstrate financial need. The average annual grant is $500.

Responsible Agency:
Office of the Governor—Education
  and Training
P.O. Box 4300
Jackson, MS 39216

Missouri

Student Grant Program. Grants of up to $900 per academic year are given to state residents for study at Missouri institutions of higher learning. Awards are based on need.

Responsible Agency:
Missouri Department of Higher Education
600 Clark Ave.
Jefferson City, MO 65101

Montana

Incentive Grant Program. Grants of up to $300 per year may be awarded to Montana residents who demonstrate financial need and are enrolled as full-time students at institutions within the state.

Responsible Agency:
Commissioner of Higher Education
33 South Last Chance Gulch
Helena, MT 59601

Nebraska

Incentive Grant Program. Grants of up to $1,500 per academic year may be awarded to financially needy students who are studying full-time at state-supported institutions.

Responsible Agency:
Nebraska Coordinating Commission
  for Post-Secondary Education
301 Centennial Mall South
P.O. Box 95005
Lincoln, NB 68509

Nevada

Incentive Grant Program. An average annual grant of $290 is given to financially needy state residents attending Nevada state-supported institutions.

Responsible Agency:
Chancellor's Office
405 Marsh Ave.
Reno, NV 89509

New Hampshire

Incentive Grant Program. Residents at

degree-granting institutions in New Hampshire may be awarded between $100 and $1,500 per year. Eligibility is determined by academic achievement and financial need.

Responsible Agency:
New Hampshire Higher Education
   Assistance Foundation
61 South Spring St.
Concord, NH 03301

New Jersey

Competitive Scholarship Program. New Jersey residents who are full-time undergraduates may apply for state scholarships. Awards are based on Scholastic Aptitude Test scores and financial need. The maximum award for a student attending a New Jersey institution is $1,000 per year; for those going to out-of-state schools, the top award is $500.

Tuition Aid Grants. Grants of $200 to $1,000 per year are made to New Jersey residents attending private institutions within the state. Awards are based on the student's financial need and the institution's tuition charges.

Educational Opportunity Grants. For students who are attending New Jersey colleges full time and who are from educationally and financially deprived backgrounds. Grants for undergraduates may range as high as $1,000 per year, and for graduate students, the awards may be as much as $1,500 per year.

Responsible Agency:
Department of Higher Education
State Scholarship Commission
225 West State St.
Trenton, NJ 08625

New Mexico

Incentive Grants. Grants in varying amounts, based on financial need, are made to New Mexico residents attending public or private degree-granting institutions within the state.

State Tuition Scholarships. Awards in varying amounts are given New Mexico residents attending the University of New Mexico or New Mexico State University. Eligibility is based partly on financial need and partly on the interest of the two institutions in aiding the applicant.

Responsible Agency:
Board of Educational Finance
Legislative-Executive Building
Santa Fe, NM 67503

New York

Tuition Assistance Program. Awards of up to $1,800 per year are given to state residents enrolled in New York colleges or universities. Grants, based on family income, may be applied to undergraduate or graduate school costs.

Regents Scholarships. Awards are made on the basis of competitive examinations taken by high school seniors within the state. Scholarships of $250 per year are granted to winners attending undergraduate institutions in New York State.

Responsible Agency:
New York State Higher Education
   Services Corporation
Tower Building
Empire State Plaza
Albany, NY 12255

North Carolina

Student Incentive Grants. Needy students who are residents of the state may be eligible for grants of up to $1,500 per year at in-state public institutions.

Independent College Grants. State residents at in-state private institutions are granted $550 for freshman year upon application. Grants are renewable at the discretion of the college financial aid officer.

Contractual Grants. Awards in widely varying amounts are granted to North Carolina residents at in-state private institutions. Grants are renewable at the discretion of the school's financial aid officer.

Responsible Agency:
North Carolina State Education
 Assistance Authority
Box 2688, University Square West
Chapel Hill, NC 27514

North Dakota
Student Financial Assistance Program. Residents of North Dakota who are enrolled on at least a half-time basis in undergraduate institutions within the state may be awarded annual grants of $250 to $350 depending on financial need.

Responsible Agency:
North Dakota Student Financial
 Assistance Agency
State Capitol
Bismarck, ND 58505

Ohio
Instructional Grants Program. Ohio residents who can demonstrate financial need and are attending state-supported institutions of higher education are eligible for yearly grants of $90 to $1,500. The awards are made on the basis of the student's financial situation and the established costs at the college he or she is attending.

Responsible Agency:
Ohio Board of Regents, Student
 Assistance Office
30 East Broad St.
Columbus, OH 43215

Oklahoma
Tuition and Grants Program. Residents of the state enrolled in undergraduate institutions within Oklahoma may receive yearly awards of up to $500. Only full-time students who can demonstrate financial need are eligible.

Responsible Agency:
Oklahoma State Regents for Higher
 Education
500 Education Building
State Capitol Complex
Oklahoma City, OK 73105

Oregon
Need Grant Program. Oregon residents who are full-time undergraduates at in-state institutions and can demonstrate financial need may qualify for annual awards of up to $1,500.

Cash Award Program. Awards of up to $1,000 are made to Oregon residents of demonstrated academic ability and financial need who attend in-state institutions of higher learning.

Responsible Agency:
Oregon State Scholarship Commission
1445 Willamette St.
Eugene, OR 97401

Pennsylvania
Higher Education Grant Program. Residents of Pennsylvania who are enrolled in approved academic programs within or outside the state may be eligible for yearly assistance of $100 to $1,200. Awards are made on the basis of academic ability—as indicated by scores on the Scholastic Aptitude Test or the American College Test—and financial need. Higher awards are generally granted to students studying at Pennsylvania institutions. Students at two-year community colleges or vocational, business and nursing schools are eligible for these grants as well as those students who are attending four-year degree-granting institutions.

Responsible Agency:
Pennsylvania Higher Education
 Assistance Agency
Towne House
Harrisburg, PA 17102

Rhode Island

Grant and Scholarship Program. Awards of $250 to $1,000 are made annually to Rhode Island residents studying at public or private degree-granting institutions anywhere in the United States. Eligibility is based on a combination of Scholastic Aptitude Test scores and demonstrated financial need.

Responsible Agency:
Rhode Island Higher Education
    Assistance Authority
274 Weybosset St.
Providence, RI 02903

South Carolina

Tuition Grants Program. Residents of the state who attend private colleges in South Carolina are eligible for grants of up to $1,500 per year. Financial need and academic records are considered in making the awards.

Non-Contract Grants. Residents of South Carolina studying at out-of-state institutions may be awarded up to $500 per year if their program of study is not available within the state. Awards are made on the basis of academic achievement; financial need is not necessarily considered.

Responsible Agency:
South Carolina Tuition Grants Agency
411 Keenan Building
Columbia, SC 29201

South Dakota

Incentive Grants Program. From $200 to $1,000 may be awarded annually to needy residents of South Dakota who are enrolled in undergraduate programs at a state college.

Responsible Agency:
Department of Education and
    Cultural Affairs
State Capitol
Pierre, SD 57501

Tennessee

Student Assistance Awards. Annual awards of $100 to $1,200, depending on need, are granted to Tennessee residents attending accredited institutions within the state.

Responsible Agency:
Tennessee Student Assistance Corporation
707 Main St.
Nashville, TN 37206

Texas

Tuition Equalization Grants. Residents of Texas enrolled in private institutions of higher education within the state are eligible for yearly grants of up to $600 if the students can demonstrate financial need.

State Scholarships. Tuition and fees at state-supported institutions may be waived for students who can show financial need.

Low-Income Scholarships. Tuition and fees at state-supported colleges may be waived for Texas residents whose family incomes are below $4,800 per year and who have graduated in the top quarter of their high school classes.

Responsible Agency:
Student Services Division
Texas College and University System
P.O. Box 12788
Capitol Station
Austin, TX 78711

Utah

Incentive Grant Program. Average awards of $700 per year are made to Utah residents enrolled in state higher education institutions. Financial need must be demonstrated.

Responsible Agency:
Utah System of Higher Education
University Club Building
136 East South Temple
Salt Lake City, UT 84111

Vermont
Incentive Grant Program. Awards are made to Vermont residents who can show financial need and are studying for undergraduate degrees at institutions within the state. Grants range from $200 to $1,150 per academic year.

Responsible Agency:
Vermont Student Assistance Corporation
5 Burlington Square
Burlington, VT 05401

Virginia
College Scholarship Assistance Program. Aid may be awarded in the form of a grant or loan to needy Virginia residents enrolled in undergraduate programs within the state. Average award is about $300.

Tuition Assistance Grant and Loan Program. Grants or loans are awarded to full-time students at private colleges in Virginia. Financial need is not a deciding factor in making the awards. The size of the awards depends on the amount of money appropriated each year by the state legislature, and the number of students applying from each of the participating private colleges.

Responsible Agency:
State Council of Higher Education
700 Fidelity Building
Ninth and Main Sts.
Richmond, VA 23219

Washington
Need Grant Program. For Washington residents attending private or public colleges within the state and needing some form of financial assistance. The amount of each award varies from year to year according to the appropriations of the state legislature and the number of applicants. Write or call the address below for current information.

Tuition Waiver Program. Tuition fees may be waived in whole or in part for needy Washington residents who are students at publicly supported two- or four-year institutions within the state.

Work-Study Program. A state-subsidized program to allow colleges in Washington to employ students. Participating students must carry at least half a normal course load. The program is open to undergraduates, graduate students and those studying at professional schools.

Responsible Agency:
Council for Post-Secondary Education
Division of Student Financial Aid
908 East Fifth St.
Olympia, WA 98504

West Virginia
Higher Education Grant Program. Grants averaging less than $600 per academic year are awarded to West Virginia residents studying at undergraduate schools within the state. Financial need and academic ability must be demonstrated. The only applicants considered for these awards are those who have also requested the federal Basic Education Opportunity Grants.

Responsible Agency:
West Virginia Board of Regents
West Virginia Higher Education
   Grant Program
950 Kanawha Blvd., East
Charleston, WV 25301

Wisconsin
Higher Education Grants. Wisconsin residents enrolled at the University of Wisconsin or at state-supported vocational and adult institutions who can demonstrate financial need are eligible for grants of up to $1,800 annually.

Tuition Grant Program. Needy Wisconsin residents may qualify for annual grants of up to $1,800 if they are enrolled in in-state private institutions.

Responsible Agency:
State of Wisconsin Higher Educational
    Aids Board
Division of Student Support
150 East Gilman St.
Madison, WI 53703

Wyoming
High School Honor Scholarships. Full
tuition scholarships are granted the valedictori-
an and runner-up in the graduating class of
every Wyoming high school. Awards must be
used at a degree-granting public or private
institution within the state.

Responsible Agency:
Wyoming Higher Education Council
1720 Carey Ave.
Cheyenne, WY 82002

Other U.S. Jurisdictions
The District of Columbia, overseas territories
and commonwealths of the United States all
offer a variety of financial aid to local residents
attending institutions of higher education. The
responsible agencies are:

District of Columbia
Government of the District of Columbia
Educational Services Division
1329 East St. NW
Washington, DC 20004

American Samoa
Department of Education
Pago Pago
American Samoa 96799

Guam
Board of Regents
University of Guam
P.O. Box EX
Agana, GU 96910

Puerto Rico
University of Puerto Rico
Central Administration
G.P.O. Box 4-984-G
San Juan, PR 00936

Trust Territory
Student Assistance Office
Headquarters, Department of Education
Saipan, Mariana Islands 96950

Virgin Islands
Virgin Islands Department of Education
P.O. Box 630, Charlotte Amalie
St. Thomas, VI 00801

Special Awards by the States
Many states offer awards to students in such
specialized categories as awards to children of
servicemen killed or permanently disabled
while on active duty with the armed forces; to
children of policemen or firemen killed or disabled in the line of duty; to blind or otherwise
physically impaired students; to students at
nursing schools; to students enrolled in programs qualifying them for jobs in which critical manpower shortages exist; to students
studying to become physicians or dentists; or
to children of prisoners of war or servicemen
missing in action.

If you fall into any of the above categories,
you should, by all means, make inquiries.

A high school guidance counselor or a college financial aid officer may be aware of these
awards. If not, call or write the agency in your
home state that is responsible for state grants
and loans to college students. The addresses
may be found on pages 46–48.

Directories

At the end of most chapters in this book you will find directories of the various federal and state offices you can write to or call for action, assistance and/or information. The number of the page on which the applicable office is listed is given in the main text. If you are calling, you can get the telephone number from your local directory or "Information."

In dealing with the federal government, service is often faster if your request is made directly to the state or regional office rather than to Washington, D.C. Getting what you want from a bureaucracy is frequently frustrating and time consuming, but you will probably find the experience less so by making full use of the directories in this book.

Directory of State Departments of Education

Alabama
State Department of Education
State Office Building
501 Dexter Ave.
Montgomery, AL 36130

Alaska
State Department of Education
Pouch F, State Office Building
Juneau, AK 99811

Arizona
Department of Education
1535 W. Jefferson St.
Phoenix, AZ 85007

Arkansas
State Department of Education
State Capitol Grounds
Little Rock, AR 72201

California
State Department of Education
721 Capitol Mall
Sacramento, CA 95814

Colorado
Department of Education
State Office Building
201 E. Colfax St.
Denver, CO 80203

Connecticut
State Department of Education
P.O. Box 2219
Hartford, CT 06115

Delaware
State Department of Public Instruction
Townsend Building, P.O. Box 1402
Dover, DE 19901

District of Columbia Public Schools
415 12th St., NW
Washington, DC 20004

Florida
State Department of Education
Knott Education Building
Tallahassee, FL 32304

Georgia
State Department of Education
State Office Building
Atlanta, GA 30334

Hawaii
State Department of Education
P.O. Box 2360
Honolulu, HI 96804

Idaho
State Department of Education
Len B. Jordan Office Building
Boise, ID 83720

Illinois
Office of Education
100 N. First St.
Springfield, IL 62777

Indiana
State Department of Public Instruction
State House
Indianapolis, IN 46204

Iowa
State Department of Education
Grimes State Office Building
Des Moines, IA 50319

Kansas
State Department of Education
120 E. 10th St.
Topeka, KS 66612

Kentucky
State Department of Education
Frankfort, KY 40601

Louisiana
State Department of Education
626 N. 4th St.
P.O. Box 44064
Baton Rouge, LA 70804

Maine
State Department of Educational and Cultural
    Services
Augusta, ME 04330

Maryland
State Department of Education
BWI Airport
P.O. Box 8717
Baltimore, MD 21240

Massachusetts
State Department of Education
31 St. James Ave.
Boston, MA 02116

Michigan
State Department of Education
P.O. Box 30008
Lansing, MI 48909

Minnesota
State Department of Education
Capitol Square Building
St. Paul, MN 55101

Mississippi
State Department of Education
Sillers State Office Building
P.O. Box 771
Jackson, MS 39205

Missouri
Department of Elementary and Secondary
  Education
P.O. Box 480, 100 E. Capitol
Jefferson City, MO 65102

Montana
Office of Public Instruction
State Capitol Building Room 106
Helena, MT 59601

Nebraska
State Department of Education
P.O. Box 94987
Lincoln, NE 68509

Nevada
Department of Education
Capitol Complex
400 W. King St.
Carson City, NV 89710

New Hampshire
State Department of Education
State House Annex
64 N. Main St.
Concord, NH 03301

New Jersey
State Department of Education
225 W. State St.
Trenton, NJ 08625

New Mexico
Education and Cultural Affairs Departments
State Capitol Complex
Santa Fe, NM 87503

New York
State Education Department
Education Building
Albany, NY 12234

North Carolina
State Department of Education
Education Building
Raleigh, NC 27611

North Dakota
State Department of Public Instruction
State Capitol
Bismarck, ND 58501

Ohio
State Department of Education
65 S. Front St.
Columbus, OH 43215

Oklahoma
State Department of Education
Oliver Hodge Memorial Education Building
Oklahoma City, OK 73105

Oregon
Department of Education
942 Lancaster Drive NE
Salem, OR 97310

Pennsylvania
State Department of Education
Box 911
Harrisburg, PA 17126

Rhode Island
State Department of Education
199 Promenade St.
Providence, RI 02908

South Carolina
State Department of Education
Rutledge Building
1429 Senate St.
Columbia, SC 29201

South Dakota
Department of Education and Cultural Affairs
Kneip Office Building
Pierre, SD 57501

Tennessee
State Department of Education
100 Cordell Hull Building
Nashville, TN 37219

Texas
Texas Education Agency
201 E. 11th St.
Austin, TX 78701

Utah
State Board of Education
250 E. Fifth South St.
Salt Lake City, UT 84111

Vermont
State Department of Education
Montpelier, VT 05602

Virginia
Department of Education
Box 6Q
Richmond, VA 23216

Washington
State Superintendent of Public Instruction
Old Capitol Building FG-11
Olympia, WA 98501

West Virginia
State Department of Education
1900 Washington St., E.
Charleston, WV 25305

Wisconsin
State Department of Public Instruction
126 Langdon St.
Madison, WI 53702

Wyoming
State Department of Education
Hathaway Building
Cheyenne, WY 82002

American Samoa
Department of Education
Education Building
Pago Pago, American Samoa 96799

Guam
Department of Education
P.O. Box DE
Agana, GU 96910

Northern Mariana Islands
Department of Education
Education Building
Saipan, Mariana Islands 96950

Puerto Rico
Department of Education

P.O. Box 759
Hato Rey, PR 00910

U.S. Virgin Islands
State Department of Education
P.O. Box 630
St. Thomas, VI 00801

Chapter I Coordinators

Alabama
Coordinator, Chapter I
State Department of Education
State Office Building
Montgomery, AL 36104

Alaska
Coordinator, Chapter I
State Department of Education
Pouch F, State Office Building
Juneau, AK 99811

Arizona
Education Program Director, Chapter I
State Department of Education
1535 W. Jefferson St.
Phoenix, AZ 85007

Arkansas
Associate Director for Federal Programs
State Department of Education
Arch Ford Education Building
Little Rock, AR 72201

California
Assistant Superintendent for Compensatory Education
State Department of Education
721 Capitol Mall
Sacramento, CA 95814

Colorado
Supervisor, Chapter I
State Department of Education
State Office Building
Denver, CO 80203

Connecticut
Coordinator, Chapter I
State Department of Education
P.O. Box 2219
Hartford, CT 06115

Delaware
State Supervisor, Chapter I
State Department of Public Instruction
Townsend Building
Dover, DE 19901

District of Columbia
Coordinator, Chapter I
Public Schools of the District of Columbia
415 12th St., NW
Washington, DC 20004

Florida
Coordinator, Compensatory Education
State Department of Education
Knott Education Building
Tallahassee, FL 32304

Georgia
Director, Chapter I
State Department of Education
Atlanta, GA 30334

Hawaii
Administrator, Compensatory Education Section
State Department of Education
1270 Queen Emma St.
Honolulu, HI 96813

Idaho
Chief, Bureau of Compensatory Education
State Department of Education
Len B. Jordan Office Building
Boise, ID 83720

Illinois
Director, Chapter I
State Office of Education
100 N. First St.
Springfield, IL 62777

Indiana
Director, Division of Compensatory Education
State Department of Public Instruction
State House
Indianapolis, IN 46204

Iowa
Chief of Chapter I
State Department of Public Instruction
Grimes State Office Building
Des Moines, IA 50319

Kansas
Director, Chapter I
State Department of Education
120 E. Tenth St.
Topeka, KS 66612

Kentucky
Director, Division of Compensatory Education
State Department of Education
Frankfort, KY 40601

Louisiana
Coordinator, Chapter I
State Department of Education
Baton Rouge, LA 70804

Maine
Coordinator, Chapter I
State Department of Educational and Cultural Services
Augusta, ME 04330

Maryland
Chief, Chapter I
State Department of Education
BWI Airport, P.O. Box 8717
Baltimore, MD 21240

Massachusetts
Director, Chapter I
State Department of Education
31 St. James Ave.
Boston, MA 02116

Michigan
Director, Compensatory Education Services
State Department of Education
P.O. Box 420
Lansing, MI 48902

Minnesota
Coordinator, Chapter I
State Department of Education
Capitol Square Building
St. Paul, MN 55101

Mississippi
Coordinator, Chapter I
State Department of Education
P.O. Box 771
Jackson, MS 39205

Missouri
Director, Chapter I
Department of Elementary and Secondary Education
P.O. Box 480, 100 E. Capitol
Jefferson City, MO 65102

Montana
Manager, Chapter I
Office of the State Superintendent of Public Instruction
State Capitol Building
Helena, MT 59601

Nebraska
Director, Chapter I
State Department of Education
233 S. Tenth St.
Lincoln, NE 68508

Nevada
Federal Liaison and Coordination
State Department of Education
400 W. King St.
Carson City, NV 89710

New Hampshire
Coordinator, Chapter I
State Department of Education
64 N. Main St.
Concord, NH 03301

New Jersey
Coordinator, Chapter I
State Department of Education
225 W. State St.
Trenton, NJ 08625

New Mexico
Director, Chapter I
State Department of Education
Santa Fe, NM 87503

New York
Director, Division of Federal Education Opportunity
    Programs
State Education Department
Albany, NY 12234

North Carolina
Director of Compensatory Education
State Department of Public Instruction
Raleigh, NC 27611

North Dakota
Coordinator, Chapter I
State Department of Public Instruction
Bismarck, ND 58501

Ohio
Coordinator, Chapter I
State Department of Education
933 High St.
Worthington, OH 43085

Oklahoma
Administrator, Compensatory Education
State Department of Education
2500 N. Lincoln Blvd.
Oklahoma City, OK 73105

Oregon
Coordinator, Chapter I
State Department of Education
942 Lancaster Dr., NE
Salem, OR 97310

Pennsylvania
Chief of Compensatory Programs
Bureau of Special and Compensatory Education
State Department of Education
P.O. Box 911
Harrisburg, PA 17126

Rhode Island
Coordinator, Compensatory Education
State Department of Education
235 Promenade St.
Providence, RI 02908

South Carolina
Coordinator, Chapter I
State Department of Education
1429 Senate St.
Columbia, SC 29201

South Dakota
Acting Coordinator, Chapter I
Division of Elementary and Secondary Education
Pierre, SD 57501

Tennessee
Director, Compensatory Education
State Department of Education
221 Cordell Hull Building
Nashville, TN 37219

Texas
Director, Division of Federal Funding
Texas Education Agency
201 E. 11th St.
Austin, TX 78701

Utah
Director, Chapter I
State Board of Education
250 E. Fifth South St.
Salt Lake City, UT 84111

Vermont
Director, Division of Federal Assistance
State Department of Education
State Office Building
Montpelier, VT 05602

Virginia
Director, Chapter I
State Department of Education
Box 6Q
Richmond, VA 23216

Washington
Assistant Superintendent, Division of Special Programs
  and Equal Educational Opportunity
State Superintendent of Public Instruction
Old Capitol Building
Olympia, WA 98504

West Virginia
Director of Compensatory Education
State Department of Education
Charleston, WV 25305

Wisconsin
Administrator, Chapter I
State Department of Public Instruction
126 Langdon St.
Madison, WI 53702

Wyoming
Coordinator, Program Services for
  the Educationally Disadvantaged
State Department of Education
Cheyenne, WY 82002

American Samoa
Federal Grants Manager
Department of Education
Pago Pago, American Samoa, 96799

Guam
Administrator, Federal Programs
Department of Education
P.O. Box DE
Agana, GU 96910

Northern Mariana Islands
Assistant Director of Education
Department of Education
Education Building
Saipan, North Mariana Islands 96950

Puerto Rico
State Chapter I Coordinator
Department of Education
Hato Rey, PR 00919

Trust Territory of Pacific Islands
Fiscal/Federal Programs Coordinator
Department of Education
Office of the High Commissioner
Trust Territory of the Pacific Islands
Saipan, Mariana Islands 96950

U.S. Virgin Islands
Chapter I Coordinator
Department of Education
P.O. Box 630
St. Thomas, VI 00801

Bureau of Indian Affairs
Chief, Division of Educational Assistance
Bureau of Indian Affairs
P.O. Box 1788
Albuquerque, NM 87103

United States Catholic Conference
Representative for Federal Assistance Programs
Division of Elementary and Secondary Education
1312 Massachusetts Ave., NW
Washington, DC 20005

Council for American Private Education
Executive Director
Council for American Private Education
1625 Eye Street, NW
Washington, DC 20006

National Advisory Council on the Education of
  Disadvantaged Children
425 13th Street, NW
Washington, DC 20004

Guaranteed Loan Agencies

Alabama
Regional Administrator
Office of Education, Region IV
50 Seventh St., NE
Atlanta, GA 30323

Alaska
Student Aid Office
State Education Department
Pouch F,
State Office Building
Juneau, AK 99811

Arizona
Regional Administrator
Office of Education, Region IX
50 United Nations Plaza
San Francisco, CA 94102

Arkansas
Student Loan Guarantee Foundation of Arkansas
1515 West 7th St.
Little Rock, AR 72202

California
Regional Administrator
Office of Education, Region IX
50 United Nations Plaza
San Francisco, CA 94102

Colorado
Regional Administrator
Office of Education, Region VIII
11037 Federal Office Building
19th and Stout Sts.
Denver, CO 80202

Connecticut
Connecticut Student Loan Foundation
25 Pratt St.
Hartford, CT 06103

Delaware
Delaware Higher Education Loan Program
c/o Brandywine College
P.O. Box 7139
Wilmington, DE 19803

District of Columbia
D.C. Student Loan Insurance Program
1329 E St., NW
Washington, DC 20004

Florida
Florida Student Financial Assistance Commission
Knott Building
Tallahassee, FL 32304

Georgia
Georgia Higher Education Assistance Corporation
9 LaVusta Perimeter Park
2187 Northlake Pkwy.
Tucker, GA 30084

Hawaii
Regional Administrator
Office of Education, Region IX
50 United Nations Plaza
San Francisco, CA 94102

Idaho
Regional Administrator
Office of Education, Region X
1321 Second Ave.
Seattle, WA 98101

Illinois
Illinois Guaranteed Loan Program
102 Wilmot Rd.
Deerfield, IL 60015

Indiana
State Student Assistance Commission
219 N. Senate Ave.
Indianapolis, IN 46202

Iowa
Regional Administrator
Office of Education, Region VII
601 E. 12th St.
Kansas City, MO 64106

Kansas
Higher Education Assistance Foundation
51 Corporate Woods
9393 W. 110th St.
Overland Park, KS 66210

Kentucky
Kentucky Higher Assistance Authority
691 Teton Trail
Frankfort, KY 40601

Louisiana
Louisiana Higher Education Assistance Commission
P.O. Box 44127
Capitol Station
Baton Rouge, LA 70804

Maine
State Department of Education and Cultural
  Services
Augusta, ME 04330

Maryland
Maryland Higher Education Loan Corporation
2100 Guilford Ave.
Baltimore, MD 21218

Massachusetts
Massachusetts Higher Education Assistance
  Corporation
1010 Park Square Building
Boston, MA 02116

Michigan
Michigan Higher Education Assistance Authority
309 North Washington Ave.
Lansing, MI 48902

Minnesota
Higher Education Assistance Foundation
1100 Northwestern Bank Building
55 E. 5th St.
St. Paul, MN 55101

Mississippi
Regional Administrator
Office of Education, Region VII
50 Seventh St., NE
Atlanta, GA 30323

Missouri
Regional Administrator
Office of Education, Region VII
601 E. 12th St.
Kansas City, MO 64106

Montana
Regional Administrator
Office of Education, Region VIII
11037 Federal Office Building
19th and Stout Sts.
Denver, CO 80202

Nebraska
Regional Administrator
Office of Education, Region VII
601 E. 12th St.
Kansas City, MO 64106

Nevada
State Department of Education
400 W. King St.
Carson City, NV 89701

New Hampshire
New Hampshire Higher Education Assistance
  Foundation
61 S. Spring St.
Concord, NH 03301

New Jersey
New Jersey Higher Education Assistance Authority
1474 Prospect St.
P.O. Box 1417
Trenton, NJ 08625

New Mexico
Regional Administrator
Office of Education, Region VI
1200 Main Tower Building
Dallas, TX 75202

New York
New York State Higher Education Services
  Corporation
Tower Building
Empire State Plaza
Albany, NY 12255

North Carolina
North Carolina Assistance Authority
P.O. Box 2688
Chapel Hill, NC 27514

North Dakota
Regional Administrator
Office of Education, Region VIII
11037 Federal Office Building
19th and Stout Sts.
Denver, CO 80202

Ohio
Ohio Student Loan Commission
34 North High St.
Columbus, OH 43215

Oklahoma
Oklahoma State Regents for Higher Education
500 Education Building
State Capitol Complex
Oklahoma City, OK 73105

Oregon
State of Oregon Scholarship Commission
1445 Willamette St.
Eugene, OR 97401

Pennsylvania
Pennsylvania Higher Education Assistance Agency
Towne House
660 Boas St.
Harrisburg, PA 17102

Puerto Rico
Regional Administrator
Office of Education, Region II
26 Federal Plaza
New York, NY 10022

Rhode Island
Rhode Island Higher Education Assistance Corporation
274 Weybosset St.
Providence, RI 02903

South Carolina
Regional Administrator
Office of Education, Region IV
50 Seventh St., NE
Atlanta, GA 30323

South Dakota
Regional Administrator
Office of Education, Region VIII
11037 Federal Office Building
19th and Stout Sts.
Denver, CO 80202

Tennessee
Tennessee Student Assistance Corporation
707 Main St.
Nashville, TN 37206

Texas
Regional Administrator
Office of Education, Region VI
1200 Main Tower Building
Dallas, TX 75201

Utah
Utah Higher Education Assistance Authority
807 East South Temple
Salt Lake City, UT 84103

Vermont
Vermont Student Assistance Corporation
156 College St.
Burlington, VT 05401

Virginia
Virginia State Educational Assistance Authority
501 E. Franklin St.
Professional Building
Richmond, VA 23219

Washington
Regional Administrator
Office of Education, Region X
1321 Second Ave.
Seattle, WA 98101

West Virginia
Regional Administrator
Office of Education, Region III
P.O. Box 13716
3535 Market St.
Philadelphia, PA 19101

Wisconsin
Wisconsin Higher Education Corporation
123 W. Washington Ave.
Madison, WI 53703

Wyoming
Regional Administrator
Office of Education, Region VIII
11037 Federal Office Building
19th and Stout Sts.
Denver, CO 80202

Chapter 2

Your Job:
When You Have One
and When You Don't

Through the years, Congress and the state legislatures have enacted a
series of laws to assure U.S. wage earners a reasonable standard of living
and enable them to enjoy the fruits of their labors. Included among
these measures have been the minimum wage; protection against discrimination
in hiring, promotions and firing; provisions for job safety and health;
and compensation for illness, injury and unemployment.
As a working person, you are entitled to the full protection of these laws.
This chapter takes you through your working life—from the day you start
looking for a job until you are ready to retire—explaining the benefits,
services and protections that you are entitled to, and telling you how
to avail yourself of them. You'll also be told about some of the pitfalls
you may encounter. The chapter concludes with a discussion of the government
help you may be able to claim if you decide to go into business for yourself.

Contents

Finding a Job

The federal government and the 50 states maintain a nationwide network of 2,600 employment offices. Supported by funds drawn from unemployment insurance payroll deductions, these offices bear a variety of names. Most of them are called Job Service offices, but some go under the names of State Employment Commission, State Employment Service, or Employment Security Commission. (See page 89 for a listing of main offices of state employment agencies. For local offices, see the state government listing in your telephone book.)

Regardless of their names, the employment offices are designed to serve a common purpose: to help employees and employers by matching qualified candidates with employment opportunities. To accomplish this assignment, the employment offices offer a broad variety of services, all of which are available to the job seeker and employer free of charge.

If you go to your local office during a recession or an economic downturn, you will probably see long lines of people waiting to sign for their unemployment compensation checks. But this is only one of the many important functions performed by the employment offices.

The most important, perhaps, are the interviewing and placement of job service applicants. The interviews are conducted by trained professionals who will question you about your education, training and job experience. You will be classified according to your occupational skills and aptitudes and assigned a number from the U.S. Labor Department's *Dictionary of Occupational Titles.*

The interviewer will then study a computer printout or punch out your number on a keyboard and scan the job listings that appear on the screen of a computer terminal. Gathered from employers, the job listings afford in capsule form a quick rundown on the specific employment opportunities that are available in the area.

If one of the capsule descriptions matches your qualifications, the interviewer may pick up the phone, call the employer and arrange an appointment for you to be interviewed for the job.

Counseling and Advice

If you have never held a job before, or are not sure what line of work you are suited for, professional counselors at the employment office can test your aptitudes and skills and recommend a course of action. Particular attention is given to job seekers with special problems: youngsters who have dropped out of school; veterans returning to civilian life; people who are in deadend jobs and want to make a move; women who are looking for jobs after time out for childbearing and family raising; handicapped people; and older workers whose training and skills may be obsolete in the current job market.

In addition to the counseling and advice, the skilled professionals may be able to plot a course that will make up for the job candidate's shortcomings in education, training and experience. And if the applicant has had trouble in adjusting to a working environment or getting along with superiors and fellow employees, the counselor can refer him or her to the appropriate agencies for psychological or rehabilitation aid.

Special Help for Veterans

A federal law requires that veterans be accorded top preference in job referrals. Each government employment office is staffed by a special veterans' representative to assist men and women who have served in the armed forces. Job centers in the nation's 100 largest cities also maintain a staff of disabled veterans who are charged with seeking out other disabled vets and informing them of their education and employment rights. In addition, the federal government operates a variety of programs to aid veterans in making the transition from military service to civilian jobs. These programs are described in Chapter 6.

Aid for the Handicapped

Every government employment office is required by federal law to maintain at least one staff member who specializes in counseling the handicapped and aiding them in acquiring needed skills and finding jobs. Applicants with physical, mental or emotional disabilities are eligible for this aid. Alcoholism, drug addiction, orthopedic disabilities, visual, speech and hearing impairments and psychiatric problems are included in this category for which assistance is available.

After the counseling and testing have been completed, the employment office may then arrange a job interview, or refer the handicapped applicant to outside agencies for training or rehabilitation. (A full discussion of job assistance for the handicapped appears in Chapter 5.)

High Marks for the Employment Office

Among the more systematic approaches to job hunting, government employment offices are second in effectiveness only to newspaper help-wanted ads. There are, of course, other approaches to job hunting. Most people find employment by word of mouth from friends or relatives. A direct approach to the employer—going to the office or plant and applying on the spot—is also a sound method. Private employment agencies, too, can often be helpful. If you are truly eager to find a job, the best approach is to combine as many methods as possible. Ask your friends and acquaintances whether they know of any job openings. Study the newspaper ads; list yourself with a government employment office and perhaps a private employment agency. Attack on as many fronts as possible, and follow up every lead.

Tips for a Job Interview

When you are interviewed for a job, you will be judged by your appearance, your record and the clarity and quickness of your answers. The interviewer will probably be seeing dozens of people and will have to size you up in a hurry.

It is essential, therefore, that you show yourself in the best light and not make careless or foolish mistakes.

Here are some tips from the U.S. Department of Labor on how to conduct yourself in a job interview.

They were designed for young people seeking summer employment, but much of the advice applies to anyone who is being interviewed for a job.

1. Find out about the company where you are going for an interview. (Ask the personnel or business office for printed material or consult the employees.) Knowing about the company's jobs may help you decide what to say about yourself.

2. Take along your work record and references.

3. Dress conservatively—in a dress or pantsuit if you are a girl, in trousers and a neat shirt if you are a boy. Do not wear "fad" or flamboyant clothes.

4. Report for your interview promptly—and alone. Don't bring anyone along.

5. Answer the employer's questions honestly and briefly. Don't talk about personal matters unless you are asked. Do tell about your qualifications completely—without exaggeration. Your job is to show why the company should hire you instead of another applicant.

6. If your first interview does not lead to a job offer, don't be discouraged. Few people get the first job they apply for—and often not the second or third either. Think over each interview and decide what you did that made a good impression—and what you might do better. Then try again.

Whether you find a job through a government employment office or not, you should be aware of the many kinds of assistance that this office can provide for you. The variety of free services—job counseling, testing and job advice, for example—cannot be matched elsewhere except at a considerable cost.

Recessions and Downturns

Government employment offices are, of course, at the mercy of the economy. In times of recessions or economic downturns, the pickings are likely to be slim. But even then the employment offices have an important mission to perform. By keeping in close touch with employers, the offices can list available job opportunities as quickly as possible and make it easier for unemployed workers to find the job openings that do exist. "The thing that we do best," says an official of the employment service, "is to minimize or shorten the duration that a job is unfilled."

Out-of-State Jobs

If you have an unusual or highly developed skill, the government employment office may be able to find you a job in another part of the country through its interstate clearance system. The state of Iowa, for example, might have a job opening for which no one in the state has applied. The Iowa office may then transmit the job description to other states, and applicants in any part of the country may apply for the job.

The Job Information Service

If you have no luck on your first visit to the state employment office, you can go back as often as you like and bring yourself up to date on the job opportunities. Most employment offices have a special section called the Job Information Service, where you can study the latest job openings on computer printouts, microfilm, microfiche viewers or bulletin boards. Videotapes offer you valuable tips on how to dress for a job interview and how to go about applying for a job.

The People Who Get Jobs

In a recent year, 80 million "job transactions" occurred in the U.S. This means that there were 80 million hirings in the country, but it does *not* mean that 80 million people were involved. Not all of the transactions represented new job opportunities; some involved seasonal hirings or the end of layoffs or similar situations in which the same people were rehired for the same jobs.

Out of these 80 million transactions, 6.4 million people found their jobs through state employment offices. A breakdown of this figure throws some light on your chance of finding employment. The largest group of successful job hunters were young people entering the labor market for the first time. Next came women who were returning to work, or finding jobs after time out for pregnancies and family raising. More than two-fifths of the job finders were under 22, nearly a third were from minority groups and one out of six was a veteran.

The jobs that were obtained through state employment offices were mostly in manufacturing, clerical, service and sales areas, and the top salary range was $20,000 to $25,000. The people who found their jobs through government employment offices generally tended to earn more than those with similar backgrounds who found employment through other routes.

Employers and Government Employment Offices

The profile of the successful job seeker suggested by the figures just cited indicates who is most likely to find employment through government offices. The kinds of employers who use these offices provide additional clues.

A study of job hunting and recruitment through government employment offices shows that in cities of 100,000 to 250,000 population, the state employment offices are used with much greater frequency by large, older firms than by smaller, new ones. The study also showed that manufacturing establishments rely heavily on these offices. Service industries, machine and benchwork trades also use them frequently. Construction firms and financial institutions, however, rarely use state employment offices.

The Offices' Value to Employers

Government employment offices perform valuable services for employers by providing a ready source of free information concerning the availability of workers and their special aptitudes and skills. The employer who needs a trained clerical worker or machinist, for example, can list the job opening with the state employment office and hope to find a worker without making an independent, expensive search. For those who are setting up new businesses, the state office can organize a task force to find trained workers. If unusual skills are required, the employer can draw upon the nationwide clearance service to bring in specially qualified workers.

The services provided by the state offices can result in substantial savings for employers. By listing job openings with the offices, a business executive can cut down on the staff, time and money that would be needed to find new workers. By taking advantage of the employment offices' resources, the prudent manager can draw upon a larger reservoir of talents and skills than would otherwise be available. Moreover, the employer may take satisfaction from the fact that the government aid is simply a return on an investment, because the service is supported by unemployment-insurance payroll deductions.

Tax Breaks for Employers

In an effort to reduce hard-core unemployment, Congress decided in 1978 to provide tax breaks for employers who hire certain categories of workers. Included are nine groups of workers who have traditionally had a hard time finding employment:

Handicapped workers referred from rehabilitation programs of the Veterans Administration.

Young people aged 18 through 24 from low-income families.

Supplemental Security Income recipients (U.S. citizens or legally admitted aliens who are aged, blind or disabled and have little or no income or financial resources).

Economically disadvantaged veterans from the Vietnam era.

People who have been on welfare for 30 days or more.

Economically disadvantaged young people aged 16 through 18 who are participating in cooperative educational courses conducted by high schools or other agencies.

Ex-felons from low-income families.

Former holders of state and local public assistance (CETA) jobs.

People who qualify for the Work Incentive (WIN) Program (page 63) or Aid to Families with Dependent Children (AFDC).

The tax-credit allowance amounts to 50 percent of the first $6,000 in wages paid during the first year of employment and 25 percent of the first $6,000 during the second year. Vouchers are issued to eligible workers by the state employment offices. When hired for a new job, the worker gives the voucher to the employer, who fills it out and mails it to the state employment office. The employment office then sends the employer a certificate to be used in claiming the tax credit with the Internal Revenue Service (IRS).

Detailed information on the tax-credit program may be obtained from the state employment office or the IRS.

Federal, State and Local Governments as Employers

The nation's largest employer is the U.S. government, which has nearly three million people, not including military personnel, on its payroll. More than 90 percent of all federal jobs are located outside Washington, D.C., and almost every kind of skill is utilized.

Government agencies hire computer programmers, forest rangers, editors, home econ-

Federal Government Salaries for White Collar Workers

White collar workers for the federal government are paid on a graduated scale based upon their skills, responsibilities and length of service. Salaries range from $8342 for entry level clerical workers to a ceiling of $50,112.50 imposed by Congress on supervisory and managerial jobs at GS-15 through GS-18 levels. Raises in grade occur over 10 different steps. Promotions from grade to grade also carry raises. Senior appointive officials are paid on a different scale, with salaries ranging up to $69,630 for cabinet level positions.

General Schedule – 1981
Annual Rates and Steps

	1	2	3	4	5	6	7	8	9	10
GS-1	8342	8620	8898	9175	9453	9615	9890	10165	10178	10439
2	9381	9603	9913	10178	10292	10595	10898	11201	11504	11807
3	10235	10576	10917	11258	11599	11940	12281	12622	12963	13304
4	11490	11873	12256	12639	13022	13405	13788	14171	14554	14937
5	12854	13282	13710	14138	14566	14994	15422	15850	16278	16706
6	14328	14806	15284	15762	16240	16718	17196	17674	18152	18630
7	15922	16453	16984	17515	18046	18577	19108	19639	20170	20701
8	17634	18222	18810	19398	19986	20574	21162	21750	22338	22926
9	19477	20126	20775	21424	22073	22722	23371	24020	24669	25318
10	21449	22164	22879	23594	24309	25024	25739	26454	27169	27884
11	23566	24352	25138	25924	26710	27496	28282	29068	29854	30640
12	28245	29187	30129	31071	32013	32955	33897	34839	35781	36723
13	33586	34706	35826	36946	38066	39186	40306	41426	42546	43666
14	39689	41012	42335	43658	44981	46304	47627	48950	50273	51596
15	46685	48241	49797	50112	. . . .	. . . .	. . . .	. . . .	. . . .	. . . .
16	54755	56580	. . . .	. . . .	. . . .	. . . .	. . . .	. . . .	. . . .	. . . .
17	. . . .	. . . .	. . . .	. . . .	. . . .					
18	. . . .									

omists, secretaries, clerks, bookkeepers, engineers, geologists—the list is almost endless. Salaries are generally comparable to those in the private sector, vacation time is generous and promotion programs are systematically used to encourage employees to make their careers with the federal government.

How to Find a Federal Government Job

Most federal jobs are competitive and in great demand. Applicants must vie with one another for the openings and be evaluated by the government's main hiring agency, the Office of Personnel Management, which succeeded the Civil Service Commission in 1979. Standards are usually high.

The place to start looking for a government job is one of the Federal Job Information Centers (FJICs) in major cities of every state. (A list of the cities appears on page 90; the FJICs are listed in telephone directories under "U.S. Government.") Information specialists in these offices can provide you with up-to-date information on the job prospects, occupations in demand and application and examination procedures (where applicable). Employment counseling services are also available at the federal job centers.

If you find a job opening that interests you, the information specialist will supply you with an application form and a description of the qualifications needed. If you lack the training and qualifications that are called for, there is no point in applying. Your application will not be accepted.

Most federal jobs do not require written tests, but there are exceptions, mainly for clerical and administrative positions. If you are applying for the first time, or for certain specified categories at the entry level, you may be required to take the Professional and Administrative Career Examination (PACE), or a similar test. The test will measure your general ability and aptitude in the kind of work you are applying for. It is not the kind of examination you can prepare for by taking a "cram course" or enrolling in a special school.

After you have taken the test, you will be informed of your score, and you will be placed on the civil service list in keeping with that score. If the job is not one that requires a test, you will be evaluated by the Office of Personnel Management on the basis of your education, experience and training, and your name will be placed on the list.

The General Schedule of Government Ratings

The government grades its employees on a General Schedule, with ratings ranging from GS-1 to GS-18. Clerical workers are usually rated GS-1, 2 or 3. Guards are GS-4, and white-collar workers with experience or education equal to a college degree start at GS-5. The top ratings are reserved for managerial and supervisory jobs.

A job opening suited to your qualifications and experience may not exist when you apply. In that case, your name will be placed on a list and will remain there until a job opening occurs. When that happens, "the rule of three" will apply. The Office of Personnel Management will forward the names of the top three applicants to the government agency that is doing the hiring.

The law does not require the agency to select the top job candidate. The agency will interview the applicants, and it may choose any one of the three provided that none is a veteran. If one of them *is* a veteran, the law specifies that he or she may not be passed over for a non-veteran.

When the choice has been made and an applicant has been hired, the two people who were not chosen go back on the Office of Personnel Management's list and may be hired when another opening occurs.

Anyone who believes he or she was not treated fairly in the selection process may appeal to the Office of Personnel Management within 15 days after the announcement of the results. Those who think that they were discriminated against because of race, creed, color, sex, national origin or physical or mental handicaps are allowed 30 days to file a written complaint.

Credits for Veterans. Veterans are favored for federal jobs not only under the "rule of three" but also by a system of special credits. A veteran receives points for his military service; a Purple Heart or service-connected disability entitles him to additional points. Widows and widowers of veterans with wartime service or service-connected disabilities also receive points. Spouses of veterans with service-connected disabilities, and the mothers of some veterans, are also favored under the point system.

Temporary and Permanent Federal Employment. Federal job appointments may be limited to a definite number of years, or they may be "career-conditional," meaning that they can lead to permanent employment after a probationary period.

Temporary workers are hired for a year or less. They may not transfer to other government jobs and are not eligible for health and life insurance benefits.

Some employees are hired for special projects that will last more than a year but less than four years. They may be promoted or assigned to different jobs on the project for which they were hired. These employees are eligible for health and life insurance but are not covered by the government's retirement program.

Sample Questions for Clerk-Typist Test

Applicants for most federal jobs do not have to take qualifying tests, but there are some exceptions to the rule. Clerk-typists may be required to demonstrate their ability to type and their basic skills in spelling, grammar and language comprehension. Reprinted below is a sample from a test given to applicants for federal clerk-typist jobs in New York.

The following sample questions show types of questions found in the written test you will take. They also show how your answers to the questions are to be recorded on a separate answer sheet. The questions on the test may be harder or easier than those shown here, but a sample of each *kind* of question on the test is given.

Read these directions, then look at the sample questions and try to answer them. Each question has several suggested answers lettered A, B, C, etc. Decide which one is the best answer to the question. Then, in the Sample Answer Sheet box, find the answer space that is numbered the same as the number of the question, and darken completely the oval that is lettered the same as the letter of your answer. Then compare your answers with those given in the Correct Answers to Sample Questions box. For some questions an explanation of the correct answer is given immediately following the sample question.

Vocabulary. For each question like 1 through 3, choose the one of the four suggested answers that means most nearly the same as the word in *italics.*

1. *Option* means most nearly
   A) use   C) value
   B) choice   D) blame

2. *Innate* means most nearly
   A) eternal   C) native
   B) well-developed   D) prospective

3. To *confine* means most nearly to
   A) restrict   C) eliminate
   B) hide   D) punish

Grammar. In questions 4, 5, and 6, decide which sentence is preferable with respect to grammar and usage suitable for a formal letter or report.

4. A) If properly addressed, the letter will reach my mother and I.
   B) The letter had been addressed to myself and my mother.
   C) I believe the letter was addressed to either my mother or I.
   D) My mother's name, as well as mine, was on the letter.

The answer to question 4 is D. The answer is not A because the word *me* (reach . . . me) should have been used, not the word *I.* The answer is not B. The expression, *to myself,* is sometimes used in spoken English, but it is not acceptable in a formal letter or report. The answer is not C, because the word *I* has been used incorrectly, just as it was in A.

5. A) Most all these statements have been supported by persons who are reliable and can be depended upon.
   B) The persons which have guaranteed these statements are reliable.
   C) Reliable persons guarantee the facts with regards to the truth of these statements.
   D) These statements can be depended on, for their truth has been guaranteed by reliable persons.

6. A) Brown's & Company employees have recently received increases in salary.
   B) Brown & Company recently increased the salaries of all its employees.
   C) Recently Brown & Company has increased their employees' salaries.
   D) Brown & Company have recently increased the salaries of all its employees.

Spelling. In questions 7 through 9, find the correct spelling of the word among the choices lettered A, B, or C and darken the proper answer space. If no suggested spelling is correct, darken space D.

7. A) athalete   C) athlete
   B) athelete   D) none of these

In question 7 an extra letter has been added to both A and B. The fourth letter in A makes that spelling of *athlete* wrong. The fourth letter in B makes that spelling of *athlete* wrong. Spelling C is correct.

8. A) predesessor   C) predecesser
   B) predecesar   D) none of these

All three spellings of the word are wrong. The correct answer, therefore, is D because none of the printed spellings of *predecessor* is right.

The career-conditional appointment begins with a probationary period in which you must demonstrate your competence. You may be dismissed on general grounds for poor job performance during the first year, but when that period has passed, specific evidence of misconduct, delinquency or inefficiency must be shown. You can achieve career status after three years. Then you will be the last to be laid off when cutbacks occur. New employees rarely receive career appointments unless they have already served satisfactorily for three years in another agency.

Fingerprinting and Investigations. If you are chosen for a federal job, you will be fingerprinted and your fingerprints will be checked against those on file with the FBI. You will also be investigated by the Office of Personnel Management or the government agency that hires you. The nature of the investigation will be determined by the sensitivity of your duties. If the job is sensitive in terms of national security, your friends, former employers, teachers and other acquaintances will probably be interviewed, and your employment records checked *before* you start work. If the position is not sensitive, your records, employers and references will be checked *after* you are on the job.

The Summer Job Program for Students
Most federal agencies hire college and high school students in clerical, administrative and other sub-professional jobs during the summer months. The jobs pay at the regular federal rate and are available not only in Washington but in government offices across the country. In a recent year, approximately 45,000 students availed themselves of these job opportunities.

The federal government's Office of Personnel Management publishes an announcement of the job possibilities every year. Appearing early in December, it is known as Announcement 414, and may be obtained at any of the Federal Job Information Centers listed on page 90.

Students may apply for as many jobs as they like. Written tests may be required for clerical positions.

The federal government formerly maintained a summer intern program for campus leaders in colleges and universities across the country, but that program has recently been discontinued.

State and Municipal Jobs
State and local governments employ some 13 million people in clerical jobs, elementary and secondary education, police and fire departments, public utilities, sewer and sanitation services, libraries, colleges, universities, public housing and a host of other activities. Approximately 36 percent of the state jobs are concentrated in seven states: California, Illinois, Michigan, New York, Ohio, Pennsylvania and Texas. The ratio of public employees to population in these states is, however, among the lowest in the nation. In a recent year, for example, Illinois employed 101 people per 10,000 population, whereas the sparsely populated state of Alaska had 389 state employees for every 10,000 people. (A chart of numbers of state and local employees appears in the box on page 62.)

Most of these state and local jobs are civil service positions. Special qualifications are needed to fill many of them, and tests or proof of aptitudes and skills may be required. You can find out about these requirements from the appropriate agencies when you apply for a job.

If you are interested in working for the state, you should apply at a state employment office. But if you are interested in a teaching job—the largest single category of occupations on state payrolls—you should apply to the local Board of Education in your state.

Most municipalities have their own personnel offices. Application should be made there or at the particular office or department where you want to work.

Special Work Programs
The federal government supports a broad spec-

Federal, State and Local Employees

One worker out of six in the United States is a federal, state or local government employee. The U.S. government, with 2.9 million workers, is the nation's largest employer. State and municipal governments, with responsibility for education, highways, fire and police protection and other local services, employ a total of 13.3 million people.

October 1980

Function	All governments	Federal Government (civilian)	State and local governments
Employees (thousands)			
Full-time and part-time	16,222	2,907	13,315
National defense			
and international relations	976	976	. . .
Postal service	664	664	. . .
Space research and technology	24	24	. . .
Education	6,867	26	6,841
Highways	563	5	559
Health and hospitals	1,675	266	1,408
Police protection	716	56	659
Natural resources	519	291	228
Financial administration	426	110	316
General control	621	65	555
All other	3,173	424	2,749

trum of work programs for people with special employment problems. Among the beneficiaries are the young, handicapped individuals, veterans, members of low-income families and older workers.

Employment Opportunities for Young People

The U.S. Department of Labor's Employment and Training Administration sponsors a variety of youth-oriented work programs. Best known, perhaps, is the Job Corps, which was authorized under the Comprehensive Employment and Training Act and is aimed at young people from low-income families who are in the age group of 16 through 21.

The Job Corps maintains a network of 104 centers across the country where educational, health-care and vocational training plus counseling are available for young people. Courses are taught in carpentry, auto repair, masonry, painting, nursing, clerical work, electronics and other skills.

Job Corps trainees are provided with room and board, clothing, books and cash allowances. Training is conducted by experienced workers and professional instructors. In addition to instruction in job skills, courses are offered in reading, mathematics, the social sciences, hygiene, grooming and getting along on the job.

Enrollment in the Job Corps usually extends over a year, but some trainees remain in the program for up to two years. Application may be made at state employment offices (see page 89).

Before the Reagan Administration came into

office, the federal government maintained a variety of other job training programs for disadvantaged young people under the Comprehensive Employment and Training Act. These programs were aimed at equipping young people with vocational skills and work experience that would enable them to enter the job market, whether specific employment opportunities were available or not.

The Reagan Administration decided to alter the approach by tying the training to specific job opportunities in the private sector. Under the new approach, the U.S. Department of Labor allocates funds to 475 city and county governments. These agencies, in turn, subcontract job-training assignments to schools, companies and other centers where job skills are taught.

Further information may be obtained from the state employment offices listed on page 89.

State and Local Summer Jobs

State and municipal governments frequently have available summer jobs in parks, playgrounds, offices and other facilities. The best place to find out about these jobs is through state employment offices or at the facilities themselves.

Private employers often have summer jobs in camps, resorts, amusement parks, ice cream and soft drink plants, theaters, motels, stores, business offices and factories. Temporary employees may be needed to fill in for vacationing full-time workers, or to help out with seasonal summer business. Some of these facilities may not start hiring until the season is about to begin, but it won't hurt to get in touch with them beforehand, get your name on the job list and find out what the prospects are.

Apprenticeship Programs

The Labor Department's Bureau of Apprenticeship and Training combines with private industry and labor unions to provide unskilled young men and women with on-the-job training in more than 700 lines of work. Job cate-

gories in the program include automobile mechanics, bricklayers, carpenters, electricians, machinists, structural steel workers and tool and die makers.

Young people who have reached the age of 16 are eligible to apply. Wage rates start at about half the trained worker's pay, climbing to approximately 95 percent of full pay toward the end of the courses. Training periods range from one to six years. Entry examinations are required for some occupations, and high school diplomas or general education certificates are a prerequisite for others.

Further information of the apprenticeship programs can be obtained at state employment offices across the country (see page 89).

Aid for Older Workers

The Office of National Programs for Older Workers of the U.S. Labor Department's Employment and Training Division administers the Senior Community Service Employment Program (SCSEP), providing part-time jobs for economically disadvantaged older workers. Participants in this program are employed approximately 20 hours per week in day care centers, schools, hospitals, libraries and almost every kind of public facility where help is needed. Many of the older workers are also used in conservation, restoration and beautification projects. Such work can be especially beneficial for those retired men and women who are incapable of holding full-time jobs, but need to supplement their income.

Services available to the older workers include annual physical examinations, counseling, training and job placements. SCSEP projects can be found in every state and territory of the United States. Information on these programs may be obtained from state employment agencies, or from state and area agencies on aging (see Chapter 8).

The Work Incentive (WIN) Program

People who qualify for Aid to Families with Dependent Children (AFDC) receive job help under the Work Incentive Program, operated jointly by the Labor Department and the Department of Health and Human Services (formerly HEW) through state employment offices and welfare agencies. The program provides job information, aid in finding employment, child care and medical services.

Anyone who receives AFDC is required to register with the local WIN representative unless specifically exempted. WIN activities also include conferences on job qualifications and openings and preparations for employment. Registrants are required to take part in these activities and to accept appropriate jobs. Refusal without cause may result in loss of AFDC benefits.

Child Labor Laws

In the early days of our history, child labor was widespread. The Industrial Revolution created labor shortages, and children were used in great numbers in factories. The diary of George Washington recorded that in a Boston duck-cloth factory "each spinner has a small girl to turn the wheel."

Corporal punishment was administered to keep the children awake. Testimony heard in the Pennsylvania legislature in 1837 indicated that factory children were frequently whipped. In Rhode Island, "the whipping room" was regarded as "an indispensable appendage to a cotton mill."

Children were frequently injured or maimed. As child labor became more widespread and the hours more oppressive, popular concern for the young people's welfare grew, and fear that their education was being neglected led to action.

The state of Massachusetts passed the first child labor law in 1836, ordering that "no child under the age of 15 years shall be employed to labor in any manufacturing establishment, unless such child shall have attended some public or private day school . . . at least three months of the 12 months next preceding

any and every year, in which such child shall be employed."

Other states adopted laws limiting the number of hours worked by children and setting age limits for youngsters employed in factories. A federal Children's Bureau was established in 1912 with orders to "investigate and report upon all matters pertaining to the welfare of children." A year later the U.S. Labor Department was formed, and the Children's Bureau was placed under its jurisdiction.

By that time the basic principles of child labor laws were widely accepted. All except nine states had set 14 as the minimum age for factory work. Protection against dangerous and unhealthful work conditions had been incorporated into the penal codes of many states. The Walsh-Healey Public Contracts Act, passed by Congress in 1936, prohibited the employment of boys under 16 or girls under 18 on all government contracts of more than $10,000.

The Fair Labor Standards Act

In 1938 Congress enacted the Fair Labor Standards Act, setting 16 as the minimum age for most jobs and empowering the Labor Department to establish 18 years as the lower limit for hazardous occupations. Today, young people are protected by a combination of federal and state laws. When these laws differ, the stricter standard prevails.

The federal law allows 18-year-olds to work at all kinds of jobs. Youngsters who are 16 may hold jobs that have not been specifically declared hazardous by the Secretary of Labor.

Working hours for 14- and 15-year-olds are carefully limited. Youngsters of these ages may work in non-hazardous occupations for no more than 3 hours on a school day, or 18 hours during a school week. The total number of hours may be raised to 8 hours on non-school days, and 40 hours during non-school weeks.

Children of any age may deliver newspapers and appear in television, radio or theatrical productions. They may also work for their parents in businesses except manufacturing and hazardous occupations.

Selected State Child Labor Standards Affecting Minors Under 18

Child labor laws are designed to protect the health of children and to enable them to attend school to a minimum age of 16. The provisions vary from one state to another, but the hours are generally controlled to minimize interference with school work. Limits are lowered for farm work. Shown below is a representative sampling of states with major child labor provisions.

State or other jurisdiction	Documentary proof of age required up to age indicated	Maximum daily and weekly hours and days per week for minors under 16 unless other age indicated	Nightwork prohibited for minors under 16 unless other age indicated	Minimum age for agricultural employment outside school hours
Alabama	17; 19 in mines and quarries.	8-40-6. Schoolday/week: 4-28.	8 p.m. to 7 a.m.	
California	18	8-48-6, under 18. Schoolday: 4, under 18 if required to attend school 4 or more hours.	10 p.m. (12:30 a.m. before nonschoolday) to 5 a.m., under 18.	14 (12 during vacation and on regular school holidays).
Florida	18	10-40-6. Schoolday: 4 when followed by schoolday, except if enrolled in vocational program.	9 p.m. (11 p.m. before non-schoolday) to 6:30 a.m. 11 p.m. (1 a.m. before non-schoolday to 5 a.m. (may be extended under certain conditions), 16 and 17.	...
Illinois	16	8-48-6. Schoolday: 3 [8h].	7 p.m. (9 p.m. June 1-Labor Day) to 7 a.m.	10
Massachusetts	18	8-48-6. 4-24 in farmwork, under 14. 9-48-6, 16 and 17.	6 p.m. to 6:30 a.m. 10 p.m. (midnight in restaurants on Friday, Saturday and vacation) to 6 a.m., 16 and 17.	...
Michigan	18	10-48-6, under 18. Schoolweek: 48, under 18.	9 p.m. to 7 a.m. 10:30 p.m. to 6 a.m., 16 and 17 if attending school. 11:30 p.m. to 6 a.m., 16 and 17 if not attending school.	...
New York	18	8-40-6. 8-48-6, 16 and 17. Schoolday/week: 3-23, under 16. 4-28, 16 if attending school.	7 p.m. to 7 a.m. Midnight to 6 a.m., 16 and 17.	14 (12 on home farm for parents, and in hand harvest of berries, fruits and vegetables with parental consent under specified hours standards.)
Ohio	18	8-40 Schoolday/week: 3-18.	7 p.m. (9 p.m. June 1 through September 1 or during school holidays of 5 days of more) to 7 a.m.	...
Texas	15	8-48, under 15	10 p.m. to 5 a.m., under 15.	14 (no minimum from June 1 to September 1).
Wisconsin	18	8-24-6 when school in session and 8-40-6 in non-schoolweek. 8-40-6 when school in session and 8-48-6 in nonschoolweek (voluntary overtime per day and week permitted up to 50-hour week), 16 and 17 if required to attend school.	8 p.m. (9:30 before nonschoolday) to 7 a.m. 12:30 a.m. to 6 a.m., except where under direct adult supervision, and with 8 hours rest between end of work and schoolday, 16 and 17 if required to attend school.	12

Enforcement of these laws is overseen by wage and hour inspectors across the United States. Violations may result in fines of up to $1,000 for each offense.

Farm Work for Children

Youngsters may engage in any kind of farm work, hazardous or not, when they have reached the age of 16. Employment for 15-year-olds or younger is limited to non-hazardous work that does not conflict with school hours. For those who are 12 or 13, the labor must be performed on farms where the children's parents are owners or employees, or with the written consent of the parents if the work is to be done elsewhere.

Trends in State Laws

Child labor laws in most states are directly tied to school attendance. All states have compulsory school-attendance laws, and most of them require children to be in school for the entire session. In some cases, however, children who work may be excused from school if they are 14 and have completed the eighth grade.

In recent years, state legislatures have tended to relax some child labor requirements. Protection against hazardous work and the exploitation of youngsters has been maintained, but provisions affecting night work, maximum hours and certification for jobs have grown more lenient. Restrictions on night work for 16- and 17-year-olds, for example, have been eliminated in North Carolina, Ohio, Tennessee and Virginia. (Major provisions of state child labor laws are shown on page 65.)

Right-to-Work Laws

Whether you will have to join a labor union when you take a new job will depend on where you work. In 1935 Congress passed the National Labor Relations Act (known as the Wagner Act, after Senator Robert F. Wagner of New York), guaranteeing workers the right to organize and bargain collectively. Several kinds of union agreements emerged:

1. The closed shop: In which the employer agrees to hire only union members, and continuous membership is an essential condition of employment.

2. The union shop: The worker is not required to belong to a union when he or she takes a job, but must join the union in 30 days (7 days in the construction industry) and remain a member for the duration of the employment.

3. The agency shop: The worker does not have to belong to the union, but must pay union dues after joining the company.

States With Right-To-Work Laws

In the past 40 years, more than a third of the states have enacted "right-to-work" laws or constitutional amendments barring the requirement that workers must join labor unions as a condition of obtaining or holding their jobs. The states with right-to-work laws are listed below.

Alabama	Iowa	Nevada	Tennessee
Arizona	Kansas	North Carolina	Texas
Arkansas	Louisiana	North Dakota	Utah
Florida	Mississippi	South Carolina	Virginia
Georgia	Nebraska	South Dakota	Wyoming

4. Maintenance of membership: Employees may join or refuse to join the union at the time of the signing of the contract. Those who join then or subsequently must maintain their membership as a condition of employment.

The Taft-Hartley law, enacted by Congress in 1947, outlawed the closed shop. The act also prohibited the union shop, but Congress overrode that provision in 1951 with an amendment to Taft-Hartley allowing the union shop if it has been approved by a majority vote of the employees.

Since World War II, 20 states have adopted "right-to-work" laws outlawing the requirement that employees join a union or pay union dues in order to hold their jobs. The states with right-to-work laws are shown on page 66.

Equal Job Opportunities

Discrimination in employment based on race, color, religion, sex or national origin is prohibited by Title VII of the 1964 Civil Rights Act and its admendments. All private employers, federal, state and local governments, labor unions, educational institutions and apprentice programs are covered by the provisions of that act.

Under Title VII, the Equal Employment Opportunity Commission (EEOC) was created to eliminate discrimination in public offices, and by private employers of 15 or more employees.

The U.S. Department of Labor's Office of Federal Contracts Compliance Programs (OFCCP) is charged with the responsibility for eliminating discrimination among contractors and subcontractors doing business with the federal government. Under the Carter Administration, contractors doing $10,000 of business per year with the federal government were affected. The Reagan Administration proposed to raise the figure to $1 million per year. A clause in the contracts of these businesses and corporations bars discrimination in recruitment, hiring, training, pay, seniority, promo-

tions and benefits. Protection is especially aimed at minorities, women, handicapped people, Vietnam era veterans (those who served at home or overseas during the Vietnam war) and disabled veterans of all wars.

The responsibilities of EEOC and OFCCP overlap to some degree. As a practical matter, however, the EEOC handles complaints of discrimination by individuals, whereas the OFCCP concerns itself mainly with *patterns* of discrimination and may initiate reviews without complaint.

Affirmative Action Programs

In the 1970s, Affirmative Action programs were established to encourage employers to make up for the effects of past discrimination against certain groups and individuals.

Targeted under these programs were the traditional victims of discrimination: women, minorities, veterans, certain religious and ethnic groups and handicapped individuals. Contractors and subcontractors doing business with the federal government were required, under certain circumstances, to prepare written Affirmative Action programs and implement them to the satisfaction of federal employers.

In cases where women and members of minority groups were under-represented, employers were ordered to set timetables for the hiring and promotion of members of these groups. Special training programs were required of some employers and, in some instances, employers had to satisfy federal inspectors that workers who appeared to be stuck in low-level or mid-level positions would be afforded opportunities for advancement in the future.

The Reagan Administration announced that it would concentrate its efforts on the elimination of discrimination, rather than the implementation of Affirmative Action programs. Efforts to establish quotas for the hiring and promotion of members of minorities and other affected groups amounted to "fighting dis-

Dubious Questions on Job Forms and in Interviews

The Economic Employment Opportunity Commission (EEOC) and the courts have held that certain questions may be discriminatory and should not be asked in job interviews or on application forms unless it can clearly be shown that the requested information is directly related to the performance of the job.

The following subjects impose upon the employer the burden of showing "through statistical evidence" that the information being sought is directly related to the performance of the job. The EEOC's reasons for including each topic are presented under each heading.

1. *Age:* The Age Discrimination in Employment Act of 1967 prohibits discrimination on the basis of age against people between the ages of 40 and 70. EEOC guidelines hold that "because the request that an applicant state his age may tend to deter older applicants or otherwise indicate a discrimination based on age, employment application forms which request such information . . . will be closely scrutinized to assure that the request is for a permissible purpose and not for purposes proscribed by the statute."

2. *Race, Color, Religion, Sex or National Origin:* Inquiries on an application form about race, color, religion, sex or national origin are not considered violations of the federal law in and of themselves, but may constitute evidence of discrimination.

However, some state laws expressly prohibit such inquiries on employment applications. In certain states it is sometimes illegal to request a photograph, former name, past residence, names of relatives, birthplace, citizenship, education, organizational activities or color of the eyes and hair.

3. *Height and Weight:* The EEOC and the courts have held that minimum height and weight requirements are illegal *if* they screen out a disproportionate number of minority-group individuals (e.g., Spanish-surnamed or Asian Americans) or women, and the employer cannot show that these standards are essential to the safe performance of the job.

4. *Citizenship:* EEOC guidelines hold that consideration of an applicant's citizenship may constitute evidence of discrimination on the basis of national origin.

5. *English Language Skill:* Testing or scoring an individual in English language proficiency when English language skill is not a requirement of work to be performed is a violation of Title VII of the 1964 Civil Rights Act.

6. *Education:* The U.S. Supreme Court has held that an employer's requirement of a high school education was discriminatory where statistics showed that the requirement tended to disqualify blacks at a substantially higher rate than whites and there was no evidence that it was significantly related to successful job performance.

7. *Availability for Work on Weekends or Holidays:* Questions relating to availability for work on Friday evenings, Saturdays, Sundays or holidays are not automatically considered violations of the law, but employers and unions have an obligation to accommodate the religious beliefs of employees and applicants unless undue economic hardship will be caused.

8. *Marital Status, Number of Children and Provision for Child Care:* Questions about marital status, pregnancy, future childbearing plans and number and ages of children may be a violation of Title VII of the 1964 Civil Rights Act if used to deny or limit employment of women. It is illegal to require pre-employment information about child care arrangements from female applicants only. The U.S. Supreme Court has held that an employer may not have different hiring prac-

tices for men and for women with pre-school children.

9. *Economic Status:* Rejection of job applicants because of poor credit ratings has been held to be unlawful by the EEOC unless a business necessity can be shown. Inquiries about bankruptcy, car ownership, rental or ownership of a house, length of residence at an address or past garnishment of wages may be illegal if used in making employment decisions.

10. *Arrest Records:* Because members of some minority groups are arrested substantially more often than whites in proportion to their number in the population, the courts and EEOC have held that without proof of a business necessity it is unlawful to use arrest records to disqualify job applicants.

11. *Conviction Records:* Federal courts have held that a conviction for a felony or a misdemeanor may not by itself constitute an absolute bar to employment, but an employer may give fair consideration to the relationship between a conviction and an applicant's fitness for a particular job.

12. *Friends or Relatives Working for the Employer:* EEOC holds that information regarding friends or relatives working for an employer is irrelevant to an applicant's competence. Requests for such information may be unlawful if they indicate a preference for friends or relatives of present employees.

The EEOC believes that much of the information that might be discriminatory—such as the date of birth, marital status, number and ages of children—can be asked after a person has been employed rather than before, if it is needed for legitimate business purposes such as Social Security, insurance or other reporting requirements.

crimination with discrimination," a spokesman for the Reagan Administration said. Such efforts would be downplayed in favor of an attack on existing patterns of discrimination.

Bringing a Discrimination Charge

Any individual or group of employees who feel that their rights have been violated may file a complaint with the Equal Employment Opportunity Commission or the Office of Federal Contract Compliance. A complaint filed by an individual with the OFCCP is, however, likely to wind up with the EEOC.

Complaints must be filed within 180 days of the alleged incidents of discrimination. The EEOC maintains 49 field offices (a list of these offices and their addresses appears on page 91) around the country, and charges may be lodged with any of these offices by a telephone call, letter or personal visit. If the allegation appears to be valid, the EEOC will draft a formal letter to the employer setting forth the charges.

The employer is invited to respond to these charges at a fact-finding conference at the EEOC field office, where an attempt will be made to iron out the differences. Nearly half of the conferences result in settlements that are acceptable to both sides.

The commission may decide that a charge lacks merit, or it may confirm the allegations brought by the employee. In the latter case, the commission will send a letter to the employer setting forth the steps that must be taken to correct the abuses within a given period.

Compliance reviews are held from time to time to determine whether the proscribed practices have been eliminated.

Failure to comply with the commission's orders may result in the loss of government contracts, and the commission may bring suit in a federal court. The suit may be brought in the name of an individual or as a "class action" on behalf of a group of employees.

Many states and municipalities have fair employment offices. These agencies work in close conjunction with the EEOC, and may also handle discrimination charges.

Equal Pay Act

In 1963 Congress passed the Equal Pay Act, barring the payment of different wages to men and women who are doing substantially the same work in the same place of employment. The act also prohibits employers from cutting back on the wages of either sex in order to achieve equality.

The law is not intended to affect pay differences based on seniority, merit or productivity. The legislation was designed to eliminate discrimination based solely on sex.

Enforcement of the Equal Pay Act for employees of private firms and of state and local governments is carried out by the EEOC. Complaints may be filed with any EEOC office.

The Women's Bureau

Nearly half of the civilian workers in the United States are women. To protect their job rights and promote their economic advancement, the U.S. Labor Department maintains a separate Women's Bureau.

The Bureau focuses mainly on the elimination of sex discrimination in employment and training, job stereotyping of women, occupational safety for women and the dissemination of information concerning women's job opportunities. It serves as an advocate and adviser to special categories of women who have experienced unusual difficulties in obtaining employment or who have been the victims of discrimination on the job. Included in these categories are minority women; older women who are attempting to find jobs or to re-enter the work force after time out for childbearing or family raising; women who are divorced, separated or widowed; young women seeking work for the first time; physically abused women in need of employment counseling, training and job-search help; ex-offenders; low-income women; rural women; and women who are going into business for themselves.

The bureau provides technical advice for working women. It serves as an advocate for women's causes but is not an employment office and is not empowered to enforce its policies.

Aid from the Women's Bureau can be obtained from its national headquarters at the U.S. Labor Department, 200 Constitution Ave. NW, Washington, DC 20210, or through any of the regional labor department offices listed on page 89.

Age Discrimination

The law protects people between 40 and 70 against age discrimination. All public and private employers with 20 or more employees and labor unions with at least 25 members are covered. The protection of the law extends to hiring, firing, pay rates and promotions.

Exceptions are made where age can be shown to be relevant to the job—for example, young actors may be hired for youthful roles, or young women for a "Junior Miss" fashion show.

The law forbidding age discrimination is enforced by the Equal Employment Opportunity Commission. Complaints may be filed at any EEOC office (page 91). The commission investigates complaints and brings court actions when they appear to be called for. If the EEOC does not act, the employee may file suit on his or her own.

The Minimum Wage

In the early part of the century, many American workers, including women and children, toiled in sweatshops and factories where wages were barely sufficient to keep them alive. In 1911, the state of Massachusetts decided to form a committee to study the pay scales for women and children in retail stores, laundries and candy factories. In 1912 the state passed the country's first minimum wage law for these two groups.

In the next decade, 14 states followed suit. In 1923, however, the U.S. Supreme Court declared a minimum wage law for the District of Columbia unconstitutional, thereby undermining all such laws. The decision was overturned in 1937, and the following year the Congress passed the Fair Labor Standards Act, calling for a minimum wage of 25 cents per hour with an increase to 40 cents after seven years on the job. By the early part of 1981, the minimum wage had risen to $3.35 per hour.

Most workers engaged in producing, handling, selling or working on goods or materials in interstate commerce are covered by the federal minimum wage. This includes retail or service enterprises doing a gross annual business of not less than $362,500 per year and all other businesses with a gross annual sales of $250,000 or more. Laundry and dry cleaning establishments, construction firms, hospitals, homes for the aged, mentally or physically handicapped, kindergartens, elementary and high schools and colleges and universities are also included. The federal minimum wage applies as well to communications and transportation workers, people engaged in shipping or handling goods in interstate commerce, clerical workers or others who regularly use the mails, telephone and telegraph workers and others who regularly cross state lines in the course of their work.

Tips as Part of the Minimum Wage

Waiters, porters, hairdressers, cab drivers and others who regularly receive tips should expect that a part of this income will be counted toward the minimum wage. The law allows the employer to take 40 percent of the gratuities into account in figuring the minimum wage. The law also provides that the reasonable value of board, lodging and other facilities furnished by an employer may be counted, provided that payments to the employee do not fall below the minimum wage.

Exceptions to the Minimum Wage

In certain situations, learners, apprentices and handicapped workers may be paid less than the minimum wage. The employer who wishes to take advantage of these exceptions must obtain a special certificate from the Wage and Hour Division of the U.S. Labor Department.

State Minimum Wages

State minimum wages are in effect in 41 states plus Puerto Rico and the District of Columbia. (A chart of minimum wages appears on pages 72–73.)

These wage rates apply to all businesses not covered by the federal minimum wage. Mainly affected by the wage rates are small retail and service businesses.

In 1980, 16 states had minimum wage rates equal to or higher than the federal rates for some or all occupations. Where state and federal minimum wages come into conflict, the employer must pay the higher minimum wage. This will assure compliance with both the state and federal laws.

The Workweek and Overtime

The Fair Labor Standards Act sets a basic workweek of 40 hours, with time and a half for overtime for all workers covered by the federal minimum wage. Hospitals and nursing homes are exempted. With the agreement of the employees, these institutions may adopt a basic 14-day work period. The employees must be paid time and a half for working more than 8 hours in a day or more than 80 hours during the 14-day period. Federal, state and local employees are covered by the minimum wage and the overtime provisions of the Fair Labor Standards Act.

People Not Covered by Overtime

Overtime coverage does not extend to employees in schools, hospitals, fire departments, sanitation departments, public health jobs, parks or other recreational facilities. Employees of airlines and railroads, taxi drivers, seamen on U.S. vessels, domestic workers living at their places of employment, farm workers, employ-

71

Changes in Federal and State Minimum Wages From 1965 to 1981

State or other jurisdiction	1965(a)	1968(a)	1970(a)	1972
Federal (FLSA)	$1.15 & $1.25	$1.15 & $1.60	$1.30 & $1.60	$1.60
Alaska	1.75	2.10	2.10	2.10
Arizona	18.72-26.40/wk.(b)	18.72-26.40/wk.(b)	18.72-26.40/wk.(b)	18.72-26.40/wk.(b)
Arkansas	1.25/day(b)	1.25/day(b)	1.10	1.20
California	1.30(b)	1.65(b)	1.65(b)	1.65(b)
Colorado	.60-1.00(b)	1.00-1.25(b)	1.00-1.25(b)	1.00-1.25(b)
Connecticut	1.25	1.40	1.60	1.85
Delaware	...	1.25	1.25	1.60
Florida	...	...	...	...
Georgia	...	...	...	1.25
Guam	...	...	...	...
Hawaii	1.25	1.25	1.60	1.60
Idaho	1.00	1.15	1.25	1.40
Illinois	...	...	...	1.40
Indiana	...	1.15	1.25	1.25
Iowa	...	...	...	...
Kansas	...	...	...	...
Kentucky	.65-.75(b)	.65-.75(b)	.65-.75(b)	.65-.75(b)
Louisiana	...	...	...	...
Maine	1.00	1.40	1.60	1.40-1.80
Maryland	...	1.00 & 1.15	1.30	1.60
Massachusetts	1.25	1.60	1.60	1.75
Michigan	1.00	1.25	1.25	1.60
Minnesota	.70-1.15(b)	.70-1.15(b)	.75-1.60(b)	.75-1.60
Mississippi	...	...	...	...
Missouri	...	...	...	...
Montana	...	...	...	1.60
Nebraska	...	1.00	1.00	1.00
Nevada	1.15(b)	1.25	1.30	1.60
New Hampshire	1.25	1.40	1.45-1.60	1.60
New Jersey	1.00-1.50(b)	1.40	1.50	1.50
New Mexico	.70-.80	1.15-1.40	1.30-1.60	1.30-1.60
New York	1.25	1.60	1.60	1.85
North Carolina	.85	1.00	1.25	1.45
North Dakota	.75-.85(b)	1.00-1.25	1.00-1.45	1.00-1.45
Ohio	.70-1.00(b)	.75-1.25(b)	.75-1.25(b)	.75-1.25(b)
Oklahoma	...	1.00	1.00	1.40
Oregon	.75-1.00	1.25	1.25	1.25
Pennsylvania	1.00	1.15	1.30	1.60
Rhode Island	1.25	1.40	1.60	1.60
South Carolina	...	...	...	...
South Dakota	17.00-20.00/wk.(b)	17.00-20.00/wk.	1.00	1.00
Tennessee	...	...	...	...
Texas	...	...	...	1.40
Utah	.95-1.10(b)	1.00-1.15(b)	1.00-1.15(b)	1.20-1.35(b)
Vermont	1.00	1.40	1.60	1.60
Virginia	...	...	...	...
Washington	1.25	1.60	1.60	1.60
West Virginia	...	1.00	1.00	1.20
Wisconsin	1.00-1.10(b)	1.25(b)	1.30(b)	1.45(b)
Wyoming	.75	1.20	1.30	1.50
Dist. of Col.	40.00-46.00/wk.(b)	1.25-1.40	1.60-2.00	1.60-2.25
Puerto Rico	.35-1.25	.43-1.60	.43-1.60	.65-1.60
Virgin Islands	...	...	...	...

*Prepared by the Division of State Employment Standards, Employment Standards Administration, U.S. Department of Labor. Rates are for January 1 of each year, except in 1968 and 1972 which show rates as of February. The rates are per hour unless otherwise indicated. A range of rates, as in North Dakota and a few other states, reflects rates which differ by industry, occupation, geographic zone, or other factors, as established under wage-board type laws.

(a) Under the federal Fair Labor Standards Act (FLSA), the two rates shown in 1965, 1970, and 1976 reflect the former multiple-track minimum wage system in

Most U.S. workers are covered by the federal minimum wage. Others, mostly in small businesses, are covered by state laws. States not listed below do not have minimum wage laws.

1976(a)	1979	1981
$2.20 & $2.30	$2.90	$3.35
2.80	3.40	3.85
...	...	...
1.90	2.30	2.70
2.00	2.90	3.35
1.00-1.25(b)	1.90	1.90
2.21 & 2.31	2.91	3.37
2.00	2.00	2.00
...	...	...
1.25	1.25	1.25
...	...	3.35
2.40	2.65	3.35
1.60	2.30	2.30
2.10	2.30	2.30
1.25	2.00	2.00
...	1.60	1.60
1.60	2.00	2.15
...	...	...
2.30	2.90	3.35
2.20 & 2.30	2.90	3.35
2.10	2.90	3.35
2.20	2.90	3.35
1.80	2.30	3.10
...	...	...
...	...	...
1.80	2.00	2.50
1.60	1.60	1.60
2.20 & 2.30	2.75	2.75
2.20-2.30	2.90	3.35
2.20	2.50	3.35
2.00	2.30	3.35
2.30	2.90	3.35
2.00	2.50	2.90
2.00-2.20	2.10-2.30	2.80 to 3.10
1.60	2.30	1.50 to 2.30
1.80	2.00	1.00 to 3.10
2.30	2.30	3.10
2.20	2.90	3.35
2.30	2.30	3.10
...	...	...
2.00	2.30	2.30
...	...	...
1.40	1.40	1.40
1.55-1.70(b)	2.20-2.45(b)	2.50 to 2.75
2.30	2.90	3.35
2.00	2.35	2.65
2.20-2.30	2.30	2.30
2.00	2.20	2.75
2.10	2.80	3.25
1.60	1.60	1.60
2.25-2.75	2.46-3.00	2.50 to 3.90
.76-2.50	1.20-2.50	1.20 to 2.50
...	...	3.35

effect from 1961 to 1978. The lower rate applied to newly covered persons brought under the act by amendments, whose rates were gradually phased in. A similar dual-track system was also in effect in certain years under the laws in Connecticut, Maryland, and Nevada.

(b) The law applies only to women and minors.

ees in motion picture theaters, TV and radio announcers and news editors and chief engineers of certain non-metropolitan broadcasting stations are exempted from the overtime provisions. Also excluded are some retail and service establishment employees who are on commission, as well as auto, aircraft, farm implement and boat sales-people, plus mechanics and parts suppliers for automobiles, trucks and farm implements.

Payment of Wages and Record Keeping

Wages must be paid at regular intervals on days that are known to the employees. Employers are obligated by law to keep detailed records of employees' attendance and earnings. Records do not have to be kept in a prescribed form, and time clocks are not required, but the following information must be compiled:

Name, home address, occupation, sex and birth date of employee (if under 19).

The hour and the day when the workweek begins.

Total number of hours worked each day and each week.

Daily and weekly earnings.

Deductions or additions to wages.

Regular weekly pay and overtime owed worker.

Total wages per pay period, date of payment and period covered.

Enforcement of Wage and Hour Standards

The U.S. Labor Department's Wage and Hour Division is charged with the responsibility for enforcing the provisions of the Fair Labor Standards Act with respect to private employers, state and local governments, the Library of Congress, the U.S. Postal Service, the Postal Rate Commission and the Tennessee Valley Authority. (Other federal agencies come under the jurisdiction of the Office of Personnel Management.)

Compliance officers of the Wage and Hour Division are empowered to carry out on-the-spot investigations, gather information on wages, hours and other aspects of employment and recommend changes in existing practices. Violators may be prosecuted and fined up to $10,000.

The law prohibits firing or penalizing an employee who brings a complaint or takes part in a hearing that follows.

Safety on the Job

Before the first occupational safety laws were enacted in the United States during the second half of the 19th century, fatalities and crippling injuries on the job were commonplace. Coal mining claimed an appalling number of victims. Hundreds of laborers in steel plants were killed or maimed by crane accidents, falls or explosions. Track workers on railroads were frequent accident victims. Employees engaged in manufacturing matches fell victim to a deadly disease known as "phossy jaw," caused by the white phosphorus used in making match heads.

In 1867 Massachusetts took the lead in attempting to reduce the toll of injured workers by designating factory safety inspectors, and later by requiring that potentially dangerous machinery be covered or protected. A survey of mine disasters was ordered in 1908, and federal action was subsequently urged to limit the use of explosives in mines, cut down on coal dust and require the use of safety lamps and electricity.

Three years later, pressure for safety action was intensified when a fire broke out among highly combustible rags, silks and cottons of the three-story Triangle Shirtwaist Company in New York. In the holocaust that followed, 146 employees—mostly young women immigrants—were killed.

The disaster paved the way for the enactment of safety laws in New York, California, Massachusetts, Ohio and Pennsylvania. Today most states have safety codes protecting employees against fire and covering such hazards as boilers, dust, gases, rickety floors and stairways, abrasive wheels, flammable liquids,

spray paints and welding. Safeguards against toxic chemicals and cancer-producing agents have been put into effect. Inspections and emergency procedures for nuclear facilities have been strengthened in recent years.

Occupational Safety and Health Legislation

Federal protection for workers was ordered under the Occupational Safety and Health Act, which was passed by Congress in 1970 "to assure so far as possible every working man and woman in the nation safe and healthful working conditions and to preserve our human resources."

Under the act, the Occupational Safety and Health Administration (OSHA) was created as a part of the Department of Labor to help reduce hazards in workplaces, promote better health and safety conditions, establish safety and health standards and organize recording and reporting procedures for job-related accidents and illnesses.

OSHA Standards

The federal law requires that an employer "shall furnish to each of his employees, employment and a place of employment which are free from the recognized hazards that are causing or are likely to cause death or serious physical harm to his employees."

OSHA sets legally enforceable standards to implement this order. The standards apply to three major work areas: general industry and the maritime and construction businesses. Published in the Federal Register, these standards are available in single copies at the nearest OSHA offices (page 92). In addition, the OSHA subscription service regularly updates standards, regulations and procedures. Published in loose-leaf form that can be assembled in three-ring binders, the service may be obtained from the Superintendent of Documents, U.S. Government Printing Office, Washington, DC 20402. Ask for: OSHA Standards and Regulations, Volume I, General Industry Standards and Interpretations. The current price of the service can be obtained from the nearest OSHA office (page 92).

OSHA also sets emergency standards to protect the health and lives of workers against newly discovered health threats. In recent years asbestos and other cancer-producing agents have been the subject of strict regulations. Studies have shown cancer death rates of 40 to 45 percent among some workers who were exposed to asbestos. Lung abnormalities have been discovered in 38 percent of the families of some employees. Workers who smoke and are exposed to asbestos have been found to be much more likely to develop cancer than those who do not smoke or work with this fibrous material.

OSHA has issued health standards to reduce asbestos levels in workplaces. Employers are required to provide asbestos workers with medical examinations within 30 days of their employment. The examinations must include chest X-rays and lung capacity tests, and are required to be repeated at least once every year.

Safety and Health Inspections

Approximately five million workplaces are covered by the Occupational Safety and Health Act. OSHA inspectors have established a system of priorities for their inspections. The highest priority is given to places where an imminent danger is believed to exist—one that might reasonably be expected to result in death or serious physical harm if no immediate corrective measures are taken. Next comes the investigation of fatalities and serious accidents, and a third priority is given to inspections in response to employee complaints of unsafe or unhealthful conditions. Periodic inspections are also made of workplaces where high death, casualty or illness rates are found. Businesses run by self-employed workers, and certain other categories, including railroads, nuclear facilities, airlines and mines, are exempt.

OSHA inspectors are empowered to "enter without delay and at reasonable times any factory, plant or establishment, construction site

or other area, workplace, or environment where work is performed by an employee of an employer." Most inspections are conducted without prior notice, and alerting an employer to an impending inspection may bring a fine of up to $1,000 and/or a six-month sentence in jail.

There are exceptions to the no-warning rule, however. In some instances a prior notification of not more than 24 hours will be given to the employer. These situations include emergencies where there is an immediate need for corrective action, inspections after business hours, inspections where the presence of the employer or employees is required and occasions where advance notice will assure a more thorough and effective inspection.

The Ground Rules for an OSHA Visit

OSHA inspectors must carry valid warrants, identify themselves on arrival at the workplace and explain the reason for their visits, the areas to be inspected and the standards that will be checked. The employer is entitled to send a representative along with the inspector during the visit. An authorized representative of the employees, chosen by the union or the plant safety committee, may also go along.

On the inspection tour, the OSHA representative may visit the plant freely, talk with employees, take pictures, make instrument readings and examine records relevant to the purpose of the visit. After the inspection, a conference will normally be held to discuss the inspector's findings and inform the employer of violations that may be cited. The employer is entitled to an opportunity to show evidence of corrective measures and to indicate how long it will take to eliminate the safety violation or health problem.

The inspector then reports to the area director, who will determine the action to be taken. A citation may then be issued, informing the employer and employees of alleged violations and setting a timetable for their elimination. The employer is required to post a copy of the citation at the spot where the alleged violation occurred and leave it there for three days or until the problem has been remedied. Failure to post OSHA notices may draw a fine of up to $1,000.

Assaulting, resisting or intimidating compliance officers, or interfering with the performance of their duties, is a criminal offense bearing a fine of up to $5,000 and imprisonment of up to three years.

Minor violations of safety or health standards may carry fines of up to $1,000. For more serious violations a fine of up to $1,000 is mandatory. Willful or repeated violations may bring fines of up to $10,000. A willful violation of an OSHA standard involving the death of an employee may result in a fine of $10,000 and imprisonment of up to six months.

Employee Action

Employees who believe that their safety or health is threatened should notify their employers. If no action results, employees may then get in touch with the nearest OSHA office. (The law prohibits discrimination, firing, demotion or penalizing of employees for reporting hazardous or unhealthful working conditions.)

An inspector from OSHA may then make an inspection of the premises. If a violation exists, the inspector first requests the employer to eliminate the hazard.

If the danger appears to be imminent and the employer takes no corrective action, the employees may refuse to expose themselves to further risk. Whether an employee may walk off the job, however, is a point on which court opinions have disagreed.

Employee Appeals

If an employee is dissatisfied because of delays by OSHA, he or she may file a written objection with the regional director within 15 days. The regional director will forward the objection to the Occupational Safety and Health Review Commission, an independent government agency, for a final determination. Employers may appeal the findings, the penalty or

the schedule of compliance with the Review Commission.

Workers' Compensation

Various states entered the field of labor law long before the U.S. Labor Department was created in 1913. As a result, compensation for job-related injuries and illnesses has traditionally been mainly a matter of concern for the states. All states have compensation laws providing benefits for workers and their survivors for job-related injuries and illnesses. The benefits, however, vary widely from state to state. Coverage is compulsory in more than half the states, but the method of insuring, amounts of coverage, occupational diseases included and waiting periods for payments differ greatly. (A list of state benefits appears on the opposite page.)

The employee who is injured or stricken with a job-related illness should report the disablement to his or her employer, who will then file a claim with the company that insures the employees. If the worker is not satisfied with the compensation, he or she may file a complaint with the compensation office of the state Labor or Industrial Relations department.

Federal Employees

Injured civilian employees of the U.S. government are covered by the Federal Employees' Compensation Act, which provides payments for medical, surgical, hospital and transportation costs plus rehabilitation services. The act also calls for payment of benefits to survivors if the injury or illness is fatal.

The injured or disabled employee may go on sick or annual leave, or request a continuation of pay for 45 days. If the employee is still not able to return to work, three days must elapse—without pay—before payment from the federal compensation fund will begin. If the disability then lasts more than 14 days, the employee will be reimbursed for the three-day no-pay period.

Maximum Benefits for Temporary Total Disability Provided by Workers' Compensation Statutes in the U.S.

The majority of workers' compensation cases involve "temporary total disability," meaning that the worker is incapacitated, but expects to return to the job. Benefits vary from state to state. Some states limit the number of weeks; others pay for duration of the disability.

State or other Jurisdiction	Maximum percentage of wages	Maximum Period
Alabama	66-2/3	300 weeks
Alaska	66-2/3	Duration of disability
Arizona	66-2/3	Duration of disability
Arkansas	66-2/3	450 weeks
California	66-2/3	Duration of disability
Colorado	66-2/3	Duration of disability
Connecticut	66-2/3	Duration of disability
Delaware	66-2/3	Duration of disability
District of Columbia	66-2/3	Duration of disability
Florida	66-2/3	350 weeks
Georgia	66-2/3	Duration of disability
Hawaii	66-2/3	Duration of disability
Idaho	60-90	52 weeks, thereafter 60% of SAWW for duration of disability
Illinois	66-2/3	Duration of disability
Indiana	66-2/3	500 weeks
Iowa	80	Duration of disability
Kansas	66-2/3	Duration of disability
Kentucky	66-2/3	Duration of disability
Louisiana	66-2/3	Duration of disability
Maine	66-2/3	Duration of disability
Maryland	66-2/3	Duration of disability
Massachusetts	66-2/3	Duration of disability
Michigan	66-2/3	Duration of disability
Minnesota	66-2/3	Duration of disability
Mississippi	66-2/3	450 weeks
Missouri	66-2/3	400 weeks
Montana	66-2/3	Duration of disability
Nebraska	66-2/3	Duration of disability
Nevada	66-2/3	Duration of disability
New Hampshire	Max $92 first 138; 66-2/3 after that	Duration of disability
New Jersey	70	400 weeks
New Mexico	66-2/3	600 weeks
New York	66-2/3	Duration of disability
North Carolina	66-2/3	Duration of disability
North Dakota	66-2/3	Duration of disability
Ohio	72 for first 12 weeks; thereafter, 66-2/3	Duration of disability
Oklahoma	66-2/3	300 weeks
Oregon	66-2/3	Duration of disability
Pennsylvania	66-2/3	Duration of disability
Puerto Rico	66-2/3	312 weeks
Rhode Island	66-2/3	Duration of disability
South Carolina	66-2/3	500 weeks
South Dakota	66-2/3	Duration of disability
Tennessee	66-2/3	Duration of disability
Texas	66-2/3	401 weeks
Utah	66-2/3	312 weeks
Vermont	66-2/3	Duration of disability
Virginia	66-2/3	500 weeks
Washington	60-75	Duration of disability
West Virginia	70	208 weeks
Wisconsin	66-2/3	Duration of disability
Wyoming	66-2/3	Duration of disability
U.S. Employees	66-2/3-75	Duration of disability

SAWW = State's Average Weekly Wage

Death Payments

When a childless federal employee dies as a result of work-related illness or injury, the widow or widower is entitled to 50 percent of the salary at the time of death. If there are children under 18, the widow or widower will receive 45 percent of the salary, and each child will be paid 15 percent. Parents, brothers, sisters, grandparents and grandchildren who were dependent on the employee may also receive death payments.

Compensation for a widow or widower will continue until the survivor's death or remarriage. A widow or widower under the age of 60 will receive a lump sum (24 times the monthly compensation) when remarried. If the survivor is over 60, the monthly payments will continue. Payments to children end when they reach 18, unless they are students or are physically incapable of supporting themselves.

Appeals of Compensation Amounts

Federal workers' compensation is handled by the Office of Workers' Compensation Programs (OWCP) in the U.S. Labor Department. An employee or survivor who wants to contest the findings of this office may request a review by OWCP. If this does not produce satisfactory results, an appeal may be lodged with the Employees' Compensation Appeals Board.

Longshoremen and Harbor Workers

Injuries and disabilities incurred in the line of duty by "non-seamen" in the navigable waters of the U.S. are covered by the Longshoremen's and Harbor Workers' Compensation Act, as amended. Approximately a million workers are covered. Benefits include medical, surgical and hospital expenses. Survivors are also covered, and are compensated for death or disability traceable to a job-related injury or disease. The coverage comes under the Office of Workers' Compensation Programs. Appeals from their rulings may be made before an administrative law judge. Further appeals may be made to the Benefits Review Board and then to the U.S. Court of Appeals.

Black Lung Benefits

Coal miners totally disabled by black lung disease (pneumonoconiosis) contracted in mines are entitled to monthly benefits and medical treatment under the Black Lung Benefits Reform Act of 1977. The program is administered by the U.S. Labor Department's Division of Coal Mine Workers' Compensation Programs. Appeals may be taken to the Benefits Review Board and the U.S. Court of Appeals.

Unemployment Insurance

In the Great Depression of the 1930s, 16 million Americans were unemployed—approximately one worker out of three. To soften the impact of this experience on individual workers and on the nation's economy, a federal-state unemployment insurance program was inaugurated under the Social Security Act of 1935. The heart of that program is the payment of weekly cash benefits to unemployed workers who have lost their jobs involuntarily. (Employees who quit are not covered.) Payments are generally made for an initial period of 26 weeks. Benefits usually end at that point, but may be extended for an additional 13 weeks in times of severe economic need. Congressional action is required for a still further extension. The initial 26-week period is paid out of payroll deductions made by the state. The 13-week extension is paid for jointly out of state payroll deductions and Federal Unemployment Tax funds.

Approximately 97 percent of all wage earners are eligible for the payments. Included are all workers who are subject to state unemployment taxes, former federal employees or members of the armed forces, as well as state and local government employees, domestic workers and certain special categories of agricultural workers.

The benefits vary from state to state, but are determined by the earnings of the employee and the number of weeks of service. To receive

Significant Provisions of State Unemployment Insurance Laws

Unemployment compensation varies from state to state. Payments are made for a 26-week period only in some states, but may be extended in others if the economy indicates the need. Waiting periods for the payments and the compensation amounts also vary. Major provisions of a cross section of states are reprinted below.

| STATE | QUALIFYING WAGE OR EMPLOYMENT | WAITING WEEKS | WEEKLY BENEFIT ALLOWANCE | | DURATION IN 52 WEEK PERIOD Benefit weeks for Total Unemployment | |
			Minimum	Maximum	Minimum	Maximum
Ala.	Not less than $522.01		$15	$90	11+	26
Calif.	$1100	1	30	130	12+-15	26
Fla.	20 weeks employment at average of $20 or more	1	10	105	10	26
Ind.	Not less than $1500; $900 in last 2 quarters	1	40	84-141	9	26
Mich.	18 weeks employment at $23.35 or more	0	16-18	182-221	11	26
Nebr.	$600; $200 in each of two quarters	1	12	106	17	26
N.H.	$1,200; 600 in each of two quarters	0	21	114	26	26
N.Y.	20 weeks employment at average of $40 or more	1	25	125	26	26
Oreg.	18 weeks employment at not more than $1000. in base period	1	41	150	6	26
Tenn.	$494.01 in 1 quarter	1	20	110	12	26
Tex.	Not less than $500	3	21	126	9	26
Utah	19 weeks employment at $20 or more; not less than $700	1	10	166	10-22	36
Wash.	680 hrs.	1	45	163	16+-25+	30
Wyo.	Not less than $600 in 1 quarter	1	24	165	12-26	26

these payments, the worker must have been employed for a specified period and must have earned a specified amount during a base period established by the state. The claimant must be registered for a job at the state employment office. He or she must be available for work, and some states require that the claimant must be actively seeking a job.

Payments are made by state employment offices. A chart of state unemployment payments in a representative selection of states appears on page 79.

Pension Plans

The law does not require employers to maintain pension programs for their employees, but companies that have pension plans must run them according to strict legal standards. In 1974, Congress, recognizing the "growth in size, scope, and number of employee benefit plans in recent years," passed the Employee Retirement Income Security Act (ERISA), which regulates the establishment, operation and administration of pension plans. Responsibility for implementing the law is shared by the U.S. Labor Department, the Internal Revenue Service and a non-profit agency called the Pension Benefit Guaranty Corporation (PBGC).

Qualifying for Pension Benefits
Eligibility requirements for pension programs vary greatly, but in most cases participation may not be denied to any employee who has reached the age of 25 and has completed one year of service with the company. In some instances the required term of service may be increased to three years.

The Basic Pension Programs
There are two major types of pension programs. One is the *Defined Benefit Plan,* under which benefits accumulate according to a clearly determined formula and can be estimated in advance of retirement. The other is the *Defined*

Contribution Plan, in which money is contributed to the participant's account and invested in various securities such as stocks and bonds. The benefits available at retirement, therefore, depend on the value of the investments at that time, and cannot be estimated in advance.

Contributions to Pension Plans
In some plans the employer alone contributes to the pension fund, and in others both the employer and employee make contributions. The employee's contributions may be required or voluntary.

"Vesting" of Pension Rights
A term that crops up repeatedly in discussions of pension plans is "vesting." It means simply that at a certain point you become fully entitled to a percentage of your pension benefits. That percentage is yours; it cannot be taken away from you even if you resign.

There are three kinds of vesting:

1. "Cliff vesting"—You are fully vested after 10 years, but have no pension rights up to then.

2. "Graded vesting"—You are entitled to 25 percent of your pension after 5 years of service. You then receive an additional 5 percent for each of the next 5 years. After that you receive 10 percent a year. By this method, you will be 50 percent vested after 10 years, and 100 percent vested after 15 years.

3. The "rule of 45"—This approach is based on age and service. You become 50 percent vested after 5 years service, if your age and service add up to 45. After that you receive an additional 10 percent for each of the next 5 years.

No matter which method is used, the employee must be 50 percent vested after 10 years of service and 100 percent vested after 15 years.

Breaks in Service with an Employer
If you work only 500 hours or less for an employer during a year, you will be regarded as having a break in service with that employer.

The effect on your pension will depend on the particular plan and whether you are vested. If you decide to leave the company or work fewer than the minimum number of hours required for continuous service, be sure to check your plan and determine the effect of this action.

If you are fully vested before leaving, you will be entitled to certain benefits when you reach retirement age, no matter what happens. If some of your benefits are vested before the break, they will count toward your pension, no matter how long the break may be. But if your benefits depend entirely on the employer's contributions to the plan, you may lose all of your non-vested benefits after a break that runs as long as a year. Service before the break may also be lost if the interruption is longer than the total number of years you have worked for the company.

Social Security and Your Pension

Some pension plans are directly tied to Social Security benefits. A percentage of the Social Security payment is deducted from the monthly pension benefit to determine the amount the participant will receive. These are known as "integrated plans." Payments by a pension program may not, however, be reduced because of increases in Social Security payments.

When the Payments Start

Most pensions begin at 65. Many plans permit the participants to take "early retirement," with payments starting before 65 and the retiree receiving reduced amounts.

Disability payments are included in some plans. The plans vary as to the disability definitions and the benefits that are paid.

Pensions are normally paid every month, but some plans provide for payments in lump sums. Cost-of-living increases may or may not be included in pension payments.

Survivors' Rights

Widows and widowers are covered in most pension plans, and are protected by the Employee Retirement Income Security Act.

Protection is afforded by a "joint and survivor annuity" provision. The employee may reject or accept this part of the pension plan. If accepted, the monthly payments after retirement may be reduced. After the recipient's death the spouse will receive monthly payments amounting to at least half the amount that the retired employee received.

The joint and survivor annuity may be subject to certain conditions. For example, the plan may stipulate that the employee and spouse must have been married at least one year before the pension starts.

Mishandling of Pension Funds

The law protects pension programs against mismanagement or misuse of funds. The fiduciary or administrator of the plan may not be paid for services rendered while receiving full-time pay from the employer or from a union whose members are participating in the plan. The administrator must act in the interest of the beneficiaries and is accountable for managing the assets of the plan with care, skill and diligence. Investments of the plan's funds must be diversified in order to minimize the risk to the participants.

The law also protects defined benefit plans against inadequate financing; severe penalties are provided for underfunding the plans. The participants are protected against insolvency of the employer of the plan by the Pension Benefit Guaranty Corporation, which insures vested pension benefits up to the legally established amounts and guarantees payment of these benefits if the employer becomes insolvent. In addition, the law also provides that vested benefits will not be affected by a corporate merger or a transfer of the assets of the plan to another plan.

Filing Claims for Benefits

Pension benefits are not automatic. You may have to file a claim, and your employer must let you know within 90 days whether the claim has been accepted or denied, or whether more time is needed to review the claim. The additional time may not exceed 90 days. If the claim is denied, you are entitled to a written explanation, and you must be given a reasonable opportunity for a full and fair review of the claim.

If you still are not satisfied, you may bring a civil action to obtain your rights or recover benefits under the plan. Civil actions may also be brought to force the plan's administrator to supply documents you have requested to clarify your future rights, to halt practices that are in violation of the provisions of the plan and to afford relief from a breach of duty by the plan's administrator.

Your Right to Know Your Pension Plan

By law you are entitled to be informed of the major provisions of your pension plan. You are also entitled to see the basic documents pertaining to the pension plan, and to obtain copies of them at a reasonable cost.

When you join a pension plan, you must be furnished a copy of the plan within 90 days. If the plan is subsequently changed, you must be so informed. An updated version of the plan, incorporating all of the changes, must be furnished to you every five years.

If you request it, the administrator must supply you with an accounting of the total benefits to which you are entitled at any point. The administrator must also indicate when the benefits become vested.

When you leave the job or retire, the administrator must furnish you with an up-to-date statement of your benefits and the percentage that is vested.

A description of the plan must be filed with the Department of Labor. The plan and other

What You Should Know About Your Pension Plan

In order to understand your rights and to make sure you get what is coming to you after you retire, you should familiarize yourself with the main provisions of your pension program. Here is a checklist of the things you should know, compiled by the U.S. Department of Labor.

My plan is a
☐ DEFINED BENEFIT PLAN
   ☐ integrated with Social Security
   ☐ non-integrated
☐ DEFINED CONTRIBUTION PLAN
   ☐ integrated with Social Security
   ☐ non-integrated

My pension plan is financed by
☐ employer contributions only.
☐ employer and employee contributions.
☐ union dues and assessments.

I contribute to my pension plan at the rate of
$ _____ per ☐ month ☐ week ☐ hour or _____ percent of my compensation.

My plan provides
☐ full and immediate vesting.
☐ cliff vesting.
☐ graded vesting.
☐ rule-of-45 vesting.
☐ other (specify).

I need ___ more years of service to be fully vested.

I will have a year of service under my pension plan
☐ if I work ___ hours in a 12-consecutive-month period.
☐ if I meet other requirements (specify).

The plan year (12-month period for which plan records are kept) ends on _____ of each year.

I will be credited for work performed
☐ before I became a participant in the plan.
☐ after the plan's normal retirement age.

As of now, _____, I have earned
continued

82

_____ years of service toward my pension. My plan's break-in-service rules are as follows:

I may begin to receive full normal retirement benefits at age ___.

If I work beyond the normal retirement age, it ☐ will ☐ will not increase the pension that will be paid to me when I retire.

I may retire at age ___ if I have completed ___ years of service. Apart from the age requirement, I need ___ years more of service to be eligible for early retirement benefits.

The amount of my normal retirement benefit is computed as follows:

The amount of my early retirement benefit is computed as follows:

My Social Security benefit
☐ will not be deducted from my plan benefit.
☐ will be deducted from my plan benefit to the extent of ___ percent of the Social Security benefit I am due to receive at retirement.

My retirement benefit
☐ will be paid monthly for life.
☐ will be paid to me in a lump sum.
☐ will be adjusted to the cost of living.
☐ will be paid to my survivor in the event of my death.

My plan ☐ *does* ☐ *does not* provide disability benefits.

My plan defines "disability" as follows:

To be eligible for disability retirement benefits, I must be ___ years old and must have _____ years of service.

I will not be eligible for disability retirement benefits if I become disabled because of
☐ mental incompetence.
☐ drug addiction.
☐ alcoholism.
☐ self-inflicted injury.

☐ other reason (specify).

A determination as to whether my condition meets my plan's definition of disability is made by
☐ a doctor chosen by me.
☐ a doctor designated by the plan administrator.

The amount of my disability retirement benefit is computed as follows:

I must send my application for disability retirement benefits to _____ within ___ months after I stop working.

If I qualify for disability benefits, I will continue to receive benefits
☐ for life, if I remain disabled.
☐ until retirement age.
☐ until I return to my former job.
☐ until I am able to work.

My pension plan ☐ provides ☐ does not provide a joint and survivor option or a similar provision for death benefits.

I ☐ *have* ☐ *have not* rejected in writing the joint and survivor option.

By electing the option, my pension benefit will be reduced to _____.

My survivor will receive _____ per month for life if the following conditions are met (specify):

My employer ☐ *will* ☐ *will not* automatically submit my pension application for me.

I must apply for my pension benefits on a special form I get from _____ within _____ months ☐ *before* ☐ *after* I retire.

My application for pension benefits should be sent to _____.

I must furnish the following documents when applying for my pension:

If my application for benefits is denied, I may appeal in writing to _____ _____ within _____ days.

pertinent documents will be made available for public inspection at the U.S. Labor Department at 200 Constitution Avenue NW, Washington, DC 20210.

Unlawful Pressures Against Pension Rights

The law stipulates that employees may not be discharged from their jobs, fined, suspended or discriminated against for exercising their rights with respect to pensions. They also may not be penalized for giving testimony in regard to pension plans.

Penalties for Violations of Pension Laws

A willful violation of reporting and disclosure provisions of the pension law may be punished by a fine of up to $5,000 and a prison term of up to one year—or both. Corporations may be fined up to $100,000. Interference with an employee's pension rights by fraud or coercion may draw a fine of up to $10,000 and a prison term of one year. Actions may be brought by the Secretary of Labor, the participants in the plan or the administrator.

Pension Plans for Self-Employed Workers

There are two kinds of plans for workers who are not covered by pension programs. One is the "Keogh plan," under which a self-employed worker is permitted to set aside 15 percent of his or her earned income every year (with a limit of $15,000) and put it in a pension fund. Both the amount deposited and the income earned by the fund are tax free until payments begin at retirement. If you set aside income for your own retirement and you are an employer of others, you are required by law to do the same thing for all of your full-time employees with three or more years of uninterrupted service. The employees must match these contributions, and the money they contribute is vested immediately.

Whether your company maintains a pension plan or not, you may set up your own tax-deferred Individual Retirement Account (IRA). Up to 15 percent of wages (with a limit of $2,000 per year) may be put into the IRA

plan. The standards for IRA are set by the Internal Revenue Service. Information about this plan may be obtained from the District Director of Internal Revenue or from the Pension Benefit Guaranty Corporation at 2020 K Street NW, Washington, DC 20006; Attention: Office of Communications.

Where to Get Further Information About Pension Plans

For additional information about pension plans and government protection for the participants, write to the Administration Area Offices of the U.S. Labor Department's Labor Management Services Administration (listed on page 93).

Starting Your Own Business

The answer to your job problems may be to go into business for yourself. But be sure to look very carefully before you leap. Starting your own business is a risky proposition. More than half of the people who try it fail within the first five years.

Ask yourself the questions on page 85, and if you still think you are qualified to run your own business, get yourself a good lawyer. You are going to need one in the coming months to help you with the paperwork, red tape and loan applications that lie ahead.

The Small Business Administration (SBA) may be able to help you. Founded in 1953, the SBA was designed to aid both fledgling and established members of the small-business community by providing financial aid, management training and advice. The agency also helps small businesses obtain a fair share of government contracts.

A word of warning about the SBA. The agency was rocked by scandals in the 1970s, and if you approach it directly for financial aid without knowing precisely what kind of business you want to go into, you may find yourself drowning in a sea of frustration and red tape.

But the SBA publishes a wealth of informa-

Rating Yourself as Operator of a Small Business

To help people decide whether they should go into business for themselves, the Small Business Administration prepared the check-list of questions below. On the next page, check-lists for two other vital steps appear: deciding on a single ownership, partnership or corporation, and selecting a site for the business.

Rating Scale for Personal Traits Important to a Business Proprietor

INSTRUCTIONS: After each question place a check mark on the line at the point closest to your answer. The check mark need not be placed directly over one of the suggested answers because your rating may lie somewhere between two answers. Be honest with yourself.

ARE YOU SELF-STARTER?

I do things my own way. Nobody needs to tell me to get going.	If someone gets me started, I keep going all right.	Easy does it. I don't put myself out until I have to.

HOW DO YOU FEEL ABOUT OTHER PEOPLE?

I like people. I can get along with just about anybody.	I have plenty of friends. I don't need anyone else.	Most people bug me.

CAN YOU LEAD OTHERS?

I can get most people to go along without much difficulty.	I can get people to do things if I drive them.	I let someone else get things moving.

CAN YOU TAKE RESPONSIBILITY?

I like to take charge of and see things through.	I'll take over if I have to, but I'd rather let someone else be responsible.	There's always some eager beaver around wanting to show off. I say let him.

HOW GOOD AN ORGANIZER ARE YOU?

I like to have a plan before I start. I'm usually the one to get things lined up.	I do all right unless things get too goofed up. Then I cop out.	I just take things as they come.

HOW GOOD A WORKER ARE YOU?

I can keep going as long as necessary. I don't mind working hard.	I'll work hard for a while, but when I've had enough, that's it!	I can't see that hard work gets you anywhere.

CAN YOU MAKE DECISIONS?

I can make up my mind in a hurry if necessary, and my decision is usually o.k.	I can if I have plenty of time. If I have to make up my mind fast, I usually regret it.	I don't like to be the one who decides things. I'd probably blow it.

CAN PEOPLE TRUST WHAT YOU SAY?

They sure can. I don't say things I don't mean.	I try to be on the level, but sometimes I just say what's easiest.	What's the sweat if the other fellow doesn't know the difference?

CAN YOU STICK WITH IT?

If I make up my mind to do something, I don't let anything stop me.	I usually finish what I start.	If a job doesn't go right, I turn off. Why beat your brains out?

HOW GOOD IS YOUR HEALTH?

I never run down.	I have enough energy for most things I want to do.	I run out of juice sooner than most of my friends seem to.

Selecting an Organization and a Site

WHAT FORM OF BUSINESS ORGANIZATION?

SINGLE PROPRIETORSHIP

ADVANTAGES
1. Low start-up costs
2. Greatest freedom from regulation
3. Owner in direct control
4. Minimal working capital requirements
5. Tax advantage to small owner
6. All profits to owner

DISADVANTAGES
1. Unlimited liability
2. Lack of continuity
3. Difficult to raise capital

PARTNERSHIP

ADVANTAGES
1. Ease of formation
2. Low start-up costs
3. Additional sources of venture capital
4. Broader management base
5. Possible tax advantage
6. Limited outside regulation

DISADVANTAGES
1. Unlimited liability
2. Lack of continuity
3. Divided authority
4. Difficulty in raising additional capital
5. Hard to find suitable partners

CORPORATION

ADVANTAGES
1. Limited liability
2. Specialized management
3. Ownership is transferrable
4. Continuous existence
5. Legal entity
6. Possible tax advantages
7. Easier to raise capital

DISADVANTAGES
1. Closely regulated
2. Most expensive form to organize.
3. Charter restrictions
4. Extensive record keeping necessary
5. Double taxation

Score Sheet on Sites

Grade each factor: "A" for excellent, "B" for good, "C" for fair and "D" for poor.

Factor	Grade
1. Centrally located to reach my market	_____
2. Merchandise or raw materials available readily	_____
3. Nearby competition situation	_____
4. Transportation availability and rates	_____
5. Quantity of available employees	_____
6. Prevailing rates of employee pay	_____
7. Parking facilities	_____
8. Adequacy of utilities (sewer, water, power, gas)	_____
9. Traffic flow	_____
10. Taxation burden	_____
11. Quality of police and fire protection	_____
12. Housing availability for employees	_____
13. Environmental factors (schools, cultural, community activites, enterprise of businessmen)	_____
14. Physical suitability of building	_____
15. Type and cost of lease	_____
16. Provision for future expansion	_____
17. Overall estimate of quality of site in 10 years	_____

tion that can be helpful to almost anyone who is just starting out in business. Get in touch with an SBA representative at the agency's nearest district office. (Look under "United States Government Offices" in cities listed on page 93.) The SBA representative may be able to arrange for you to attend one of the agency's workshops—held at the local office or close by—where the kinds of problems you are going to be facing will be discussed: financing new businesses, different kinds of businesses, business organization and the selection of a business site.

Once you have decided what kind of business you want to get into, gather as much information as possible about the amount of capital you will need. If you can't finance the undertaking on your own, visit a bank and see whether it will make you a loan. If the bank is not willing to make a loan on its own, it may ask the Small Business Administration to guarantee a loan. Approximately 85 percent of SBA's business is in guaranteed loans.

SBA loans are designed to meet a variety of financial needs. Some are start-up loans for new businesses; women, minorities, handicapped people and veterans get special aid. Under its 503 program, the SBA helps finance the purchase of land and equipment and the start-up or revitalization of small businesses to create jobs where the need is felt. A ceiling of $500,000 or 50 percent of the financing applies to each application.

The SBA also makes loans to displaced businesses forced out of their locations by urban renewal or other construction projects. Small firms that suffer from the closing or contraction of U.S. military installations, or from abrupt federal government cutbacks on orders, may also be aided by SBA loans. Loans are sometimes made to tide over companies suffering from shortages of fuel, or from requirements to retool or modify their equipment and plant facilities as a result of changes in federal laws and regulations. The SBA also makes bonding available to small businesses that cannot get this service from private companies.

Disaster Loans

If the President of the United States or the Small Business Administrator designates a section of the country a disaster area after a hurricane, flood, tornado or other natural disaster, the SBA offers two types of loans. One is the Physical Damage Natural Disaster Recovery Loan—for property owners, renters, businesses and non-profit organizations in the area. These loans are designed to repair or replace damaged and destroyed homes, personal property and business establishments.

Economic Injury Natural Disaster Loans are specifically designed to help small businesses that suffer economic damage because of natural disasters that affect a relatively small region. These loans may be used to provide working capital and to pay debts that could not otherwise be met. When disaster strikes, the SBA usually establishes on-site offices to provide loan information.

Government Contract Procurement

About one-third of the total federal procurement in recent years has been obtained by small businesses. The SBA helps small businesses get their share of federal contracts through its 10 regional offices and more than 100 local offices around the country. Federal procurement specialists in these offices offer advice to small businessmen on how to prepare bids for federal contracts and subcontracts. They also help the small businesses get their names on bidders' lists. If a firm's ability to perform the contract is questioned, the SBA can study the company's facilities and performance and, if satisfied, provide a Certificate of Competency.

Surplus Property and Technical Aid

Every year the federal government disposes of large quantities of surplus property and natural resources. SBA works with other government agencies to see that small businesses are afforded a chance to buy a fair share of these properties. It also attempts to assure small businesses a reasonable share of federal research and development contracts—amounting to billions of dollars in underseas exploration, health-and-welfare programs and defense projects—and it makes an effort to see that useful technology developed by the government is made available to small businesses.

Management Tips

Advice and counseling to small-business managers is a major part of the SBA's effort. The Management and Technical Assistance Program features free counseling by retired and active business executives and other trained professionals. The program offers special courses, workshops and a wide range of publications.

The agency's Small Business Institute also provides on-site counseling by senior and graduate business students. Professional consulting firms, under contract with the SBA, provide advice and assistance through the Call Contracts Program. In conjunction with educational and business institutions, SBA sponsors courses in planning, organizing and directing businesses.

Women in Business

Women who are starting new businesses, or already established in enterprises of their own, are eligible for the full range of programs and services of the Small Business Administration. An assistant administrator for Women's Business Enterprise was appointed to the agency's managerial staff in 1980, and each SBA office now has a special women's representative. Workshops and seminars are held around the country to instruct women on how to go into business and to sharpen their managerial skills. Information on these programs and other forms of aid for women may be obtained from any of the SBA's field offices that are listed on page 93.

Special Aid for Minority Businesses

Members of minority groups who need advice in starting or operating small businesses are aided by the Minority Business Development Agency (MBDA) in the U.S. Department of Commerce. Technical and managerial expertise are afforded on marketing, site selection, production, personnel management, negotiation of leases, mergers and divestitures and a variety of other important subjects.

Further information can be obtained from the MBDA Information Clearing House, Department of Commerce, Washington, D.C. 20230, or at any of MBDA's regional offices located in San Francisco, Atlanta, Chicago, New York City, Dallas, and Washington D.C. Regional offices are listed in telephone directories in these cities under "U.S. Government, Department of Commerce, Minority Business Development Agency."

Directory of Government Offices For Jobs, Benefits and Services

U.S. Department of Labor
200 Constitution Ave., NW
Washington, DC 20210

Regional Offices

Region I
(Connecticut, Maine, Massachusetts, New Hampshire.
Rhode Island, Vermont)
John F. Kennedy Federal Building
Boston, MA 02203

Region II
(New Jersey, New York, Puerto Rico, Virgin Islands)
1515 Broadway
New York, NY 10036

Region III
(Delaware, District of Columbia, Maryland, Pennsylvania,
Virginia, West Virginia)
P.O. Box 8796
Philadelphia, PA 19101

Region IV
(Alabama, Florida, Georgia, Kentucky, Mississippi, North
Carolina, South Carolina, Tennessee)
1371 Peachtree St. NE
Atlanta, GA 30309

Region V
(Illinois, Indiana, Michigan, Minnesota, Ohio, Wisconsin)
230 S. Dearborn St.
Chicago, IL 60604

Region VI
(Arkansas, Louisiana, New Mexico, Oklahoma, Texas)
555 Griffin Sq. Bldg.
Dallas, TX 75202

Region VII
(Iowa, Kansas, Missouri, Nebraska)
911 Walnut St.
Kansas City, MO 64106

Region VIII
(Colorado, Montana, North Dakota, South Dakota, Utah,
Wyoming)
1961 Stout St.
Denver, CO 80294

Region IX
(Arizona, California, Guam, Hawaii, Nevada)
450 Golden Gate Ave.
San Francisco, CA 94102

Region X
(Alaska, Idaho, Oregon, Washington)
909 First Ave
Seattle, WA 98174

State Employment Offices

Alabama: Dept. of Industrial Relations, Headquarters of,
649 Monroe St., Montgomery, AL 36120

Alaska: Employment Security Division, Department of
Labor, P.O. Box 3-7000, Juneau, AK 99811

Arizona: Department of Economic Security, P.O. Box
6123, Phoenix, AZ 85005

Arkansas: Employment Security Division, P.O. Box
2981, Little Rock, AR 72203

California: Employment Development Department, 800
Capitol Mall, Sacramento, CA 95814

Colorado: Division of Employment and Training, 251 E.
12th Ave., Denver, CO 80203

Connecticut: Connecticut Labor Department, 200 Folly
Brook Blvd., Wethersfield, CT 06109

Delaware: Department of Labor, 820 N. French St.,
Wilmington, DE 19801

District of Columbia: Department of Employment
Services, 500 C St., NW Washington, D.C. 20001

Florida: Dept. of Labor and Employment Security, 201
Caldwell Building, Tallahassee, FL 32304

Georgia: Employment Security Agency, 254 Washington
St., SW, Atlanta, GA 30334

Guam: Dept. of Labor, P.O. Box 2950, Agana, GU
96910

Hawaii: Dept. of Labor and Industrial Relations, 825
Miliani St., Honolulu, HI 96813

Idaho: Dept. of Employment, 317 Main St., P.O. Box
35, Boise, ID 83735

Illinois: Bureau of Employment Security, 910 Michigan
Ave., Chicago, IL 60605

Indiana: Employment Security Div., 10 N. Senate Ave.,
Indianapolis, IN 46304

Iowa: Dept. of Job Service, 1000 E. Grand Ave., Des
Moines, IA 50319

Kansas: Div. of Employment, Dept. of Human
Resources, 401 Topeka Ave., Topeka, KS 66603

Kentucky: Dept. for Human Resources, New Capitol
Annex, Frankfort, KY 40601

Louisiana: Office of Employment Security, 1001 N.
23rd., P.O. Box 44094, Baton Rouge, LA 70804

Maine: Dept. of Manpower Affairs, P.O. Box 309,
Augusta, ME 04330

Maryland: Employment Security Administration, 1100
N. Eutaw St., Baltimore, MD 21201

Massachusetts: Div. of Employment Security, Charles F.
Hurley Bldg., Boston, MA 02114

Michigan: Employment Security Commission, 7310
Woodward Ave., Detroit, MI 48202

Minnesota: Dept. of Economic Security, 390 N. Robert St., St. Paul, MN 55101

Mississippi: Employment Security Commission, 1520 W. Capital St., PO 1699, Jackson, MS 39205

Missouri: Div. of Employment Security, 421 E. Dunklin St., Jefferson City, MO 65104

Montana: Employment Security Div., P.O. Box 1728, Helena, MT 59601

Nebraska: Div. of Employment, P.O. Box 94600, Lincoln, NE 68509

Nevada: Employment Security Dept., 500 E. Third St., Carson City, NV 89713

New Hampshire: Dept. of Employment Security, 32 S. Main St., Concord, NH 03301

New Jersey: Dept. of Labor and Industry, Labor and Industry Bldg., John Fitch Plaza, Trenton, NJ 08625

New Mexico: Employment Security Dept., P.O. Box 1928, Albuquerque, NM 87103

New York: State Dept. of Labor, Bldg. 12, State Campus, Albany, NY 12240

North Carolina: Employment Security Commission, P.O. Box 25903, Raleigh, NC 27611

North Dakota: Job Service North Dakota, P.O. Box 1537, Bismarck, ND 58505

Ohio: Bureau of Employment Services, 145 S. Front St., Columbus, OH 43216

Oklahoma: Employment Security Commission, Will Rogers Memorial Office Bldg., Oklahoma City, OK 73105

Oregon: Employment Div., 875 Union St., NE., Salem, OR 97311

Pennsylvania: Bureau of Employment Security, Labor and Industry Bldg., 7th and Forster Sts., Harrisburg, PA 17121

Puerto Rico: Bureau of Employment Security, 505 Munoz Rivera Ave., Hato Rey, PR 00918

Rhode Island: Dept. of Employment Security, 24 Mason St., Providence, RI 02903

South Carolina: Employment Security Commission, P.O. 995, Columbia, SC 29202

South Dakota: Dept. of Labor, Capitol Lake Plaza, P.O. Box 307, Pierre, SD 57501

Tennessee: Dept. of Employment Security, Cordell Hull Bldg., Nashville, TN 37219

Texas: Employment Commission, 638 TEC Bldg., 15th and Congress Ave., Austin, TX 78778

Utah: Dept. of Employment Security, P.O. Box 11249, Salt Lake City, UT 84147

Vermont: Dept. of Employment Security, P.O. Box 488, Montpelier, VT 05602

Virginia: Employment Commission, P.O. Box 1358, Richmond, VA 23211

Virgin Islands: Employment Security Agency, P.O. Box 1092, Charlotte Amalie, St. Thomas, VI 00801

Washington: Employment Security Department, P.O. Box 367, Olympia, WA 98504

West Virginia: Department of Employment Security, 112 California Ave., Charleston, WV 25305

Wisconsin: Job Service, P.O. Box 7903, Madison, WI 53707

Wyoming: Employment Security Commission, P.O. Box 2760, Casper, WY 82602

Federal Job Information Centers

Alabama: Southerland Bldg., 806 Governors Dr., NW, Huntsville, AL 35801

Alaska: Federal Bldg. & U.S. Courthouse, 701 C St., P.O. Box 22, Anchorage, AK 99513

Arizona: 522 N. Central Ave., Phoenix, AZ 85004

Arkansas: Federal Bldg., 700 W. Capitol Ave., Little Rock, AR 72201

California:
Los Angeles: Linder Bldg., 845 S. Figueroa, CA 90017
Sacramento: Federal Bldg., 650 Capitol Mall, CA 95814
San Diego: 880 Front St., CA 92188
San Francisco: Federal Bldg., 450 Golden Ave., CA 94102

Colorado: 1845 Sherman St., Denver, CO 80203

Connecticut: Federal Bldg., 450 Main St., Hartford, CT 06103

Delaware: Federal Bldg., 844 King St., Wilmington, DE 19801

District of Columbia: 1900 E St. NW, Washington, DC 20415

Florida:
Miami: 330 Biscayne Blvd., FL 33131
Orlando: 80 N. Hughey Ave., FL 32801

Georgia: Richard B. Russell Federal Bldg., 75 Spring St., SW, Atlanta, GA 30303

Guam: 238 O'Hara St., Agana, GU 96910

Hawaii: Federal Bldg., 300 Ala Moana Blvd., Honolulu, HI 96850

Illinois: Dirksen Bldg., 219 S. Dearborn St., Chicago, IL 60604

Indiana: 46 E. Ohio St., Indianapolis, IN 46204

Iowa: 210 Walnut St., Des Moines, IA 50309

Kansas: One-Twenty Bldg., 120 S. Market St., Wichita, KS 67202

Kentucky: Federal Bldg., 600 Federal Pl., Louisville, KY 40202

Louisiana: F. Edward Herbert Bldg., 610 South St., New Orleans, LA 70130

Maine: Federal Bldg., Sewall St. & Western Ave., Augusta, ME 04330

Maryland:
Baltimore: Garmatz Federal Bldg., 101 W. Lombard St., MD 21201
DC Metro Area: 1900 E. St. NW, Washington, DC 20415

Massachusetts: 3 Center Plaza, Boston, MA 02108

Michigan: 477 Michigan Ave., Detroit, MI 48226

Minnesota: Federal Bldg., Ft. Snelling, Twin Cities, MN 55111

Mississippi: 100 W. Capitol St., Jackson, MS 39201

Missouri:

Kansas City: Federal Bldg., 601 E. 12th St., MO 64106

St. Louis: Federal Bldg., 1520 Market St., MO 63103

Montana: Federal Bldg. & Courthouse, 301 S. Park, Helena, MT 59601

Nebraska: U.S. Courthouse and Post Office Bldg., 215 N. 17th St., Omaha, NE 68102

Nevada: Mill & S. Virginia Sts., P.O. Box 3296, Reno, NV 89505

New Hampshire: Federal Bldg., Daniel & Penhallow Sts., Portsmouth, NH 03801

New Jersey: Federal Bldg., 970 Broad St., Newark, NJ 07102

New Mexico: Federal Bldg., 421 Gold Ave. SW, Albuquerque, NM 87102

New York:

Bronx: 590 Grand Concourse, NY 10451

Buffalo: 111 W. Huron St., NY 14202

Jamaica: 90-04 161st St., NY 11432

New York City: Federal Bldg., 26 Federal Plaza, NY 10007

Syracuse: 100 S. Clinton St., NY 13260

North Carolina: Federal Bldg., 310 New Bern Ave., P.O. Box 25069, Raleigh, NC 27611

North Dakota: Federal Bldg., 657 Second Ave. N., Fargo, ND 58102

Ohio:

Cleveland: Federal Bldg., 1240 E. 9th St., OH 44199

Dayton: Federal Bldg., 200 W. 2nd St., OH 45402

Oklahoma: 200 NW Fifth St., Oklahoma City, OK 73102

Oregon: Federal Bldg., 1220 SW Third St., Portland OR 97204

Pennsylvania:

Harrisburg: Federal Bldg., PA 17108

Philadelphia: Wm. J. Green, Jr. Fed. Bldg., 600 Arch St., PA 19106

Pittsburgh: Federal Bldg., 1000 Liberty Ave., PA 15222

Puerto Rico: Federico Degetau Federal Bldg., Carlos E. Chardon St., Hato Rey, PR 00918

Rhode Island: Federal & P.O. Bldg., Kennedy Plaza, Providence, RI 02903

South Carolina: Federal Bldg., 334 Meeting St., Charleston, SC 29403

South Dakota: Federal Bldg., U.S. Court House, 515 9th St., Rapid City, SD 57701

Tennessee: Federal Bldg., 167 N. Main St., Memphis, TN 38103

Texas:

Dallas: 1100 Commerce St., TX 75242

El Paso: Property Trust Bldg., 2211 E. Missouri Ave., TX 79903

Houston: 701 San Jacinto, TX 77002

San Antonio: 643 E. Durango Blvd., TX 78205

Utah: 1234 South Main St., Salt Lake City, UT 84101

Vermont: Federal Bldg., P.O. Box 489, Elmwood Ave. & Pearl St., Burlington, VT 05402

Virginia:

Norfolk: Federal Bldg., 200 Granby Mall, VA 23510

DC Metro Area: 1900 E St., NW, Washington, DC 20415

Washington: Federal Bldg., 915 Second Ave., Seattle, WA 98174

West Virginia: Federal Bldg., 500 Quarrier St., Charleston, WV 25301

Wisconsin: Plankinton Bldg., 161 W. Wisconsin Ave., Milwaukee, WI 53203

Wyoming: 2120 Capitol Ave., P.O. Box 967, Cheyenne, WY 82001

Field Offices—Equal Employment Opportunity Commission

(For addresses and phone numbers, see listings in telephone directories under "U.S. Government").

Albuquerque, New Mexico
Atlanta, Georgia
Baltimore, Maryland
Birmingham, Alabama
Boston, Massachusetts
Buffalo, New York
Charlotte, North Carolina
Chicago, Illinois
Cincinnati, Ohio
Cleveland, Ohio
Dallas, Texas
Dayton, Ohio
Denver, Colorado
Detroit, Michigan

El Paso, Texas
Fresno, California
Greensboro, North Carolina
Greenville, South Carolina
Houston, Texas
Indianapolis, Indiana
Jackson, Mississippi
Kansas City, Missouri
Little Rock, Arkansas
Los Angeles, California
Louisville, Kentucky
Memphis, Tennessee
Miami, Florida
Milwaukee, Wisconsin

Minneapolis, Minnesota
Nashville, Tennessee
Newark, New Jersey
New Orleans, Louisiana
New York, New York
Norfolk, Virginia
Oakland, California
Oklahoma City, Oklahoma
Philadelphia, Pennsylvania
Phoenix, Arizona
Pittsburgh, Pennsylvania
Raleigh, North Carolina
Richmond, Virginia
St. Louis, Missouri

San Antonio, Texas
San Diego, California
San Francisco, California

San Jose, California
Seattle, Washington
Tampa, Florida

Washington, D.C.

Area Offices for Occupational Safety and Health Administration

Alabama:
Birmingham: 2047 Canyon Rd., Todd Mall, AL 35216
Mobile: Commerce Bldg., 118 N Royal St., AL 36602

Alaska: Federal Bldg., U.S. Courthouse, 701 C St., Anchorage, AK 99501

Arizona: Amerco Towers, 2721 N Central Ave., Phoenix, AZ 85004

Arkansas: West Mark Bldg., 4120 West Markham, Little Rock, AR 72205

California:
Long Beach: 400 Oceangate, CA 90802
San Francisco: 211 Main St., CA 94105

Colorado: Tremont Center, 333 W. Colfax, Lakewood, CO 80204

Connecticut: 555 Main St., Hartford, CT 06103

District of Columbia: 400 First St., NW, Washington, DC 20215

Florida:
Fort Lauderdale: 299 E. Broward Blvd., FL 33301
Jacksonville: Art Museum Plaza, 2809 Art Museum Dr., FL 32207
Tampa: 700 Twiggs St., FL 33602

Georgia:
Macon: 152 New St., GA 31201
Savannah: Enterprise Bldg., 6605 Abercorn St., GA 31405
Tucker: Building 10, La Vista Perimeter Office Park, GA 30084

Hawaii: 300 Ala Moana Blvd., Honolulu, HI 96850

Idaho: 1315 W. Idaho St., Boise, ID 83706

Illinois:
Calumet City: 1400 Torrence Ave., IL 60409
Niles: 6000 W. Touhy Ave., IL 60648
Aurora: 344 Smoke Tree Business Park, IL 60542
Peoria: 228 NE Jefferson, IL 61603

Indiana: U.S. Post Office and Courthouse, 46 E. Ohio St., Indianapolis, IN 46204

Iowa: 210 Walnut St., Des Moines, IA 50309

Kansas: 216 N. Waco, Wichita, KS 67202

Kentucky: 600 Federal Pl., Louisville, KY 40202

Louisiana:
Baton Rouge: 2156 Wooddale Blvd., Hoover Annex, LA 70806
New Orleans: 600 South St., LA 70130

Maine: U.S. Federal Bldg., 40 Western Ave., Augusta, ME 04330

Maryland: Federal Bldg., Charles Center, 31 Hopkins Plaza, Baltimore, MD 21201

Massachusetts:
Springfield: 1200 Main St., MA 01103
Waltham: 400-2 Totten Pond Rd., MA 02154

Michigan: 231 W. Lafayette, Detroit, MI 48226

Minnesota: 100 N. 6th St., Minneapolis, MN 55403

Mississippi: Federal Bldg., 100 W. Capitol St., Jackson, MS 39201

Missouri:
Kansas City: 1150 Grand Ave., 12 Grand Bldg., MO 64106
St. Louis: 210 N. 12th Blvd., MO 63101

Montana: Petroleum Bldg., 2812 1st Ave. N., Billings, MT 59101

Nebraska: Overland-Wolf Bldg., 6910 Pacific St., Omaha, NE 68106

Nevada: 1100 E. William St., Carson City, NV 89701

New Hampshire: Federal Bldg., 55 Pleasant St., Concord, NH 03301

New Jersey:
Belle Mead: Belle Mead GSA Depot, NJ 08502
Camden: 2101 Ferry Ave., NJ 08104
Dover: 2 E. Blackwell St., NJ 07801
Hasbrouck Heights: Teterboro Airport Professional Bldg., 377 Route 17, NJ 07604
Newark: 970 Broad St., NJ 07102

New Mexico: Western Bank Bldg., 505 Marquette Ave. NW, Albuquerque, NM 87102

New York:
Albany: Leo W. O'Brien Federal Bldg., Clinton Ave. & Pearl St., NY 12207
Brooklyn: 185 Montague St., NY 11201
Buffalo: 220 Delaware Ave., NY 14202
Flushing: 136-21 Roosevelt Ave., NY 11354
New York: 90 Church St., NY 10007
Rochester: Federal Office Bldg., 100 State St., NY 14614
Syracuse: 100 S. Clinton St., NY 13260
Westbury: 990 Westbury Rd., NY 11590
White Plains: 200 Mamaroneck Ave., NY 10601

North Carolina: Federal Office Bldg., 310 New Bern Ave., Raleigh, NC 27601

North Dakota: Federal Bldg., P.O. Box 2439, Bismarck, ND 58501

Ohio:
Cincinnati: Federal Office Bldg., 550 Main St., OH 45202
Cleveland: Federal Office Bldg., 1240 E. 9th St., OH 44199
Columbus: Federal Office Bldg., 200 N. High St., OH 43215
Toledo: Federal Office Bldg., 234 N. Summit St., OH 43604

Oklahoma:
Oklahoma City: 50 Penn Place, OK 73118
Tulsa: 717 S. Houston, OK 74127

Oregon: 1220 SW Third St., Portland, OR 97204

Pennsylvania:
Erie: 147 W. 18th St., PA 16501
Harrisburg: Progress Plaza, 49 N. Progress Ave., PA 17109
Philadelphia: Wm. J. Green, Jr. Federal Bldg., 600 Arch St., PA 19106
Pittsburgh: 400 Penn Center Blvd., PA 15235
Wilkes-Barre: Penn Place, 20 N. Pennsylvania Ave., PA 18701
Puerto Rico: U.S. Courthouse & FOB, Carlos Chardon, Hato Rey, PR 00918
Rhode Island: Federal Bldg. & U.S. Post Office, Providence, RI 02903
South Carolina: Kittrell Center, 2711 Middleburg Dr., Columbia, SC 29204
Tennessee: 1600 Hayes St., Nashville, TN 37203
Texas
Austin: American Bank Tower, 221 W 6th St., TX 78701
Fort Worth: Fort Worth Federal Center, 4900 Hemphill Bldg., 24, TX 76115

Harlingen: Riverview Professional Bldg., 1325 S. 77 Sunshine Strip, TX 78550
Houston: 1100 NASA Road I, TX 77058
2320 La Branch St., TX 77004
Irving: 1425 W. Pioneer Dr., TX 75061
Lubbock: Federal Bldg., 1205 Texas Ave., TX 79401
Tyler: FOB-USPO & Courthouse, 211 W. Ferguson St., TX 75702
Utah: U.S. Post Office Bldg., 350 S. Main St., Salt Lake City, UT 84101
Virginia: Federal Bldg., 400 N. 8th St., Richmond, VA 23240
Washington: 121 107th St., NE, Bellevue, WA 98004
West Virginia: Charleston National Plaza, 700 Virginia St., Charleston, WV 25301
Wisconsin:
Appleton: 2618 N Ballard Rd., WI 54911
Milwaukee: Clark Bldg., 633 W. Wisconsin Ave., WI 53203

Labor-Management Services Administration Area Offices (For Pension Information)

California:
Los Angeles: 300 N. Los Angeles St., CA 90012
San Francisco: 211 Main St., CA 94105
Colorado: 1961 Stout St., Denver, CO 80294
District of Columbia: 1111 20th St. NW, Washington, D.C. 20036
Florida: 111 NW 183rd St., Miami, FL 33169
Georgia: 1365 Peachtree St. NE, Atlanta, GA 30309
Hawaii: 300 Ala Moana, Honolulu, HI 96850
Illinois: 175 W. Jackson Blvd., Chicago, IL 60604
Louisiana: 600 South St., New Orleans, LA 70130
Massachusetts: 110 Tremont St., Boston, MA 02108
Michigan: 231 W. Lafayette St., Detroit, MI 48226
Minnesota: 100 N. 6th St., Minneapolis, MN 55401
Missouri:
Kansas City: 911 Walnut St., MO 64106
St. Louis: 210 N. 12th Blvd., MO 63101

New Jersey: 744 Broad St., Newark, NJ 07102
New York:
Buffalo: 111 West Huron St., NY 14202
New York: 26 Federal Plaza, NY 10007
Ohio: 1240 E. 9th St., Cleveland, OH 44199
Pennsylvania:
Philadelphia: 601 Market St., PA 19106
Pittsburgh: 1000 Liberty Ave., PA 15222
Puerto Rico: Carlos Chardon St., Hato Rey, PR 00918
Tennessee: 1808 W. End Bldg., Nashville, TN 37203
Texas: 555 Griffin Square Bldg., Dallas, TX 75202
Washington: 909 First Ave., Seattle, WA 98174

Small Business Administration Field Offices

For address and telephone numbers of the field offices,
look under "United States Government" in the appropriate telephone directories.

Agana, Guam
Albany, New York
Albuquerque, New Mexico
Anchorage, Alaska
Atlanta, Georgia
Augusta, Maine
Austin, Texas
Baltimore, Maryland

Biloxi, Mississippi
Birmingham, Alabama
Boise, Idaho
Boston, Massachusetts
Buffalo, New York
Camden, New Jersey
Casper, Wyoming
Cedar Rapids, Iowa

Charleston, West Virginia
Charlotte, North Carolina
Chicago, Illinois
Cincinnati, Ohio
Clarksburg, West Virginia
Cleveland, Ohio
Columbia, South Carolina
Columbus, Ohio

Concord, New Hampshire
Corpus Christi, Texas
Dallas, Texas
Denver, Colorado
Des Moines, Iowa
Detroit, Michigan
Eau Claire, Wisconsin
Elmira, New York
El Paso, Texas
Fairbanks, Alaska
Fargo, North Dakota
Fort Worth, Texas
Fresno, California
Greenville, North Carolina
Harrisburg, Pennsylvania
Hartford, Connecticut
Hato Rey, Puerto Rico
Helena, Montana
Holyoke, Massachusetts
Honolulu, Hawaii
Houston, Texas
Indianapolis, Indiana
Jackson, Mississippi
Jacksonville, Florida
Kansas City, Missouri
Knoxville, Tennessee
Las Vegas, Nevada
Little Rock, Arkansas

Los Angeles, California
Louisville, Kentucky
Lubbock, Texas
Madison, Wisconsin
Marquette, Michigan
Marshall, Texas
Melville, New York
Memphis, Tennessee
Miami, Florida
Milwaukee, Wisconsin
Minneapolis, Minnesota
Montpelier, Vermont
Nashville, Tennessee
Newark, New Jersey
New Orleans, Louisiana
New York, New York
Norfolk, Virginia
Oakland, California
Oklahoma City, Oklahoma
Omaha, Nebraska
Philadelphia, Pennsylvania
Phoenix, Arizona
Pittsburgh, Pennsylvania
Portland, Oregon
Providence, Rhode Island
Rapid City, South Dakota
Reno, Nevada
Richmond, Virginia

Rochester, New York
Sacramento, California
St. Louis, Missouri
Salt Lake City, Utah
Santa Ana, California
San Antonio, Texas
San Diego, California
San Francisco, California
Seattle, Washington
Shreveport, Louisiana
Sikeston, Missouri
Sioux Falls, South Dakota
South Bend, Indiana
Spokane, Washington
Springfield, Illinois
Springfield, Missouri
Statesboro, Georgia
Syracuse, New York
Tampa, Florida
Tulsa, Oklahoma
Tucson, Arizona
Washington, D.C.
West Palm Beach, Florida
Wichita, Kansas
Wilkes-Barre, Pennsylvania
Wilmington, Delaware

Chapter 3

Help for Your Home and Your Neighborhood

When you have completed your schooling and settled into a job, you probably
will want to start thinking about getting married and finding a home to suit
your needs. The first of these steps is, of course, a private matter,
but the government may be able to help you with the second.
The Department of Housing and Urban Development (HUD) guarantees mortgages
for single or multi-family homes. It subsidizes public housing and maintains
a rental assistance program for low- and moderate-income families, awards
block grants for the revitalization of neighborhoods and communities and makes
rundown houses available for sale at as little as $1 each to people who
promise to fix them up. Other government agencies allow tax credits for
energy-saving devices in the home, offer insurance protection against crime,
floods and riots, and furnish a broad range of assistance to the victims of
natural disasters. Apart from these services, the government
provides a wealth of valuable information on everything from
solar heating to the control of cockroaches in the home.

Contents

The Decision to Rent or Buy

The purchase of a house may be the biggest investment of your life. Before making such a commitment, you should consider all of the ramifications. Can you afford the down payment, the closing costs and the monthly carrying charges? How high is the interest rate? Is it likely to be come down if you wait awhile? How long do you expect to be in the house? In the first few years, your mortgage payments will go almost entirely toward paying off the interest; you will earn very little equity in the house. If you are going to be there for only a few years, it may make more sense for you to rent now and buy later.

On the other hand, a house is often a good investment. You may want to buy a small house now, and "trade up" to a larger one when you are making more money. And when the children are grown and you are tired of car pools and crab grass, you can sell the house, move into a smaller one or rent an apartment. You may be able to make some money that way, a nest egg for the day when you have retired and your income has declined.

It's not an easy decision, and before making it you might want to talk with a counselor at one of the field offices of the Department of Housing and Urban Development (listed on page 124) or at any of the nearly 18,000 HUD-approved lending agencies.

Failing that, you might want to ponder the advice that follows. Compiled by HUD, it includes the arguments pro and con for buying and renting. There may be some points that would not otherwise occur to you.

In Favor of Buying:

1. Home ownership can be an incentive to save and therefore serve as a measure of your economic progress.

2. Monthly mortgage payments may be less expensive than rent for comparable space and convenience.

3. The interest charges and the real estate taxes included in your mortgage payments are deductible from your income tax.

4. A home-owning family gains independence and a sense of pride from the new responsibility as property owners and members of a community.

5. Your equity in a home will improve your credit rating. This will be an advantage when you decide to move to a larger home.

6. A house is an investment that may weather the ups and downs of the economy better than anything else.

In Favor of Renting:

1. You retain your mobility and avoid the necessity for disposing of a house if you have to move.

2. You can leave the upkeep problems and repairs to a landlord or a janitor, saving your time and energy for other matters.

3. You can avoid expensive maintenance costs or an unexpected loss in case the property values drop in your area.

4. You may be able to have the best of both worlds by renting now with an option to buy later on. In this case, your rental contract should state that a portion of your rent is being credited toward the purchase price.

Buying a House

If you lean toward buying a house, figure out how much you can afford to spend on it without getting in over your head. A good rule of thumb, provided by HUD, is that the price of the house should not be more than two- and-a-half times your total family income for a year. This means that if the total family income is $25,000, you should not go higher than about $63,000 for the house. Young couples, just starting out, probably shouldn't go that high.

Another way of looking at the obligation you are assuming is that your total monthly expenses for the house, including the mortgage payment, heat, utilities, repairs and upkeep should not exceed 35 percent of your total monthly income.

Choosing Between an
Old House and a New One

Statistics gathered by HUD show that two out of three home buyers in the United States purchase previously occupied houses. There are good reasons for this. Older houses usually have more space per dollar cost than new ones. Moreover, they are likely to be found in settled communities with trees, shrubs and paved streets, near shopping areas and schools.

There are disadvantages, of course. Older houses may be in need of repair, and the services in older neighborhoods—garbage collection, police protection and utilities—may be declining.

It's a good idea to check the house carefully before making up your mind. Be sure the wiring, the plumbing and the furnace are in good working order. If the house has a septic tank, have an expert check it.

If you don't trust your expertise on the plumbing, the furnace or wiring, you may want to hire a professional inspector. Firms that specialize in inspecting houses are listed in the Yellow Pages in most cities. A detailed report will cost you a fee, but it may save you a lot of money later on.

Making an Offer for the House

When you are ready to make an offer for a house, don't immediately agree to the seller's asking price. "Start by taking at least 10 percent off the asking price," HUD advises. "Bargaining is an accepted practice in home-buying." You may go back and forth several times before you hit the rock-bottom figure. When you reach that point, you or your agent will probably know it by the firmness with which the seller holds to the price.

Getting a Mortgage
for Your House

Once you have decided on a house, the next step, of course, is to find a way to finance it. If you are like most people, you will need a mortgage, and you will be looking for the best bargain you can find.

Shop around. Mortgages are financed by savings banks, savings and loan associations, mortgage bankers and insurance companies. Try some of these lenders. If you are a veteran, get in touch with the Veterans Administration; a GI mortgage may be your best bet. (See Chapter 6, for the details.)

You may find that none of these loans suits you as well as an FHA mortgage. These government-backed loans get their name from the Federal Housing Administration, which had been an independent government agency but was incorporated as a part of HUD in 1965. The mortgages are available to anyone who has a good credit record and can afford a relatively low down payment. The monthly charges typically are stretched out over periods of up to 30 years, and the interest rate on the FHA mortgage usually is lower than on conventional housing loans.

How FHA Mortgages Work

The government does not make housing loans. It insures loans made by other institutions, thereby protecting the lenders against default and making it possible for people to obtain financing that would not otherwise be available to them.

The FHA mortgages are designed to finance the purchase of single-family, two-family, three-family and four-family houses. In most areas, the maximum amounts are as indicated below in the column in the middle. The allowable amounts run higher in high-cost areas, as shown in the column at the right. The figures were compiled in 1981 and are subject to change.

Dwelling	Normal Amount	High-Cost Areas
Single-family houses	$67,500	$90,000
Two-family houses	76,000	101,300
Three-family houses	92,000	122,650
Four-family houses	107,000	142,650

The mortgage figures are also limited by HUD's appraisal of the houses. The total amount of the loan may not exceed 97 percent of the first $25,000 plus 95 percent of the remainder of the appraisal.

To obtain an FHA mortgage, you should apply at a bank, a savings and loan association or any other HUD-approved lending institution. The lender will supply you with the forms and help you complete them. The papers will then be forwarded to the nearest HUD field office. A HUD representative will inspect the property and appraise it. Your credit will be checked, and HUD will inform the lender when the mortgage has been approved. You will deal with the bank or other lending institution. It will deal with HUD.

The Meaning of the HUD Inspection

It is important to understand the meaning of the HUD inspection of the house. The government agency is merely making sure the property meets its standards for a loan. It does not guarantee the condition of the house. If you move in and the plumbing leaks, the furnace breaks down or you discover major structural weaknesses, it will not help for you to go to HUD and say, "But you inspected the house and said it was OK." Their inspection is *not* a warranty for the condition of the house.

On the other hand, if you plan to build a new house with an FHA mortgage, the plans must be approved by HUD before the construction begins. The builder must sign a warranty that the house will conform to the specifications agreed upon. The warranty lasts a year, dating from the time you take title to the house, or the house is occupied, whichever occurs first. Major defects that come to light during that year are the responsibility of the builder. If the builder refuses to correct them, you should get in touch with HUD and request the agency's help in enforcing the warranty.

If the builder can get a private warranty corporation to insure the condition of the property, it will not be necessary to obtain HUD approval before construction starts.

The Disadvantages of an FHA Mortgage

As indicated earlier in this chapter, the amounts that may be borrowed on an FHA mortgage are limited. If the mortgage amounts do not suit your needs, you will have to look elsewhere for your financing.

Also, it takes longer to arrange an FHA mortgage than a conventional loan. You have to go to the bank or other lending institution first. It will want to run a credit check on you and consider your application carefully. Then the institution will apply to HUD for the department's approval. Like most transactions with government agencies, this takes time.

Still another problem stems from the fact that the interest rates on FHA mortgages usually are lower than on conventional loans. The lenders may charge "discount points" to make up for the loss. Normally, a discount point is 1 percent of the mortgage. If the mortgage amounts to $60,000, three points would come to $1,800. The first $600 is paid by the purchaser as an "origination fee," and the remaining $1,200 normally is charged to the seller.

Not many sellers are pleased by that prospect. Some will raise the price of the house to offset the loss under the point system.

The Graduated Payment Mortgage

Suppose you find a house that suits you perfectly. You'd like to move right in, but you can't afford the mortgage payments. You hate to pass up the house; in a few years, you'll be making more money and you'll be able to manage the payments easily.

The government has a program that may be the answer to your problem. It's called the Graduated Payment Mortgage, and it enables you to buy a house with lower initial monthly payments than you would normally be able to obtain. The payments rise gradually; then they level off at an amount that you should be able to meet.

Payment Plans for Graduated Mortgages

There are several variations of the Graduated

Payment Mortgage plan, depending on the term and the rate at which the payments are increased. The number of years varies from five to ten, and the rate at which the payments are increased ranges from 2 to 7½ percent.

Below is a comparison between a regular FHA mortgage and a graduated payment plan. The figures are subject to change, but they show the basic difference between standard and graduated payment mortgages. In the examples cited here, the amount of the loan is $50,000, and the term is 30 years. The regular mortgage payments are $693 throughout the 30-year term. The payment on the graduated plan starts at $565 and increases every year before leveling off at $811.

Here is how the regular and graduated monthly payments compare:

Year	Regular FHA Mortgage	Graduated Payments
1	$693	$565
2	693	607
3	693	652
4	693	701
5	693	754
6	693	811
Remaining Payments	693	811

Anyone who can afford the down payment and the carrying charges is eligible for the graduated payment plan.

Closing the Deal for Your House

When all of the obstacles have been cleared, you will meet with the seller, representatives of the lending institution and of the title company, real estate brokers and lawyers. This meeting is the "closing"; it is here that the formal transfer of the property occurs. (There are exceptions in some states, where the entire transaction is handled by an "escrow agent." The procedure described here, however, applies in most parts of the country.)

It's a good idea to have your lawyer with you at this session because a lot of legal documents will be passed back and forth. Moreover, you will be called on to write a stream of checks for the "closing costs." The lawyer can verify the charges for you and help you preserve your equanimity as your bank account diminishes. The closing costs are legitimate, but they may be a shock if you do not know what to expect.

Condominiums and Co-ops

If you live in a metropolitan area, a condominium or a cooperative may suit you better than a house. These housing arrangements have become so popular that real estate experts predict half of the people in the United States may be living in them by the end of the century.

The differences between condominiums and cooperatives are mainly technical. In a "condo," as it is commonly called, the occupants own the apartment or housing unit they live in. In a "co-op," people own shares in the housing project. The shares entitle them to a certain amount of living space and an equity in the mortgage, but they do not *own* particular apartments or housing units.

In both arrangements the occupants have a right to such common facilities as parking spaces, laundry areas and recreation rooms. These facilities, and the housing units themselves, are run by boards or management companies selected by the occupants. Everyone who lives in a condo or co-op has a say in the running of the place. In a condominium, the occupants usually vote on a proportional basis, depending on the size or value of their housing units. In a co-op, each owner usually has one vote, regardless of the size or value of the housing unit.

Mortgages for Condos and Co-ops

The FHA guarantees mortgages for the construction of condominiums and cooperatives. The people who buy these housing units have no obligation under the construction mortgages. They may, however, finance the purchase of their apartments or co-op shares with FHA mortgages or conventional loans.

Occupants of the apartments or housing units in condos or co-ops make monthly payments to the condominium or cooperative associations to cover the maintenance of the buildings and common facilities. In condominiums, they pay their taxes separately and, like other home owners, may deduct mortgage interest and real estate taxes from their federal income taxes. In co-ops the taxes are included in the monthly maintenance payments. Occupants of both kinds of housing may deduct mortgage interest and real estate taxes from their federal income taxes.

Mobile Homes

If you can't afford any of the possibilities that have already been discussed, you might consider buying a mobile home. More and more people are doing that today (approximately 11.5 million people were living in mobile homes in the United States at the beginning of the decade), and you may be surprised at the space and luxury of these housing units.

To qualify for an FHA loan, a mobile home must be at least 10 feet wide and 40 feet long, or be comprised of units with a total floor space of 400 square feet. But some mobile homes are up to 28 feet by 70 feet, with living rooms, bedrooms, kitchens and baths.

The FHA guarantees loans of up to $22,500 on single-unit mobile homes, and $35,000 on two or more unit homes. The mortgagor has 15 years to repay the loan on a single unit, and 20 years for larger models. The down payment includes a minimum of 5 percent on the first $3,000 and 10 percent on any amount over that figure. For an $18,000 loan, that would come to $1,650 annually.

To qualify for an FHA mortgage, a mobile home must meet federal safety and construction standards. Moreover, it must be new, or have been financed previously with an FHA mortgage.

Mobile Home Parks

Most people who buy mobile homes park them in one place and remain there. Spaces are hard to find in some areas, owing to local zoning restrictions, but the government finances the development of mobile home parks where suitable sites can be found.

The FHA normally insures mortgages on mobile home plots up to $9,000 per space. In some areas, where prices are especially high, that amount may be increased by as much as 90 percent. The term is up to 40 years, and normal FHA interest rates apply.

The park must comply with standards set by HUD. (These standards are set forth in a publication called *Minimum Design Standards for Mobile Home Parks,* HUD Handbook 4940.5.) Before the loan will be approved, an FHA inspector will visit the mobile home park to make sure the standards are going to be met. The inspector checks on the location, the layout and the availability of utilities, and makes certain that each mobile home has a space for a car.

The FHA will also want to be sure that the sponsor of the mobile home park is sufficiently qualified from a managerial standpoint and has the financial resources to undertake the development and operation of the facility. Construction must also be in accordance with FHA regulations.

Developers who are interested in obtaining FHA mortgage insurance for mobile home parks should visit the nearest HUD office and go over the plans with a qualified representative of the department. The developer can learn what must be done to meet the FHA requirements, and will obtain expert advice on planning, cost-cutting and budget preparation. The developer then goes to a HUD-approved lender and applies for a loan. The lender, in turn, applies to HUD for the government guarantee.

Owners of mobile homes rent their spaces in the parks. For information on HUD-approved parks, get in touch with the nearest HUD office.

Home Improvements and Repairs

When you have taken possession of your house, you may want to add one or more rooms, or make improvements on the existing structure. You can obtain a HUD-insured loan for such purposes. The loans cover everything from alterations, repairs and new construction to the purchase of built-in dishwashers, refrigerators, ovens, freezers and solar heating units.

The ceiling on these loans is $15,000, and you can borrow up to $7,500 with no security. All you need is a good credit rating, title to the property or a long-term lease and an income large enough to handle the payments. A word of warning: be sure to check on the interest rates. Nowadays, they are high even on HUD loans.

Tax Credits for Energy Savers

With dishwashers whirring, furnaces running full blast through the winter, and air conditioners humming through the summer, American homes account for 20 percent of all the energy consumed in the United States. To encourage energy conservation, Congress has enacted a series of tax credits.

The tax credits fall into two categories. The first is fuel conservation. It includes thermostat control, insulation, furnace modifications, weather stripping, installing storm windows and doors and caulking cracks and other leaky areas. The second category covers the addition of new energy sources, such as solar heating, geothermal heat and windmills.

Tax credits of up to 15 percent on the first $2,000 are allowed for energy-conserving measures in the first category. Second-category improvements, such as solar heating units, geothermal heat or other new energy sources entitle the homeowner to a credit of up to 40 percent on the first $10,000.

These are tax credits, *not* deductions. When you have figured out your federal income tax, you may subtract the tax credit from the amount that you owe. An example appears on page 102.

Energy-Saving Advice

Along with the tax credits, the government offers an abundance of practical information on energy saving in the home. During the energy crisis of the late 1970s, the Department of Energy compiled a check-list of energy savers, which is reprinted on page 104.

The department also reminded consumers that substantial savings (in energy and fuel bills) can be achieved by such simple expedients as wearing warmer clothing in winter, rinsing laundry in cold water, turning dishwashers off when they reach the drying cycle and letting the dishes dry by air, and making sure the lights and TV sets are off in empty rooms.

Solar Heating in the Home

If you are considering the installation of a solar heating system in your home, shop around carefully before making your selection. Solar heating units vary greatly in quality and cost, and an effective system is an expensive proposition. It will, however, not only conserve energy but save you money in the long run. Moreover, with energy costs constantly rising, it may enhance the resale value of your home.

Don't expect a solar unit to solve all your heating problems. The heat in the storage unit will not last more than a few days. If the weather turns cloudy for an extended period, you will have to rely on conventional heat sources.

At best, most solar systems probably will not satisfy more than 50 to 75 percent of your heating needs. Before investing in a unit, you should study the equipment costs and weigh them carefully against the potential savings. Take into account the tax credits allowed by the Internal Revenue Service (page 102), plus the tax incentives allowed in many states to

Form 5695

Department of the Treasury
Internal Revenue Service

Energy Credits

► Attach to Form 1040.   ► See Instructions on back.

1980

34

Name(s) as shown on Form 1040   BOB AND MARY BROWN

Your social security number   111 11 1111

Enter in the space below the address of your principal residence on which the credit is claimed if it is different from the address shown on Form 1040.

Part I   Fill in your energy conservation costs (but do not include **repair or maintenance costs**).
If you have an energy credit carryover from a previous tax year and no energy savings costs this year, skip to Part III, line 16.

A. Answer the following question: Was your principal residence substantially completed before April 20, 1977? . . . ☑ Yes ☐ No

B. If you checked the "NO" box, you CANNOT claim an energy credit for conservation cost. Do NOT fill in lines 1 through 7 of this form.

1 **Energy Conservation Items:**			
a Insulation	1a		
b Storm (or thermal) windows or doors	1b	600	00
c Caulking or weatherstripping	1c		
d A furnace replacement burner that reduces the amount of fuel used . . .	1d		
e A device for modifying flue openings to make a heating system more efficient .	1e		
f An electrical or mechanical furnace ignition system that replaces a gas pilot light	1f		
g A thermostat with an automatic setback	1g		
h A meter that shows the cost of energy used	1h		
2 Total (add lines 1a through 1h)	2	600	00
3 Maximum amount	3	$2,000	00
4 Enter the total energy conservation costs for this residence from your 1978 and 1979 Form 5695, line 2 .	4	1,700	00
5 Subtract line 4 from line 3 (If line 4 is more than line 3, do not complete any more of this part. You cannot claim any more energy conservation credit for this residence.)	5	300	00
6 Enter the amount on line 2 or line 5, whichever is less	6	300	00
7 Enter 15% of line 6 here and include in amount on line 15 below	7	45	00

Part II   Fill in your renewable energy source costs (but do not include **repair or maintenance costs**).
If you have an energy credit carryover from a previous tax year and no energy savings costs this year, skip to Part III, line 16.

8 **Renewable Energy Source Items:**			
a Solar	8a	3,000	00
b Geothermal	8b		
c Wind	8c		
9 Total (add lines 8a through 8c)	9	3,000	00
10 Maximum amount	10	$10,000	00
11 Enter the total renewable energy source costs for this residence from your 1978 Form 5695, line 5 and 1979 Form 5695, line 9	11	3,000	00
12 Subtract line 11 from line 10 (If line 11 is more than line 10, do not complete any more of this part. You cannot claim any more renewable energy source cost credit for this residence.)	12	7,000	00
13 Enter amount on line 9 or line 12, whichever is less	13	3,000	00
14 Enter 40% of line 13 here and include in amount on line 15 below	14	1,200	00

Part III   Fill in this part to figure the limitation

15 Add line 7 and line 14. *If less than $10, enter zero*	15	1,245	00
16 *Enter your energy credit carryover from a previous tax year*	16	150	00
17 Add lines 15 and 16	17	1,395	00
18 Enter the amount of tax shown on Form 1040, line 37	18	1,895	00
19 Add lines 38 through 44 from Form 1040 and enter the total	19	275	00
20 Subtract line 19 from line 18. If zero or less, enter zero	20	1,620	00
21 Residential energy credit. Enter the amount on line 17 or line 20, whichever is less. Also, enter this amount on Form 1040, line 45	21	1,395	00

For sale by the Superintendent of Documents, U.S. Government Printing Office

Sample Tax Form

Energy credits on federal income tax returns may be claimed for conservation measures such as the installation of storm windows and doors or for the addition of new solar, geothermal or wind-driven energy units. In the hypothetical tax return on the opposite page, Bob and Mary Brown spent $600 on storm windows and doors. The maximum credit for such energy conservation measures was $2,000, but they had already claimed $1,700 in previous years. They could therefore claim only $300 in 1980. Their tax credit, computed at the prevailing rate of 15 percent, was $45. They spent $3,000 on a solar heating unit, and were allowed the full amount, since it did not exceed the maximum allowance of $10,000 for renewable energy sources. Computed at the rate of 40 percent, this gave them an additional credit of $1,200, bringing their total to $1,245. A carryover credit of $150 from a previous year increased the total to $1,395. After figuring their income tax on the 1040 form, they owed the goverment $1,895, but they were entitled to another, unrelated tax credit of $275, reducing the amount they owed to $1,620. To compute their final tax figure, they simply subtracted the energy tax credit of $1,395 from the $1,620, which meant they owed the government $225.

encourage the use of solar energy. The incentives vary from state to state, but they include property tax exemptions, income tax deductions and sales tax exemptions.

You can find out about the tax situation in your state from the state taxation and finance department.

For basic information on solar heating manufacturers write to:

Renewal Energy Information
P.O. Box 8900
Silver Spring, MD 20907

Or call toll-free between the hours of 9 AM and 6 PM (Eastern time):

800-523-2929.
If you live in Pennsylvania, call:
800-462-4983.
If you live in Alaska or Hawaii, call:
800-523-4700.

Crime and Natural Disaster Insurance

If you live in a high-crime area, or a section of the country where floods, hurricanes or other natural disasters frequently occur, you may not be able to get insurance protection for your property from private companies, or the rates may be excessive. Under such circumstances, the Federal Emergency Management Agency (FEMA), which offers such insurance in many parts of the country, may be able to help you. The government also has an elaborate program of emergency assistance for the victims of natural disasters.

Crime Insurance

In 1970, Congress authorized the Federal Insurance Administration (a part of FEMA) to make low-cost burglary and robbery insurance available to property owners, tenants and business people in areas where such protection is not provided by private insurance companies.

Crime insurance can be obtained in the District of Columbia, Puerto Rico, the Virgin Islands and 26 states through brokers and agents designated by the Federal Insurance Administration. States included are:

Alabama	Iowa	North Carolina
Arkansas	Kansas	Ohio
California	Maryland	Pennsylvania
Colorado	Massachusetts	Rhode Island
Connecticut	Minnesota	Tennessee
Delaware	Missouri	Virginia
Florida	New Jersey	Washington
Georgia	New Mexico	Wisconsin
Illinois	New York	

Energy-Saving Checklist
for Home Builders, Buyers, and Owners

This checklist contains many items that you should consider when building, renovating, or improving the energy efficiency of your home.

Building Shell	Yes	No	NA
1. Are storm windows and storm doors installed?			
2. Are window panes and frames properly caulked? Do windows open for natural ventilation?			
3. Are exterior doors weatherstripped? Are door frames caulked?			
4. Are ceilings and walls insulated to the highest level recommended for your geographic location?			
5. Does the home have a vapor barrier in the walls to prevent water vapor from passing through and condensing into the insulation?			
6. Are floors insulated over unheated basements, crawl spaces, and garages?			
7. Do basement walls contain 2″ x 2″ furring with R-7 insulation?			
8. Have you considered 6″ walls with studs on 24″ centers to allow maximum space for insulation?			
9. Has a clock thermostat been installed to reduce, automatically, evening temperatures?			
10. In colder climates, is window space on the north side of the house at a minimum?			
11. Is the home efficiently shaped to limit heat loss, avoiding L-, T-, and H-shaped configurations?			
12. Does the house have an overhang for the south wall which will protect it from summer sun, but allow exposure to winter sun?			
13. Does the fireplace have a heat exchanger to collect unused heat?			
14. Is the fireplace a high-efficiency type with a tight damper?			
15. Is fluorescent rather than incandescent lighting used in the kitchen and bathroom?			

	Yes	No	NA
16. Are outdoor gas lamps essential for safety or merely decorative?			
17. Does the landscaping shade the house in summer and let in winter sun?			
Appliances	**Yes**	**No**	**NA**
1. Do appliances have the highest Energy Efficiency Rating?			
2. Is the hot water heater well insulated? Is the water temperature at a reasonably low level?			
Heating, Ventilating, and Air Conditioning	**Yes**	**No**	**NA**
1. Are hot water pipes or hot air ducts insulated in unheated passages?			
2. Are air leaks in ductwork sealed?			
3. Are exposed hot water pipes and hot water storage tank insulated to reduce heat loss?			
4. Have you considered a heat-recovery pipe which preheats outside air with exhaust air from the ventilation system?			
5. Are window or whole-house ventilating fans adequate for comfort?			
6. If home has air-conditioning units or a central compressor, are they shaded from the sun to increase efficiency and reduce energy use?			
7. Does cooling equipment have the highest Energy Efficiency Rating?			
8. Is cooling equipment the smallest size possible to do the job adequately?			
9. Is the heating system the most efficient? Is it the appropriate size? Oversized systems waste a great deal of energy. Is the oil furnace serviced regularly?			
10. Do heating and cooling systems provide for continuous fan operation, which often provides comfort without using the full system capacity?			
11. Does the attic have 1 square foot of ventilation for each 300 square feet of ceiling? This reduces the air-conditioning load, and should be done even with insulation having a vapor barrier in the ceiling.			
12. Have fuel costs and supplies been evaluated to select equipment and fuel on a lifetime cost efficiency basis?			

Residences may be insured in amounts from $1,000 to $10,000 against losses through burglary or robbery. Residential coverage includes cash losses up to $100. Jewelry and furs may be insured for up to $500 per break-in or robbery. Claims are subject to a deduction of $50 or 5 percent of the value of the loss, whichever is larger.

Coverage for business establishments ranges from $1,000 to $15,000. Losses occurring off the premises may be insured up to $5,000. Claims by businesses with less than $100,000 in gross receipts are subject to a deduction of $50 or 5 percent of the value of the loss. Businesses with larger gross receipts are subject to higher deductions.

The residential protection against burglary and robbery cost between $20 and $80 in 1981, depending on the crime rate in the area and the nature of the coverage maintained by the home owner. Premiums on business establishments ran anywhere from $35 per $1,000 coverage in low-crime areas to $748 for a $15,000 policy in high-crime areas. Increases should be expected in all of these categories.

To qualify for the coverage, an applicant must take a number of security precautions. Exterior doors must be equipped with deadbolt locks or self-locking dead latches. Sliding doors and windows providing easy access to the interior of the house must also be equipped with locks.

Commercial establishments are inspected before the policy is written (the federal government pays for the inspection). The inspector will check to see that all doors, transoms and other means of access are adequately protected during non-business hours.

An application for a residential crime insurance policy appears on page 107.

Flood Insurance

Protection against floods was formerly limited to dams, dikes, seawalls and disaster loans. But the scope of the protection was broadened considerably in 1968 when Congress passed the National Flood Insurance Act, authorizing flood insurance for property owners at reasonable rates.

The program is managed by the Federal Insurance Administration (FIA). Single-family residences may be insured up to $185,000 (half of the coverage is government subsidized). Non-residential properties are insured up to $250,000. The contents of residences may be insured for an additional $60,000, and the contents of non-residential properties up to $200,000.

Almost every kind of building, public or private, may be insured. Residences, religious establishments, industrial, commercial and agricultural installations are included.

In order for residents to obtain flood insurance, the community must first submit an application to FIA, including a flood plan for the area, an estimate of the population and a list of buildings in flood-prone areas. FIA will review the application and determine whether the community is eligible. If the community qualifies, residents may then purchase flood insurance from licensed property or casualty insurance agents.

To find out whether your property qualifies for the coverage, call or write to your community officials, insurance agents in the community or a regional office of FEMA, listed on page 125.

Riot Insurance

The government also guarantees property insurance in areas that may be threatened by riots or civil disturbances. The insurance is available in 16 states and the District of Columbia. Losses directly attributable to riots or civil disturbances are covered. To qualify for the government guarantees, an insurance company must cooperate with state insurance authorities in their Fair Access to Insurance Requirements (FAIR) plan, an arrangement designed to assure urban dwellers access to basic insurance.

If you live in a threatened area, you can find out about the riot insurance from your insurance agent or broker.

Form Approved
OMB No. 026-R-0034

FEDERAL EMERGENCY MANAGEMENT AGENCY
FEDERAL CRIME INSURANCE

APPLICATION FOR RESIDENTIAL CRIME INSURANCE POLICY
CAREFULLY FILL OUT FORM. CLEARLY PRINT ALL ENTRIES

APPLICANT'S SOCIAL SECURITY NO.
(This will be the Policy Number)

1 2 3 - 4 5 - 6 7 8 9

Coverage under this Policy *(of which this application is a part)* will become effective at Noon on the day following the date of a U.S. Post Office affixed postmark. In the absence of such a postmark the effective date will be the day following receipt of application and payment unless a later date is requested. **(PLEASE READ PRIVACY ACT STATEMENT ON REVERSE)**

FOR OFFICIAL USE ONLY

EFFECTIVE DATE	EXPIRATION DATE *(One year from effective date)*
DEC. 1, 1980	DEC 1, 1981

ENTER NAME AND ADDRESS ▶

NAME JAMES J. JONES

TELEPHONE NUMBER
(Area Code)

NUMBER AND STREET
1 MAIN

APARTMENT NO.

CITY NEW YORK

COUNTY

STATE N.Y

ZIP CODE 11111

LOCATION TO BE INSURED IF DIFFERENT FROM THAT SHOWN ABOVE, IF SAME ENTER "SAME AS ABOVE"

NUMBER AND STREET
SAME AS ABOVE

APARTMENT NO.

CITY

COUNTY

STATE

ZIP CODE

SELECT AMOUNT OF COVERAGE DESIRED ▶

☐ $1000   ☐ $3000   ☐ $5000   ☐ $7000   ☒ $10,000

PLACE AN "X" IN THE APPROPRIATE BOX TO ANSWER EACH QUESTION. ▶

TYPE OF PREMISES TO BE INSURED

☐ Single Family Residence
☒ An Apartment
☐ Other *(Specify)* _____

HAS APPLICANT EVER PREVIOUSLY BEEN INSURED UNDER A FEDERAL CRIME INSURANCE POLICY?

☐ YES ☒ NO

(a) When was coverage last in force? _____
(b) What was previous policy number? _____

ENTER THE CORRECT PREMIUM FOR THE AMOUNT OF COVERAGE DESIRED, AND ENTER AMOUNT OF THE CHECK YOU ARE ENCLOSING. ▶

AT LEAST ONE HALF OF THE ANNUAL PREMIUM MUST ACCOMPANY THIS APPLICATION IN THE FORM OF A CHECK OR MONEY ORDER MADE PAYABLE TO THE "FEDERAL INSURANCE ADMINISTRATION".

AMOUNT OF ANNUAL PREMIUM	AMOUNT SUBMITTED	TERRITORY *(Check One)*		
$ 80 .00	$ 40.00	☐ 1	☐ 2	☒ 3

CERTIFICATION BY APPLICANT

READ CERTIFICATION, IF YOU HAVE ANY QUESTIONS, CALL NUMBER SHOWN AT BOTTOM, OTHERWISE SIGN, DATE, AND MAIL IMMEDIATELY. COVERAGE CANNOT BEGIN UNTIL FORM AND CHECK ARE RECEIVED ▶

"I certify under penalty of Federal law for fraud or intentional misrepresentation as set forth in 18 U.S.C. 1001 (1) that the statements I have made in the Application, are true and correct to the best of my knowledge and belief, (2) that I have read the information on the back of this application."

Policy is subject to the crime insurance provisions of Title VI of the Housing and Urban Development Act of 1970 (P.L. 91-609, December 31, 1970; 12 U.S.C. 1749 bbb-10a et seq.) and the Regulations of the Federal Insurance Administration issued pursuant thereto (24C.F.R. 80 et. seq.). Renewals of this coverage (and deductibles) shall be subject to the Regulations in force at the time of such renewals.

SIGNATURE OF APPLICANT James J. Jones

DATE Nov. 14, 1980

THE FOLLOWING IS TO BE COMPLETED WHEN APPLICATION IS BEING SUBMITTED FOR AN APPLICANT BY A LICENSED PROPERTY INSURANCE AGENT OR BROKER.

AGENTS/BROKERS, PLEASE BE SURE TO SIGN, DATE, AND FILL IN ALL OF THE INFORMATION REQUESTED. ▶

CERTIFICATION BY AGENT OR BROKER:
"I certify under penalty of Federal law (1) that I am an agent or broker licensed in the State in which the premises are located, (2) that the date of my signature is correct, and (3) I have explained to the Applicant that compliance with protective device requirements is a prerequisite for coverage under this Policy. I also agree that in the event of cancellation of a policy, I shall ratably refund to the Federal Insurance Administration commissions on the unearned portion of premiums at the same rate at which such commission was originally paid."

(Signature of Agent or Broker)

(Date)

(Federal Crime Producer Code)

NAME

(Agent's Tax Number)

ADDRESS

(Property Insurance License Number)

TELEPHONE NO.

SEND TO: FEDERAL CRIME INSURANCE, P.O. Box 41033, WASHINGTON, D.C. 20014

FOR ADDITIONAL INFORMATION OR TO REPORT CLAIMS, CALL TOLL FREE 800-638-8780. If you call from the DISTRICT OF COLUMBIA METRO-POLITAN AREA *(District of Columbia, Alexandria, Arlington, Va.: Prince Georges and Montgomery Counties, Md.)* you must call 652-2637. From all other communities in MARYLAND, you should call COLLECT (301) 652-2637. From Puerto Rico and the Virgin Islands call toll free 800-638-6830.

Replaces HUD-1621 (7-78) and all previous editions

FEMA-81-12 (5-80)

Disaster Relief

When a tornado, hurricane, flood or other natural disaster looms, local and state officials are the first to act. Residents of the threatened area are warned, and evacuated if necessary. If help is needed, the governor may order emergency measures put into effect, including the commitment of state police, National Guardsmen and all other resources at the disposal of the state.

If the situation appears to be too much for state and local authorities to handle, the governor may ask the President to declare the existence of a major disaster. Almost every kind of natural calamity may qualify. The Disaster Relief Act of 1974 defines a major disaster as a "hurricane, tornado, storm, flood, high water, wind-driven water, tidal wave, tsunami, earth-

How To Foil Burglars and Robbers

The Federal Insurance Administration (FIA) has published a leaflet called "Protecting Your Home Against Theft" containing valuable advice on burglar-proofing the home.

Here are some tips from that publication:

1. A good lock serves little purpose if the thief can break a pane of glass and unlock the door or window from the inside. One method of foiling such action is to replace glass near a lock with plastic pressed between two sheets of glass, which is virtually indestructible. Since an accomplished burglar will usually have a tool of some kind to extend his reach, it would be wise to replace more than just the panes closest to the lock with plastic glass.

On windows where appearance is of secondary importance, iron bars or a heavy grille might be used instead of plastic glass. If these windows might be needed as a fire escape, the grille or bars should be equipped with hinges and a padlock.

2. Most burglars will not enter a house that is occupied. A burglar alarm will usually protect you against forced entry. All doors and windows should be a part of this system.

3. To help create the impression that someone is at home, leave a radio or air conditioner running when you go out. Also leave several lights on; one light probably will not fool a burglar. A barking dog will scare away most burglars.

4. Leave the outside lights on to eliminate shadows around the house. The cost in electric light bills will be small, and the added protection will be of great value.

5. Leave the shades or blinds in the same position they would be in if you were at home. If all window shades and blinds are drawn, it will look as though nobody is there.

6. Be sure to close the garage door before leaving the house. If the car is gone, the burglar will conclude that you are away. Also, if the garage is open, a thief can go in, close the door behind him, and be protected while breaking into the house through the door leading from the garage.

7. Don't forget those little obvious things that give away your absence to burglars. If you go away, stop the newspaper, milk and mail deliveries so that tell-tale evidence will not pile up at the door and call attention to the fact that nobody is there. Ask your neighbors and the police to keep an eye on the house. Don't try to hide the key outdoors. Most of the places you can hide it are obvious. Also, don't go off leaving a lot of money or other valuables hidden somewhere in the house. Burglars are hard to fool at this sort of thing. If no one is there, and they have all the time they want, they will manage to find just about anything.

Operation Identification

To discourage the theft of radios, stereo sets, jewelry, electric typewriters, silverware and other items in the home, most major cities in the United States have adopted a program known as "Operation Identification." The key to the program is the marking of valuable personal items with identifying numbers that will make them easier to trace.

The program varies from one location to another, but the broad outlines are the same. In New York City, for example, the property owner may obtain registration forms, decals bearing the word "Operation Identification" and an electric etching tool at local precinct station houses.

The property owner uses the etching tool to mark the valuables with his or her Social Security number, plus the letters "N.Y.C." (Some cities prefer the number from the owner's driver's license.) The etching tool must be returned to the police within three days. The forms are filled out and also returned to the police, and the decals are placed on doors and windows where they will be seen by anyone who is tempted to burglarize the house.

Operation Identification is not, of course, a foolproof system. But the decals may discourage burglars from breaking into the house and if they do enter, the identifying numbers will make stolen goods harder to dispose of and easier to recover.

For best results, the system should be combined with as many protective measures as possible. Photograph all of the valuable items that cannot be marked with the identifying numbers. When you go away, leave your jewelry, silverware and other expensive belongings in a safe deposit box or the custody of a friend. Use timers with some of the lights in your house so that they will be on at normal hours. And if you have a tape recorder, rig it to go off when the doorbell is pushed. (A recording of a barking dog will do very nicely.) Thieves often try the doorbell to determine if anyone is at home.

The object of all these precautions is quite simple. By making it look as though someone is at home, you may cause the burglars to decide not to take a chance on breaking into your house.

POLICE DEPARTMENT CITY OF NEW YORK

CRIME PREVENTION PROGRAM

WE HAVE JOINED...

OPERATION IDENTIFICATION

ALL ITEMS OF VALUE ON THESE PREMISES HAVE BEEN MARKED FOR READY IDENTIFICATION BY THE NEW YORK CITY POLICE DEPT.

quake, volcanic eruption, landslide, mudslide, snowstorm, drought, fire, explosion, or other catastrophe in any part of the United States, which in the determination of the President, causes damage of sufficient severity and magnitude to warrant major disaster assistance above and beyond emergency services by the federal government to supplement the efforts and available resources of states, local governments, and private relief organizations in alleviating the damage, loss, hardship or suffering caused by a disaster."

When the President makes his declaration, the governor or an authorized representative applies for assistance through a coordinating officer of the Federal Emergency Management Agency. Disaster assistance centers are established in the affected area by FEMA and the state, and a broad range of relief measures is set in motion. Included are:

1. Temporary housing for disaster victims.

2. Unemployment and job-placement assistance for people who are thrown out of work by the disaster.

3. Low-interest loans to property owners, businessmen and farmers for repair and rehabilitation or replacement of damaged properties.

4. Grants of up to $5,000 to individuals and families for disaster-related expenses not otherwise covered.

5. Farm assistance for a wide range of needs, including crop insurance, debris removal, clearance of clogged streams, and loans for crops, equipment and machinery.

6. Food coupons for disaster victims.

7. Legal assistance for low-income disaster victims.

8. Insurance counseling and assistance for property owners.

9. Counseling and aid to relieve mental anguish and stress incurred by the victims.

10. Help for Social Security recipients and survivors to make sure their checks are forwarded to the correct addresses.

11. Veteran's aid, including survivor payments, pensions, insurance settlements and mortgage adjustments on VA-insured houses.

When a disaster occurs federal engineers will move in promptly to prepare a damage survey and make an estimate of the scope and costs of repairs. Within 90 days, eligible states, communities or authorized organizations may submit applications to the FEMA regional director for cleanup, construction and repair projects. Included in these projects are the removal of wreckage and debris; repair of roads, streets and bridges; repair or replacement of dikes, levees, irrigation works and drainage facilities; restoration or replacement of public buildings; repair of schools, utilities, recreational facilities, parks, hospitals, nursing homes and other publicly-owned medical installations.

Applications may also include requests for financial grants to supplement state and local aid for repairs on damaged installations or the construction of related new facilities. Federal help may also include loans to communities needing financial assistance, aid to public elementary and secondary schools and the use of federal equipment and resources for disaster relief or rehabilitation.

The President may simply declare an *emergency*. In this case, many different forms of aid will still be available. Included are emergency shelters, food, water, medicine and medical care; search and rescue aid, emergency communications and transportation; and repairs to essential utilities and facilities.

Even if the President does not declare a major disaster or an emergency, government agencies may provide a broad range of help. Some of these agencies and the kinds of aid they may provide are listed below.

1. The U.S. Coast Guard and the U.S. Air Force. Search and rescue missions, evacuation of disaster victims, transportation of supplies and equipment.

2. The U.S. Army Corps of Engineers. Flood fighting and rescue operations, rebuilding and repair of federally constructed flood-control works.

3. Federal Emergency Management Administration. This agency provides grants, equipment, supplies and personnel for fighting forest and grassland fires on public or private lands.

4. Department of Health and Human Services. Assistance to welfare and vocational rehabilitation agencies. The department's Public Health Service provides emergency health and sanitation help. The Food and Drug Administration aids in the decontamination or condemnation of contaminated food and drugs.

5. Agricultural Stabilization and Conservation Service (U.S. Agriculture Department). Grants for rehabilitation of damaged farm lands.

6. Farmers Home Administration. Guarantees emergency loans to farmers, ranchers and oyster planters for damage to farm property, crops, livestock and equipment. (Further information may be obtained from the local offices of the Farmers Home Administration, which are usually located in county seats and listed in telephone directories under U.S. Government, Agriculture.)

7. The Small Business Administration. Disaster loans designed to assist businesses and homeowners.

The loans may be used to repair or replace personal property, damaged real estate, machinery and equipment. Damage—as a result of natural disasters, riots or civil disturbances—must have occurred in an area officially declared by the executive branch of the government to be eligible for assistance.

Home loans run as high as $55,000. The ceiling on business loans is $500,000. Applications may be made to field offices of the Small Business Administration, which are listed on page 93 of this book and appear in telephone directories in major cities under U.S. Government.

8. Federal Highway Administration (Department of Transportation). Assistance for the restoration of highways and bridges.

9. Internal Revenue Service. Tax refunds for losses resulting from natural disasters.

10. Food and Nutrition Service (U.S. Department of Agriculture). Foods from storage supplies for group feeding of disaster victims.

Aid from Non-Government Organizations

Working in close cooperation with government agencies are a number of non-profit organizations that provide indispensable services in time of emergency. The leading voluntary organizations and the services that they render are listed below.

The American Red Cross. Provides mass care for disaster victims, including food, shelter, medical treatment, blood. Makes grants for repair or rebuilding of homes and replacement of goods for families not eligible for government assistance, or in emergencies where there is no official disaster declaration.

The Salvation Army. Provides housing, food, clothing, counseling and other personal services for disaster victims.

Church Organizations. Local and national branches of many of the country's churches offer various types of assistance, including mass feeding, shelter, clothing, bedding, used furniture, technical and financial aid.

A comprehensive list of these and other organizations that play important roles in disaster relief, together with the kinds of aid provided, has been compiled by the National Governors' Association. Titled *National Emergency Assistance Programs, A Governor's Guide,* the publication is distributed in looseleaf form and is updated on a quarterly basis. Copies can be found in state civil defense or emergency offices.

A Decision to Rent

If mortgage interest rates are too high for you, or you can't afford to buy the kind of house you need, your best bet may be to find a place to rent. You can get some good advice, and perhaps a lead or two, from the nearest HUD area office. The department publishes a booklet called *Wise Rental Practices,* which is crammed with useful information on topics such as "Where To Look"; "How To Approach a Landlord"; "Inspect the Premises Before Renting"; "Some Provisions Every Normal Lease Should Contain"; "Rules and Regulations"; "Deposits"; "Landlords' Rights and Responsibilities"; and "Receiving Greater Satisfaction from Renting."

Here's a sample from the booklet, explaining how to calculate the amount you can afford to spend on the rent:

"In attempting to determine what may be considered a reasonable rent, you should try to keep your total monthly housing cost equal to one week's gross pay. . . . As costs rise, it may be more difficult for you to achieve this goal, but it is one to aim towards. Some states and localities have rent controls. Check the local laws to determine if rent controls affect your area."

You can obtain a copy of *Wise Rental Practices* by writing to: Consumer Information Center, Dept. 579 K, Pueblo, Colorado, 81009.

Low- and Moderate-Income Rentals

In the aftermath of World War II, the Congress of the United States passed the Housing Act of 1949, calling for an end to "the serious housing shortage, the elimination of substandard and other inadequate housing through the clearance of slums and blighted areas, and the realization as soon as feasible of a goal of a decent home in a suitable living environment for every American family."

The program was mainly directed toward slum clearance, and in 1954 the concept was expanded to include urban renewal, aimed at the rehabilitation and conservation of declining areas. Progress was made in the years that followed, but the efforts fell far short of the objective of a decent home and suitable environment for every American family. A housing census in 1960 declared that one housing unit out of four in the United States was sub-standard.

The government has attempted to alleviate the housing shortage by a system of subsidies for the construction, rehabilitation and financing of rental housing.

Mortgages for the construction and rehabilitation of multi-family rental housing are guaranteed by HUD. The department also insures mortgages for the financing of rental or co-operative multi-family housing. It offers technical assistance and loans for housing for the elderly and the handicapped.

Public Housing

To provide decent rental housing for low-income families, HUD furnishes operating subsidies and technical assistance to local public housing agencies. The local agencies develop, own and operate the housing. It comes into their possession by three routes:

1. The "turnkey" approach, by which a public housing agency invites proposals from private developers, then selects the best proposal and purchases the project upon completion.

2. The public housing agency acts as its own developer, acquiring the site, drawing up plans and accepting private bids for construction.

3. The local housing agency purchases existing housing, rehabilitates it or simply makes it available to low-income families.

HUD finances improvements in the locally owned public housing, and provides subsidies to the public housing agencies for the maintenance and operation of their projects. The operating subsidies are calculated through a formula based on what it costs a well-run housing agency to operate its projects. The object of these subsidies is to make sure that rents will be reasonable and services adequate.

Applications for living space in public housing are made to the local agencies, which are listed in telephone directories under the city government. In fiscal 1982, the number of new public housing starts was cut back from 24,000 to 22,500. Public housing will therefore be harder to find in some areas.

The Section 8 Rental Assistance Program

The government's multi-billion-dollar rental subsidy program is known as Section 8, after the authorizing provision in the Housing Act of 1937. Described by former HUD Secretary Moon Landrieu as "the backbone" of his department's housing effort, the rent subsidies are designed to make up the difference between government-approved rents and the amounts that low-income people are able to pay.

To be eligible for the housing assistance, tenants must be able to show that their incomes are between 50 and 80 percent of the median incomes for their areas. (The median is not the average; it is the figure at the middle of the income ladder for the area. Median is used rather than the average to prevent high incomes at the top of the ladder from unduly influencing the result.) Adjustments are allowed to take into account the number of people in the family.

Tenants were formerly required to pay no more than 25 percent of their incomes for the rent. Beginning in 1982, the tenant contribution is being increased by one percent per year over a five-year period, until it reaches 30 percent of the tenant's adjusted income. The subsidy takes care of the rest.

The rental units may be existing, newly constructed or rehabilitated structures. Rentals in existing units are administered by public housing agencies, which certify the tenants for the program, inspect the rental units and enter into contractual arrangements with the owners. The tenants sign leases with the owners for their portions of the rents. The subsidy is paid by HUD to the public housing agencies, which in turn pay the owners.

The program provides only rental assistance; construction costs and mortgages are not within its scope. But when new housing is constructed for the program, HUD imposes a limit on the cost. (The ceilings vary in different parts of the country. The figure is lower in Biloxi, Mississippi, for example, than in New York.) The agency also reviews each project to see that it does not exceed the limits.

When housing is being constructed or rehabilitated, developers are invited by HUD to submit proposals. (The proposals may also come to HUD by way of state financing agencies or the Farmers Home Administration.) If the agency grants a preliminary approval, the developer goes to an FHA-approved lender for a loan. The developer then submits a more detailed proposal, setting forth the cost, design, financing arrangements and management setup. HUD reviews this detailed proposal before signing an agreement with the developer. When the project is completed to HUD's satisfaction, the department enters into a contract with the developer for payment of rental subsidies over a period of from 20 to 40 years.

The program expanded so rapidly and became so expensive that the Reagan Administration decided to slow down its growth and explore new ways to house low-income people. This means that the number of new housing contracts for the Section 8 program will be substantially cut back.

Housing for the Handicapped and the Elderly

Under Section 202 of the Housing Act of 1959, HUD makes low-interest loans to finance the development and rehabilitation of housing for the elderly and the handicapped. To make sure that low-income people have access to this housing, a minimum of 20 percent of the Section 202 housing units must be set aside for the Section 8 rental assistance program. As explained above, the Section 8 program pays the difference between the contract rent and the contribution that is made by the tenant.

Single people who are 62 or over are eligible for this housing, as well as two or more related people, including a head of household who is 62 or handicapped. Unrelated people may qualify if a doctor certifies that the presence of one is needed for the care and keeping of the other. Physically handicapped individuals who are 18 or more may also qualify.

Further information about the Section 202 program may be obtained from area HUD offices (listed on page 124).

Housing for the handicapped is discussed in detail in Chapter 5. A more detailed discussion of housing for the elderly may be found in Chapter 8.

Fair Housing in the United States
Under Title VIII of the Civil Rights Act of 1968, discrimination in housing on the basis of race, color, age, religion, sex or national origin is forbidden. Responsibility for the administration of the law is charged to HUD. Complaints of discrimination are usually investigated by the department. But where state and local agencies afford protection comparable to that of the federal law, HUD refers complaints to those agencies.

The Department of Housing and Urban Development is also responsible for enforcing Executive Order 11063 forbidding discrimination in housing and related facilities owned or operated by the federal government.

Individuals who believe that they have been victimized by discrimination should file their

The New Look at Niagara Falls

Housing rehabilitation projects in America's declining cities may draw upon a variety of programs for funding. Niagara Falls, New York, is a good example.

Until the 1960s, the celebrated tourist area was steadily growing in population, reaching a peak of 102,000 residents. But the city fell into a decline, plagued by many of the ills that have beset older industrial cities throughout the northeast. The population dwindled and grew older; middle-class residents moved to the suburbs; commercial areas decayed; unemployment soared, and the city's older neighborhoods were afflicted by such a severe housing blight that only 28 percent of all the residences could be classified as sound.

Community Block Grants totaling approximately $3 million a year were allocated to Niagara Falls. But only about a third of each year's allocation was set aside for housing. With nearly 10,000 housing units in need of rehabilitation or repair, the Block Grants were inadequate for the task at hand.

In the fall of 1977, Mrs. Nancy Correa was brought to Niagara Falls from the town of Newburgh, New York, in the Hudson Valley, near West Point. Mrs. Correa had lived in Newburgh for 22 years, and had run the community's housing rehabilitation program there so effectively that the Department of Housing and Urban Development in an unusual departure from normal bureaucratic procedure, had permitted her to approve loan applications without waiting for the agency's assent.

In Niagara Falls, Mrs. Correa was appointed to the position of Community Development Director, charged with the responsibility for creating an effective housing rehabilitation program. Under her direction, a Community Development Program was devised. Niagara Falls' housing needs were surveyed, and four neighborhoods were targeted for top priority action. Public notices were placed in the newspapers inviting local residents to meetings where citizen advisory committees would be formed to participate in the planning, execution and supervision of strategies for the neighborhood.

114

complaints with any HUD office. The department will attempt to eliminate the alleged abuse by conciliation, or refer it to the Attorney General for legal action, if necessary.

Revitalization of Neighborhoods and Communities

With the passage of the Housing and Development Act of 1974, Congress signaled a new approach to the revitalization of declining urban areas. All federal programs would be consolidated under one gigantic umbrella known as Community Development Block Grants. The federal government would fund urban projects, but spending priorities would be determined at the local level.

Under the block-grant approach, 70 percent of the funds are provided to cities with at least 50,000 population and urban counties of 200,000 or more. Grants are calculated on the basis of need according to a weighted formula in which poverty counts for 50 percent, and population and overcrowding are assigned a value of 25 percent each. The formula varies for more severely distressed cities: here the age of the housing counts 50 percent, poverty is rated at 30 percent and population growth counts 20 percent.

Neighborhood corporations, including business people and residents, were formed, and comprehensive plans for the rehabilitation of the targeted neighborhoods were devised. To finance the undertakings, a flexible funding strategy was adopted. Community Development Block Grants and HUD's Rehabilitation loan program would be used to help finance this program. Section 8 housing assistance contracts would be utilized to encourage landlords with dilapidated multi-unit structures to rehabilitate their housing.

Basic grants of up to $7,500 were allowed for qualified property owners, and those who were not eligible were permitted to apply for loans of up to $27,000 per housing unit. Action was speeded when HUD again empowered Nancy Correa to approve the loans without waiting for concurrence from the department.

Home repairs and rehabilitation were undertaken, as well as public works, commercial revitalization, site clearance and demolition, the development of urban parks and community facilities. In the first three years, 350 houses were rehabilitated. In the central city's North Main Street district, business people and property owners undertook the refurbishing of their buildings. New sidewalks, curbs, trees and a canopied walkway appeared. In the Highland Avenue neighborhood, long one of the city's roughest areas, where prostitution, street gambling and violence had flourished, blighted buildings were demolished and dilapidated housing was rehabilitated. A painting and siding campaign was instituted to spruce up many of the rundown dwellings.

The task of rehabilitating the housing in Niagara Falls would be long and arduous. But as the work progressed, a new look and a new spirit emerged.

Reflecting that spirit, John Brewer, the owner of a refurbished house in the Highland Avenue neighborhood proudly exclaimed, "This program is making our neighborhood a better place to live. People are starting to care about the neighborhood. I get a lot of compliments for my house. Before, nobody would have cared."

Urban Homestead Loans

Because people in marginal residential areas frequently default on their mortgages, HUD usually has an inventory of thousands of unoccupied houses. To reduce this inventory, and to encourage the revitalization of rundown neighborhoods, HUD transfers some of the vacant properties to local governments and permits them to be sold for sums as low as one dollar, to "urban homesteaders," who promise to move in and restore the property. The sales of these houses are publicized in the newspapers, on television and the radio.

If you would like to buy a house for a token amount and fix it up, call your local housing agency and find out whether any homesteading properties are available. Before making a bid, you will have to visit the city housing agency and complete an application designed mainly to show that you can afford the home ownership and the repairs that are needed to restore the property.

A credit check will be done on you, and if your application is approved, you will be permitted to look over the available properties and place your name in contention for the house you want. HUD requires that the houses be awarded fairly. Therefore the "bidding" normally takes the form of a lottery. The names of the applicants are usually placed in a hat or a fishbowl, and the mayor or another public official will draw the winners. A first choice and an alternate are picked for each house. If, for some reason, the winner fails to qualify or backs out, the alternate will become the owner of the house.

It is possible to bid on more than one house at a time, but if a bidder's name is drawn twice, it will be discarded the second time around. After the drawing, a warranty deed will be issued, transferring the property from HUD to the local housing agency, and the winner will be furnished with a conditional deed for a payment as low as one dollar.

If you win one of these houses, you must repair it sufficiently to meet the local building-code standards before moving in. After you have occupied the house, you must bring it up to local standards for decent, safe and sanitary housing within a period of 18 months. You may be able to get an FHA-insured or conventional loan to restore the property and make the necessary repairs.

You must live in the house a minimum of three years (in some places the requirement is five years). Then you can get a quit-claim deed making you the outright owner. At that point, you should have a livable house, purchased for a small amount of money and restored to good condition by dint of your own labors. There's an appropriate term for that kind of investment: "Sweat Equity."

Action Grants

Adopted in 1977, the Action Grant program represents a partnership between government, local agencies and private interests. The program's distinctive feature is its use of government funds to stimulate private investment in the revitalization of neighborhoods and communities.

Before the Urban Development Action Grant (UDAG) funds are committed, plans for the projects and their financing are drawn up by local agencies. The government then reviews the plans and selects the projects to be funded on a competitive basis, with the major emphasis on the physical and economic deterioration of the project areas.

The projects may include rehabilitation and new construction. Central business districts, aging neighborhoods and declining industrial areas are targeted for rejuvenation. New shopping centers, hotels, office buildings and housing units may be built. Government funding for the program serves as a catalyst, and is heavily outweighed by private investment. In the first four years of the plan's operation, 1,200 projects were funded. Private investment amounted to $13 billion, and the contributions of the federal government totaled $2.1 billion.

How Action Grant Funds Are Obtained

Applications for action grants for major cities and urban counties are accepted by HUD during the first month of each quarter. Small cities should apply during the second month of each quarter. A separate application must be submitted for each project, and HUD normally expects the projects to be completed within four years. Applications should be made on forms obtainable from HUD area offices.

Action at the Local Level

In recent years, community residents have been playing an ever-larger role in the revitalization of neighborhoods. In some cases, they work independently, and in others they cooperate with government agencies at the local, state and federal level.

In 1978, HUD formed the Office of Neighborhood Development to support local groups in their rehabilitation efforts. The purpose of that office, as described at the time by President Carter, is "to draw upon the sense of community and voluntary effort that is alive in America and on the loyalty that Americans feel for their neighborhoods."

Some outstanding examples of local initiatives are cited below. The projects vary widely, both in terms of geography and the nature of the activities. But they all have one thing in common: they came about because people cared about their neighborhoods and took action to prevent them from going to ruin.

Baltimore, Maryland

Baltimore has served as a pacesetter in the revitalization of neighborhoods. The city's Federal Hill section, with its modest row houses, is a melting pot in which people from many ethnic groups have lived for generations. From the mid nineteenth century until the post-World War II years, the Cross Street Market was the hub of everyday life, where many people shopped at stalls laden with fish, poultry, meat and baked goods.

But as Baltimore expanded and shopping malls mushroomed, the market lost most of its customers. Then, in the mid 1970s, residents, businessmen and city planners got together to devise a strategy for the market's revival.

A revitalization plan was submitted to the City Council, and an ordinance was passed delineating the area to be restored, the timetable, the role and obligations of the city, business establishments and area residents.

A private developer bought five dilapidated buildings and converted them into attractive town houses to stimulate action on the project. The city decided to make loans available at a 7 percent interest rate over a term of 20 years.

Streets were repaired and the lighting improved. Shop owners promised to refurbish their establishments. Storefronts were cleaned and painted. Neon lights and over-sized signs were removed. Boarded windows were repaired and shutters were added where needed.

The result was the transformation of a dying neighborhood into one of the city's most bustling and attractive areas. The Cross Street Market is now thriving, and people have started moving back into the adjacent areas.

Madison, Wisconsin

When workmen started pouring concrete in a hole in the ground where a filling station had stood on Williamson Street in Madison, neighborhood residents watched warily. A few days later, a truck drove up to the location and workmen unloaded a taco stand and bolted it to the ground. Williamson Street residents were outraged. The neighborhood was run-down, a 10-block corridor of faded wooden houses and shabby storefronts. But there was hope for it. The Madison Development Corporation, a non-profit organization, had decided that it could be revived and had prevailed upon the city for a feasibility study.

The arrival of the taco stand, however, led neighborhood residents to conclude that the area was going to be converted into a commercial strip with fast-food drive-ins and never-ending traffic jams.

117

Action Grants in Action

There are many kinds of Action Grants. They may be designed to expand or rejuvenate business sections, or rehabilitate outmoded housing, or for a variety of other purposes. Some of the major categories follow, together with examples of the Action Grants in action.

Restoration of Historic Districts

Savannah, Georgia. In the 1950s, a group of interested citizens organized the Historic Savannah Foundation and saved the old quarter of the city, which had been laid out by James Oglethorpe in the 18th century. The refurbished section with its lovely green squares became one of the showplaces of the South. Tourists flocked to Savannah, swelling the city's coffers by $100 million a year.

As the project neared completion, Savannah turned its attention to the rehabilitation of surrounding neighborhoods. A 60-block area known as the Victorian District, with brick sidewalks and tree-lined streets a mile and a half from the center of the city, became the focal point of the new revitalization efforts.

Bordering on an old Civil War parade ground, the area had been developed toward the end of the 19th century with spacious single-family Victorian houses made of brick or wood with turrets and gingerbread ornamentation. But the neighborhood had gone into a decline years ago. When plans for its restoration were initiated in the mid-1970s, it was little more than a slum, with abandoned buildings, dilapidated houses, sidewalks and streets in disrepair.

The projected restoration of the Victorian District had a two-fold objective. Residences and business establishments would be refurbished and upgraded, but the essential Victorian character of the neighborhood would be retained.

The city of Savannah was unable to finance the project, and local investors could go only part of the way. Outside help was needed if the undertaking was to become a reality, and that was where the Action Grant program came in. By providing $650,000 for street and sidewalk repairs, lighting, landscaping and park improvements, the government made it possible for the city to obtain commitments of $1,945,000 from Savannah banks for rehabilitation loans to the owners of 53 homes. HUD funds from Section 8 were obtained for 500 rental units in the area and the Historic Savannah Foundation assumed responsibility for the rehabilitation of 25 vacant properties.

As the project moved forward, an Action Grant of $5 million, earmarked for subsequent phases, was expected to stimulate an additional $220 million in private investments. By the end of the 1980s, Savannah's Victorian District will be a revitalized residential quarter where people of all races and economic levels can live.

Adaptive Use

Akron, Ohio. When the Quaker Oats Company moved out of downtown Akron in 1970, it left behind a complex of 101 tall silos that had been used to store corn, oats and other grains. Logic dictated that all of the abandoned, odd-looking structures be torn down, but the city of Akron and a private organization called the Quaker Square Association came up with an alternative solution. A cluster of 36 of the largest silos would be saved and converted into a hotel.

An Action Grant of $1 million made possible the raising of nearly $5.5 million in private funds. With a hydraulic, diamond-tipped saw, panels were cut through the silos, concrete floors were poured; hotel rooms, baths, connecting corridors and elevators were installed.

In the summer of 1980, the new 144-room hotel—known as the Quaker Square Hilton—opened for business, providing Akron with 168 new jobs, tax revenues of approximately $25,000 a year, and a showpiece that had architects in all parts of the country buzzing with interest.

Historic Buildings

Birmingham, Alabama's, experience had been repeated many times over in America. While the city's outer edge sprouted shopping centers, automobile dealerships, filling stations and fast food eateries, the central city was depressed and partially abandoned.

The proud old four-story Steiner Bank Building had lain vacant for more than a decade. Built in 1890, the gaudy Romanesque structure with its stone arches and lintels, and its vividly contrasting colors, was at the time of its construction the tallest building in Birmingham, and the only one with an elevator.

In the 1970s, Birmingham initiated a massive redevelopment program. Substandard housing would be rehabilitated, and residential neighborhoods revitalized with Community Development Block Grant funds. But these projects left no money for smaller undertakings like the renovation of the Steiner Bank Building and the development of badly needed parking space nearby.

An Action Grant of $300,000 served as a catalyst to encourage the investment of nearly $1.4 million in private funds. The grant was earmarked for the purchase and development of two parking lots. Two local firms then secured funds for the restoration of the bank building, and the city contributed $3,000 to the project, all it could afford at the time.

Triggered by the Action Grant, the project went forward. The historic old building was preserved; a warehouse behind it was restored and occupied by an accounting firm, and a badly needed stimulus provided for the revitalization of the downtown area.

New Construction

Troy, New York, was an aging, depressed city, its downtown area dotted with dilapidated, vacant buildings. As the exodus to the suburbs gained momentum, Denby's department store remained behind, an island in a trash-littered *cul-de-sac,* surrounded by abandoned, decaying buildings.

The store's owners did not want to move, but sales were slumping, and talk of the downtown area revitalization project had come to nothing. Relocation of the store, as contemplated by the owners, sounded what the city's mayor described as "the death knell for an already devastated central business district."

A developer named Carl Grimm scoured up private funds for the construction and operation of a shopping mall in the area around Denby's. But leases for spaces in the buildings were contingent upon adequate parking space and the enclosure of the shopping mall to seal it off from traffic.

With an Action Grant of $1.75 million, and $6,150,944 in private funds, the new Uncle Sam Mall and the parking spaces were developed. Shops were leased; a refurbished Denby's opened for business in time for the Christmas season of 1978, and reported record sales.

The project served a dual purpose for Troy. Care was taken in the rehabilitation to preserve the city's historic character, and the new development served as a catalyst for the downtown area's recovery.

Angered by this development, 50 residents met with their alderman and the developer who had set up the taco stand. When the developer refused to accede to their request to take the stand down, they decided to go before the City Council. The council ruled in their favor, and the taco stand was removed. The owner of a motorcycle shop next door planted dahlias, marigolds and hollyhocks where the eyesore had stood.

To celebrate their victory over the developer, the residents of Williamson Street decided to hold a fair. They blocked off the street, hired musicians, dancers and a puppeteer, and set up booths to serve food and beverages. Six-foot maps of the neighborhood were distributed, so people could mark the stores and houses they wanted to keep, point out where additional facilities were needed and indicate structures to be repaired or torn down. The suggestions were forwarded to a local development corporation, where the most promising ideas were selected and incorporated into a plan for revitalizing the area. Today, new housing projects and business establishments have emerged, and the Williamson Street area is a bustling community.

New Haven, Connecticut

In the Hill Section of New Haven, buildings were boarded up, and vacant lots were choked with weeds. More than 200 houses were abandoned, and the neighborhood appeared to be on an irreversible downward slide. Then some of the residents got together and formed the Home Maintenance Corporation. They planned to rehabilitate some of the 17 abandoned houses along Ann Street, but the corporation could raise only $5,000, and it wasn't enough for the job.

The residents decided to start a tool-lending library, so people could borrow tools and do some of the repair work themselves. They got a grant of $4,800 from a local development agency and began to look around for other sources of funds. The city of New Haven was getting $17 million in Community Development Block Grants, but only $250,000 of the amount was being set aside for home owners assistance.

A delegation from the neighborhood went downtown to interest City Hall in housing rehabilitation and preservation. It was election year, and at the urging of Hill Section residents, a candidate for mayor decided to make neighborhood preservation a campaign issue. The candidate was elected, and the $250,000 housing appropriation was increased to a total of $3 million.

A block-by-block revitalization of the Ann Street area was initiated. Seven of the abandoned houses belonged to HUD, and had been offered to the city of New Haven, but the city had turned them down. Now, the Home Maintenance Corporation prevailed upon the city to accept the houses and transfer them to the community. Sales of the remaining ten abandoned houses to members of the corporation were negotiated with the owners.

The houses were repaired by the new owners, with tools borrowed from the Home Maintenance Corporation. Design assistance, financial consultations, budgets, on-site supervision and recycled building materials were also made available.

From Ann Street, the corporation expanded its efforts to take in adjacent areas. In conjunction with the city of New Haven and the Yale Medical Center, a comprehensive plan for the revitalization of the entire Hill Section was devised. Housing units for one, two and three families were earmarked for rehabilitation, and ground was broken for 80 new units of Section 8 housing.

As the revitalization spread through the Hill Street section, the feeling of the residents was well expressed by Dolly Wilson. "There isn't a night or morning goes by that I don't get on my knees and pray to God about how he blessed me with this house," she said.

David, Kentucky

Tucked away in the green hills of Kentucky, David was a town of fewer than 200 inhabitants, "so beautiful," a resident recalled, "the people used to go out of their way just to drive through it."

The town had a movie house, a swimming pool and a company store with clothing, hardware, groceries, a post office and beauty shop. There were no other stores, and no neon signs, for David was a mining town, where the company owned everything.

If you needed a plumber or a carpenter, the company supplied one. "If you wanted a roast for supper," Dorothy Clarke, director of the David Community Development Corporation, recalled, "you called the company store, and at 11:00 the truck would make its first run. The driver would put your groceries on your front porch, and at 3:00 he would do the same thing."

In 1968, the mine closed. The company store shut down; there were no services and, even worse, no jobs. The town was sold to a developer, then to a buyer who was interested in it as a tax write-off. The buyer sold some of the houses to people who lived in a neighboring county, and they came and hauled them away.

David appeared to be doomed. The local water supply was contaminated; an outbreak of hepatitis struck the town, and people had to drive to Prestonburg, eight miles away, to fill jugs with water.

Local residents organized the David Community Development Corporation. The Appalachian Regional Commission (a federal-state development agency) and HUD put up the money to pipe water in from a neighboring community. Residents raised $110,000, with the help of the local Catholic Mission, the Housing Assistance Council in Washington, DC, and a loan from a local bank, and bought the town from the developer.

A planning grant from the Appalachian Regional Commission enabled the residents to work out a five-year plan for the town's revival. A craft center, two community parks and a 28-unit complex of Section 8 housing were developed, and a new air of confidence emerged in David. "We know exactly where we are

going," said Dorothy Clarke. She added some practical advice for others who may find themselves in the predicament that David faced in 1968: "If you ask me what you have to do to form a community development corporation that's successful, I'd tell you, first, excite and unite your people. If there's something in your town or your community you don't like, don't put up with it. Get your people mad."

The key is persistence and commitment, she says. "Once the people are committed, incorporate the organization, assess your resources and needs, find money, address your immediate problems, and set up a plan. . . . Once people make up their minds to change things, they find a way. David was almost a ghost town, but I can promise you, it will never die again. Never. The people won't let it."

Rural Housing Aid

More than three-fifths of all the sub-standard housing in the United States is located in rural areas. In an effort to alleviate the housing shortage, the Farmers Home Administration (FmHA) maintains a variety of programs. A summary of the key features follows.

Home Ownership Loans. The FmHA makes loans to low- and moderate- income families living in rural areas. The loans are designed to enable families to purchase, build, improve or relocate their homes.

Individuals, corporations or partnerships may also obtain "conditional commitments" for the construction or rehabilitation of single-family housing in rural areas. The commitments are not contracts, but assurances to builders or sellers that FmHA will make loans to qualified applicants, provided that the houses meet the agency's specifications.

Applicants must be qualified builders who own the sites where the housing will be located and can show that they are financially able to complete the projects. The builders must certify that there will be no discrimination in the sale of the housing on the basis of race, creed, color, sex, marital status or national origin.

The conditional commitment is valid for 12 months, but may be extended for an additional 6 months if delays are caused by bad weather, shortages of material or other uncontrollable circumstances.

Applications are made at county offices of the FmHA, usually located in the county seats.

Repair and Improvement Loans. The FmHA makes loans to low-income homeowners to bring houses to minimum property standards. Grants are made to remove safety or health hazards.

Repair loans and grants may be used to repair roofs, provide sanitary water and waste disposal systems, install screens, windows and insulation or make other repairs intended to improve the safety of the houses.

Home improvement loans may include the addition of an extra room, remodeling of the kitchen and other measures to modernize the house.

The form and amounts of assistance vary. Loans are made to families that do not need or cannot afford a new house, but need repair work to bring their property to minimum standards. Grants are made only to low-income homeowners who are 62 or older and cannot afford the full cost of the repairs. Very low-income families may receive up to $5,000 in loans or grants.

Higher income families may borrow up to $7,000 for home improvement. Most loans are for up to 25 years. Interest rates are based on the family's adjusted income.

Home Weatherization Loans. Energy-saving devices and modifications designed to make houses more comfortable may be financed by loans from electric co-ops in rural areas. Insulation, weather-stripping, storm windows and doors and repairs of deteriorating or substandard parts of the houses are included. Applicants must be members of rural electric co-ops;

they must have good credit ratings and be in need of the loans to make the improvements. Loans are limited to low- and moderate-income families.

Application should be made at the local electric co-op.

Rental Assistance Program. The FmHA maintains a rental assistance program similar to HUD's Section 8 housing assistance payments. Low-income families are helped with their rent payments by the program. An income ceiling is applied to applicants for assistance from the program. The amount depends upon the part of the country where the transaction occurs.

Application should be made at the county FmHA office.

Construction and Repair Loans for Rental Housing. Loans for the construction, purchase or repair of rental housing in rural areas are made by the FmHA. Duplexes, apartment houses and other multi-unit dwellings are included.

The loans are made in communities of up to 20,000 people. Funds may be used for the purchase of land, construction or improvement of streets and water and waste disposal systems, recreation and service facilities, installation of laundry equipment and landscaping. Lawn seeding, shrubbery and tree planting are also included.

The FmHA determines the eligibility of the borrowers. Application should be made to a county FmHA office.

Self-Help Housing Loans. Low-income families may qualify for FmHA loans for the construction of modest houses if they are unable to obtain financing elsewhere. In order to apply, an applicant must find from 6 to 10 families in the area who are interested in the program. They must agree to work together as a group under the supervision of a construction expert. The houses must be built in the same community. Group members must attend all pre-construction meetings and fulfill their responsibilities as homeowners once the construction is completed.

Up to $100,000 may be borrowed; the exact amount is determined by FmHA.

Housing for the Elderly and Handicapped. Communal rental housing for the elderly and handicapped is financed by the FmHA. The purpose of the program is to afford senior citizens housing with dining facilities and supporting services. Transportation to health clinics and shopping centers, housekeeping and personal care are also provided.

Loans cover the construction and repair of apartment-style housing, mainly in towns of up to 10,000 population, but communities of as many as 20,000 people are sometimes included.

Applicants must be able to operate the housing projects effectively. Individuals, trusts, consumer co-ops, associations, partnerships, profit and non-profit corporations and state or local public agencies are eligible for the loans. A maximum repayment period of 50 years is allowed. Details of the project's location and construction must be included. Plans for meal service, housekeeping, personal care, transportation, social and recreational activities must be explained.

Applications for the construction and repair loans should be made to the county FmHA office or FmHA district office.

For further information, or to apply for a loan, get in touch with the county FmHA office or write to:

The Farmers Home Administration
U.S. Department of Agriculture
Washington, DC 20250

Directory of Government Housing Offices

U.S. Department of Housing and Urban Development, Washington, DC 20410

HUD Regional Offices

Region I
(Connecticut, Maine, Massachusetts, New Hampshire, Rhode Island, Vermont)
John F. Kennedy Federal Building
Boston, MA 02203

Region II
(New Jersey, New York, Caribbean)
26 Federal Plaza
New York, NY 10278

Region III
(Delaware, Maryland, Pennsylvania, Virginia, West Virginia)
Curtis Building
6th and Walnut Sts.
Philadelphia, PA 19106

Region IV
(Alabama, Florida, Georgia, Kentucky, Mississippi, North Carolina, South Carolina, Tennessee)
Richard B. Russell Federal Building
75 Spring St., SW
Atlanta, GA 30303

Region V
(Illinois, Indiana, Michigan, Minnesota, Ohio, Wisconsin)
300 South Wacker Dr.
Chicago, IL 60606

Region VI
(Arkansas, Louisiana, New Mexico, Oklahoma, Texas)
221 West Lancaster Ave.
Fort Worth, TX 76113

Region VII
(Iowa, Kansas, Missouri, Nebraska)
Professional Building
1103 Grand St.
Kansas City, MO 64106

Region VIII
(Colorado, Montana, North Dakota, South Dakota, Utah, Wyoming)
Executive Tower
1405 Curtis St.
Denver, CO 80202

Region IX
(Arizona, California, Hawaii, Nevada)
450 Golden Gate Ave.
P. O. Box 36003
San Francisco, CA 94102

Region X
(Alaska, Idaho, Oregon, Washington)
Arcade Plaza Building
1321 Second Ave.
Seattle, WA 98101

HUD Area Offices

(Note: States not listed do not have area offices. Residents of those states should contact regional offices indicated above.)

Alabama:
Daniel Building
15 South 20th St.
Birmingham, AL 35233

Alaska:
701 C St.
Anchorage, AK 99513

Arkansas:
One Union National Plaza
Little Rock, AR 72201

California:
2500 Wilshire Blvd.
Los Angeles, CA 90057

1 Embarcadero Center
San Francisco, CA 94111

Connecticut:
One Hartford Square West
Hartford, CT 06106

District of Columbia:
1875 Connecticut Ave., NW
Washington, DC 20009

Florida:
Peninsular Plaza
661 Riverside Ave.
Jacksonville, FL 32204

Georgia:
Richard B. Russell Federal Building
75 Spring St., SW
Atlanta, GA 30303

Hawaii:
300 Ala Moana Blvd.
Honolulu, HI 96850

Illinois
1 North Dearborn St.
Chicago, IL 60602

Indiana:
151 North Delaware St.
Indianapolis, IN 46207

Kentucky:
539 River City Mall
Louisville, KY 40202

Louisiana:
Plaza Tower
1001 Howard Ave.
New Orleans, LA 70113

Maryland:
Two Hopkins Plaza
10 North Calvert St.
Baltimore, MD 21202

Massachusetts:
Bullfinch Building
15 New Chardon St.
Boston, MA 02114

Michigan:
McNamara Federal Building
477 Michigan Ave.
Detroit, MI 48226

Minnesota:
220 Second St. South
Minneapolis, MN 55401

Mississippi:
U.S. Federal Building
100 West Capitol St.
Jackson, MS 39201

Missouri:
Professional Building
1103 Grand St.
Kansas City, MO 63101

210 North Tucker Blvd.
St. Louis, MO 63101

Montana:
Federal Office Building
Drawer 10095
301 South Park
Helena, MT 59601

Nebraska:
Univac Building
7100 West Center Rd.
Omaha, NE 68106

New Jersey:
Gateway Building No. 1
Raymond Plaza
Newark, NJ 07102

New York:
Statler Building
107 Delaware Ave.
Buffalo, NY 14202

26 Federal Plaza
New York City, NY 10278

North Carolina:
415 North Edgewood St.
Greensboro, NC 27401

Ohio:
200 North High St.
Columbus, OH 43251

Oklahoma:
200 North West 5th St.
Oklahoma City, OK 73102

Oregon:
520 Southwest 6th Ave.
Portland, OR 97204

Pennsylvania:
Curtis Building
625 Walnut St.
Philadelphia, PA 19106

Fort Pitt Commons
445 Fort Pitt Blvd.
Pittsburgh, PA 15219

Puerto Rico and the Caribbean
U.S. Courthouse
Carlos E. Chardon Ave.
Hato Rey, PR 00918

South Carolina:
Strom Thurmond Building
1835-45 Assembly St.
Columbia, SC 29201

Tennessee:
One Northshore Building
1111 Northshore Dr.
Knoxville, TN 37919

Texas:
2001 Bryan Tower
Dallas, TX 75201

Washington Square
700 Dolorosa
P. O. Box 9163
San Antonio, TX 78285

Utah:
125 South State St.
Salt Lake City, UT 84111

Virginia:
701 East Franklin St.
Richmond, VA 23219

Washington:
Arcade Plaza Building
1321 Second Ave.
Seattle, WA 98101

Wisconsin:
744 North 4th St.
Milwaukee, WI 53203

Federal Emergency Management Agency (FEMA) Offices

National Office

Federal Emergency Management Agency
Disaster Response and Recovery
Washington, DC 20472

Regional Offices

Region I
(Connecticut, Maine, Massachusetts, New Hampshire,
Rhode Island, Vermont)
Federal Emergency Management Agency
442 J.W. McCormack
Boston, MA 02109

Region II
(New Jersey, New York, Puerto Rico, Virgin Islands)
Federal Emergency Management Agency
26 Federal Plaza
New York, NY 10278

Region III
(Delaware, District of Columbia, Maryland, Pennsylvania,
Virginia, West Virginia)
Federal Emergency Management Agency

Curtis Building
Sixth and Walnut Sts.
Philadelphia, PA 19106

Region IV
(Alabama, Florida, Georgia, Kentucky, Mississippi,
North Carolina, South Carolina, Tennessee)
Federal Emergency Management Agency
1375 Peachtree St., NE
Atlanta, GA 30309

Region V
(Illinois, Indiana, Michigan, Minnesota, Ohio, Wisconsin)
Federal Emergency Management Agency
1 North Dearborn
Chicago, IL 60602

Region VI
(Arkansas, Louisiana, New Mexico, Oklahoma, Texas)
Federal Emergency Management Agency
Federal Regional Center
Denton, TX 76201

Region VII
(Iowa, Kansas, Missouri, Nebraska)
Federal Emergency Management Agency
Old Federal Building
Kansas City, MO 64106

Region VIII
(Colorado, Montana, North Dakota, South Dakota, Utah,
Wyoming)
Federal Emergency Management Agency
Federal Regional Center
Denver, CO 80225

Region IX
(American Samoa, Arizona, California, Guam, Hawaii,
Nevada, Trust Territory of the Pacific Islands,
Commonwealth of the Northern Mariana Islands)
Federal Emergency Management Agency
211 Main St.
San Francisco, CA 94105

Region X
(Alaska, Idaho, Oregon, Washington)
Federal Emergency Management Agency
Federal Regional Center
130 228th St., SW
Bothell, WA 98011

Chapter 4

Maintaining Your Family's Health and Well-Being

Government involvement in protecting the health and well-being of U.S. citizens goes back to the early days of the Republic. The Public Health Service was founded in 1798, but in those days, the agency's responsibility was limited mainly to caring for the well-being of America's merchant seamen. Slowly, the government began to assume a larger role, concerning itself with controlling epidemics and searching out the causes and cures of chronic ailments affecting large segments of the population. In the Great Depression of the 1930s, new programs were launched to feed the hungry, make surplus food commodities available to schools, provide the indigent with basic medical care and investigate major health threats and diseases. Today, the government supports a vast array of health and nutritional programs. This chapter explores the basic benefits and services, starting with those that are aimed specifically at the young, then taking up diseases and health threats that affect people of all ages and winding up with Medicare and Medicaid, the hospital and medical benefits for older people and those who cannot afford the proper care.

Contents

Pre-Natal and Early Childhood Care

In recent years, government on all levels has been providing a broad array of services to pregnant women, new mothers, infants and small children. Sometimes these services come directly from state, federal or local governmental agencies; at other times, voluntary organizations, aided by government, furnish the services. Whatever the source of help, the purpose is to assure the health of the mother and child or the creation of a secure environment for the infant. Some of these benefits are offered free; other services are provided at a very low cost or are billed according to the recipient's ability to pay.

Supplemental Food Program for Women, Infants and Children (WIC)

Sponsored by the United States Department of Agriculture (USDA), this program is intended to assure adequate nourishment for those American children whose parents do not have enough money to buy them proper food. Eligible women and their young children receive considerable quantities of food free of charge. The food is intended for the specific needs of these groups, and the contributions are not considered a substitute for, but a supplement to, other nutritional programs—such as food stamps (see page 144)—in which the recipient of the WIC aid may also be participating.

Eligibility for Participation in WIC. Pregnant women, new mothers and children up to the age of five may receive supplemental food if they live in an area where an active WIC program is in effect. They must also be certified by competent professionals (such as physicians, nurses or nutritionists) to be health risks because of inability to afford adequate food for themselves or their children. Currently there are more than 1,500 WIC programs in the 50 states, the District of Columbia, Puerto Rico and the Virgin Islands.

How WIC Is Administered. At the local level, agencies of city government or tax-exempt community groups set up and administer WIC programs. State health departments oversee the programs and, in turn, report to the Food and Nutrition Service of the federal Department of Agriculture.

Starting a WIC Program. Any group of concerned citizens or voluntary organization may apply to its state department of health (see page 164 for addresses) for a contract to operate a WIC program. Because funds for WIC are limited, preference is given to proposals that would establish the service where the need is greatest, such as in underserved rural areas and in poor urban neighborhoods.

Food Distribution Procedures. Recipients of WIC aid are given monthly (occasionally weekly) allotments of coupons that can be exchanged at grocery stores and supermarkets for such basic items as milk, cheese, eggs, fruit, cereals and baby formulas.

For More Information. Anyone who would like to participate in a WIC program or establish one should write to the appropriate regional office of the Department of Agriculture's Food and Nutrition Service (addresses, page 163), to the state department of health (addresses, page 164) or to:

The Children's Foundation
1420 New York Ave., NW
Washington, DC 20005

Maternal and Child Health Care

Maternal and child health programs that were once operated by the federal government are now primarily administered by state departments of health, but much of the financing continues to come from Washington through block grants. Each state determines the extent to which it will maintain the various services that had previously been mandated by the federal government.

Among services generally offered are pre-natal medical examinations, delivery, infant care and family counseling. Stress is laid on services that will reduce infant mortality and prevent diseases or crippling handicaps among newborns. Other programs that are often offered include diagnosis and treatment for crippled and blind children under the age of 16 who are entitled to Supplemental Security Income. Funds are also supplied to programs dealing with sudden infant death syndrome (SIDS), genetic screening and counseling, adolescent pregnancy prevention, hemophilia treatment and the prevention of lead-paint poisoning.

For more information, write to your state department of health (addresses, pages 164–166) or to:

Health Services Administration
5600 Fishers Lane
Rockville, MD 20857

Birth Defects

Long renowned for its successful campaign to wipe out infantile paralysis, the March of Dimes Foundation has turned its attention to genetically based diseases and birth defects. In addition to financing research in these fields, the Foundation offers free and low-cost prenatal care to pregnant women who are believed to be likely to give birth to babies with genetically transmitted defects. In cases of extreme hardship, the March of Dimes sometimes provides direct financial assistance to children suffering from birth defects, and to expectant mothers who may transmit genetic diseases. For more information, write to:

The March of Dimes Birth Defects
   Foundation
1275 Mamaroneck Ave.
White Plains, NY 10605

Counseling Services for Expectant Parents

Many community mental health services (see page 154) offer psychological counseling to expectant parents. One organization that specializes in this service is the Maternity Center Association. The Association also publishes numerous pamphlets on childbirth and pregnancy, and in some communities it offers courses on natural childbirth. Another voluntary agency that provides similar services is the International Childbirth Education Association. In cities across America, this organization conducts classes on all aspects of pregnancy, childbirth and infant care. For more information, write to:

Maternity Center Association
48 East 92nd St.
New York, NY 10028
   or
International Childbirth Education
   Association
P.O. Box 20852
Milwaukee, WI 53220

Pre-School Care

Mothers of children under the age of six are the fastest-growing category of workers in the United States. Approximately 47 percent of the women in this group are now in the work force. In addition, about 65 percent of the women with children between the ages of 6 and 13 now work outside their homes. Given these figures, it is hardly surprising that competent child-care services have become a major concern for millions of American families. Today, about one million children under the age of 14 spend part or all of each weekday at licensed day-care centers, normally large, professionally staffed facilities run by voluntary organizations. Another 300,000 are looked after in what are known as licensed family day-care homes—usually smaller installations under state supervision—where qualified workers watch over the children.

Licensed Day-Care and Family Day-Care Programs

Licensed day-care centers may be found in schools, churches, public buildings and a variety of other places. Most of these facilities receive subsidies from state or local governments, and about 44 percent receive some federal funding. In fact, about 400,000 children in day-care centers are subsidized by federal monies through the Department of Health and Human Services' Administration for Children, Youth and Families (ACYF).

Family day-care homes tend to be smaller than licensed day-care facilities, and usually are not as well equipped. As federal funding of day-care centers and homes is channeled through state agencies via social service block grants, the states themselves decide the amount of financing they will provide, draw up their own regulations and enforce their own standards on these facilities. Local governmental agencies may also impose their own sets of rules and regulations. Thus, day-care facilities may vary widely—in terms of staff-to-child ratio and in such matters as minimum playground equipment—not only from state to state but also from town to town. And, of course, different day-care centers have different philosophies of teaching. By and large, however, states enforce stringent health and safety standards upon all day-care centers, and in instances where the children receive meals, these too must conform to state standards. In addition, local fire and safety codes must be observed. And parents, of course, must ensure that their children have received all immunizations required by state law before they enroll their children in a day-care center.

States also determine minimum staffing requirements for day-care facilities that receive government subsidies. The federal government has been working on a model day-care code that it hopes will be adopted by the states. This code will include suggested regulations on such matters as health, nutrition and staffing requirements. The states, however, will be under no obligation to adopt the model code as their own.

Workers in subsidized licensed day-care centers are generally certified by the state in which they work or are required to enroll in training that will lead to certification. The goal of federal officials is to work with the states so that all day-care programs meet the "needs of children to foster their social, intellectual, emotional and physical development." Parents in search of a suitable day-care center for their children might consult the box on the opposite page for some hints on selecting a facility.

Choosing a Day-Care Facility
Before enrolling your pre-school child in a day-care program, it's a good idea to check out the Head Start project in your area. Even though your family may not meet the residential and financial requirements for Head Start, you can learn a lot about the quality of the day-care operation by spending a few hours watching this program in action and comparing it with those in other facilities.

You probably will discover that the licensed centers offer better services and a greater variety of activities than the more informal family day-care homes. You may, however, have trouble finding a handy day-care center for your child. There simply are not enough licensed programs to meet the demand, and many children are turned away for lack of space. But persistence often pays off.

Further Information on Day-Care Centers. If you are interested in obtaining more information on federally supported day-care facilities, write to your state social service agency (addresses are on page 166) or to the appropriate office of the ACYF (the addresses are on page 163).

A private agency that offers information on day-care facilities all over America is:
Day Care Council of America, Inc.
711 14th St., NW
Washington, DC 20005

Head Start's Health and Nutrition Programs

The extensive educational opportunities offered by Head Start have already been discussed in

A Day Care Checklist

If you are looking for a day care facility for your child, this checklist—adapted from a government pamphlet—will help you evaluate a particular center or home. Positive answers to all of the questions are most unlikely. There probably are no perfect day care facilities, but there may be a center in your community that comes reasonably close to meeting all of the requirements. The checklist reprinted here was compiled by the Department of Health and Human Services. It will service as a yardstick for measuring the quality of day care centers in your area.

Do the Caregivers . . .	Yes	No
Appear to be warm and friendly?		
Seem calm and gentle?		
Seem to be people with whom you can develop a warm, relaxed and sharing relationship?		
Seem to be people your child will enjoy being with?		
Have child-rearing attitudes similar to your own?		
Treat each child as a special person?		
Have the right equipment on hand to help children learn and grow mentally and physically?		
Patiently help children solve their problems?		
Encourage good health habits, such as washing hands before eating?		
Talk to children and encourage them to express themselves through words?		
Encourage children to express themselves in creative ways?		
Have art and music supplies?		
Provide a routine and rules the children can understand and follow?		
Accept and respect your family's cultural values?		
Have previous experience or training in working with children?		
Have a yearly physical exam and TB test?		

Does the Day Care Home or Center Have . . .	Yes	No
An up-to-date license, if one is required?		
A clean and comfortable look?		
Enough space indoors and out so that all the children can move freely and safely?		
Enough caregivers to give attention to all the children in their care?		
Enough furniture, playthings and equipment for the needs of the children?		
Equipment and materials that are suitable for the ages of the children being cared for?		
Enough cots or cribs so that the children can nap?		

	Yes	No
Enough clean bathrooms for all the children in care?		
Safety caps on electrical outlets?		
A safe place to store medicines, household chemicals, matches, sharp instruments and the like?		
Alternate exits in case of fire?		
A safety plan to follow in case of emergencies?		
An outdoor play area that is safe, fenced and free of litter?		
Enough heat, light and ventilation?		
Nutritious meals and snacks made with foods you want your child to eat?		
A separate place to care for sick children where they can be watched?		
A first-aid kit?		
Fire extinguishers?		
A sprinkler system?		
Smoke detectors?		
Covered radiators and protected heaters?		
Strong screens or bars on windows above the first floor?		

Are There Opportunities for Children . . .	Yes	No
To play quietly and actively, indoors and out?		
To play alone at times and with friends at other times?		
To learn to get along, to share and to respect themselves and others?		
To learn about their own and others' cultures through art, music, books, songs, games and so forth?		
To use materials and equipment that help them learn new physical skills and exercise their muscles?		
To speak both English and their family's native language?		
(Adapted from HHS's *A Parent's Guide To Day Care*.)		

Chapter 1, and the day-care facilities at these institutions have just been mentioned. As indicated in Chapter 1, health, nutritional and social services are also a major part of Head Start's effort to enable disadvantaged children to begin their lives on equal footing with youngsters from more favored families. Each Head Start installation must provide hot meals every day, physical and dental examinations, medical treatment and psychological testing and counseling. As with Head Start education programs, all Head Start health and nutrition projects must include a minimum 10 percent enrollment of children who have been diagnosed as handicapped.

The Role of Parents

A goal of Head Start is to involve parents as closely as possible in every aspect of the program. Parents of Head Start children play a major role in the management and policy-making bodies. Many work as paid aides and volunteers, and because the program recognizes the importance of improving home life for Head Start youngsters, thousands of parents receive training in child care and nutrition from Head Start professionals.

Head Start Demonstration Programs

In an effort to expand and improve the services offered by Head Start, a number of demonstration programs have been established in various towns and cities. Among the special programs are:

Parent-Child Centers. These facilities are designed to help families with children who are too young to enter Head Start centers. Parents are instructed on their children's health and nutritional needs. Services are limited to low-income families with children under the age of three.

Child and Family Resource Program. Counseling for families with children up to the age of eight is offered under this program. In situations where treatment of one sort or another is required, professional staff members refer families to appropriate organizations within the communities where they live.

The Child and Family Mental Health Project. Emerging emotional problems of Head Start children are identified under this program, and family counseling is offered with the objective of preventing problems from developing into serious disturbances.

Home Start Training Centers. Head Start programs are brought directly into the homes of qualified children through regular visits by social work para-professionals in the field of health and education.

The Child Development Associate Program. Training for adults—often the parents of Head Start children—is provided so they may become qualified professional workers in the child-care field.

For More Information. Because each program operates under its own locally chosen name, you may not find a listing under "Head Start" in your phone book. If you are interested in enrolling a child or joining with your neighbors to organize a Head Start program in your community, write to the appropriate regional office of the ACYF (addresses on page 163) or to:

> Administration for Children, Youth and Families/Head Start
> Office of Human Development Services
> P.O. Box 1182
> Washington, DC 20013

Health Services for Young People

The physical, mental and emotional health of America's children and adolescents is a major concern of government. Many programs have been established to provide free or inexpensive basic health care for young people. The services include treatment and preventive medicine for youngsters whose families cannot afford the rising costs of private medical care. Below are some of the major programs.

Early and Periodic Screening, Diagnosis and Treatment Program (EPSDT)

EPSDT is part of the Medicaid program (see page 162). On the federal level it is administered by the Health Care Financing Administration. A joint federal-state effort, it is aimed at protecting the health of America's needy children. As the name of the program implies, the emphasis is on early diagnosis and preventive medicine. Basic to EPSDT is the screening of eligible children to discover medical problems at an early age. Vision, hearing and general physical condition of children are checked. Early diagnosis generally makes treatment relatively simple and inexpensive. Follow-up care is provided for children who need it.

Unfortunately, of the 11 million children who are eligible for this program, fewer than

30 percent have participated in it. To improve this record, the federal government, in cooperation with the states, has embarked on a campaign to make EPSDT services more widely known. This involves using schools, community health or social service agencies and other federal projects to alert eligible parents to the EPSDT program.

As part of the Medicaid program, EPSDT is primarily intended for the long-term poor, but families who are temporarily unable to meet medical expenses may also be eligible for help under federal and state Medicaid regulations.

For more information on EPSDT, write to your state's social service agency (addresses, page 166) or to:

Office of Child Health
Health Care Financing Administration
Department of Health and Human
  Services
Dogwood West Blvd.
1848 Gwynn Oak Ave.
Baltimore, MD 21207

Immunization Programs

Most of the ailments generally known as childhood diseases—such as measles, mumps, polio, German measles and diphtheria may now be prevented through inoculations. In many areas of the country, schools refuse to admit children who have not been vaccinated against these diseases. Though private physicians often perform the inoculations, in many states free or low-cost immunization is offered by clinics of local boards of health or the state departments of health. If you would like your child to be inoculated at one of these public facilities, call your local school or board of health or write to your state's department of health (addresses page 164).

Food and Nutrition Programs for Children

Since the Great Depression of the 1930's, the Department of Agriculture has been involved in providing free and low-cost nutritious meals for America's children. Today, millions of federally subsidized meals are served in day-care centers, public and private schools and to children on vacation. Summaries of the major food programs for children from the pre-school years through high school are presented below.

The Child Care Food Program

This program provides food for children in day-care centers and may include youths up to the age of 18 who are enrolled in programs meeting after school hours. But most children who benefit from the program are pre-schoolers. Meals are served to these children, and the sponsoring institutions are reimbursed for their expenses once a month. Breakfasts, lunches, suppers and snacks may be included. The Department of Agriculture frequently provides the food.

The sponsoring organization may be a day-care facility itself, or a local, non-profit, tax-exempt service group which administers the program for a day-care facility. Meals must meet the Agriculture Department's standards. A lunch or supper, for example, must include milk, a meat dish or a protein-rich alternative, vegetables or fruits and bread.

Anyone who would like to establish a Child Care Food Program should write to the appropriate regional food and nutrition service office (addresses on page 163) for necessary forms and instructions.

School Breakfast Program

Any public or private non-profit school in the United States may participate in the Department of Agriculture's School Breakfast Program. The program has not been well publicized, however, and only about 30,000 schools have signed up. In schools that do participate, a nourishing breakfast—including fruit, milk and a main dish such as pancakes, granola or corn muffins—is offered to children. For youngsters whose families are at or below the poverty line, the service is free; for families with incomes somewhat above the poverty level, breakfast is offered at a very low price. Even middle-class children benefit. They pay "full price" for the meals, but that price actually is a fraction of the cost of such a breakfast in a restaurant or even at home. The low prices are possible because all of the breakfasts—even those selling at full price—are subsidized by the Department of Agriculture. Typically, schools receive 8 cents for every full-priced breakfast they serve; almost 29 cents for each reduced-price breakfast, and a bit over 50 cents for every free breakfast. Federal aid comes in two forms: cash payments for the breakfasts served; and direct distribution of commodities to the schools.

In some states the state department of education operates the school breakfast program; in others, direct authority is in the hands of the regional office of the Department of Agriculture's Food and Nutrition Service. In all instances, however, information on the program is available through the Food and Nutrition Service. Anyone interested in establishing a school breakfast program should write to that agency's appropriate regional office (addresses, page 163).

School Lunch Program

The Reagan Administration cut back on the subsidies for school lunches and modified the eligibility requirements, but this remains the major federal nutritional program for America's school children. Each year approximately 25 million students in more than 90,000 public and non-profit private schools around the nation benefit from this program. All children attending these schools may receive the lunches. The meals are free to children from very low-income families, but youngsters from families that are not considered poor must pay for the meals on a sliding scale. Children from relatively low-income families pay only a small

Income Limits for Meals Program

The table below shows the income limits that families must meet if their children are to qualify for free or reduced-price breakfasts and lunches. Income eligibility for free or reduced-price meals is determined by guidelines established by the Secretary of Agriculture. For example a family of four may not have a monthly income higher than $1,303, to qualify for reduced-price meals. Parents who believe their children may be entitled to free or reduced-price meals should call the principal of their children's school or their local board of education.

Your Child Qualifies for Free Meals if . . .		Your Child Qualifies for Reduced-Price Meals if . . .	
Your Family Size Is	Your Family's Monthly Income Is No More Than	Your Family Size Is	Your Family's Monthly Income Is No More Than
2	$ 617	2	$ 878
3	766	3	1,090
4	916	4	1,303
5	1,065	5	1,516
6	1,214	6	1,728
7	1,364	7	1,941
8	1,513	8	2,153

price, usually about 40 cents, while those from higher income families are often charged between 90 cents and $1.00. However, local school districts are permitted considerable latitude in their fees and some may charge more than the amounts cited here.

All meals served under this program must be in conformity with strict government nutrition standards. Lunch includes the following: meat or an alternative protein source (usually fish or cheese); vegetables and fruit; enriched or whole-grain bread; and a glass of milk.

In most schools with adequate kitchen facilities, meals are prepared on the spot. In some areas, however, the school system employs a central kitchen to prepare the lunches and a delivery truck then transports them to the participating schools. Other school systems may employ qualified caterers to prepare TV-type lunches that are warmed on site.

If your child's school is among the relatively few that do not offer the School Lunch Program, or if you desire more information, write to the appropriate regional office of the Department of Agriculture's Food and Nutrition Service (addresses, page 163).

Summer Food Service Program for Children (SFSPC)

This service supplements the national school lunch and breakfast programs by providing free meals for children from low-income families during periods when school is not in session. The SFSPC is run by local sponsors, including government agencies, summer residential camps, private and non-profit community organizations and schools. These agencies are reimbursed for meals served to eligible children. The recipients are youngsters who receive free or reduced-price meals under the School Lunch Program or who live in areas where at least 50 percent of the families are at or below the poverty level.

Anyone who would like to locate the nearest sponsor, or who belongs to an organization that would like to start a summer food program, should write to the appropriate regional office

of the Department of Agriculture's Food and Nutrition Service (addresses on page 163).

The Children's Bureau

A wide range of child-oriented programs is supported by the Children's Bureau of the Department of Health and Human Services. Aimed at providing a healthy and emotionally stable environment for youngsters, these services are designed to meet a broad variety of problems that threaten the integrity of the family or the well-being of the child.

Such problems may include serious financial difficulties, major illnesses, severe emotional crises, or other situations likely to result in the break-up of the family. Help is also afforded for cases involving runaway teenagers, instances of child abuse or neglect, and alcohol or drug abuse by a child.

In some cases the aid is provided directly by an agency of the Children's Bureau. In others, the Bureau may merely support a state, local or voluntary agency. In any case, help may be obtained by writing to the appropriate regional office of the ACYF (addresses, page 163) or to:

Administration for Children, Youth and Families
Children's Bureau
Office of Human Development Services
P.O. Box 1182
Washington, DC 20013

What follows is a brief summary of the major services provided by the Children's Bureau, beginning at the outset of the child's life.

Child Adoption Services

People who are qualified to be good parents and who would like to adopt a child can be helped by the Children's Bureau. Each state has its own adoption laws and supervises the voluntary agencies within its borders. The Children's Bureau supplements the work of these state and voluntary agencies through its 10 regional Adoption Resource Centers (see pages 173–174 for addresses). These centers provide assistance in the form of grants and contracts to state and local adoption agencies. The Children's Bureau, through the regional Adoption Resource Centers, also operates a National Adoption Information Exchange System that is particularly valuable to local agencies having difficulties placing certain categories of children—such as siblings who wish to remain together and children with mental or physical handicaps. Indeed, many of the approximately 100,000 youngsters available for adoption fall into these categories.

The Children's Bureau advocates the passage of a Model Adoption Act, which the individual states may copy or modify, that will eliminate many of the legal and procedural barriers to the adoption of parentless children. Already, more than two-thirds of the states conform to an Interstate Compact on the Placement of Children, an act that is promoted and periodically modified by the Bureau.

Partly because of this Interstate Compact, a number of states have greatly eased restrictions on adoption. Inter-religious and inter-racial couples, couples over the age of 40 and single adults used to be routinely barred from adopting children, but today, in some states, people in these categories are considered suitable candidates.

If you are interested in adopting a child, you probably should start by calling or writing to the government department in your state that supervises adoption agencies. In most cases, this will be your state's social service agency (the addresses are on page 166) or your regional adoption resource center (see pages 173–174). An alternate route is to write to one of the national voluntary organizations that deal with adoption. These agencies can put you in touch with an adoption agency in your area and answer questions concerning qualifications for adoptive parents, their rights and responsibilities. Following are descriptions of two of the more important agencies.

The Child Welfare League of America. This organization has more than 170 offices around the nation. Among the many services it offers is a wealth of information on adoption procedures and qualifications, and the referral of adoptive parents to the proper agencies in their areas. The address is:

Child Welfare League of America, Inc.
67 Irving Place
New York, NY 10003

Birthright. This organization offers help and referrals to people who want to adopt a child. The agency also helps unwed mothers place their infants for adoption. The address is:

Birthright
11055 South St. Louis Ave.
Chicago, IL 60655

National Center on Child Abuse and Neglect

According to government statistics, at least one million American children are victims of abuse or neglect each year. In 1974, Congress established within the Children's Bureau the National Center on Child Abuse and Neglect. This organization works with state and local authorities and voluntary agencies to improve services to abused children and their families. The goal of the Center is not to punish parents who mistreat or neglect their children, but to provide them with the means of rehabilitation. Major activities of the Center include:

Demonstration, Research and Service Improvement Program. Approximately 50 percent of the National Center's funds are devoted to demonstration and research projects, many of which are located in rural areas not generally served by other child-protection agencies. These projects offer social services for abused children and their families and test new means of dealing with the victims and perpetrators of child abuse. A major effort is made to steer those guilty of child abuse to therapy programs that will help them deal with the stresses that led to their maltreatment of the young.

Grants to the States. Child neglect and treatment programs at the state and local level are supported by federal grants. State social service departments pass on federal funds to both local government and private agencies that deal with child abuse. A goal is to establish 24-hour-a-day, seven-day-a-week emergency aid facilities for abused and neglected children and their families. This type of funding is usually limited to a three-year grant to enable local groups to initiate child abuse projects. At the end of the grant period, the project, if it is to continue, must be funded by the state, by the locality or through private contributions.

National Clearinghouse on Child Abuse. This federal office provides a wide range of information—including pamphlets, booklets, flyers and the like—on programs to prevent child abuse and neglect. Individuals or professional groups desiring advice or information on securing grants should write to:

National Clearinghouse on Child Abuse
Central Register of Information
Children's Bureau
P.O. Box 1182
Washington, DC 20013

Voluntary Agencies Dealing with Child Abuse

A number of voluntary groups work with the victims of child abuse or their parents. Some of these organizations receive federal or state aid. The goal is to lessen the effects of past abuses and to prevent their recurrence. Among these organizations and their activities are:

Parents Anonymous Self-help group therapy sessions are organized for parents who have abused their children or believe that they are in danger of doing so. The address is:

Parents Anonymous
22330 Hawthorne Blvd.
Torrance, CA 90505

National Committee for the Prevention of Child Abuse. Programs are established throughout the country to create an awareness of the scope of the problem and to disseminate treatment information. The members of the Committee may also direct parents who are anxious about their potential for child abuse to local treatment centers. The address is:

National Committee for the Prevention of Child Abuse
111 West Wacker Dr.
Chicago, IL 60601

Center for Women's Policy Studies. Information and referral services are offered to the victims of child abuse and to parents who are concerned about becoming abusers. The address is:

Center for Women's Policy Studies
2000 P St. NW
Washington, DC 20036

Family Crisis Management

A major goal of the Children's Bureau is to help local and state social service agencies establish programs to ameliorate family crises. Such crises may involve divorce, severe illness, drug abuse or alcoholism, and often lead to situations in which there is a complete disintegration of the family and the placement of children in foster homes.

The Children's Bureau has established an excellent demonstration project, called the Comprehensive Emergency Services Program, in Nashville, Tennessee. Families caught up in crises are aided by trained professionals who go into homes every day and try to resolve or ameliorate potentially explosive situations. Supporting services, such as referrals to local community medical and mental health clinics, are also offered.

The demonstration project has proved so successful that a number of state and local agencies, aided by federal grants, have established their own programs based upon the Nashville model.

As with all projects supported by the Children's Bureau, the well-being of the young receives major emphasis.

Any family that faces a crisis it cannot cope with may be helped by writing to the national office of the Children's Bureau (address on page 136) or the appropriate regional office of the ACYF (addresses on page 163). An inquiry should bring detailed information as to how and where to apply for help within your community or county.

Voluntary Family Crisis Management Agencies

Many non-profit organizations also help families threatened by crises. Among them are:

The Salvation Army. Day-care centers for children and temporary shelters or foster homes for the young are offered while parents attempt to work out their problems with or without professional assistance. For further information, write to:

The Salvation Army
National Information Service
50 West 23rd St.
New York, NY 10010

The National Council for Homemaker-Home Health Aide Services, Inc. Temporary homemaker services for families facing crisis situations are provided by this agency. Communities are aided in developing their own services to assist families in times of emergency. Children in need of help are a special concern. For information and referrals, write to:

National Council for Homemaker-Home Health Aide Services, Inc.
67 Irving Place
New York, NY 10003

The Family Service Association of America. This nationwide agency helps local agencies conduct programs to strengthen family life. Some of the branches offer family counseling. For more information, write to:

Family Service Association of America
44 East 23rd St.
New York, NY 10010

Special Programs for Runaways and Pregnant Teenagers

The federal government, together with state and local authorities and voluntary agencies, has established special programs to help youths between the ages of 10 and 21. One of the most important, desperately needed services is aid to runaway children and pregnant teenagers.

Runaway Children

Each year more than half a million American teenagers run away from home. Many of them fall into the drug culture and criminal activities such as prostitution and petty thievery. To aid these children, the ACYF's Youth Development Bureau finances about 170 centers for runaways. The purpose of these shelters is not to treat the children as criminals, but to offer food, housing, clothing, training, counseling and medical care. Whenever possible, the centers try to reunite the children with their families. The Youth Development Bureau also offers information on local counseling services. Parents and teenagers are aided in solving problems that might otherwise result in a child's running away from home. For more information, write to:

Administration for Children, Youth and Families / Youth Development Bureau
Office of Human Development Services
P.O. Box 1182
Washington, DC 20013

Runaway Hotline: The Youth Development Bureau operates a "hotline" that provides a channel of communication between runaways and their parents. The hotline also provides counseling and referral of both parents and their runaway children to local agencies that may help them resolve their difficulties. The runaways' hotline toll-free number is: 800-621-4000.

Voluntary Agencies

Among the non-profit organizations that help runaway children and their families are:

The National Network of Runaway and Youth Services. This nationwide organization works with local social service agencies to trace runaway youngsters and help them. Its publications provide information on funding and operating services for runaways and their families. For more information, write to:

> The National Network of Runaway and
> Youth Services
> 1705 De Sales St., NW
> Washington, DC 20036

Public Affairs Committee, Inc. A "hotline" operated by this agency enables runaways and their parents to make contact. The Committee also publishes a number of pamphlets on the problems of adolescence, including one on runaways. For more information, write to:

> Public Affairs Committee, Inc.
> 381 Park Avenue South
> New York, NY 10016

Adolescent Pregnancy

Approximately one million American girls between the ages of 15 and 19 become pregnant each year. About 40 percent of these girls are under 17. In addition, some 11,000 girls 14 or under become mothers each year, a situation that social workers describe as "children giving birth to children." Though the vast majority of teenage mothers face enormous health, education, economic and social problems, all of these difficulties are compounded among the girls in the youngest group. Many people believe that the problem of teenage pregnancy is largely restricted to poor urban areas; in fact, it cuts across all economic boundaries, extending to the affluent suburbs, small towns and rural areas as well as the city slums.

To deal with the problems of teenage pregnancy and motherhood, the Public Health Service's Office of Adolescent Family Life Programs awards funds to the states and private voluntary agencies. The funds are used to establish demonstration programs that deal with problems associated with teenage sexuality. Agencies that qualify for federal funding usually offer the following services:

*Pregnancy testing and maternity counseling.

*Adoption counseling and referral services which present adoption as a realistic course for prospective teenage mothers.

*Continuing health monitoring to assure the physical well-being of both mother and fetus, and post-natal care for parent and child.

*Nutritional information and counseling, and counseling on drug abuse, alcohol and smoking and their effects on the fetus.

*Referral for screening and treatment of venereal disease.

*Referral services for pediatric care for the new-born.

*Education services relating to family life and problems associated with teenage sexuality.

*Referral to educational and vocational services. Every effort must be made to keep the pregnant teenager or young mother in school.

*Referral to mental health services or other appropriate health services.

*Child care services that will make it possible for the teenager to continue her education or gain employment.

*Consumer education and homemaking skills.

*Counseling for the teenager's family.

*Assistance and advice to parents, schools, youth agencies and health providers for the education of adolescents and pre-adolescents in responsible sexual behavior.

*Transportation. When services are scattered over large geographic areas, school buses or vans are furnished to transport clients from one service to another.

Great stress is placed on services designed to enable the teenage mother to complete her education. The federal government looks with particular favor upon pregnancy programs that have been established by local high schools or maintain strong links with these institutions.

Financing a Teenage Pregnancy Program. The federal government does not expect that its financial support for a local teenage pregnancy program will be permanent. For the first two years that a federally approved project is in operation, the Office of Adolescent Pregnancy Programs will provide 70 percent of the funding, with the rest of the financing coming from the state or local government or from voluntary sources. Over a five-year period the federal presence will gradually be reduced until the program is funded entirely from other sources. There are, however, exceptions to this rule. The Secretary of Health and Human Services may decide to continue federal financing after the five-year period if the existence of an essential pregnancy program would be threatened by a cutoff of federal aid.

Adolescent pregnancy programs are not required to provide all of their services free of charge. But teenagers who cannot afford to pay, or whose parents refuse to pay, may be treated free of charge.

For More Information. People who are interested in establishing teenage pregnancy programs in their communities or would like to know about these programs should write to their state's social service department (addresses page 166), or to:

Office of Adolescent Pregnancy Programs
Public Health Service
Department of Health and Human
  Services
200 Independence Ave., SW
Washington, DC 20201

Voluntary Agencies Concerned with Teenage Pregnancy. Among the many private, non-profit organizations that deal with teenage sexuality or offer services to pregnant teenagers, adolescent mothers and their children are the following:
The Children's Foundation

1420 New York Ave., NW
Washington, DC 20005

Child Welfare League of America, Inc.
67 Irving Place
New York, NY 10003

Coalition for Children and Youth
815 15th St., NW
Washington, DC 20005

March of Dimes Birth Defects Foundation
1275 Mamaroneck Ave.,
White Plains, NY 10605

Planned Parenthood Federation of America,
  Inc.
810 Seventh Ave.
New York, NY 10019

The Salvation Army, Inc.
50 West 23rd St.
New York, NY 10010

Sex Information and Education Council of
  the United States (SIECUS)
84 Fifth Ave.
New York, NY 10011

Birthright
11055 South St. Louis Ave.
Chicago, IL 60655

Services for People of All Ages

Beyond the many programs aimed specifically at young people, the federal, state and local governments offer an abundance of health and nutritional services for people of all ages. These services cover a broad range of health problems, including alcoholism and drug abuse, heart disease, mental health, home nursing care and the food stamp programs, to mention some of the most important ones.

In keeping with the American federal system, the national government offers relatively few *direct* consumer services in the health, mental health and social service fields. (There are a number of exceptions, which will be mentioned in the following pages.) This does not mean, however, that the federal government plays only a marginal role. On the contrary, through its research facilities, its grants to states, localities and voluntary agencies and its informational resources, the federal government provides a vital underpinning for health agencies dealing directly with the public. For example, the federal government does not directly operate family-planning clinics, but federal funds support both public and privately operated birth control clinics around the country that offer counseling and clinical services to the public. The federal government also serves as an information clearinghouse, offering advice and a wealth of knowledge to professionals and the general public.

In most cases, the various agencies, bureaus and divisions of the Department of Health and Human Services play the dominant federal role in supporting state and local organizations. But the Department of Agriculture, through its Food and Nutrition Service and its Cooperative Extension Service, is also an important source of federal aid, particularly in areas relating to nutrition.

In the pages that follow, the major federal health and nutritional agencies and services are described. After that, the chapter focuses on specific health problems, coupling them with summaries of the services offered by government agencies and voluntary organizations.

The Public Health Service (PHS)

A branch of the Department of Health and Human Services, the Public Health Service is the federal government's front-line agency in protecting the health and well-being of Americans. The PHS includes six divisions.

The National Institutes of Health. One of the world's most prestigious medical research organizations, the NIH is headquartered in Bethesda, Maryland. Most of the 12,000 employees of the NIH work there, more than half of them in research laboratories and clinics. In terms of direct health service to the public, the 500-bed NIH Clinical Center at Bethesda is the most important facility. This is not a hospital open to the general public. To gain admission, a patient must be referred by a physician and must be suffering from an ailment being studied at one of the Institutes.

Among the ailments being constantly studied at the NIH are cancer; diseases of the heart, lungs and blood; ailments common to the elderly; allergies and infectious diseases; arthritis, metabolism and digestive diseases; eye ailments; and dental problems. For more information on the NIH, write to:

Division of Public Information
National Institutes of Health
Building #1
Bethesda, MD 20205

The Food and Drug Administration. The FDA reviews the testing and certifies many of the foods and all of the pharmacological drugs and cosmetics available to the American public. It also oversees the implementation of the Fair Packaging and Labeling Act as it applies to food, drugs, medical devices and cosmetics. This Act entitles purchasers to know exactly what is inside a package and enables them to compare values from one brand to the next. Another of the FDA's functions is to protect consumers against unnecessary radiation from X-ray machines, microwave ovens and color television sets. Although the FDA plays a major role in maintaining the health and safety of Americans, its direct relationship with the general public is limited. FDA consumer affairs and safety officers, however, are always ready to listen to and investigate complaints from the public. Write to:

The Food and Drug Administration
HFI-10
5600 Fishers Lane
Rockville, MD 20857

142

The Centers for Disease Control. The Centers are primarily concerned with preventive medicine, the dissemination of the latest knowledge of new treatment and prevention procedures to health professionals, the control and eradication of epidemics and the elimination of safety and health hazards at America's work sites. Based in Atlanta, Georgia, the Centers are primarily research facilities, but their professional personnel are available to states and localities when epidemics threaten or become a reality. In recent years, for example, the Centers have played a major role in determining the nature of Legionnaire's Disease and combatting that killer ailment.

In addition, the Centers are responsible for paying the federal preventive health care block grant to the states. This money, or a portion of it, may be used by any of the states to continue a service known as the Home Health Program. Traditionally, the funds from this program have been used to establish or upgrade community health facilities and to provide such services as visiting nurses and physicians.

The Centers for Disease Control also offer advice and technical assistance to those states that wish to use a portion of their preventive health care block grants to establish emergency medical services. About half of America's communities lack even a telephone number to call when a medical emergency arises. Approximately two-thirds of all ambulances in the country lack the equipment to deal with many emergencies, and three-quarters of all ambulance personnel have not received the minimum training recommended for emergency technicians. In addition, only about 1 hospital in 10 has emergency facilities in operation 24 hours a day, 7 days a week. It is to rectify such situations that the Centers offer their advice to states engaged in upgrading emergency medical facilities.

Anyone who is interested in knowing more about the Centers may write to:

Office of Public Affairs
The Centers for Disease Control
Atlanta, GA 30333

The Health Resources Administration (HRA). Financial aid and professional advice are provided by this agency for America's medical, dental, pharmaceutical and nursing schools, particularly in the area of training students in family medicine. HRA also helps the states organize their health facilities effectively and facilitates fund raising by hospitals engaged in modernization projects. For more information, write to:

Office of Communications
Health Resources Administration
3700 East-West Hwy.
Hyattsville, MD 20782

The Health Services Administration. This is the branch of the Public Health Service that offers the most direct health care service to the American public. Through its Bureau of Community Health Services, the HSA subsidizes and helps establish locally operated health facilities in cities and rural areas around the country. Physicians, nurses and others in the health field who have received federal financial aid during their training may be assigned to the HSA's National Health Service Corps to provide health care for people living in medically underserved areas. A goal of the Service Corps is to match staff members with assignments that are sufficiently attractive that the workers will remain in the assigned areas after their contracts have been fulfilled. In a recent year, approximately 2,000 health care professionals were assigned to medically underserved areas where they were charged with the responsibility for almost 1.5 million people.

The HSA's Appalachian Health Program is designed to improve health services in 12 states, from southwestern New York to northeastern Mississippi. The Administration's Office of Migrant Health provides medical services for approximately 600,000 seasonal farm workers (including diagnostic, treatment and preventive services) in the United States. In addition, the HSA, through its Indian Health Service, offers a wide range of health care services to American Indians and Alaskan Eskimos. The Maternal and Child Health Care program is largely financed by HSA (see page 128). A major effort of the HSA is to help provide facilities for voluntary birth control and family planning. In a recent year the agency subsidized nearly 5,000 family planning clinics that provided services for some 3.5 million clients.

For further information on this branch of the Public Health Service, write to:

Office of Communications and Public Affairs
Health Services Administration
5600 Fishers Lane
Rockville, MD 20857

The Alcohol, Drug Abuse and Mental Health Administration. The ADAMHA conducts and supports research in the prevention, causes and possible cures for alcoholism, drug abuse and mental and emotional illness. It also subsidizes the treatment of these conditions at local, state and community levels. Currently, ADAMHA subsidizes some 850 health centers (for addresses, contact state agencies on page 171) and scores of rehabilitation centers for alcoholics and drug addicts. Through its clearinghouses for alcohol and drug abuse information, ADAMHA makes available to the general public and professionals a wealth of up-to-date research on health problems affecting millions of Americans. For more information, write to:

Office of Communications and
  Public Affairs
Alcohol, Drug Abuse and Mental Health
Administration
5600 Fishers Lane
Rockville, MD 20857

The Food Stamp Program

The Food and Nutrition Service of the Department of Agriculture administers and finances the Food Stamp Program, subsidizing the food purchases of millions of low-income Americans. Participants in the program receive food stamps worth a specific dollar amount, the amount varying with family income and family size. (Tobacco and alcohol may not be purchased with food stamps.)

Eligibility Requirements. Under current regulations, for example, a family of four may receive food stamps if its gross income is not more than $916 per month. A person living alone may have a gross monthly income of up to $467 and be eligible.

When a family applies for food stamps, an employee of a state agency—usually the state social service agency—conducts an interview and establishes the family's net worth. In arriving at that figure, the official is required by law to take into account a family's savings, its motor vehicles and other assets that are easily converted into cash. Cars and trucks are not counted when these are necessary for work, nor is the value of a family's home included. In addition, some other forms of income are excluded. Among these are wages of young people under 18 who are attending school at least half-time; money received for alimony or child support; portions of education loans and grants, scholarships, veterans' educational benefits used for tuition and school fees; and money used by the self-employed to operate a business. However, a family with more than $1,500 in readily available assets will be required to use them up before becoming eligible for food stamps. Households with at least one member who is 60 or older are excepted. They may maintain cashable assets of up to $3,000 and remain eligible for the food stamp program.

Eligibility for food stamps is not limited to the long-term poor. Families faced with temporary financial difficulties—stemming, for example, from the fact that the principal wage earner has been laid off from a job—may qualify if they meet other eligibility requirements.

Applying for Food Stamps. Anyone who is interested in securing food stamps should call the local food stamp office and set up an appointment. An interview will follow in which the family's eligibility for the program will be determined. Food stamp offices are listed alphabetically in phone books or under the heading "U.S. Government." If an application for food stamps is approved, the coupons will be received within 30 days. As eligibility requirements are frequently altered, it is a good idea to check with a Food Stamp office even if you think you may not qualify.

For More Information. The best source of general information on the program is the Department of Agriculture's Food and Nutrition Service. Write to the appropriate regional office (addresses, page 163) or to:

Food and Nutrition Service
Department of Agriculture
Washington, DC 20250

Cooperative Extension Service (County Agent System)

Though best known for providing technical assistance to America's farmers, the Agricultural Extension Service actually does far more. It advises suburban gardeners on plantings and helps interested families plan nutritious menus and buy food at the best market prices. Through its visiting homemaker program, the Extension Service also helps both rural and urban families deal with child-raising problems. Special emphasis is placed on care for babies and general nutritional and health care for youngsters. Workers in the program also refer clients to other social services and health agencies, such as community mental health or health clinics. The Service, as well, helps those in need of food stamps, Medicare, Medicaid and other benefits.

For More Information. If you are interested in the programs of the Cooperative Extension Service, check the white pages of your phone book under the name of your county. There will be a listing for "agricultural agents," "county agents" or "Cooperative Extension Service." Listings may also be found under state universities, since the Cooperative Extension Service is administratively attached to these institutions.

Comprehensive Care Across the Country

The federal government supports approximately 800 clinics in rural, inner city and other medically underserved areas. Comprehensive health care is offered at these centers, and fees are based on the ability to pay. Counseling and immunization programs and diagnostic and treatment services are offered. The staffs of many of the centers include physicians, nurses, dentists, pharmacists, laboratory technicians, nutritionists, social and family-health workers. In rural areas, these facilities are often called "Rural Health Centers." In the inner cities, the term "Community Health Centers" is generally used. Some of the smaller rural centers are staffed by nurses, medical technicians and paramedics, but physicians are on call and transportation is available to take patients to larger centers or hospitals for intensive care. These centers, which had been funded by categorical grants, will come under primary care block grants with funding that may be supplemented by the states. Some states, however, may prefer to use their health care block grants for other purposes and, in such instances, the federal government may, at its option, continue to fund community health facilities, at least temporarily. For information on the program in general or on the center nearest you, write to:

Community Health Centers
Bureau of Community Health Services
5600 Fishers Lane
Rockville, MD 20857

Health Maintenance Organizations (HMOs)

Comprehensive medical services are provided by the HMOs. Dental care and mental health services are sometimes included. The federal

Non-Federal Physicians per 100,000 Population

Maldistribution of physicians is one of the basic, long-term health problems that Americans face. As the map below shows, physicians tend to congregate in wealthy and industrialized areas, leaving some Far West states and much of the South badly underserved. The National Health Service Corps is trying to alleviate this problem by offering financial aid to medical students in exchange for their agreement to work for a period of years in medically underserved sections of the nation.

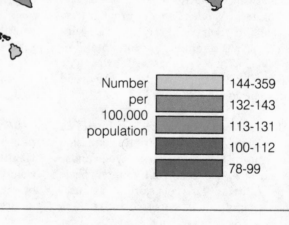

Number per 100,000 population	
	144-359
	132-143
	113-131
	100-112
	78-99

Addresses and Phone Numbers

Your Telephone Book. A primary source of help for a great many services offered by the various levels of government and private voluntary agencies, your telephone book offers immediate information in the form of addresses and phone numbers. In many areas of the country, local telephone directories have a page near the front listing community-service numbers. In addition to this, the yellow pages will probably have a heading "Community Service Organizations." A quick perusal of this list should enable you to get in touch with an organization offering the kind of service you need.

Government agencies may be found in telephone directories, under the heading "United States," or under the name of your state, county or town, depending upon the level of government to which that agency is responsible.

government frequently makes loans to these organizations in the belief that they can provide quality care to large numbers of subscribers at relatively low cost. Subscribers—employers or institutions such as colleges and labor unions—pay a yearly fee, which may be billed on a monthly basis. In exchange, patients on the rolls of the HMOs may use the medical services of the organization as needed for diagnosis, treatment and rehabilitation. HMO services usually are performed at a central location, but some member physicians are allowed to practice individually and work out of their own offices. The subscriber is thereby provided with a greater choice of physicians. In situations where the services of a specialist, not on the rolls of the HMO, are needed, the patient is referred to that professional. The fee is covered by the contract between the patient and the Health Maintenance Organization.

In some instances, the contracting organization may not pay the complete cost for the HMO's services. An employer, for example, may pay only a portion of the contract costs and charge his employees the rest through payroll deductions.

There are currently about 250 HMOs in the United States that serve approximately 10 million Americans. Under new regulations, a significant number of Americans who receive Medicare or Medicaid benefits may now be treated by Health Maintenance Organizations.

For more information on HMOs, write to:

Office of Health Maintenance
Organizations
Department of Health and Human
Services
12420 Parklawn Dr.
Rockville, MD 20857

Major Illnesses and Health Threats

State, local and federal governments provide a host of services aimed at curing or alleviating specific health and social problems. These are supplemented by private, non-profit agencies, many of which receive a portion of their financial support from the various levels of government. The specific services range from the diagnosis and treatment of diseases to aid for a family whose breadwinner is suffering from cancer to help for a child whose parents are alcoholics. Anyone who needs help for a specific health or social problem should write to the state department of health (addresses, page 164). Direct aid or referral to a local agency may be offered. To learn if a particular service is available in your community, write to:

The Alliance of Information and Referral
Services
P.O. Box 10705
Phoenix, AZ 85064

Do You Have a Drinking Problem?

According to many authorities in the field, about one-tenth of those who drink alcohol are, or are in danger of becoming, alcoholics. The National Council on Alcoholism has devised questionnaire checklists to help people who are concerned about their drinking habits. "Yes" answers to several of the questions below indicate that there is a problem. In general terms questions 1 through 8 relate to the early stages of alcoholism; 9 through 21 to the middle stages; and 22 through 27 to the beginning of the final and often life-threatening stage. However, symptoms are not always experienced in the order listed, and it is possible to skip over some of the early-stage symptoms altogether.

1. Do you sometimes drink heavily after a disappointment or quarrel, or when the boss gives you a hard time?

2. When you have troubles or feel you are under pressure, do you drink more heavily than usual?

3. Have you noticed that you are now able to handle more liquor than you did when you first started drinking?

4. Do you ever wake up the "morning after" and discover that you cannot remember part of the night before, even though friends tell you that you did not pass out?

5. When drinking socially, do you have a few extra drinks when others will not know it? Do you ever gulp your drinks?

6. Do you avoid social occasions in which alcohol is not available, or plan your life around occasions when it will be?

7. Have you noticed that you are now in a greater hurry to get the first drink of the day than you used to be?

8. Do you feel preoccupied with, or guilty about, your drinking?

9. Do you become irritated when friends or family members discuss your drinking?

10. Have family members, friends or coworkers ever told you that your personality

An alphabetical list of major health and social problems follows, together with descriptions of helpful agencies and their activities.

Alcoholism

The National Clearinghouse for Alcohol Information. This agency is a primary source of information on alcoholism both for specialists and ordinary citizens. The Clearinghouse can recommend local treatment facilities for problem drinkers. The address is:

The National Clearinghouse for Alcohol
Information
P.O. Box 2345
Rockville, MD 20852

Alcoholics Anonymous. A voluntary self-help organization, AA provides aid for people with severe drinking problems. Through its meetings and personal services, alcoholics help one another to overcome their addiction. Branches of AA function all over the United States. For information, call your local chapter of AA or write to:

Alcoholics Anonymous World Services,
Inc.
P.O. Box 459, Grand Central Station
New York, NY 10017

The National Council on Alcoholism. An educational and referral service, the Council subsidizes research into the causes and treatment of alcoholism, and refers those in need of treatment to appropriate facilities. For more information, write to:

The National Council on Alcoholism
733 Third Ave.
New York, NY 10017

changes when you drink?

11. Have you recently noticed an increase in the frequency of your memory "blackouts"?

12. Do you often wish to continue drinking after others say they have had enough?

13. Do you usually have an excuse for the occasions when you drink heavily?

14. When you are sober, do you often regret things you have said or done while drinking?

15. Have you tried switching brands, switching from hard liquor to beer, or similar measures to control your drinking?

16. Have you ever tried to control your drinking by changing jobs or schools, or moving to a new location?

17. Have you often failed to keep a promise to yourself or others to stop drinking?

18. Do you try to avoid family or close friends while drinking?

19. Are you having a growing number of financial, work or school problems that might be connected to your drinking?

20. Do you increasingly resent other people's treatment of you?

21. Do you eat very little or irregularly when drinking?

22. Do you sometimes have the "shakes" in the morning and find that it helps to have a drink?

23. Have you recently noticed that you cannot drink as much as you once did without getting drunk?

24. Do you sometimes stay drunk for several days at a time?

25. Do you ever feel very depressed and wonder whether life is worth living?

26. Sometimes, after periods of drinking, do you see or hear things that aren't there?

27. Do you ever get terribly frightened after you have been drinking heavily?

Answer all questions honestly.

Al-Anon and Ala-Teen. These agencies follow Alcoholics Anonymous self-help practices to aid the families of active alcoholics and people who are recovering from the disease. All family members may join Al-Anon, but Ala-Teen is primarily for adolescents. For more information, write to:

Al-Anon Family Group Headquarters and Ala-Teen
P.O. Box 182, Madison Square Station
New York, NY 10010

Arthritis

The Arthritis Foundation. The major voluntary organization offering medical treatment, information and rehabilitation services to victims of this crippling disease and to their families. Chapters are spread throughout the country. For more information write to:

The Arthritis Foundation
3400 Peachtree Rd., NW
Atlanta, GA 30326

Asthma

The Asthma and Allergy Foundation of America. Referral services are provided for victims of asthma or severe allergies. For information and help concerning diagnosis or treatment of these conditions, write to:

The Asthma and Allergy Foundation of America
801 Second Ave.
New York, NY 10017

The American Allergy Association. Victims of severe allergies are aided with day-to-day problems. Advice is offered on creating meals and a home environment free of allergy-producing substances. For information, write to:

American Allergy Association
P.O. Box 7273
Menlo Park, CA 94025

Autism (see Chapter 5)

Blind, Services for the (see Chapter 5)

Blood Transfusions
The American Association of Blood Banks. The Association acts as a clearinghouse for blood donations and transfusions. Through this service, people in areas where blood is in short supply receive "credits" for donations made by friends or relatives who live in distant parts of the country. Approximately 2,000 hospitals participate in the program. For further information, write to:

The American Association of Blood Banks
1828 L St., NW
Washington, DC 20036

Brain Tumors and Associated Ailments
The Brain Research Foundation. The "Helping Hand" program, run by the Foundation, refers victims of brain disorders and their families to local agencies for help. The Foundation also operates services on its own, including various forms of medical, vocational and educational aid. For more information, write to:

The Brain Research Foundation
343 South Dearborn St.
Chicago, IL 60604

The Association for Brain Tumor Research. Primarily concerned with investigations into the causes and cures of the illness, the Association operates a referral service for patients who want to participate in experimental procedures. It also provides helpful information for families of individuals suffering from brain tumors. The address is:

The Association for Brain Tumor Research
6232 North Pulaski Rd.
Chicago, IL 60646

Cancer
The American Cancer Society operates a large number of programs dealing with cancer prevention and treatment. Patients and their families are urged to call local chapters of the Society for help in coping with the trauma produced by this disease. Among the services offered by the society are the following:

Gifts and loans of hospital beds, surgical dressings, crutches and other equipment needed by cancer patients;

Medications and nursing care;

Rehabilitation services for cancer patients;

Community-wide detection programs;

Low-cost and free clinics for financially needy patients;

Transportation services to and from treatment facilities;

Emergency financial aid for especially needy patients.

For more information, write to:

The American Cancer Society
777 Third Ave.
New York, NY 10017

The Cancer Information Service. Information, counseling and referral help for victims of cancer and their families are provided by the Service. It also operates a nationwide "hotline" offering immediate aid to callers. For current hotline phone numbers and general information on the Service, write to:

Cancer Information Service
1825 Connecticut Ave., NW
Washington, DC 20009

Deafness and Hearing Impairment (see Chapter 5)

Diabetes
The American Diabetes Association. Research and special services for diabetes sufferers are offered by the Association. Included are cookbooks and menu-planning aids for diabetics and their families, educational programs on how to deal with the disease, physician referrals, information on free and low-cost care and

on summer camps for diabetic children. The Association conducts an annual diagnostic drive aimed at detecting diabetes. A diagnostic kit is offered to help people determine whether they may be contracting the disease. For more information, write to:

The American Diabetes Association
600 Fifth Ave.
New York, NY 10020

Drug Abuse

The National Clearinghouse for Drug Abuse Information. A service of the Alcohol, Drug Abuse and Mental Health Administration (see page 144), the agency operates an information service concerning drug treatment facilities and answers questions dealing with drug abuse. For information, write to:

National Clearinghouse for Drug Abuse
    Information
P.O. Box 1635
Rockville, MD 20850

State Agencies on Drug Abuse. The executive branch of every state government includes a drug abuse agency. Working with the federal government, these agencies help finance and guide local, county and state facilities in dealing with drug addicts.

Alcoholics are also aided by many of these same organizations. The state agencies offer advice, support facilities and, in many cases, financial aid for community programs dealing with the prevention and treatment of drug and alcohol abuse. Addresses of agencies appear on page 171.

Narcotics Anonymous. The self-help techniques pioneered by Alcoholics Anonymous are employed in group meetings and personal counseling for addicts and people who are recovering from drug addiction. For the name and address of an NA group in your area, write to:

Narcotics Anonymous
P.O. Box 622
Sun Valley, CA 91352

Alcoholics Anonymous. Many chapters of Alcoholics Anonymous also welcome people who have been addicted to such drugs as heroin, amphetamines and tranquilizers.

The Salvation Army. Clinics around the country are operated for addicts who want to be cured of their drug dependence. Among the facilities are places where addicts may go for counseling; halfway houses where people who have recently come off drugs can put their lives in order; and family service facilities that offer aid and counseling to the relatives of addicts or former addicts. For more information about these programs, write to:

The Salvation Army
National Information Service
50 West 23rd St.
New York, NY 10010

Nar-Anon Family Group. Families of active and former drug addicts are served by this mutual-support association. Meeting in public buildings and churches, the relatives of former addicts share helpful experiences and offer advice to one another. For more information, write to:

Nar-Anon Family Group
P.O. Box 2562
Palos Verdes Peninsula, CA 90274

Epilepsy (see Chapter 5)

Eye Care

New Eyes for the Needy. Financial assistance is provided for those who need eye glasses or artificial eyes but lack sufficient funds to pay for them. For information, write to:

New Eyes for the Needy
Short Hills, NJ 07078

Lions Clubs. These organizations help people who cannot afford to buy eye glasses. Free eye examinations, information and referral services for the diagnosis and treatment of glaucoma are also offered. For more information, check the white pages of your telephone book for the

What Your Community Can Do About

Chances are that some of the members of your community are having problems with drugs—problems that may affect everyone in the community. There is no "cure-all," nor is there any one program that has all the answers. One thing is certain, however: the problem must be approached at the local level with the support and assistance of the entire community. Though major results may take years, a cooperative community effort can get the job done. Here is some practical advice, adapted from a report by the Special Action Office for Drug Abuse Prevention.

Start today. Discuss the problem with other people. Find out what resources are being brought to bear in your area. Drug abuse should be approached on a comprehensive basis that deals with the entire community. Government, educational institutions, health groups, law enforcement agencies and the courts, drug abuse programs, business and professional groups must work together. Broad community understanding of the scope of the problem, a knowledge of existing pro-grams that help prevent drug abuse, and an understanding of the new programs that are needed are essential if you are to come to grips with the issue.

How to Get Organized. A drug coordinating council is the starting point for effective action. It can serve as the primary vehicle for mobilizing community understanding and commitment. If your community does not already have such a group, enlist the help of others in organizing one.

A coordinating council should be:

* Representative of the entire community and include in its membership public officials, professionals, civic leaders, agency officials who have services to offer, community group members, people already involved in the drug abuse fields and representatives of all racial, national and religious groups.

* Open in approach, i.e. making use of all kinds of programs and methods that have proved effective in helping people in their problems.

Lions Club nearest you, or write to:

Lions International
300 22nd St.
Oakbrook, IL 60521

Family Planning

The Office of Family Planning. Part of the U.S. Health Services Administration, the Office of Family Planning provides grants to the states, local governments and private voluntary agencies to help establish and operate clinics around the country. More than 5,000 family planning clinics are now aided by federal funds. Their purpose is to make birth control information and devices available to people who need and want such services. In addition they offer information and treatment of infer-tility to those couples who are having difficulty conceiving. Clinics receiving federal aid generally offer a wide range of health-screening procedures to their clients. For more information or the address of a federally subsidized family planning clinic near you, write to:

The Family Planning Office
Bureau of Community Health Services
500 Fishers Lane
Rockville, MD 20857

The National Clearinghouse for Family Planning Information. Up-to-date information on all aspects of family planning may be obtained from this federal agency. The address is:

National Clearinghouse for Family Planning

Drug Abuse Prevention

* Action-oriented. Effective programs should be quickly developed to help drug abusers and to prevent others from becoming addicted to drugs.

Successful Coordinating Efforts. Sustained enlightened action is required if efforts to combat drug abuses are to succeed. Here are the essential ingredients of a successful program:

* Leadership: The most important single factor is leadership that can organize community support, obtain private and governmental funds and other resources, stimulate the development of quality programs and keep them moving forward.

* Goals: The overall focus must be broader than the immediate issue of drug abuse. Effective action must also deal with related problems, such as insufficient recreational and developmental programs for youth, poverty, discrimination, general health, and police-community relations.

* Publicity: Broad media coverage and open community meetings are needed to create a greater public awareness of drug abuse and related problems.

* Broad Representation: All community groups, including minorities and youth, should be represented on the coordinating council. Law enforcement agencies should also be involved. In drawing up action plans, make use of the experiences of former drug abusers.

* Operating Style: Visitors should be welcome at council meetings and their opinions should be sought. But once action programs have been established, no one should interfere with their day-by-day operations.

* Resource Utilization: The council should attempt to use all community resources, such as neighborhood organizations, schools and city agencies. The council should seek financial support from private as well as government agencies.

P.O. Box 2225
Rockville, MD 20852

The Planned Parenthood Federation of America. A nationwide network of counseling services and birth control clinics, this organization offers information and clinical help on all aspects of family planning and sexual problems. Treatments for venereal diseases are included. Services are sometimes offered without fee or in keeping with the client's ability to pay. Local chapters or clinics are listed in the white pages of telephone books or may be reached by mail by writing to:

Planned Parenthood Federation of America
810 7th Ave.
New York, NY 10019

The Couple to Couple League. This organization offers information and classes on natural family planning, such as the rhythm method of birth control favored by those who seek alternatives to artificial (chemical and mechanical) birth control devices. For further information, write to:

The Couple to Couple League
P.O. Box 11084
Cincinnati, OH 45211

Handicapped, Services for the (see Chapter 5)

Heart Disease
The American Heart Association. The leading agency dealing with heart disease, the

American Heart Association offers a variety of services that include educational programs, aid to schools and local health facilities, counseling for individuals and institutions to encourage the adoption of healthful diets and exercise programs, and literature on the prevention and treatment of heart problems.

The American Heart Association also maintains a nationwide high blood pressure screening program. It provides rehabilitation services for the victims of heart disease and strokes, and offers counseling for the families of victims. In conjunction with local hospitals, voluntary ambulance corps and other agencies, the Association prepares courses for the general public in cardio-pulmonary resuscitation and other life-saving techniques. Further information may be obtained by calling the Association's local chapter, or by writing to:

The American Heart Association
205 East 42nd St.
New York, NY 10017

Kidney Disease

The National Kidney Foundation. Chapters across the country offer a variety of services, including: screening procedures for early diagnosis of kidney disease; blood for kidney surgery or dialysis patients; referral to health care facilities or physicians specializing in kidney ailments; low-cost drugs for patients whose doctors are members of the Foundation; financial aid for patients on dialysis; summer camp for children undergoing dialysis treatments; and recruitment of kidney donors. For more information, check the white pages of your phone book for the local chapter of the Foundation, or write to:

The National Kidney Foundation
2 Park Ave.
New York, NY 10016

Mental and Emotional Health Services

Community Mental Health Centers. Jointly funded by federal, state and local governments, these agencies offer a broad variety of mental health services. A typical center employs psy-

chiatrists, psychologists and social workers, and deals with the full range of mental and emotional problems, including alcoholism and drug addiction. Short- and long-term therapy and counseling are provided. Therapy sessions may involve family members individually or in groups. The emphasis is on outpatient care, but when necessary, short-term intensive hospital care or partial hospitalization may be provided. Most centers offer 24-hour-a-day, 7-day-a-week emergency services. Patients generally pay according to their ability.

Because the centers may operate under almost any name, your local center may be difficult to locate through the pages of your phone book. A call to your local health department, the state department of health (addresses, page 164) or the local chapter of the Mental Health Association (see below) will enable you to locate the address and phone number of your closest community mental health center. For more information on the program, write to:

National Institute of Mental Health
Public Inquiries Office
5600 Fishers Lane
Rockville, MD 20857

The Mental Health Association. Chapters in cities and towns throughout the country provide referral services for those in need of counseling or therapy. Staff members are knowledgeable about federally funded community mental-health centers, and other low-cost, community supported facilities offering a broad range of counseling services. For more information, check the white pages of the telephone directory for the local Mental Health Association chapter, or write to:

The Mental Health Association
1800 North Kent St.
Arlington, VA 22209

Halfway Houses and Community Residences. Live-in facilities for people with severe emotional problems who do not require hospitalization are provided at these institutions. Residents learn how to cope with day-to-day life in a protected environment. Round-the-clock staffs provide help to the residents and, where needed, psychological therapy is offered. Most halfway houses and community residences are financed by state, local and federal funds, but some are operated by local voluntary agencies. For more information on halfway houses, write to your state's mental health agency (addresses page 169), call your local chapter of the Mental Health Association or write to:

The National Institute of Mental Health
5600 Fishers Lane
Rockville, MD 20857

Mental Retardation (see Chapter 5)

Multiple Sclerosis

The National Multiple Sclerosis Society. Counseling services, medical equipment and therapy programs are provided for multiple sclerosis victims. The Society also helps finance clinics where the disease is diagnosed and aid is provided. Check the white pages of your phone book for the address and phone number of your local chapter, or write to:

The National Multiple Sclerosis Society
205 East 42nd St.
New York, NY 10017

Muscular Dystrophy

The Muscular Dystrophy Association. Local chapters offer diagnostic services and physical therapy free of charge to victims of this disease. They also lend orthopedic devices to sufferers and provide transportation to doctors and dentists' offices, schools and work places. Check your phone book's white pages for your local chapter or write to:

The Muscular Dystrophy Association
810 7th Ave.
New York, NY 10019

Nursing Homes (see Chapter 8)

Poisonings

The National Poison Center Network. A 24-hour, 7-day-a-week phone service is maintained by the Center. If you know or suspect that someone has taken poison, call the number immediately and a staff member will tell you what emergency steps to take. The staff member will also tell you where to take the victim and will notify the treatment facility that you and the victim are on the way.

To obtain the phone number of the Poison Center "hotline" in your area, check the white pages in your phone book under "poison." If there is no listing, call the National Center at: 412-681-6669. To obtain the number in your area in advance, write to:

National Poison Center Network
Children's Hospital of Pittsburgh
125 DeSoto St.
Pittsburgh, PA 15213

Venereal Disease

The American Social Health Association. Under a contract from The Centers for Disease Control, this organization operates a nationwide "hotline" service that provides information and referral on venereal disease. People who suspect they may have contracted a venereal disease are referred to one of 5,000 clinics where free or low-cost diagnosis and treatment are provided. The hotline number is 800-227-8922. The address is:

American Social Health Association
260 Sheridan Ave.
Palo Alto, CA 94306

Medicare

Americans 65 years old and older are protected against the soaring costs of hospital, nursing-home care and other medical expenses by the federally financed Medicare program. Established under the Social Security Act, the program is administered by the Health Care Financing Administration of the Health and Human Services Department. Medicare does not cover all expenses, but provides subscribers with significant benefits described below.

Filling Out Your Medicare Form

REQUEST FOR MEDICARE PAYMENT

Form Approved

MEDICAL INSURANCE BENEFITS—SOCIAL SECURITY ACT (See Instructions on Back — **Type or Print Information**) OMB No. 066-R-0012

No Part B Medicare benefits may be paid unless this form is received as required by existing law and regulations (20 CFR 422.510)

NOTICE—Anyone who misrepresents or falsifies essential information requested by this form may upon conviction be subject to fine and imprisonment under Federal Law.

PART I—PATIENT TO FILL IN ITEMS 1 THROUGH 6 ONLY

A

Copy from
YOUR OWN
HEALTH
INSURANCE
CARD
*(See example
on back)*

1 Name of patient (First name, Middle initial, Last name)

2 Health insurance claim number
(Include all letters)

☐ Male ☐ Female

B

3 Patient's complete mailing address (including Apt. no.)   City, State, ZIP Code

Telephone Number

4 Describe the illness or injury for which you received treatment *(Always fill in this item if your doctor does not complete Part II below)*

C

Was your illness or injury connected with your employment?

☐ Yes ☐ No

5 If any of your medical expenses will be or could be paid by another insurance organization or government agency, show below

Name and address of organization or agency

Policy or Identification Number

D

Note: If you **Do Not** want information about this Medicare claim released to the above upon its request, check (X) the following block ☐

6 I authorize any holder of medical or other information about me to release to the Social Security Administration and Health Care Financing Administration or its intermediaries or carriers any information needed for this or a related Medicare claim. I permit a copy of this authorization to be used in place of the original, and request payment of medical insurance benefits either to myself or to the party who accepts assignment below.

Signature of patient *(See instructions on reverse where patient is unable to sign)*

Date signed

E

SIGN HERE ►

PART II—PHYSICIAN OR SUPPLIER TO FILL IN 7 THROUGH 14

7 A. Date of each service	B. Place of service (*See Codes below)	C. Fully describe surgical or medical procedures and other services or supplies furnished for each date given (if lab service, indicate if automated)	Procedure Code	D. Nature of illness or injury requiring services or supplies	E. Charges (if related to unusual circumstances explain in 7C)	Leave Blank
					$	

F

8 Name and address of physician or supplier *(Number and street, city, State, ZIP code)*

Telephone No.

9 Total charges $

Physician or supplier code

10 Amount paid $

11 Any unpaid balance due $

12 Assignment of patient's bill

☐ I accept assignment *(See reverse)*   ☐ I do not accept assignment.

13 Name and address of person or facility where services were furnished *(Complete if outside your own office or patient's residence)*.

14 Signature of physician or supplier (I certify that the statements under Physicians' Notes on the reverse apply to this bill and are made a part hereof.)

Date Signed

O—Doctor's Office   H—Patient's Home (If portable X-ray services, identify the supplier)   SNF—Skilled Nursing Facility   OL—Other Locations
IL—Independent Laboratory   IH—Inpatient Hospital   OH—Outpatient Hospital   NH—Nursing Home

Form HCFA-1490 (2) (5-78) (Formerly SSA-1490 (2))

Department of Health Education and Welfare—Health Care Financing Administration

A. Print your health insurance number *exactly* as it's shown on your Medicare card. Be sure to include any letter either at the beginning or the end of the number.

B. Print your complete address—street, city, state, and ZIP code.

C. Briefly describe the condition (illness or injury) for which you were treated. If you were treated for different conditions, describe each.

D. If you have private health insurance or are covered under a state medical assistance program (such as Medicaid), print the name and address of the insurance company or state program.

E. Sign your name. (Do not print.)

F. If Part II (items 7 through 14) is completed by the doctor or supplier, you do not have to attach itemized bills. If your doctor or supplier does not complete Part II, you *must* attach itemized bills.

G. Print your name *exactly* as it's shown on your Medicare card.

H. Check the box next to male or female.

I. Print the telephone number where you can be reached.

J. Check the box marked "yes" or "no."

K. Print your private insurance policy number or state medical assistance number.

L. Check this box *only if* you do *not* want information about this Medicare claim given to your private insurance company or state medical assistance program.

M. Print the date you signed this form.

A Medicare payment form is easy for both the patient and doctor to fill out. Just follow directions, as above.

Eligibility Requirements

Any citizen or long-term U.S. resident who is 65 or over and has worked long enough (or is the spouse of someone who has worked long enough) to qualify for Social Security retirement benefits is eligible for Medicare. Contrary to widespread belief, it is not essential to be retired in order to receive Medicare benefits. Once you are 65 or older, you are eligible, regardless of your work status. In addition, people under 65 who are disabled and have been entitled to Social Security disability payments for 24 months, or those of any age who require dialysis treatments or kidney transplants, are entitled to Medicare hospital coverage. Wives, husbands and children of Medicare beneficiaries who require dialysis or kidney transplants are also eligible. People who have reached 65 but have not worked long enough to be eligible for Social Security benefits may purchase Medicare hospital coverage. The cost in the early 1980s was $89 per month.

The Two Parts of Medicare

Medicare consists of two elements: hospital insurance and medical insurance. Hospital insurance is provided free to subscribers; medical insurance costs $12.10 a month beginning in July 1982.

The Benefits of Hospital Insurance

If you are a Medicare hospital insurance subscriber, you are entitled to up to 90 days of hospital care, in any one "benefit period," with the government paying most of the expenses. For your first 60 days in the hospital, the government will pay all expenses except a $260 deductible which you must pay. For the next 30 days, you pay $65 per day and the government pays the rest of your expenses.

The Meaning of "Benefit Period"

A benefit period of 90 days begins the first time you enter a hospital. A new 90-day period begins after you have been out of the hospital and, if used, a follow-up care facility (such as a participating nursing home) for 60 days. Suppose, for example, you entered a hospital in early January, remained for three weeks, then were discharged, but in June, you had to return to the hospital. A new period would begin in June because you have been out of the hospital for more than 60 days. On the other hand, if your January stay at the hospital was for, say, 75 days, followed by a 15-day confinement in a nursing home, your new period would not begin until you had been out of the nursing home for at least 60 days. There is no limit on the number of benefit periods to which you are entitled, but you will not get full or partial coverage in the hospital for any one period lasting more than 90 days.

An Exception to the Benefit Period Rule. Every Medicare subscriber has a total of 60 reserve days. If you are in the hospital for a condition that requires you to be there more than 90 days, the reserve-day clause comes into effect, and coverage will continue through the additional 60 days on a reduced benefit basis. You will have to pay $90 per day toward the cost of hospitalization. Once you have used up the 60 reserve days, they are gone forever. If, for example, you are in the hospital for 150 consecutive days, your costs will be totally paid (minus the $260 deductible) during the first 60 days; you will pay $65 per day from the 61st through the 90th day; and $90 per day from the 91st day through the 150th day.

Suppose you are sent home at this point, but a year later you are required to return to the hospital for another extended period. Your costs will be the same as before for the first 90 days. But at the end of the 90th day you will have no more reserve days, and from that time until the end of your hospital stay you will have to bear the full cost of hospitalization unless you have private insurance coverage to fill the gap (see box page 160).

Nursing Home Services Under Medicare
Your hospitalization coverage also includes up to 100 days in a participating nursing facility during each benefit period. For the first 20 days, your costs will be completely covered; for the last 80 you must pay $32.50 per day. The nursing home must meet federal standards by maintaining a skilled nursing and rehabilitation program and related health services. To obtain nursing home coverage you must meet the following conditions:

*You must have been hospitalized for at least three consecutive days before entering the nursing home.

*The condition for which you were treated in the hospital must require that you be in a nursing home.

*You must enter the nursing home no more than 14 days after leaving the hospital.

*You must be receiving medically necessary nursing or rehabilitative care every day.

*Your stay in the nursing facility must be approved by Medicare's local Professional Standards Review Organization.

Home Health Visits
In addition to your hospital and nursing home benefits, you are entitled to an unlimited number of visits from professional workers employed by home-health agencies during each benefit period. These visits must come within 12 months of your most recent discharge from a hospital or participating nursing care facility if they are to be paid for by Medicare. In addition, the following conditions must be met:

*You must have been in a hospital for at least three consecutive days (not counting the day you were discharged).

*The condition for which you are being treated must be the same one for which you were treated in the hospital or skilled nursing facility.

*Home health care must be medical in nature. Physician's care, skilled nursing, physical or speech therapy will be included, but non-medical expenses will not be paid.

*Your condition makes it impossible for you to leave home.

*The visiting services must be required by a physician who has established a formal home health schedule for you within 14 days of your discharge from the hospital or nursing home.

*The agency or agencies providing the home health care must have been approved by Medicare.

What Medicare's Hospitalization Plan Covers

Services in a hospital or participating nursing facility include the following:

*A semi-private (two to four beds) room.

*All meals, including special diets.

*Nursing services and fees for necessary special care, such as an intensive care unit.

*Drugs, supplies, appliances, equipment and other services required by the subscriber. Services of home health agencies include:

*Part-time skilled nursing care.

*Fees charged by physical, speech and occupational therapists.

*Medical and social services (not including drugs), and medical equipment provided by the agencies.

What Medicare's Hospitalization Plan Does Not Cover

A number of services that may be desired or needed by the subscriber are not covered by the hospitalization plan. These include:

*All services and supplies not necessary to the treatment of the patient's ailment.

*Physician's bills. (These are covered by Medicare's medical-insurance plan—see the explanation below.)

*Private nurses.

*The first three pints of blood a patient receives during a benefit period.

*Convenience items such as television set or a telephone in your room.

*Custodial care, such as help with bathing, walking or dressing.

*Homemaker services such as those provided by a housekeeper or a cook, or meals delivered to your home.

Hospital Services Outside the United States

By and large, Medicare hospitalization coverage is limited to facilities in the 50 states, the District of Columbia, U.S. possessions and commonwealths overseas. In certain instances, coverage may extend to Canadian and Mexican hospitals. If, for example, you are traveling in Canada or Mexico and require immediate hospitalization, your costs will be covered.

Medicare Medical Insurance: Eligibility

If you are 65 or older or are otherwise entitled to Medicare hospital insurance, you may participate in the Medicare medical coverage plan. The plan starts automatically if you receive Social Security or railroad retirement benefits, but you may refuse to participate if you do not want to pay the $12.10 monthly fee. Enrollment occurs when your coverage in the hospital plan begins. About 90 days before that date, you will receive information on the medical program and be provided with a form that you must return if you *do not* want to be enrolled.

Exceptions to the Automatic Enrollment Provisions

You will not be automatically enrolled in the medical plan under the following circumstances:

*If you are 65 or older but have not worked long enough to be eligible for the hospital plan.

*You have a permanent kidney disease requiring dialysis or a transplant.

*You live in Puerto Rico or a foreign country.

*If you fall into one of these categories, you must apply at a Social Security office for enrollment in the medical plan.

Enrollment Periods

You may enroll in the medical plan during the three months before and the four months after you first become eligible. If you decide not to enroll during this period, then change your mind, enrollments are accepted again from January 1 to March 31 of the following year. You may enroll during any of these general enrollment periods, even 10 or 20 years after you first become eligible for the medical plan. However, if you delay enrollment until after the time when you are initially eligible, benefits will not begin until July of the year when you join, and you will pay higher monthly premiums—in some cases, much higher.

What Medicare's Medical Insurance Covers

Medical insurance under the plan will pay for the following medically necessary services:

*Most of the costs associated with physicians' services performed in the United States, including diagnosis and treatment in a physician's office, a hospital, a participating nursing care facility, your home or anywhere else. (Maximum rates for all such services are, however, set by Medicare. If charges are higher, you must pay the difference.)

*Hospital emergency room and out-patient treatment and diagnosis.

*An unlimited number of home health visits every year, provided that a physician determines that you need the services and establishes a formal health-care plan for you; you need part-time nursing or physical and speech therapy; you are unable to leave your home; and the agencies providing the services are approved by Medicare.

*Physical and speech therapy performed in a physician's office, in a hospital out-patient clinic, at a participating nursing home facility; at an approved rehabilitation agency such as a community health service or rural health clinic. Such services must be in accord with your physician's formal treatment plan. They must also be reviewed periodically by the attending physician.

*Other medically necessary services such as X-ray and radiation treatments; surgical dressings, splints, casts, braces and the like; and the rental or purchase of other necessary items such as oxygen equipment and wheel chairs to be used in the home.

Plugging the Medicare Insurance Gap

Because of the limitations of Medicare insurance, a beneficiary may be faced with a large medical bill. A number of private insurance companies have instituted plans that wholly or partially cover situations that are not covered by Medicare. These plans are popularly known as "Medigap" insurance. You must pay premiums for them, but they may well be worth the cost. Some of the plans can be purchased by individuals, others are available only on a group basis through employers or associations, such as lodges, labor unions or clubs. There are three major categories of coverage:

* **Medicare Supplement Plans.** Coverage is provided for some or all of the deductibles and co-payments charged by Medicare.

* **Catastrophic or Major Medical Plans.** Payments are made for long-term conditions after Medicare benefits cease. These plans usually have their own deductibles and maximum benefit payments, but they may be useful in protecting you when Medicare benefits run out.

* **Health Maintenance Organizations. (HMOs).** Comprehensive care is offered for a set fee each year (see page 145). If there is an HMO in your area that participates in the Medicare program, it may charge you only a relatively small amount to provide necessary supplementary services.

When considering Medigap insurance, there are a number of things to watch for, among them:

*Some ambulance services.

*Some limited chiropractic services.

*Home care and office services performed by licensed Medicare-certified therapists. The amounts paid by the plan are limited.

How Much Medicare's Medical Insurance Pays

Under current regulations subscribers are charged a $75 deductible each year. After this fee has been met, Medicare's medical insurance will pay 80 percent of the fees that are judged to be "reasonable and customary." The following exceptions are made.

*During a hospital stay, the medical plan will pay 100 percent of the reasonable charges of pathologists and radiologists whether or not the $75 deductible has been paid.

*Exclusive of the deductible, the plan will pay all of the reasonable charges of home care specialists.

*The plan pays only a maximum of $80 in any one year toward the fees of independent physical therapists (those not associated with an approved home-care agency). A maximum of $250 will be paid toward the fees charged by physician-psychiatrists for treatment outside the hospital.

Services Not Covered by the Plan

Medicare's medical insurance will not pay for the following:

*Services and supplies unnecessary for the diagnosis or treatment of an illness or injury.

*Routine physical examinations and tests.

*Prescription drugs and patent medicines.

*Hearing aids and examinations for hearing loss.

*Glasses and eye examinations.

*Dental care and dentures.

*Custodial services performed while you are ill, such as housekeeping, cooking and meal deliveries.

*Full-time home nursing care.

* Check the policy carefully. Determine exactly what the plan will cover or not cover. Compare it with policies offered by competing insurance companies in terms of benefits and premium costs.

* If a policy is offered on an individual basis, delay signing up until you have checked with all organizations to which you belong to see if they offer similar coverage at group rates. Group rates are often far less expensive than rates offered to individuals. You might even consider joining a particular organization in order to qualify for its health insurance plan.

* Don't purchase more policies than you absolutely need. Overlapping coverage will not benefit you. One comprehensive policy is usually better than several policies, each covering a specific set of circumstances.

* Check carefully for exclusions. Many policies will not cover pre-existing conditions or will require a long waiting period before they will pay benefits on such ailments.

* Beware of the insurance salesman who suggests that you give up a policy you already have. Consider very carefully the benefits and costs of a new policy. Does it really offer more than the old one at competitive premiums? Is there a waiting period between the time you start paying premiums and the time when benefits are available?

* Check the maximum benefits. Most policies will not go on paying interminably for treatment of a particular condition. Try to determine if the maximum benefits are reasonable in terms of today's medical costs.

*Orthopedic shoes.

*Items used essentially for purposes of comfort or convenience.

How Medicare Payments Are Made

Payments for medical services are made by the federal government through third-party carriers (insurance companies). The payments are based upon formulas that take into account the "reasonable and customary" charges for such services. The government will pay 80 percent of these "reasonable and customary" fees. You will pay the rest. However, physicians and others providing services may charge whatever they please.

All amounts beyond the government-approved fees must be borne by the subscriber. To be certain that you will not be required to pay an excessive fee, have a frank discussion with your physician, nurse or therapist to determine if he or she will accept "assignment." This means that the provider accepts Medicare's definition of a reasonable fee and will not charge you more.

Two Methods of Payment

Assignment. The physician or provider fills out the necessary forms and is paid directly by the third-party carrier.

Non-assignment. The patient fills out at least a portion of the "Request for Medicare Payment" form. The physician or supplier fills out the rest of the form or, failing that, the patient attaches all itemized bills to the form. (See the sample form on page 156.)

Under the non-assignment plan, the patient is responsible for all medical charges in excess of those that are deemed reasonable by Medicare administrators.

For More Information

The best source of information on Medicare is your local Social Security office. Check the white pages of your telephone directory, both under "S" and under "U.S. Government" for the office nearest you.

Medicaid

Medicaid is intended to provide basic medical, hospital and health services for low-income individuals and families. Authorized under the Social Security Act, the program is jointly funded by federal and state governments. States have the option of joining the program or refusing to participate. Currently, Arizona is the only state without a Medicaid program.

The federal government establishes basic guidelines for Medicaid and requires that certain services be provided free of charge, but each state administers its own Medicaid program. Once the basic guidelines have been met, the states have a large degree of autonomy in running the service.

Eligibility Requirements

There are two broad categories of eligibility for Medicaid. The first is the "categorically needy." This includes individuals and families receiving some form of federally subsidized welfare payments. With minor exceptions, anyone who receives these payments is entitled to all of the benefits of Medicaid. A second category of people, defined as the "medically needy," may also be entitled to receive all or some Medicaid benefits, depending upon the regulations in effect in their states. The medically needy are normally defined as individuals or families who are ineligible for welfare but lack the funds to pay for medical care. It is up to the individual states to decide whether these people are entitled to all or some Medicaid's many services.

For More Information

Each state participating in the program has its own Medicaid offices listed in the telephone directory. For general information on the program, write to:

Office of Beneficiary Services
Health Care Financing Administration
200 Independence Ave., SW
Washington, DC 20201

Directory of Government Health and Social Service Agencies

U.S. Department of Health and Human Services
200 Independence Ave., SW
Washington, DC 20201

Food and Nutrition Service
United States Department of Agriculture
3101 Park Center Dr.
Alexandria, VA 22302

Regional Offices

New England Regional Office
(Connecticut, Maine, Massachusetts, New Hampshire,
Rhode Island, Vermont)
Food and Nutrition Service
U.S. Department of Agriculture
33 North Ave.
Burlington, MA 01803

Mid-Atlantic Regional Office
(Delaware, Maryland, New Jersey, New York,
Pennsylvania, District of Columbia, Virginia, West
Virginia, Puerto Rico, Virgin Islands)
Food and Nutrition Service
U.S. Department of Agriculture
One Vahlsing Center
Robbinsville, NJ 08691

Southeast Regional Office
(Alabama, Florida, Georgia, Kentucky, Mississippi,
North Carolina, South Carolina, Tennessee)
Food and Nutrition Service
U.S. Department of Agriculture
1100 Spring St., NW
Atlanta, GA 30367

Midwest Regional Office
(Illinois, Indiana, Michigan, Minnesota, Ohio, Wisconsin)
Food and Nutrition Service
U.S. Department of Agriculture
536 South Clark St.
Chicago, IL 60605

Mountain Plains Regional Office
(Colorado, Iowa, Kansas, Missouri, Montana, Nebraska,
North Dakota, South Dakota, Utah, Wyoming)
Food and Nutrition Service
U.S. Department of Agriculture
2420 West 26th Ave.
Denver, CO 80211

Southwest Regional Office
(Arkansas, Louisiana, New Mexico, Oklahoma, Texas)
Food and Nutrition Service
U.S. Department of Agriculture
1100 Commerce St.
Dallas, TX 75242

Western Regional Office
(Alaska, American Samoa, Arizona, California, Guam,
Hawaii, Idaho, Nevada, Oregon, Pacific Trust Territories,
Washington)
Food and Nutrition Service
U.S. Department of Agriculture
550 Kearny St.
San Francisco, CA 94108

Administration for Children, Youth and Families

Includes:
  Head Start
  Children's Bureau
  Youth Development Bureau

Office of Human Development Services
Administration for Children, Youth and Families
P.O. Box 1182
Washington, DC 20013

Regional Offices

Region I
(Connecticut, Maine, Massachusetts, New Hampshire,
Vermont, Rhode Island)
Administration for Children, Youth and Families
Federal Building
Government Center
Boston, MA 02203

Region II
(New York, New Jersey, Puerto Rico, Virgin Islands)

Administration for Children, Youth and Families
26 Federal Plaza
New York, NY 10007

Region III
(Delaware, District of Columbia, Maryland, Pennsylvania,
Virginia, West Virginia)
Administration for Children, Youth and Families
3535 Market St.
P.O. Box 13716
Philadelphia, PA 19101

Region IV
(Alabama, Florida, Georgia, Kentucky, Mississippi,
North Carolina, South Carolina, Tennessee)
Administration for Children, Youth and Families
Peachtree-Seventh Building
50 7th St., NE
Atlanta, GA 30323

Region V
(Illinois, Indiana, Michigan, Minnesota, Ohio, Wisconsin)

Administration for Children, Youth and Families
300 South Wacker Dr.
Chicago, IL 60606

Region VI
(Arkansas, Louisiana, New Mexico, Oklahoma, Texas)
Administration for Children, Youth and Families
1200 Main Tower Building
Dallas, TX 75202

Region VII
(Iowa, Kansas, Missouri, Nebraska)
Administration for Children, Youth and Families
3rd Floor, Federal Building
601 East 12th St.
Kansas City, MO 64106

Region VIII
(Colorado, Montana, North Dakota, South Dakota, Utah, Wyoming)
Administration for Children, Youth and Families
1961 Stout St.
Denver, CO 80294

Region IX
(Arizona, California, Hawaii, Nevada, Pacific Trust Territories)

Administration for Children, Youth and Families
Federal Building
50 United Nations Plaza
San Francisco, CA 94102

Region X
(Alaska, Idaho, Oregon, Washington)
Administration for Children, Youth and Families
Arcade Plaza Building
1321 2nd Ave.
Seattle, WA 98101

Indian and Migrant Programs Division
Head Start Bureau, Administration for Children, Youth and Families
Department of Health and Human Services
Room 5550, Donohoe Building
P.O. Box 1182
Washington, DC 20013

State Departments of Health

Alabama
Department of Public Health
State Office Building
Montgomery, AL 36130

Alaska
Division of Public Health
Pouch H-06
Department of Health and Social Services
Juneau, AK 99811

Arizona
Department of Health Services
1740 West Adams
Phoenix, AZ 85007

Arkansas
Department of Health
4815 West Markham St.
Little Rock, AR 72201

California
Department of Health Services
Health and Welfare Agency
714 P St.
Sacramento, CA 95814

Colorado
State Department of Health
4210 East 11th Ave.
Denver, CO 80220

Connecticut
State Department of Health
79 Elm St.
Hartford, CT 06115

Delaware
State Department of Health and Social Services
Division of Health
Jesse Cooper Building
Dover, DE 19901

District of Columbia
Community Health and Hospital Administration
1875 Connecticut Ave., NW
Washington, DC 20009

Florida
Department of Health and Rehabilitative Services
1323 Winewood Blvd.
Tallahassee, FL 32301

Georgia
Department of Human Resources
47 Trinity Ave., SW
Atlanta, GA 30334

Hawaii
State Department of Health
P.O. Box 3378
Honolulu, HI 96801

Idaho
State Department of Health and Welfare
Statehouse
Boise, ID 83720

Illinois
State Department of Public Health
535 West Jefferson
Springfield, IL 62761

Indiana
State Board of Health
1330 West Michigan St.
Indianapolis, IN 46206

Iowa
State Department of Health
Robert Lucas State Office Building
Des Moines, IA 50319

Kansas
State Department of Health and Environment
Forbes AFB
Topeka, KS 66620

Kentucky
Department for Human Resources
275 East Main St.
Frankfort, KY 40621

Louisiana
State Department of Health and Human Resources
P.O. Box 60630
New Orleans, LA 70160

Maine
State Department of Human Services
Bureau of Health
221 State St.
Augusta, ME 04333

Maryland
State Department of Health and Mental Hygiene
201 West Preston St.
Baltimore, MD 21201

Massachusetts
Department of Public Health
600 Washington St.
Boston, MA 02111

Michigan
State Department of Public Health
P.O. Box 30035
Lansing, MI 48909

Minnesota
State Department of Health
717 Delaware St., SE
Minneapolis, MN 55440

Mississippi
State Board of Health
Felix J. Underwood Building
P.O. Box 1700
Jackson, MS 39205

Missouri
Division of Health
Department of Social Services
P.O. Box 570
Jefferson City, MO 65102

Montana
State Department of Health and Environmental
 Sciences
W.F. Cogswell Building
Helena, MT 59601

Nebraska
State Department of Health

P.O. Box 95007
Lincoln, NE 68509

Nevada
State Department of Human Resources
Division of Health
Capitol Complex
505 East King St.
Carson City, NV 89710

New Hampshire
State Department of Health and Welfare
Hazan Dr.
Concord, NH 03301

New Jersey
State Department of Health
John Fitch Plaza
P.O. Box 1540
Trenton, NJ 08625

New Mexico
Department of Health and Environment
Health Services Division
P.O. Box 968
Santa Fe, NM 87503

New York State
Department of Health
Tower Building
Empire State Plaza
Albany, NY 12237

New York City
City Department of Health
125 Worth St.
New York, NY 10013

North Carolina
State Department of Human Resources
Division of Health Services
P.O. Box 2091
Raleigh, NC 27602

North Dakota
State Department of Health
State Capitol
Bismarck, ND 58505

Ohio
State Department of Health
246 North High St.
Columbus, OH 43215

Oklahoma
State Department of Health
1000 NE 10th St.
Oklahoma City, OK 73152

Oregon
Department of Human Resources
State Health Division
1400 SW Fifth Ave.
Portland, OR 97201

Pennsylvania
State Department of Health
P.O. Box 90
Harrisburg, PA 17120

Rhode Island
State Department of Health

75 Davis St.
Providence, RI 02908

South Carolina
State Department of Health and Environmental Control
J. Marion Sims Building
2600 Bull St.
Columbia, SC 29201

South Dakota
State Department of Health
Joe Foss Building
Pierre, SD 57501

Tennessee
Department of Public Health
Cordell Hull Building
Nashville, TN 37219

Texas
State Department of Health
1100 West 49th St.
Austin, TX 78756

Utah
Department of Health
Division of Community Health Services
150 West North Temple
Salt Lake City, UT 84103

Vermont
State Department of Health
60 Main St.
Burlington, VT 05401

Virginia
State Department of Health
The James Madison Building
109 Governor St.
Richmond, VA 23219

Washington
Health Services Division
Department of Social and Health Services
Office Building 2
Olympia, WA 98504

West Virginia
Department of Health
Building 3, State Capitol Complex
1800 Washington St., E
Charleston, WV 25305

Wisconsin
State Department of Health and Social Services
Division of Health
West Wilson St.
Madison, WI 53702

Wyoming
State Department of Health and Social Services
Division of Health and Medical Services
Hathaway Building
Cheyenne, WY 82002

Guam
Department of Public Health and Social Services
Government of Guam
P.O. Box 2816
Agana, Guam 96910

Commonwealth of Northern Mariana Islands
Department of Public Health and Environmental Services
Saipan, Mariana Islands 96950

Federated States of Micronesia
Department of Health Services
Office of the High Commissioner
Saipan, Mariana Islands 96950

Puerto Rico
Department of Health, Edificio "A"
Call Box 70184
San Juan, PR 00936

Virgin Islands
Department of Health
Division of Community Health Services
P.O. Box 7309
St. Thomas, VI 00801

State Departments of Social Services

Alabama
State Agency of Social Security
Public Safety Building
Montgomery, AL 36130

Alaska
Division of Social Services
Pouch H-05
Department of Health and Social Services
Juneau, AK 99811

Arizona
Department of Economic Security
1717 West Jefferson
Phoenix, AZ 85007

Arkansas
Social Services Division
Department of Human Services
P.O. Box 1437
Little Rock, AR 72201

California
Adult and Family Services
Department of Social Services
Health and Welfare Agency
744 P St.
Sacramento, CA 95814

Colorado
Department of Social Services

1575 Sherman St.
Denver, CO 80203

Connecticut
Department of Human Resources
1179 Main St.
Hartford, CT 06115

Delaware
Department of Health and Social Services
Division of Social Services
P.O. Box 309
Wilmington, DE 19899

District of Columbia
Department of Human Resources
415 12th St., NW
Washington, DC 20004

Florida
Social and Economic Services Program Office
Department of Health and Rehabilitative Services
1323 Winewood Blvd.
Tallahassee, FL 32301

Georgia
Family and Children Services Division
Department of Human Resources
47 Trinity Ave., SW
Atlanta, GA 30334

Hawaii
Department of Social Services and Housing
Liliuokalani Building
1390 Miller St.
Honolulu, HI 96813

Idaho
Bureau of Social Services
Division of Welfare
Department of Health and Welfare
700 West State St.
Boise, ID 83720

Illinois
Social Services Division
Department of Public Aid
316 South Second
Springfield, IL 62762

Indiana
Department of Public Welfare
701 State Office Building
Indianapolis, IN 46204

Iowa
Department of Social Services
Hoover Building
Des Moines, IA 50319

Kansas
Division of Social Services
Department of Social and Rehabilitation Services
State Office Building
Topeka, KS 66612

Kentucky
Department for Human Resources
275 East Main St.
Frankfort, KY 40601

Louisiana
Office of Human Development
Department of Health and Human Resources
P.O. Box 44367
Baton Rouge, LA 70804

Maine
Bureau of Social Welfare
Department of Human Services
State House
Augusta, ME 04333

Maryland
Social Services Administration
Department of Human Resources
11 South St.
Baltimore, MD 21202

Massachusetts
Executive Office of Human Services
State House
Boston, MA 02133

Michigan
Department of Social Services
Commerce Center
P.O. Box 30037
Lansing, MI 48909

Minnesota
Bureau of Social Services
Department of Public Welfare
Centennial Office Building
St. Paul, MN 55155

Mississippi
Office of Human Resources
Barefield Complex #407
455 North Lamar St.
Jackson, MS 39201

Missouri
Department of Social Services
Broadway State Office Building
Jefferson City, MO 65101

Montana
Department of Social and Rehabilitation Services
SRS Building
111 Sanders
Helena, MT 59601

Nebraska
Social Services Division
Department of Public Welfare
P.O. Box 95026
Lincoln, NE 68509

Nevada
Department of Human Resources
505 East King St.
Carson City, NV 89710

New Hampshire
Division of Human Resources
Office of the Governor
15 North Main St.
Concord, NH 03301

New Jersey
Department of Human Services
Capitol Place One
222 South Warren St.
Trenton, NJ 08625

New Mexico
Social Services Division
Human Services Department
P.E.R.A. Building
Santa Fe, NM 87503

New York
Department of Social Services
40 North Pearl St.
Albany, NY 12243

North Carolina
Division of Social Services
Department of Human Resources
Albemarle Building
Raleigh, NC 27611

North Dakota
Social Service Board
State Capitol
Bismarck, ND 58505

Ohio
Division of Social Services
Department of Public Welfare
30 East Broad St.
Columbus, OH 43215

Oklahoma
Department of Institutions, Social and Rehabilitative
    Services
Sequoyah Building
State Capitol Complex
Oklahoma City, OK 73105

Oregon
Department of Human Resources
318 Public Service Building
Salem, OR 97310

Pennsylvania
Secretary for Social Services
Department of Public Welfare
432 Health and Welfare Building
Harrisburg, PA 17120

Rhode Island
Department of Social and Rehabilitative Services
600 New London Ave.
Cranston, RI 02920

South Carolina
Department of Social Services
1535 Confederate Ave. Extension
North Tower Complex
P.O. Box 1520
Columbia, SC 29202

South Dakota
Division of Human Development
Department of Social Services
Knelp Building
Illinois Ave.
Pierre, SD 57501

Tennessee
Division of Social Services
Department of Human Services
111 Seventh Avenue, N
Nashville, TN 37203

Texas
Social and Financial Programs Division
Department of Human Resources
John H. Reagan Building
Austin, TX 78701

Utah
Department of Social Services
150 West North Temple
P.O. Box 2500
Salt Lake City, UT 84110

Vermont
Department of Social and Rehabilitation Services
Agency of Human Services
State Office Building
Montpelier, VT 05602

Virginia
Division of Social Services
Department of Welfare
8007 Discovery Dr.
Richmond, VA 23229

Washington
Division of Community Services
Department of Social and Health Services
Office Building, 2
Olympia, WA 98504

West Virginia
Social Services Division
Department of Welfare
Building 6
State Capitol Complex
Charleston, WV 25305

Wisconsin
Department of Health and Social Services
State Office Building
1 West Wilson St.
Madison, WI 53702

Wyoming
Department of Health and Social Services
Hathaway Building
Cheyenne, WY 82002

Guam
Agency for Human Resources and Development
P.O. Box 2950
Agana, GU 96910

Puerto Rico
Department of Social Services
Box 11398
Santurce, PR 00910

Virgin Islands
Social Services
Department of Social Welfare
P.O. Box 539
St. Thomas, VI 00801

State Mental Health Authorities

Alabama
State Department of Mental Health
135 South Union St.
Montgomery, AL 36130

Alaska
Alaska Department of Health and Social Services
Pouch H-01, Health and Welfare Building
Juneau, AK 99811

Arizona
Arizona Department of Health Services
Division of Behavioral Health Services
1740 West Adams St.
Phoenix, AZ 85007

Arkansas
Arkansas State Hospital
Division of Mental Health Services
Department of Social and Rehabilitative Services
4313 West Markham St.
Little Rock, AR 72201

California
California Department of Mental Health
1600 9th St.
Sacramento, CA 95814

Colorado
Colorado Department of Institutions
3550 West Oxford Ave.
Denver, CO 80236

Connecticut
Connecticut Department of Mental Health
90 Washington St.
Hartford, CT 06115

Delaware
Department of Health and Social Services
1901 N. DuPont Hwy.
New Castle, DE 19720

District of Columbia
Department of Human Resources
801 N. Capitol St., NE
Washington, DC 20004

Florida
Florida Department of Health and Rehabilitative
   Services
1323 Winewood Blvd.
Tallahassee, FL 32301

Georgia
Department of Human Resources
State Office Building
47 Trinity Ave., SW
Atlanta, GA 30334

Hawaii
State Department of Health
P.O. Box 3378
Honolulu, HI 96801

Idaho
Department of Health and Welfare
Bureau of Mental Health
Statehouse
Boise, ID 83720

Illinois
Illinois Department of Mental Health and Developmental Disabilities
160 North LaSalle St.
Chicago, IL 60601

Indiana
Indiana Department of Mental Health
5 Indiana Square
Indianapolis, IN 46204

Iowa
Division of Mental Health Resources
Department of Social Services
Hoover State Office Building
Des Moines, IA 50319

Kansas
State Department of Social and Rehabilitative
   Services
State Office Building
Topeka, KS 66612

Kentucky
Department of Human Resources
275 East Main St.
Frankfort, KY 40601

Louisiana
Department of Health and Human Resources
P.O. Box 3776
Baton Rouge, LA 70821

Maine
Maine Department of Mental Health and Corrections
State Office Building
Augusta, ME 04330

Maryland
Maryland Department of Health and Mental Hygiene
State Office Building
201 West Preston St.
Baltimore, MD 21201

Massachusetts
Massachusetts Department of Mental Health
160 North Washington St.
Boston, MA 02114

Michigan
Michigan Department of Mental Health
Lewis Cass Building
Lansing, MI 48926

Minnesota
Department of Public Welfare
Centennial Office Building
St. Paul, MN 55155

Mississippi
State Department of Mental Health

1100 Robert E. Lee Building
Jackson, MS 39201

Missouri
Department of Mental Health
2002 Missouri Blvd.
Jefferson City, MO 65102

Montana
Montana State Department of Institutions
1539 11th Ave.
Helena, MT 59620

Nebraska
State Department of Public Institutions
801 West Van Dorn
P.O. Box 94728
Lincoln, NE 68509

Nevada
Department of Human Resources
Kinkead Building
505 East King St.
Carson City, NV 89710

New Hampshire
Department of Health and Welfare
Division of Mental Health
Health and Welfare Building
Hazen Dr.
Concord, NH 03301

New Jersey
Department of Human Services
222 South Warren St.
Trenton, NJ 08625

New Mexico
New Mexico Department of Health and Environment
P.O. Box 968
Santa Fe, NM 87503

New York
New York State Office of Mental Health
44 Holland Ave.
Albany, NY 12229

North Carolina
North Carolina Department of Human Resources
Division of Mental Health/Mental Retardation
325 North Salisbury St.
Raleigh, NC 27611

North Dakota
State Department of Health
North Dakota Division of Mental Health and Mental Retardation
Capitol Building
Bismarck, ND 58505

Ohio
Ohio Department of Mental Health and Mental Retardation
30 East Broad St.
Columbus, OH 43215

Oklahoma
State Department of Mental Health
P.O. Box 53277

Capitol Station
Oklahoma City, OK 73152

Oregon
Mental Health Division
2575 Bittern St., NE
Salem, OR 97310

Pennsylvania
State Department of Public Welfare
Health and Welfare Building
Harrisburg, PA 17120

Rhode Island
Rhode Island Department of Mental Health, Retardation and Hospitals
600 New London Ave.
Cranston, RI 02920

South Carolina
State Department of Mental Health
P.O. Box 485
Columbia, SC 29202

South Dakota
Division of Mental Health and Mental Retardation
Kneip Building
Illinois Ave.
Pierre, SD 57501

Tennessee
State Department of Mental Health and Mental Retardation
505 Deaderick St.
Nashville, TN 37219

Texas
Texas Department of Mental Health and Mental Retardation
Capitol Station
P.O. Box 12668
Austin, TX 78711

Utah
State Department of Social Resources
P.O. Box 2500
Salt Lake City, UT 84110

Vermont
Vermont Department of Mental Health
Waterbury Office Complex
103 South Main St.
Waterbury VT 05676

Virginia
State Department of Mental Health and Mental Retardation
P.O. Box 1797
Richmond, VA 23214

Washington
Department of Social Services
Mental Health Division
Mail Stop OB-42F
Olympia, WA 98504

West Virginia
State Department of Mental Health
State Capitol Complex

1800 Washington St., East
Charleston, WV 25305

Wisconsin
Wisconsin Department of Health and Social Services
State Office Building
1 West Wilson St.
Madison, WI 53707

Wyoming
Department of Social Services
Division of Health and Medical Services
Hathaway Building
Cheyenne, WY 82002

Guam
Division of Mental Health
Guam Memorial Hospital
P.O. Box 20999
Agana, GU 96921

American Samoa
Department of Health
LBJ Tropical Medical Center
Pago Pago, Tutuila, AS 96799

Northern Marianas
Department of Health Services
Trust Territory of the Pacific Islands
Saipan, Mariana Islands 96950

Puerto Rico
Department of Health
Call Box 70184
San Juan, PR 00936

Virgin Islands
Virgin Islands Department of Health
P.O. 7309
St. Thomas, VI 00801

State Alcohol and Drug Agencies

Alabama
Drug Abuse Program Section
Division of Alcoholism and Drug Abuse
Department of Mental Health
135 South Union St.
Montgomery, AL 36130

Alaska
Office of Alcoholism and Drug Abuse
Pouch H-05F
Department of Health and Social Services
Juneau, AK 99811

Arizona
Drug Abuse Programs
Division of Behavioral Health Services
Department of Health Services
2500 East Van Buren
Phoenix, AZ 85008

Arkansas
Office of Drug and Alcohol Abuse Prevention
Department of Social and Rehabilitative Services
Seventh and Main Sts.
Little Rock, AR 72201

California
California Department of Health
Department of Alcohol and Drug Programs
111 Capitol Mall
Sacramento, CA 95814

Colorado
Alcohol and Drug Abuse Division
Department of Health
4210 East 11th Ave.
Denver, CO 80220

Connecticut
Connecticut Alcohol and Drug Abuse Commission
Department of Mental Health
999 Asylum Ave.
Hartford, CT 06105

Delaware
Bureau of Alcoholism and Drug Abuse
Governor Bacon Health Center
1901 N. DuPont Hwy.
New Casrle, DE 19720

District of Columbia
Alcohol and Drug Abuse Services Administration
1875 Connecticut Ave., NW
Washington, DC 20009

Florida
Bureau of Drug Abuse Prevention
Division of Mental Health
Department of Health and Rehabilitative Services
1323 Winewood Blvd.
Tallahassee, FL 32301

Georgia
Alcohol and Drug Abuse Section
Division of Mental Health and Retardation
Department of Human Resources
47 Trinity Ave., SW
Atlanta, GA 30334

Hawaii
Alcohol and Drug Abuse Branch
Department of Health
1270 Queen Emma St.
Honolulu, HI 96813

Idaho
Bureau of Substance Abuse
Division of Community Rehabilitation
Department of Health and Welfare
450 West State St.
Boise, ID 83720

Illinois
Dangerous Drugs Commission
160 North LaSalle St.
Chicago, IL 60601

Indiana
Division of Addiction Services
Department of Mental Health
5 Indiana Square
Indianapolis, IN 46204

Iowa
Iowa Department of Substance Abuse
505 Fifth Ave.
Des Moines, IA 50319

Kansas
Alcohol and Drug Abuse Services
Department of Social and Rehabilitative Services
Biddle Building
2700 West 6th St.
Topeka, KS 66606

Kentucky
Alcohol and Drug Abuse Branch
Division for Prevention Services
Bureau of Health Services
Department of Human Resources
275 East Main St.
Frankfort, KY 40621

Louisiana
Bureau of Substance Abuse
Louisiana Health and Human Resource Administration
P.O. Box 4049
Baton Rouge, LA 70801

Maine
Office of Alcoholism and Drug Abuse Prevention
Bureau of Rehabilitation
221 State St.
Augusta, ME 04330

Maryland
Drug Abuse Administration
Department of Health and Mental Hygiene
Herbert O'Conor Office Building
201 West Preston St.
Baltimore, MD 21201

Massachusetts
Division of Drug Rehabilitation
Department of Public Health
600 Washington St.
Boston, MA 02111

Michigan
Office of Substance Abuse Services
3500 North Logan St.
P.O. Box 30035
Lansing, MI 48909

Minnesota
Drug and Alcohol Authority
Chemical Dependency Division
Department of Public Welfare
Centennial Office Building
St. Paul, MN 55155

Mississippi
Division of Alcohol and Drug Abuse
Department of Mental Health
1100 Robert E. Lee Building
Jackson, MS 39201

Missouri
Division of Alcoholism and Drug Abuse
Department of Mental Health
2002 Missouri Blvd.
Jefferson City, MO 65102

Montana
Addictive Diseases Division
Department of Institutions
1539 11th Ave.
Helena, MT 59620

Nebraska
Nebraska Commission on Drugs
P.O. Box 94728
State Capitol Building
Lincoln, NE 68509

Nevada
Bureau of Alcohol and Drug Abuse
Rehabilitation Division
Department of Human Resources
505 East King St.
Carson City, NV 89710

New Hampshire
Office of Alcohol and Drug Abuse Prevention
Hazen Dr.
Concord, NH 03301

New Jersey
Division of Alcohol, Narcotic and Drug Abuse Control
Department of Health
CN360 John Fitch Plaza
Trenton, NJ 08625

New Mexico
Substance Abuse Bureau
Division of Behavioral Health Services
P.O. Box 968
Santa Fe, NM 87503

New York
Office of Drug Abuse Services
194 Washington Ave.
Albany, NY 12210

North Carolina
North Carolina Drug Commission
325 North Salisbury St.
Raleigh, NC 27611

North Dakota
Division of Alcoholism and Drug Abuse
Department of Health
Capitol Building
Bismarck, ND 58505

Ohio
Ohio Bureau of Drug Abuse
Division of Mental Health
Department of Mental Health and Mental Retardation
246 North High St.
Columbus, OH 43216

Oklahoma
Division of Drug Abuse Services
Department of Mental Health
P.O. Box 53277, Capitol Station
Oklahoma City, OK 73152

Oregon
Programs for Alcohol and Drug Problems
Mental Health Division
Department of Human Resources
2575 Bittern St., NE
Salem, OR 97310

Pennsylvania
State Department of Health
Office of Drug and Alcohol Programs
2101 North Front St.
Harrisburg, PA 17120

Rhode Island
Rhode Island Drug Abuse Program
Department of Mental Health and Retardation and
  Hospitals
303 General Hospital
Rhode Island Medical Center
Cranston, RI 02920

South Carolina
South Carolina Commission on Alcohol and Drug
  Abuse
3700 Forest Dr.
P.O. Box 4616
Columbia, SC 29204

South Dakota
Division of Alcohol, Drugs and Substance Control
Department of Health
Joe Foss Building
Pierre, SD 57501

Tennessee
Alcohol and Drug Abuse Section
Department of Mental Health
505 Deaderick St.
Nashville, TN 37219

Texas
Drug Abuse Division
Sam Houston State Office Bldg.
201 E. 14th St.
Austin, TX 78711

Utah
Division of Alcoholism and Drugs
150 West North Temple
P.O. Box 2500
Salt Lake City, UT 84110

Vermont
Alcohol and Drug Abuse Division
Department of Social And Rehabilitative Services
103 South Main St.
Waterbury, VT 05676

Virginia
Department of Mental Health/Mental Retardation
Division of Substance Abuse Control
P.O. Box 1797
Richmond, VA 23214

Washington
Office of Drug Abuse Prevention
Community Services Division
Department of Social and Health Services, OB 44W
Olympia, WA 98504

West Virginia
Division of Alcoholism and Drug Abuse
Department of Mental Health
1800 Washington St., East
Charleston, WV 25305

Wisconsin
Bureau of Alcohol and Other Drug Abuse
Division of Mental Hygiene
Department of Health and Social Services
One West Wilson St.
Madison, WI 53707

Wyoming
Drug Abuse Programs
457 Hathaway Building
2300 Capitol Ave.
Cheyenne, WY 82002

Regional Adoption Resource Centers

Region I
(Connecticut, Maine, Massachusetts, New Hampshire, Rhode Island, Vermont)
61 Batterymarch St.
Boston, MA 02110

Region II
(New Jersey, New York, Puerto Rico, Virgin Islands)
605 West 113th St.
New York, NY 10025

Region III
(Delaware, District of Columbia, Maryland, Pennsylvania, Virginia, West Virginia)
1218 Chestnut St.
Philadelphia, PA 19107

Region IV
(Alabama, Florida, Georgia, Kentucky, Mississippi, North Carolina, South Carolina, Tennessee)
143 West Franklin
Chapel Hill, NC 27514

Region V
(Illinois, Indiana, Michigan, Minnesota, Ohio, Wisconsin)
1015 East Huron St.
Social Work Center Building
Ann Arbor, MI 48109

Region VI
(Arkansas, Louisiana, New Mexico, Oklahoma, Texas)
2609 University Ave.
Austin, TX 78712

Region VII
(Iowa, Kansas, Missouri, Nebraska)
124 Clark Hall
School of Social Work
University of Missouri
Columbia, MO 65201

Region VIII
(Colorado, Montana, North Dakota, South Dakota, Utah, Wyoming)
P.O. Box 38031
Denver, CO 80238

Region IX
(American Samoa, Arizona, California, Hawaii, Nevada, Pacific Trust Territory)
2117 West Temple St.
Los Angeles, CA 90026

Region X
(Alaska, Idaho, Oregon, Washington)
157 Yesler Way
Seattle, WA 98104

Chapter 5

Special Programs
for the Handicapped

The census of 1970 showed that one person in 11 in the United States
was significantly handicapped. In the employable age range of 16 to 64 years,
more than 11 million persons, exclusive of those in institutions, were
in this category. The census found that as a group these Americans had less
income, less education, less employment and a greater incidence of
poverty than their fellow citizens.

In the intervening years, however, the government and many private
organizations and advocacy groups have been taking important steps to better
the status of the handicapped. At the same time, disabled people themselves
have become more articulate in their demands for needed services. This chapter
is intended to help the handicapped, their families and guardians to a better
understanding of the educational, financial, medical, rehabilitation,
institutional and legal resources that are available to them.

The basic rights of the handicapped are explained. Pre-natal care and
early education of the handicapped are discussed, and then the chapter takes
up aid for specific major handicaps. After that, it turns to ways that
the handicapped can go about leading more normal lives, holding down
regular jobs, adapting their houses to their special needs and enjoying
some of the pleasures and avocations that other people take for granted.

Contents

The Bill of Rights for the Handicapped

In the 1970s, Congress passed a series of laws affecting the rights of disabled persons. Taken together, these laws have greatly expanded the horizons for handicapped people. They spell out the end of second-class citizenship for those who have suffered from discriminatory practices in schools, in jobs, in mass transportation and even in finding accessible public washrooms.

The most comprehensive of these laws is Section 504, Title V of the Rehabilitation Act of 1973, which states that "No otherwise qualified handicapped individual in the United States . . . shall, solely by reason of his handicap, be excluded from participation in, be denied the benefits of, or be subjected to discrimination under any program or activity receiving Federal financial assistance." A further regulation, issued in April 1977, covers all recipients of federal health, education and welfare funds, including elementary and secondary schools, colleges, hospitals, social service agencies and, in some instances, doctors.

The new regulation provides that all such programs must be accessible to handicapped persons and that no one shall be excluded from public or post-secondary education because of a disability. The law also requires that health, welfare and social service institutions must find ways to provide services for the handicapped equal in quality to those afforded other members of society.

What Section 504 Can Do for You

If you are otherwise qualified for a job, college, welfare or other activity or service, your disability may not be used to bar you from that entitlement or position. This may mean that an employer will have to install an elevator for people who are unable to climb the stairs, or a hospital will have to provide an emergency room interpreter or make other provisions for deaf patients. An employer may be required to make certain that there is adequate workspace and access for an employee who uses a wheelchair, and a college may have to provide readers for a blind student if the assigned text is not available in record or cassette form.

Sources of Information and Aid

The many forms of aid for the handicapped come from a broad variety of sources, and the great number of programs being run by government and private agencies compounds the problem of finding the specific kinds of aid that may be needed. Moreover, each state and local community has wide latitude as to how government funds will be used and in determining which agencies will dispense which kinds of help. Even the dollar amounts can vary depending upon the amount of the state or local contribution to the federal funds. The many different private agencies that deal with specific handicaps further complicate the picture, for these may be national (in which case you will probably find them listed in this chapter) or they may exist at the state or local level (in which case they may be listed in your telephone directory).

If used imaginatively, your telephone may be crucial in locating the help you need in your community.

You may have to make several calls. You won't always find exactly the kind of service you are looking for, but if you call an agency that handles similar services, it may refer you to the appropriate person, office or institution. Moreover, you may find the right agency by trying several, closely related titles. If, for instance, you need financial assistance in buying a hearing aid and find no listings under "deaf" or "hearing aids," you might try calling an agency that works with blind persons. A vocational rehabilitation agency or the local Medicare or Medicaid office may be able to help you. The personnel there can probably tell you whom to call, but if the individual answering the phone does not know, ask to speak to the supervisor or head of the agency. A bit of aggressiveness may appreciably shorten the time it takes to find the appropriate resource. Be persistent.

Special Phone Services for Handicapped Persons

The telephone company can help you in other ways as well. People who find it difficult or impossible to use the directory can make arrangements through the phone company for directory assistance, for which there is no charge. Moreover, simply telling the operator that you are handicapped usually assures free operator assistance in placing a call.

There are many kinds of telephone equipment that may be helpful to you: extra loud bells for those with impaired hearing; or light signals for the totally deaf; speaker phones activated by a puff of breath for persons who have lost the use of their arms and hands; hearing and speech amplifiers; extra large dials for people whose vision is impaired; teletypewriters for individuals with speech and hearing impairments. In some areas, those with a speech or hearing impairment who use a teletypewriter are eligible for a 25 percent discount on toll calls within the state. These and many other kinds of equipment are available, some on a lease basis, others for sale at cost. If there is no standard equipment that will solve your problem, the phone company has pledged to try to design a special system for you.

The following regional phone offices have set up special Handicapped Services Centers: New York Telephone; Chesapeake and Potomac Bell Telephone Co.; Pennsylvania Bell; Illinois Bell; Northwestern Bell; Pacific Bell.

The Office for Handicapped Individuals

Another important source of information is the Office for Handicapped Individuals (OHI), which was specifically established by Congress to broaden communication about all government programs for handicapped individuals. OHI does this through a national clearinghouse that responds to inquiries from individuals seeking information about federal programs and those of state and local agencies. OHI is also a source of information about federal legislation, funding and assistance for programs serving the handicapped.

Although OHI provides no direct services to individuals, it will answer mail or phone inquiries and put you in touch with relevant information sources and local and state agencies that can deal with your problems. If you need help, write to:

Office for Handicapped Individuals
400 Maryland Ave., SW
Washington, DC 20202

Pre-Natal Care and Early Screening

Some handicapping conditions can be prevented by proper pre-natal care and early screening. Current knowledge about the value of good nutrition during pregnancy, the effects of some maternal diseases, the potential damage of environmental and drug hazards on the developing fetus, and other conditions that threaten the unborn child make it imperative that every prospective mother receive proper medical care from early in her pregnancy.

The care may be provided by private physicians, state health agencies, maternity clinics, visits of public health nurses, family planning agencies and pediatric clinics. A more detailed discussion of health resources available to the pregnant woman and her newborn child appears in Chapter 4.

Genetic and Pre-Natal Counseling

Many persons with congenital handicapping conditions worry about whether their children will inherit their disabilities. For such individuals, the advice of a genetic counselor is vital in delineating areas of legitimate concern and alleviating unnecessary fears. Here are some sources of information:

National Genetics Foundation. This organization sponsors a network of genetic diagnostic and counseling centers at 60 locations across the country where parents and prospective parents can obtain advice about the risk to their children of genetic disorders. The Foundation counselors will help assemble your family medical history and forward it to the nearest center where you will be referred for diagnosis and counseling, and your physician can utilize extensive computerized data on birth defects and draw upon the expertise of a national network of genetic specialists. There is no fee for information or referral services, but there usually is a charge for lab work and direct counseling services at the local center. For the center nearest you write to:

National Genetics Foundation
555 West 57th St.
New York City, NY 10019

March of Dimes Birth Defects Foundation. The Foundation funds 48 clinical centers in the United States where genetic medicine is practiced and counseling is available. Early diagnosis and treatment for pregnant women with high-risk conditions and intensive care for unhealthy babies are offered at these centers. The March of Dimes, like the National Genetics Foundation, has compiled extensive computerized data on birth defects which can be used by genetic counselors and physicians in answering prospective parents' questions about the risks of genetic disorders in their offspring. For information call or write:

March of Dimes Birth Defects Foundation
1275 Mamaroneck Ave.
White Plains, NY 10605

National Foundation for Jewish Genetic Diseases. This group provides information upon request about genetic disorders such as Tay Sachs disease, which afflicts Jews whose ancestors came from eastern and central Europe. Write to:

National Foundation for Jewish Genetic
  Diseases
609 Fifth Ave.
New York, NY 10017

Sickle Cell Screening and Counseling. Sickle cell anemia is a heredity disorder in which the blood cells become deformed into shapes resembling a sickle. Circulation is impaired by the inability of the misshapen cells to pass normally through capillaries, small veins and arteries. Severe pain in the abdomen and the joints may result. In the United States, the disease occurs mainly among black people.

The National Association for Sickle Cell Disease offers a variety of services for sufferers, including sickle cell screening, and counseling to parents who possess the sickle cell trait. There are 77 community sickle cell programs located throughout the United States and the Bahamas. For the program closest to you write:

National Association for
  Sickle Cell Disease, Inc.
3460 Wilshire Blvd.
Los Angeles, CA 90010

Education for the Handicapped

Public Law 94-142, passed by Congress in November 1975, requires each state to provide a specifically designed, free education and related services for every handicapped student. Thus, education is now officially recognized as the handicapped person's fundamental right, a right that cannot be denied even on the grounds that a state does not have the necessary funds or facilities to meet the requirements.

Analyzing the Child's Needs

The following provisions of PL 94-142 are especially important. First, the law states that all children in need of special education are to be identified, located and evaluated, which is crucial if the children are to be adequately assisted at an early age when they can benefit most from special services. The law further specifies that each handicapped child be educated in accordance with a plan tailored to his or her special needs and capacities. This indi-

Constructive Attitude Toward a Disabled Child

Left a paraplegic after a childhood bout of polio, Itzhak Perlman has transcended his disability to become a renowned violinist, playing with the finest orchestras and chamber-music groups in the world. Perlman's warm, radiant personality and brilliant musical talent so command the stage during his performances that it comes as a bit of a shock to the audience when he leaves the stage on crutches. The young artist credits his parents for encouraging him to accept his disability and lead a full, "normal" life. "Tragedy," he says, "occurs when a child is disabled and the parents don't know how to handle it."

Parents of disabled children may be helped by the advice that follows. Taken from an article by June Fine in *American Rehabilitation* magazine, it explains how to avoid the tragedy that can flow from not knowing how to deal with a handicapped child.

*Look at the child's disability objectively. You must be free of "hangups" if you are to pass on a positive attitude.

*Don't try to hide the fact that the child is disabled, either from the child or from society, but seek to "mainstream" his or her social and educational life to the fullest extent possible.

*Encourage the child to develop his or her potential, but be careful not to give the impression that your love is dependent upon the youngster's achievements.

*Give the child responsibilities to build a sense of accomplishment and independence.

vidualized educational program must be set forth in a written statement, jointly developed by the school authorities, the child's parents or guardian and, if possible, by the child as well. It should include an analysis of the child's present achievement level, a list of short-term and long-range goals, an indication of the extent to which the child will be able to participate in the school's regular programs, and provisions for checking on the progress being made by the child and for revising the plan when necessary. Changes in an educational program may not be made except in consultation with the parents.

Tailoring the Instruction to the Child

Specially designed instruction must be available, including physical education, classroom instruction, home instruction and, if necessary, instruction in hospitals and institutions. Transportation, recreation, counseling and all the varied support services that may be required to enable the handicapped child to benefit from education must also be made available.

Placing the Child in the Right School

The law provides for grants to the states to educate handicapped children, starting at age 3. If the state cannot provide the appropriate educational facilities in the public schools, the child must be placed in or referred to a private school at no cost to the parents, even if the appropriate school is out of state.

The Parents' Rights

Under the law, parents or guardians have a right to examine school records that bear on the child's handicap, and schools must give written notice prior to changing a child's placement. If the parent objects to a school's decision on educational planning for the child, there must be a hearing with adequate legal safeguards.

Problems in Special Education

Of course, problems remain in implementing the education of the handicapped. Some states are further along than others in construction of programs and suitable facilities. Teachers trained in "special education" are much in demand, and some school districts haven't yet been able to find the experienced personnel to implement their good intentions. Moreover, the issue of "mainstreaming" (placing youngsters in regular classrooms to the extent consistent with their best interests) has divided both educators and parents. Many experts think that the handicapped child will benefit from as much contact as possible with children of the same age, but some educators and parents are concerned that this course of action will impose too much strain on students and teachers.

Parents or guardians of handicapped children should be in touch with the local Board of Education well before the child's third birthday so that a plan can be set up for the child's entry into the schools. If you have a handicapped child who, in your opinion, is not being well served by the school system, you have a right to an impartial hearing conducted by the state education agency. You may be accompanied and advised at this hearing by a legal counsel or a specialist who deals with the problems of handicapped children.

Within the federal government, the Civil Rights Division of the U.S. Department of Justice is charged with the responsibility for enforcing the laws against discrimination, including access to education. The address is:

The Civil Rights Division
U.S. Department of Justice
Washington, DC 20530

Head Start

In addition to other educational and instructional programs, described in Chapters 1 and 4, Head Start is mandated to reserve no less than 10 percent of its enrollment openings for handicapped children. In accordance with PL 94-142, Head Start must provide places for handicapped students, assure physical access, and supply speech therapy, physical therapy and other special services as needed. It must act in consultation with the parents to draw up an educational plan for each handicapped child. The handicapped children must not be segregated from others in Head Start groups.

Even though your income exceeds the poverty guidelines, it might still be worth your while to investigate the possibility of entering your child in the Head Start program. Ten percent of the admissions may be allotted to children from families above the poverty level.

Admittance to Head Start is for children who will be three by the end of December of the current school year. Because there usually is a waiting list, however, parents are advised to apply before the child's second birthday. Further information may be obtained from the local Head Start office.

Vocational Education

Under the Vocational Education Amendments of 1968, 10 percent of the federal funds granted to the states must be used in serving the handicapped. Although the program is federally funded, it depends in large measure upon the resources and commitment of local districts. Planning and implementation are decided at the local level.

Special help is provided for high school students, those who have completed high school and require further preparation to enter the labor market, working people who need training or retraining to keep their jobs or advance, those with special needs and handicaps and those in post-secondary schools.

Parents should insist that there be provision for vocational education of a kind suited to the child's abilities and interests. Local boards of education should have cooperative arrangements with the state employment service and state agencies for the education of handicapped persons to provide up-to-date occupational information.

Finding a College
to Suit Your Needs

Choosing a college is never easy, but for the handicapped person the choice includes a number of complicating factors. In addition to determining whether a given institution can serve the student's academic needs and geographical preference, the following special concerns for the handicapped must be satisfied:

* Access for mobility-impaired students— (ramps, wheelchair-width aisles, elevators and toilet facilities).
* Adequate counseling in such crucial areas as financial aid, career development, proper academic-skills preparation and academic advisement.
* Policy flexibility with regard to schedules, location of classes, testing arrangements, guide dogs allowed on campus.
* Special services for blind or deaf students, including readers, note takers, books in Braille, tape recordings and interpreters.
* Dormitory and dining facilities designed for safety and accessibility.
* The presence on campus of a disabled student's organization.

A useful publication for beginning your search is *Getting Through College With a Disability* (available without charge from The President's Committee on Employment of the Handicapped, 1111 20th St., NW, Washington, DC 20210). This directory includes a summary of services on 500 campuses for handicapped students. However, many good institutions have been omitted, and because colleges are rapidly adapting their facilities to accommodate handicapped students, much of the information is now out of date. You should write to the prospective college of your choice requesting current information about its facilities and services for the handicapped.

Financial Aid for College Students

There is at this time no federal financial-aid program specifically designed to enable handicapped individuals to attend college, but the four kinds of federal financial-aid programs available to all students are, of course, available to the handicapped as well. Broadly stated these fall into four categories:

* grants on the basis of financial need—do not have to be repaid;
* loans which must be repaid;
* work-study programs in which the student is given a part-time job to help him or her through school;
* benefits such as the GI Bill and Social Security which do not have to be repaid.

Further information on college aid programs can be found in Chapter 1.

Vocational Education Assistance

Education is a primary component of many rehabilitation programs. When a vocational rehabilitation agency determines that particular individuals need a college education, it may provide financial assistance to those in need of help. If you have the will and aptitude for teaching, accounting or social service work, for example, a college education is mandatory, and the vocational rehabilitation agency probably will support your education (see page 213). Help may also be provided by organizations geared to help people with specific handicaps. Churches and service clubs also frequently respond to the need for scholarship funds.

Adult Education Programs

Federal funds are provided to the states for the education of handicapped persons 16 and older who wish to continue their education to the high school level or to gain training that will make them more employable. These programs are usually run by local school boards in cooperation with state educational or health agencies. Most of the programs concentrate on basic skills (reading, writing, math) and job-related subjects. Up to 20 percent of allocated federal funds may be used for instruction of people who are confined to institutions, enabling many persons with severe handicaps to receive the benefits of education in hospitals and residential facilities.

The primary focus of the federal adult education projects is to reach persons with less than an eighth-grade education and those who live in geographical areas (such as the inner cities) where the need is most acute. These programs may be particularly useful to older dis-

Colleges Welcome Handicapped Students

Two colleges have led the way in making campus facilities physically accessible to the handicapped and providing a warm, supportive atmosphere in which disabled students can enjoy as normal a college experience as possible.

In the fall of 1977, Rhode Island College in Providence decided to make a special effort to implement state and federal regulations on non-discrimination for handicapped persons, and to facilitate the successful integration of the disabled into college life. Classroom buildings, residence halls, the library and other key facilities are now equipped with ramps or elevators to make things easier for handicapped students. Special washrooms and sloping curbs have been installed. Drawings and maps of the campus are now included in the handicapped student's *Handbook*, locating special facilities, indicating which sections of buildings are still accessible by stairs only and explaining the easiest way to get around the campus.

Through the Dean of Students' Office, parking arrangements have been made for the handicapped, and vans are provided for those who cannot reach the campus by public transportation. Other special services include personal and academic counseling by persons familiar with the problems of handicapped students; flexible class scheduling; arrangements for readers, note takers and tape recorders. Special reading, writing and math workshops have been organized. Library aides are available to retrieve books from upper shelves, help with the card catalogue and perform other services for handicapped library users.

The student group called The Handicapped Awareness Organization provides special services for the disabled. Membership in this organization is open to *all* students interested in working for the concerns of the handicapped, their physical, recreational, educational, vocational, psychological and emotional needs.

At Boston University, steps have been taken to make the campus as accessible as possible for the handicapped and to provide services similar to those at Rhode Island College. A recorded program titled "Boston University on Tape; a Resource/Directory for Sight-Impaired Students, Faculty and Staff" has been prepared. It consists of two 90-minute tapes describing campus services for disabled people, introducing the library of tapes covering more than 200 university-related topics, and including a walking tour of the campus. A blind or near-blind student needing information on registration procedures or special events can also use the large-type directory or Braille directory at the school's library, and be guided by a special "beep-tone" index to specific sections.

abled persons whose education was impaired or interrupted by the failure of schools of a bygone era to address themselves to the special needs of the handicapped. Because adult education programs are run locally by many different schools and a broad variety of agencies, you can probably receive the most accurate information by getting in touch with a school administrator in your locality or from your state education office.

Home-Study Programs

For people who are confined to institutions, or those whose mobility is seriously limited by their disabilities, home-study instruction may provide the opportunity to learn a skill, train for a job or pursue knowledge for personal gratification. Traditionally, home study has meant study by mail through a correspondence school, but in recent years, the concept has been broadened to include special phone hookups to classrooms, radio and television instruction, and tutoring by faculties in innovative college programs that operate on an individual rather than a classroom basis.

Home study is available at varying educational levels: for those without a high school education, students who have completed high school and those with college backgrounds.

The quality of home-study programs is the concern of the Accrediting Commission of the National Home Study Council, which evaluates both private and non-private home-study schools. In order to meet NHSC accrediting standards, each school must have a competent faculty and offer educationally sound, up-to-date courses. The NHSC *Directory of Accredited Home Study Schools* is available free from the National Home Study Council, 1601 18th St., NW, Washington, DC 20009.

Further information about the varying programs and courses that are available may be obtained from educational, vocational or rehabilitation counselors or from the National University Continuing Education Association's *Guide to Independent Study Through Correspondence Instruction* ($4.50 plus postage). The address is Peterson's Guides Book Order Department, Box 978, Edison, NJ 08817.

Financial aid is available for some accredited home-study courses on the same basis as for conventional instruction. However, the programs supported by certain funding sources, such as the Veterans Administration, require class attendance and do not include instruction by correspondence. It is best to check with individual schools and colleges about their eligibility requirements for specific types of funding assistance.

Library Services for the Disabled and the Blind

No blind or disabled U.S. citizen need be cut off from the world of information, entertainment, beauty and intellectual fulfillment to be found in the printed word. The Library of Congress maintains an extensive collection of Braille and recorded books and magazines that are loaned free to individuals who cannot hold, handle or read conventional printed materials. The library also operates the National Library Service for the Blind and Physically Handicapped (NLS), which distributes reading materials through a network of 56 regional and more than 100 sub-regional (local) libraries. Books and other publications may be borrowed and returned by postage-free mail. Among the kinds of services and materials available are the following:

*An extensive collection of Braille and recorded books, including best sellers, classics, mysteries, poetry, history, biographies, religious literature, children's books and foreign language materials.

*Seventy popular magazines in Braille and recorded formats. Readers may request free subscriptions to such popular magazines as *U.S. News, Jack and Jill, Sports Illustrated, Consumer Reports* and many others. Current issues are mailed to readers after the print issues appear.

*Special library publications such as *Braille Book Review* (in print and Braille) and *Talking Book Topics* (in print and on records) as well as numerous catalogs and subject bibliographies.

*Music scores in Braille and large type; cassette recordings of elementary instruction for piano, organ and guitar.

*Information services on various aspects of blindness and physical handicaps.

*Special equipment loaned free to readers while library materials are being borrowed; machines for recorded books and magazines; cassette machines; earphones and auxiliary amplifiers for those who are hearing impaired.

Eligibility for Library Services

The following persons are eligible for the Library of Congress program:

*Blind or visually impaired persons whose vision is 20/200 or less in the better eye with correcting lenses, or whose visual field is no greater than 20 degrees.

*Persons whose visual disability with correction is certified by a competent authority as leaving them unable to read standard printed material.

*Persons certified by competent authority as unable to use standard printed material as a result of physical limitations.

*Persons certified as having a reading disability of sufficient severity to prevent their reading most printed material normally.

If you wish to participate in the Library of Congress program ask your local public librarian for more information or write for an "Application for Free Library Service" and the name of a cooperating library to:

The Library of Congress
National Library Service for the
   Blind and Physically Handicapped
Washington, DC 20542

Local Libraries

Most local libraries have such special services for disabled persons as Braille, tape and record collections, special magnifying devices, volunteer or paid readers to the blind and "Books on Wheels" (vans that bring library materials to convenient locations in the community). In some communities books are delivered directly to disabled persons who are housebound. Call the special services librarian in your local library for further information.

Aid for the Developmentally Disabled

The 1975 Developmentally Disabled Assistance and Bill of Rights Act defines developmental disability as "attributable to mental retardation, cerebral palsy, epilepsy, autism (or dyslexia resulting from these), or any other conditions closely related to mental retardation in terms of intellectual and adaptive problems." The definition further stipulates that the developmental disability must originate before age 18 and can be expected to continue indefinitely. Statistics on the numbers of developmentally disabled individuals vary according to the measuring scales used, but it has been estimated that mental retardation alone affects some 6 million Americans.

The Developmental Disabilities Program of 1978 is a joint federal-state effort offering assistance in health, welfare, education and rehabilitation. The availability of services varies widely from one community to another, however. Each state has a special agency to administer the program and a protection and advocacy office where parents of developmentally disabled persons can turn if they can't find help on the local level. If these agencies cannot be located or further help is needed, inquiries should be addressed to:

Administration on Developmental Disabilities
Department of Health and Human Services
330 Independence Ave., SW
Washington, DC 20201

A great deal of research is currently being carried on to better understand the causes of developmental disabilities, to prevent them when possible and to ameliorate their effects through early screening and special medical and educational techniques. For example, with the knowledge that more than half the incidence of Down's Syndrome (Mongolism) births occur to women over 35, analysis of a sample of amniotic fluid during the pregnancies of older women is becoming routine and gives them a choice of terminating the pregnancy when the condition is present in the fetus. Similarly, today most children born in the United States are screened for Phenylketonuria (PKU), a condition that causes mental retardation. A simple test, done routinely at birth in most hospitals, can detect PKU, and treatment can be given to mitigate the effects of the condition.

Research has shown that poverty and some forms of mental retardation frequently go hand in hand. The effect can be reduced by improved nutrition and health care and by helping the parents to encourage the motor and language skills of their children and provide better emotional support for them.

Educating the Developmentally Disabled

The early education of children with diagnosed or suspected developmental disabilities is crucial in enabling the youngsters to develop their potential skills and abilities.

The guarantees of the Education for All Handicapped Children Act of 1975 are particularly important to children with developmental disabilities. In the past these children frequently were denied access to public schools on the grounds that they were too difficult to manage. Under the act, the schools not only accept responsibility for their education but must, if possible, integrate them into regular classrooms and make provision for special services and therapies.

Learning Disabilities

If your child does not seem to be able to keep up with the class or to take things in as quickly as you would expect, you should request that the child be tested at the school he or she is attending. The law requires the school to provide this service.

Learning disabilities are defined by Public Law 94–142 as disorders that may manifest themselves "in an imperfect ability to listen, think, speak, read, write, spell, or do mathematical calculations." Disabilities stemming from *perceptual* handicaps, brain injury, minimal brain dysfunction, dyslexia and developmental aphasia are included. Learning handicaps caused by visual, motor or hearing handicaps, mental retardation, emotional disturbances or cultural, economic or environmental disadvantages are not included.

The school may be able to recommend a course of action. If you are not satisfied, you may want to get a second opinion at a clinic or a hospital in the area. For further information, write to:

Association for Children and Adults with Learning Disabilities

4156 Library Road
Pittsburgh, PA 15234

The association has 787 local chapters across the country. They vary greatly; some are not even listed in telephone directories. The association can put you in touch with the nearest chapter, and it can help you decide what action should be taken or where you should go for help for your child.

Aphasia. This disability manifests itself in the loss or impairment of the ability to express oneself through speech, writing or signs, or the inability to understand spoken or written language. The disability may result from a brain injury, or a disease affecting one of the brain centers. If present at an early age, it may constitute a serious learning disability. Information and help may be obtained from the Association for Children and Adults with Learning Disabilities, already cited.

Dyslexia. If a child forms the letters "p" or "b" backwards, makes the letter "w" upside down or has trouble recognizing and spelling such simple words as "cat," the problem may be a brain disorder called dyslexia, which is sometimes known as "word blindness." The disability is not uncommon, and the victims are usually of average or higher intelligence. (Nelson Rockefeller and General George S. Patton, Jr., for example, were among the sufferers.) Moreover, the handicap can be overcome, if the particular case is not too severe.

When a parent or a teacher notices the problem, the child should be tested at school, if proper facilities are available. Otherwise, the child should be taken to a hospital or clinic where the testing can be done. The school or testing authority should then be able to recommend a course of action. If not, advice may be obtained from The Orton Society at 8415 Bellona Lane, Towson, MD 21204. This organization is devoted exclusively to disseminating information about dyslexia and to diagnosing, treating and tutoring the victims. There are 24 branch offices around the country, and the main office can put you in touch with one of them for further aid.

Speech and Language Disorders

Speech disorders fall into three major categories: articulation problems, or difficulties in making or forming sounds and putting them together; stuttering (or stammering), an uncontrollable interruption in the rhythm of speech; and voice disorders, which have to do with loudness, improper pitch or inappropriate voice control.

Language disorders may include aphasia; delayed language development, or slowness in learning to express oneself through language; and learning disabilities related to the inability to understand language.

The parents of a child who suffers from any of these disabilities should get in touch with a speech pathologist or audiologist at a local clinic or hospital. Look under "speech" in the telephone directory, or call the main hospital in your area. If further help is needed, write to the following address:

American Speech-Language-Hearing
   Association

Symptoms of Learning Disabilities

The symptoms of learning disabilities are a diverse set of characteristics which affect development and achievement. It is important to note that some of these symptoms can be found in all children at some time during their development. However, *a learning disability person has a cluster of these symptoms* which do not disappear with advancement in age. The most frequently displayed symptoms are: short attention span, poor memory, difficulty following directions, inadequate ability to discriminate between and among letters, numerals or sounds, poor reading ability, eye-hand coordination problems, difficulties with sequencing, disorganization and numerous other problems which may affect all of the sensory systems. An expanded list of symptoms is included below:

☐ performs differently from day to day
☐ responds inappropriately in many instances
☐ restless, can't stay interested in anything very long, easily distracted
☐ says one thing, means another
☐ difficult to discipline
☐ doesn't adjust well to change
☐ immature speech
☐ doesn't listen well or remember

☐ can't follow multiple directions
☐ forgets easily
☐ has difficulty telling time and telling right from left
☐ has trouble naming familiar people or things
☐ has difficulty sounding out words
☐ writes poorly
☐ reverses letters or places them in incorrect sequences—for example, "d" for "b" and "gril" for "girl"
☐ reads poorly if at all
☐ poorly coordinated
☐ trouble understanding words or concepts
☐ late speech development
☐ late gross or fine motor development
☐ impulsive

A child is not necessarily learning disabled if he or she exhibits only a few of these symptoms, since most children show some of them at one time or another. However, a child who has a cluster of these problems needs examination of his or her possible disability.

Reprinted from *Taking the First Step to Solving Learning Problems,* by the Association for Children and Adults with Learning Disabilities.

10801 Rockville Pike
Rockville, MD 20852

Children or adults who are handicapped by stuttering or stammering may be helped by the National Council of Stutterers. The organization has 10 local councils across the United States where stutterers or stammerers (the council makes no distinction between the two) may share their problems and learn techniques of control from each other. The address is:

National Council of Stutterers
Speech and Hearing Clinic
The Catholic University of America
Washington, DC 20064

Other Developmental Disturbances

Autism. This mental disturbance is characterized by an extreme absorption with one's self and an obliviousness to the outer world. Symptoms of the disturbance may appear in early childhood. The child may drop things, fail to respond to normal stimuli, show no sensitivity to pain or even be unable to relate to his or her mother, normally the center of a small child's world.

Adults may be similarly afflicted. They may withdraw from reality, fail to react to normal stimuli and even revert to childlike behavior.

Treatment is not easy to prescribe; different cases respond to different approaches. Parents of autistic children who need help and information about treatment facilities should write to:

National Society for Autistic Children
1234 Massachusetts Ave., NW
Washington, DC 20005

The society maintains an information and referral service that can supply the names and addresses of public schools and day and residential camps where autistic children are admitted. Sources of public and private funds for the treatment and care of autistic patients are also available, as well as advice on how to organize effective action to obtain community services for autistic children; a list of colleges and universities offering training in the field of autism; and income tax information for the parents of autistic children.

Cerebral Palsy. This disabling affliction is caused by damage to the brain before, during or after birth. The most frequent symptoms are a lack of coordination, spasms, weakness of the muscles and speech impairment.

The disorder is not uncommon; approximately 750,000 people in North America are afflicted. About a third are under the age of 21. The severity varies greatly, but cerebral palsy is not progressive. Youngsters who are affected may appear sub-normal, but their intelligence frequently is equal to that of normal children. Treatment varies, depending upon the severity of the cases. Some children with cerebral palsy are able to lead reasonably normal lives; others will show signs of progress through training and encouragement. Speech training may be needed, and psychological testing may be required to determine whether mental retardation is present and to plan treatment and education. The best source of information is:

United Cerebral Palsy Associations, Inc.
66 East 34th St.
New York, NY 10016

The organization has branches throughout the country. These may be located in telephone directories, under United Cerebral Palsy, or by referral from the national headquarters.

Epilepsy. This is a neurological condition in which temporary disturbances of the brain impulses cause minor or major seizures that may range from brief loss of consciousness to violent convulsive movement. Although the condition usually manifests itself before adulthood, it sometimes does not appear until maturity. Experts are, therefore, divided over classifying it as a developmental disability. Whether it is regarded as such depends on the severity of the case and the age at which it first appears.

Sufferers from epilepsy should be under medical supervision. With proper medication some 80 percent of cases can be fully or partially controlled.

The Epilepsy Foundation of America serves as an advocate for epileptics and fosters a number of special programs designed to improve school environments for epileptic children, encourage research and promote self-help groups. The foundation also provides information on employment, health, vocational rehabilitation, transportation and the civil rights of epileptics. For further information, write to The Epilepsy Foundation of America, 1828 L St., NW, Washington, DC 20036. Free information about its publications and the addresses of affiliated chapters may be obtained.

Special Institutions for the Developmentally Handicapped

If public schools cannot adequately meet the needs of developmentally disturbed youngsters, the children may be placed in private institutions where special education will be provided at no cost. The parents are guaranteed a role in setting up a plan for their child's education, and may question screening and placement procedures that appear to be unfair or likely to lead to false labeling of the boy or girl.

One of the most emotion-laden problems facing a parent or guardian is the decision to place a severely retarded, disturbed or autistic child in a special institution or school. Media coverage of the shocking conditions in many public and private institutions in recent years has sensitized the public to the need for careful investigation of the schools and hospitals to which their children are entrusted. Physicians, psychologists and social workers can be helpful in deciding whether institutionalization is in the child's best interest, but all too often adequate professional guidance is lacking when the choice has to be made.

A useful guide is the directory *U.S. Facilities and Programs for Children with Severe Mental Illnesses* (available from the U.S. Government Printing Office, Washington, DC 20402 for $5.50). The directory lists public and private schools with special programs for children with disabilities, mental health centers, hospitals and child-guidance centers throughout the 50 states. The book includes information on the number of children admitted, whether there are waiting lists, admissions' criteria, fees, programs, staffs, physical descriptions of the facilities and the extent to which parent participation is encouraged. No attempt is made to evaluate the facilities, however, and the inclusion of an institution does not mean that it is accredited.

Because the number of institutions devoted to caring for children with mental problems is growing rapidly, new facilities may not always be included. Information in the directory can be supplemented by checking such agencies as local child-guidance centers, community health centers, medical school clinics, private physicians and departments of special education or vocational rehabilitation. The parent or guardian probably will want to visit the facility to see what sort of environment the child will be living in.

Additional help in choosing a school or residential facility is available from the Accreditation Council for Services for Mentally Retarded and Other Developmentally Disabled Persons at 5101 Wisconsin Ave., NW, Washington, DC 20016. The National Association of Private Residential Facilities for the Mentally Retarded also offers placement advice. The address is 6269 Leesburg Pike, Falls Church, VA 22044.

More Normal Lives for the Retarded

It has been estimated that at least a third of the 200,000 persons in state institutions in the United States could live outside these facilities if enlightened programs of training and support were available. In many states, programs are underway to enable retarded people to live on their own or in group or foster homes, to work in special workshops or at jobs tailored to their capabilities, to marry, pay taxes and enjoy more normal lives. As a result of these efforts, the population in public residential facilities declined 9.8 percent over a five-year period.

Vocational Education

The law requires that 10 percent of all vocational education funds must be spent to help the physically or mentally handicapped. Most states therefore are now providing expanded vocational opportunities for developmentally disabled people. Work-study programs, workshops and on-the-job training programs are enabling disabled individuals to make the transition to useful jobs. Good leads on job opportunities can be provided by state governors' committees on employment for the handicapped, similar local committees and retarded citizens associations.

The federal government has a special program for mentally retarded people enabling them to be hired directly by federal agencies without taking Civil Service tests or being placed on the Civil Service register. Only certification for the work by vocational rehabilitation counselors is necessary. The jobs range from agricultural aides to operators of photocopy machines, and under this program, more than 10,000 retarded workers have been employed in federal offices in every state in the Union.

The National Association for Retarded Citizens (NARC). In cooperation with the U.S. Department of Labor, this organization operates an on-the-job training program for mentally retarded people. Referral agencies locate employers willing to train and hire mentally retarded people. To offset the employers' training costs, NARC will pay half the wages for the first four weeks and one-fourth of the wages for the second four weeks.

NARC is also an important source of service and information concerned with research on the prevention and cure of mental retardation; the training of volunteers to work with the mentally retarded; the development of demonstration models for educational, training and residential facilities; the establishment of effective advocacy systems; and the expansion of employment opportunities for the mentally retarded. NARC has 1,900 state and local branches that

provide day-care centers, special workshops, pre-school programs and transportation for the retarded. The organization works closely with the President's Committee on Mental Retardation, and it serves on national, state and local levels as an advocate and interpreter for the needs of the mentally retarded. Information about direct services may be obtained from the state or local organizations, listed in telephone directories under the Association for Retarded Citizens. For a list of publications, write to the National Association for Retarded Citizens, 2709 Avenue E East, Arlington, TX 76011.

Personal and Legal Rights of the Developmentally Disabled

Developmentally disabled persons frequently are unable to speak out on their own behalf and assert their rights as citizens. Often they are powerless to act for themselves in such vital matters as education, jobs, marriage, child bearing, contract signing, inheritance and property rights. The severely disabled frequently are unable to protect their interests on such critical issues as guardianship, commitment to institutions and allegations of criminal offenses.

The Developmental Disabilities Assistance and Bill of Rights Act, passed in 1978, is designed to strengthen services and safeguard the rights of the developmentally handicapped. The Administration on Developmental Disabilities is charged with the responsibility for administering the act. Specific information regarding legal advocacy services and programs available in your state may be obtained from:

Administration on Developmental
   Disabilities
Department of Health and Human Services
330 Independence Ave., SW
Washington, DC 20201

Organizations Serving the Developmentally Disabled

The President's Committee on Mental Retardation. (PCMR). A federal agency established to serve as an advocate for this "silent minority," the committee coordinates and reviews federal, state and local programs to meet the needs of mentally retarded people and their families. It works toward the prevention of mental retardation, improved services, public acceptance of and full citizenship rights for those who are disabled. Publications are free of charge on a single-copy basis. Write to PCMR, Public Information Office, Washington, DC 20201.

The Association for the Severely Handicapped. (TASH). This is another important organization devoted to the advancement of the interests of the developmentally disabled. The agency works toward the goal of making quality education and needed services available for the severely handicapped. It promotes the integration of living, working and learning environments for the developmentally disabled, and has organized a parent-to-parent communications network to provide mutual support for the mothers and fathers of severely handicapped children. For further information or a bibliography of publications, write TASH, 1600 West Armory Way, Seattle, WA 98119.

Programs and Services for the Blind

Despite progress in the prevention of blindness, approximately 500,000 Americans are totally blind, and approximately 35,000 people in the United States lose their sight each year. In addition, more than a million people are legally blind, meaning that their vision is so badly impaired that they cannot read a newspaper. These people have not completely lost their sight, but even with corrective lenses, their vision is 20/200 or less in the better eye. A large number of programs and organizations have been established to meet their special needs.

Education for the Visually Impaired
Approximately one percent of students in the United States today are visually impaired. Of these, 6,000 are totally blind. The rest have limited vision, which they are encouraged to use to the fullest possible extent with the help of large-type print and special optical devices. Experts in educating the blind have advocated keeping these students in regular classrooms, realizing that they will make better adjustments to the everyday world if they are treated like everyone else. Some 75 percent of legally blind students are therefore now in public schools. Specialized private schools are usually considered preferable for students with multiple handicaps, such as the deaf-blind.

Educational Materials for the Blind
To assist in the education of visually impaired students, the American Printing House for the Blind distributes textbooks and other materials in large print, recordings and books in Braille. The institution is partially supported by federal funds, and the materials are free of charge. (See page 208 for the address.)

Among other sources of educational materials are the Library of Congress (see page 183), The American Foundation for the Blind (see page 208), the Jewish Guild for the Blind (15 West 65th St., NYC 10023), The National Braille Association (654-A Godwin Ave., Midland, NJ 07432) and Recording for the Blind (215 East 58th St., NYC 10022).

Schools for the Blind
There are over 55 special schools for blind children in the United States, providing education and training from kindergarten through the 12th grade. Local school districts can supply information on these institutions. Inquiries may also be directed by phone or letter to the American Council of the Blind or the American Foundation for the Blind (see page 208).

One of the oldest and best known institutions for the blind is the Perkins School in Watertown, Massachusetts, which accepts not only blind children, but those who are both

New Products for the Blind

In the recent marketing growth of high-technology toys, games and ingenious products for the home, the blind have not been forgotten. Many of the advances have resulted in products that contribute directly to the safety, convenience and enjoyment of visually impaired individuals. There are talking clocks that tell the time on command. Talking scales are equipped to call out the user's weight in a matter of seconds. Tape measures and rulers with Braille markings, saws, soldering irons, drills and simple measuring spoons have been specially adapted for the use of the blind.

The American Foundation for the Blind has compiled a mail-order catalogue of talking books, shop tools and other instruments for blind persons. Entitled "Products for People with Vision Problems" the catalog covers everything from bingo to audible basketballs with bells inside them, and is available free of charge in large type, in Braille or on cassette. Write to the foundation at 15 West 16th St., New York, NY 10011.

deaf and blind. Originally chartered in 1829, Perkins is a private residential school, but tuition usually is paid by the state or local agency that refers the student. High school diplomas are awarded, and there is also a rehabilitation program in which Perkins graduates and older people learn daily living and employment skills. The address is Perkins School for the Blind, 175 North Beacon St., Watertown, MA 02172.

The Hadley School for the Blind in Winnetka, Illinois, offers a high school diploma, accredited courses and self-improvement courses by mail. The courses are provided without charge to blind and deaf-blind students who receive their lessons in Braille or on cassettes supplemented by tutoring through correspondence or on the phone. College courses are given in cooperation with the extension services of selected colleges and universities. A two-week intensive training course is offered on site in the use of a print-reading device called Optacon. The address is Hadley School, 700 Elm St., Winnetka, IL 60093.

Vocational Rehabilitation for the Blind

In 30 states a special commission has been created to deal with services to the blind (see page 215). In the remaining 20 states, vocational rehabilitation units provide services for the blind. Trained counselors offer aid in developing the practical skills of daily living, mobility training, instruction in filling out job-application forms and in arranging for medical examinations to assess the extent of disabilities and other rehabilitation needs. These units also provide funding for reader services for blind students who are taking vocational training.

The rehabilitation of the blind has achieved impressive results. Blind people have taken their place in the work force as physicians, lawyers, teachers, engineers, machine operators, agricultural workers, salesmen, clerks and computer technicians. Two federal laws have been enacted to help blind persons achieve financial independence. The Randolph-Sheppard Act, passed in 1936, established a priority for blind persons to operate vending machines on federal property. The arrangements vary somewhat from state to state. In some cases the blind persons may own the vending machines. In other states, they may be licensed as operators. Similar arrangements provide for the operation of vending facilities on state government property, and there is a growing movement to permit the establishment of such businesses on private property. Further information may be obtained from state vocational rehabilitation agencies.

The Javits-Wagner-O'Day Act provides for

the purchase by the federal government of certain products that have been manufactured by the blind or severely handicapped. The products must be made in qualified workshops and must be sold at a fair market price. For further information, write to National Industries for the Blind at 1455 Broad St., Bloomfield, NJ 07003, or National Industries for the Severely Handicapped at 4350 East West Highway, Washington, DC 20014.

Guide Dogs for the Blind
Whether a blind person chooses to use a guide dog is a personal matter, depending upon the individual's particular preference and need. Some individuals are greatly helped by the dogs, and others find it impossible to make the adjustment satisfactorily. Guide dog agencies can help with the decision and the adjustment. Most of the agencies listed below charge no fees except for the purchase of the dog. Others may charge according to the ability to pay. All of these schools carefully match the animals and their owners and provide thorough training in the use of the dogs.

Guide Dog Foundation for the Blind
109–19 72nd Ave.
Forest Hills, NY 11375
Guide Dogs for the Blind
P.O. Box 1200
San Rafael, CA 49463
Guiding Eyes for the Blind (GEB)
250 East Hartsdale Ave.
Hartsdale, NY 10530
International Guiding Eyes (IGE)
5431 Denny Ave.
North Hollywood, CA 91603
Leader Dogs for the Blind
1039 South Rochester Rd.
Rochester, MI 48063
Pilot Guide Dog Foundation
33 East Congress Parkway
Chicago, IL 60605
Seeing Eye
Washington Valley Rd.
Morristown, NJ 07960

Programs and Services for the Deaf

More than 15 million people in the United States have serious hearing problems. Of these, 1.8 million are totally deaf. Their deafness cannot be reversed by operations, hearing aids or medical treatment.

These people are severely handicapped, not only by their deafness, but by their inability to develop their language skills, which impedes their social and psychological development and frequently results in the neglect of their abilities and skills.

Age is a critical factor in determining the extent of the deafness handicap. People who become deaf after their basic speech and language patterns are established can adjust far more easily to the world of the hearing than those who were afflicted at a very early age. For those in the latter group, communication frequently remains a lifelong problem. Early detection of deafness and training to offset the handicap are, therefore, vital. Most experts believe that in the years from two to four, the deaf child should have intensive pre-school training.

There are 62 public residential schools in the United States where deaf children receive speech therapy and training in lip reading, sign language and the use of hearing aids. Local or state boards of education can supply information on the locations of these schools.

The federal government supports post-secondary education for deaf or deaf-blind students at major centers across the country. A directory of these state agencies appears on page 216. For further information on the programs at these centers, write: Office of Special Education, 400 Maryland Ave., SW, Washington, DC 20202.

Gallaudet: The College for the Deaf
The only accredited liberal arts college for the deaf in the world is Gallaudet College in Washington, DC. Established by an act of

Congress in 1864, Gallaudet from the beginning has pioneered teaching methods and educational research for the deaf. The college offers bachelor degree programs in 26 fields, master's programs in 5 and a doctorate in special education administration.

Admission is by examination. Modest fees are charged for tuition, room, board and other services. Financial aid of one kind or another is received by 85 percent of the students, either through their state vocational rehabilitation services or through conventional student loans and grants.

Gallaudet also operates the Kendall Demonstration Elementary School for the Deaf and the Model Secondary School for the Deaf. Funded by Congress, these schools are located on the Gallaudet campus and are concerned with developing and evaluating innovative teaching methods, curricula and educational technology for the training of deaf children. Kendall serves day students from the metropolitan Washington, DC, area, but the Model Secondary School is equipped with residential facilities and accepts students from anywhere in the nation.

Gallaudet also maintains an education program for adults and offers special instruction in sign language for interpreters. Its National Center for Law and the Deaf provides free legal services for the deaf and hearing impaired, with a special emphasis on employment problems, income maintenance, insurance and tax benefits and civil rights. For further information write to:

Gallaudet College
7th and Florida Ave., NE
Washington, DC 20002

Technical Education for the Deaf

The National Technical Institute for the Deaf (NTID) in Rochester, New York, is a special technical college supported by funds from the U.S. government. Established in 1968, the institute accepts deaf students from all over the United States.

Over 80 percent of the students receive financial support from state vocational rehabilitation agencies. Students may pursue business, science, engineering or visual communications courses, and are awarded a certificate, diploma or associate degree. If qualified, they may cross-register at the Rochester Institute of Technology, which is affiliated with NTID, for courses leading to a bachelor's or master's degree.

NTID's National Center on Employment of the Deaf offers special services in matching the skills of the deaf to the needs of government, business and industry. Employee development and the training of professionals who work with the deaf are also a part of NTID's program. For information write to NTID, One Lomb Memorial Dr., Rochester, NY 14623.

Employment Opportunities for the Deaf

All too often deaf people are underemployed or hired for menial and repetitive tasks that isolate them from their fellow workers and make little use of their talents. Such jobs are gradually being eliminated by automation; and there is an urgent need to move deaf employees into areas where their special capacity for concentration can be utilized. Accounting, printing and computer programming are among the skills now enjoying a high priority in most rehabilitation agencies. The prospects of deaf persons are enhanced by the fact that they usually rate higher than their fellow employees in safety, concentration, job stability and productivity.

Each of the 10 regional offices of the Department of Health and Human Services is staffed by a specialist in deafness reahabilitation, and counselors who are trained to work with deaf people. The Rehabilitation Services Administration (under the Office of Special Education, page 196) also funds 11 special projects around the country to assist deaf people in achieving their maximum potential.

Hearing Dogs for the Deaf

Dogs have been trained to help the deaf and protect them by responding to such sounds as a crying child, a doorbell, a smoke detector, a car horn or even the sound of boiling water. The dog is trained to nudge his master, run to the source of the sound and then come back. Training courses are conducted at the American Humane Association in Denver in cooperation with the National Association of the Deaf. Anyone who is interested in acquiring a "hearing" dog should write to NAD, 814 Thayer Ave., Silver Spring, MD 20910.

The Helen Keller National Center for Deaf-Blind Youths and Adults

This organization, with headquarters in Sands Point, New York, provides evaluation and rehabilitation services for the approximately 4,500 deaf-blind people in the United States. The center offers individual training in mobility, communication and daily living for deaf-blind youths and adults. Whenever possible, training is accompanied by job placement and travel orientation. The center also carries on research, trains professional personnel to work with deaf-blind persons and conducts public education programs on the needs of the deaf-blind. The address of the headquarters is 111 Middle Neck Rd., Sands Point, NY 11050.

In addition, eight field offices provide referral services, assist the deaf-blind with resettlement in their communities, and recruit trainees for the personnel-training program. Located in Sands Point, New York; Philadelphia, Pennsylvania; Atlanta, Georgia; Chicago, Illinois; Dallas, Texas; Denver, Colorado; Seattle, Washington; Glendale, California, these offices are listed in local phone directories under the Helen Keller Center.

Other Major Disabilities

Arthritis. See Chapter 4, page 149.

Asthma. See Chapter 4, page 149.

Crippled Children's Services. The federal government provides financial support to the states to implement and improve diagnostic services and hospital and out-patient care for crippled children. The beneficiaries are children under 21 who are crippled or suffering from a disease or condition that might lead to crippling. To participate in the program, state crippled-children's agencies must submit evidence of satisfactory services. In a recent year, approximately 560,000 crippled children were aided through this program. Included in that number were 97,000 children with multiple handicaps, and 41,000 with congenital heart disease.

Cystic Fibrosis. This is a hereditary disease, affecting children and adolescents, that causes malfunction of the sweat and mucus-secreting glands. Infection of the lungs, bronchitis, pneumonia and emphysema are likely. Enzymes from the pancreas fail to reach the intestine, resulting in malnutrition and underweight. The loss of salt in body sweat also makes the victim susceptible to heat exhaustion when exposed to excessively hot weather or body fevers. For further information, write to:

Cystic Fibrosis Foundation
6000 Executive Blvd.
Rockville, MD 20852

Diabetes. See Chapter 4, page 150.

Kidney Disease. See Chapter 4, page 154.

Multiple Sclerosis. See Chapter 4, page 155.

Muscular Dystrophy. See Chapter 4, page 155.

Parkinson's Disease. A chronic, progressive brain disorder resulting in a loss of muscular coordination and control. Most commonly appearing after the ages of 50 or 60, the disease advances slowly and may result in tremors of the whole body, speech impediment, rolling of the eyes and impairment of the balance. General information about the disease may be obtained from:

Parkinson's Disease Foundation, Inc.
William Black Medical Research Bldg.
Columbia University Medical Center
640 West 168th St.
New York, NY 10032

Poliomyelitis. A crippling infection of the central nervous system. The disease has largely been brought under control since the introduction of polio vaccines and the widespread immunization programs in the 1960s. People of all ages may be affected, but polio is most commonly reported in young children. Symptoms include fever, headache, vomiting, drowsiness, sore throat and stiffness in the back and neck. Children should be immunized with the Sabin oral polio vaccine. The family doctor can provide the vaccine.

Spinal Cord Injuries. Comprehensive care for paraplegics and quadraplegics is the objective of the National Spinal Cord Injury Foundation, founded by the Paralyzed Veterans of America in 1948. The foundation works through 67 local chapters that offer individual consultations, advice for the newly injured or referrals to agencies providing direct services for paralysis victims.

Information on independent living rehabilitation, self-help devices, equipment, transportation, employment, education and personal care is offered by the national office and local chapters. The foundation also publishes a bimonthly magazine called *Paraplegia Life* and distributes handbooks on nursing, personal care and nutrition.

Local chapters may be located in telephone directories under "National Spinal Cord Injury Foundation." The address of the headquarters is:

National Spinal Cord Injury Foundation
369 Eliot St.
Newton Upper Falls, MA 02164

Paralyzed Veterans of America. A national organization, the PVA has offices in each of the Veterans Administration's Spinal Cord Injury Centers (See Chapter 6 directory), 30 VA regional offices and out-patient clinics. The PVA is an information and advocacy agency, supporting research in the treatment and understanding of spinal cord injuries and the championing of programs for the improvement of transportation facilities, the removal of architectural barriers to mobility of the paralyzed, and the refinement of wheelchair design to aid victims of paralysis. It also pleads claims for paralyzed veterans before government agencies. The agency's publications include: *An Introduction to Paraplegia, Wheelchair in a Home* and *Highway Rest Areas for Handicapped Travelers*. The address is:

Paralyzed Veterans of America
4350 East West Highway
Washington, DC 20014

Handicapped Veterans

Veterans with service-connected disabilities are entitled to a wide range of benefits and services, including monthly compensation payments, treatment in VA hospitals, vocational rehabilitation and preference in employment, grants toward the purchase of "wheelchair homes" and specially adapted automobiles, clothing allowances and compensation to survivors after death. The full range of benefits for disabled veterans is covered in Chapter 6.

Civilian Health and Medical Program of the Uniformed Services (CHAMPUS). Congress established the CHAMPUS program to provide health benefits for the dependents of active service personnel (see Chapter 6, p. 239). The coverage includes the Handicapped Dependent Program, which is designed to help care for physically and mentally handicapped spouses and children of men and women in the armed forces. Services include diagnosis, in-patient and out-patient treatment, special education, training and rehabilitation, and residential care in a federal, state or private facility.

The Handicapped Dependent Program is not intended to supplant other forms of health care but to supplement them when necessary. Thus, if the family of someone who has been in the armed service is entitled to Medicare, they will transfer to that program. If they are entitled to insurance benefits, these must be used before CHAMPUS can make any payments. Moreover, in any case in which CHAMPUS funds are used, a percentage of the cost must be borne by the beneficiary.

All benefits under the CHAMPUS program except initial diagnostic services must be approved before they will be paid. Approval can be obtained by filling out CHAMPUS form 190A, which is obtainable from the CHAMPUS adviser at most military installations, or by writing to CHAMPUS, Denver, CO 80240.

The Civilian Health and Medical Program of the Veterans Administration (CHAMP-VA). This program provides medical care for spouses or children of totally disabled veterans who are not entitled to similar care from CHAMPUS. The benefits are essentially the same.

Learning to Live with the Handicaps

The growing awareness of the problems of the disabled, the gradual erosion of uninformed and unsympathetic attitudes toward the handicapped and the passage of such landmark legislation as the Bill of Rights for All the Handicapped have broadened the opportunity for handicapped individuals to take their place in the mainstream of American life. If the disability is not too severe, an individual who formerly would have been consigned to a life of isolation can now acquire a first-class education, find a home and a job that are suited to his or her needs and enjoy many of the pleasures and a vocation that were denied those who were physically or developmentally disabled.

Learning to overcome or offset the handicap requires, of course, a great effort on the part of the disabled individual. Many obstacles and frustrations must be overcome. But there is more help and more understanding for the handicapped now, and more opportunities for those who are able to make the adjustment.

Rehabilitation Services for the Disabled
The federal Rehabilitation Services Administration, working through state rehabilitation agencies, offers a series of services to enable the handicapped to develop the skills and work habits that are needed to obtain jobs and live more independent, productive lives. Here are some of the services that are included:

1. Counseling to evaluate disabled persons' needs and potential, understand their problems, develop individualized rehabilitation plans and assure that all necessary services are provided. The evaluation period may take up to 18 months.
2. Medical, surgical and hospital care to limit the effects of disabilities; prosthetics, braces and other devices plus fitting and training in their use; recreational, physical and occupational therapy; speech and hearing therapy.
3. Vocational training services in occupations in which there is a reasonable chance of employment.
4. Maintenance and transportation during rehabilitation, as well as tools, equipment and licenses for work on a job or in establishing a small business.
5. Aid in arranging suitable employment for individuals who cannot readily make their way in the competitive labor market.
6. Reader services for the blind and interpreter services for the deaf.
7. Initial stock, supplies and management services for small businesses.
8. Help for families of handicapped persons that will facilitate the rehabilitation of the disabled.
9. Job placement and follow-up services to help disabled persons hold their jobs.

Eligibility. The Rehabilitation Services Administration requires that "applicants must have a physical or mental disability which constitutes a substantial handicap to employment, with a reasonable expectation that vocational rehabilitation services will benefit the person in obtaining and sustaining employment."

Priorities for Job Placements

In federal-state programs, severely handicapped people are assigned a priority over those with less serious disabilities. Special attention is accorded to applicants with the following problems:

*Severely handicapped persons with disabilities stemming from amputations and orthopedic injuries, blindness and visual impairment, cancer, cerebral palsy, cystic fibrosis, deafness, acute kidney disease, epilepsy, heart disease and stroke, mental illness, mental retardation, multiple sclerosis, muscular dystrophy, respiratory or pulmonary problems and spinal cord injuries.

*Homebound or institutionalized people who can be trained for employment.

*People who are receiving Supplemental Security Income (see Chapter 7, p. 282).

The state vocational rehabilitation agencies are not equipped to furnish all of these services. But they can provide access to the resources of other public and private organizations to implement rehabilitation plans worked out by handicapped individuals and their counselors.

Job Placements for the Disabled

A special program, known as Projects with Industry, trains and places disabled persons in such private-industry jobs as computer technology, optical technology, information systems and other technically oriented and managerial positions.

The Rehabilitation Services Administration works closely with the Helen Keller National Center for Deaf-Blind Youth and Adults (see p. 194) and also administers the licensing of vending facilities on federal and other property to qualified blind persons.

Financial Eligibility for Rehabilitation Programs

The following services are provided free by state vocational rehabilitation agencies to eligible individuals regardless of financial need:

* evaluation of rehabilitation potential.
* counseling, guidance and referral services.
* job placement.

For other services, the state agency may consider the client's financial need as well as the availability of similar benefits through insurance or other programs. People who are eligible for Social Security Disability Insurance (SSDI) or Supplemental Security Income (SSI) may have their rehabilitation services paid for by the Social Security Administration.

Further information on the rehabilitation programs may be obtained from the nearest local office of the state vocational rehabilitation agency (see page 213 for list), or from the federal Rehabilitation Services Administration at 400 Maryland Ave., SW, Washington, DC 20202.

Goodwill Workshops

Since 1902 Goodwill Industries of America has been operating workshops where handicapped persons renovate or recondition donated clothing, furniture and appliances for resale in the Goodwill outlet stores. Working relationships are maintained with state vocational rehabilitation agencies and other community resources, providing the participants with an industrial atmosphere supplemented by a program of rehabilitation services, counseling, work training, social and medical evaluation and job placement. Goodwill also does contract work for private manufacturers and government agencies. For information, call your local Goodwill Industries or write to:

Goodwill Industries of America
92 Wisconsin Ave., NW
Washington, DC 20014

Rehabilitation for Veterans

For veterans whose disabilities are service connected, the Veterans Administration should be the primary resource for getting started on a rehabilitation program (see Chapter 6 directory). A veteran is provided counseling and training for up to 48 months, during which time the recipient may obtain help in identifying jobs that he or she can perform, receive tuition for special schooling and be helped in job placement and follow-up assistance. The VA also advises on and arranges for special equipment needed by handicapped persons to perform their jobs. The 48-month period may be extended if necessary. If placement in a training institution is required, the costs are paid to the institution, and the veteran receives a monthly subsistence allowance. Necessary medical, dental, hospital and out-patient treatment may also be furnished.

In addition to providing counselors and rehabilitation staffs, the VA uses the services of the state rehabilitation agencies as well as private rehabilitation organizations. For addresses of VA regional offices, see Chapter 6.

The Right to Gainful Employment

Among the rights of handicapped persons, none is more vital than that of gainful employment. But, until recently the one out of 11 U.S. citizens who are handicapped were frequently unemployed or employed at jobs below their capabilities. A survey, made late in the 1970s, showed that of the estimated 7.2 million disabled individuals 16 to 64 years old and able to work, only about 42 percent were employed as opposed to 53 percent of the non-handicapped.

Affirmative Action Programs
Three major government programs are beginning to change the employment outlook for handicapped persons:

1. Section 503 of the Rehabilitation Act of 1973 states that every employer doing business with the federal government under a contract for more than $2,500 must take affirmative action not only in hiring qualified handicapped persons but in job assignments, promotion, training, transfers, accessibility and working conditions. About half of the nation's three million private businesses are covered by this provision.

2. Section 504 requires every institution (school, college, hospital, social service agency) receiving federal financial assistance to take steps to assure that handicapped persons are not discriminated against in employment.

3. The Vietnam Era Veterans Readjustment Assistance Act stipulates that any employer with a federal government contract of $10,000 or more must take affirmative action to hire disabled veterans of all wars as well as veterans of the Vietnam era.

How Affirmative Action Works for the Handicapped
A "handicapped person" is interpreted to mean anyone who:

1. has a physical or mental impairment that substantially limits one or more of his or her major life activites (such as communication, movement, self-care, education or socialization);

2. has a record of such impairment;

3. is regarded as having such an impairment even though he or she actually is not disabled (a person who appears to be mentally retarded, but is not, might be eligible).

In the context of Section 503, "qualified" means that a person must be capable of performing a particular job—with a reasonable accommodation to his or her handicapping condition.

"Reasonable accommodation" means making facilities accessible, changing work schedules to enable a paraplegic to avoid rush hours, modifying the job so that a deaf typist is not responsible for answering the phone, providing a reader when needed by a blind worker.

Not all handicaps are obvious. Some, such as epilepsy, mental illness, heart disease may not

Hiring the Handicapped Can Be Good for Business

Many employers fear that hiring the handicapped will increase their insurance costs, jeopardize their safety records, involve expensive adjustments for access and threaten the morale of other employees who will resent the special "privileges" granted to the disabled. But James H. Sears, coordinator of industry education activities for E. I. duPont de Nemours and Company, America's 16th largest employer, convinced his company that hiring the handicapped is good business. A long-time member of the President's Committee on Employment of the Handicapped, Sears was responsible for a study that examined the job performance of 1,452 company workers with handicaps ranging from orthopedic disabilities to total blindness. The workers were engaged in a wide variety of jobs at duPont. Craftsmen were the largest category (562), but professional, technical and managerial posts were included, as well as office and clerical workers, and factory laborers.

The study revealed not only that employers' fears are unfounded, but that there seems to be a direct correlation between the job performance of the handicapped and the severity of their impairment, with amputees, blind persons, paraplegics and epileptics coming out on top of the job-performance list. For most of the handicapped workers, the physical adjustments to the job were minimal. No special work arrangements were required, nor was there an increase in compensation costs. The safety record of handicapped workers was impressive, with 96 percent rated average or better on and off the job and more than half rated above average. Moreover, 91 percent rated average or better on job performance, 93 percent rated average or better on job stability and 79 percent rated average or better on attendance.

In another survey, prepared by the U.S. Office of Vocational Rehabilitation from reports of more than 100 large corporations, 66 percent of the employers reported no difference between the handicapped and the able-bodied in productivity, while 24 percent rated the handicapped higher. More than half of the employers said the accident rate for the handicapped was lower, and 41 percent reported that the rate was the same for handicapped and able-bodied workers. Turnover rates were appreciably lower for the handicapped in 83 percent of the cases, and absenteeism was lower in 55 percent. The message seems loud and clear. All handicapped persons need is a chance to prove themselves in an atmosphere in which they are encouraged to compete as individuals and are given the opportunity to utilize their skills and abilities to the fullest.

---

be apparent. You do not have to provide your prospective employer with information about your handicap if you do not want to. However, if you want to avail yourself of the protections of Sections 503 and 504, you will need to explain your handicap in order to be eligible. Employers must respect the confidentiality of such information, but your supervisor or manager may be informed about any necessary work restrictions or needed accommodations, and first-aid people will be informed about the possible need for emergency services.

Complaints of
Unfair Treatment by Employers

Affirmative action programs are designed to aid the disabled and to persuade employers who do business with the government to hire more qualified handicapped persons. The programs are not meant to be punitive. However, if you feel that you have been denied employment on the basis of your handicap, or if you are convinced that your special needs have not been reasonably accommodated or you have unfairly been passed over for promotion, you have recourse to legal action because of these discriminatory practices.

You, or your representative, may file a written complaint, explaining the nature of your handicap, specifying the acts of discrimination that are charged and setting forth the efforts that have been made to resolve the complaint. The written complaint, and pertinent documents, should be forwarded to:

The Office of Federal Contracts Compliance Programs
U.S. Department of Labor
Washington, DC 20210

If the initial investigation by the Office of Federal Contracts concludes that there was no violation, you can ask for a review of the case. If a violation is eventually shown, efforts will be made to encourage the employer to state in writing that corrective action will be taken. If efforts to settle the problem are to no avail, the Department of Labor will intervene. Penalties may be instituted or the government contract may be terminated.

Federal Jobs for the Handicapped
The federal government, conscious of its role as the nation's largest employer, and mandated to serve in this area as a model for state and local governments and private employers, has taken the lead in developing and implementing affirmative action practices to protect the handicapped. Within the federal Civil Service, agency coordinators and counselors are charged with the responsibility for recruiting, hiring, promoting and retaining handicapped persons, eliminating physical, attitudinal and procedural barriers and smoothing the way toward successful employment.

Special Testing for Civil Service Jobs
Special procedures are available for certain severely disabled individuals. These include arrangements for individual testing for blind or deaf persons or people with poor dexterity or coordination when such a test is clearly job related and there is no reasonable alternative. (Federal agencies may not use any test that screens out handicapped individuals unless the test is clearly job related, such as typing or taking shorthand.)

Trial Appointments in the Government Service
A temporary trial appointment may enable a severely handicapped person to show how well he or she can perform in a particular job. The usual trial appointment is for 700 hours (approximately four months). Some persons may come in as "excepted" employees, which means that they are hired for specific jobs tailored to their abilities, without competing with other applicants. In some cases, unpaid work experience may be arranged as part of a rehabilitation program through the state vocational rehabilitation agencies or through the Veterans Administration.

To learn more about how to apply for employment with the federal government, see Chapter 2. A list of federal job information centers appears on p. 90. Each center has a specialist who provides assistance to handicapped individuals.

State Job Services
Under the terms of the Wagner Labor Relations Act, every local office of the state employment service is required to maintain at least one staff member who can help handicapped persons find training or employment. The program seeks to place persons in jobs utilizing their highest skills, and attempts to insure that they receive equal opportunity and equal pay in competition with other applicants. Aptitude testing, counseling and appraisal of employability may be provided.

The state job service offices also provide veterans with special interviewing, counseling, job preparation and job-placement assistance. The veterans employment representative in each office is specially trained to work with government agencies, the Veterans Administration and business groups in seeking job opportunities for veterans.

The VA also sponsors "job fairs" in different cities throughout the year at which employers and people who want to work are encouraged to get together. Your local VA office can give you more information about the possibility of a job fair in your locality.

Minimum Wage
Exceptions for the Handicapped

When handicapped persons are unable to earn the minimum wage, the Employment Standards Administration of the U.S. Department of Labor may allow employers to pay less than the legally prescribed rate. For example, if a mentally retarded person could do an assembly-line job in a small factory, but would be substantially slower than the other workers, the employer might be able to obtain a wage exception for the job. Because of the danger of abuses to avoid paying fair wages, the exceptions are not granted without careful study. The initial request for information about subminimum wage exceptions should go to:

Wage and Hour Division
Employment Standards Administration
U.S. Department of Labor
Washington, DC 20210

Small Business Loans for the Handicapped

Suppose that you are handicapped and you have the chance to buy an established store in the local shopping center but the owner is asking for a $2,500 down payment. You may be thinking of opening an electrical repair shop but you would need money to finance the first six month's rent, refurbish the building and order the initial stock. The Small Business Administration may be able to help you (see Chapter 2, pp. 00). The SBA's Handicapped Assistance Loans Program provides assistance for the establishment, acquisition or operation of small businesses that are 100 percent owned by handicapped persons. The loans will not be made for speculation, non-profit enterprises, publishing ventures or the financing of real property held for sale or investment. Loan applications must be related to projects of such sound value that repayment will be reasonably certain. For further information write to the:

Director, Office of Financing
Small Business Administration
1441 L St., NW
Washington, DC 20416

As an alternative, you may want to contact your local Small Business Administration field office. (A list appears on p. 93.)

President's Committee
on Employment of the Handicapped

The committee cooperates with the state governors' committees for employment of the handicapped and with local committees to promote employment opportunities for physically and mentally handicapped people. It also works to advance the cause of affirmative action and the elimination of discrimination in hiring practices. The committee's publications are widely circulated and provide useful information for those who are interested in promoting job opportunities for the handicapped. The address is:

PCEH
1111 20th St., NW
Washington, DC 20210

Compensation Programs
for Work-Related Disabilities

A handicapped person whose disability was incurred in the performance of his or her work may be entitled to compensation as well as medical and rehabilitative services. Workers' compensation programs are covered in detail in Chapter 2.

Social Security Programs for the Disabled

The Social Security Administration operates two programs that provide financial aid for handicapped persons. These are Social Security Disability Insurance (SSDI) and Supplemental Security Income (SSI).

Under the SSDI program, disabled workers who have not reached 65, unmarried children under 18, children attending school full-time, and those who are disabled before the age of 22 are eligible for financial aid. The benefits are payable when a parent (or in some cases a grandparent) receives Social Security retirement benefits, or when an insured parent dies.

Disabled widows, widowers and, under certain circumstances, disabled surviving divorced wives of workers who were insured at death are also eligible. The payments may begin as early as age 50.

The Supplemental Security Income (SSI) program provides monthly cash payments for blind, aged or disabled persons at or below the poverty level. The amount of the payments depends on the individual's financial status and need. In certain circumstances, a small allowance of up to $25 per month may also be paid for the recipient's personal use.

Definition of "Disabled"

For purposes of Social Security you are considered "disabled" if you have a physical or mental impairment that is expected to last at least 12 months, and prevents you from doing any substantial gainful work during this period.

"Blindness" is defined in Social Security law as a visual rating of 20/200 or less in the better eye with the use of corrective lenses, or a visual field of 20 degrees or less.

Mental retardation in children under 18 (or under 22 and attending school) is defined as an IQ of 59 or less; an IQ of 60-69 with marked dependence upon others for meeting basic personal needs; or an achievement of certain developmental abilities no greater than those reasonably expected of a child half the applicant's age. For adults, the definition is an IQ of less than 50 or an IQ of 50-69 with an inability to perform routine, repetitive tasks. A severe mental and social incapacity resulting in a dependence on others for meeting personal needs may also be sufficient evidence of mental retardation. The inability to understand the spoken word, to avoid physical danger or follow directions, or to read, write or perform simple calculations also come within the definition of mental retardation.

The applicant or guardian will be required to provide medical evidence of retardation, and the handicapped person may be asked to undergo special examinations and tests.

Eligibility for the SSDI program, the disabilities covered, payment plans and the filing of claims and appeals are discussed in detail in Chapter 7. The SSI program is also covered in Chapter 7.

Housing for the Handicapped

At the present time there are no federal funds specifically designated for enabling handicapped individuals to purchase homes. The handicapped are, of course, eligible for all the standard federal housing loans and mortgage insurance programs available to other citizens. Moreover, they may be helped by special barrier-removal loans and rent subsidies.

If you are handicapped and need to modify your home to remove architectural barriers, install ramps, special bathroom facilities, railings or lower light switches, you may be eligible for an FHA-insured loan of up to $10,000 per home or $5,000 per apartment. The loans are applied for through your local bank or other financial lending institution, and the lender is insured against possible loss by the FHA.

If you live on a farm or in a rural area, you may be eligible for a Farmers Home Administration loan to purchase or repair your home. Write to:

Farmers Home Administration
Department of Agriculture
Washington, DC 20250

Rental Assistance

Low-income handicapped persons living alone or with their families may be eligible for U.S. Housing and Urban Development (HUD) rent subsidies under Section 202 of the Housing

Act of 1959 (see Chapter 3). HUD grants subsidies in the form of direct payments to the owners of rental units for the benefit of needy persons renting privately owned apartments, houses and mobile homes. The payments are intended to make up the difference between the HUD-approved rental amount and the portion of the rent that the tenant is required to pay (between 15 percent and 25 percent of the family's adjusted income). Rental assistance may also be obtained for independent group residences with supervised living arrangements for the physically or mentally handicapped. The residents are assigned one or two persons to a bedroom, and share bathing, cooking and dining facilities.

For further information on rental assistance, call or write to an area HUD office (see directory, Chapter 3).

Other Housing Possibilities

Federally sponsored community block grants have been used in some urban communities to provide group homes and halfway houses for the handicapped. The funds go directly toward construction costs, and not to individuals. There is no requirement that a given proportion of the money be spent on housing for the handicapped. It is, therefore, important that individuals and organizations interested in the welfare of the handicapped make their needs known to the city officials responsible for setting priorities for the use of such funds.

Many communities have also sponsored public housing projects that are designed to accommodate handicapped persons. Because the availability of public and rent-subsidized housing varies widely from city to city, inquiries about existing or planned projects should be directed to local housing authorities. Information may also be obtained from:

Office of Independent Living for the
  Disabled
Department of Housing and Urban
  Development
451 7th St., SW
Washington, DC 20410

Wheelchair Homes

If you are a veteran with a service-connected disability necessitating the use of a wheelchair, up to 50 percent of the cost of building, buying, remodeling or paying off the indebtedness on a home suited to your needs may be granted by the Veterans Administration. A maximum figure of $32,500 applies (see discussion in Chapter 6).

Tax Benefits for the Disabled

Many of the expenses that handicapped persons or their parents incur in caring for their physical needs, providing for their education or adapting to their employment may be deducted from federal income-tax payments. According to the Internal Revenue Service regulations, these may include:

*special equipment such as motorized wheelchairs, specially equipped automobiles, the cost and repair of special telephones for deaf or hearing-disabled persons;

*special equipment, including artificial limbs, eyeglasses, hearing aids, crutches and dogs for the use of the blind or deaf;

*payments to special schools for mentally or physically handicapped persons if the principal reason for attendance is the institution's resources for dealing with or relieving the handicap.

Tax credits may be allowed in some circumstances for payments to relatives who provide special care. There are also tax credits for costs incurred in caring for disabled spouses or dependents.

The tax law allows an additional personal exemption for blind persons. For further information, contact your local IRS office.

Access to Public Buildings and Transportation

In recent years, physical access to public buildings and mass transportation has become a major issue for the handicapped. Some 250,000 people in wheelchairs, a similar number wearing leg braces and many persons with other disabilities are affected. No matter what your handicap, you have a right to access to any building or facility constructed, leased or altered since 1969 by or for the federal government with federal funds. Similarly, you have a right to use any mass transportation system. These rights are guaranteed by the 1964 Urban Mass Transit Act and the 1968 Architectural Barriers Act. Since 1973, these acts have been enforced by the U.S. Architectural and Transportation Barriers Compliance Board (A&TBCB).

The organization's goal is to set up guidelines for compliance with the law and to serve as a watch dog over federal, state and local governments and public and private groups in their efforts to eliminate barriers. The board also proposes specific ways to eliminate barriers and thereby provide easy access to transportation, housing and public buildings. It seeks to establish minimum standards requiring at least one ramp or level entrance per building, wheelchair-accessible restrooms, lower light switches, elevator buttons within reach, audible and visual fire alarm signals, lowered wall pay phones and chair lifts where elevators are not architecturally feasible. These and other aids, many of them ingenious responses to recurrent problems, are gradually opening up a world of mobility for the handicapped.

The board handles written complaints about the inaccessibility of public facilities and transportation systems. The address is:

Architectural and Transportation
  Barriers Compliance Board
Switzer Bldg.
330 C St., SW
Washington, DC 20202

The Removal of Architectural Barriers

The Architectural Barriers Act does not apply to buildings built before 1969, but a climate has been created in which many organizations, including those that are privately owned, have become more sensitive to the needs of the physically disabled and have begun on their own to remodel their facilities in accordance with the A&TBCB's guidelines.

Some supermarkets have installed wide check-out aisles with lower counters for wheelchair patrons, and some theaters have begun providing designated wheelchair spaces as well as amplifiers for the deaf. Ramps, guide rails and special restrooms are appearing as profit-making organizations realize that making their facilities available to the handicapped is good business.

Complaints about Exclusion from Federally Funded Facilities

Most hospitals, schools, libraries, museums and other public institutions are probably at least partially dependent upon public funding and thereby fall under the provisions of the federal law. If you believe you have been denied your right of access to a federally owned, leased or funded facility, send your complaint to the Executive Director of the A&TBCB at the above address. Include the following information: your name, address and phone number; a brief statement of the barrier-related problem; the name and location of the building or facility; the name of the person or agency responsible for the building or facility; the owner and the tenant; the name of the federal agency occupying the building or providing funds for its lease, alteration or construction; your suggestion for solving the problem.

Travel by Public Conveyances

Today's mass-transportation system, while far more responsive to the needs of the handicapped than formerly, has not yet solved all its problems. Moreover, local transportation systems vary widely in the speed with which they are making accommodations. If you are planning to travel, make your arrangements well in advance and ask detailed questions of the travel agent, airline, bus or train sales representative to whom you speak regarding the services that

International Symbol of Access

This symbol tells a handicapped person, particularly one using a wheelchair, that a building or facility is accessible and can be entered and used without fear of being blocked by architectural barriers. It should be displayed only on those buildings intended for public use. Used throughout the world, the symbol is recognized for its special meaning.

will be available and the obstacles you may encounter. If you give these people enough notice, they may be able to smooth your way by making certain that the necessary personnel and equipment will be on hand to serve your needs.

Going by Train

Amtrak is making an effort to accommodate handicapped passengers, but is hampered by antiquated stations and outmoded equipment. Limited clearance through certain tunnels in the East has prevented the purchase of new cars with better accommodations for the handicapped. The new superliner cars running west out of Chicago are, however, equipped for wheelchairs.

Complete bedroom, daytime seating and dining facilities are available for passengers who are confined to wheelchairs. Even in the East, most trains can accommodate people in wheelchairs in their lounges or dining cars, and every train has at least one restroom that has been adapted for wheelchair users.

Special fares are in effect in some areas. Handicapped persons who can produce identification verifying their handicaps receive a 25 percent discount on all one-way fares that exceed $40. In addition, handicapped children from two to 11 who are traveling alone pay ³/₈ of the full adult fare, but they must be able to show some verification of their handicaps (from the National Association for the Blind, an appropriate state or local agency or a physician). Guide dogs or hearing dogs ride free of charge as long as they do not occupy a seat.

At most stations there are elevators which disabled persons may use, and wheelchairs are generally available. It is advisable to inquire ahead about the specific facilities and possible obstacles, both at the station from which you will depart and the one at which you will arrive. Moreover, if your sight or hearing is impaired or you suffer from any other disability, the journey will be safer and more comfortable if you notify the conductor ahead of time about your special needs. You may wish, for instance, to be told when you are about to arrive at your station, or you may need help in getting to the dining car or the restroom.

Getting There by Bus

Travel by bus may also pose special problems for the handicapped. Although some communities are using new buses with specially designed steps for the disabled (the so-called "kneeling" buses), most long-distance vehicles are not equipped with these devices. Moreover, the facilities vary from up-to-date big-city terminals with elevators, access ramps, restrooms and attendants on duty 24 hours a day to multipurpose outdoor platforms in outlying areas where no one is in attendance.

The bus companies are aware of the problems, however, and if the traveler calls ahead, an effort will be made at most stops to have someone on hand to assist the bus driver in helping the handicapped person. Wheelchairs may be carried with the luggage. Guide dogs are permitted on board free, and special help can be obtained for blind, deaf, physically or developmentally disabled persons.

When you make your travel plans, find out about the facilities at both ends of your trip, and be sure to inquire about special fares. Greyhound has what it calls a "helping hand" fare; if you need help, there is no charge for an attendant who accompanies you. Trailways also charges full fare for a handicapped person traveling alone, but allows an attendant to go along for no extra charge. To take advantage of these and other discounts, you will have to show a valid identification of yourself as a handicapped person when you pay for your fare.

Travel by Plane

If you are planning to fly, it is essential that you tell the reservation agent exactly what help you will need and what special problems your disability poses. Because of stringent air-safety rules, you may be asked to furnish a medical certificate from your doctor attesting that it is safe for you to fly.

Airlines can reserve a special seat for you near an exit and a lavatory. They can furnish special meals and provide elevator-type vehicles to lift wheelchairs onto planes. On any flight, however, the number of unaccompanied persons who are incapable of evacuating themselves in an emergency may be limited by the number of attendants who will be available to help them.

If you use a wheelchair, you will be taken aboard the plane before the other passengers, and the wheelchair will be carried free in the baggage compartment. The layout of the aircraft will be explained to blind passengers. Locations of call buttons, audio outlets and lavatories will be indicated and they will be told when the No Smoking or Fasten Seat Belt signs are illuminated or turned off. Deaf passengers will have safety procedures and signs brought to their attention.

If you are a frequent air traveler, you should obtain a copy of the A&TBCB's *Access Travel: A Guide to Accessibility of Airport Terminals*. This publication lists 282 terminals in 40 countries,

Making Art Accessible

The 1980 Picasso show at the Museum of Modern Art in New York City showed how sensitive planning and preparation can enable vast numbers of handicapped persons to take advantage of a major cultural event. Anticipating the show's popularity and wishing to encourage participation by handicapped persons, the museum made a great effort to assure their comfort and enjoyment. Two restrooms were remodeled to accommodate the physically disabled. Access to the exhibit was provided through the main entrance rather than the garden, which was used by other patrons. Ramps were placed where necessary, and additional wheelchairs were rented. A guidebook to the show was prepared in large type and in Braille for the visually impaired. The audio tour was made available in an amplified version for those with hearing difficulties, and the transcription was prepared by a writer who herself was hearing impaired and aware of the language problems experienced by some deaf persons. Moreover, advance notices for the show announced that these provisions were being made. Even the ticket envelopes included a printed notice telling wheelchair users which entrance to use.

Because of the desire to treat the handicapped like everybody else, the museum did not keep a tally on the numbers of disabled individuals who visited the Picasso show. But members of the staff and many visitors to the show later recalled they could not remember ever seeing so many persons in wheelchairs in an American museum.

with pertinent information about parking, boarding facilities, ramps and elevators. Single copies are free from A&TBCB.

Guidebooks and Hotel Accommodations

The Society for the Advancement of Travel for the Handicapped can supply listings of accessible hotels and sightseeing attractions as well as names of travel agents who are knowledgeable about the needs of travelers with disabilities. The society is located at 26 Court St., Brooklyn, NY 11242.

The National Park Service will provide information on camping and recreational facilities available to handicapped people through the Division of Special Programs and Populations, National Park Service, Department of the Interior, 18th and C St., NW, Washington, DC 20240.

For a worldwide master list of guides for the handicapped traveler, write to Rehabilitation International USA, 20 West 40th St., New York, NY 10018. Ask them for the *International Directory of Access Guides*.

A Directory of National Organizations That Help the Handicapped

Alexander Graham Bell Association for the Deaf
3417 Volta Place, NW
Washington, DC 20007

American Association on Mental Deficiency
5101 Wisconsin Ave., NW
Washington, DC 20016

American Coalition of Citizens with Disabilities
1200 15th St., NW
Washington, DC 20005

American Council of the Blind
1211 Connecticut Ave., NW
Washington, DC 20036

American Foundation for the Blind, Inc.
15 West 16th St.
New York, NY 10011

American Printing House for the Blind, Inc.
1839 Frankfort Ave.
Louisville, KY 40206

Association for Children and Adults with Learning
Disabilities
4156 Library Rd.
Pittsburgh, PA 15234

Association for the Severely Handicapped
1600 West Armory Way
Seattle, WA 98119

Blinded Veterans Association
1735 DeSales St., NW
Washington, DC 20036

Center for Independent Living
2539 Telegraph Ave.
Berkeley, CA 94704

Council for Exceptional Children
1920 Association Dr.
Reston, VA 22091

Council of Organizations Serving the Deaf
P.O. Box 894
Columbia, MD 21044

Disabled American Veterans National Service and
Legislation Headquarters
807 Maine Ave., SW
Washington, DC 20024

Epilepsy Foundation of America
1828 L St., NW
Washington, DC 20036

International Committee Against Mental Illness
418 East 76 St.
New York, NY 10021

Junior National Association of the Deaf (Student
Organization)
Gallaudet College
7th and Florida Ave., NE
Washington, DC 20002

March of Dimes Birth Defects Foundation
1275 Mamaroneck Ave.
White Plains, NY 10605

National Amputation Foundation
12–45 150th St.
Whitestone, NY 11357

National Association of the Deaf
814 Thayer Ave.
Silver Spring, MD 20910

The National Association for Mental Health, Inc.
1800 North Kent St.
Arlington, VA 22209

National Association of the Physically Handicapped,
Inc.
2810 Terrace Rd., SW
Washington, DC 20020

National Association for Retarded Citizens
2709 Avenue E East
P.O. Box 6109
Arlington, TX 76011

National Congress of Organizations of the Physically
Handicapped, Inc.
101 Lincoln Park Blvd.
Rockford, IL 61102

National Easter Seal Society for Crippled Children and
Adults
2023 West Ogden Ave.
Chicago, IL 60612

National Federation of the Blind
1800 Johnson St.
Baltimore, Md 21230

National Genetics Foundation, Inc.
555 West 57th St.
New York, NY 10019

National Industries for the Blind
1455 Broad St.
Bloomfield, NJ 07003

National Rehabilitation Association
1522 K St., NW
Washington, DC 20005

National Society to Prevent Blindness
79 Madison Ave.
New York, NY 10016

National Spinal Cord Injury Foundation
369 Elliot St.
Newton Upper Falls, MA 02164

Paralyzed Veterans of America
4350 East West Hghwy.
Washington, DC 20014

Parkinson's Disease Foundation
640 West 168th St.
New York, NY 10032

President's Committee on Employment of the
  Handicapped
  Washington, DC 20210

Society for the Rehabilitation of the Facially
  Disfigured, Inc.

550 First Ave.
New York, NY 10016

State Agencies Serving Handicapped Individuals

CRIPPLED CHILDREN'S STATE SERVICES

Alabama Crippled Children's Services
  2129 East South Blvd.
  Montgomery, AL 36111

Alaska State Department of Health and Social
  Services
  Family Health Section
  Pouch H, Health and Welfare Building
  Juneau, AK 99801

Arizona State Crippled Children's Hospital
  200 North Curry Rd.
  Tempe, AZ 85281

Arkansas Department of Social and Rehabilitative
  Services
  Arkansas Social Services
  Crippled Children's Section
  P.O. Box 1437
  Little Rock, AR 72203

California State Department of Health
  Crippled Children's Services Section
  741–744 P St.
  Sacramento, CA 95814

Colorado Department of Health
  Handicapped Children's Program
  4210 East 11th Ave.
  Denver, CO 80220

Connecticut State Department of Health
  Crippled Children's Section
  79 Elm St.
  Hartford, CT 06115

Delaware Bureau of Personal Health Services
  Division of Public Health
  Jesse Cooper Memorial Building
  Capital Square
  Dover, DE 19901

District of Columbia Department of Human
  Resources
  Maternal and Child Health and Crippled Children's
  Services
  1875 Connecticut Ave., NW
  Washington, DC 20001

Florida Department of Health and Rehabilitative
  Services
  Children's Medical Services Program
  Building 5, 1323 Winewood Blvd.
  Tallahassee, FL 32301

Georgia Department of Human Resources
  Division of Physical Health

Crippled Children's Unit
  618 Ponce de Leon Ave., NE
  Atlanta, GA 30308

Hawaii State Department of Health
  Crippled Children's Services Branch
  P.O. Box 3378
  Honolulu, HI 96801

Idaho State Department of Health and Welfare
  Bureau of Child Health
  Crippled Children's Services
  State House
  700 West State St.
  Boise, ID 83270

Illinois Division of Services for Crippled Children
  540 Iles Park Place
  Springfield, IL 62718

Indiana State Department of Public Welfare
  Division of Services for Crippled Children
  100 North Senate Ave.
  Indianapolis, IN 46204

Iowa State Services for Crippled Children
  University of Iowa
  Iowa City, IA 52242

Kansas State Department of Health and Environment
  Bureau of Maternal and Child Health
  Topeka, KS 66620

Kentucky State Department of Human Resources
  Bureau for Health Services
  275 East Main St.
  Frankfort, KY 40601

Louisiana Department of Health/Human Resources
  Handicapped Children's Program
  P.O. Box 60630
  New Orleans, LA 70160

Maine Division of Child Health
  Department of Human Resources
  State House
  Augusta, ME 04330

Maryland Department of Health and Mental Hygiene
  Preventative Medicine Administration
  Division of Crippled Children
  201 West Preston St.
  Baltimore, MD 21201

Massachusetts State Department of Public Health
  Division of Family Health
  39 Boylston St.
  Boston, MA 02116

Michigan Department of Public Health
Bureau of Maternal and Child Health
3500 North Logan St.
Lansing, MI 48914

Minnesota Department of Health
Crippled Children's Services
717 Delaware Street, SE
Minneapolis, MN 55440

Mississippi State Board of Health
Bureau of Family Health Services
Crippled Children's Services
P.O. Box 1700
Jackson, MS 39205

Missouri Department of Social Services
Division of Health
Crippled Children's Services
P.O. Box 570
Broadway State Office Building
Jefferson City, MO 65101

Montana Department of Health and Environmental
Sciences
Health Services Division
Maternal and Child Health
Cogswell Building
Helena, MT 59601

Nebraska Department of Public Welfare
Services for Crippled Children
301 Centennial Mall
Lincoln, NE 68509

Nevada State Department of Human Resources
Division of Public Health
505 East King St.
Carson City, NV 89010

New Hampshire State Department of Health/Welfare
Division of Public Health
61 South Spring St.
Concord, NH 03301

New Jersey State Department of Health
Crippled Children's Program
Health and Agricultural Building
Trenton, NJ 08625

New Mexico State Health Agency
Health and Environment Department
P.O. Box 968
Sante Fe, NM 87501

New York State Department of Health
Bureau of Medical Rehabilitation
Empire State Plaza
Tower Building
Albany, NY 12237

North Carolina Department of Human Resources
Crippled Children's Section
Division of Health Services
P.O. Box 2091
Raleigh, NC 27602

North Dakota Social Service Board
State Capitol Building
Bismarck, ND 58501

Ohio State Department of Health
Division of Maternal and Child Health
P.O. Box 118
450 East Town St.
Columbus, OH 43215

Oklahoma Department of Institutions, Social and
Rehabilitative Services
Crippled Children's Unit
P.O. Box 25352
Oklahoma City, OK 73125

Oregon Crippled Children's Division
University of Oregon Medical School
3181 Southwest Sam Jackson Park Rd.
Portland, OR 97201

Pennsylvania State Department of Health
Bureau of Children's Services
Children's Rehabilitation Services
407 South Cameron St.
Harrisburg, PA 17120

Rhode Island Department of Health
Division of Child Health
75 Davis St.
Providence, RI 02908

South Carolina Department of Health and
Environmental Control
Children's Services
J. Marion Sims Building
Columbia, SC 29201

South Dakota State Department of Health
Division of Health Services
Joe Foss Building
Pierre, SD 57501

Tennessee State Department of Public Health
Crippled Children's Services
347 Cordell Hull Building
Nashville, TN 37219

Texas Department of Health
Crippled Children's Program
1100 West 49th St.
Austin, TX 78576

Utah State Division of Health
Crippled Children's Services
44 Medical Dr.
Salt Lake City, UT 84113

Vermont Department of Health
Child Health Services
115 Colchester Ave.
Burlington, VT 05402

Virginia State Department of Health
Division of Hospital Medical Services
Bureau of Crippled Children's Services
109 Governor St.
Richmond, VA 23219

Washington Department of Social and Health Services
Division of Health Services
Child Health Section
Olympia, WA 98504

West Virginia State Department of Welfare
Division of Crippled Children's Services

1212 Lewis St., Morris Square
Charleston, WV 25301

Wisconsin State Department of Public Instruction
Bureau for Crippled Children
126 Langdon St.
Madison, WI 53702

Wyoming State Department of Health/Social Services
Division of Health and Medical Services
Hathaway Office Building
Cheyenne, WY 82002

STATE DEVELOPMENTAL DISABILITIES AGENCIES

Alabama Department of Mental Health
Developmental Disabilities Program
502 Washington St.
Montgomery, AL 36130

Alaska Department Health and Social Services
Developmental Disabilities Program
Pouch H-04
Juneau, AK 99811

Arizona Department of Economic Security
Developmental Disabilities Program
P.O. Box 6123
Phoenix, AZ 85005

Arkansas Department of Social and Rehabilitation Services Developmental Disabilities Program
Waldon Building
7th and Main
Little Rock, AR 72201

California State Health and Welfare Agency
Developmental Disabilities Program
915 Capitol Mall
Sacramento, CA 95814

Colorado Dept of Institutions
Developmental Disabilities Program
4150 South Lowell Blvd.
Denver, CO 80236

Connecticut Department of Retardation
Developmental Disabilities Program
79 Elm St.
Hartford, CT 06115

Delaware Department of Health and Social Services
Developmental Disabilities Program
Delaware State Hospital
New Castle, DE 19720

District Office of Social Services
Developmental Disabilities Program
122 C St., NW
Washington, DC 20004

Florida Department of Health and Rehabilitation Services
Developmental Disabilities Program
1311 Winewood Blvd.
Tallahassee, FL 32301

Georgia Department of Human Resources
Division of Mental Health and Mental Retardation
Developmental Disabilities Program
47 Trinity Ave., SW
Atlanta, GA 30334

Hawaii State Department of Health
Children's Health Services Division
Developmental Disabilities Program
P.O. Box 3378
Honolulu, HI 96801

Idaho Department of Health and Welfare
Developmental Disabilities Program
State House
Boise, ID 83720

Illinois Department of Mental Health
Developmental Disabilities Program
401 South Spring St.
Springfield, IL 62706

Indiana Department of Mental Health
Division of Mental Retardation and Other Development Disabilities
5 Indiana Square
Indianapolis, IN 46204

Iowa Office for Planning and Programs
Developmental Disabilities Program
523 East 12th St.
Des Moines, IA 50319

Kansas Department of Social and Rehabilitation Services
Director of Institutions
Developmental Disabilities Program
State Office Building
Topeka, KS 66612

Kentucky Bureau for Health Services
Developmental Disabilities Program
275 East Main St.
Frankfort, KY 40601

Louisiana Health and Human Resources Administration
Division of Mental Retardation Developmental Disabilities Program
P.O. Box 44215
Baton Rouge, LA 70802

Maine Department of Mental Health and Correction
Bureau of Mental Retardation
Developmental Disabilities Program
State Office Building
Augusta, ME 04330

Maryland Department of Health and Mental Hygiene
Developmental Disabilities Program
301 West Preston St.
Baltimore, MD 21201

Massachusetts Division of Physical Affairs
Developmental Disabilities Program
1 Ashburton Place
Boston, MA 02108

Michigan Department of Mental Health
Developmental Disabilities Program
Lewis-Cass Building
Lansing, MI 48926

Minnesota State Planning Agency
Developmental Disabilities Program

200 Capitol Square Building
550 Cedar St.
St. Paul, MN 55101

Mississippi Department of Mental Health
Developmental Disabilities Program
607 Lee Building
Jackson, MS 39201

Missouri Department of Mental Health
Developmental Disabilities Program
2002 Missouri Blvd., P.O. Box 687
Jefferson City, MO 65101

Montana Department of Social and Rehabilitation Services
Developmental Disabilities Program
P.O. Box 4210
Helena, MT 59601

Nebraska Department of Health
Developmental Disabilities Program
P.O. Box 95007
Lincoln, NE 68509

Nevada Department of Human Resources
Developmental Disabilities Program
600 Kinkead Building
Carson City, NV 89710

New Hampshire Department of Health and Welfare
Division of Mental Health
Developmental Disabilities Program
105 Pleasant St.
Concord, NH 03301

New Jersey Department of Human Resources
Division of Mental Retardation
Developmental Disabilities Program
222 South Warren St.
Capitol Place 1
Trenton, NJ 08625

New Mexico Department of Education
Division of Vocational Rehabilitation
Developmental Disabilities Program
P.O. Box 1830
Santa Fe. NM 87503

New York Office of Mental Retardation and Developmental Disabilities
Developmental Disabilities Program
44 Holland Ave.
Albany, NY 12208

North Carolina Developmental
Disabilities Council Staff
325 North Salisbury St.
Raleigh, NC 27611

North Dakota Department of Health
Developmental Disabilities Program
909 Basin Ave.
Bismarck, ND 58505

Ohio Department of Mental Health and Mental Retardation
Developmental Disabilities Program
30 East Broad St.
Columbus, OH 43215

Oklahoma Department of Institutions, Social and Rehabilitation Services
Developmental Disabilities Program
Sequoyah Memorial Office Building
P.O. Box 25352
Oklahoma City, OK 73125

Oregon Mental Retardation Services and Developmental Disabilities
Mental Health Division Developmental Disabilities Program
2575 Bittern St., NE
Salem, OR 97310

Pennsylvania Developmental Disabilities State Administration Agency
Developmental Disabilities Program
2101 North Front St.
Harrisburg, PA 17110

Rhode Island Department of Mental Health, Retardation and Hospitals
Developmental Disabilities Program
600 New London Ave.
Cranston, RI 02920

South Carolina Office of the Governor
Division of Health and Social Development
Developmental Disabilities Program
Edgar Brown Building
Columbia, SC 29240

South Dakota Division of Mental Health and Mental Retardation
Developmental Disabilities Program
State Office Building
Pierre. SD 57501

Tennessee Department of Mental Health and Mental Retardation
Developmental Disabilities Program
501 Union Building
Nashville, TN 37219

Texas Department of Mental Health and Mental Retardation
Developmental Disabilities Program
Box 12668, Capitol Station
Austin, TX 78711

Utah Department of Social Services
Division of Family Services
Developmental Disabilities Program
151 North Temple
Salt Lake City, UT 84103

Vermont Agency of Human Services
Developmental Disabilities Program
79 River St., State Office Building
Montpelier, VT 05602

Virginia State Department of Mental Health and Mental Retardation
Developmental Disabilities Program
109 Governor St.
Richmond, VA 23219

Washington Department of Social and Health Services
Developmental Disabilities Program

Mail Stop OB-42-C
Olympia, WA 98504

West Virginia Department of Health
Developmental Disabilities Program
State Capitol
Charleston, WV 25305

Wisconsin Department of Health and Social Services
Developmental Disabilities Program
1 West Wilson St.
Madison, WI 53702

Wyoming Department of Health and Social Services
Division of Mental Health/Mental Retardation
Developmental Disabilities Program
Hathaway Building
Cheyenne, WY 82002

STATE VOCATIONAL REHABILITATION PROGRAMS

Alabama Rehabilitation and Crippled Children Services
P.O. Box 11586
Montgomery, AL 36111

Alaska Office of Vocational Rehabilitation
Pouch F, Mail Station 0581
Juneau, AK 99811

Arizona Rehabilitation Services Bureau
Department of Economic Security
1400 West Washington St.
Phoenix, AZ 85007

Arkansas Department of Human Services
Rehabilitation Services Division
1801 Rebsamen Park Rd.
P.O. Box 3781
Little Rock, AR 72203

California Department of Rehabilitation
830 K St. Mall
Sacramento, CA 98514

Colorado Department of Social Services
Division of Rehabilitation
1571 Sherman St.
Denver, CO 80203

Connecticut State Department of Education
Division of Vocational Rehabilitation
600 Asylum Ave.
Hartford, CT 06105

Delaware Department of Labor
Division of Vocational Rehabilitation
820 North French St.
Wilmington, DE 19801

District of Columbia Department of Human Resources
Vocational Rehabilitation Services Administration
122 C. St., NW
Washington, D.C. 20001

Florida Department of Health and Rehabilitation Services
Office of Vocational Rehabilitation

1323 Winewood Blvd.
Tallahassee, FL 32301

Georgia Department of Human Resources
Division of Vocational Rehabilitation
629 State Office Building
Atlanta, GA 30334

Guam Department of Vocational Rehabilitation
P.O. Box 10-C
Agana, GU 96910

Hawaii Department of Social Services
Vocational Rehabilitation and Services for the Blind
Queen Liliuokalani Building
P.O. Box 339
Honolulu, HI 96809

Idaho Division of Vocational Rehabilitation
1501 McKinney
Boise, ID 83704

Illinois Department of Rehabilitation Services
623 East Adams St.
P.O. Box 1587
Springfield, IL 62706

Indiana Rehabilitation Services
P.O. Box 7070
Indianapolis, IN 46204

Iowa Department of Public Instruction
Rehabilitation Education and Services Branch
510 East 12th St.
Des Moines, IA 50316

Kansas Department of Social and Rehabilitation Services
Division of Vocational Rehabilitation
2700 West 6th, Biddle Building
Topeka, KS 66606

Kentucky Department of Education
Bureau of Vocational Rehabilitation Services
Capital Plaza Office Tower
Frankfort, KY 40601

Louisiana Department of Health and Human Services
Division of Rehabilitation Services
P.O. Box 44371
Baton Rouge, LA 70804

Maine Bureau of Rehabilitation
32 Winthrop St.
Augusta, ME 04330

Maryland Division of Vocational Rehabilitation
Box 8717, BWI Airport
Baltimore, MD 21240

Massachusetts Rehabilitation Commission
20 Providence St.
Statler Office Building
Boston, MA 02116

Michigan Department of Education
Vocational Rehabilitation Service
P.O. Box 30010
Lansing, MI 48909

Minnesota Division of Vocational Rehabilitation
Department of Economic Security
444 Lafayette Rd.

Space Center
St. Paul, MN 55101

Mississippi Division of Vocational Rehabilitation
932 North State St.
P.O. Box 1698
Jackson, MS 39205

Missouri State Department of Education
Division of Vocational Rehabilitation
2401 East McCarty
Jefferson City, MO 65101

Montana Social and Rehabilitation Services
Rehabilitation Services Division
P.O. Box 4210
Helena, MT 59601

Nebraska State Department of Education
Division of Rehabilitation Services
301 Centennial Mall
Lincoln, NE 68509

Nevada Department of Human Resources
Rehabilitation Division
Kinkead Building
505 East King St.
Carson City, NV 89701

New Hampshire State Department of Education
Division of Vocational Rehabilitation
105 Loudon Rd.
Concord, NH 03301

New Jersey Department of Labor and Industry
Division of Vocational Rehabilitation Services
Labor and Industry Building
John Fitch Plaza
Trenton, NJ 08625

New Mexico Department of Education
Vocational Rehabilitation
231 Washington Ave.
P.O. Box 1830
Santa Fe, NM 87503

New York Department of Education
Office of Vocational Rehabilitation
99 Washington Ave.
Albany, NY 12230

North Carolina Department of Human Resources
Division of Vocational Rehabilitation
State Office
620 North West St., Box 26053
Raleigh, NC 27611

North Dakota Division of Vocational Rehabilitation
1025 North 3rd St., Box 1037
Bismarck, ND 58501

Ohio Rehabilitation Services Commission
4656 Heaton Rd.
Columbus, OH 43229

Oklahoma Department of Institutions, Rehabilitation Services
Division of Rehabilitation and Visual Services
P.O. Box 25352
Oklahoma City, OK 73125

Oregon Department of Human Resources
Vocational Rehabilitation Division
2045 Silverton Rd., NE
Salem, OR 97310

Pennsylvania Bureau of Vocational Rehabilitation
Labor and Industry Building
7th & Forster Sts.
Harrisburg, PA 17120

Puerto Rico Department of Social Services
Vocational Rehabilitation Services
P.O. Box 118
Hato Rey, PR 00919

Rhode Island Vocational Rehabilitation Division
40 Fountain St.
Providence, RI 02903

South Carolina Vocational Rehabilitation Department
3600 Forest Dr.
P.O. Box 4945
Columbia, SC 29240

South Dakota Department of Vocational Rehabilitation
Richard F. Kneip Building
Illinois St.
Pierre, SD 57501

Tennessee Division of Vocational Rehabilitation
1808 West End Building
Nashville, TN 37203

Texas Rehabilitation Commission
118 East Riverdale Dr.
Austin, TX 78704

Utah State Office of Education
Division of Rehabilitation Sevices
250 East Fifth South
Salt Lake City, UT 84111

Vermont Department of Social and Rehabilitation Services
Vocational Rehabilitation Division
103 South Main St.
Montpelier, VT 05676

Virginia Department of Rehabilitation Services
4901 Fitzhugh Ave.
P.O. Box 11045
Richmond, VA 23230

Virgin Islands Department of Social Welfare
Division of Vocational Rehabilitation
P.O. Box 539
St. Thomas, VI 00801

Washington Department of Social and Health Services
Division of Vocational Rehabilitation
P.O. Box 1788 (Mail Stop 31-C)
Olympia, WA 98504

West Virginia State Board of Education
State Captiol Complex
Charleston, WV 25305

Wisconsin Department of Health and Social Services
131 West Wilson St.
Madison, WI 53702

Wyoming Department of Health and Social Services
Hathaway Building West
Cheyenne, WY 82002

STATE VOCATIONAL REHABILITATION PROGRAMS
Serving the Blind and Visually Impaired

Arizona Department of Economic Security
Rehabilitation Services Bureau
Section of Rehabilitation for the Blind and Visually Impaired
P.O. Box 6123
Phoenix, AZ 85005

Arkansas Department of Social and Rehabilitation Services
Office for Blind/Visually Impaired
411 Victory Street, P.O. Box 3237
Little Rock, AR 72203

Connecticut Board of Education
Services for the Blind
170 Ridge Rd.
Wethersfield, CT 06109

Delaware Department of Health and Social Services
305 West Eighth St.
Wilmington, DE 19801

Florida Department of Education
Office of Blind Services
2571 Executive Center Circle, East
Howard Building
Tallahassee, FL 32301

Idaho Commission for the Blind
Statehouse
Boise, ID 83704

Iowa Commission for the Blind
Fourth and Keosauqua
Des Moines, IA 50309

Kansas Department of Social and Rehabilitation Services
Services for the Blind and Visually Handicapped
Biddle Building
2700 West 6th St.
Topeka, KS 66606

Kentucky Bureau of Blind Services
State Office Building Annex
Frankfort, KY 40601

Louisiana Department of Health and Human Resources
Office of Human Development Services
Blind Services Program
1755 Florida St.
Baton Rouge, LA 70821

Massachusetts Commission for the Blind
110 Tremont St.
Boston, MA 02108

Michigan Department of Labor
Commission for the Blind
309 North Washington Ave.
Lansing, MI 48909

Minnesota Department of Public Welfare
1745 University Ave.
St. Paul, MN 55104

Mississippi Board of Education
Vocational Rehabilitation for the Blind
P.O. Box 4872
Jackson, MS 39125

Missouri Bureau for the Blind
Division of Family Services
619 East Capital
Jefferson City, MO 65101

Montana Department of Social and Rehabilitation Services
Visual Services Division
P.O. Box 4210
Helena, MT 59601

Nebraska Department of Education
Division of Rehabilitation
Services for the Visually Impaired
1047 South St.
Lincoln, NE 68502

New Jersey Commission for the Blind and Visually Impaired
1100 Raymond Blvd.
Newark, NJ 07102

New York Commission for the Visually Handicapped
State Department of Social Services
40 North Pearl St.
Albany, NY 12243

North Carolina Department of Human Resources
Division of Services for the Blind
410 North Boylan Ave.
P.O. Box 2658
Raleigh, NC 27602

Oregon Commission for the Blind
535 South East 12th Ave.
Portland, OR 97214

Pennsylvania Department of Public Welfare
Bureau for the Visually Handicapped
P.O. Box 2675
Harrisburg, PA 17120

Rhode Island Department of Social and Rehabilitation Services
Services for the Blind and Visually Impaired
46 Aborn St.
Providence, RI 02003

South Carolina Commission for the Blind
1430 Confederate Ave.
Columbia, SC 29201

Tennessee Department of Human Services
303–304 State Office Building
Nashville, TN 37219

Texas State Commission for the Blind
P.O. Box 12866, Capitol Station
Austin, TX 78711

Utah State Office of Education
309 East First South
Salt Lake City, UT 84111

Vermont Department of Social and Rehabilitation
Services
Division for the Blind and Visually Handicapped
Osgood Building, Waterbury Complex
103 South Main St.
Waterbury, VT 05676

Virginia Commission for the Visually Handicapped
3003 Parkwood Ave.
P.O. Box 7388
Richmond, VA 23221

Washington State Commission for the Blind
3411 South Alaska St.
Seattle, WA 98118

MULTI-STATE CENTERS FOR DEAF-BLIND CHILDREN
(States not included are listed in Single State Centers for
the Deaf, Blind, below.)

New England Region
Connecticut, Maine, Massachusetts, New Hampshire,
Rhode Island, Vermont
Perkins School for the Blind
175 North Beacon St.
Watertown, MA 02172

Midwest Region
Indiana, Michigan, Minnesota, Wisconsin
Michigan Department of Education
Davenport Building
Ottawa and Capitol Sts.
Lansing, MI 48933

South Atlantic Region
District of Columbia, Maryland, North Carolina, South
Carolina, Virginia, West Virginia
North Carolina Department of Public Instruction
Bunn-Hatch Building.
327 Hillsboro St.
Raleigh, NC 27611

Mid-Atlantic Region
Delaware, New Jersey, New York, Puerto Rico, Virgin
Islands
New York Institute for Education of the Blind
999 Pelham Pkwy.
Bronx, NY 10469

South Central Region
Arkansas, Iowa, Louisiana, Missouri, Oklahoma
South Central Regional Deaf-Blind Center
2930 Turtle Creek Plaza
Dallas, TX 75204

Southeast Region
Alabama, Florida, Georgia, Kentucky, Mississippi,
Tennessee

Alabama Institute for the Deaf-Blind
Box 698
Talladega, AL 35160

Southwest Region
Arizona, California, Guam, Hawaii, Nevada, Trust
Territories
California Department of Education
721 Capitol Mall
Sacramento, CA 96814

Mountain Plains Region
Idaho, Kansas, Montana, Nebraska, New Mexico,
North Dakota, South Dakota, Utah, Wyoming
165 Cook St.
Denver, CO 80203

SINGLE-STATE CENTERS FOR DEAF-BLIND

Alaska
Alaska State Center for Deaf-Blind Children
1111 Dowling Rd.
Anchorage 99502

Colorado
Colorado Department of Education
State Office Building
201 East Colfax
Denver 80203

Illinois
Illinois Office of Education
100 North 1st St.
Springfield 62777

Ohio
Ohio Department of Education
Division of Special Education
933 High St.
Worthington 43085

Oregon
University of Oregon
Health, Science and Child Development Center
707 Gaines Rd.
Portland 97210

Pennsylvania
Pennsylvania Department of Education
P.O. Box 911
Harrisburg 17126

Texas
Texas Education Agency
201 East 11th St.
Austin 78701

Washington
Educational School District 121
1410 South 200th
Seattle 98148

Chapter 6

Veterans' Benefits and Services

In gratitude for their service to the nation, the United States offers more help of all kinds to ex-members of its armed forces than any other country in the world. Included among the many benefits and services are: financial compensation; vocational rehabilitation and counseling for disabled veterans; education allowances under the GI Bill; preference in hiring for federal, state and municipal jobs; help in getting employment or re-employment in private industry; low-cost life insurance; government-guaranteed housing loans; free medical and dental services for eligible veterans; care in veterans' hospitals and nursing homes; funeral and burial assistance and continuing aid for survivors.

The major benefits and services are examined in detail in this chapter. Federal, state and local programs are included. The chapter concludes with a section on the voluntary veterans' organizations that have been recognized by Congress and the Veterans Administration as official representatives of ex-service members in obtaining the various forms of aid.

Almost every man and woman who has served in the armed forces will find new and valuable information in this section.

Contents

The Veterans Administration: What It Is and Does

The major share of veterans' benefits and services is administered by a single federal agency, the Veterans Administration (VA), with headquarters in Washington, DC, and offices all over the country. Established in 1930, the VA was designed to bring together under a single agency all the various veterans' programs put into motion since the first pensions were authorized by the Continental Congress in 1776 for men disabled during the Revolutionary War. Over the years the VA and its predecessor agencies have spent an estimated $350 billion for benefits and services to veterans, their dependents and survivors. Of that figure, $155 billion was generated by World War II alone.

Today the VA has become the largest of all independent federal agencies, with 203,000 full-time and 31,000 part-time employees (including nearly 87,000 veterans). Only the Department of Defense has a larger manpower pool. Some 90 percent of those who work for the VA are associated with what is undoubtedly its most visible service, the veterans' health-care system, the largest medical organization in the nation (see page 237). The balance of the VA employees staff the agency's Washington, DC, headquarters, its 72 field offices and the 108 units of the National Cemetery System, which the VA took over from the Department of the Army in 1973. A directory of VA regional offices appears on page 251. National cemeteries are listed on page 254.

With a budget of over $20 billion a year—more than twice the amount Congress appropriated to operate the entire federal government in 1940—the VA ranks behind only the Departments of Defense, Health and Human Services, Labor, and Treasury in annual expenditures. Some 66 percent of the agency's outlays go for direct benefits such as disability compensation, pensions and education checks; 30 percent is spent on hospital and medical care. (Of the remainder, 1 percent is allotted to hospital and cemetery construction and 3 percent to general operations.)

In a typical recent year, a total of more than 5 million veterans, their widows, their children and the parents of deceased veterans received compensation or pension payments. Of these, 178,000 were survivors of the Vietnam era, more than 2.6 million were World War II veterans and their dependents, and approximately 200 were survivors of men who served in the Civil War more than a century ago. During that same year, VA hospitals treated more than 1.3 million patients; VA nursing homes and domiciliaries cared for 78,000 veterans; outpatient clinics registered more than 15 million visits. Burial plots were provided for 40,000 veterans in VA cemeteries, and financial assistance was given to thousands of families who chose to bury deceased veterans elsewhere.

Eligibility for Veterans' Benefits

To qualify for a particular Veterans Administration benefit, you must have served on active duty for a specified time in a regular or reserve component of one of the following branches of the services of the United States: the Army, Navy, Air Force, Marine Corps, Coast Guard, National Oceanic and Atmospheric Administration Corps, or the Public Health Service. Certain civilian employees of the armed forces also qualify for limited benefits. The Women's Air Service Pilots of the World War II era, for example, receive limited medical benefits and burial allowances.

All benefits payable to veterans or their dependents, with the exception of insurance and certain medical programs, require the veteran to have been separated or retired from the service under conditions "other than dishonorable." Thus, an *honorable discharge* or a *general discharge* qualifies a veteran; a *dishonorable discharge* does not. A veteran with a *bad conduct discharge* may or may not qualify for benefits, depending upon a special determination by the VA of the circumstances of the veteran's separation from the service.

Review of Discharges

Each of the services maintains a Discharge Review Board which has authority to change or modify all discharges except those that are medical in origin or awarded by a general court-martial. A dissatisfied veteran (or the surviving spouse, next of kin or legal representative if the veteran is deceased or incompetent to act in his or her own behalf) may apply for a review of discharge by writing to the military department concerned. The application should be made on Department of Defense Form 293, obtainable at any VA office.

A veteran discharged for unauthorized absence from duty in excess of 180 days is ineligible for VA benefits regardless of any action taken by a Discharge Review Board, unless strong, mitigating evidence is given.

Veterans with disabilities incurred in or aggravated during active service may qualify for medical or related benefits if the conditions under which they were discharged were "other than dishonorable."

How to Apply for Benefits

For information or assistance in applying for any of the benefits described in this chapter, veterans (or their dependents or survivors) should call, visit or write to a Veterans Benefits Counselor at the nearest office of the Veterans Administration listed under "U.S. Government" in telephone directories. Application for medical or dental care can be made directly at any VA hospital or VA station with medical facilities. Or you can call the local representative of a major veterans' organization—such as the American Legion; the Veterans of Foreign Wars; American Veterans of World War II,

Korea and Viet Nam; or the Disabled American Veterans—for information and application forms. The American Red Cross can also help you. Veterans living or traveling in foreign countries (except the Philippines, where there is a VA office) should call or write a letter to the nearest U.S. embassy or consulate.

In processing any application for benefits, the VA will need the following information: the veteran's full name; VA file number or Social Security number; military service number; dates of service; date and place of birth, and current address.

When to Apply for Benefits

Some veterans' benefits may be applied for any time after separation from service, but others must be acted on within certain time limits, as shown on page 223.

If you intend to go back to your old civilian job, for example, you must apply to your former employer within 90 days of separation from active duty in order to come within the protection of federal re-employment legislation. If you expect to be out of work for a while, either awaiting rehiring by your former company or searching for a new job, you can qualify for unemployment compensation and receive a weekly income to meet your basic living needs. Because the amounts and duration of payments vary widely from state to state (see Chapter 2), it is wise to inquire immediately after separation at your nearest state employment office.

Servicemen's Group Life Insurance, which is automatically issued to all members of the uniformed services, may be converted to Veterans Group Life Insurance after separation. SGLI coverage continues without cost for 120 days. Application for conversion to VGLI (accompanied by initial premium) requires no health statement if submitted within 120 days. An application may be submitted past that time—up to a one-year limit—but must be accompanied with the initial premium payment and evidence of insurability.

You may take advantage of the GI Bill to

America's Wars Total

The magnitude of the task of compensating and caring for the nation's veterans and their dependents is indicated by the figures shown here and on the opposite page. Nearly 39 million Americans have served in the nation's wars. More than 65 percent of them were alive in 1981, and at that time, approximately 93 million persons—veterans, dependents and survivors of deceased veterans—were potentially eligible for VA benefits and services. Moreover, as past experience has shown, the care of veterans and their dependents spans the centuries. The last Revolutionary War veteran did not die until 1911. The last widow of a veteran of the War of 1812 lived until 1936, and the last dependent from that war did not pass away until 1946, more than 130 years after that conflict ended.

War Participants* 38,924,000
Deaths in Service 1,081,000
Living War Veterans 25,789,000
Living Ex-Servicemembers 30,083,000

Veterans and Dependents on the
Compensation and Pension Rolls as of October 1, 1981

VETERANS		CHILDREN	PARENTS	SURVIVING SPOUSES
Civil War (approx. 75% Union, 25% Confederate)		118		48
Indian Wars		9		29
Spanish-American War	86	1,013		10,578
World War I	166,497	18,869	94	452,653
World War II	1,800,760	195,298	63,943	493,496
Korean Conflict	316,758	109,162	17,395	57,561
Vietnam Era	585,645	93,758	20,054	52,410
Total (as of October 1, 1981)	3,154.029[a]	432,319[b]	112,523[c]	1,107,135[d]

FOOTNOTES:
*Persons who served in more than one war period are counted only once.
(a) Includes 284,283 peacetime veterans with service between January 31, 1955 and August 5, 1964 and veterans with Mexican Border Service between May 9, 1916 and April 5, 1917, and peacetime veterans with service beginning after May 7, 1975.
(b) Includes 14,092 children of deceased peacetime veterans;
(c) Includes 11,037 parents of deceased peacetime veterans;
(d) Includes 40,360 surviving spouses of deceased peacetime veterans;

AMERICAN REVOLUTION
(1775-1784)
Participants 290,000
Deaths in Service 4,000
Last Veteran, Daniel F. Blakeman, died
4/5/1869, age 109
Last Widow, Catherine S. Damon, died
11/11/06, age 92
Last Dependent, Phoebe M. Palmeter, died
4/25/11, age 90

WAR OF 1812 (1812-1815)
Participants 287,000
Deaths in Service 2,000
Last Veteran, Hiram Cronk, died 5/13/05,
age 105
Last Widow, Carolina King, died 6/28/36,
age not available
Last Dependent, Esther A.H. Morgan, died
3/12/46, age 89

MEXICAN WAR (1846-1848)
Participants 79,000
Deaths in Service 13,000
Last Veteran, Owen Thomas Edgar, died
9/3/29, age 98
Last Widow, Lena James Theobald, died
6/20/63, age 89
Last Dependent, Jesse G. Bivens, died
11/1/62, age 94

INDIAN WARS
(Approx. 1817-1898)
Participants 106,000
Deaths in Service 1,000
Last Veteran, Fredrak Fraske, died 6/18/73,
age 101

CIVIL WAR (1861-1865)
Participants (Union) 2,213,000
Deaths in Service (Union) 364,000

Participants (Confederate) 1,000,000*
Deaths in Service (Confederate) . . 133,821*
Last Union Veteran, Albert Woolson, died
8/2/56, age 109

*Authoritative statistics for Confederate
Forces not available. Estimated 28,000 Confederate personnel died in Union prisons.

SPANISH-AMERICAN WAR
(1898-1902)
Participants 392,000
Deaths in Service 11,000
Living Veterans 86

WORLD WAR I (1917-1918)
Participants 4,744,000
Deaths in Service 116,000
Living Veterans 449,000

WORLD WAR II
(9/16/40 thru 7/25/47)
Participants . . . . 16,535,000(e)
Deaths in Service 406,000
Living Veterans . . . . 12,170,000(f)

KOREAN CONFLICT
(6/27/50 thru 1/31/55)
Participants . . . . 6,807,000(e)
Deaths in Service 55,000
Living Veterans . . . . 5,781,000(fh)

VIETNAM ERA
(8/5/64 thru 5/7/75)
Participants . . . . 9,834,000(g)
Deaths in Service
Due to hostile forces 47,000
Due to other causes 62,000
Living Veterans . . . . 9,087,000(h)

(e) 1,476,000 served in WW II and Korean Conflict.
(f) 1,167,000 served in WW II and Korean Conflict.
(g) 887,000 served in Korean Conflict.
(h) 552,000 served in Korean Conflict and Vietnam Era.

complete high school or college or to learn a trade at any time up to 10 years after separation from service, but remember that coverage under the current law expires on December 31, 1989. There are no limits on GI housing loans, medical care, disability compensation or assistance in finding a job. You may apply for these benefits at any time.

Appealing a Benefits Claim

If you are dissatisfied with a ruling regarding a claim for benefits, you may present your case to the final authority in such matters, the VA's Board of Veterans Appeals. The Board seeks to resolve all reasonable doubts in the veteran's favor. Personal hearings are scheduled on request. An appellant may be represented, without charge, by an accredited representative of a veterans' organization or other service organization recognized by the Administrator of Veterans Affairs (see list under "National Service Organizations," page 250). An attorney may be employed to assist in the claim; but by law, such legal services are subject to a maximum fee.

Education and Training Programs

Among the most popular and productive benefits for veterans have been the various programs collectively known as the GI Bill. Since 1944, when the first such program became law, some 18 million Americans have taken advantage of its major provision: government-sponsored education costing a total of more than $54 billion—$18 billion more than the United States spent to fight World War I. The recipients have gained knowledge, skills and degrees that have enabled them to obtain better jobs, and the government sees the money as well spent, noting that the additional income taxes from veterans whose earning capacities have been increased by the GI Bill amount to several times the government's original investment in education.

Of the total number of beneficiaries of the GI Bill, some 7.8 million have been World War II veterans, 2.4 million have been veterans of the Korean conflict and 7.8 million have been veterans of the post-Korean and Vietnam era, as well as service personnel on active duty. More than 8 million veterans have used the GI Bill to attend college, including 4.7 million post-Korean and Vietnam vets and active service personnel. Proportionately, Vietnam-era servicemen and women have been the most active beneficiaries of the program, with 65 percent of those eligible taking some form of training, compared with about 50 percent for World War II veterans and 43 percent for Korean vets. In addition, more than 800,000 veterans who have suffered service-connected disabilities have been given counseling and training under vocational rehabilitation programs to enable them to hold productive jobs in civilian life. Also assisted by the VA in furthering their education have been nearly 400,000 sons, daughters, widows and wives of veterans who died or were totally disabled as a result of their military service.

Two Basic Educational Plans

The VA administers two basic programs for those who are seeking assistance in education or vocational training. If your period of service occurred at any time from 1955 through 1976, you may qualify for the current GI Bill, under which VA payments largely cover educational costs. If you entered the service in 1977 or later, you are eligible for the newer Veterans Educational Assistance Program, under which the U.S. government pays $2 for every $1 you contribute.

The GI Bill

To be eligible for the GI Bill now in effect, you must have had at least 181 days of continuous service on active duty. Part of your service must have occurred after January 31, 1955, and all of it must have been completed by January 1, 1977. Your discharge must have occurred under conditions that were not dis-

Deadlines for Veterans' Benefits

Veterans just released from active duty have:

90 days	To apply to a former employer for reemployment.
120 days	To retain insurance protection by converting Servicemen's Group Life Insurance to Veterans' Group Life Insurance without meeting health requirements. If totally disabled at time of separation, conversion may be made within one year from discharge.
1 year	From date of notice of VA disability rating to obtain GI life insurance because of service connected disability.
90 days	To file for VA dental treatment. No time limit for trauma or combat caused conditions, or for former prisoners of war.
3 years	To apply for correction of military records believed to contain an error or injustice.
12 years	To complete Vocational Rehabilitation, except for certain cases of serious disability or delay in establishing eligibility.
10 years	To complete GI Bill education. Course must be started in time to finish in ten years. The final entry date for the program was December 31, 1981.
15 years	To apply for review of discharge.
Limited Time	To receive unemployment compensation. Amount of benefit and payment period vary between states. Apply immediately after separation.
No Limit	To obtain VA-guaranteed housing loans.
No Limit	To file a pension claim that is not service-connected.
No Limit	To file a compensation claim for injury or disease.
No Limit	To file for Federal Civil Service Veterans Preference.
No Limit	To obtain VA hospital care.
No Limit	To obtain special assistance in finding employment or a place in a job training program.
No Limit	To convert term life insurance to permanent insurance.

Monthly Allowances Under the G.I. Bill

TYPE OF EDUCATION	No. Deps.	1 Dep.	2 Deps.	Each Add. Dep.
Institutional				
Full-time	$342	$407	$464	$29
Three-quarter	257	305	348	22
Half-time	171	204	232	15
Cooperative	276	323	367	21
Apprenticeship				
Or On-The-Job Training				
1st 6 Months	249	279	305	13
2nd 6 Months	186	217	243	13
3rd 6 Months	124	155	180	13
4th and Any Succeeding				
6-Month Period	62	92	119	13
Farm Cooperative				
Full-time	276	323	367	21
Three-quarter	207	242		15
Half-time	126	147	167	10

Correspondence . . . . Entitlement charged at rate of one month for each $342 paid.

Flight . . . . Entitlement charged at rate of one month for each $317 paid.

Service personnel on Active Duty or less than Half time . . . . Tuition cost, not to exceed rate of $342 for full-time; $257 for ¾ time; $171 for ½ time or less but more than ¼ time; $86 for ¼ time or less.

honorable. (A veteran with less than 181 days' service may be eligible if he or she has been released because of a service-connected disability.) You are also eligible if you enlisted in, or were assigned to, a reserve unit before January 1, 1977, started your active duty tour before January 1, 1978, and served on active duty for at least 181 days. (Servicemen and women who meet the requirements and continue on active duty may also qualify under the GI Bill.)

The 181 days cannot include time served as a cadet or midshipman in a service academy. Any period when you were assigned full-time by your service to a civilian institution for substantially civilian courses is also excluded. Time spent in training in the Reserves or

National Guard does not count unless you subsequently served on active duty for one year or more (in which case your reserve training-time counts as active duty in computing benefits).

Where You May Study

Almost any accredited institution providing education at the elementary school level or above that finds you qualified to undertake its curriculum may be approved for training under the GI Bill. This includes elementary or secondary schools, private as well as public; vocational, correspondence, business or flight schools; colleges, junior colleges, teachers' colleges and universities; professional, scientific and technical institutions; medical, law, business and other graduate schools. Flight training is restricted to veterans who enrolled prior to September 1, 1981, and who remain in the same program continuously.

Generally speaking, programs of education outside the United States may be pursued only at approved institutions at college or higher levels. Information concerning the approval of particular schools or courses may be obtained through your local VA office. Educational counseling will also be provided on request.

How Long You May Study

Any eligible veteran with 18 months or more of continuous active duty is entitled to receive 45 months of full-time educational benefits, or the equivalent in part-time benefits if the veteran is not attending school full-time. This amounts to nearly five full years at institutions that take a summer break. Veterans with less than 18 months' active duty receive 1.5 months of full-time educational benefits for each month of active duty served.

Benefits take the form of monthly education assistance allowances, which are paid directly to the veterans and out of which they pay for their tuition, fees, books and other educational and living costs. Monthly allowances are higher than normal for veterans with dependents. They are correspondingly lower for those on cooperative, apprenticeship or farm-training

programs because individuals in such programs receive pay for the hours they work.

For example, let's say that you are a veteran with two dependents: your spouse and a child. If you had 12 months of continuous service, you are entitled to 18 months of full-time benefits, or 1.5 months of benefits for every service month. If you attend an educational institution full-time, Uncle Sam will cover your expenses to the extent of $464 a month up to a total of 18 months, or roughly two school years. If you attend only half-time while holding down a job, you will receive $232 a month for a total of 36 months, or roughly four school years. (The VA considers full-time education to consist of 14 hours per semester, unless the school has certified to the agency that 12 hours is its normal full course load.)

Under the law, you are entitled to one major change in your educational program. Subsequent changes may or may not be approved by the VA. A progression from one course or program to another when the first is a prerequisite for the second is not considered a program change.

Except in special circumstances, your eligibility for educational benefits ceases 10 years from the date of your final release from active duty, or on December 31, 1989, whichever comes first. This means that you must *complete* your course of study by that time in order to receive all of the benefits coming to you. (Veterans prevented from beginning or completing a chosen program of education because of a physical or mental disability, which does not result from their own willful misconduct, may receive an extension on their limiting date.)

Veterans who must complete their high school educations or pass qualifying examinations to enter college may receive monthly educational assistance allowances without charge against their basic entitlements. Veterans who have not yet completed the eighth grade are also eligible for monthly assistance, and those who have already qualified in a program of education may receive allowances to take refresher courses in order to update their skills.

Special Programs Under the GI Bill

Correspondence courses may qualify under the GI Bill. The allowance paid by the VA is computed at 55 percent of the tuition.

If you choose an on-the-job or apprentice training program, it must be approved by the appropriate state agency and you must pursue it full-time. Your starting wage must be at least one-half that normally paid for the job, and your pay must be increased regularly until you are receiving 85 percent of the standard wage by the last month of the training period. (A two-year limit applies to the training period, but it does not affect apprenticeships.) The VA allowances are payable regardless of the wages paid by your employer.

Veterans who enroll in a school offering a farm cooperative program will receive the allowances shown in the table on page 224, but they must be employed full-time in agricultural jobs related to their courses of study.

The GI Bill will pay for flight training if it is directed toward a vocational goal in aviation. The veteran must have a private pilot's license and meet the medical requirements for a commercial pilot's license. The allowance is computed at 60 percent of the established charge for tuition. If the flight training is part of a college program, the allowance is payable at the regular institutional rates.

Tutoring and Work-Study Plans

A veteran who is taking courses above the high school level on at least a half-time basis may be reimbursed for expenses incurred for individual tutoring to make up a deficiency in a required course. Reimbursements are subject to monthly and overall maximums, $76 a month in the early 1980s, with a total limit of $911.

Under a special work-study program, veterans enrolled as full-time students may earn additional income to live on by performing part-time services for the VA itself, including helping out in VA medical centers, processing paperwork or working in the VA "outreach" program to help other veterans. Disabled veterans are given preference in the work-study program. Participants may work up to a maximum of 250 hours per enrollment term; they receive at least the hourly minimum wage prescribed by law and may be paid 40 percent of their wages in advance.

Vocational Rehabilitation

A veteran with a service-connected disability which entitles him or her to VA compensation may be eligible for the vocational rehabilitation program if the VA determines that training or other available services are needed to overcome the veteran's handicaps to employment. Once the veteran is determined eligible for the program, he or she is evaluated for rehabilitation potential. The veteran and the VA staff then work out a detailed plan to achieve the rehabilitation goal.

For some veterans, particularly the more seriously handicapped, the goal might well be greater independence in daily living. For most veterans, however, the goal will be suitable employment. They will enroll in a school or college, on-job or on-farm training or a program that combines both education and training.

During the active training phase of the rehabilitation program, and for two months afterward, the veteran will receive a subsistence allowance in addition to any VA disability compensation or military retirement pay being received. The Veterans Administration will pay all costs of tuition, books, supplies and fees for the program. Following participation in vocational rehabilitation training, the veteran may be provided further services to aid in the search for and adjustment to a job. Generally, a veteran is eligible for vocational rehabilitation for twelve years after separation from service, though extensions may be granted under certain conditions.

The Veterans Educational Assistance Program

For veterans who entered the service after December 31, 1976, the GI Bill has been replaced by the Veterans Educational Assistance Program, familiarly known as VEAP. Under this program, individuals in the service may participate in a contributory plan by setting aside from $25 to $100 each month in an educational fund. A maximum of $2,700 may be reserved. The U.S. government matches each $1 contributed by the individual with $2 of its own. Participants may make lump sum contributions while on active duty. Generally, an individual must participate in the program for at least 12 consecutive months.

A veteran who has served at least 181 days or has been released for a service-connected disability may use the money to pay educational expenses at a VA-approved institution. Service personnel who remain in the service after completing their first tour of duty may also start using their VEAP benefits. Veterans who decide not to continue their education may have their share refunded by notifying the VA. If they attend school for a while and decide to stop, the remainder of the fund may be withdrawn or left in the account for future use.

Checklist for Veterans, Dependents and Survivors

1. **Keep your address up to date:** Promptly notify the Veterans Administration, the VA insurance center that keeps your records and any other benefits sources of any change of address. This will ensure that you will continue to receive compensation checks, notices of premiums due and other communications.

2. **Safeguard your records:** Keep copies of your service record, discharge or retirement papers, insurance and benefit records and other documents in a safe and orderly file. If it is not possible to keep them all together, make a list with the title of each document and where it is located, and give the list to a family member or friend. The best place to keep valuable originals is in a safe deposit box; these should include not only service-related documents but such records as your original marriage certificate, divorce decree, spouse's death certificate, will, power of attorney, income tax returns, house deed, automobile title, commercial insurance policies and any securities you may hold for investment purposes. List the safe deposit box jointly in your name and that of your spouse or other survivor; otherwise it may be necessary to obtain a court order

before the box can be opened following your death.

3. **Keep your beneficiaries current:** When there is a change in your family picture as a result of marriage, birth, divorce or death, notify all appropriate agencies, including the Veterans Administration, the center that administers your life insurance and the source of any retirement pay or survivor benefit plans.

4. **Use the proper identification in all communications:** In any correspondence involving benefits, changes of beneficiary or claims, the veteran's full name, rank, branch and service number should appear. In correspondence with the VA, the veteran's C number should be included as well.

5. **Run a periodic check on your status:** Look over your GI and other insurance policies from time to time to make sure coverage is adequate and beneficiaries are up to date; if you hold term insurance, you may want to consider a permanent plan that may be better suited to your needs when the term expires. Every two or three years, evaluate your Social Security status and the benefits you can expect by specific retirement dates.

Matching funds are paid directly to students while they are attending school full-time. Monthly payments are determined by dividing an individual's total accumulated educational fund by the number of months in VEAP. For example, if an individual contributed $75 for 24 months, the VEAP fund would have accumulated $1,800 from the beneficiary plus $3,600 in government contributions, for a total of $5,400. Over a two-year period, this would come to $225 a month in educational assistance payments. Students attending school part-time receive proportionately smaller amounts, but the payments extend over a longer period. Benefits must be used within 10 years of release from active duty.

In recent years, many foresighted veterans-to-be have set aside at least part of the money needed to complete their education. By contributing $75 a month for three years, and having the accumulated $2,700 matched by $5,400 from Uncle Sam, an $8,100 bank account can be established.

Educational Loans

Veterans who are using their GI Bill benefits or were enrolled in VEAP prior to October 1, 1981, but are still having trouble meeting educational costs, may apply for direct loans from the Veterans Administration, provided they can show the need for such assistance based on the total resources available to them. An eligible veteran, under the non-contributory program, may borrow up to $2,500 per academic year to continue to pursue a full-time course leading to a standard college degree, or if enrolled in a course leading to a professional or vocational objective that requires at least six months to complete. Veterans enrolled in flight training, reimbursed at the rate of 60 percent, also may apply for an educational loan.

No interest accrues on the loan until repayment begins, nine months after the veteran ceases to be at least a half-time student. Interest on the unpaid balance is then payable at a modest rate (recently around 7 percent); the veteran has up to 10 years and 9 months to repay the loan, and may repay all or any part of it before the loan becomes due.

Veterans may also be eligible for other federally supported programs of financial aid, including Basic Educational Opportunity Grants, the National Direct Student Loan program, the Federal Work-Study program, the Guaranteed Student Loan program and the Supplemental Educational Opportunity Grant program. For further information on these, see Chapter 1.

Survivors' and Dependents' Education

The full range of educational benefits is available to both the survivors and the dependents of veterans whose death or permanent, total disability was service-connected, or who are listed as missing in action, captured or interned in the line of duty.

Spouses and children of such veterans may receive up to 45 months of schooling (or the equivalent of 45 months if enrolled part-time) at any VA-approved institution, including secondary schools, colleges, business or vocational schools, farm cooperatives and on-the-job programs. Monthly payments are the same as for a single veteran with no dependents (table, page 224). Persons who can demonstrate financial need may also borrow up to $2,500 per academic year under the VA loan program.

Deceased or disabled veterans' children who are between the ages of 18 and 26 are eligible for these educational benefits. Sons or daughters under 18 may qualify, provided they have completed high school or are above the prescribed age for compulsory school attendance in their states. Spouses must complete their training within ten years from the date of their eligibility. Eligible children may receive educational counseling from the VA. A child who marries continues to receive benefits, but a spouse who remarries does not (unless the remarriage is terminated by death or divorce).

Survivors of deceased veterans may also receive other benefits: monthly income under the Survivor Benefit Plan, home loans and mortgage guarantees, preference in government jobs, benefits from state veterans' agencies, privileges in Army and Navy officers' and enlisted men's messes, appointments to service academies or relief from federal income taxes for the year in which the death of the veteran occurred. (See the section on Survivor's Benefits starting on page 240, and other sections such as the one on home loans on page 233.)

Other Educational Benefits

In addition to GI educational allowances and federally sponsored loans, some states waive tuition charges for veterans at state and community colleges. Some also provide educational assistance for dependents of deceased or totally disabled veterans.

Each year a limited number of appointments to the major service academies is reserved for the sons or daughters of service people who died of war injuries. For further information, write to: Registrar, U.S. Military Academy, West Point, NY 10996; Director of Admissions, U.S. Air Force Academy, CO 80840; or Office of Candidate Guidance, U.S. Naval Academy, Annapolis, MD 21402.

Getting Your Old Job Back, or Finding a New One

If you decide to go to work rather than to school after leaving the service, you are entitled to certain well-defined rights and privileges of employment under federal law. These include the right to get your old job back with the same seniority, pay and benefits you would have had if you had not been away; assistance in finding a new job; and preference over non-veterans in qualifying for employment in federal, state and local agencies.

Re-employment Rights

The basic concept of veterans' re-employment rights was expressed by Senator Elbert Thomas of Utah during 1940 Congressional hearings on the peacetime draft. "If it is constitutional to require a man to serve in the armed forces," the Senator said, "it is not unreasonable to require the employers of such men to rehire them upon the completion of their service, since the lives and property of the employers as well as everyone else in the United States are defended by such service."

This concept, enacted into law and subsequently broadened, now applies to all veterans of the uniformed services, whether drafted or enlisted, as well as to members of military reserve units and the National Guard. All employees in private businesses and organizations are covered, as well as all holders of jobs in federal, state and local governments.

To be entitled to re-employment, you must meet certain requirements. First, you must have left a position "other than temporary" to go into service. The law does not define this phrase, but court decisions have made it clear that it covers employment expected to be continuous for an indefinite period, rather than casual and non-recurring.

Second, you will not be allowed more than a total of four years on active duty away from your job since August 1, 1961 (December 2, 1974, in the case of state or local government employees). The limitation is extended to five years if the additional time is served "at the request and for the convenience of the Federal Government."

Third, you must have satisfactorily completed your period of service, and you must have a certificate to that effect. If you were discharged, your release must have occurred under honorable conditions.

Fourth, you must be qualified to perform the duties of your former position or, if disabled while in the service, be capable of filling another job of comparable seniority, status and pay. If your skills have lapsed from disuse while you were in the service, but you can be expected to regain your former proficiency within a reasonable time after re-employment, you meet the statutory requirements. If the requirements of the job itself have changed,

Useful Publications for Veterans

Federal Benefits for Veterans and Dependents (IS-1 Fact Sheet, Veterans Administration). For sale by the Superintendent of Documents, U.S. Government Printing Office, Washington, DC 20402. Information, eligibility, current rates of compensation and allowances for most federal benefits available to veterans, their dependents and survivors.

Veterans' Re-employment Rights Handbook, U.S. Department of Labor, Labor-Management Services Administration, Government Printing Office, Washington, DC 20402. Detailed coverage of veterans' lawful rights in getting their old jobs back.

Veterans Preference in Federal Employment (EV 2). U.S. Office of Personnel Management, Government Printing Office.

Questions and Answers on Servicemen's Group Life Insurance (VA Pamphlet 29-78-1). Veterans Administration, Washington, DC 20420.

Information Pamphlet for Veterans

Group Life Insurance (VA Pamphlet 29-74-3). Veterans Administration, Washington, DC 20420.

Uniformed Services Almanac, National Guard Almanac, Reserve Forces Almanac, Retired Military Almanac. Published by Uniformed Services Almanac, Inc., P.O. Box 76, Dept. A, Washington, DC 20044. Information and advice on all aspects of service and post-retirement life, rights, benefits, restrictions and compensation rates. These handbooks, published and updated annually by a private firm, are tailored to four specific readerships, as their titles indicate, but they contain material of interest to everyone who has served in the armed forces.

Many other pamphlets and handbooks on special subjects of interest to ex-service people are available through the armed services, the Veterans Administration, the Social Security Administration, the U.S. Department of Labor and various veterans' organizations. (Addresses of the veterans' organizations are given on page 250.)

---

you must be able to meet them within a reasonable period after you return to work. If you have the minimum qualifications needed for the job, the fact that someone else who currently holds it is better qualified than you does not preclude your right to it. If it is established that the job's requirements have been increased beyond your skills, or the skills you could be expected to attain within a reasonable period, you are entitled to a job requiring skills comparable to those called for by your former job at the time you left it.

Fifth—and in many ways most important—

you must apply to your old employer *within 90 days* after separation from active duty, or if you are hospitalized following your discharge, within a minimum of a year. Reservists and National Guardsmen returning from active-duty training of three months or more, and members of the Selected Reserve returning from active-duty tours of not more than 90 days, must apply within 31 days.

Your former employer must rehire you in the position you would have attained if you had remained on the job instead of entering the service, or in a position of similar status, rather than at the level you held before going away. You must be paid at the wage scale you would have reached if your employment had not been interrupted, including all general, cost-of-living and periodic "step" increases you would have received. You are entitled to the same working conditions, pension and other benefits you would be enjoying if your employment had been continuous. Your employer must retain you on the job for at least a year, unless you are discharged for cause or laid off in order of seniority. In fairness, however, your employer's obligations may be modified by factors such as changes in the nature of the business, collective bargaining agreements and non-discriminatory personnel policies. In some instances, you may have to meet special work requirements under a collective bargaining agreement or established practice before your seniority can be adjusted.

Similar job protection is provided for National Guard and Reserve members who take leaves of absence to perform military training. This protection applies whether they are employed in private industry or by federal, state or local governments, but they must request such leaves, and be granted them, by their employers. The law provides that an employee cannot be discharged or denied any benefits of employment—including promotion, vacation time or the opportunity to make up lost overtime—solely because of his or her reserve obligation.

If you have any problems or questions concerning your re-employment rights, call or write to the Office of Veterans Re-employment Rights listed under the Labor Management Services Administration of the U.S. Department of Labor (see the "U.S. Government" section of your telephone directory, or the offices listed in Chapter 2). Detailed information and case-history examples are given in the 196-page *Veterans' Re-employment Rights Handbook* which was prepared by the Department of Labor. The helpful handbook is available at Labor Department area offices or for sale through the Superintendent of Documents, U.S. Government Printing Office, Washington, DC 20402.

Job Counseling and Placement

Veterans who need help in finding a job, or advice about career opportunities, can obtain assistance at any state employment office through a program supervised by the U.S. Department of Labor. A Veterans Employment Representative can provide job counseling, testing and information about job markets and on-the-job and apprentice training programs. Priority in referral to current employment and training opportunities is given to veterans over non-veterans, with first consideration for disabled veterans.

A list of state employment offices may be found in the directory that appears at the end of Chapter 2.

Unemployment Compensation

State employment offices also adminster the Department of Labor's unemployment compensation program for veterans. Its purpose is to provide a weekly income for a limited period to help newly discharged veterans meet basic needs while they are looking for employment. Benefits are paid from federal funds, but the actual amount and duration of payments is governed by individual state laws, which vary considerably.

To be eligible, you must have had 90 days or more of continuous active service (unless separated earlier because of a service-connected disability). You must have been released under conditions that were not dishonorable, and must be willing and able to work. Generally, unemployment benefits are not paid to veterans who are already receiving educational or vocational training allowances from the Veterans Administration.

To avoid possible loss of benefits, you should apply immediately after leaving the service at your nearest state employment office—*not* at a VA office—and present Copy #4 of your DD Form 214 to establish your type of separation from the service.

Jobs in Government

All levels of government—federal agencies and departments, as well as state, county and municipal—give veterans preferential consideration for jobs, and in certain cases that preference is extended to spouses or survivors. The advantages of this policy include additional points added to passing scores in civil service examinations, waivers of certain physical requirements for disabled veterans, first consideration for some jobs and priority for retention in case of layoffs.

Under the Veterans Preference Act of 1944, as amended, ex-servicemen and women applying for federal jobs are entitled to have five points added to their examination scores, provided they were separated under honorable conditions after service in wartime, in peacetime campaigns for which service medals were authorized or after 180 consecutive days of active duty between January 31, 1955, and October 15, 1976. (Effective October 1, 1980, veterans' preference was eliminated for non-disabled veterans who retire from service at or above the rank of major or its equivalent.)

Veterans with service-connected disabilities, and all those who were awarded the Purple Heart for wounds, are entitled to have 10 points added to their scores. Veterans with disabilities rated at 30 percent or more qualify for additional benefits. They may be appointed to federal jobs without taking competitive examinations. They are entitled to have their positions converted to career appointments, and are given preference over other veterans and non-veterans in case of layoffs. They also have the right to be notified in advance about, and to respond to, any decision in which they are deemed ineligible for a job because of the job's physical requirements.

Similar benefits, including the 10-point preference in federal exams, are extended to the wives or husbands of disabled veterans who are no longer able to work in their normal occupations. The same benefits apply to a veterans' widow or widower, provided the veteran served on active duty in wartime or under the other conditions of the Veterans Preference Act cited above. The mother of a veteran may also claim the 10-point preference if her son or daughter died while on active duty in wartime, or incurred a total service-connected disability that precludes a federal job in his or her accustomed line of work.

Many states accord veterans or members of their families similar—in some cases even greater—advantages in employment. California, for example, gives a 10-point preference in state civil service exams—15 points in the case of disabled veterans. Veterans in that state also have retention rights on employment lists. They are entitled to civil service credit for applicable military experience. They are accorded preference over non-veterans in examinations for local and state police officers and other security personnel and may be granted leaves of absence for education. For further information with respect to special benefits, check with your own state's Department of Veterans Affairs (see also "State and Local Benefits," page 247).

Affirmative Action Programs

Under the terms of the Vietnam Era Veterans' Readjustment Assistance Act of 1974, all agencies of the federal government are required to maintain affirmative action plans for the hiring and promotion of veterans who served during the Vietnam period as well as for disabled veterans of any era. A non-disabled veteran of the Vietnam era who has completed no more than 14 years of education may be hired by a federal agency without having to compete in a regular civil service examination, provided the veteran agrees to participate in a program of education or training that will qualify him or her for the job.

The act also prohibits private employers who hold federal contracts or subcontracts of $10,000 or more from discriminating against Vietnam-era and disabled veterans. The employers are, in fact, required to take positive steps toward hiring and promoting these veterans. Vietnam vets are covered by this program during the first four years after their discharge; veterans with a disability of 30 percent or more are covered throughout their working lives. Complaints may be filed with the U.S. Labor Department's Office of Federal Contract Compliance Programs, or with the Veterans' Employment Representative at a local state employment office.

The Department of Labor places disabled veterans in state employment offices, VA regional offices and at other locations in the state; their task is to locate jobless disabled veterans and inform them about training and employment opportunities. Under this "outreach" program, these staff members work with Veterans Administration personnel, veterans' organizations and community groups. The resources of state employment offices are at the staff's disposal, including "job banks" that list and describe positions available locally.

Going Into Business for Yourself

The federal government's Small Business Administration offers a number of programs designed to help individuals, including veterans, to become owners and operators of their own business enterprises. The SBA will guarantee loans from private lenders up to 90 percent of the total amount, and in certain cases make direct loans itself. The agency also provides assistance in financial, management and other business techniques. For further information, see Chapter 2 which provides a list of local SBA offices.

GI Housing and Home Improvement Loans

Veterans, and certain surviving spouses of veterans, can obtain special VA-guaranteed loans to help them with their housing needs. The loan guaranties are available for many purposes: to buy a house or condominium unit; to build a new house; to repair, alter or improve an existing house, improve a house through weatherproofing or installation of a solar heating and cooling system; to purchase a house and improve it by installing energy-saving systems; to refinance an existing home loan; to buy a mobile home with or without a lot, or to purchase a lot for a mobile home a veteran already owns. The major advantages of such VA (or "GI") mortgages are that they require little or no down payment, have generally moderate interest rates and generous repayment periods, and allow a veteran to pay off all or any part of a loan at any time without incurring a penalty.

How the Housing Loans Work

VA financing takes the form of a guarantee on a mortgage loan secured by the veteran from a mortgage company, bank, savings and loan association or other private lending institution. Both the applicant and his or her spouse must be satisfactory credit risks and have sufficient income to meet the mortgage payments along with their other expenses. The VA guarantee is limited to 60 percent of the amount of the loan for a house or condominium, up to a maximum of $27,500, and to 50 percent of a loan for a mobile home and lot, up to a maximum of $20,000.

Generally speaking, you are eligible for a loan if you served a total of 90 days on active duty during wartime, or 181 continuous days in peacetime. If you are separated from enlisted service which began after September 7, 1980, or service as an officer which began after October 16, 1981, in most cases you must have served two years to be eligible. The surviving spouse of a veteran who died as a result of a service-connected injury or disability, or who has been officially listed as missing in action or a prisoner of war for 90 days, may also obtain a GI housing loan, provided he or she has not remarried. There is no expiration date for applications.

Before seeking a loan from lenders in your community, you should obtain a Certificate of Eligibility (if one has not already been mailed to you after separation). Call or write to any VA office and present a copy of your discharge or DD form 214. Your certificate will show the exact amount of your entitlement, up to the maximum of $27,500. If you have already used up a lower maximum entitlement, you will be allowed the difference between the amount that you have used and $27,500.

Although the VA limits the portion of the loan that it will guarantee, it does not attempt to fix a ceiling on the total amount that the veteran may borrow from the bank or other lender. As long as the loan does not exceed the property's reasonable value as determined by the VA appraisal, the VA places no limit on the amount.

Some lenders, however, limit the amount of their loans to four times a veteran's entitlement; in such a case, if you have the full $27,500 entitlement, you might be able to obtain a $110,000 loan—provided, of course, your income and credit rating permit you to qualify for the loan. If you do not use all your entitlement, you can save what remains and use it later for any eligible purpose, such as acquiring a second home or covering remodeling costs. (The only restriction is that if you bought one mobile home with VA financing, you cannot buy a second one until you dispose of the first.) You can sell your home and let the buyer assume your VA loan. If the loan has been fully paid or a qualified veteran agrees to substitute his or her entitlement and assume your current obligation, you can request to have your entitlement restored for subsequent use.

Conditions of GI Loan Guaranties

Before a VA loan guaranty is approved, a professional appraisal must be made of the property to determine its reasonable value in the prevailing market. In the case of most new houses, the VA requires inspections to determine whether the house meets accepted construction standards and conforms to the plans and specifications submitted to the VA. The VA does not supervise construction, act as an attorney for the buyer or guarantee that the house is a good investment or free of defects. On new houses or mobile homes, however, the builder is required to give the veteran a one-year warranty certifying that construction is in conformity with the plans and specifications. Houses completed less than a year before purchase must meet VA minimum requirements for planning, construction and general acceptability. In cases of new construction completed under VA or HUD inspection, the VA may compensate a veteran for the correction of serious structural defects that develop within four years.

Protection against Discrimination. The VA may suspend from participation in its loan guaranty program anyone who takes unfair advantage of veterans, or who declines to sell a new house or make a loan to an eligible and credit-worthy veteran because of race, color, religion, sex or national origin.

Terms of Purchase. Down payments are not required unless requested by the lender, or unless the purchase price exceeds the reasonable value of the house as determined by the VA. In the latter case, the veteran must certify that the difference is being paid in cash from the veteran's own resources. Closing costs, including title search and recording, insurance premiums, prepaid taxes and any lender's origination fees may not be included in the loan. Veterans must also certify that they intend to live in the house they are buying or building with a GI loan; if they wish to refinance or improve a home, they must be occupying it at the time of application. They are also required to certify that they will not discriminate because of race, color, religion or national origin in the resale of their homes.

FHA-Insured Home Loans

Older veterans with at least 90 days' active service, whether they are eligible to apply for VA-guaranteed loans or not, may seek government-insured home loans through the Home Mortgage Insurance Program for veterans, administered by the Federal Housing Administration (FHA). If you are separated from enlisted service which began after September 7, 1980, in most cases, you must have served at least two years to be eligible. The maximum mortgage amount the FHA normally insures for a single-family house is $67,500. (In high-cost areas, the figure runs as high as $90,000.) Loans are made by private lending institutions at FHA-fixed interest rates, which may vary in accordance with fluctuations in the mortgage market. To apply for an FHA-insured loan, you should obtain a certificate of status from any VA office and present it to the prospective bank or other lender for submission to the FHA. For further details on FHA loans, see Chapter 3 of this book.

Farm and Rural Loans

Veterans interested in buying, improving or operating farms, or running other businesses in rural areas, receive preference from the Farmers Home Administration (FmHA), which can provide both guaranteed loans and management advice. For further information, apply at local FmHA offices, usually located in county seats, or write to the Farmers Home Administration, U.S. Department of Agriculture, Washington, DC 20250.

GI Life Insurance

During this century, the federal government has authorized a wide variety of life insurance programs to protect the men and women who served their country. The United States Government Life Insurance program (USGLI) was established during World War I; National Service Life Insurance (NSLI) was instituted in World War II; Veterans Special Life Insurance (VSLI) and Service Disabled Veterans Insurance (SDVI) were inaugurated during the Korean conflict; and Veterans Reopened Insurance (VRI) was initiated in 1965. Shortly after that, the current program of Servicemen's Group Life Insurance (SGLI) was established.

Converting or Increasing Your Insurance

Holders of World War II National Service Life Insurance, Veterans Special Life Insurance (Korean conflict) or the newer Veterans Reopened Insurance were previously limited to $10,000 in insurance coverage. Veterans may now increase their coverage by using their dividends to purchase paid-up additions to their policies. The dividends may also be paid in cash to the insured; held as credit, with interest, to prevent the insurance from lapsing; used to pay premiums in advance; placed on deposit with interest (only on permanent plans); or applied to reduce an outstanding loan on the policy.

Coverage Under SGLI

All members of the uniformed services are now automatically insured under SGLI to a maximum amount of $35,000, unless they decide to carry lesser amounts or no insurance at all. The automatic coverage continues for 120 days following separation from the service.

Since 1974, veterans leaving the service have been able to extend the advantages of GI life insurance by means of Veterans Group Life Insurance (VGLI), a low-cost form of term insurance that runs for five years and is not renewable. At the end of the five-year term, anyone insured under VGLI has the right to convert his or her coverage to an individual commercial policy, at standard premium rates, with any of the participating companies licensed to do business in his or her state. No evidence of insurability is required.

Coverage under veterans' insurance may be in amounts ranging from $35,000 down to $5,000, but in any event it may not exceed the amount of insurance the veteran maintained while in service. Application and the initial premium should be submitted within 120 days of separation or release from active duty. After that, application may still be made within a year of the termination of SGLI coverage, but the applicant must submit medical evidence of insurability. Applications submitted after the one-year and 120-day period will not be considered. Veterans who are totally disabled at the time of separation retain their SGLI coverage at no additional cost for one year, or until their disability ceases to be total, whichever comes first. They may then convert to VGLI.

The Veterans Administration attempts to mail information and applications for insurance to all veterans within 30 days of separation, with a follow-up in about six months. If you do not receive an application for some reason, call or write any VA office within the specified period. You can also write to the Office of Servicemen's Group Life Insurance, 212 Washington St., Newark, NJ 07102, which administers the program under VA supervision.

Reservists may qualify for coverage under VGLI, SGLI or both, depending on their circumstances, as long as the combined amount of coverage does not exceed $35,000. Members of the Ready Reserve, including National Guard units, may be covered by SGLI while on active duty or training, including travel time. If a reservist suffers an injury during this period that makes him or her uninsurable at standard rates, the SGLI remains in force for an additional 120 days, during which time the holder may be eligible to apply for VGLI. Veterans eligible for assignment to the Retired Reserve who have completed 20 years of satisfactory service may continue to be insured under SGLI until their 61st birthday or on receipt of their first retirement paycheck, whichever occurs first. Though they are not eligible for Veterans Group Life Insurance, they may apply within 120 days for continuing insurance in the form of an individual policy from one of the companies participating in the program.

Borrowing on Your Insurance Policy

A veteran who needs to raise money and is holding GI life insurance is generally better off borrowing on the policy than cashing it in. Protection ceases forever when a policy is surrendered for cash. Up to 94 percent of the cash surrender value may be borrowed on a permanent policy, but term insurance has no loan value. Annual interest on a policy loan is due on the anniversary date of the loan, and if not paid, the interest becomes part of the loan principal. If a veteran dies before repaying the loan in full, the unpaid balance is deducted from the proceeds of the policy before the beneficiary is paid.

Keeping Your Policy Up to Date

Because provisions on individual policies vary, it is wise to check with your local VA office if you have any questions about your insurance. It is also important to read your policy so that you understand its specific provisions and benefits, and to review your beneficiary designations from time to time to keep them up to date. You should know whether your dividends are being used in the most effective way and whether it would make sense for you to convert your policy from term to permanent insurance, if you have not already done so. Also, you should investigate the advantages of modifying your coverage when you are 65 or 70 if your financial picture and family situation have changed. Discuss your insurance with family members or other beneficiaries, and leave a letter for them indicating the benefits and payment plans that will be available to them. Be sure to keep your policy in a safe place; duplicate copies can be obtained if the policy is lost or destroyed, but not without some inconvenience and delay.

Information and Help With Your Policy

Your local VA office can supply information and insurance forms, but specific inquiries, changes of beneficiary, requests for policy conversions and claims for death benefits should be addressed to the center where the records are actually kept. Where your records are maintained depends on your address and the policy you hold.

Records for Older Insurance Policies

All U.S. Government Life Insurance records, as well as all National Service Life Insurance and retired pay records, are kept at the VA Regional Office and Insurance Center, P.O. Box 8079, Philadelphia, PA 19101. If you pay your premiums directly, however, your records may be either in Philadelphia or at the VA Regional Office and Insurance Center, Federal Building, Fort Snelling, St. Paul, MN 55111. Generally speaking, St. Paul handles the records of those living west of the Mississippi River, and Philadelphia, those living to the east, but insurance records are no longer transferred from one center to another because of a change of address.

Records for More Recent Policies
Holders of the Servicemen's Group Life insurance policies and Veterans Group Life Insurance policies should address correspondence and premiums to the Office of Servicemen's Group Life Insurance, 212 Washington St., Newark, NJ 07102.

In any correspondence, be sure to include the full name of the insured, together with the policy number. If the policy number is not known, the veteran should be identified by name, file number, Social Security number and military serial number, as well as the branch and dates of service and date of birth.

Medical Insurance
Members of the armed services are entitled to free medical care while on active duty. To avoid a sudden lapse of coverage for major health problems, a service member should look into commercial medical insurance plans before being discharged. As a stopgap, a temporary medical insurance policy is available from a major insurance company through an agreement with the Department of Defense. Called Majorcare 90, it covers ex-service members for 90 days while they establish permanent policies. The coverage includes part of hospitalization costs and physicians' fees for illnesses or accidents occurring within this three-month period. Total premiums are moderate; in a recent year, the charges were $25 for a veteran, $25 for a spouse and $10 for each child. The policy is limited to veterans who served on active duty for 30 days or more; it excludes retirees and those who served less than four

months in training programs. It does not cover childbirth, dental care, eye or ear examinations for glasses or hearing aids, or congenital or preexisting conditions, nor does it pay for care covered by other forms of compensation. To apply for Majorcare, talk to your personnel officer before separation.

Hospital and Medical Care

The Veterans Administration operates the nation's largest health-care system. Scattered across the country are 172 hospitals, 226 outpatient clinics, 92 nursing homes, 16 domiciliaries, 18 spinal-cord-injury centers, two rehabilitative-engineering research and development centers and other installations (see directory, page 251 for VA offices, Alcohol or Drug Treatment Centers, Spinal Cord Injury Centers and Cemeteries).

Out of the total number of hospitals, 137 are affiliated with medical schools. The VA employs 11,391 doctors and 30,233 nurses, 918 dentists and 159,000 other specialists and service personnel. An additional 80,000 members of the VA Voluntary Service donate more than 10 million hours of their time each year to bringing companionship and additional care to hospitalized veterans. Approximately 100,000 people are trained every year by the VA in various health specialities, and more than 5,000 research projects are under way at any given time, many of them in rehabilitative techniques. Worldwide recognition came to the research programs in 1977 when two VA career scientists were awarded the Nobel Prize in Medicine (see box on pages 238-239).

Each year the VA provides treatment for more than 1.3 million inpatients and 18 million outpatients. There are close to 70,000 patients in VA hospitals on any given day, about 15 percent of them Vietnam veterans. In addition to routine medical care, the VA offers special treatment not readily available elsewhere, including care of persons paralyzed due to spinal-cord injury and disease, rehabilitation for the blind and hard of hearing, speech training, training in the use of artificial limbs, occupational therapy, family counseling, driver education for the disabled and a variety of other services, all provided to needy veterans without cost. Because the proportion of older veterans in the population is steadily increasing, the VA expects its total number of patients to become even greater over the years ahead.

Who Qualifies for Medical Care

First priority for treatment and admission at VA health facilities is given to veterans with injuries or illnesses incurred or aggravated in the course of their military service. Second priority goes to those with service-connected disabilities who also need treatment for ailments not related to service. Other veterans may be treated or admitted when professional help and beds are available, if they are financially unable to get the necessary care elsewhere. (The ability-to-pay requirement does not apply to veterans over 65, to those who hold a VA pension or to recipients of the Medal of Honor.) In recent years, some 70 percent of VA medical care has been provided to veterans who do not have service-connected disabilities, but are 65 or older, or whose financial situations and lack of health insurance make it impossible for them to pay private institutions for the health care they require.

Outpatient Care

Eligible veterans who do not require hospitalization can obtain treatment on an outpatient basis, including medical examinations, consultations, counseling, mental health services, prosthetic devices and prescription drugs. Also included are health services and installation of necessary facilities in disabled veterans' homes. Blind veterans may receive training in adjusting to their blindness, as well as mechanical aids, guide dogs and talking books, tapes and

Medicine, VA Style

The medical branch of the Veterans Administration is not only one of the largest health-care systems in the world, it is also one of the most innovative.

While some VA hospitals provide mainly routine care, others offer notable special services and conduct advanced research in various fields. VA hospitals that are affiliated with outstanding medical schools attract many top-flight younger physicians from among the estimated one-third of all the country's medical graduates receiving training in VA medical facilities each year.

Of the thousands of research projects developed in VA laboratories and hospital wards, not a few have resulted in significant breakthroughs. Years ago, the treatment of tuberculosis by means of drug therapy, rather than the traditional "cure" of rest in a mountain or desert climate, was instituted by the VA. The agency's medical center in Denver was the site of the world's first successful liver transplant; and pioneering work in lowering the body temperature for open-heart surgery was done in the VA hospital in Coral Gables, Florida. Techniques of laser surgery have been explored in VA centers in West Roxbury, Massachusetts, Pittsburgh, Pennsylvania, and Washington, DC. VA research into cell-typing helped make Dr. Christiaan Barnard's first heart transplant possible. And the first successful implant of a heart pacemaker was accomplished at the VA hospital in Buffalo, New York.

In dealing with the problems of disabled veterans, VA experts have come up with many useful aids for the handicapped. Madge Skelly, a VA speech therapist and former

Braille literature from the Library of Congress. Veterans with service-connected dental problems receive free dental care.

Nursing Homes and Domiciliaries
Veterans who are convalescing after hospitalization, or who are not ill enough to require hospital care, may be admitted to VA nursing homes, or to private nursing homes at VA expense. Aging or disabled veterans who do not need skilled hospital or nursing-home care may live in a VA domiciliary, where a residential setting and basic care for ambulatory patients are provided. In addition, some 31 states operate homes for incapacitated veterans who have little or no income; these facilities are supplemented by the U.S. Soldiers' and Airmen's Home in Washington, DC, and the U.S. Naval Home in Gulfport, Mississippi.

Under the Uniformed Services Health Benefits Program (USHBP), retired service members, their families and their survivors—as well as survivors of personnel who died while on active duty—may receive medical care at little or no cost at armed forces and Public Health Service hospitals, provided adequate space and staff care are available. When no such facilities exist in the area where the retired service members or their families live, individuals may be partially reimbursed for medical expenses incurred at civilian hospitals or clinics under a complementary plan called the Civilian Health and Medical Program of the Uniformed Services (CHAMPUS). For more specific information, inquire at any service hospital, or the medical office or health-benefits counselor of any military command.

Alcohol and Drug Treatment
A veteran who has a problem with alcoholism or drug dependence, and who was separated from the service under other than dishonorable conditions, may apply for treatment, including hospitalization and follow-up outpatient care if

actress, developed a simple sign language for stroke victims—based on Indian signals she had learned from her grandfather. Prosthetics specialists pioneered a "laser cane" for the blind, which signals information about the distance, size and shape of objects; these scientists also invented a "myoelectric hand"—a sensitive battery-powered artificial hand that works by means of muscle signals transmitted by electrodes placed in contact with the stump of an amputee's arm. Among other VA-developed aids for persons with spinal-cord injuries are breath-activated mechanisms that direct powered wheelchairs, turn the pages of a book and change channels on a television set. A recent development is a computer that answers voice commands given by people who have lost the use of both arms and legs; it can turn lights on and off, adjust a power-driven bed for greater comfort and dial numbers on a telephone.

Probably the agency's greatest public recognition came in 1977 when two Veterans Administration doctors won the Nobel Prize in Medicine. Dr. Rosalyn S. Yalow, an endocrinologist at the Bronx, New York, VA hospital, received half the $145,000 award for her role in the development of the radioimmunoassay, a technique using radioactive materials to measure minute quantities of substances in the body that influence the balance between normal health and disease. The other half of the prize went to Dr. Andrew V. Schally, a senior medical investigator at the New Orleans VA hospital, for his research into the brain's production of peptide hormones and their role in controlling the body's chemistry.

needed. Although patients may be admitted to any VA hospital, the VA maintains specialized treatment facilities for veterans who are dependent on alcohol or other drugs. (See list of cities, page 252.) Inquire at the nearest VA office or VA medical installation for referral to the nearest appropriate facility.

Care for Dependents and Survivors

The Veterans Administration provides medical care for the spouses and children of veterans totally disabled by service-connected injuries or illnesses, and for the widows, widowers and children of veterans who died because of service-connected disabilities. Normally, such care is offered in non-VA facilities under the Civilian Health and Medical Program of the Veterans Administration (CHAMPVA). For authorized inpatient care, CHAMPVA pays 75 percent of hospital and professional fees. The patient pays the other 25 percent. The same percentages apply to outpatient charges, after the patient has paid a modest deduction ($50 a year in recent years). VA facilities may be used for specialized treatment when such use does not interfere with the treatment of other veterans. Mental-health services and professional counseling are also available to families of veterans who are under treatment in VA facilities. For further information and applications, call or write your nearest VA medical facility.

Disabled Veterans and Their Survivors

Disabled veterans are entitled to a wide range of benefits over and above those accorded to other veterans. In addition to priority treatment in VA health facilities, vocational rehabilitation and preference in employment— already described in preceding sections—these benefits include monthly disability compensation payments; pensions for non-service disabilities; special life insurance; "wheelchair" homes, grants toward the purchase of automobiles, with special adaptive equipment installed if necessary; special clothing allowances; and continuing compensation to survivors after death. Totally disabled veterans, their eligible dependents and surviving spouses who have not remarried are also entitled to unlimited privileges at post exchanges and commissary stores in the United States.

Disability Payments

The Veterans Administration pays compensation to veterans who have been disabled by injury or disease incurred in, or aggravated in, the line of duty during either wartime or peacetime, provided these veterans were separated from service under other than dishonorable conditions.

The compensation takes the form of monthly payments based on the degree of disability. In 1981, these payments ranged from $58 a month for a veteran with a disability rated at 10 percent to $1,130 a month for a veteran with a total disability, or one rated at 100 percent. In addition, specific payments ranging up to a maximum of $3,223 a month are made to veterans who have suffered certain severe disabilities, including multiple loss of limbs, blindness, deafness or combinations of these. All such payments are decided on an individual basis.

Veterans with disabilities rated at 30 percent or more are entitled to additional monthly allowances for their dependents, including spouses, children and parents. Actual amounts are based on the number of dependents and the degree of disability. A veteran with a 30 percent disability who has a wife and no children, for example, receives an additional $21 a month; a totally disabled veteran with a wife and three children receives an additional $192 a month.

Some 2.3 million veterans are currently receiving monthly compensation checks for service-connected disabilities.

Pensions for Non-Service Disabilities

Veterans of wartime service who are judged to

be permanently and totally disabled for reasons *not* traceable to their service are eligible for pensions, provided their income does not exceed certain limits. In cases where the disability is less than 100 percent, requirements are based on age.

If a veteran is under 60, a disability rated at 60 percent must be shown; from 60 to 65, only 50 percent is required. At age 65, the veteran may be eligible for a pension whether he or she is disabled or not. The key factor is the veteran's income.

This is the situation under the improved program that went into effect on January 1, 1979. In the absence of other income, pensions paid range from $4,960 a year for a healthy veteran without a dependent spouse or child to $9,474 a year for a veteran who has one dependent and is in need of regular medical or nursing aid. For each additional dependent child, $840 is added, and if the veteran saw service in World War I, the figure comes to $1,119. Veterans who came on the pension rolls before January 1, 1979, may continue to receive payments under the system in which they were previously enrolled, or they may elect to receive pensions under the improved program, whichever happens to be more advantageous to them.

Pensions are generally paid in monthly installments.

Disabled Veterans' Life Insurance

A veteran who was separated from service on or after April 25, 1951, with a service-connected disability may apply to the VA for a special policy. This insurance, which is designated National Service Life Insurance, is subsidized by the government, but the veteran pays the premiums, and there are no dividends. The veteran must be in good health apart from the disability. Application must be made within one year from the date the VA notifies the veteran that the disability has been rated as service-connected. Insurance is available in several plans, including term, ordinary life and endowment.

Waiver of Premiums for the Totally Disabled

All NSLI policies contain a provision for waiving payment of premiums if the insured becomes totally disabled before reaching the age of 65 (in some cases 60). Holders of NSLI policies who become totally disabled and are likely to remain so for six months or more should consult the VA about their entitlement to the waiver of premiums. USGLI policyholders who become totally disabled are entitled to receive the proceeds of their policies in monthly payments, and should consult the VA about these benefits.

"Wheelchair" Homes

In addition to GI or FHA loans, seriously disabled veterans may be entitled to VA grants for "wheelchair" homes especially adapted to their needs. Such a grant, provided outright on a one-time basis, covers up to 50 percent of the cost (to a maximum of $32,500) of building or buying a suitable house or remodeling an existing one to include special features and equipment. Veterans holding these grants automatically receive special Veterans Mortgage Life Insurance up to $40,000 or the amount of the mortgage, whichever is less. The insurance is designed to pay off the mortgage in the event of the veteran's death. The veteran pays the standard rate for the mortgage insurance. The government bears the administrative costs and the cost attributable to higher mortality rates stemming from specific disabilities. Premiums are deducted from VA disability compensation payments if the veteran is receiving them. The deductions continue until the mortgage is paid off, the house is sold, or the veteran reaches the age of 70 or dies.

Automobiles and Special Equipment

Veterans who have permanently lost the use of one or both hands or feet may receive a one-time maximum payment ($4,400 in recent years) toward the purchase of an automobile, truck or other conveyance. The VA will also pay for the installation and maintenance of adaptive equipment to enable the veteran to operate the vehicle successfully and safely. The adaptive features include modifications of the controls, power assists and special equipment to help the veteran in and out of the vehicle.

Other Aids for the Disabled

As part of its medical benefits (pages 237–240), the VA furnishes certain necessary aids for disabled veterans—such as artificial limbs, braces, orthopedic shoes, wheelchairs, hearing aids and invalid lifts—as well as training the veterans in their use and authorizing their repair at VA expense. If a veteran must use equipment that tends to wear out or tear the user's clothing, an annual replacement allowance is also supplied. Blind veterans receive special assistance such as visual aids or guide dogs, and help in adapting to these devices.

Compensation for Disabled Veterans' Survivors

Surviving spouses, children and parents of a disabled veteran may be entitled to monthly compensation payments after the veteran's death. Under the Dependency and Indemnity Compensation program (DIC), the survivors are eligible if the veteran (or service member on active duty) died on or after January 1, 1957, from: 1) a disease or injury incurred or aggravated in the line of duty; 2) an injury incurred or aggravated in the course of inactive duty training; or 3) a disability otherwise compensable under laws administered by the VA. DIC payments may also be made to survivors of veterans whose deaths were not related to military service but who at the time of death had suffered from a total service-connected disability for 10 or more years.

The basic rate of payment for a surviving spouse is determined by the military grade of the deceased person (in a recent year it ranged from $415 to $1,138 a month). The amount is increased by $48 monthly for each child under 18. If the survivor is in need of assistance because of a disability, he or she may be paid an additional amount.

If the surviving spouse is ineligible for any reason—the most common one is remarriage—the veteran's children may still qualify for DIC in their own right. A lower schedule of payments applies, ranging from $210 monthly for one child to $389 for three children, plus $79 for each additional child.

Payments to dependent parents of a deceased veteran may also be made. Recently these have ranged from $5 to $230 a month, plus an additional $121 a month to those in need of regular nursing care, provided total income for each does not exceed $5,642 a year, or $7,587 for parents living together.

Survivors of veterans who died before January 1, 1957, from service-connected causes may continue to receive benefits under previous programs or switch to the DIC program. Generally it's to their advantage to elect the greater benefits of DIC.

Survivor Pensions for Non-Service Deaths

Widows, widowers and children of veterans who served during wartime, including the Korean and Vietnam eras, may receive pensions even if the veteran died of causes not related to service. The veteran must have served honorably for at least 90 days (unless separated or retired sooner for a service-connected disability); if the veteran died in service but not in line of duty, benefits are payable provided the veteran completed at least two years of honorable active service.

Under the improved pension program that took effect on January 1, 1979, pensions, in the absence of income from other sources, are currently payable to survivors at maximum rates, ranging from $3,324 for a surviving spouse with no dependent children to $6,347 for a surviving spouse who is in need of regular nursing care and has one dependent child. A further payment of $840 a year is allowed for each additional child. Paid monthly, the pensions are reduced by the amount of annual income received by the surviving spouse and children from other sources. Pensioners under older programs may continue to receive bene-

Residences for Widows and Retirees

The services have established foundations designed to provide housing for widows, survivors and dependents of career officers. The Army Distaff Hall, a 282-unit facility in Washington, DC, is open to widows, mothers, daughters, sisters and daughters-in-law of career Army officers, as well as to retired female officers. For information as to eligibility requirements and the availability of living spaces, write the Army Distaff Foundation, Inc., 6200 Oregon Ave. NW, Washington, DC 20015.

Carl Vinson Hall is a similar residence of 250 units in Fairfax County, Virginia, for survivors of Navy, Marine and Coast Guard officers. For information, apply to the Navy-Marine-Coast Guard Residence Foundation, Inc., U.S. Naval Observatory, Washington, DC 20390.

Widows of Air Force officers, as well as retired Air Force officers themselves, may apply for residence in Air Force Village, San Antonio, Texas, by writing to the Air Force Village Foundation, Inc., 4917 Ravenswood Drive, San Antonio, TX 78227.

Widows and widowers of retired enlisted members of the Air Force, including the Air National Guard and Air Force Reserve, may be admitted to Teresa Village, a 96-unit complex in Fort Walton Beach, Florida. Applications should be addressed to the Air Force Enlisted Men's Widows Home Foundation, Inc., 354 Woodraw St., Fort Walton Beach, FL 32548.

fits under those programs or convert to the improved pension plan.

Survivor Benefit Plan for Retirees

All career members of the uniformed services who reach retirement eligibility can leave a portion of their retirement pay to their survivors at reasonable cost under the Survivor Benefit Plan (SBP). (This program replaced the older Retired Serviceman's Family Protection Plan as of September 21, 1972.) All retirees are automatically enrolled in the SBP for maximum coverage at the time of their retirement, unless they decline to enroll or request lesser coverage. Reservists are included, and can qualify at age 60.

SBP enables the retiree to provide his or her beneficiaries with a monthly income equal to 55 percent of the ex-service member's retirement pay, and to purchase additional benefits. The cost to the retiree of benefits to a husband or wife is 2.5 percent of the first $300 of retirement pay, plus 10 percent of any amount over $300. A retiree receiving $700 a month, for example, can guarantee his widow a monthly income of $385 by paying in $47.50 a month. Coverage for a spouse, children or other dependents can also be provided at varying rates. SBP payments may be reduced by payments from government programs, including Dependency and Indemnity Compensation from the Veterans Administration (page 242) and any portion of Social Security benefits derived from the retiree's active-duty earnings. Retiring service members are urged to check with their personnel officers and familiarize themselves with the options available under the Survivor Benefit Plan well ahead of actual retirement; once retired pay starts, most choices cannot be changed.

Social Security Benefits for Veterans

Like all working citizens, veterans are eligible for Social Security benefits when they reach retirement age, based on their average earnings over a period of years. These include retirement benefits payable to a retired worker and spouse, generally at 62 or later; benefits for severe disabilities, payable to workers under 65 and their families; the lump-sum death payment to a widow or widower to help defray burial expenses; and continuing monthly benefits to survivors.

Since January 1, 1957, servicemen and women have earned regular Social Security credits for their entire periods of duty. Social Security contributions have been deducted from their pay, just as they are deducted from the wages of civilian workers. Since January 1, 1968, service personnel have also received extra earnings credits ($100 a month in recent years) that take into account the value of room, board and other non-monetary benefits supplied by the services in addition to pay. People who served on active duty before 1957 did not earn regular Social Security credits, but with certain exceptions they are eligible for credits ($160 a month in recent years) for each month of active service between September 16, 1940, and December 31, 1956.

Veterans and members of their families who reach the age of 65 are, of course, eligible for the federal health program of Medicare. They automatically receive hospital insurance when they apply for Social Security benefits, and may at the same time take out insurance for other medical expenses at low, federally subsidized rates. For detailed information on both Social Security and Medicare, check with your local office of the Social Security Administration, and see Chapters 4 and 7 of this book.

Death and Burial Allowances

A veteran of honorable service is entitled to certain final honors, including burial allowances, a headstone, an American flag and a Presidential certificate for the next of kin expressing the nation's gratitude.

Lump-Sum Allowances
The government will pay a maxiumum of $300 toward burial expenses for veterans eligible for

VA pensions or compensation and those who die in VA medical facilities, and for peacetime veterans who die of service-connected disabilities, or were receiving a pension or compensation. In addition, the cost of transporting the remains to the place of burial may be borne by the government if the death occurred while the veteran was hospitalized or domiciled under VA care.

A further sum ($150 in recent years) is payable to the next of kin as a plot or interment allowance when the veteran is not buried in a national cemetery. If the veteran dies of a service-connected disability, a larger amount (up to $1,100) is paid in lieu of the basic burial reimbursement and plot allowance. If the veteran had a compensable service-connected disability at the time of death, the VA will also pay the cost of transporting the remains to the nearest national cemetery in which grave space is available.

The Social Security Administration will make an additional lump-sum payment ($255 in recent years) toward funeral and burial costs for veterans with Social Security credits.

When a member of the armed services dies on active duty, in training or in a military hospital, the survivors are entitled to benefits that include preparation, transportation and interment of the remains. A lump-sum death payment of $3,000 is also made if a service member dies in the line of duty, or from a service-connected cause within 120 days following separation. The income of an individual who dies in a combat zone is exempt from federal income taxes for the year in which the death occurred.

Burial in National Cemeteries
The National Cemetery System, supervised by the Veterans Administration, includes 108 cemeteries: 82 transferred from the Department of the Army, 21 VA hospital cemeteries and five new ones in California, Massachusetts, New York, Pennsylvania and Virginia, each of which is as large as or larger than the famed Arlington National Cemetery across the river

A Special Community for Children and Widows

A unique facility designed for family members of veterans is the Veterans of Foreign Wars National Home in Eaton Rapids, Michigan, which provides a homelike suburban community for sons, daughters, wives and widows of deceased or totally disabled VFW members.

Founded in 1925, the home now has some 50 units, including a modern hospital, community center, day nursery, guest lodge, chapel, and clothing and grocery store, all located on a 60-acre campus.

Children live in small groups, six or eight to a home unit, often with their own mothers acting as housemothers. They attend regular public schools and community churches, and participate in the normal social life of Eaton Rapids.

If you would like to have additional information about the National Home, you can write to the VFW National Home, Eaton Rapids, MI 48827; or to a VFW representative or VFW ladies' auxiliary member in your community.

from Washington, DC. Development is under way on three more national cemeteries, in Michigan, Alabama and Florida. (See page 254 for a list of national cemeteries.)

Depending on the availability of grave space, any deceased veteran of wartime or peacetime active duty may be buried in a national cemetery. Members of the Reserves and National Guard who die on active duty are also eligible. Upon death, the spouse or minor child of a deceased veteran may be buried in the same cemetery as the veteran, usually in the same plot. Burial in Arlington National Cemetery, which remains under the jurisdiction of the Army, is limited to Medal of Honor winners, those who die on active duty in the armed services, retired career military personnel and other special categories. For further information, contact the Superintendent, Arlington National Cemetery, Arlington, VA 22211.

Burial at Sea

If a veteran wishes to be buried at sea, or to have his or her ashes scattered over the ocean, that wish should be indicated in writing. Upon the veteran's death, the family member or friend designated to dispose of the remains should notify the District Medical Officer at the nearest district headquarters of the U.S. Navy.

Headstones or Memorial Markers

The government inscribes headstones or memorial markers for all veterans who are buried in national cemeteries. A headstone or marker will be shipped without charge to the gravesite when a veteran is buried in a private cemetery. Memorial markers will also be furnished for veterans whose remains have not been recovered; whose remains were buried at sea, whether by the veteran's own choice or otherwise; whose remains were donated to science; or whose remains were cremated and the ashes scattered. The cost of installing any marker in a private cemetery must be borne by the applicant. If the next of kin choose to have their own headstone made and inscribed for a private plot, the VA will reimburse them in an amount not to exeed the average cost of a government-supplied headstone.

Burial Flags

The government will supply, without charge, an American flag that may be used to drape the casket of a veteran at his funeral. Eligible veterans include those who served in wartime, who served after January 31, 1955, or who served at least one enlistment during peacetime (unless released earlier for disability incurred in the line of duty). Flags may be obtained at any VA office or national cemetery, and at most

Tributes to Fallen Heroes

Twice each year, in the spring and fall, Americans gather to pay honor to more than a million compatriots who gave their lives in the nation's wars.

The first of these observances, originally known as Decoration Day, started spontaneously more than a century ago when women in both Northern and Southern communities began to place flowers on the still-fresh graves of their Civil War dead. Backed by the Grand Army of the Republic, an organization of Union veterans, the idea spread to the country as a whole, eventually becoming known as Memorial Day.

The date of May 30, a few days after the surrender of the last Confederate army, became traditional, but in 1971 a federal law designated the last Monday in May as the day of official observance in order to yield a long weekend. In parts of the South, a separate Confederate Memorial Day is observed, either in place of, or in addition to, the national holiday. The observance occurs on April 26 in Florida and Georgia, commemorating Johnston's surrender to Sherman. In the Carolinas it is May 10, the anniversary of Jefferson Davis' capture in 1865. In Kentucky and Louisiana, Davis' birthday, June 3, is the date. Communities in Virginia and elsewhere mark the observance on other dates to commemorate the deaths of local heroes or heroic actions in the war.

Ceremonies vary from one part of the country to another, but generally flags are flown at half mast and parades wend their way to local cemeteries, where wreaths and bouquets are laid on the graves of the combat victims and others who served their country in time of war.

Similar tributes are paid on November 11, which was first officially observed in 1919 as Armistice Day, on the first anniversary of the end of World War I. A year earlier on November 9, 1918, there had been premature and short-lived rejoicing when a surrender was mistakenly reported in the New York papers and denied the same day. On the 11th, however, in a railroad car in the Forest of Compiègne, representatives of the Allied and German armies signed the armistice at 5

post offices. After burial, the flag may be given to the veteran's next of kin or to a close friend or associate. A flag may also be issued later to the next of kin if one was not available at the time of burial, or if the death occurred in the service and the remains were buried at sea or not recovered.

Presidential Memorial Certificates

The next of kin of any deceased veteran of honorable service is entitled to a certificate expressing the country's grateful recognition of the veteran's service in the armed forces, and bearing the signature of the President of the United States. When notice of an eligible veteran's death is received in one of the VA offices, that office automatically identifies the next of kin from the veteran's records and arranges for a certificate to be mailed out in a White House envelope. The definition of next of kin is determined in the following order: surviving spouse, oldest child, mother, father, oldest sister, oldest brother. When no certificate has been issued to a relative, a request for one from a close friend or associate of the deceased will be honored.

Gold Star lapel buttons are also issued without cost to survivors of those who died in service during wartime.

State Burial Benefits

A number of states have set aside cemeteries for the burial of their veterans, and some will arrange for other honors. Information may be

A.M., and it became effective with a cease-fire at 11 A.M. The news was genuine this time. It reached the United States in the predawn stillness, setting off an explosion of joy as sirens wailed, whistles tooted, bonfires were lit and people marched, weeping and laughing, through the streets.

At precisely 11 A.M. on November 11, 1921, President Warren G. Harding and other officials watched as the body of an unidentified American, who had fallen in the fields of France, was lowered to its final resting place in the Tomb of the Unknown Soldier at Arlington National Cemetery in Virginia. During the 1920s, observance of Armistice Day (Remembrance Day in England and Canada) became a tradition on both sides of the Atlantic, and in 1938 the day was made an official federal holiday in the United States. In 1954 Congress passed a bill changing the name to Veterans Day, to include those who had fought in subsequent wars, and in 1958 the bodies of two servicemen, one killed in World War II and the other in Korea, were buried in the crypt at Arlington,

which was renamed the Tomb of the Unknowns. In 1971 a federal law designated the fourth Monday in October as Veterans Day—again, to give Americans an additional three-day weekend—but after several years of confusion and the opposition of veterans' groups it was switched back to the original date of November 11.

The national focus on both Veterans Day and Memorial Day is still the Tomb of the Unknowns at Arlington, where sentries keep a 24-hour vigil and an eternal flame burns. At 11 A.M. each Veterans Day, dignitaries and spectators watch as a color guard of the combined military services presents arms; after a moment of silence, a bugler plays "Taps" and a Presidential wreath is laid upon the tomb.

Elsewhere around the country, local parades, speeches and religious observances are held. Veterans' groups, churchmen, town officials, high school bands, Boy Scouts and other volunteers join in, and a brief silence is observed in tribute to those who died in the service of their country.

obtained from state departments of veterans' affairs.

State and Local Benefits

Many states, counties and municipalities offer veterans special aid and privileges. Among these are partial exemptions from property taxes, preference points on civil service job examinations, and scholarships or other educational assistance for dependents of deceased or totally disabled veterans. Some states, like California, provide long-term, low-interest loans to their veterans to enable them to purchase houses, farms or mobile homes.

In many states, disabled veterans are entitled

to free hunting and fishing licenses, free use of public parks and campsites, exemption from payment of motor vehicle registration fees, and unlimited parking meter privileges. Some states pay blinded veterans annual allowances, and a few (Illinois, Massachusetts and Vermont) still pay a modest, one-time bonus to any veteran of active service, with higher amounts for those who served in wartime or overseas.

Many states maintain veterans' homes that provide hospitalization, nursing-home care or residential facilities for aged or infirm veterans who are state residents. To determine specific benefits in your area, call or write your local government or state department of veterans' affairs.

Retired Service Personnel

Career members of the armed services who have retired, as well as their dependents and survivors, are entitled to certain benefits and privileges not available to other veterans. In addition to retirement pay and the Survivor Benefit Plan (page 243), the benefits include travel, shipment and storage of household goods incident to retirement; medical care at military and civilian facilities; privileges at base facilities such as post exchanges, commissary stores and officers' and enlisted messes; moderate-cost accommodations near bases; and stand-by space on military airlift flights. Inquiries should be directed to the appropriate military base or armed service involved.

Added Payments for Heroism

Veterans who have been credited with extraordinary heroism in the line of duty are entitled to additional income beyond any other benefits they may receive. Any person who has been awarded the Medal of Honor may apply to the Secretary of the Army, Navy or other department making the award for certification to the Veterans Administration, which will pay the veteran (or serviceman, if he continues on active duty) a Medal of Honor pension, set at the rate of $200 a month in recent years.

Enlisted personnel who have displayed extraordinary heroism and who retire after 20 or more years of active service are entitled to a 10 percent increase in their retirement pay. Normally, recipients of the Medal of Honor, the Distinguished Service Cross and the Navy Cross are included; others may be credited by the secretary of the appropriate service if the heroism displayed can be shown to have been equivalent to that required for the award of the latter two medals.

Veterans' Organizations

Veterans not only receive help from government agencies and programs, but from a variety of organizations that have been recognized by Congress and the VA as officially representing veterans. These organizations can provide information on benefits, help adjust claims, seek legislation favorable to veterans, support community activities and serve as social centers for ex-service people. The three largest are discussed below. In the box on page 250 is a complete list of organizations that have been authorized to present veterans' claims.

The American Legion

The Legion is the largest of the nation's veterans' groups, with some 2.6 million members, plus a million-member auxiliary. It is organized into 58 departments and 15,800 local posts in the United States and abroad. Membership is open only to those veterans who served during periods of armed hostilities, including both World Wars and the Korean and Vietnam conflicts.

Each year the American Legion helps tens of thousands of veterans without charge, whether they are members or not, in obtaining medical, educational and other benefits; in correcting military records, upgrading discharges and obtaining back pay or missing checks; and in getting job training or employment. Volunteers from the Legion, its auxiliary and its junior volunteer program visit hospitalized veterans; service officers attached to VA medical facilities also provide professional help and counseling for patients.

Much of the Legion's effort is exerted at the community level, with an accent on the nation's youth. More than $25 million is raised annually to help American youngsters achieve their potential. American Legion School Awards for honor, courage, scholarship, leadership and service are presented to some 27,000 boys and girls annually. Legion posts sponsor 1,500 Boy Scout troops, conduct summer education programs in government, distribute handbooks on opportunies for high school students, disburse grants to children's organizations, award scholarships to college candidates and high school orators, run blood-donor programs and raise funds for the Special

Olympics for the handicapped and retarded.

Members keep up with local and national veterans' affairs through a monthly publication, *The American Legion* magazine, and women members of the auxiliary receive its bimonthly *National News*. For other information about membership, apply to your local post or American Legion National Headquarters, P.O. Box 1055, Indianapolis, IN 46206.

Veterans of Foreign Wars of the United States

The VFW, one of the faster-growing veterans' groups, claims more than 1.9 million members in 10,000 posts scattered across the United States and in such places as Paris, Berlin, Tokyo, Okinawa, Taiwan and Bangkok. Membership is open to those who served honorably overseas in time of emergency in any engagements for which campaign badges or medals have been authorized.

The Veterans of Foreign Wars takes pride in the fact that it has either initiated or supported every major veterans' law now on the books. It maintains a nationwide Veterans Service, staffed by legal and medical experts, to aid all veterans, regardless of membership, in filing claims for benefits. The organization also sponsors numerous community activities.

The VFW structure, which includes a ladies' auxiliary, is organized at post, county, district, departmental and national levels; officers are elected annually and a national convention is held in a major American city each year. A monthly publication, *VFW Magazine,* goes to all members; a newsletter, *Washington Action Reporter,* is circulated widely to cover news of current programs, issues and legislation. Information on membership is available at any local VFW post or from National Headquarters. The address is: Veterans of Foreign Wars of the United States, 34th and Broadway, Kansas City, MO 64111.

Disabled American Veterans

The DAV is an association of some 670,000 disabled veterans who have joined together to provide assistance to the country's 2.5 million disabled vets, their families and survivors. To qualify for membership, an individual must have been honorably discharged, and must have incurred a disability during wartime military service or under conditions simulating war, such as maneuvers.

About 25 percent of DAV members are of the Vietnam era, roughly the same percentage of Vietnam vets as in the veteran population at large. Seriously disabled veterans make up more than 90 percent of the DAV professional staff, both in the organization's Cincinnati headquarters and in the field force of 300 National Service Officers in 68 cities across the United States. In a recent year, these NSOs helped disabled veterans and their families, regardless of DAV membership, to secure nearly three-quarters of a billion dollars in benefits by functioning as legal counselors, assembling evidence, preparing claims forms and presenting briefs before hearing boards. With a fleet of office-equipped vans, DAV representatives have brought their services to the doorsteps of a quarter of a million veterans, dependents and survivors in towns distant from the organization's regular field offices.

One of DAV's most notable efforts has been its Vietnam Vet Outreach Program, which enlists the volunteer aid of psychiatrists, guidance counselors and other community professionals in assisting thousands of survivors of the Vietnam experience to cope with delayed and continuing stress reactions, including loneliness, depression, alcohol and drug abuse and legal, marital and employment problems. The organization also maintains relief funds to assist disabled veterans who need help in coping with financial emergencies or natural catastrophes, and it provides 60 scholarships a year to children of disabled vets unable to afford the cost of higher education. The DAV helps employers place disabled veterans in jobs and job training programs, files complaints about job discrimination and encourages the elimination of architectural barriers to the handi-

National Service Organizations Chartered by Congress

American Legion	Indianapolis, IN 46206
American Red Cross	Washington, DC 20006
AMVETS	Washington, DC 20036
Blinded Veterans Association	Washington DC 20037
Congressional Medal of Honor Society of the U.S.A.	Braintree, MA 02184
Disabled American Veterans	Cincinnati, OH 45214
Legion of Valor of the United States of America, Inc.	Arlington, VA 22204
Marine Corps League	Arlington, VA 22201
Military Order of the Purple Heart	Washington, DC 20013
Paralyzed Veterans of America, Inc.	Washington, DC 20420
United Spanish War Veterans	Washington, DC 20420
Veterans of Foreign Wars of the United States	Kansas City, MO 64111
Veterans of World War I of the U.S.A. Inc.	Alexandria, VA 22314

Other National Service Organizations Recognized by the VA

American Veterans Committee	Washington, DC 20036
Army and Navy Union, U.S.A.	Lakemore, OH 44250
Army Mutual Aid Association	Arlington, VA 22211
Catholic War Veterans of the U.S.A.	Washington, DC 20001
Coast Guard League	Washington, DC 20591
Disabled Officers Association	Washington, DC 20006
Fleet Reserve Association	Washington, DC 20036
Gold Star Wives of America	Skokie, IL 60077
Jewish War Veterans of the United States	Washington, DC 20009
Military Order of the World Wars	Washington, DC 20006
National Jewish Welfare Board	New York, NY 10010
National Tribune	Washington, DC 20013
Navy Mutual Aid Association	Washington, DC 20370
Polish Legion of American Veterans	Dearborn, MI 48127
Regular Veterans Association	Washington, DC 20015
Swords to Plowshares	San Francisco, CA 94102
United Indian War Veterans, U.S.A.	San Francisco, CA 94103

capped. It also sponsors some 200 Boy Scout troops for handicapped children. Members of DAV and its ladies' auxiliary donate more than a million hours and nearly a million dollars a year to help sick and disabled veterans in VA hospitals.

The organization, which maintains chapters across the United States, elects a National Commander and other officers at a national convention held each year. A monthly magazine, *DAV,* brings members news of local and national goings-on. For further information, apply to the DAV chapter in your area or Disabled American Veterans, National Headquarters, P.O. Box 14301, Cincinnati, OH 45214.

Directory of Veterans Administration and Other Facilities

The Veterans Administration has hundreds of facilities across the country. The best way to find the office nearest you is to look in the telephone directory under "U.S. Government—Veterans Administration," or contact one of the offices of the VA listed below.

National Office
Veterans Administration
Washington DC 20420

Regional Offices

Alabama
474 South Court St.
Montgomery, AL 36104
Alaska
235 East 8th Ave.
Anchorage, AK 99501
Arizona
3225 North Central Ave.
Phoenix, AZ 85012
Arkansas
1200 West 3rd St.
Little Rock, AR 72201
California
Federal Building
11000 Wilshire Blvd.
Los Angeles, CA 90024
also:

211 Main St.
San Francisco, CA 94105
Colorado
Building 20
Denver Federal Center
Denver, CO 80225
Connecticut
450 Main St.
Hartford, CT 06103
Delaware
1601 Kirkwood Hwy.
Wilmington, DE 19805
District of Columbia
941 North Capitol St., NE
Washington, DC 20421
Florida
144 1st Ave. South
St. Petersburg, FL 33731
Georgia
730 Peachtree St., NE
Atlanta, GA 30365
Hawaii
PJKK Federal Building
300 Ala Moana Blvd.
Honolulu, HI 96813
Idaho
Federal Building and U.S. Courthouse
550 West Fort St.
Boise, ID 83724

Illinois
536 South Clark St.
Chicago, IL 60680
Indiana
575 North Pennsylvania St.
Indianapolis, IN 46204
Iowa
210 Walnut St.
Des Moines, IO 50309
Kansas
Boulevard Office Park
901 George Washington Blvd.
Wichita, KS 67211
Kentucky
600 Federal Place
Louisville, KY 40202
Louisiana
701 Loyola Ave.
New Orleans, LA 70113
Maine
Togus, ME 04330
Maryland
Counties of Montgomery and Prince Georges
941 North Capitol St., NE
Washington, DC 20421

All other Maryland counties
31 Hopkins Plaza
Federal Building
Baltimore, MD 21201
Massachusetts
Towns of Fall River and New Bedford and counties of Barnstable, Dukes, Nantucket, part of Plymouth, and Bristol are served by:
321 South Main St.
Providence, RI 02903

Remaining Massachusetts counties served by:
John Fitzgerald Kennedy Federal Building
Government Center
Boston, MA 02203
Michigan
Patrick V. McNamara Federal Building
477 Michigan Ave.
Detroit, MI 48226

Minnesota
Counties of Becker, Beltrami, Clay, Clearwater, Kittson, Lake of the Woods, Mahnomen, Marshall, Norman, Otter Tail, Pennington, Polk, Red Lake, Roseau and Wilkin are served by:
21st Ave. & Elm St.
Fargo, ND 58102

all other counties served by:

Federal Building, Fort Snelling
St. Paul, MN 55111
Mississippi
100 West Capitol St.
Jackson, MS 39201

Missouri
Federal Building
1520 Market St.
St. Louis, MO 63103
Montana
Fort Harrison, MT 59636
Nebraska
Federal Building
100 Centennial Mall North
Lincoln, NE 68508
Nevada
245 East Liberty St.
Reno, NV 89520
New Hampshire
Norris Cotton Federal Building
275 Chestnut St.
Manchester, NH 03101
New Jersey
20 Washington Place
Newark, NJ 07102
New Mexico
Dennis Chavez Federal Building
U.S. Courthouse
500 Gold Ave., SW
Albuquerque, NM 87102
New York
Federal Building
111 West Huron St.
Buffalo, NY 14202

252 Seventh Ave.
New York City, NY 10001
North Carolina
Federal Building
251 North Main St.
Winston-Salem, NC 27102
North Dakota
21st Ave. and Elm St.
Fargo, ND 58102
Ohio
Anthony J. Celebrezze Federal Building
1240 East 9th St.
Cleveland, OH 44199
Oklahoma
Federal Building
125 South Main St.
Muskogee, OK 74401
Oregon
Federal Building
1220 South West 3rd Ave.
Portland, OR 97204
Pennsylvania
P.O. Box 8079
5000 Wissahickon Ave.
Philadelphia, PA 19101

1000 Liberty Ave.
Pittsburgh, PA 15222
Philippines
1131 Roxas Blvd.
Manila, PI 96528
Puerto Rico
U.S. Courthouse and Federal Building
Carlos E. Chardon St.
Hato Rey
San Juan, PR 00918
Rhode Island
321 South Main St.
Providence, RI 02903
South Carolina
1801 Assembly St.
Columbia, SC 29201
South Dakota
Courthouse Plaza Building
300 North Dakota Ave.
Sioux Falls, SD 57101
Tennessee
110 9th Ave. South
Nashville, TN 37203
Texas
2515 Murworth Dr.
Houston, TX 77054

1400 North Valley Mills Dr.
Waco, TX 76799
Utah
Federal Building
125 South State St.
Salt Lake City, UT 84138
Vermont
White River Junction, VT 05001
Virginia
For Arlington or Fairfax counties
210 Franklin Rd., SW
Roanoke, VA 24011

941 North Capitol St., NE
Washington, DC 20421
Washington
Federal Building
915 2nd Ave.
Seattle, WA 98174
West Virginia
640 Fourth Ave.
Huntington, WV 25701
Wisconsin
342 North Water St.
Milwaukee, WI 53202
Wyoming
2360 East Pershing Blvd.
Cheyenne, WY 82001

Where To Apply for Alcohol or Drug Dependence Treatment

ALCOHOL AND DRUG DEPENDENCE TREATMENT PROGRAMS

Arizona
Tucson

Arkansas
Little Rock

California
Long Beach, Los Angeles (Brentwood and Sepulveda)
Martinez, Palo Alto, San Diego, San Francisco

Colorado
Denver

District of Columbia
Washington, DC

Florida
Miami

Georgia
Decatur

Illinois
Chicago (West Side), Hines, North Chicago

Indiana
Indianapolis

Louisiana
New Orleans

Maryland
Baltimore

Massachusetts
Bedford, Boston

Michigan
Allen Park, Battle Creek

Minnesota
Minneapolis

Missouri
St. Louis

New Jersey
East Orange

New York City
Bronx, Brooklyn

New York
Albany, Buffalo, Montrose

Ohio
Cincinnati, Cleveland

Oklahoma
Oklahoma City

Pennsylvania
Coatesville, Philadelphia

Puerto Rico
San Juan

Rhode Island
Providence

Tennessee
Memphis

Texas
Dallas, Houston

Utah
Salt Lake City

Washington
American Lake (Tacoma), Seattle

Wisconsin
Milwaukee

ALCOHOL DEPENDENCE TREATMENT PROGRAMS ONLY

Alabama
Birmingham, Tuscaloosa

Alaska
Anchorage

Arizona
Phoenix, Prescott

California
Fresno, Loma Linda

Colorado
Ft. Lyon

Connecticut
West Haven

Florida
Bay Pines, Gainesville

Georgia
Augusta

Illinois
Danville

Indiana
Marion

Iowa
Knoxville, Des Moines

Kansas
Leavenworth, Topeka

Kentucky
Lexington

Maine
Togus

Maryland
Ft. Howard

Massachusetts
Brockton, Northampton

Minnesota
St. Cloud

Mississippi
Biloxi, Jackson

Missouri
Kansas City

Nebraska
Lincoln, Omaha

New Hampshire
Manchester

New Jersey
Lyons

New Mexico
Albuquerque

New York
Canandaigua

Ohio
Cleveland

Oregon
Roseburg, White City

Pennsylvania
Pittsburgh

South Carolina
Charleston, Columbia

South Dakota
Ft. Meade, Hot Springs

Tennessee
Mountain Home, Murfreesboro, Nashville

Texas
Big Spring, Temple, Waco

Vermont
White River Junction

Virginia
Hampton, Salem

West Virginia
   Martinsburg
Wisconsin
   Tomah

**DRUG DEPENDENCE TREATMENT PROGRAMS
ONLY**

California
   Los Angeles
Massachusetts
   Boston

New York
   New York City
Oklahoma
   Tulsa
Pennsylvania
   Pittsburgh
Virginia
   Richmond
Washington
   Vancouver

Spinal Cord Injury Centers

California
VA Medical Center
5901 E. Seventh St.
Long Beach, CA 90822

VA Medical Center
3801 Miranda Ave.
Palo Alto, CA 94304

VA Medical Center
Sepulveda, CA 91343

Florida
VA Medical Center
1201 Northwest 16th St.
Miami, FL 33125

VA Medical Center
1300 North 30th St.
Tampa, FL 33612

Georgia
VA Medical Center
Augusta, GA 30904

Illinois
VA Medical Center
Hines, IL 60141

Massachusetts
VA Medical Center

940 Belmont St.
Brockton, MA 02401

VA Medical Center
1400 Veterans of Foreign Wars Pkwy.
West Roxbury, MA 02132

Missouri
VA Medical Center
St. Louis, MO 63125

New Jersey
VA Medical Center
East Orange, NJ 07019

New York
VA Medical Center
130 West Kingsbridge Rd.
Bronx, NY 10468

VA Medical Center
Castle Point, NY 12511

Ohio
VA Medical Center
10701 East Blvd.
Cleveland, OH 44106

Puerto Rico
VA Medical Center
San Juan, PR 00936

Tennessee
VA Medical Center
1030 Jefferson Ave.
Memphis, TN 38104

Texas
VA Medical Center
2002 Holcombe Blvd.
Houston, TX 77031

Virginia
VA Medical Center
Hampton, VA 23667

VA Medical Center
1201 Broad Rock Rd.
Richmond, VA 23249

Wisconsin
VA Medical Center
5000 West National Ave.
Wood, WI 53196

Veterans Administration National Cemeteries

Alabama
Mobile National Cemetery
1202 Virginia St.
Mobile 36604

**Fort Mitchell National Cemetery
Phenix City 36867

Alaska
*Sitka National Cemetery
P.O. Box 1065
Sitka 99835

Arizona
Prescott National Cemetery

VA Medical Center
Prescott 86313

Arkansas
*Fayetteville National Cemetery
700 Government Ave.
Fayetteville 72701

*Fort Smith National Cemetery
522 Garland Ave. and South 6th St.
Fort Smith 72901

*Little Rock National Cemetery
2523 Confederate Blvd.
Little Rock 72206

California
Fort Rosecrans National Cemetery
Point Loma, P.O. Box 6237
San Diego 92106

Golden Gate National Cemetery
P.O. Box 185
San Bruno 94066

Los Angeles National Cemetery
950 South Sepulveda Blvd.
Los Angeles 90049

*Riverside National Cemetery
22495 Van Buren Blvd.
Riverside 92508

San Francisco National Cemetery
P.O. Box 9012
Presidio of San Francisco
San Francisco 94129

Colorado
*Fort Logan National Cemetery
3698 South Sheridan Blvd.
Denver 80235

*Fort Lyon National Cemetery
Veterans Administration Medical Center
Fort Lyon 81038

Florida
*Barrancas National Cemetery
Naval Air Station
Pensacola 32508

Bay Pines National Cemetery
VA Medical Center
Bay Pines 33504

St. Augustine National Cemetery
104 Marine St.
St. Augustine 32084

Georgia
Marietta National Cemetery
500 Washington Ave.
Marietta 30060

Hawaii
*National Memorial Cemetery of the Pacific
2177 Puowaina Dr.
Honolulu 96813

Illinois
Alton National Cemetery
600 Pearl St.
Alton
(Contact Jefferson Barracks National Cemetery, St.
Louis, Missouri, for information)

*Camp Butler National Cemetery
R.F.D. No. 1
Springfield 62707

*Danville National Cemetery
1900 East Main St.
Danville 61832

*Mound City National Cemetery
P.O. Box 128
Mound City 62963

*Quincy National Cemetery
36th and Maine St.

Quincy
(Contact Keokuk National Cemetery, Keokuk, Iowa,
for information)

*Rock Island National Cemetery
Rock Island Arsenal
Rock Island 61299

Indiana
Crown Hill National Cemetery
3402 Boulevard Pl.
Indianapolis 46208

*Marion National Cemetery
VA Administration Medical Center
Marion 46952

New Albany National Cemetery
1943 Ekin Ave.
New Albany 47150

Iowa
*Keokuk National Cemetery
18th and Ridge Sts.
Keokuk 52632

Kansas
*Fort Leavenworth National Cemetery
Fort Leavenworth 66027

*Fort Scott National Cemetery
P.O. Box 917
Fort Scott 66701

*Leavenworth National Cemetery
VA Medical Center
Leavenworth
(Contact Fort Leavenworth National Cemetery for
information)

Kentucky
*Camp Nelson National Cemetery
RR No. 3
Nicholasville 40356

Cave Hill National Cemetery
701 Baxter Ave.
Louisville
(Contact Zachary Taylor National Cemetery Louisville,
for information)

Danville National Cemetery
377 North First St.
Danville
(Contact Camp Nelson National Cemetery
Nicholasville, for information)

*Lebanon National Cemetery
Lebanon 40033

Lexington National Cemetery
833 West Main St.
Lexington
(Contact Camp Nelson National Cemetery
Nicholasville, for information)

*Mill Springs National Cemetery
R.D. No. 1, Box 172
Nancy 42544

Zachary Taylor National Cemetery
4701 Brownsboro Rd.
Louisville 40207

Louisiana
*Alexandria National Cemetery
209 Shamrock Ave.
Pineville 71360

Baton Rouge National Cemetery
220 North 19th St.
Baton Rouge 70806

*Port Hudson National Cemetery
Route 1, Box 185
Zachary 70791

Maine
Togus National Cemetery
Veterans Medical and Regional Office Center
Togus 04330

Maryland
Annapolis National Cemetery
800 West St.
Annapolis 21401

Baltimore National Cemetery
5501 Frederick Ave.
Baltimore 21228

Loudon Park National Cemetery
3445 Frederick Ave.
Baltimore
(Contact Baltimore National Cemetery for information)

Massachusetts
*Massachusetts National Cemetery
Bourne 02532

Michigan
**Fort Custer National Cemetery
Battle Creek

Minnesota
*Fort Snelling National Cemetery
34th Ave. South
St. Paul 55111

Mississippi
*Biloxi National Cemetery
VA Hospital
Biloxi 39531

*Corinth National Cemetery
1551 Horton St.
Corinth 38834

*Natchez National Cemetery
61 Cemetery Rd.
Natchez 39120

Missouri
*Jefferson Barracks National Cemetery
101 Memorial Dr.
St. Louis 63125

Jefferson City National Cemetery
1024 East McCarty St.
Jefferson City 65101

*Springfield National Cemetery
1702 East Seminole St.
Springfield 65804

Nebraska
*Fort McPherson National Cemetery
Maxwell 69151

New Jersey
Beverly National Cemetery

Beverly 08010

Finn's Point National Cemetery
R.F.D. No. 3, Fort Mott Rd.
Salem 08079

New Mexico
*Fort Bayard National Cemetery
Fort Bayard 88306

*Sante Fe National Cemetery
Box 88
Santa Fe 87501

New York
*Bath National Cemetery
VA Medical Center
Bath 14810

*Calverton National Cemetery
Route 25
P.O. Box 144
Calverton 11933

Cypress Hills National Cemetery
625 Jamaica Ave.
Brooklyn 11208

Long Island National Cemetery
Farmingdale 11735

Woodlawn National Cemetery
1825 Davis St.
Elmira 14901

North Carolina
*New Bern National Cemetery
1711 National Ave.
New Bern 28560

*Raleigh National Cemetery
501 Rock Quarry Rd.
Raleigh 27610

*Salisbury National Cemetery
202 Government Rd.
Salisbury 28144

*Wilmington National Cemetery
2011 Market St.
Wilmington 28401

Ohio
*Dayton National Cemetery
VA Medical Center
4100 West Third St.
Dayton 45428

Oklahoma
*Fort Gibson National Cemetery
Fort Gibson 74434

Oregon
Roseburg National Cemetery
VA Medical Center
Roseburg 97470

*White City National Cemetery
VA Domiciliary
White City 97501

*Willamette National Cemetery
11800 South East Mt. Scott Blvd.
P.O. Box 66147
Portland 97266

Pennsylvania
****Indiantown Gap National Cemetery
Annville 17003

Philadelphia National Cemetery
Haines St. and Limekiln Pike
Philadelphia 19138
Puerto Rico
*Puerto Rico National Cemetery
Box 1298
Bayamon 00619
South Carolina
*Beaufort National Cemetery
1601 Boundary St.
Beaufort 29902

*Florence National Cemetery
803 East National Cemetery Rd.
Florence 29501
South Dakota
*Black Hills National Cemetery
P. O. Box 640
Sturgis 57785

Fort Meade National Cemetery
VA Medical Center
Fort Meade
(Contact Black Hills National Cemetery for
information)

Hot Springs National Cemetery
VA Medical Center
Hot Springs 57747
Tennessee
*Chattanooga National Cemetery
1200 Bailey Ave.
Chattanooga 37404

Knoxville National Cemetery
939 Tyson Street, NW
Knoxville 37917

*Memphis National Cemetery
3568 Townes Ave.
Memphis 38122

*Mountain Home National Cemetery
P.O. Box 8
Mountain Home 37684

*Nashville National Cemetery
1420 South Gallatin Rd.
Madison 37115
Texas
*Fort Bliss National Cemetery
P.O. Box 6342
Fort Bliss 79906

*Fort Sam Houston National Cemetery
1520 Harry Wurzbach Rd.
San Antonio 78209

*Houston National Cemetery
10410 Stuebner Airline Dr.
Houston 77038

Kerrville National Cemetery
VA Medical Center
Spur Rt. 100
Kerrville 78028

San Antonio National Cemetery
517 Paso Hondo St.
San Antonio
(Contact Fort Sam Houston National Cemetery, San
Antonia, for information)
Virginia
Alexandria National Cemtery
1450 Wilkes St.
Alexandria 22314

Balls Bluff National Cemetery
Leesburg
(Contact Winchester National Cemetery for
information)

City Point National Cemetery
10th Ave. and Davis St.
Hopewell
(Contact Richmond National Cemetery for information)

Cold Harbor National Cemetery
R.F.D. No. 4, Box 155
(Contact Richmond National Cemetery for information)

Culpeper National Cemetery
305 U.S. Ave.
Culpeper 22701

Danville National Cemetery
721 Lee St.
Danville 24541

Fort Harrison National Cemetery
R.F.D. No. 5, Box 174
Varina Rd.
Richmond
(Contact Richmond National Cemetery for information)

Glendale National Cemetery
R.F.D. No. 5, Box 272
Richmond
(Contact Richmond National Cemetery for information)

Hampton National Cemetery
Cemetery Rd. at Marshall Ave.
Hampton 23669

Quantico National Cemetery
Quantico 22134

Richmond National Cemetery
1701 Williamsburg Rd.
Richmond 23231

Seven Pines National Cemetery
400 East Williamsburg Rd.
Sandston
(Contact Richmond National Cemetery for information)

Staunton National Cemetery
901 Richmond Ave.
Staunton 24401

Winchester National Cemetery
401 National Ave.
Winchester 22601
West Virginia
Grafton National Cemetery
Grafton 26354
Wisconsin
Wood National Cemetery

VA Medical Center
5000 West National Ave.
Wood 53193

*Grave Space Available
**New Cemetery Not Yet Open for Interment

Department of the Army National Cemeteries

District of Columbia
Soldiers' Home National Cemetery
21 Harewood Rd., NW
Washington 20011

Virginia
Arlington National Cemetery
Arlington 22211

Department of the Interior National Cemeteries

District of Columbia
Battleground National Cemetery
6625 Georgia Ave., NW
(Between Whittier & Van Buren Sts.)
Washington 20012

Georgia
Andersonville National Historic Site
Andersonville 31711

Louisiana
Chalmette National Historical Park
St. Bernard Hwy.
Chalmette 70043

Maryland
Antietam National Battlefield Site
Box 158
Sharpsburg 21782

Mississippi
Vicksburg National Military Park
Vicksburg 39180

Montana
Custer Battlefield National Monument
P.O. Box 39
Crow Agency 59022

Pennsylvania
Gettysburg National Military Park
P.O. Box 70
Gettysburg 17325

Tennessee
Andrew Johnson National Historic Site
Depot St.
Greeneville 37743

Fort Donelson National Military Park
P.O. Box F
Dover 37058

Shiloh National Military Park
Shiloh 38376

Stones River National Battlefield
Rt. 10, Box 401, Old Nashville Hwy.
Murfreesboro 37130

Virginia
Fredericksburg and Spotsylvania County Battlefields
Memorial National Military Park
1013 Lafayette Blvd.
P.O. Box 679
Fredericksburg 22401

Poplar Grove National Cemetery
Petersburg National Battlefield
P.O. Box 549
Petersburg 23803

Yorktown Battlefield
Colonial National Historical Park
Box 210
Yorktown 23690

Chapter 7

The Broad Coverage
of Social Security

In 1935, when President Franklin D. Roosevelt signed the
Social Security bill into law, our society undertook to accept a degree of
responsibility for the well-being of the elderly. At first, relatively
few Americans were enrolled in the Social Security system, and both the
benefits and the taxes to pay for them were miniscule. Today, however,
more than 115 million Americans—over 90 percent of the work force—
pay into the Social Security trust funds, and 36 million retirees, disabled
workers, their dependents or survivors receive substantial benefits.
Retirement checks are the largest item, but the coverage also includes
disability compensation, survivors' benefits and Medicare.
The Supplemental Security Income payments program, financed by
general revenues, is also administered by the Social Security Administration.
In this chapter, the types of benefits available under Social Security are
described, and the eligibility requirements are explained. You are told how
Social Security credits are counted; what typical wage earners in various income brackets can expect in the way of Social Security payments; and what
disabled people, survivors and dependents are entitled to under the program. Where possible, examples are given to show how the benefits are
computed.

Contents

The Concept of Social Security

When Americans think about Social Security, the word "retirement" almost automatically comes to mind. Indeed, the original purpose—and still the primary function—of the program was to provide a modest income for the elderly when their working days were over. Yet Social Security, as it has evolved during more than four decades, has come to be a federally administered insurance program that protects tens of millions of American workers and their families from many of the vicissitudes of modern life. The term "insurance" is used advisedly, for Social Security differs in many important respects from ordinary private insurance plans. For example, if you buy a retirement insurance plan on the private market, the money you pay into the plan during your working years is placed in an account in your name and is then paid out to you at a predetermined rate. Under the Social Security system, however, the money you and your employer contribute in your name does not lie fallow—or collect interest—until you retire. It is used to pay *current* recipients of Social Security benefits. When you retire (or become disabled) the money that is then being collected from those in the work force will be employed to pay *you* the benefits you have earned. Their benefits, in turn, will come from the next generation of workers.

The entire system is based on the ability of the U.S. government to continue to collect Social Security taxes (euphemistically called "contributions") generation after generation, thus keeping the program solvent. Social Security also differs from some insurance plans in another respect: there is no limit on the number of payments you will receive. Under some—but not all—private annuity plans and even GI insurance, you may begin receiving benefits at, say, age 65, with monthly payments being made to you for a specific number of years. If you live beyond that predetermined time limit, the payments stop. Under Social Security, payments continue as long as you live. Even if you live to be over 100, you will continue to receive your monthly checks, as will all eligible dependents. Another major benefit that Social Security offers is that it is pegged to inflation. By law, every year that inflation rises by 3 percent or more, monthly payments are adjusted to reflect the higher cost of living. Finally, funds from private pension plans are taxable; income from Social Security is not. This is no small consideration, given today's tax rates.

The fact that Social Security differs in many important respects from private insurance plans does not mean, however, that it is not insurance. When you enroll in the Social Security system, usually at the time you get your first job, you begin making contributions and gaining credits that will protect you, or your dependents and survivors in the event of your death, disability or retirement, just as you would if you were enrolled in a private insurance plan. Indeed, the basic benefits offered by Social Security are summed up in one of the official names the system uses to describe itself: Old Age, Survivors, Disability and Hospital Insurance (OASDHI).

In this chapter, we will not be concerned with the hospital insurance aspects (Medicare) of Social Security; these are explained in detail in Chapter 4. The other major components of the program may be briefly described as:

*Old Age Insurance. Benefits are paid to those 65 and over (reduced benefits may be obtained by those as young as 62). These benefits are based in part on the earnings that were covered under the system during the working years. Benefits are weighted in favor of those who had relatively low earnings. A worker whose income was low, and who therefore earned a relatively small amount during his or her financially productive years, will receive a somewhat greater proportion of the working income than will a person who was highly paid. Retirement benefits are also paid to the

The Growing Cost of Social Security

The alarming increase in the cost of the Social Security program as America grows older, is reflected in the chart below. Compiled at the start of the present decade, it shows the percentages of the federal budget that would be needed to meet Social Security payments in the coming decades if eligibility requirements remained unchanged. As the chart indicates, Social Security would claim an additional six percent of the federal budget by the year 2000. The figure would increase a further ten percent by 2010, and by 2020, 63 percent of the federal budget would be needed for Social Security payments. The change stems from the rapid increase in the numbers of Americans who are over 65. In 1970, 20 million people in the United States were over 65. By the year 2000, the figure will have increased to 32 million, and by 2020, it will have soared to nearly 53 million people.

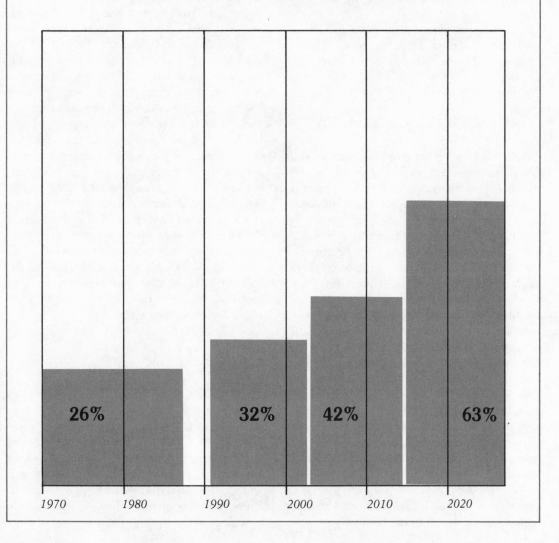

1970	1980	1990	2000	2010	2020
26%		32%	42%		63%

worker's spouse—even if that husband or wife never worked in a job that was covered by the system—and to a retiree's minor or disabled children.

*Survivors' Insurance.** These are monthly payments made to a spouse and other dependents (usually minor children) of a deceased retiree or a deceased worker who was covered by Social Security.

*Disability Insurance.** These are monthly benefits paid to the permanently or long-term disabled and their dependents.

All these categories of insurance, as well as lesser benefits offered by the Social Security system, will be described in detail later in the chapter.

Your Social Security Card

Your ticket to the system's benefits is your Social Security card or, more precisely, the number that appears on that card. Your earnings, reflected in your payroll taxes, are credited to that number.

Once you receive a number it will be exclusively yours. It will be listed in your name for the rest of your life, and you will be constantly referring to it for a variety of purposes.

Getting Your Social Security Card

Few, if any, employers will hire a person without a Social Security card—or at least a number. Most people, therefore, apply for a card shortly before they begin looking for their first job. Any resident of the United States, even a child, can have a Social Security card and number. In certain circumstances—as when a parent or grandparent sets up a trust fund for a minor—the child is required by law to have a card.

To apply for a card and number, just go to your nearest Social Security office. There are approximately 1,300 in the United States. For the nearest one, check under the headings "U.S. Government" or "Social Security" in the white pages of your phone book. If you are 18 or over, you must apply in person. Children may be represented by a parent or guardian at the Social Security office. You must bring along proof of identity, such as a birth certificate or a driver's license. The form you will be required to fill out is short and simple. Once completed, the form will be mailed to Social Security headquarters in Baltimore, and in six to eight weeks you will receive a card.

If You Lose Your Card

When you receive your Social Security card, you will notice that there are two parts to it: the card itself and the stub. Each will have printed on it your name and number. Tear off the stub and file it in some safe, convenient place where you can find it. Carry the card itself in your wallet or purse, and memorize the number or write it down and keep it in a safe but handy place. If you lose your card, take the stub, along with proof of identity, to your Social Security office and apply for a new card. If you have lost the stub as well as the card but remember your number, just give the number to a Social Security worker. Though the stub or the number will facilitate replacement of your lost card, neither is absolutely necessary. The Social Security Administration has cross-indexed files, and if they know your name and date of birth, they can turn up your number and issue you a new card.

How Social Security Is Financed

The federal government has established three trust funds from which it distributes Social Security benefits: the Old Age and Survivors Insurance Fund; the Disability Insurance Fund; and the Hospital Insurance Fund (Medicare). These funds are financed through a payroll tax that is entirely separate from the income tax

Change of Name and Social Security

Should you change your name because of marriage, divorce or for any other reason, be sure to notify your local Social Security office. You set this process in motion by merely making a phone call to Teleservice (see page 279), but you must appear in person to complete the application. Be sure to bring with you proof of your old name and new. Birth certificates, marriage licenses, passports and drivers' licenses constitute proof. After your application is processed, you will receive a new Social Security card. The number will be the same as on your old card, but the name will be your new one.

that finances most other government activities. Money from the income tax as well as from the sale of government bonds and treasury bills goes under the heading "general revenues." Social Security, on the other hand, is financed through taxes imposed under the Federal Insurance Contributions Act—known to most workers through the initials "FICA" that appear on the stubs of millions of paychecks. Beneath these initials is listed a sum of money withheld from the worker's salary to pay his or her share of Social Security. Not appearing on the paycheck, however, is the amount that the worker's employer must contribute in that employee's name. In almost all instances, the amount matches the sum contributed by the worker.

Increasing Benefits and Costs

There was a time, in the years before 1950, when Social Security benefits were minimal, and a worker hardly noticed the Social Security tax. In those days the combined contribution of worker and employer amounted to only 2 percent of the employee's first $3,000 of annual income. In other words, the total contribution was $60, with the worker contributing $30 per year, and his company contributing a like amount. Of course, if the worker earned under $3,000—as most did—contributions were even smaller.

Inflation and a rising standard of living have led to a vast increase in Social Security benefits. Consequently, Social Security taxes have risen at a rate that could hardly have been imagined by the founders of the system. (They would also be stunned by the percentage of Americans currently covered by the system and by the generosity of the benefits.) By 1980, for example, the first $25,900 of a person's annual income was subject to Social Security contributions at a rate of 6.13 percent, with the employer paying a like amount. That means that in 1980 a person who earned more than the maximum covered amount ($25,900 at that time) paid $1,587 in Social Security taxes. The employer was required, of course, to contribute an equal amount in the employee's name.

If current projections are accurate, by 1990 the maximum income covered under Social Security will be $60,600. For those earning this sum or more, the combined employer and employee contribution will amount to $9,271.80. The tax rate for Social Security will then be 7.65 percent. This projection takes into account continuing inflation of both wages and prices and the growing number of Social Security beneficiaries (mostly retirees) in proportion to the working population. Remember, these are maximum figures. People earning less than the top amount covered by Social Security will pay less money into the system, while those who earn more than the top amount will pay only on the maximum amount. The rest of their earnings will not be subject to Social Security taxes. The *rate* of Social Security taxes will be the same for the

The Social Security Funding Problem

When speaking of Social Security benefits, people often refer to the "trust fund." By that, they mean the money collected by the Social Security Administration through payroll taxes and then distributed to beneficiaries. Actually, there are three trust funds, separately administered within the Social Security Administration. Far and away the largest of these funds is the Old Age and Survivors Fund. The bulk of Social Security taxes goes into this fund, and most benefits are paid through it. The other two trusts are the disability insurance fund and the hospital insurance fund, which pays for hospital benefits under Medicare. An authorization by Congress is required to shift money from one of the funds to another, and the transfer is made only under compelling circumstances.

In 1980, for example, when demands on the Old Age and Survivors Fund were higher than had been anticipated, and payments through the disability fund fell below expectations, Congress authorized the shifting of $8 billion from the disability trust to the old age trust. There is, however, no guarantee that in the future there will be a surplus in one fund that will permit it to come to the rescue of another. A much-talked-about solution to this problem would remove hospital insurance from the Social Security tax (presumably without lowering that tax) and transfer responsibility for hospital benefits to general revenues. This would free large amounts collected through the Social Security tax and make them available for the disability and old age funds.

worker earning $10,000 and for the more fortunate fellow citizen who earns the maximum: 6.13 percent in 1980, 7.65 percent in 1990.

The Tax Break for Employers
At first glance it would seem that the employer's contribution to the worker's Social Security accounts would amount to an enormous financial burden. The burden, in most instances, is more apparent than real. Employers are permitted to deduct these contributions as necessary business expenses, thus greatly reducing their companies' tax liability. For most employers, the actual out-of-pocket expenditures associated with contributions to employees' Social Security accounts are only 50 cents on the dollar.

Contributions of the Self-Employed
Over six million workers who contribute to the Social Security system are self-employed. They are taxed somewhat differently from other employees, because there is no employer

involved to pay a share of the contributions. In assessing the self-employed, a compromise has been reached. These people pay more than they would if they were employed at the same salary by somebody else, but they do not pay a double rate. This has come about because the government recognizes that it would be unfair to require them to contribute the full amount for the employer and the employee when they are not permitted to write off a share of their contributions as business expenses. A self-employed person in 1980 paid 138 percent of what an employee paid for the cash benefit programs of Social Security (retirement, disability and survivors' benefits) and the same percentage that the employee paid for Medicare hospital insurance. The maximum amount on which the self-employed may be taxed is the same as the maximum amount on which an employee is taxed.

Tips as a Part of Income
Many people in the United States—such as

waiters, waitresses, bellmen and taxi drivers—earn a large proportion of their incomes in tips. Under the law, they are required to report their tips, for both Social Security and income tax purposes if the tips come to more than $20 in any one month. A waiter, for example, must file a written report with his employer before the 10th of each month, listing the tips he collected in the preceding month. The employer must then deduct from the waiter's wages the appropriate amount to cover Social Security contributions. The amount will be based on the waiter's combined salary and tips. Employers, however, are not required to make contributions on their employees' tips. But they are required to make contributions on the salary. The contributions must equal the amount they would pay if the worker was employed at the federal minimum wage.

Income Exempt from Social Security Taxes
As already indicated, income above the maximum amount is not taxed for Social Security. In addition, certain types of income that the government classifies as "unearned" are exempt from Social Security contributions. Interest and dividends on stocks, bonds and bank accounts, for example, are not taxed, nor are profits realized from the sale of a house (unless real estate is your business), and such windfalls as inheritances.

Persons Exempt from Social Security
The overwhelming majority of American workers and their families are covered by Social Security, but some segments of the working population are not included. The largest single group of people who do not participate in the program are civilian employees of the federal government, most of whom are covered by special retirement and disability plans. (Members of the armed forces are covered under Social Security and have their own retirement plan as well.) In addition, railroad workers—past and present—have a retirement program which, though not part of Social Security, is closely associated with the system.

Until 1951, many state and local government employees were exempt from Social Security taxes and received no Social Security benefits. At the time the Social Security system was established, it was believed that, under the Constitution, the federal government could not levy the Social Security employers' tax on state and local governments. For a long time following the establishment of Social Security, both state and local governments and their civil servants preferred to remain outside the system, relying instead on their own pension and disability plans. But all states have now entered into voluntary agreements with the federal government to bring most of their workers into the Social Security program. Today, only 3.3 million of the nation's 13.3 million state and local government employees remain outside the system. In many parts of the country, state and local civil servants are covered by both Social Security and their own retirement programs.

Another category that is not automatically covered by Social Security is the clergy, for it has been felt that to require clergymen to join the system would violate the Constitutional mandate concerning the separation of church and state. Clergymen, however, are now routinely covered unless they elect to be excluded. Though they may receive salaries from their congregations, they are taxed on the same basis as the self-employed. A few other categories of people also have traditionally been exempted from Social Security. Some religious denominations, most notably the Amish, objected so fiercely to the program as a violation of their consciences that self-employed members of these groups may choose not to be covered if their denominations make reasonable alternative provisions.

Many people outside of federal employment have objected to the exclusion of federal employees from the system. But by and large, these employees have resisted inclusion, for their own retirement and disability programs are superior to those offered by Social Security. There is, however, increasing public pressure to require federal employees to contribute to Social Security on the same basis as the rest of the population.

Accumulating Credits for Social Security Protection

To be insured under Social Security, you must accumulate a certain number of work credits or, to put it another way, you must have been paying Social Security taxes for a certain number of years. The number of credits you need varies according to your age and the type of benefit in question. For example, the credits needed for disability benefits (see pages 274–278) may be quite different from the number required for retirement or survivors' benefits. In all instances, however, there is a minimum requirement of work credits. Suppose, for purposes of illustration, that you entered the labor market at the age of 18 and got a job as a clerk. After two months of working, the proverbial "long-lost uncle" died and left you his entire fortune of $10 million. You decide, on the strength of this windfall, that the humdrum work-a-day world is no longer for you. You quit your job and go into permanent retirement, drawing on income from your investments, monies not taxable by the Social Security Administration. Although you don't really need it, at 65 you apply for retirement benefits under Social Security to augment your income. You will not get any, for two months of work under this system is not long enough.

Retirement Benefit Credits

Under current regulations, the number of credits, or years worked in a Social Security covered job, needed to qualify you for retirement benefits varies according to the year at which you reach the age of 62. If, for example, you reached 62 in 1975, you would have needed only six years of covered employment. On the other hand, anyone who reaches 62 in 1991 or later will need credit for 10 years. The chart

below tells you how many years of credit for covered employment are needed for retirement benefits from the years 1975 to 1991 and beyond.

If You Reach (or Reached) Age 62 in	Years of Credit You Need
1975	6
1976	6¼
1977	6½
1978	6¾
1979	7
1980	7¼
1981	7½
1982	7¾
1983	8
1984	8¼
1985	8½
1986	8¾
1987	9
1988	9¼
1989	9½
1990	9¾
1991 or later	10

Quarters of Coverage. Social Security credits are often expressed in "quarters," with four quarters equaling one year of coverage. Before 1978 an employee was credited with a quarter of coverage for each calendar quarter, in which a total of $50 or more in wages was earned. Starting in 1978, however, a quarter of coverage was credited for each $250 in annual earnings. By 1981, the amount had risen to $310. Thus you received a quarter of coverage (or credit) for each $310 you earned in calendar 1981, up to a maximum of four quarters of credit. Even if you earned $1,240 or more, all in one month, you would receive four quarters of credit.

If you were self-employed, however, you must have earned at least $400 net during the year to receive any Social Security credit. Before 1978, $400 in net earnings from self-employment provided four quarters of coverage. In 1978 and after, the figures for earning credits are the same as for those who are not self-employed. A self-employed person who, in 1981, earned $1,240 or more, would receive four quarters of credit. For both the self-employed and those who work for others, the amount of earnings needed to earn a quarter's credit will probably continue to rise, to take into account general increases in average wages.

Family Businesses. Husbands and wives who work together in partnership arrangements should each report their respective shares of profits. In this way, each will have a separate Social Security record, and each will receive full credit for retirement benefits. Each will be regarded as a self-employed worker, and as explained above, each must have a minimum of $400 in net income during a given year in order to receive credit. In addition, if both are to report income for Social Security purposes, the partnership must be a real one. For example, a husband or wife who merely holds the title of "partner" in a spouse's business but makes no significant contribution to the enterprise is not considered a true partner by the Social Security Administration on the basis of that titular relationship.

This in no way prevents one spouse or the other from maintaining a Social Security record on the basis of other income. For example, suppose Mrs. Jones sets up a boutique with her husband listed as partner. Her husband actually does nothing to contribute to the success of the boutique, but he does work full-time as a drill-press operator. Mr. Jones' record will be maintained through his factory job, while Mrs. Jones' separate record will be based on the income she makes through her boutique.

How Credits Are Translated into Benefits

Anyone who is fully insured for retirement purposes under Social Security may apply for full benefits at the age of 65, or may choose to retire as early as age 62 with permanently reduced benefits. On the other hand, workers may defer retirement—if they wish and if their situation allows it—and get higher retirement benefits. A person who retires at age 62 will receive monthly cash benefits equal to about 80 percent of the amount he or she would have received at the age of 65. The closer that person is to 65 at retirement time, the greater will be the retirement income. The longer a person works beyond the age of 65 (up to 72, or 70 starting in 1983), the greater his or her benefits will be. A covered worker who reaches age 62 in 1979 or later and delays retirement beyond the age of 65 will receive 3 percent more in monthly cash benefits for each year that he or she continues on the job. Workers who reached age 62 before 1979, and decided to delay retirement after reaching age 65, receive only a 1 percent addition to their monthly benefits for each year that they continued to work. To take a specific example, suppose a worker reaches age 62 in 1982. That worker will be 65 in 1985, but decides to continue on the job until 1990 when he or she turns 70. That person will receive an additional 15 percent or more in retirement benefits. The additional sum is merely a recognition of two facts: that the worker has contributed taxes to the Social Security funds for five extra years and that the delayed retirement reduces the number of years that he or she will draw benefits.

Factors that Determine Benefit Amounts

The specific amount of money you will receive each month after retiring is based upon a number of factors, the major ones being:

*Your earnings record during your years of employment.
*Your family situation.
*The income, if any, that you continue to earn up to the age of 72 (or 70 starting in 1983).
*Cost-of-living increases in benefits based on the Consumer Price Index.
*The age at which you retire.

Earnings Record. Your monthly retirement check is directly linked to the amount you earned under Social Security. Remember that if, in some or all of those years, you earned more than the covered maximum, only that maximum was credited for Social Security purposes. A distinction should be re-emphasized here between your entitlement to retirement benefits and the amount you will receive. Your entitlement derives from your accumulation of the required number of credits (see page 266) and your having reached retirement age. Once entitlement is secured, however, the actual dollar amount you will receive each month is based, in large measure, upon the amount of your covered earnings over your working lifetime, and the number of years, beyond the minimum, that you worked. As a rule of thumb, it is safe to say that the larger your covered earnings and the longer you work, the greater will be your Social Security retirement income.

The ratio between earnings and benefits, however, is far from an absolute one. If George Carter, for example, earned twice as much in his 50 years on the job as Richard Gross, this does not necessarily mean that George's monthly retirement check will be twice as large as Richard's. There are other factors involved, including the fundamental consideration that Social Security benefits be sufficiently high to permit those who were relatively low-paid during their working years to achieve a decent standard of living in retirement.

Direct Deposit of Checks

If you are a Social Security beneficiary, the Administration offers a major convenience through the direct deposit of your monthly checks into your savings or checking account. All you have to do is ask your bank for Form SF-1199, fill it in and ask an officer of the financial institution to mail it. Processing of the application usually takes three to four months. Meanwhile, you will continue to receive your checks at home. When the checks begin arriving at your bank or savings and loan association you will be informed. Procedures vary greatly from one institution to another, however, and it's a good idea to check with your bank or savings and loan association to determine how they will keep you informed of the status of your account. Some banks send out a notice whenever a Social Security check is received; others make no special arrangements for notifying direct deposit customers (other than the usual monthly or quarterly statements); still others will credit your account for the amount of your usual benefit on a specified day whether or not the check has actually been received; and some notify customers *only* if a check has not been received on the day it is due.

You may end a direct deposit arrangement or switch banks at any time merely by notifying your local Social Security office. If you transfer your account to another bank, you must submit a new SF-1199 form. Again, be sure to allow three to four months for processing before closing out your old account.

The advantages of direct deposit are numerous, among them the following:

* The possibility of your check being lost or stolen is greatly minimized.
* You can leave home for several days, weeks or months and know that money for your expenses is being paid directly into your bank account.
* You save time and transportation costs by being relieved of the responsibility for depositing your own check.
* Your bank statements will provide you with a written record of Social Security check deposits.

Payments for Dependents. A retiree with dependents—a wife or husband without his or her own Social Security benefit, children under the age of 18 or children over the age of 18 who became disabled before the age of 22—will receive benefits. (Children between the ages of 18 and 22 who are enrolled in college have also been receiving benefits, but this program is to be phased out over the next several years.) A wife of retirement age, for example, who did not work long enough to receive her own Social Security benefits—or whose benefit based solely on her own record would be small—will receive a monthly check equal to half her husband's full benefit.

Maximum Family Benefits. There is a limit to the amount that will be paid each month to the members of one family whose benefits derive from the earnings of a single person. In general, the absolute maximum is 188 percent of the former wage earner's own check, but the figure may be less, because of the need to hold down soaring Social Security costs. Suppose a worker named Jim Smith with four dependents—a wife and three minor children—retires at the age of 65 with a Social Security benefit of $300.70 per month. If each family member were entitled to a full dependent's allowance of 50 percent ($150.35), the total family income would be $902.10 per month. Social Security just cannot be that generous. In this situation, under a complex formula, taking into account Smith's earnings record, each dependent is permitted a payment of $47 per month, for a family total of $488.70. This comes to approximately 162 percent of the primary insurance amount. As each child gets older and loses the dependent status, the individual checks for the spouse and remaining children will grow larger, though the total family payment will never be larger than approximately 162 percent of the primary benefit. Finally, when all three children are on their own, the former wage earner will continue to receive a full payment and the dependent spouse will get a benefit 50 percent as large.

The Inflation Factor

Benefits under Social Security are linked to inflation and, to some extent, to the rising standard of living Americans have enjoyed over the past few decades. The linkage is accomplished through two mathematical concepts: wage indexing and price indexing.

Wage Indexing. Because retirement benefits under the Social Security system reflect earnings over a long period of time, some provision must be made for the years when wages and covered earnings were relatively low in terms of today's dollars. Many people approaching retirement age today were working in the 1940s and paying into Social Security. In those days the maximum covered income was $3,000 and the tax was a mere 1 percent. Yet, that $3,000 represents a much higher income than $3,000 earned by a worker today. To allow for the general rise in incomes over the decades, the Social Security Administration adjusts or "indexes" a person's wages at the time of retirement so that the salary that the worker earned during the low-income years of the 1940s reflects today's economic realities.

Perhaps the best way to explain wage indexing is by means of an example. Suppose that Paul Rogers began his working career in 1951. That year his salary was $2,200, all of which was covered by Social Security. When Paul retires at age 62 in 1984, the $2,200 on which he paid Social Security contributions more than a quarter of a century before will be counted as $11,825 in figuring his retirement benefits, if government projections of inflation hold true over the next few years. Similarly, Paul's earnings of $10,000 in 1979 will be translated as $13,106 in 1984 terms. Paul's earnings of $14,000 the year before his retirement will not be indexed, however, since all wages received after age 60 are counted at face value.

By indexing in this manner, the government manages to link earnings throughout the working life of a Social Security subscriber to the wage levels that exist in the year when the person becomes eligible for retirement benefits.

Price Indexing. Once the worker becomes eligible to retire, wage indexing stops and price indexing takes over. This is simply a means of pegging Social Security benefits to the cost of living. To accomplish this result, the law requires that in any year when prices, as measured by the Consumer Price Index, rise by 3 percent or more, Social Security benefits must rise by the same amount.

Retirement Benefits Under Social Security

Because of the many variables involved in calculating retirement benefits, it is impossible to predict long in advance, with any assurance of accuracy, precisely what an individual or family will receive. Current benefits can, of course, be established for typical situations. Below are several examples of what workers in different categories would have received as their initial benefits had they retired at age 65 on January 1, 1981. All are assumed to have been covered for three decades.

A Low-Paid Worker. Assuming this person always earned the minimum wage ($3.35 per hour as of January 1, 1981) the monthly check would be $345.70, for a replacement rate of 69 percent of his last year's earnings. If the former worker is married, and his wife is also 65, but has not built up her own Social Security record, she will be entitled to a monthly benefit half as large as his, or $172.85. Together, their total monthly income from Social Security will be $518.55 per month.

A Worker Who Earned Average Wages. The average wage of persons covered by Social Security was about $12,500 in 1980. A single worker who had received the equivalent of this wage through the years would receive a monthly benefit of $532.80, computed from the previous gross earnings, as a retirement

benefit. If the retiree is married and the spouse is the same age, the couple will receive a second monthly check equal to half the basic benefits, or $266.40, for a total monthly benefit of $799.20. (Remember, this amount may be increased if the spouse was not a dependent but had established an earnings record under Social Security.)

A High-Paid Worker. A worker whose income was always above the covered maximum ($25,900 in 1980) would receive a monthly benefit of $677—based upon the maximum coverage. The check for a dependent spouse—if that spouse is also 65—would be $388.50, for a total monthly income of $1,015.50.

Other Retirement Benefits

Although the examples offered here are typical of the benefits that retired Americans receive under Social Security, they may not tell the whole story. It is worth reiterating that the benefits just listed represent initial payments, and will probably rise year by year to keep pace with inflation. Add to this the fact that Social Security benefits are not taxable by any level of government and it becomes clear that even if family members have only their Social Security checks to rely upon, it is often possible for them to retain a style of living at least close to that of pre-retirement days. Retirees may also benefit from other aspects of Social Security, listed below.

Dependent Childrens' Benefits. If the retiree has dependent children under 18, each child will receive a monthly check based on half of the former wage earner's full benefit.

Disabled Childrens' Benefits. If the retiree has children over the age of 18 who are permanently disabled, each one will receive a monthly check half as large as the retiree's full benefit. The condition causing the disability must have occurred before the child or children reached the age of 22.

Grandparents Caring for Children. Retirees who are contributing to the support of dependent grandchildren may, in certain cases, claim Social Security benefits for these minors. Generally these benefits are allowed only when the children's own parents are dead or disabled and the minors have been legally adopted by the grandparents.

Medicare. All Americans who are 65 or older, whether or not they are retired, are eligible for Medicare. Also, disabled persons who are not yet 65 but have been on the Social Security program's rolls for 24 months may participate.

Spouses' Benefits. When the Social Security Act was amended in 1939 to include spouses, the assumption was that in the overwhelming majority of families, the husband was the sole breadwinner, and that the wife stayed home, cared for the children and earned no salary. A wife's benefit was considered to be a payment related to her husband's contributions to the Social Security system. Her benefit was set at 50 percent of her husband's. She would begin receiving her payments when she reached retirement age (assuming her husband was already retired). Upon her husband's death, she would receive the full amount of her husband's monthly benefit as long as she lived.

In large measure, Social Security retirement benefits still work in this manner, even though in the past couple of decades increasing numbers of women have entered the work force and have established their own employment records covered by Social Security. In situations where the woman has established her own earnings record, and the payments that she has earned are higher than those she would receive as a dependent of her husband, she has a right to the higher payment. Yet even today this is not the usual pattern. Although a woman may have been in the work force for a considerable number of years, past discrimination in pay scales, plus time out for bearing and raising children, have left most women with earnings records that are insufficient to entitle them to an independent benefit greater than the one they would receive as dependent wives.

During the next few decades this situation is likely to change quite radically. More and more women are entering high-paying jobs; equal pay for equal work is gradually becoming a reality; and increasingly women are taking shorter leaves for bearing and rearing children. When the time comes for couples now in their 20s and 30s to retire, it may well be that many, if not a majority, of the women will have established earnings records that entitle them to monthly payments considerably higher than the 50 percent now offered to dependent wives.

Benefits for the Divorced. When a couple is divorced, the wife—or, for that matter, the husband—does not automatically lose retirement benefits as a dependent. In fact, if the couple has been married for 10 years or more, the spouse retains full rights so long as he or she remains unmarried. Suppose, for example, that Tom and Susan Cartwright (who, like the other sample beneficiaries in this chapter, are fictitious) were divorced after 11 years together. At the time of the divorce, Tom was 37 and Susan 34. Tom retires from his job when he is 65, Susan is then 62. Like others her age, she will collect nothing until she is 65, unless she chooses to accept reduced benefits. When she reaches 65, however, she will get a monthly check equal to half her ex-husband's payment, just as she would if they had never been divorced. Susan does, of course, have the option of collecting benefits based on her own work record—provided she has built up a Social Security account that would pay her more.

Suppose Tom remarried? His wife as well as his ex-wife would be entitled to dependents' benefits. If Tom were to die before either of the women, both his widow and his surviving divorced wife could collect the full amount of his monthly check. In fact, even if Tom had wed several women and had been married to each for more than 10 years, all would be entitled to benefits as Tom's dependents, so long as they have not remarried or if their subsequent marriages had ended.

Remarriage Among the Elderly. Until fairly recently, when a retired widow remarried after age 60, she automatically lost the full benefit check she had been receiving as the widow of a deceased recipient of Social Security payments. Instead, she became the dependent of her new husband and began receiving a check equal to 50 percent of his retirement benefit. This situation often imposed a considerable financial burden on the newlyweds, for more often than not the woman's new benefit was considerably lower than her old one. The solution was simple, if unpalatable for many of the elderly: instead of marrying, they just lived together, and each continued to receive full retirement benefits. But both the federal government and many of the retirees began to feel that this was socially unacceptable. In a recent reform of the Social Security Act, the problem was resolved by permitting each of the retired parties to retain the benefits to which they were entitled before they wed. Remarriage before the age of 60, however, precludes widows' benefits, unless the new marriage ends.

Working After Retirement

The stated purpose of Social Security retirement benefits at its inception was to provide those no longer working with a base income on which to live out their retirement years. Benefits were not intended as a supplement to income received through one's job or profession. Over the years, however, this purpose has been greatly modified, and the earned-income provisions of the Social Security Act have been much liberalized. A beneficiary aged 65 to 72 may now earn up to $6,000 per year and still retain the full amount of his or her Social Security check. If, however, the beneficiary earns more than $6,000, he or she loses $1 in benefits for every $2 in earned income above $6,000. (Remember, income derived from private pension arrangements, stocks, bonds,

bank interest and the like is not considered earned income and does not count against Social Security benefits.) Those who are 72 or older (70, starting in 1983) may earn as much as they can and still retain the full amount of their Social Security benefits. Dependents of those receiving retirement benefits who are between the ages of 65 and 72 (70, starting in 1983) will have their checks reduced if they earn more than the allowable maximum.

For beneficiaries from age 62 through 64 and for dependents under 65, allowable outside earnings are somewhat less liberal. In 1982 they can earn only $4,440. Any earnings above that amount cost them $1 in benefits for every $2 earned. The amounts beneficiaries can earn are updated annually to conform with the rising cost of living.

There is a special rule about earned income that relates only to the year of retirement. Under this regulation, even though earnings in that year may exceed the annual exempted amount, a benefit can be paid for any month in which a person's wages do not exceed 1/12 the permissible amount for the year. Suppose, for example, that Anne Flax retires at age 62 in May 1982. Her salary for the first four months of the year was $5,000. After that she received no wages. She will be entitled to retirement benefits for the last eight months of the year without incurring a penalty, even though her total earned income for the year was $560 above the limit.

Estimating Social Security Retirement Benefits

People often ask: "What will my Social Security payment be?" If you are 20 or 30 years away from retirement, the question is virtually impossible to answer. Even if you are only seven or eight years short of 62 or 65 the answer can only be in the form of an estimate; there are just too many variables to take into account. These include what your future salary will be, your family situation at the time of retirement and the Social Security Administration's estimate of future benefits.

Your salary next year or the year after, or 10 years down the line, depends in large measure upon the course of inflation, as does the dollar amount of benefits in the years 1990 or 2000. The variables diminish, of course, as you get closer to retirement age, and if you are 56 or older, the Social Security Administration will estimate your initial benefits for you. All you have to do is obtain form OAR-7004 from your local Social Security office and mail it to the address shown. In several weeks you will receive an estimate of your initial retirement benefits. Don't accept this as the final word, however. Your wages may go up or down significantly in the years before you retire. Inflation may increase, decrease or continue at its current rate. The status of your dependents may change. All these factors can greatly influence your future benefits.

Retirement Benefits in the Next Two Decades

The Social Security Administration does, of course, make predictions of future retirement benefits for broad categories of people. These estimates are based upon the best economic projections available, concerning the course of inflation, tomorrow's wage rates and other variables. Such projections are also based upon the assumption that there will be no radical changes in the Social Security law itself. The table below, prepared by the Social Security Administration, predicts such benefits for different years up to the year 2000.

These figures project a single person's retirement benefits under Social Security. Married workers with dependent spouses of retirement age will receive half again as much as a single retiree. And in cases in which both spouses have established their own Social Security records, the sums will be larger yet. For example, let's examine the situation of a couple we will call Bill and Jane Davenport. Both reach the age of 65 and retire in 1995. Bill's working career has been spent as a highly paid engineer; Jane has been a school teacher. As Bill's income has always been above the maximum amount covered by Social Security, his initial retirement benefits, as projected in the table will be $18,847 annually (to be adjusted each year to reflect the rising cost of living). Jane earned an average income over the years, and her initial benefit will be $13,695. Thus the couple's total income will be $32,542. Given the fact that this Social Security income will not be taxable at any level of government, and that a large share of the couple's medical expenses and hospital bills will be paid for by Medicare, their real income will be considerably larger than it appears to be on paper.

Estimated Benefits for Those Retiring at 65
(Estimate made in October 1981)

Year	Earnings in Previous Years			Annual Benefits		
	low	average	maximum	low	average	maximum
1982	$ 6,968	$13,728	$29,700	$4,498	$ 6,784	$ 8,610
1983	7,636	15,045	32,100	4,769	7,144	9,150
1984	8,379	16,508	35,400	4,930	7,394	9,539
1985	9,117	17,961	38,700	5,228	7,788	10,118
1990	12,647	24,917	57,000	7,013	10,553	14,146
1995	16,512	32,532	74,700	9,078	13,695	18,847
2000	21,581	42,518	97,500	11,853	17,902	25,541

Now suppose that Jane had held a low-paying job over the years—say, as a clerk in a department store—and her wage record entitled her to an initial payment of only $9,078, an amount based upon her earnings record. This is slightly less than half the amount her husband receives. Therefore, she will receive an additional payment each month of $346 to bring her check up to 50 percent of his. Thus Bill and Jane together will have a tax-free income of $28,275 for the year 1995. If Jane had never worked at all, her own check would be exactly the same, but by having had an earnings record she gains two advantages. Were she to become disabled before retirement age, she would be entitled to draw Social Security disability benefits; were she to die before retirement age, her minor children could draw survivors' benefits while Bill continues to work.

Applying for Retirement Benefits

Securing retirement benefits is usually a cut-and-dried affair. Either you are old enough to receive payments or you are not, and either you have earned sufficient credits or you have not. If you have reached the age of 62—assuming you are free to decide whether or not to continue working—the only questions you have to ask yourself are: "Shall I retire between my 62nd and 65th birthdays at somewhat reduced benefits? Shall I wait until I am 65 to get full benefits? Or shall I continue to work after 65 so that I can increase my benefits by three percent a year?"

Once you have made up your mind on these points, all you have to do is apply for retirement benefits at your local Social Security office. To be certain that your checks begin arriving as soon as you retire, make your application for benefits at least three months before your retirement date. Aside from your Social Security card, the only document you are likely to be required to show is your birth certificate. If your birth certificate is not available, a baptismal certificate or immigration papers normally will be accepted. To get immediate credit for your last year's earnings, bring along a copy of your W-2 form. If you are applying at the same time for dependents' benefits for a spouse, your husband or wife should also appear with a birth certificate and proof of marriage. If you are applying for dependents' benefits for minor children, take their birth certificates along as well.

Disability and Social Security

Among the most important benefits that Social Security offers are those for disabled workers and their families—Social Security Disability Insurance (SSDI). About 2.8 million workers and 1.8 million of their dependents now collect monthly checks, which amounted to a total of $14 billion in 1979. This represented about 11 percent of Social Security's expenditures for that year.

Defining the Disabled

Because it has long been feared that many reasonably healthy people would claim disability merely to qualify for Social Security payments, the law is clear on what constitutes disabling conditions. People claiming disabilities must be able to prove that their condition is such that they will be prevented from performing any work that will bring them substantial sums for a period of at least a year; or the condition must be of such severity that it will result in death. Furthermore, no one claiming disability receives a benefit until he or she has served a five-month waiting period.

Verifying Claims. The responsibility for making the disability determination on claims for Social Security disability benefits rests with the Disability Determination Services (DDS), an agency in each of the 50 states, the District of Columbia, Puerto Rico and Guam. The DDS develops the medical evidence needed to determine whether an applicant is disabled within the meaning of the Social Security law. In making this determination, the DDS relies on medical information furnished by the applicant, reports from the treating physician, hospital records and other available sources of information. If the DDS requires additional medical information, it will arrange a consultative examination at no expense to the applicant.

Eligibilty for Disability Benefits. Aside from the mere fact of being disabled, a claimant must have been covered by Social Security for a specific number of years in order to be eligible for disability benefits. Those between the ages of 31 and 42, for example, are required to have accumulated 20 quarters of coverage (five full years of credit) during the 10 years preceding the quarter in which they were adjudged to be disabled.

Workers below the age of 31, who presumably have had less chance to acquire coverage credits, are granted somewhat easier terms. By and large, these people must have been covered by Social Security for half the time between their 21st birthdays and the calendar quarter in which they were judged to be disabled. For those 24 and younger, a minimum of six quarters of coverage is required. The six quarters must have been accumulated in the 12-quarter period (three years) immediately preceding the disability. Thus, someone who began working at 22 and was disabled a year later would be ineligible for disability benefits.

Disabled Widows and Widowers. Disabled widows and widowers of former Social Security beneficiaries will not receive disability benefits unless they are at least 50 years old. To cite an example: suppose a man named Richard Smathers, age 67, dies two years after his retirement benefits under Social Security began. He leaves behind a wife, Clare, who is totally disabled because of an automobile accident that occurred three years before. Clare is only 48, and she will not be eligible for disability benefits until she is 50. If the Smathers had minor children, Clare and the youngsters would have been eligible for survivors' benefits

immediately. However, this was not the case, and Clare will have to wait. Even if Clare were not disabled, as a survivor she will be eligible for reduced retirement benefits at age 60, two years earlier than the wife of a living retiree.

Conditions Considered Disabling

To qualify for disability benefits, you must prove that the condition you claim exists, and that it is indeed totally disabling. Among the impairments that the Social Security Administration considers disabling are the following:

* Loss of major function in both arms, both legs or one arm and leg.
* Severe arthritis that causes recurrent inflammation, pain and deformity in major joints, so that the ability to walk or use one's hands is greatly impaired.
* Diseases of the heart, lungs or blood vessels resulting in serious loss of heart or lung functions, as revealed by medical tests. Symptoms of pain, fatigue and breathlessness must not be amenable to medical treatment.
* Diseases of the digestive system that result in severe malnutrition, weakness and anemia.
* Serious loss of kidney function.
* Cancer that cannot be controlled or cured.
* Severe brain damage.
* Severe mental illness or retardation.
* Total inability to speak.

The above are impairments that are generally considered to be disabling. Many other conditions may be equally disabling in individual circumstances, and if a claimant can prove disability, he or she may be entitled to benefits. (For a further discussion of physical and mental disabilities covered by Social Security, see Chapter 5, page 201.)

Applying for Disability Benefits

Of all Social Security regulations, those concerning disability benefits are the most stringent. The burden of proof rests heavily with the applicant, who must be able to show that the disability is total and that his or her inability to work stems directly from the injury or illness itself and not from such factors as an employer's unwillingness to make special arrangements that would facilitate gainful employment. The process of gaining disability benefits may be long and arduous, as is often the case when the Social Security Administration entertains some doubts as to the extent or seriousness of the injury or illness. On the other hand, in clear-cut situations—as with a paraplegic—approval of the claim may be swift.

Making an Initial Application

As with all other questions relating to Social Security, the place to make initial inquiries and file an application for disability benefits is the nearest Social Security office. Should you be applying for these benefits, you should come prepared to provide the following items of information.

* Your Social Security number.
* Year, month and day of your last employment along with a copy of your latest W-2 form.
* The nature of your illness or injury.
* Names, addresses and telephone numbers of physicians, hospitals or clinics that provided treatment for your ailment, and the dates on which examinations or treatments were performed.
* If you are a veteran and have received medical attention in an armed forces or VA hospital for the disabling ailment, provide your service serial number and VA claims number.
* A list of your employers over the last 10 years.
* Names, Social Security numbers and dates of birth of your husband or wife and children.
* If you have filed for workers' compensation, you will need your workers' compensation number.
* A telephone number at which you can be reached.

Processing Disability Claims

In a recent year, some 1.2 million Americans applied for disability benefits. Almost half a million of the claims were quickly approved, but more than 700,000 were initially turned down. All of those who had been refused benefits had the right to appeal the initial decision, and many of them did. About 100,000 of those originally turned down eventually received benefits through the appeals process.

Appealing a Disability Claims Denial. A person whose claim is denied may request a reconsideration of the decision through the local Social Security office. Additional medical evidence may be required. If your claim is denied for a second time, you may take the following steps:

* Request a hearing before an administrative law judge employed by the Social Security Administration. After hearing your case, the judge will reach a decision. If he or she decides against you, the next step is to . . .
* Seek redress from the Social Security Appeals Council, the next appellate step.
* If this body rejects your claim, you will have exhausted all administrative remedies and you may take your case to a federal district court, and from there all the way to the U.S. Supreme Court if necessary. Relatively few cases ever make their way even to the district court level, as the process is both time consuming and expensive. Nonetheless, judicial remedies are available to those who feel strongly enough to employ them.

The Extent of Disability Coverage

As with all other Social Security coverage, the actual monthly cash allotment you and your family may receive as disability payments varies with your earnings record and your family situation. However, if you have dependents, say a wife and minor children, each one will receive a monthly check based upon the amount of your allotment as the primary beneficiary, with adjustments made for the maximum family benefit. In some instances, the total amount that a family receives may be quite close to the worker's pre-disability earnings. This is particularly true in situations involving relatively low-paid workers and their families; like retirement allotments, the disability benefits received by these workers represent a larger percentage of their earlier incomes than do those of highly paid workers. One recent reform of the Social Security Act has been to limit the total disability payment for a family to 85 percent of average monthly pre-disability earnings. Saving money was just one reason for this reform. Another was the sense that if families actually increased income through disability payments, there would be little incentive for rehabilitation.

Examples of Disability Benefits

Paul Jaspers is a single worker, age 24, who always earned an average income. In February 1980, Paul suddenly became blind. He was able to demonstrate that he could no longer earn substantial sums, and thus he qualified for disability payments under Social Security. Six months after the disability began, Paul's checks started coming in. His initial payment, pegged to his former salary, was $463.80 per month. Had Paul always earned the top amount covered by Social Security, his initial benefit would have been $674 a month. In

either instance, however, the checks will increase to reflect rises in the cost of living.

Timothy Wright, also 24, a married man with two small children, was totally disabled the same month that Paul lost his sight. He, too, earned an average income, but because of the size of his family, their overall benefits were higher than Paul's, coming to $695.70 per month.

Special Provisions for the Blind

Anyone whose corrected vision (that is, with glasses) is rated no better than 20/200, or whose field of vision is 20 degrees or less, is considered legally blind. Under the law, a worker who becomes blind before he or she reaches the age of 65 must meet all provisions of the disability regulations in order to be eligible for Social Security benefits. Specifically, that person must be judged unable to earn a substantial income in any occupation. Usually a person who becomes legally blind, though still able to perform some work, suffers a severe decline in income. Under current Social Security rules, such people may request that their income records be frozen so that only the salaries they earned in their pre-blindness years will be counted toward future benefits. As benefits depend, in considerable degree, on average earnings during the working years, these benefits may be much increased by ignoring the earnings record of the post-blindness years.

Keeping Current on Social Security

Like most other government departments, the Social Security Administration publishes dozens of pamphlets each year to apprise beneficiaries and other interested parties of the latest information concerning the program. New regulations are constantly being made, benefits are broadened or reduced and services are instituted. All of these matters, as well as information concerning basic regulations and

benefits, are explained in detail in pamphlets that are available at any Social Security office and are usually found on a rack near the entrance. If you cannot find a pamphlet that addresses itself to your particular concerns, ask the receptionist for help. The receptionist will find the pamphlet for you or direct you to someone in the office who can provide the information.

A special provision of law aids blind workers who are between the ages of 55 and 65. In order to secure disability benefits, they are required only to show that they are unable to earn significant sums in their accustomed jobs.

Benefits for Disabled Children

Under certain circumstances, disabled children—age 18 and older—of a parent drawing Social Security benefits or of an insured deceased parent may themselves receive benefit checks if their disabilities disqualify them for gainful employment. A basic rule regarding such provisions is that the child's disability must have occurred before the age of 22, with benefits first payable in the month the child reaches 18. Perhaps the best way of approaching the question of benefits for disabled children is with an example. Karl Helms was a factory worker. He was married and had one child, a severely retarded son. While Karl worked, he was always able to support his wife and son, but at 65, Karl retired. His wife, who was also 65, began drawing a dependent's benefit at the time of Karl's retirement. And although Karl's son was then 30, he had been severely retarded from birth and consequently was unemployable. This entitled the son to a dependent's benefit, pegged to his father's monthly check. The amount came to somewhat less than 50 percent of his father's monthly payment because of provisions regarding maximum family benefits. Karl died at age 70, making his wife the primary beneficiary. She began to draw benefits equal to the amount her husband would have drawn were he still alive. Her retarded son, now age 35, received a larger monthly check, approximately 75 percent as large as his mother's. When his mother dies, for the rest of his life, his monthly check will remain at 75 percent of the amount she had been receiving, after adjustments are made for inflation.

Payments to Representatives of the Disabled

In many instances where the recipient of Social Security benefits is a minor or is severely disabled (particularly in the case of the mentally handicapped), payments are made to a representative of the beneficiary rather than directly to the insured person. The person who receives the checks may be a close relative of the beneficiary, a court-appointed financial guardian or an official of a public or private institution. This person is known as a "representative payee." The representative payee is legally responsible for seeing to it that funds intended for the benefit of his or her charge are, in fact, used for that purpose. Food, clothing and shelter, as well as medical expenses, school and institutional fees are all considered proper expenditures. A small amount of pocket money for the beneficiary, where appropriate, is also proper. Under the law, representative payees must keep a record of Social Security funds received and of how they are spent. These records are subject to review by the Social Security Administration. If you, as a representative payee, should have any doubts about the legality of an expenditure, check with your local Social Security office.

Survivors' Benefits

The term "survivors' benefits" has been employed many times in this chapter, and where not self-explanatory it has been defined. For purposes of clarity, however, it may be useful to recapitulate, and place the matter of survivors' benefits within the context of Social Security as a whole.

Entitlement to Survivors' Benefits

Briefly put, as far as the Social Security system is concerned, a survivor is a close relative or spouse of a deceased worker or retiree who was covered by the system. In some instances, any or all of these survivors may be entitled to benefits. Indeed, almost eight million Americans currently receive Social Security checks as survivors. Among those covered are widows and widowers, divorced spouses, minor and dis-

Social Security Teleservice

Much of the business between Social Security and claimants or information seekers can be handled by telephone. Each Social Security office maintains special Teleservice lines for this purpose. Check the white pages (alphabetical listings) of your telephone directory under Social Security for your local Teleservice number, or call your local Social Security office. Among the uses of Teleservice are the following:

* To apply for Social Security or Supplemental Security Income payments. It is likely that such applications cannot be completed entirely by telephone, but you can save considerable time if you initiate the application process through Teleservice.
* To initiate applications for Medicare.
* To initiate the change of a name or address on Social Security records.
* To report any event—such as starting or stopping work—that might affect Social Security payments.
* To report a lost or stolen check or a delayed payment.
* To find out how to replace a lost, stolen or missing Social Security card or Medicare card.

* To find out whether a particular health facility is eligible for Medicare reimbursements.
* To get help in obtaining a review when a claim has been denied.
* To obtain information on any aspect of Social Security.

If your call concerns benefit payments under the old age, survivors' or disability programs, be sure to tell the Teleservice person your Social Security claim number. (This number appears on your benefit checks.) If the call concerns a Medicare benefit, you will need your Medicare number.

During the early part of each month, when Social Security checks are sent out, Teleservice lines are often extremely busy and you may have trouble getting through to Teleservice. If your business is not urgent, it's a good idea to wait until the second half of the month before trying to reach Teleservice. In fact, the last week of the month is probably the best time to call.

All local Social Security offices maintain Teleservice during business hours, Mondays through Fridays. Some Teleservice lines remain in operation during early evening hours and on Saturdays.

---

abled children, dependent parents and sometimes even grandchildren of deceased beneficiaries or workers who were covered at the time of death.

Widows and Widowers. This is the major category of people receiving survivors' benefits, with far more widows than widowers qualifying. To simplify matters, we shall refer here only to widows, with the understanding that the benefits listed are also applicable to widowers in instances where they qualify for survivors' benefits. An elderly widow (65 or older) is entitled to a monthly benefit equal to the

amount her late husband would be receiving were he still alive. A widow may claim a reduced benefit as early as age 60. (A widow of retirement age who has had her own earnings record may, of course, receive benefits based on that record.)

A younger widow with children under age 16 will receive a monthly benefit 75 percent as large as the amount that would be paid to her late husband were he still alive. (The children, of course, also receive benefits.)

Divorced Spouses. A divorced wife entitled to a benefit as a dependent of her former husband (see page 271) becomes eligible for a higher survivor's benefit upon her former husband's death. A man who had been a dependent of his retired, divorced wife is also entitled to a higher survivor's benefit after she dies.

Children of Deceased Beneficiaries. Generally the minor children (or children between the ages of 18 and under 22, in some instances where they are still students) of a deceased worker are eligible for monthly payments. By and large, each child will receive a payment equal to 75 percent of the amount the late parent would be receiving if still alive. Grandchildren may also be entitled to payments if the minors' own parents are dead or disabled, or the children were legally adopted by their grandparents.

Surviving Parents. If the parents of a deceased worker can demonstrate that at least one-half of their support came from the deceased, they may be entitled to benefits as survivors. In such circumstances a widowed parent receives 82.5 percent of the amount the son or daughter would be receiving if he or she were still alive. If both parents are alive and qualify, each receives 75 percent. This assumes, of course, that the parents themselves are not eligible for Social Security retirement benefits.

Survivors of Those Who Never Collected Benefits. If someone who is still in the active work force suddenly dies, the dependents (usually spouse and minor children) are entitled to survivors' benefits provided the worker had enough quarters of coverage. If the worker had at least six quarters in the three years before death, a surviving spouse and children could get benefits. There is, however, a limit on how much earned income the beneficiaries may make if they are under 72 (70, beginning in 1983).

Amount of Survivors' Benefits
As with retirement benefits, the amount survivors receive depends upon variables such as the earnings record of the late breadwinner and the size of the family. In August 1981, however, the average monthly payment awarded to an aged widow who qualified for survivors' benefits was $341 per month and to a child, $260.

Lump-Sum Payment
In addition to survivors' benefits, there is a single lump-sum payment of $225 to a spouse living with a worker at the time of his or her death. If there is no spouse who was living with the worker, the payment may be made to a spouse living elsewhere or to someone else in the family who is entitled to the survivors' benefits.

Limitations on Survivors' Earnings
One of the primary reasons for providing widows who have minor children with survivors' benefits is to permit women to remain at home and raise their youngsters. A widow under age 65 who receives such benefits is permitted to earn up to $4,440 per year (in 1982) without any loss of Social Security payments; a widow age 65 or older may earn up to $6,000. Widows who earn more than the maximum allowable amount will lose $1 in Social Security benefits for every $2 they earn. As with retirement benefits, income that is classified as "unearned"—such as dividends on stocks or interest on bonds—is allowable in any amount and will not reduce Social Security payments. And beneficiaries who are 72 or older are not limited in the amount they may earn.

Applying for Survivors' Benefits
When someone who is covered by Social Security dies, the widow or widower should apply as quickly as possible for benefits at the nearest Social Security office. If you want to apply for these payments, be sure to bring certain proofs with you. Among these are:
* Your Social Security number.
* The deceased's Social Security number.
* Proof of your age. (A birth certificate is the best document to have.)

Collecting Social Security When Abroad

If you are entitled to retirement checks under Social Security, you can continue to receive them even while you are out of the United States. Moreover, regulations for those residing abroad are the same as for those in the United States. For example, if you are living abroad and are under age 72, you may not take employment and continue to receive full benefits. In addition, if you are not a citizen of the United States, your checks will stop after six months unless you are a citizen of one of the following countries:

Argentina	Ecuador	Luxembourg	Spain
Austria	El Salvador	Malta	Sweden
Barbados	Finland	Mexico	Switzerland
Belgium	France	Micronesia	Tobago
Bolivia	Gabon	Monaco	Trinidad
Brazil	Greece	The Netherlands	Turkey
Bulgaria	Guyana	Nicaragua	United Kingdom
Canada	Ireland	Norway	Upper Volta
Chile	Israel	Panama	West Germany
Colombia	Italy	Peru	Western Samoa
Costa Rica	Ivory Coast	Philippines	Yugoslavia
Cyprus	Jamaica	Poland	Zaire
Czechoslovakia	Japan	Portugal	
Denmark	Liechtenstein	San Marino	

(This list of countries is subject to change.)

In order to receive your checks abroad, you must, of course, keep the Social Security Administration informed about your address. In addition, if you are spending an extended period abroad, you will receive an annual questionnaire concerning your status. This form must be filled out carefully and returned to the Social Security office that mailed it to you.

Although Social Security checks can be mailed to most countries, there are exceptions. These include Albania, Cuba, East Berlin, East Germany, Cambodia, North Korea, Mainland China and Vietnam. If you are a U.S citizen visiting one of these countries, you may collect your back checks after leaving that particular nation. Most non-U.S. citizens who are otherwise entitled to Social Security retirement benefits lose their eligibility for payments during periods that they reside in these countries. Thus a long visit can be expensive.

Remember that although Social Security checks are not taxable within the United States, if you are living abroad, your host country has the right to levy taxes on these payments.

* Proof of relationship to the deceased, such as a marriage certificate.
* Proof of death of the insured worker, such as a death certificate.
* The birth certificates of your children if you believe they qualify for benefits.

* If the deceased was self-employed, income tax forms for the last year in which he or she filed a return.
* In the case of a parent or grandparent filing for survivors' benefits, that person should bring some proof that the deceased

worker provided at least half of his or her income.

In addition, the Social Security Administration may require other documents, such as proof of disability or of school attendance, depending upon the exact nature of your claim.

Supplemental Security Income

Financed through general revenues, but administered by the Social Security Administration, the Supplemental Security Income (SSI) provides a base cash income for the aged, blind and disabled when other programs (such as Social Security itself) cannot offer sufficient funds to provide people in these categories with even a modest standard of living.

Most retired people have no need for SSI, but this is not always the case. People who worked in very low-paying jobs, or were covered for only a short period of time, may not have had an opportunity to build an earnings record sufficient to entitle them to a reasonable monthly benefit. In such instances, SSI is available to augment their limited resources, provided that SSI eligibility requirements can be met.

In some states, though not all, state revenues are allotted to increase benefits under SSI. The program is, in effect, a welfare arrangement, and a means test is required before benefits are paid. The maximum amount a single person can receive from the federal government under SSI is $264.70 per month. A married couple may get as much as $397 per month, if both husband and wife are eligible to receive the payments.

Eligibility Requirements for SSI
A person applying for SSI must be 65 or older, blind (see page 277 for definition of blindness) or otherwise disabled. In addition, he or she must be able to demonstrate a significant degree of poverty. A single person, for example, may not have assets worth more than $1,500, while a couple's assets may not amount to more than $2,250 if they are to qualify. Among items that the government considers to be assets are savings accounts, stocks, bonds and jewelry. For purposes of qualifying for SSI, a house in which the claimant actually lives is not considered an asset. Insurance policies and automobiles generally are not considered assets, though in some instances they may be.

Medicaid and SSI
In some states SSI recipients may be entitled to medical care under the Medicaid program (see Chapter 4).

Applying for SSI
Applications for SSI are made at the nearest Social Security office. A worker there will help the applicant fill out the required forms. Those who do not qualify for this program may find that they are eligible for other federal or state programs which are not administered by Social Security. Many such programs are described in this book, particularly in Chapters 2 and 4.

Social Security Addresses

Because all Social Security benefits are administered by a single government agency, a directory of office addresses is not included with this chapter. Further information or aid may be obtained by calling your local Social Security office, listed in the telephone directory under "U.S. Government," or "Social Security."

Chapter 8

The Retirement Years: Aid for Older Americans

Retirement can be one of the best times of your life—if you plan for it,
and if you know how to take advantage of the countless opportunities,
benefits and services available to older Americans today. Many of these
are the result of the Older Americans Act of 1965 and the myriad programs
administered under that Magna Carta for the elderly, as well as privileges
accorded by state and local governments and other organizations.
This chapter covers such basic benefits and services as protection against
job discrimination because of age; help in finding employment, paid as well
as voluntary; tax breaks for older citizens; opportunities for recreation
and continuing education; discounts and low-cost or free transportation;
food stamps and nutritious meals. It tells you how to obtain help
with housing, home care, home improvement and repairs; explains how
individual rights can be protected in nursing homes; shows how you can
combat crime, abuses and fraud; and sets forth in detail the wide range
of services, activities and friendships that are available
in organizations and community centers that are designed
specifically to serve senior citizens.

Contents

A Bill of Rights for Older Americans

In the belief that millions of elderly Americans were "suffering unnecessary harm from the lack of adequate service," Congress in 1965 passed the Older Americans Act. Combined with previous and subsequent legislation, this act has created a fountainhead of benefits and services for persons whose needs had long been slighted or even ignored.

The purpose of the 1965 act, as strengthened by amendments in 1973 and 1978, is to "make available comprehensive programs which include a full range of health, education and social services to our older citizens. . . ." As defined by the act, "social services" include a multitude of activities encompassing everything from assistance with rent payments to free transportation for those unable to drive a car.

Older Americans eligible for such services were defined by the original act as those who are 65 or above, but in the 1973 amendments the limit was lowered to include anyone 60 or older.

To implement the act, Congress, in cooperation with state and local governments, established a structure of agencies that has become popularly known as "the aging network." At the top of the pyramid is the Administration on Aging (AoA), which is charged with coordinating all federal programs for the elderly and with speaking for and acting on behalf of all Americans over the age of 60. AoA is a prime advocate of the elderly in the forums of government where policies and rules are made; it also serves as a focal point and clearinghouse for ideas and actions generated by thousands of organizations and individuals concerned in one way or another with the aging population.

From its headquarters in Washington, DC, the Administration on Aging reaches across the continental United States and beyond to provide funds and technical assistance to 57 state and territorial agencies on aging. These, in turn, channel money and ideas to approximate-

Aging's Magna Carta

The Older Americans Act—aging's "Magna Carta"—was enacted in 1965 and amended in 1973 and 1978. Its objectives, as stated by Congress, are to provide older people with:

1. An adequate income in retirement in accordance with the American standard of living.

2. The best possible physical and mental health that science can make available and without regard to economic status.

3. Suitable housing, independently selected, designed and located with reference to special needs and available at costs that older citizens can afford.

4. Full restorative services for those who require institutional care.

5. Opportunity for employment with no discriminatory personnel practices because of age.

6. Retirement in health, honor, dignity—after years of contributing to the economy.

7. Pursuit of meaningful activity within the widest range of civic, cultural and recreational opportunities.

8. Efficient community services, including access to low-cost transportation, and adequate living arrangements.

9. Immediate benefits from proven research to sustain and improve health and happiness.

10. Freedom, independence and the exercise of individual initiative in planning and managing their own lives.

ly 600 area agencies and 1,000 nutrition projects, which combine with more than 25,000 private and public agencies to provide services at the local level.

In a recent year, for example, about 155 million meals were made available to older citizens. Eighty percent of these were served at 11,000 different dining facilities, including senior centers, school lunchrooms and church halls; the balance consisted of "meals on wheels" delivered to older people unable to leave their homes.

Some 5,000 senior centers across the country provided not only meals but various other services, ranging from health checkups to discussion groups, museum and theater trips and free classes in everything from oil painting to bridge. Through senior centers and other agencies, the aging network also offers free information and referral service to individuals on almost every conceivable problem, as well as legal services, transportation and escort service, home health care, homemaker help, shopping assistance, friendly visits and daily telephone reassurance to those who cannot easily get out and move around by themselves. Most of the services depend heavily on volunteers, many of whom are older people themselves; at dining facilities for seniors, for example, volunteers outnumber paid workers by an average of seven to one.

All of these efforts are aimed at a single goal: helping older people to live independent, useful and fruitful lives for as long as possible in their own homes and communities—without being needlessly isolated from others or prematurely institutionalized.

How to Plug into the Network

Whatever your needs or interests, you can get further information simply by picking up the telephone. The Older Americans Act requires that all elderly persons in the United States be provided reasonable access to an information and referral source, and in most areas such an "I&R" service has been set up. Inquire about it at your local senior center, library or town hall,

or look under state or city government listings for agencies with "Aging," "Elderly" or "Senior Citizens" in their names.

Many states, counties and larger cities have toll-free "hot lines" or governor's information lines, some specifically established for seniors, through which inquiries can be routed to appropriate departments. In addition, each state has one or more federal information centers whose staffs are trained to answer questions and help you find the right federal agency or department. These are listed in local telephone directories under "United States Government—Federal Information."

In the front or back of many phone books there is also a list of frequently called agencies under "Community Services Numbers," ranging from food programs to legal services and opportunities for volunteer work. Since a distressing number of elderly people are not aware of, or are reluctant about pursuing, the services available to them, some communities have set up outreach programs that train volunteers, many of them older citizens themselves, to find and advise those in need of help. If you are unable to find in your community any of the programs described in this chapter, contact your state agency on aging, listed on pages 331–334.

The Decision to Retire

Retirement at age 65, 60 or even earlier is a goal that many employees look forward to. In recent years, however, it has been tempered by economic and social trends. As many retirees have discovered, inflation can eat away at fixed incomes: living costs can swell faster than they can be offset by annual Social Security adjustments, and most company pension and annuity plans do not provide for cost-of-living increases at all.

As the percentage of older people in the population increases, and fixed incomes continue to be squeezed, many authorities believe that

A Profile of Aging America

A quiet but dramatic revolution has been taking place in the United States; a nation once young is rapidly becoming old. The implications—for the economy, social programs and aging Americans themselves—are already profound, and promise to become even more so in the years to come.

Thanks to medical and scientific advances that have resulted in lower death rates and longer life spans, older Americans are now the fastest-growing segment of the population. Since 1900 the number of people over 60 has increased 4 times as fast as the number under 60. At the turn of the century 1 of every 16 Americans was over 60; today the figure is 1 of 7.

At the same time, the elderly population itself has become increasingly older. While the number of those aged 60 or more has increased nearly 7 times since 1900, the number of those 75 and over has experienced a 10-fold increase and now constitutes about a quarter of the older population.

Women—who have benefited most from medical advances, particularly during their child-bearing years—now comprise a much larger proportion of the elderly population than in the past. In 1900 older men slightly outnumbered older women; today women represent approximately 58 percent of those over 60.

The number of elderly people living alone has grown rapidly in recent decades, from one sixth of all older persons not in institutions in 1960 to about one fourth today. The greatest increase has been among women: more than one third over 60 now live alone, and nearly half over 75 live alone.

more and more older workers will consider delaying retirement as long as they can. Moreover, statistics indicate that great numbers of older people want to go on working: one poll found that 88 percent of the employees surveyed preferred to work in some capacity rather than retire, and 53 percent wished they had never quit.

Rather than encourage workers to take early retirement, employers are now being urged to persuade older employees to stay on the job, or to return to work on either a full- or part-time basis. Some companies are experimenting with gradual retirement plans in which older employees work less and less, turning over more and more of the responsibilities to successors. The older workers receive a changing mix of earned and pension income until they are completely retired, at which point they are free to enjoy a leisurely life or switch to new careers they may have been testing on the outside.

Protection Against Age Discrimination

If you are among the growing number of Americans who want to go on working past age 60 or 65, you have the law on your side. In 1967 Congress passed the Age Discrimination in Employment Act, adding age to existing prohibitions on race, color, religion, sex, handicaps and national origin as reasons for denying a person equal rights. The purpose of the act is "to promote employment of older persons based on their ability rather than age; to prohibit arbitrary age discrimination in employment; to help employers and workers find ways of meeting problems arising from the impact of age on employment."

Under the act, as amended in 1974 and 1978, it is unlawful to discriminate against a worker on the basis of age between the ages of

40 and 70 in non-federal employment. Except for a few classes of positions, compulsory retirement at any age has been abolished in federal jobs. The law states that it is illegal for an employer to discharge an employee, or to refuse to hire one, because of age, or to discriminate against a worker with respect to compensation, terms, conditions or privileges of employment. It is also unlawful for an employment agency to refuse to refer a person, or to classify a potential employee for a job, on the basis of age. Much the same restrictions apply to labor unions, which cannot exclude from membership, classify or otherwise deprive an individual of job opportunities because of age. Job notices or advertisements, whether published by employers, employment agencies or unions, may not indicate any preference or limitation based on age.

Under the law, exceptions may be made in cases where age is a "bona fide occupational qualification" for a particular job. However, the Federal Council on the Aging, a 15-member Presidential advisory body charged with reviewing national policy, has recommended that Congress should remove this provision. The council has also recommended that the present limit of age 70 be deleted from the law, and that employers no longer be permitted to disregard years of service beyond age 65 in calculating a worker's final retirement benefit.

Enforcement of the age discrimination act, once the province of the Department of Labor, has been transferred to the Equal Employment Opportunities Commission. Most states also have laws that prohibit age discrimination. If you have a complaint, it should be filed with the human rights commission or labor department of your state or the nearest local office of the EEOC (see Chapter 2).

In any case of discrimination, proof must be supplied before a government agency can move, and proof is often hard to come by; discrimination can be subtle and is sometimes skillfully disguised. For a checklist of things to look for, see "Spotting Age Discrimination" on pages 288 and 289.

Your Rights Under Pension Plans

Pension plans are discussed in detail in Chapter 2. That chapter also tells you how to make sure you are adequately covered in your pension plan.

Your Credit Rights

Many older Americans have complained of being denied credit—at banks, stores, car dealers, credit-card or finance companies or other places—just because they were over a certain age. Some have found their credit suddenly cut off or reduced when they retired. Under the Consumer Credit Protection Act of 1968, however, discrimination in credit because of age is illegal.

A creditor may ask you your age, but if you're old enough to sign a binding contract (usually 18 or 21 depending on your state law), a creditor may *not* take any of the following actions against you: 1) turn you down or decrease your credit solely because of your age; 2) ignore your retirement income in rating your application; 3) close your credit account or require you to reapply because you have reached a certain age or retired; 4) deny you credit because life insurance or other credit-related insurance is not available to persons of your age.

Because age does have economic consequences, the law permits a creditor to consider certain information related to age, such as how long it will be until you retire or how long your income will continue. An older applicant might not qualify for a large loan with a small down payment in the case of a risky venture, but the same person might well qualify for a smaller loan by securing it with good collateral and making a larger down payment.

While a declining income may be a handicap if you are older, you may be able to demonstrate a solid credit history. The creditor must look at all the facts and apply the customary standards of creditworthiness to your particular situation.

If you have a complaint about a bank in connection with federal credit laws, contact the

Spotting Age Discrimination

Despite legislation that prohibits it, older workers are often subjected to subtle, and sometimes not-so-subtle, forms of discrimination because of their age, both in present and prospective jobs. Rarely will an employer, employment agency or labor union tell you straight out that you are too old for a given position (if they did, you would have a clear-cut case). Usually the signs are less obvious, and it is up to you to put the pieces together. If you think you are being discriminated against, write down the facts, noting who said what to you and on what date. Then take your complaint to your state's fair employment practices agency or to the local office of the Equal Employment Opportunities Commission. Here is a list of things to look for, compiled for the California Department of Aging.

If You Are Presently Employed

*Does your employer have a "young" work force? How many older workers, over 40, are there in your work place? Do people seem to leave, as they get older?

*Do many workers stay long enough to become eligible for a pension? (Some employers try to save money by firing workers or easing them out before their pension rights become vested.)

*Have you been put on a "faster line," in a more physically demanding job than you feel you can handle?

*Have you been "promoted" into a job you don't want? Many old workers find themselves put in a position where they can no longer meet job requirements, although they were doing fine in a different kind of job.

*Have you been passed over for a promotion or training program you were eligible for? Did a younger worker get it?

*After years of satisfactory job performance, have you suddenly found yourself receiving bad evaluations or warnings for imaginary mistakes, or for ones that are usually overlooked?

*Have you been asked to take "early retirement" even though you had no interest in retiring?

*If you were fired, or "retired" early, were you replaced by a younger worker? Was the younger person less qualified than you?

Federal Reserve Bank for your district, or the Board of Governors of the Federal Reserve System, Washington, DC 20551. For a complaint about a mortgage banker, consumer finance company or other creditor, call or write to the regional office of the Federal Trade Commission in your area or write Federal Trade Commission, Equal Credit Opportunity, Washington, DC 20580. If the creditor falls under another federal jurisdiction these agencies can tell you which one to call. Problems with brokers and dealers should be addressed to the nearest office of the U.S. Securities and Exchange Commission; those regarding small investment companies to the local office of the U.S. Small Business Administration.

Tax Breaks for Older Americans

In general, tax laws apply equally to all taxpayers regardless of age, but certain provisions of federal and state statutes are designed to help older citizens. Not all individuals are aware of these provisions: in a recent year, the U.S. Senate Special Committee on Aging found that as many as half of older taxpayers might have overpaid their federal income taxes. Both the committee and the Internal Revenue Service urge the elderly to reduce the taxes they pay by taking advantage of all means the law permits.

If You Were Refused a Job

*Were you qualified for the job? The requirements may have been purposely fuzzy, allowing the employer or agency to pick and choose. Ask for a job description or a list of minimal qualifications.

*Why weren't you hired? If you don't get a straight answer, ask to speak to someone higher up. Ask if there is some kind of "point system," and if so, how many points did you receive? If your rejection was based on an oral interview, ask what the interviewer was looking for and what you were lacking.

*Who got the job? Was that person younger and less qualified than you?

*Were you told that you were "overqualified" for the job? (If you are qualified for a position, it is up to you, not the employer, to decide whether you would be overqualified for, and thus possibly bored with, the job.)

*Were you told the job might be too "strenuous" for you, with no medical evidence to back it up? (Employers may not make blanket assumptions about the physical qualifications of persons simply because of their age.)

*Were you asked whether you would be bothered by working with, or under, younger people? (This is a common assumption about older workers, and often is the excuse given for age discrimination.)

*What did the advertisement for the job say? Was there any reference to age or recent school graduation?

*Did the application form ask your age? Is the application biased toward a younger person (asking about your parents or school courses, for example)? Did the application mention the provisions of the age discrimination law? (It is not illegal to ask your age for legitimate purposes, but some clear indication must be made that this will not be used to discriminate against you.)

*If there was a test of any kind involved in applying for the job, was it biased toward younger people or recent school graduates? Did it test only those skills needed for the job?

*Did the employer post a notice, as required by law, in the personnel or hiring office about the Age Discrimination in Employment Act?

Federal Income Taxes

If you are a single person—never married, divorced, a widow or widower—65 years of age or older, you need not file any federal tax return at all if your total income is less than a specified amount—$4,300 in 1982 (compared with $3,300 for single individuals under 65). The amount for married persons living together and eligible to file a joint return is higher: $6,400 if one spouse is 65 or older, $7,400 if both are 65 or more (compared with $5,400 for a couple under 65). If you are married and filing a separate return, however, or were living apart from your spouse at the end of the year, you must file a return if your income was $1,000 or more; if you were self-employed

and netted $400 or more, you must also file.

You must count as income any wages, tips, commissions, fees, rents, royalties, pensions and annuities, military retirement pay and interest and dividends you received. Do *not* count as income your Social Security benefits, railroad retirement benefits, veterans' benefits, proceeds from insurance policies, gifts and inheritances. Your pension or profit-sharing plan becomes taxable income as soon as you begin to receive whatever contributions your former employer has made. If you take your pension in a lump-sum payment, you can use an averaging method that allows you to pay taxes on it as if it were spread out over 10 years' time (for details, ask the IRS for a copy of its free publication No. 575 "Pension and Annuity Income").

Exemptions, Credits and Deductions

In addition to the standard exemptions of $1,000 each for yourself, your spouse and any dependents, you may take an extra $1,000 exemption if you were 65 or older on the last day of the tax year; if your spouse is also 65 or older and you are filing a joint return, you may take an extra $1,000 exemption for your spouse as well. Beyond these personal and age exemptions you can take another $1,000 if either you or your spouse are legally blind (vision of less than 20/200 in the better eye with glasses or a field of vision not more than 20 degrees).

If you are 65 or older, or if you are under 65 and receive a taxable pension from a public retirement system, you may be eligible to claim a special credit for the elderly amounting to 15 percent of adjusted gross income or the amount received as retirement income. Ask the IRS for a free copy of its publication No. 524, "Credit for the Elderly."

Tax Credits for Dependents. If you maintained a household that included a dependent under age 15, or a dependent or spouse incapable of self-care, you may be allowed a 30 percent credit for employment-related expenses (see the instructions in IRS Form 2441). If you have a dependent child living at home and an adjusted gross income of less than $10,000, you may be able to claim a tax credit of up to $500 (see instructions for Form 1040 or 1040A).

Medical and Dental Expenses. Don't forget that medical and dental expenses not reimbursed by insurance are deductible to the extent that they exceed 3 percent of your adjusted gross income. These include not only doctors', dentists' and hospital bills and cost of medicines but also eyeglasses, dentures, arch, back or abdominal supports prescribed by a doctor. They also include hearing aids and batteries; crutches, wheelchairs and invalid chairs; and the services of opticians, psychologists and physical therapists.

Deductions for Nursing Home. If you maintained anyone in a nursing or convalescent home, and the main reason for that person's being there was the need for proper medical care, you can deduct the entire cost, including meals and lodging, as a medical expense. If the individual is in a nursing home primarily for personal or family reasons, you cannot deduct meals or lodging, but only that portion of the cost attributable to medical or nursing care.

Energy Savings. Any taxpayer, regardless of age, can also take a credit of 15 percent of the first $2,000 (a maximum of $300) spent on energy-saving items installed in his or her home, including insulation, storm or thermal windows, caulking or weatherstripping, furnace replacement burners, and meters or clock thermostats. Credits for installing solar, wind or geothermal energy-producing equipment are larger: 40 percent on the first $10,000 (a maximum of $4,000). For further information, see IRS publication 903, "Energy Credits for Individuals."

Selling Your Home

Normally, if you sell your house, you must pay a capital-gains tax on any profit. If you postpone the sale until *after* your 55th birthday, however, and if you owned and occupied the house for at least three of the five years before the sale, you can exclude from your gross income up to $125,000 of the gain or $62,500 each if you are married and are filing separately. (The $125,000 exclusion may be used only once. Any future real estate transactions are subject to the usual capital-gains tax. In addition, payment of the tax on a gain in excess of the excluded amount will be deferred if you buy and occupy another home of equal or greater sales price within 18 months of the sale. For detailed information, see IRS publication 523, "Tax Information on Selling Your Home."

Where to Get Tax Help

If you have any questions or need help on your federal taxes, call the toll-free number listed in your telephone directory under "United States Government—Internal Revenue Service" (it is also listed in the instruction booklet that comes with your tax forms). Ask for any of the free publications mentioned above, and for the more comprehensive booklet No. 554, "Tax Benefits for Older Americans."

The IRS will compute your tax for you on a short form (1040A). You simply fill in certain items as instructed on these forms and mail the forms by April 15th.

Through the Volunteer Income Tax Assistance (VITA) program, older Americans can get free help in preparing their returns from local, IRS-trained volunteers. Your local IRS office can tell you where and when to locate such help in your community. The American Association of Retired Persons (AARP) has a program called Tax-Aide especially designed for older people; counselors are available in most communities from about February 1st to April 15th. They will explain what forms are required, what information should be included and where to enter it on the forms. A counselor will also prepare the return for you on request, and may be able to give you a hand with your state tax returns as well. For information about the program in your community, write Tax-Aide, AARP, 1909 K St. NW., Washington, DC 20049. A free tax booklet, "Your Retirement Income Tax Guide," is available from AARP at P.O. Box 2400, Long Beach, CA 90801.

State Tax Relief

States also offer various programs of tax relief for older Americans. These include personal exemptions, medical deductions, special treatment of retirement income, tax credits for the elderly, property-tax concessions and special property-tax relief for low-income property owners and renters.

California, for example, has five different programs: property-tax exemption, property-tax postponement, homeowner assistance, renter assistance and renter credit. New York allows its local governments to reduce property taxes for residents 65 or older by 50 percent within certain limits. Michigan reduces the state income tax liability of persons 65 and over by the amount their property taxes exceed a certain percentage of their annual incomes. Some states exempt from taxation all or part of federal, state or local government pensions, and a handful have no income taxes at all.

The specific details of state tax structures are far too varied and complex to go into here. Obviously it is to your advantage to inquire about the total tax picture in any community where you live, or in any community or state into which you intend to move—not only income taxes, property taxes and sales taxes but also inheritance and estate taxes that will come into play when you die. Sources include local tax collectors and assessors, senior centers and area agencies on aging as well as the tax revenue department of the state. An especially useful guide, giving an overview of all taxes state by state, is "Your Retirement State Tax Guide," available from the American Association of Retired Persons, P.O. Box 2400, Long Beach, CA 90801.

Second Careers

An increasing number of retired Americans are going back to work. Many are taking paying jobs, part- or full-time, not only to stay busy and productive, but to try to keep their budgets even with inflation. Others are working as volunteers, giving their time to worthy causes, and in the process opening up new interests and discovering the rewards that come from service to others.

You can work for pay and still collect full Social Security benefits, provided your earnings do not exceed a given amount in a year ($6,000 in 1982 for persons 65 or older, $4,840 for those who are between 62 and 64. If you go above the ceiling, $1 in benefits is with-

withheld for each $2 you earn. If you are 72 or older (70, starting in 1983), you are entitled to your full Social Security check each month regardless of your earnings.

In seeking any job, remember that it is illegal for employers, employment agencies and labor unions to discriminate against applicants between 40 and 70 on the basis of age (see section on age discrimination).

Remember, too, that while you are looking for a position, you *may* be eligible for unemployment insurance. Many workers assume that once they have retired such benefits are no longer available to them, but if you are still seeking work you should check with your state employment agency, and ask them whether you are eligible for unemployment benefits.

Help in Finding Jobs

Many agencies provide older persons with assistance in finding jobs. Among them are professional and trade associations, labor unions, churches, schools, YMCAs and YWCAs and other community groups. In many communities non-profit organizations have been established specifically to help seniors. Check your local senior citizens center, area agency on aging or Chamber of Commerce, or look in the telephone directory for such names as "Senior Employment Service," "Senior Job Bank," "Senior Personnel Placement Bureau," "Forty-Plus," "Sixty-Plus," "Jobs for Older Women" and "Mature Temps."

Other local employment programs for older people are sponsored by national voluntary organizations. They include Senior Aides, administered by the National Council of Senior Citizens (925 15th St., NW, Washington, DC 20005); Senior Community Service Project, sponsored by the National Council on the Aging (600 Maryland Ave., SW, Washington, DC 20024); and Senior Community Aides, administered by the American Association of Retired Persons (1909 K St. NW, Washington, DC 20049).

Employment offices of state departments of labor also offer help; many have older worker consultants or older worker job specialists trained to aid those who have been having difficulty in finding employment because of their age.

Older people are given special consideration in filling jobs in state and area agencies on aging, in nutrition and other local service programs for the elderly. The U.S. government itself is one of the largest employers of older citizens, not only in Washington but in branch offices all over the country. For further information, call the Federal Job Information Center in your area, listed in the telephone book. Positions exist in a wide range of occupations, from secretaries and accountants to doctors and engineers.

The Administration on Aging is committed to developing and demonstrating new roles for older workers, in the belief that they represent a resource of great potential that all too often goes to waste. Countless opportunities, many of which never existed before, have been created through AoA-funded demonstration projects. In some communities senior citizens have been employed as part-time librarians, allowing libraries to stay open longer. In others, they work in local school systems as tutors or teachers' aides, in day-care centers as baby-sitters for working parents, in hospitals as office employees or nurses' aides. In still others they help out at senior centers, giving advice on home economics, nutrition, health and employment. To find out about such opportunities, or to help create new ones in your community, call your local or state agency on aging.

Major Volunteer Programs

Hundreds of thousands of retired people are putting their skills and experience to work in major programs funded by the federal government. Several of these programs are administered by ACTION, the federal agency primarily responsible for volunteer work, and some of the projects are specifically aimed at senior volunteers.

The largest of ACTION's operations is the Retired Senior Volunteer Program (RSVP). Some 250,000 RSVP volunteers, 60 years of age and older, serve in more than 680 projects around the United States, including schools, libraries, day-care centers, hospitals, nursing homes, courts, economic development agencies and Boy and Girl Scout groups. They counsel others on health, proper nutrition, how to go about claiming benefits, and how people who are living on fixed incomes can make ends meet in the face of soaring costs. Volunteers choose their assignments from lists compiled by local RSVP organizations, are given training and are reimbursed for transportation, meals and out-of-pocket expenses related to their work. For further information, call or write to the local RSVP office, the nearest regional office of ACTION (listed on page 331) or ACTION/RSVP, 806 Connecticut Ave. NW, Washington, DC 20525.

Foster Grandparents

Some 17,000 lower-income men and women age 60 and over serve in ACTION's Foster Grandparent program, which is designed to provide love and attention for children who are physically, emotionally or mentally handicapped. Foster Grandparents work four hours a day for five days a week, devoting two hours a day to each of the two children in their care, playing games, reading stories, helping to feed and dress the youngsters and aiding in speech and physical therapy sessions. Volunteers receive 40 hours of initial training, a modest, tax-free weekly stipend, a transportation allowance, hot meals, accident and liability insurance and a free annual physical exam. For more information, including income eligibility, check the local Foster Grandparent Program, the nearest regional ACTION office or write ACTION/FOSTER GRANDPARENTS, 806 Connecticut Ave. NW, Washington, DC 20525.

Senior Companions

In a program patterned after Foster Grandparents, another 4,000 low-income volunteers age 60 and over take part in ACTION's Senior Companion Program, helping adults with special needs, many of whom are frail, elderly citizens confined to their homes or to nursing homes. A Senior Companion helps two such adults, each for a total of 10 hours a week, providing conversation and companionship, aiding with budgeting and shopping, escorting them to the doctor's office when needed and putting them in touch with other community services. Like Foster Grandparents, Senior Companions receive an initial 40 hours of orientation, plus monthly in-service training; they get a modest tax-free stipend, transportation allowance, meals on the job, free accident insurance and an annual physical exam. Call or write to your local Senior Companion office, regional ACTION office or ACTION/SENIOR COMPANIONS, 806 Connecticut Ave. NW, Washington, DC 20525.

Peace Corps

In the last two decades, more than 80,000 Peace Corps volunteers of all ages have served in 60-odd Third World countries, bringing their special skills into play to solve problems of food production, water supply, health, nutrition, education and other vital resources—and in return gaining an experience few of them will forget. The Peace Corps actively recruits older people as well as younger ones, and it needs dozens of different skills: foresters, agriculturalists, fishery specialists, scientists, architects, planners, engineers, skilled carpenters, masons, plumbers, electricians, health professionals, businessmen, home economists, teachers and many more. Any healthy U.S. citizen 18 or over is eligible, and there is no upper age limit; married couples are welcome if both are willing to work, and many handicapped individuals serve overseas with great success.

Peace Corps volunteers receive training for a month to 10 weeks, generally in the countries in which they will serve, with emphasis on learning the native languages and cultures. While in training, and for a two-year period of service afterwards, volunteers are given a monthly living allowance to cover food and other essentials, as well as a little spending money. On completion of their service, they receive an additional stipend or readjustment allowance for every month served. Transportation is paid to and from overseas assignments and for family emergencies. Health care and insurance are provided. If you are interested, and would like more information, call or write to the PEACE CORPS, 806 Connecticut Avenue, NW, Washington, DC 20525.

Other Opportunities Overseas

A non-governmental agency akin to the Peace Corps is the International Executive Service Corps, which helps place skilled executives in temporary positions in developing nations around the world. IESC welcomes candidates with solid backgrounds in various fields, including manufacturing, electronics, plastics, food processing, retailing, railroad operations and foundry work. Assignments are generally for three months and volunteers are encouraged to take their spouses along. Transportation and living expenses are paid by IESC and the country in question. Write to International Executive Service Corps, 622 Third Ave., New York, NY 10022.

Many religious groups also seek volunteers for their programs overseas. Among them are the United Church Board for World Ministries, 475 Riverside Dr., New York, NY 10027, and the Commission on Voluntary Service and Action, at the same address, which serves as a clearinghouse for hundreds of programs in social work, health care, education, business, farming and the arts.

SCORE/ACE Business Volunteers

Under programs sponsored by the federal Small Business Administration, seasoned businessmen and women volunteer their management and technical expertise to the owners and managers of small businesses and community organizations around the United States. Known as the Service Corps of Retired Executives (SCORE), more than 10,000 of these volunteers are organized into 380-odd chapters. They work in their own or nearby communities to aid small factories, stores, restaurants, services and other businesses with their finances, products, marketing problems and business procedures. Performed confidentially and without charge, the counseling can be of enormous help to struggling businesses, and of great satisfaction to the volunteers themselves.

Though SCORE volunteers receive no pay, they may be reimbursed for out-of-pocket expenses on request. Special talents not available through local SCORE chapters are furnished through a companion organization, the Active Corps of Executives (ACE), whose members are still employed in their regular jobs. For further details on either group, call or write to your local SCORE/ACE chapter or the local office of the Small Business Administration, or write SCORE, Small Business Administration, 1441 L St., NW, Washington, DC 20416.

Senior Community Service Employment Program

Under the Senior Community Service Employment Program (SCSEP), administered by the U.S. Department of Labor, more than 50,000 economically disadvantaged persons who are age 55 and over, and who have poor employment prospects, work at a variety of paid, part-time community jobs. Participants may help out in schools, day-care centers, hospitals, programs for the handicapped, senior citizens' centers, nutrition, transportation and fire prevention programs or in beautification, conservation and restoration projects.

SCSEP programs operate in all of the states, the District of Columbia, Puerto Rico and U.S. territories, and are sponsored by local government units and eight national organizations: Green Thumb, Inc., an arm of the

National Farmers' Union; the National Council on the Aging; the National Council of Senior Citizens: the American Association of Retired Persons; the U.S. Department of Agriculture's Forest Service; the National Center on Black Aged; the National Urban League; and the National Association Pro Spanish Speaking Elderly.

Participants in SCSEP are paid no less than the federal or state minimum wage, or the local prevailing rate of pay for similar employment, whichever is higher, and may work up to a total of 1,300 hours a year, averaging 20 to 25 hours a week. They receive annual physical examinations, counseling, job training if necessary, and help with placement in regular, unsubsidized jobs. For further information, call or write to your local U.S. Department of Labor office or SCSEP, Employment and Training Administration, U.S. Department of Labor, 601 D St., NW, Washington, DC 20213.

Other Government-Sponsored Job Programs

Older persons may also find jobs in a variety of other capacities, geared to their interests and abilities and to community needs.

Volunteers for VA Hospitals. Greatly in demand are volunteers to work in the 172 Veterans Administration hospitals across the country. Volunteers visit with patients, read to them, help them with letter writing, errands, meals and recreation; some work in hospital admissions offices or with telephone reassurance programs for patients recently released from hospitals and confined at home. If you are interested, call the chief of voluntary service at the nearest VA hospital.

Environmental and Weather Aides. Other government agencies enlist older volunteers from time to time. Among them are state environmental agencies, which may need help in such tasks as monitoring air and water pollution; the National Weather Service, which can use local weather observers (write to the Data Acquisition Division, National Oceanic and Atmospheric Administration, Silver Spring, MD 20910); and the Treasury Department, which may welcome salesmen for U.S. Savings Bonds. (Check with the Public Affairs Office, U.S. Savings Bond Division, Treasury Department, 1111 20th St., NW, Washington, DC 20226).

Income Tax Helpers. The Internal Revenue Service gives special training to volunteers who are willing to help others, including the elderly, with their income tax returns (see the earlier section on taxes). For details, check the local office of the IRS.

Starting Your Own Business

Many Americans dream of retiring from the company they have been working for and starting a business of their own. As the figures on small-business failures all too eloquently indicate, however, setting up your own business takes sufficient capital and a lot of planning, know-how, persistence and hard work. The Small Business Administration may be able to help you with pertinent literature, counseling services and assistance in arranging loans (see Chapter 2). Among its free publications are *Checklist for Going Into Business, Sound Management and Borrowing,* and *Insurance Checklist for Small Business.*

Many other publications on various aspects of business are available free or at a modest price. Check with your nearest SBA office, listed under "U.S. Government–Small Business Administration" in the telephone book. Don't forget that the Service Corps of Retired Executives (see above) may also be a source of free and expert advice.

Job Information and Guides

In addition to the SBA and other agencies noted above, most of which will send free literature on request, various organizations offer guides to jobs and other aspects of the retirement years. A booklet, *Your Retirement Job,* published by the Association of Retired Persons, also offers similar guides to retirement activities, consumer matters, crime, driving, food, health, home repair, housing, income taxes, legal matters, money, psychology, safety, state taxes and widowhood. Free copies are available from AARP, P.O. Box 2400, Long Beach, CA 90801 (see membership and services of AARP and other national organizations later in this chapter).

Another helpful booklet is *Working in Retirement,* prepared by the editors of *50 Plus Magazine,* who also publish guides on retirement planning, money, health, law, home and leisure activities. For prices and copies, write to 50 Plus, 850 Third Ave., New York, NY 10022.

Going Back to School

An increasing number of older people—probably upwards of 2 million every year—are returning to school. The reasons are many: to pursue favorite subjects they didn't have a chance to take before; to complete a degree or begin one; to learn how to manage their personal finances or develop entirely new career skills; or simply to get out of the house, keep their minds active and make new friends. At the same time many educational institutions, recognizing this important and growing market for their services, are accommodating the demand in a variety of ways, including programs of special interest to older Americans and policies of reduced or free tuition.

Among the most popular, and convenient, services are adult education courses sponsored by local public school systems and community colleges and offered to older citizens for a modest fee or without charge. The Reagan Administration decided that the cost of such programs must be underwritten by the states and municipalities aided by block grants from the federal government.

A national survey published by the Administration on Aging showed that nearly twice as many older women as men participated in adult education. The survey also indicated, perhaps not surprisingly, that participants tended to be of higher educational attainment and income than the older population at large. Among the courses most frequently taken, in order, were 1) crafts; 2) business, particularly administration and real estate; 3) arts, particulary dancing and painting; 4) health care; and 5) home economics, with a heavy emphasis on sewing and needlework. In contrast to younger students, a high percentage of older ones did not take their courses for formal academic credit but for practical, personal or social reasons, including just plain fun.

Pre-Retirement Courses

For a growing number of senior citizens, the return to education actually starts before retirement, in the form of planning programs that help them deal with the many changes they will face when they stop work. Courses on various aspects of retirement are offered by a broad range of sources. An increasing number of employers, and some unions, sponsor pre-retirement lectures, seminars and workshops, using materials developed by universities, by gerontology centers and by such groups as the National Council on the Aging and the Manpower Education Institute. Courses in retirement planning are also offered by such diverse ogranizations as community colleges, local adult-education and recreation departments, agricultural extension services, YMCAs and YWCAs, chambers of commerce and church and social groups. For courses available in your area, check with such groups, with your employer or with the local area agency on aging.

Teaching Yourself

For those who prefer self-education, before or during retirement, many helpful publications are available. One of the best sources is the local public library. Guides to retirement are also offered by the American Association of Retired Persons and *50-Plus Magazine* as well

Mixing Young and Old

"I forget that I'm 67 years old when I'm with kids," says retired engineer Ronald Brown.

Brown is one of 50 or so older citizens who attend classes at the Harbor Springs, Michigan, high school—and who are taking part in one of a growing number of programs around the country aimed at bridging the "generation gap" while enriching the lives of old and young alike. In the beginning, some of the older students worried that they'd be "knocked down by kids in the halls"; some of the kids, in turn, thought their new classmates would be "grouchy." By the end of the first semester, however, most of the qualms had disappeared. "At first it was weird," recalled a 15-year-old. "But now it's nice—well, sort of weird and nice combined."

The idea started when members of the Harbor Springs Senior Center, who had been meeting in a church basement, began looking for a better location, one which would also meet barrier-free standards for the handicapped. They found it in the old library at the local school, which was being replaced by a new one in a major expansion program. With the help of $4,000 put up by the local Kiwanis Club and $1,313 raised by the seniors themselves, a $16,000 grant was obtained from the area Agency on Aging to renovate the old library into a "Friendship Center" with a recreation—meeting room, crafts area, kitchenette, nurse's station and counseling room.

Using the new center as their base, the senior citizens are free to take virtually any courses they wish at the school under the community's continuing education program. Some with special skills help out as teacher's assistants or instructors, and any older student is welcome to take part in activities like the school play or the school band. Old and young mingle freely in the halls and share experiences, learning from one another's point of view. "We're giving the elderly people of this community a reason to get up in the morning," says 69-year-old Ed Schnell, a founder of the center. "And what senior citizens group do you know has a whole curriculum at its disposal, plus a 340-seat auditorium, three gymnasiums, a library and an art room with five pottery wheels and two kilns?"

Much the same sort of thing is happening at an increasing number of colleges, including the University of California at Santa Cruz, the University of Wisconsin and Bucknell. One of the pioneers has been little Fairhaven College in Bellingham, Washington, where about 50 of the 500-odd students are at least three times the average age of those enrolled. Fairhaven's "Bridge Project," started in 1973, spans the generation gap nicely, drawing the older students into all aspects of campus life from crafts projects to theatrical productions and even sports. About 30 of the "Bridgers," as they are called, live on campus, either in furnished apartments or right in the undergraduate dormitories, and about half of them are working toward degrees.

Helen Warinsky, 64, for example, is a journalism major and a reporter on the college newspaper; she has her own dorm room, carries on lively conversations with younger students in the cafeteria and has sold stories on the Bridge project to national publications. Like many of the Bridgers, she wondered at first whether the youngsters and the teachers would accept her. The experience, and enthusiasm, of the seniors, however, broke the ice. More than one has been stopped in the hall and told how much the others have enjoyed having them in class.

"There ought to be more places like Fairhaven," says Helen Warinsky. "It's given me a whole new dimension; it's changed my life. Why can't it do that for others?"

as by the Administration on Aging and state and area agencies on aging and by the federal government. Among the latter are countless free or modestly priced booklets on topics of practical interest ("Know Your Pension Plan," "A Woman's Guide to Social Security," "Generic Drugs," "Watch Your Blood Pressure," "You, the Law and Retirement," "Shopping by Mail"). For a complete listing, get a free copy of the federal Consumer Information Catalog by sending a postcard to the Consumer Information Center, Pueblo, CO 81009. More than 70 federal publications dealing specifically with retirement are for sale; for a free list, write the Superintendent of Documents, U.S. Government Printing Office, Washington, DC 20402 and ask for "Retirement: Subject Bibliography SB-285."

Local School Programs

Many public school systems across the nation offer special classes for senior citizens at reduced rates or without charge. The Westport, Connecticut, public schools, for example, maintain a continuing education program under state legislation that requires all school districts to offer adult classes for at least 150 hours a year; no tuition fees are charged for students 62 years of age or over, or for handicapped adults and those who are completing their basic education by studying English as a second language or who are completing subjects for a high-school equivalency degree.

The courses, most of which are offered in the evening, cover a wide range of interests: photography, printmaking, quilting, yoga, French, Spanish, money management, ballroom dancing, guitarplaying and gourmet cooking. In addition, special day activities are scheduled for the elderly: bridge, painting, indoor gardening, rhythmic exercises and play production for amateur groups.

Community Colleges

Some 200 community colleges in America, mandated by state legislatures to assist men and women over 18, also pay special attention to the needs of older students. Under policies in many states, tuition is reduced or waived entirely for persons over a specified age. Besides offering a wide range of college-level courses—both at the colleges themselves and at off-campus senior centers, nursing homes and other community locations—programs provide support services for the elderly, including special counseling, simplified registration procedures and help with transportation.

Some colleges have established "gold card" programs that extend community privileges to the elderly. Los Angeles Valley College in Van Nuys, California, for example, has about 12,000 gold card holders who are entitled to free parking, free or reduced admission to plays, concerts and other college events and free placement aid in finding part-time jobs.

Older students have responded handsomely to such opportunities in several ways. Eighty percent of those at Los Angeles Valley College who are taking college courses for credit register a B average or better, compared with 40 percent of the student body as a whole. "They have become a real and welcome presence on campus," commented a 22-year-old officer of a student booster club. "They attend most school functions, and they make as much noise cheering at ballgames as we do." Said another young student, "I went to a disco dance the other night, and half the dancers there were Gold Card students."

Employers who have hired members of the Los Angeles Valley College effort are enthusiastic too: they have found that older workers want to work and are popular with customers. Said one store owner, "I'll take an older employee over a younger one every time."

Other College and University Programs

State colleges, technical schools and universities across the country also reduce or waive tuition for the elderly, modify admission requirements, offer retirement counseling, courses in health, legal rights and financial planning and make campus facilities accessible to the disabled and handicapped.

Some 300 colleges and universities in the United States and Canada participate in a unique summer educational experience called Elderhostel. Inspired by the youth hostels and folk schools of Europe, Elderhostel is designed specifically for older persons who are reaching out for intellectual stimulation and adventure. For a modest fee, groups of 30 or 40 persons age 60 or over meet at member colleges starting on Sunday evening and live together until the following Saturday morning, either remaining on campus or traveling elsewhere while they take informal courses, live in simple accommodations and eat in college cafeterias. For further information, inquire at local colleges or contact Elderhostel, 100 Boylston St., Boston, MA 02116.

Home Education and Free Lectures

Through its Cooperative Extension Service, which maintains 3,000 offices around the country, the U.S. Department of Agriculture offers information and instruction in agriculture and home economics, including gardening, food and nutrition, clothing, housing, home furnishings, health and safety. In many states the elderly population is a special target audience, particularly for home-economics courses. For further information, call your nearest county extension office.

The Library of Congress offers free services for persons with visual or physical handicaps. Large print materials and books on tapes, discs and in Braille are obtainable without charge through local libraries, or by writing to the National Library Service, Library of Congress, 1291 Taylor St. NW, Washington, DC 20542.

Many lecture series and other programs are held at local public libraries, museums and universities, and most are free to older persons. Check your library bulletin board or local newspaper under community events.

Correspondence, home study and television courses abound for those who want to learn at home at their own convenience and pace. Though most commercial correspondence schools are reputable, a few are not, so it is wise to check first with your local Better Business Bureau or Department of Consumer Affairs. Through its Institute of Lifetime Learning, the American Association of Retired Persons offers a series of mini-courses, with supplementary reading and questions for discussion groups. Write to the Institute at 1909 K St., NW, Washington, DC 20049. Other courses are described in the *Guide to Independent Study Through Correspondence Instruction,* available from Peterson's Guides, Box 778, Edison, NJ 00817, or the *Directory of Accredited Home Study Schools* published by the National Home Study Council, 1601 18th St., NW, Washington, DC 20009.

Recreation and Special Services for the Elderly

In many parts of the country, municipal or county recreation departments sponsor programs for the elderly or programs for people of all ages that older citizens are welcome to join, including athletic and exercise groups, arts and crafts classes, dramatic and musical organizations, hobby clubs, picnics, outings and other special events. Public museums as well as private theaters, concert halls and movie houses often give seniors a discount on admission or distribute tickets without charge.

Many states issue passes that allow elderly residents to park their cars free at state-operated recreation areas. The National Park Service of the U.S. Department of the Interior offers anyone 62 or over a Golden Age Passport, a lifetime entrance permit to parks, monuments and recreation areas administered by the federal government. The permit also entitles you to a 50 percent discount on fees charged for parking, camping, boat launching and other facilities and services. (It does not cover fees charged by private concessionaires.) It admits the holder and a carload of accompanying people; if entry is not by car, it admits the holder and his or her spouse and children. You can pick up your Golden Age Passport at most federal recreation areas where it may be used, or through any regional office of the National Park Service. Persons under 62 can apply for a "Golden Eagle Passport," which costs $10 for one calendar year and admits the holder and family group to all federal parks, monuments and recreation areas but does not provide any discount on camping, parking or other special-use fees (see Chapter 9 for specific information).

Special Transportation
One of the major problems facing the elderly is simply getting around. Many don't drive, or even have a car; taxis are expensive, and regular public transportation, if it exists at all, may be difficult for them to use. As a result they can't get to clinics and doctors' offices, visit senior centers to sample a hot meal and some companionship, or enjoy a concert or an outing in the park. Supermarkets are often too far away to walk to, especially when there are heavy packages to carry home.

To make life more manageable for older citizens, many communities offer transportation and other services, some supported by government programs and others maintained through the generosity of private organizations and volunteer groups.

Scores of cities with public transportation systems offer reduced fares for senior citizens during non-rush hours and on weekends. The National Mass Transportation Act of 1974 requires that any public transit system receiving capital assistance from the Urban Mass Transportation Administration charge half fare or less for the elderly. Thus New York City and Chicago, for example, charge half the normal amount; San Francisco charges even less, and Seattle and Tacoma charge a small sum for a monthly pass. The little town of Commerce, California, a suburb of Los Angeles, goes them one better, providing free bus service to people of all ages within its city limits: it also offers senior citizens and other groups two free char-

tered bus trips a year to any destination within 50 miles—a service older residents have enjoyed as a means of getting to ball games, museums, plays and other events.

In other communities, people have got together to organize all manner of ingenious answers to the transportation problem, many of them with the help of demonstration grants and subsidies from local and state governments and the U.S. Department of Transportation.

In most of Missouri's 115 counties, rural residents who are 55 and over or handicapped can enroll in OATS (Older Adults Transportation Service, Inc.), a low-cost transportation scheme, sponsored by the state department of aging, that operates more than one hundred 14- to 16-passenger vans. Members are asked to request service well ahead of time; a helper may accompany a member on payment of a second fare, and those unable to pay can make arrangements to ride free (see opposite page.)

San Mateo County, California, provides door-to-door minibus service far below actual cost through "Redi-Wheels," giving priority to medical trips. The city of San Diego uses a score of vans and small buses in its "Dial-A-Ride" program. Kinston, North Carolina, lacking any group transportation facilities, established KITE (Kinston Independent Transportation for the Elderly), which sells ticket books at half price for use in taxicabs and pays taxi operators full fare when the tickets are redeemed. Pennsylvania uses proceeds from its state lottery to finance state-wide free transit during off-peak hours for all persons 65 and over.

Long-Range Travel
Reduced fares for inter-city travel are also available to the elderly on many scheduled trains, buses and airplanes. In the New York area, for example, the Harlem, Hudson and New Haven divisions of Conrail offer 50 percent off to persons 65 and older during off-peak hours and on weekends. Amtrak gives senior citizens a 25 percent discount on trips in the United States costing over $40. Greyhound and Continental

Door-to-Door Rides in Missouri

"After my husband died," recalls senior citizen Alma Hodges of Bloomfield, Missouri, "I sold the car. Driving made me nervous, and I didn't know how to take care of the thing anyway." Still, she adds, she was luckier than others: "Some of my folks would take time off from work to drive me where I just *had* to go. But I sure hated to ask because it worked a hardship on them."

The state of Missouri has shown how much can be done to help people like Alma Hodges. Every month some 115 vans and minibuses belonging to the Older Adult Transportation Services (OATS), based in the city of Columbia, provide door-to-door rides for more than 100,000 senior citizens and handicapped residents of 800 communities scattered over 88 counties in the state. The vans take passengers from their homes to doctors' offices, supermarkets, shopping centers and even to friends' and relatives' homes. Riders pay only what they can afford.

OATS began in 1971 when Quinnie Benton, a 70-year-old resident of St. Joseph, got together with others to form a cooperative transportation association in Calloway County in order to help themselves and their elderly neighbors become more independent and more mobile. They convinced the Missouri Office of Aging to contribute $30,000 and started off with three county-loaned buses and an all-volunteer staff. The idea quickly spread, and in 1973 OATS was incorporated as a non-profit group.

In recent years much of OATS' budget has come from federal funds made available through the Older Americans Act, the Urban Mass Transportation Act and the Social Security Act, with the rest made up by fund-raising efforts and rider fares. There is now a staff of paid drivers and administrators, but the backbone of the organization consists of some 500 volunteers, many of them OATS riders, who schedule routes, arrange rides, plan special outings and raise money through activities like potluck dinners and quilt sales.

After using the OATS system for the first time, riders receive a monthly schedule for the vans; and when they need transportation they can call a local number to reserve a place on the pickup list. Riders can also become members of the OATS Wheel Club for a small yearly fee. They receive a monthly newsletter of activities, which include special low-cost OATS tours such as trips to St. Louis to enjoy the Cardinals' baseball games.

The transportation service not only frees its elderly users from an embarrassing dependence on neighbors and relatives, but relieves them of the expense and headaches of maintaining automobiles themselves. It also enriches their lives by enabling them to make new friends and enjoy a lively sense of camaraderie. "It's both a convenience and a pleasure when they come to pick me up," says Marie Sagler of Mendon, Missouri, a regular rider in the program. "I feel I'm part of one big family, and I realize how much it means to so many others who travel by OATS."

Trailways also offer special rates. A number of airlines give discounts averaging one third on domestic flights, and the United States tourist offices of many European countries extend discount privileges to older travelers for use abroad. Members of national seniors' organizations such as AARP (see end of chapter) receive discounts on rental cars, motels and other travel services.

Savings at Stores, Restaurants, Museums and Theaters

In many localities, shops and service establishments participate in plans to reduce prices for older patrons. The New York City Department for the Aging, for example, sponsors a program called Community Concern for Senior Citizens under which merchants are encouraged to offer discount rates. The Department then lists the names and addresses of the hundreds of participants and the discounts they give—generally 10 percent but in some cases as high as 50 percent—in a "Senior Citizens Discount Book" that is distributed to older New Yorkers without charge.

The book groups services for easy reference ("Appliances," "Banks," "Drug Stores," "Restaurants"). Merchants are provided with stickers labeled "Community Concern for Senior-Citizens," and readers of the discount book are advised to patronize places displaying the sticker. By showing their senior ID card, reduced-fare card or Medicare card they can obtain the lower rate. Also described in the discount book are many other benefits of interest to seniors: educational programs, museums, theaters and other entertainment; employment opportunities and agencies; services for the handicapped; travel and transportation; health care; food stamps; important addresses and telephone numbers through which individuals can get further information or register complaints.

Special Banking Services

Banking institutions around the country offer various services to the elderly. Connecticut's Union Trust Co., for example, advertises "Free Golden-60 Senior Checking," a typical plan that gives anyone over 60 a checking account without any minimum-balance requirement, activity charge or monthly maintenance fee. Such larger banks as New York's Chase Manhattan Bank and Citibank offer a variety of financial, referral and educational services for seniors; many of their branches have special senior citizens' advisers, bulletins and free literature, and even hold seminars for seniors on security, investments, housing and health.

Commercial banks, savings banks, credit unions and savings and loan associations also offer "Direct Deposit," a convenient and safe way to have monthly government checks automatically delivered for deposit without fear of being stolen, temporarily mislaid or lost. Under Direct Deposit, which is sponsored by the U.S. Treasury Department, you can choose the bank you want and have deposits made by the appropriate government agency directly into your personal checking or savings account. Social Security benefits, supplemental security income, veterans compensation and pension payments, civil service and railroad retirement checks may be included. Simply take your next check to your bank and say you want to sign up for Direct Deposit; the bank will help you complete the necessary form, and within 90 days Uncle Sam will begin depositing your payments for you. (If there is a change in your payment or any other important information, the government will communicate directly with you at home.)

Proper Nutrition for Older Americans

The need for proper nutrition, so strongly stressed by parents when their children are young, does not stop at any particular age. Yet a sensible diet is often neglected with the passing years, even by those who once told Junior firmly to eat his spinach or else. The result can be a downward spiral, as described in the Older Americans Act:

"Many older persons do not eat adequately because 1) they cannot afford to do so; 2) they lack the skills to select and prepare nourishing and well-balanced meals; 3) they have limited mobility, which may impair their capacity to shop and cook for themselves; and 4) they have feelings of rejection and loneliness which obliterate the incentive necessary to prepare and eat a meal alone. These and other physiological, psychological, social and economic changes that occur with aging result in a pattern of living which causes malnutrition and further physical and mental deterioration."

In attempts to correct this unhappy situation, both government and private, non-profit groups operate programs to help older people obtain access to nutritious and well-balanced meals.

Good Food at Low Cost

For those who are interested in improving their own diets, and in fighting rising food costs as well, there is an abundance of advice in popular magazines and books. In this area, as in others, the federal government also has publications to offer the consumer, many of them free. Recent ones include *Food; Nutrition and Your Health; Consumer's Guide to Food Labels; Salt; Sugar; Some Facts and Myths About Vitamins; Fats in Food and Diet,* as well as booklets on vegetable gardening and the storing, preserving and preparing of home-grown foods. For a more complete list, write for a free copy of the *Consumer Information Catalog,* Consumer Information Center, Pueblo, CO 81009, or ask your county agricultural extension agent for publications that are in stock.

To combat rising food prices, people in many localities across the United States have got together to form food cooperatives, food banks, food-buying clubs, community vegetable gardens and other schemes that offer considerable savings in return for volunteer labor and minimal dues. In Davenport, Iowa, for example, the Central Davenport Food Buying Club, under the sponsorship of a non-profit neighborhood corporation, purchases directly from wholesalers to eliminate normal packaging, distribution and retailing costs and saves up to 30 percent on fresh fruits, vegetables, meats, grains and beans. Pittsburgh's East End Food Co-op, operating out of a store front, saves its 400-odd members an average of 25 percent. In Connecticut, the New Haven Food Co-op took over an existing supermarket, enabling its 5,000 members to buy at an average of 12 percent below competing supermarket prices. On some items the savings are much greater.

While older citizens are among those participating in such plans, some projects have been started primarily by and for seniors. In California's Santa Clara County, a food bank, partly funded by the county department of social services, has a "Brown Bag Program" that provides elderly members with five or six pounds of donated surplus food each week for a $2 annual fee; in Sacramento the Senior Gleaners, an organization of some 1,700 retired volunteers, pick their own produce from farmers' fields. In North Portland, Oregon, more than 7,000 members of Senior Citizens Grocery, Inc., staffed mainly by elderly volunteers, save an average of 13 percent on their budgets for food (see box, pages 304 and 305).

Eating Together

Thousands of communities around the country participate in the Nutrition Services Program for Older Americans, which provides at least one hot meal a day, five or more days a week, to persons 60 or over, and to their spouses regardless of age. Administered by the federal Administration on Aging, which channels funds through state and area agencies, the program serves meals in congregate dining facilities—senior centers, church halls, school lunchrooms—where lonely elders not only can enjoy eating together and striking up friendships but can also play cards, attend discussion groups and get help on matters of individual concern. Though roughly two thirds of those participating are at or below the official poverty level, no means test is required in order to qualify; no one is turned away, and all are given an opportunity to contribute whatever they can afford toward the cost of the meals. In many communities, the program includes transportation to and from senior centers or other dining halls.

Meals-on-Wheels

For those who cannot get to a communal dining place because of illness, disability or transportation problems, prepared "meals-on-wheels" are delivered under the same program

A Grocery Store for Seniors

When senior citizens of North Portland, Oregon, asked the owner of a local grocery chain if he might offer them lower prices, he told them that it wasn't a practical idea. But the owner, John Piacentini, had just heard a speech by Oregon Governor Robert Straub about the heavy burden of rising food costs, particularly on elderly people with fixed incomes. And he happened to have no immediate plans for a convenience food store he had just closed. To their surprise, Piacentini offered the seniors a grocery store of their own—including the use of the space and equipment, rent free, plus $20,000 worth of merchandise to give them a start.

The organizers immediately called a public meeting of other elderly residents to make plans and spread the word. Piacentini provided a media expert who designed and distributed brochures describing the new market and created advertising skits that ran as free public-service announcements on TV. A local lawyer donated his time to draw up a constitution, bylaws and an application for a nonprofit corporation, Senior Citizens Grocery, Inc. A three-member board of directors, elected to govern the store's operations, was established.

Volunteers under the direction of the new store's manager, Wayne Henry, a retired grocer, scrubbed dusty shelves, wielded mops and paint brushes and got the merchandise in place. At the grand opening some two and a half months later, the governor hailed the new venture as a great idea. Piacentini and other private donors kicked in money to pay the store's utility and telephone bills for six months. A minimum shopper age of 60 was

up to five or more days a week. Brought by private automobiles or special vans, the food often consists of a hot meal for mid-day use and a cold one for supper later on. The meals are not only balanced and nourishing but they provide the homebound with a daily link to the outside world—someone to greet and chat with each day—and frequently a volunteer who brings the food will stay on to visit during the meal. Charges for home-delivery service vary from nothing to a few dollars a week, according to the ability of the recipient to pay.

One of the largest such programs, Baltimore's Meals-on-Wheels, is run almost entirely by volunteers. Started by an association of Jewish charities, it operates out of 9 communal kitchens and delivers two meals daily, one hot and one cold. Recipients are charged according to their ability to pay and are given a phone number to call if they want to comment or complain about meals or service, or just talk. Volunteers who deliver the meals help out by reporting their clients' other needs, which are followed up by an appropriate agency.

Food Stamps

People who are having trouble meeting basic living expenses can apply for the federally funded Food Stamp Program, which is intended to help low-income households buy the food they need for good health. Coupons, or stamps, issued to those eligible may be used to buy groceries in participating food stores that display the U.S. Department of Agriculture sign, "We Accept Food Coupons." They can also be used to pay for donations at communal dining places and for home-delivered meals sponsored by the government's Nutrition Services Program.

The food-stamp program is run by state public assistance agencies under agreement with the USDA. Low income is the primary criterion for eligibility. The elderly or disabled who live on small incomes are a specially targeted group. If you meet the eligibility tests, established and an annual membership fee of 50 cents was set. By the end of the first year, the membership had reached 6,000 and was still climbing, and the founders discovered that they had enough of an operating budget to pay the expenses.

Senior Citizens Grocery, whose success has been emulated by similar efforts across the nation, saves its elderly shoppers an average of 13 percent by taking advantage of free rent, free labor and limited stock. Manager Henry and three other older paid employees are assisted by senior volunteers. Markups on various goods average about 3 percent, well below the markups of commercial supermarkets that must pay heavier staff and advertising costs. The store, which is open seven days a week from 9 to 5, offers fruits, vegetables, dry goods, a delicatessen, sundries and a range of special products for people on low-sugar or low-salt diets.

The store's patrons find it not only a money saver, but a lively and congenial place to shop and meet friends. Any elderly resident is welcome to shop once on a trial basis before joining, and scarcely a week goes by when some new faces don't show up. "It's a delightful little store," observes Lydia Clairmore, a widow who compares prices at other area stores and finds that the labels at Senior Citizens Grocery are consistently lower. Mrs. Clairmore grows her own vegetables at home, but she pronounces the store's produce "fresh and nice." "One of the reasons," she adds with a twinkle in her eye, "is that a lot of members bring in some of their own extra vegetables and fruits to sell, or to just give away."

which involve proof of income and assets and a confidential personal interview, the value of stamps you receive will depend on a complex formula involving the number of people in your household and the amount of monthly income left after certain deductions are made for other living costs.

Food stamps, which bear different denominations and are spent in lieu of cash, can be used only for food and for plants and seeds to grow food for your household. They cannot be used to buy tobacco, alcoholic beverages, medicines, pet foods, ready-to-eat hot foods, household supplies like soap and paper products and other non-food items. Stamps cannot be sold, traded or given away. Anyone who breaks the rules may be disqualified from the program, fined, imprisoned or all three.

To apply for food stamps, contact the local office of your state welfare, social services or income-maintenance department, listed under state agencies in your telephone book. Some areas have toll-free "hotline" numbers listed under "Food Stamps" in a section of frequently used community and government services. The food stamp office will give or mail you a form on request. If you are receiving, or applying for, Supplemental Security Income (SSI) benefits, you can apply for food stamps at the same time in your Social Security District Office. If you are 65 or older or disabled and cannot find someone to go to the food stamp office for you, you can arrange for your interview at home or by telephone. For further information on the food stamp program, see Chapter 4.

Choosing a Place to Live

For many people, the most important decision of the retirement years is the choice of a place to live. The American dream, as touted in countless advertisements, is to head south or west where the climate is eternal springtime and one can enjoy endless days of swimming, fishing, playing golf or just loafing.

Buying Retirement Property

Though most land developers are reputable, and must operate under various laws, some are tempted to stretch the rules. If you are thinking of buying land for a retirement home, be careful to check out the developer's credentials as well as the terms. Never buy "blind" by mail or telephone; inspect the property in person, and if it is registered for interstate sales, ask for, and study, a copy of the property report required by law. If you are unsure of any details, consult a lawyer. Never sign any agreement until you have understood every word of it, and make sure you get a copy of it to keep. Here are some questions, prepared by HUD, you may need answers for:

* How large will the development become, and what zoning controls are specified?
* What amenities are promised (for example, lake, marina, golf course, club house, swimming pool)? Has the developer set aside money to build and maintain them, and when will they be ready? Will you be charged extra for their use?
* What provisions are there for roads, water supply, sewers, garbage collection? Who maintains them and what will they cost?
* Will you have clear title to your property? What liens, reservations or encumbrances exist?
* Will you receive a deed, or a recordable sales contract? Will your payments be placed in an escrow account to pay for your property, or will they be spent by the developer?
* When the developer moves out, is there a homeowners' association to take over management? If the developer defaults or goes bankrupt, could you lose your investment to satisfy a claim?

Watch out for these practices, which are generally shunned by reputable sales operations:
* The "hot investment" pitch. A salesman may get carried away about the area's growth potential and its effect on the value of your plot. It may even be suggested to you that the developer will resell your lot at a profit if you

But the dream may be beyond the reach of some. The expense of moving may be more than they can afford, or the move itself may be a mirage. The faraway places where the sun shines every day may be boring or hostile environments for people in their sixties. The boardwalk beside the beach may be less inviting than the old neighborhood in Chicago or New York.

As a result, while thousands of retirees do indeed move to "sunbelt" states every year, most people—an estimated 94 out of 100—stay put.

For most Americans their hometowns are their retirement towns, whether they prefer to remain in familiar surroundings among old friends or simply cannot afford to strike out for the supposedly greener pastures.

Moving to a New Community

If you are thinking about trying a new community, or a new state, be sure to check out all the particulars: cost of living, local and state taxes, exemptions and other advantages for persons over a certain age. You should also look into specific housing, cultural, recreational and medical facilities, shopping, and opportunities for part-time work, if you're interested in limited work. Before actually visiting a community, you can get much of the information you need about it by writing the local area or state agency on aging, the local chamber of commerce or the mayor's office or by subscribing for a few months to a local newspaper to get the community's "feel" (your hometown librarian can help you with names and addresses to write to for such details).

want—an unlikely prospect if the developer is still holding lots to sell later on. You are probably paying top price already, including heavy advertising costs and sales commissions, and it is doubtful that your lot's value will increase spectacularly enough to justify holding it purely as a long-term investment.

* The money-back guarantee. A long-distance telephone or mail campaign may include an offer of a refund if the property has been misrepresented or you inspect it and decide not to buy. If and when you request the refund, you may encounter arguments about the terms of the agreement, possibly an accusation that the salesman made the guarantee without the knowledge and consent of the developer.

* "Bait and switch". Lots are sometimes offered at extremely low prices, even "free." When the buyer appears, the bargains are all gone, or so obviously undesirable that the only available property is much more expensive.

* High-pressure tactics. If a salesman tells you desirable lots are selling so fast you'd better act quickly, or attempts to embarrass you into action, ask to see the boss or, better still, take your leave.

* Sales inducements. Beware of "free vacations," lavish gifts and other inducements to lure you to a sales presentation or to the site. The bonuses may never materialize, or they may go only to people who actually purchase the lots.

* Failure to deliver documents. A few salesmen withhold the detailed property report until a customer signs up for a specific lot, or bury it in a mass of promotional material and legal documents so the buyer fails to recognize it for what it is. To protect yourself, make sure that you know when all of the vital papers—the deed, title, insurance policy and other documents—are to be delivered to you under the contract—and make sure they *are* delivered as promised.

If you are considering a planned retirement community, or "retirement village," designed specifically for seniors, check the minimum entrance age, the types of housing available, other amenities and the reputation of the developer-owner. If you are thinking of buying land to build on, make sure you have the answers to some basic questions. Does the developer have clear title to the land and water rights? Does the purchase include a guarantee to put in roads, utilities, sewage lines or septic tanks? Land developers and builders must operate within local laws, including those of the state real-estate commission. Those offering land for recreation, vacation or retirement purposes across state lines are also governed by the federal Interstate Land Sales Act of 1968, a "full disclosure" law that seeks to protect consumers against fraud by assuring them access to all the information needed for a sensible, unhurried decision.

Generally, companies offering 50 or more unimproved lots for sale or lease must file a statement of record with the Department of Housing and Urban Development's Office of Interstate Land Sales Registration. They must also provide any prospective buyer with a property report prior to the time a purchase agreement is signed. The report must contain the financial statements of the developer, details of utilities, roads, soil conditions, mortgages or liens on the property and special risk factors about which the buyer should be warned. For a more complete guide, see "Buying Lots From Developers," for sale through the U.S. Government Printing Office, Washington, DC

20402, or the Consumer Information Center, Pueblo, CO 81009. A more detailed discussion of retirement property purchases appears on pages 306 and 307. If you believe you have been cheated in a transaction, contact HUD/OILSR, 451 Seventh St., SW, Washington, DC 20410. Be sure to provide details of your complaint and copies of the contract or other documents you have signed.

Staying in Your Old Community

If, like most Americans, you decide to spend your retirement in your hometown, you may want to sell your house and move to more modest, more modern or more covenient quarters in the community, whether these are in a smaller house, an apartment, a cooperative or a condominium. Don't forget that if you are 55 or older, you can exclude from your gross income on federal taxes up to $125,000 of gain on the sale (see the earlier section on selling your home). To finance your new home you may also be eligible for government-supported FHA, FmHA or VA loans (see Chapter 3 on Housing and Chapter 6 on Veterans Affairs). You may find helpful one or more of the free pamphlets distributed by the U.S. Department of Housing and Urban Development through its regional and district offices. Among them are "How to Buy Your Home Wisely," "Home Mortgage Insurance," "How to Buy a Condominium," "Let's Consider Cooperatives" and "How to Buy a Mobile Home."

Rental Assistance

The Department of Housing and Urban Development administers a number of programs to help elderly people with limited incomes to obtain decent housing they can afford. The Section 8 Rental Assistance Program (see Chapter 3) offers subsidies to lower-income persons, including the elderly, who pay up to 25 percent of their income for rent to private landlords. HUD pays the difference between what the tenant can afford and the fair-market rental for the dwelling unit. To be eligible, tenants' incomes must not exceed 80 percent of the

median income in their area. For more information, contact your local public housing agency or area HUD office.

Other Housing Programs

Under the low-income public housing program, HUD offers federal aid to local public housing authorities to construct or acquire housing for persons of limited means. Tenants, according to their financial ability, pay up to 25 percent of their adjusted incomes for rent, with the government making up the difference. About half the present public housing inventory across the nation is currently occupied by elderly people. Many older individuals also benefit from HUD's Section 202 program, designed specifically for the elderly and handicapped. Under this program HUD makes direct, low-cost, long-term loans to non-profit sponsors to finance the production of rental housing. Tenants can use government Section 8 rental assistance subsidies to help pay their rent.

HUD also administers several other programs tailored to meet the housing needs of the elderly and handicapped. The Section 231 mortgage insurance program aids the financing of new or rehabilitated housing of eight or more units. The congregate housing program helps local public-housing authorities to develop rental housing that has common kitchen, dining, recreational and other facilities built in. The Section 232 program insures mortgages for builders of nursing homes.

Also available directly to homeowners are several programs of home-ownership assistance, home improvement and home-rehabilitation loans. For further details, see Chapter 3 on housing or contact your local HUD area office (see Directory, Chapter 3).

Energy Assistance Programs

Some states have energy assistance programs designed to help low-income Americans, including the elderly, pay their rising fuel bills. Weatherstripping, insulation, storm windows and improvements to heating equipment are included in some of these programs. To find out whether your state provides this kind of aid, contact your local housing agency, or the local agency for the aging.

Homeowner and Tenant Rights

Various local laws exist to protect individuals, including the elderly, against undue disruption in the enjoyment of their homes. These laws govern leases, rent increases, security deposits, living conditions, utilities, evictions and other matters. Some state laws regulate the conversion of rental apartments into condominium units, requiring six months' advance notice, allowing elderly or handicapped persons to remain longer and helping tenants who do not wish to, or cannot afford to, buy their units to find other places to live. Since local laws vary, and are administered by different agencies, inquiries should be directed to your local community action agency, information service or senior center.

Everyday Help at Home

Many frail older persons are unable to provide for themselves at home and cannot afford the costly services of hospitals or nursing homes. Fortunately, an increasing number of community services are available to assist many of these people in their own homes, thus avoiding unnecessary institutionalization as long as possible. Such services include visiting-nurse care, homemaker assistance, escort and transportation services, meals-on-wheels, friendly visiting and telephone reassurance, able-bodied aid for the older people with occasional house repair or garden chores—not to mention the help of family, friends or neighbors who pitch in when they can.

Telephone Reassurance

Besides being lonely for the sound of another voice, older people who live by themselves often fear they may fall or be taken ill suddenly and be unable to call for help. A simple solution instituted in many communities is telephone reassurance or "Ring-A-Day," in which volunteers call every day at a pre-determined time, ask if everything is all right and perhaps chat for a while. If things are not well, or if the person does not answer, a neighbor, relative or nearby police or fire station is asked to make an immediate, personal check.

Telephone reassurance not only provides daily human contacts for older persons who might otherwise be isolated for long periods; it is frequently credited with saving lives by dispatching medical help in time. The service costs little and can be performed by callers of any age. In Nassau County, New York, for example, residents of a home for the aged make daily calls to others who live alone; in Albuquerque, New Mexico, calls are made by a hospital auxiliary and members of the business and professional women's club. In Davenport, Iowa, a popular variation on the theme is a telephone service called "Dial-A-Listener," in which a handful of older professional people take calls from stay-at-homes who need friendly advice or just want to talk.

Friendly Visiting

A logical, and even more personal, extension of telephone reassurance is Friendly Visiting, a program in which volunteers go to see isolated older persons on a regular schedule once or more a week. While there they may sit and chat, play cards, help write letters or provide companionship and an arm to lean on for a walk in the fresh air or a needed shopping trip.

Such visits have proved of priceless benefit to elderly residents who have no close relatives or friends. "She has made my life over," says one lady of her visitor; "It makes me feel like I am still somebody worth talking to," says another. Professional staff workers have noted that those visited usually take a greater interest in the world, look better, become less absorbed in their personal problems and in some cases actually experience an improvement in health.

Older persons often prove the most effective visitors. Programs generally assign a volunteer to one, sometimes two, clients. A school-bus driver in Yampa Valley, Colorado, found he enjoyed his responsibility so much that he started visiting several older people every day. After delivering the children to school, he would make his rounds to say hello until it was time to start up the bus again for the children's return trip. In Austin, Texas, the "Roadrunner" volunteers visit the residents of more than 40 nursing homes, take groups of patients on outings and provide transportation to the homes for relatives, friends and other visitors who cannot get there on their own.

In some communities Friendly Visiting knows no generation gap. Under YES (Youth Elderly Service) of Fall River, Massachusetts, more than 100 high school girls and boys have gotten together to visit elderly residents in 9 local nursing homes. In places like San Francisco and West Hartford, Connecticut, high school students take part in "Adopt-A-Grandparent" programs, stopping in on older people to talk, write letters and do errands and household chores.

Homemaker Services

In many communities older residents who are unable to keep up with household tasks can get help through homemaker services sponsored by a Visiting Nurse Association, welfare department or other social agency. These services may include dusting, laundry, meal preparation, shopping, personal care and grooming. The homemaker assigned to such duties is generally

Senior Centers: Where the Action Is

In the past decade, the number of senior citizens' centers and clubs in the United States has multiplied sevenfold, from 1,200 to more than 8,000. The centers range from small, informal groups meeting in church parish halls or other borrowed space to organizations with thousands of members who have their own buildings, complete with recreation and dining rooms, libraries, auditoriums, movies, lectures, concerts, organized classes and discussion groups. They call themselves by many names; Senior Center, Senior Circle, Golden Age Club, 60-Plus Club, Retirement or Leisure Association, Bee Hive, Young-in-Heart.

More remarkable than the increase in numbers has been the metamorphosis of the idea itself. No longer just a place where older people can get together to play cards or chat, the modern multi-purpose senior center has expanded its activities so broadly that it has been designated the major focal point for delivery of services to the elderly under the Older Americans Act. It is a veritable hub of

activity, a place where seniors can socialize over nutritious, low-cost meals; attend courses in painting, embroidery, woodcraft, creative writing or personal finances; receive education in health matters and have their blood pressure checked; talk to counselors about opportunities for employment in paid or volunteer jobs. Older citizens also join bus trips to stores, theaters, museums and scenic sites; celebrate holidays and members' birthdays with festive parties; obtain needed outside services such as door-to-door transportation, shopping escorts, friendly visits, help with household chores, home repairs, home-delivered meals. Some centers even have their own members' orchestras and stage their own amateur musicals and plays. If there is any service or information a center cannot provide—help with taxes or a legal problem, for example—it usually can suggest another agency that does.

The main purpose of senior centers is to aid older Americans in maintaining active roles in the community and to provide them with a a mature woman with skills in home management and an understanding of human behavior. She usually has some training in basic care of the sick but she is not a substitute for a professional nurse or social worker, and she is not a maid.

Home Maintenance and Repair

Home-care services often include special help with home repairs, maintenance and heavier work for those who cannot do it themselves: mowing or raking lawns, putting up and taking down storm windows, painting, fixing plumbing or leaky roofs. In the state of Washington, STEP (Service to Elderly Persons) coordinates a program in which teenagers perform heavy household and gardening chores: lifting,

reason for living and a break from the isolation of lonely rooms. The centers attempt to integrate the numerous benefits and services available to the elderly and thus make it easier for older people to take advantage of the varied resources they are entitled to. Many, if not most, of the centers around the nation enjoy some form of public support, whether it comes from local, state or federal funds or a combination thereof. And at most of these places, the door is wide open to senior citizens, with membership fees either minimal or non-existent.

To find the senior center, or centers, nearest you and discover what they have to offer, talk to friends, call your local agency on aging or consult a directory of community organizations at your public library. If you are interested in helping to start a new center or expand the programs and services of an older one, contact the National Institute of Senior Centers, c/o the National Council on the Aging, 600 Maryland Ave. SW, Washington, DC 20024.

moving, washing, spading garden beds. In Westmoreland County, Pennsylvania, senior citizens can call on a volunteer service known as Repairs-on-Wheels. In Detroit, Maintenance Central for Seniors, Inc., started with the help of a federal demonstration grant and, supported by local contributions, performs hundreds of repair jobs every month; workers range in age from 18 to 87, and retired persons are used whenever possible. Senior citizens with years of experience in construction and maintenance enjoy the chance to help other retirees who do not have their skills, and the older craftsmen are invaluable in teaching younger workers their trades.

Home Health Services

For elderly persons who have chronic conditions, or are recuperating from illnesses, various agencies such as the Visiting Nurse Association provide skilled care at home. Under such programs, licensed nurses visit clients on a regular or short-term basis to check blood pressure, administer prescribed medicines, give injections or change dressings. Care may also include physical, occupational or speech therapy and education in nutrition and health.

Older citizens in need of less attention may be visited by home health aides, paraprofessionals who combine some training in nursing with the ability to help bathe and dress patients and do light household work.

If you, or a relative or friend need health, homemaker or other home services, check with your local health department, social service agency or senior citizens' group. Further information can be obtained from the Homecaring Council, 67 Irving Place, New York, NY 10003.

Adult Day-Care Centers

Another option in many communities is Adult Day Care, of which there are more than 600 programs in operation around the United States. Under this concept, people who are able to live at home but need some attention during

A Community Checklist

Many communities offer a wide range of benefits and services for older Americans, including those listed below. If your community lacks one or more of them for which you feel there is a real need, talk to other interested citizens and to local authorities about establishing new programs to fill in the gaps.

- [ ] A citywide or areawide information and referral center on matters of interest to senior citizens.
- [ ] An area agency on aging, local council or advocate agency.
- [ ] Transportation and escort services for the elderly.
- [ ] A senior center or centers, offering social activities, recreation, education and a setting for community services.
- [ ] Health care services, including:
    - [ ] health clinic.
    - [ ] health maintenance organization.
    - [ ] health screening program.
- [ ] In-home services, including:
    - [ ] visiting nurse service.
    - [ ] home-health service.
    - [ ] homemaker service.
    - [ ] handyman service.
    - [ ] telephone reassurance.
    - [ ] friendly visiting.
    - [ ] meals-on-wheels.
- [ ] Nursing home or homes with high standards and a wide range of fees.
- [ ] Group meals program, providing a social setting for improved nutrition for older persons.
- [ ] Recreation activities for seniors.
- [ ] Library, museum, art gallery and performing arts programs for older people.
- [ ] Adult education opportunities.
- [ ] Job opportunities.
- [ ] Volunteer opportunites.
- [ ] Senior talent pool.
- [ ] Senior citizens employment service or job registry.
- [ ] Legal aid and general counseling.
- [ ] Low-rent public housing for the elderly.
- [ ] A range of moderate-income housing—for sale and rent.
- [ ] Repair and renovation program for existing "elderly housing."
- [ ] Property tax relief for older Americans.

How Seniors Used Their Clout

The Jamaica Service Program for Older Adults (JSPOA), which operates in the New York City borough of Queens, publishes a monthly calendar of activities for its members. The list usually includes such popular items as free movies, recycling workshops, yoga sessions, conferences on inflation and opportunities for older adults to provide a useful service and earn some money by becoming Foster Grandparents. In addition, JSPOA's daily operations offer medical and dental clinic services, help with Social Security and Medicare problems and aid in finding housing and employment. They also provide courses in the arts and the legislative process and offer sports programs such as swimming and golf.

This extensive and useful service did not just happen; it was the product of persistence, cooperation and political clout. When plans for a senior citizens' housing project were announced for Jamaica, various community groups got together to insure that the blueprints included a social center for the elderly. But when the project was about to be opened, word came from city hall that funds for the center had been cut. The citizens of Jamaica were distressed but not daunted. The area's older citizens organized an advisory group composed of representatives of senior clubs to work closely with a committee representing local civic organizations and churches to save the center. First they appealed directly to the city's Commissioner of Human Resources, who had been responsible for the cut. They also asked the Queens borough president and their local congressman to speak to the commissioner on their behalf, and the borough president arranged a meeting. When the delegates met with the commissioner, they were armed not only with welldocumented arguments but with the strength that comes from broad community support—in all they represented no fewer than 23 senior citizens' organizations and 48 other community groups. In the face of that much political power, the officials somehow found the money to reinstate the center.

The organization, formed first to win and then to save the center, broadened its objectives and became JSPOA, which its director, Theodora Jackson, describes as "a total community working together to assure its senior citizens a better way of life." The Senior Citizens Advisory Council that helps direct JSPOA now represents 31 senior groups, which boast a combined membership of 12,000 of Jamaica's 35,000 older adults.

the day can visit an adult day-care center for health monitoring, a nutritious noon meal and opportunities for socializing with others. The program works well in many individual cases. A 76-year-old widow in rural southern Illinois, for example, is a diabetic and amputee confined to a wheelchair. Her daughter, who lives with her, is able to prepare breakfast and help dress her mother every morning, but then must go off to her job. Since it would be dangerous to leave the mother unattended, and a nursing home is not a desirable or feasible alternative, the local adult day-care center fills the bill.

Each weekday the local department of aging provides transportation to the day-care center, where the mother can get a checkup, have lunch and meet her friends; at the end of the day she is taken back home to her daughter's personal companionship and care.

In some states, reimbursement for adult day-care services can be provided under Medicaid. For more information, call or write a letter to your local social services or health department or the Health Care Financing Administration, 1849 Gwynn Oak Ave., Baltimore, MD 21207.

Communal Living Facilities

Other alternatives for isolated older people are various kinds of group-living arrangements. These range from apartment or condominium complexes designed specifically for seniors to "retirement hotels" and smaller rooming houses that cater to an elderly clientele. In addition to a room or apartment for each resident, many offer meals, housekeeping and laundry services as well as common rooms where people can get together to eat, talk or play cards.

An interesting variation on the theme is a series of small group homes for the elderly developed by Home Care Research, Inc., a private non-profit organization in Frederick, Maryland. The first, Heather Ridge House, was opened in 1978 for three women in their 70s and 80s who because of their physical or mental handicaps would otherwise have had to be placed in a nursing home. Homemaker–health aides come in four or five hours a day to provide personal care, shopping, meal planning and preparation, laundry, transportation and yard chores; a consulting nurse is available for specialized care and to serve as a liaison with doctors. There is no overnight supervision but emergency help can be summoned by telephone. Residents of such homes are charged what it costs for maintenance and services but funding help is possible through local agencies, foundations and Medicaid.

Helping Others—and Yourself

Close to 5 million people age 65 and over, a national poll found, take part in some kind of volunteer work, as a way of helping others and at the same time enriching their own lives. Some participate in programs to provide housebound older persons with daily telephone reassurance, friendly visits, transportation or escort services. Others with special experience and skills work as aides in local schools or libraries, counsel struggling small businessmen, help direct job seekers toward second careers or advise senior-center audiences on health problems and the proper use of medicinal drugs.

Among the more vital, and lesser known, programs are those aimed at the trauma of widowhood. To aid individuals in working their way through grief and mourning, and to help them master the tasks of living alone and building a new life, the Gerontology Department of Virginia Commonwealth University and the Virginia Center on Aging, with the assistance of a federal grant, developed an unusual widow counseling service in the Richmond area. The service relies on lay counselors who are widows themselves, on the premise that those who have experienced widowhood are most likely to understand the problems and to empathize with a newly widowed individual's feelings and concerns. Knowing that the counselor is of the same generation, and has shared a common loss, helps to establish trust and a sense of acceptance. "They see that we have weathered the storm," says Margaret Atkinson, one of the counselors, "And they begin to realize that they can, too."

Before taking on their first assignments, counselors receive 24 hours of training conducted by professionals in counseling and clinical psychology, during which they are encouraged to share their own personal encounters with widowhood. Many trainees initially think of themselves as advice givers, but are gradually persuaded that it is more important to be good listeners, to encourage clients to talk about themselves, to help them make their own decisions, to provide understanding and support. "We try not to give advice," says one counselor. "A widow usu-

Nursing Homes

The different kinds of housing and services for the elderly described above are generally the most desirable and economical answers to the daily problems of growing old. In some cases, however, higher levels of care are called for. An older person may need a place to recuperate for a while after hospitalization, or may develop a chronic condition that requires round-the-clock supervision and medical care for an indefinite term. A nursing home may be the best solution.

In recent years there has been much publicity about nursing homes, and much of it has

ally gets more advice than she ever needs."

The approach has proved to be highly effective. The experience of Mrs. W., a 68-year-old retired businesswoman whose husband died in an auto accident, is a case in point. Mrs. W. did not enter the program until after she had been widowed for three years, but she still complained of depression, loneliness, insomnia and, perhaps most importantly, an inability to express her emotion, even to relatives and friends. A person who placed a high value on self-sufficiency, she had been prevented by her own sense of privacy from "ventilating" her grief.

In sessions with a peer counselor, she was assured that it was not unusual for a widow to be in a state of bereavement as long as she had been, and she was encouraged to express the things that she had previously repressed. After the last session, Mrs. W. pronounced the counseling "extremely helpful," noting that for the first time in three years she was able to talk freely about her life. Moreover, as an indication of her new attitude, she decided to become involved in volunteer work.

been bad—scandals involving cases of poor or unsafe living conditions, patient neglect or abuse. Some of the charges have proved accurate, and they have helped set in motion the tightening of regulations and movements for reform. To judge all nursing homes by the excesses of a few, however, is obviously neither fair nor helpful in finding the proper facilities for those in need of special care. Nursing homes serve an important function in society, providing special attention and living accommodations for those with nowhere else to go.

Confusion sometimes arises over the terms "nursing home," "convalescent home," "rest home," "home for the aged" and "retirement home." Whatever term individual institutions may use, the important thing is to determine the level of care they actually provide. The next step is to decide what kind of care is needed in your case—a matter in which you should first seek your doctor's advice.

All nursing homes must be licensed by the states in which they operate. In order to be reimbursed under Medicare and Medicaid (see Chapter 4), they must provide certain levels of care. Some homes may be licensed to provide more than one level of care, and are reimbursed for specific patients according to the attention those patients receive (some health insurance policies and pension plans also cover nursing-home care). Basically, there are three kinds of nursing homes.

Skilled Nursing Facilities

Skilled nursing facilities (SNFs) are for persons needing fairly intensive care on a daily basis, or the care closest to that found in a hospital, including various kinds of rehabilitative therapy. An SNF must have a medical director and offer 24-hour nursing service by registered nurses, licensed practical nurses and nurses aides as prescribed by the patient's physician. A minimum of one registered nurse (more in some states in larger facilities) must be on duty during the day shift, seven days a week; the RN works with the patient's doctor, who is required to visit once a month for the first 90

The Nursing Home Patient's Bill of Rights

In a nursing facility certified by Medicare or Medicaid, any patient has the right:

1. To be informed of his or her rights and of the rules and regulations of the nursing home.
2. To be informed of available services and of any additional charges not covered by the daily rate.
3. To be informed about his or her medical condition by a doctor, to participate in the planning of his or her medical treatment and to refuse to participate in experimental research.
4. To be transferred or discharged only for medical reasons, or for the protection of his or her welfare or that of other patients, or for non-payment. The patient must receive reasonable advance notice of any such action.
5. To voice grievances and recommend changes.
6. To manage his or her personal financial affairs, or to be given at least a quarterly accounting if the nursing home accepts the patient's written delegation of this responsibility.
7. To be free from mental and physical abuse, and free from chemical and (except for emergencies) physical restraints unless authorized by a doctor to protect

days of the patient's stay and every two months thereafter. Skilled nursing facilities may be recognized under both the Medicare and Medicaid programs. Medicare helps pay for up to 100 days in an SNF, but only if the patient has spent at least three days in a hospital beforehand and such continued daily care is recommended by a doctor and approved by Medicare. Medicaid programs in all states pay for care in an SNF if a physician decides such care is needed and the decision is duly approved under the program. Medicaid can usually pick up the charges after 100 days for those who are eligible.

Intermediate Care Facilities

For people who require less attention, Intermediate Care Facilities (ICFs) offer basic nursing care, some supervision and help with eating, dressing, walking and other personal needs. Typical patients in an ICF are those suffering from long-term chronic conditions that are not in a crisis stage. Registered nurses are not required on staff, but a part-time RN consultant is; and a licensed practical nurse must be on duty. Visits by a physician can be spaced as much as 60 days apart from the start of a

patient's stay. Medicaid pays for intermediate care if the home is licensed and the patient is eligible for this kind of attention; Medicare does not.

Residential Care Facilities

Residential care, sometimes called personal, custodial or domiciliary care, is designed for people whose physical and mental condition is reasonably good but who may need help with eating, dressing, walking or other daily tasks. Residential care facilities provide basic medical monitoring but stress the social and recreational needs of their residents. Since trained nursing care is not provided, the cost is usually less than that for a skilled or intermediate nursing home. Residential care facilities must be licensed by their states and must meet certain standards, but they do not qualify for either Medicare or Medicaid.

Choosing a Nursing Home

If you believe you or your relative requires nursing home care, first make a list of the homes in your area that seem to fit your needs. Your doctor may be able to suggest some that offer the appropriate level of care. (At the same the patient and others from injury.

8. To have his or her personal and medical records treated confidentially.
9. To be treated with consideration and respect, including privacy in treatment and care for his or her personal needs.
10. To be free from having to perform services for the facility that are not included for therapeutic purpose in his or her plan of care.
11. To associate and communicate privately with persons of his or her choice and send and receive mail unopened.
12. To participate in activites of social, religious and community groups.
13. To retain and use personal clothing and possessions as space permits.
14. If married, to have private visits with his or her spouse, and if in the same facility, to share a room.

If a patient is judged incompetent, or medically incapable of understanding these rights, or exhibits a communication barrier, rights 1–4 devolve upon the patient's guardian, next of kin or sponsoring agency. Rights 11, 12 and 13 may be denied for good cause only by the attending physician and must be documented in the patient's medical record.

From the Administration on Aging.

time determine whether your doctor can continue to care for you after admission; a person in a skilled or intermediate nursing home must be under the care of a licensed physician, and if your doctor cannot continue treating you, you will have to find another physician who can.) You can also get a list of currently licensed homes from your local health department. Further suggestions may be obtained from clergymen, hospital social workers, the local agency on aging and other social service groups, or from your state health care or nursing-home association.

Narrow down the list by making a few phone calls to find out if a given home actually provides the kind of care you are looking for and at what cost; also ask whether the home qualifies for Medicare or Medicaid and whether there is a waiting list for rooms.

When you have two or three homes that sound promising, make an appointment to visit the administrator of each and be shown around. One of the best times to visit is in mid-to-late morning, after breakfast and the morning cleanup and in time to observe, even participate, as the noon meal is served. If it is a relative or friend who will be the resident, ask if he or she would like to go along; you may want to wait until you have narrowed the choice still further to avoid depressing or confusing the potential resident, but remember who will have to live there and be sure it's that person's decision too. Plan to spend at least an hour in the home so you can do a thorough job. If you cannot get there on your own, some nursing homes will provide transportation on request.

What to Look For

You can tell something about a nursing home from the way it looks outside. Is the building in good repair, and are the grounds well kept? Where possible, do residents make use of the outdoors in good weather? Is the home convenient to public transportation? Would you feel comfortable going there at night?

Inside, is the lobby inviting? If it can be used as a lounge by residents, is it comfortable and is it enjoying active use? Here, and throughout your tour, *always observe the residents;* how they look, and act, is one of the best clues to the overall quality of the place. Are some of them up, dressed and well-groomed, talking, doing things? Or do they seem poorly

Selecting a Nursing Home

If possible the patient should participate in the choice of a home. Location is important if family or friends might want to visit.

Several resources can help compile a list of appropriate facilities in the chosen area: the patient's physician, the local medical society, social services department, community welfare or aging council or Social Security office, and the state chapters of the American Health Care Association (for proprietary homes) and the American Association of Homes for the Aging (for nonprofit homes). Ask for the names of licensed facilities that are eligible for the type of reimbursement you expect to rely on.

The next step is to visit the homes, both on an official tour and, if possible, as an ordinary visitor. The following checklist will help you evaluate what you find; take it with you. Do not hesitate to ask questions about anything that is not immediately apparent.

INSTITUTIONAL FACTORS

☐ Is the home licensed by the state or local agency? Ask to see the certificate. Is it accredited by the Joint Commission on Accreditation of Hospitals?

☐ Is a medical examination required before or immediately after admission? This is the practice in good nursing homes.

☐ Is there an arrangement with a nearby hospital for the transfer and care of patients needing hospitalization?

☐ Is the facility clean and relatively free of bad odors?

☐ What are the visiting hours and who can come?

☐ Does each bedroom have a window and open onto a corridor?

☐ Is there room for maneuvering a wheelchair?

☐ How many beds to a room? Four should be the maximum.

COSTS

☐ Is the home eligible for Medicare and/or Medicaid reimbursement?

☐ What is covered under the basic rate? What is extra? To guard against surprise charges, get a signed statement about coverage from the home you choose. Remember that while better homes tend to charge more, higher costs do not guarantee better care.

☐ Are there refunds on advance payments should the patient leave the home?

☐ Does the patient's insurance policy cover any or all charges?

SAFETY

☐ Is the building fireproof or fire-resistant, with a sprinkler system and clearly posted emergency exit routes?

☐ Are there grab bars in the halls, bathrooms and elevators and call bells at bedside and in the bathrooms? Do they work?

continued

☐ Are the floor coverings nonskid and the hallways well lighted?

☐ Are there ramps for wheelchairs and are the halls wide enough to permit chairs to pass?

STAFF

☐ Are a doctor and a registered nurse on call 24 hours a day?

☐ Is there provision for regular dental care? What about an ophthalmologist, podiatrist or other specialists the patient may need? How often are they available?

☐ Is the staff friendly and efficient in responding to patient calls? If possible, talk with a few current residents.

☐ Is the nursing staff trained in basic rehabilitation techniques? Is there a full-time physical-therapy program directed by a qualified physical or occupational therapist?

☐ Does the staff encourage patients to be independent?

☐ Are patients overtranquilized or restrained to minimize harassment of the staff? Often, the the best candidates for rehabilitation are the most heavily sedated, since they are more active and demanding than others.

FOOD

☐ Are the meals varied, well-balanced, well-cooked and appetizingly served? Are special likes and dislikes taken into account?

☐ Does a dietician prepare meals for those on special diets?

☐ Are patients encouraged to eat in a group, or do they dine alone in their rooms?

☐ Are the menus prepared a week or more in advance, and does the food served match what is on the menu?

☐ Do those who need help in eating get it? Promptly, before the food gets cold?

☐ Is the dining room attractive and accessible to patients in wheelchairs?

ACTIVITIES

☐ Is there a recreation program?

☐ Are there rooms for socializing, physical therapy and occupational therapy?

☐ Are the grounds well kept and are patients who are able to to do so encouraged to go outside daily?

☐ Do volunteers from the community work with and visit patients regularly?

☐ Are patients kept busy and occupied? Are there activities like card games, knitting and sewing, conversation?

☐ Are outings scheduled?

PERSONAL FACTORS

☐ Are patients treated with dignity and respect or are they talked down to as if they were small children?

☐ Do patients have privacy — for dressing and undressing, phone calls, visits?

☐ Are personal possessions such as a favorite rocking chair allowed and is there room for keeping personal belongings?

☐ Are there arrangements for religious observances?

☐ Are a barber and beautician available?

☐ Are patients allowed to wear their own clothing? Are they kept clean and well-groomed?

cared for, listless, staring out the window or at the walls?

Talk to the administrator or director of admissions, and the medical director or head nurse, too, if you can. Most homes display their licenses and certificates prominently; both the home *and* its administrator should have state licenses for the current year. Ask also to see the home's most recent fire safety report. A good indication that the home does its job well is a recent certificate from the Joint Commission on Accreditation or the peer review committee of the state's affiliate of the American Health Care Association, two voluntary programs whose seals of approval generally mean quality care. Don't forget to check the home's certification for Medicaid and Medicare, and any other compensation plans the potential resident may qualify for.

While you are in the office, find out precisely what the basic daily charge includes, and how much will be charged for therapy, laundry, medical supplies, special nursing, lab tests, a wheelchair, a private telephone or television in the room. Is the patient required to have prescriptions filled in the nursing home's pharmacy or can medicines be bought at another pharmacy that may charge less? Does the contract clearly state the date of admission, level of care, services to be rendered, any required advance payments, conditions of transfer or discharge if the patient no longer requires a specified level of care? Is there a refund of advance payments if the patient leaves or a penalty if the patient leaves before the end of the month? Will the nursing home take care of the patient's personal funds and give an accounting, including receipts or withdrawals? Is the "Patient's Bill of Rights" (see box on pages 316 and 317) prominently posted—and observed in all its details? During admission, nursing homes must explain these rights and obtain a signed statement that the patient is informed about them.

While you are visiting the nursing home, make sure you are given a complete tour, including patients' rooms, lounges, dining room, kitchen, bathrooms and therapy rooms. Is the atmosphere generally clean, comfortable, as homelike as possible? Does the staff seem attentive to, and friendly with, the residents? Are the menus inviting, varied? Are provisions for special diets available? Are the hallways wide, well-lighted and free of obstructions? Are fire escapes well marked and accessible to people with wheelchairs or orthopedic devices? Are there grab bars in the bathrooms and handrails in the halls that elderly people can use to support themselves? What does the place smell like? (There may be a little odor, particularly before morning cleanup, but it should not be pervasive, such as that of a strong disinfectant covering the smell of urine.) Do residents have adequate furniture and storage, and are they allowed to decorate their rooms with personal touches? Is there a barber or beautician available for appointments? Is there a well-stocked library, craft and game supplies, an active social program with a director who arranges card games, movies, music, celebrations on special days? Are religious services available? Is there a residents' council to organize activities, to make suggestions and to work with the management to iron out complaints? What are the visiting hours? Are special trips and outings arranged for residents?

A further checklist of things to look for is given on pages 318 and 319. Many communities have produced their own guides to area nursing homes. Pamphlets from other sources may be helpful. "Selecting a Nursing Home" can be obtained without charge from the American Association of Retired Persons, 1909 K St., NW, Washington, DC 20049. "Thinking About a Nursing Home?" and "Welcome to Our Nursing Home" are available at many member homes of the American Health Care Association or through the Association's headquarters at 1200 15th St., NW, Washington, DC 20005. "How to Select a Nursing Home," prepared by the U.S. Department of Health and Human Services, can be purchased through the U.S. Government Printing Office, Washington, DC 20402.

Continuing Care Contracts

Some nursing homes include purely residential facilities for elderly people who are well enough not to need nursing care, but who want to be reassured that if they do need such care in the future they can get it without having to move to entirely new surroundings. Some homes for the aging offer "continuing care" or "life-care" contracts, involving a sizeable one-time admission fee in return for a guarantee to provide living quarters, meals and varying levels of attention for the rest of a person's life. Some charge an additional monthly maintenance fee, with higher charges if the level of nursing care rises, while others require that the resident turn over most or all of his or her assets to the home. For more information about such plans, inquire locally or write the American Association of Homes for the Aging, 1050 17th St., NW, Washington, DC 20036.

Living in a Nursing Home

No matter how well you choose a nursing home, the new surroundings will require a big adjustment. Families and friends can help by visiting frequently and regularly, by taking the resident for occasional outings if possible and by observing birthdays, anniversaries and other special dates. The resident can help, too, by keeping up his or her own interests, becoming involved in the activities the home has to offer, making new friends and getting outside when the weather is nice.

If problems with the staff or service should arise, they should first be discussed with the people involved; the next line of inquiry is the administrator of the home. If there is a residents' council, it may be able to help; common complaints may be reviewed and brought to the management's attention if needed, and suggestions for improvements and innovations may be advanced to improve the overall quality of life in the home.

Reporting Serious Complaints

If a complaint is serious enough, and remains unresolved after discussion with the nursing-

home administrator, it should be reported to the state department of health. Many states require that incidents, or even suspicion, of neglect, mistreatment or physical abuse of patients be reported by the personnel of nursing homes themselves; a person found guilty of such an act—or one who fails to report the act—may be punished by a heavy fine. All states have systems of patient-care investigators or nursing-home ombudsmen who look into complaints, whether they are brought by patients, relatives, friends, doctors or nursing home personnel.

Volunteer organizations to watch over nursing-home standards also exist in many communities, and periodic inspections are made by them to check on conditions in local homes. If no such group exists in your community, and you are interested in starting one, write the National Citizens' Coalition for Nursing Home Reform, 1424 16th St., NW, Washington, DC 20036.

Terminal Illnesses

Until recent years, the American medical system had no organized way to deal with the special problems of the terminally ill and their families, with the result that many patients had to live out their final days in the costly isolation of hospitals or nursing homes. An increasing number of communities, however— some 200 or more across the United States at last count—have been developing answers under the "hospice" movement. This concept of specialized, total care helps persons, most of them dying of cancer, to live as painlessly as possible, with the support of their relatives and in their own homes.

In medieval times, hospices were way stations and sanctuaries for weary travelers, usually run by religious orders whose members also ministered to the medical and spiritual needs of the destitute. The modern hospice idea, which began in England in the 1960s, was pioneered in the United States by The Connecticut Hospice, Inc., organized in New Haven in 1971 and now located in Branford,

Connecticut. With the consent and cooperation of the physician and family, anyone diagnosed as having a terminal illness with a limited prognosis (generally six months or less) can receive the care and support of a well-rounded inter-disciplinary team, which may include not only physicians and nurses but a pharmacist, a social worker, a chaplain, a psychiatrist, a physical therapist, a financial adviser and an arts director as well as trained volunteers.

Under a plan tailored to the individual situation, team members visit the patient and his or her family regularly during the week and are on call 24 hours a day for emergency consultation. Drugs are carefully administered to control pain while leaving the patient both comfortable and alert. Volunteers sit with the patient while family members take a much-needed nap or go out on errands; they also help with household chores, take patients shopping, to the hairdresser or on other outings.

For the roughly one out of four individuals who is unable to stay at home or needs more intensive medical supervision, there are attractive modern facilities like the 44-bed hospice in Branford, Connecticut. Patients there live together in large, four-bed rooms that create a sense of community and where they can have visitors at virtually any hour. Wheelchairs and beds can be rolled into the glass-walled corridors, which resemble sunny, well-planted greenhouses, out onto patios in good weather, or into a small chapel where patients, visitors and staff members are welcome to meditate or pray. The unique building, made possible by funds from the state and the federal government as well as foundations, corporations and individuals, has been in use since the summer of 1980.

In Connecticut and other states, patients are admitted to hospice programs on the basis of need rather than ability to pay. Reimbursement for services is available from Medicare, Medicaid, Blue Cross and private insurance companies (the General Electric Company, headquartered in Connecticut, led the way in granting full coverage for its employees, and

other companies have followed suit). Many hospice demonstration projects around the nation have received assistance from the Health Care Financing Administration of the U.S. Department of Health and Human Services. The emphasis wherever possible is on home rather than hospital care, considerably reducing the financial burden that traditionally adds to the anxiety of the terminally ill.

Further information can be obtained from the Hospice Institute for Education, Training and Research, Inc., 61 Burban Dr., Branford, CT 06405 and the National Hospice Organization, 1311-A Dolley Madison Blvd., McLean, VA 22101.

Preventing Crime Against the Elderly

Older people are particularly vulnerable to the effects of crime and fraud, ranging from purse snatchings and home burglaries to deceptive mail-order schemes. Because so many live on fixed incomes, the loss of a televison set or a Social Security check can be a heavy blow; a roughing up at the hands of a street robber can be psychologically devastating even if it does not result in serious physical harm. In a national survey commissioned by the National Council on the Aging, the problem of greatest concern cited by those 65 and older was fear of crime; it was named by 23 percent of those surveyed, with poor health ranking second at 21 percent.

Mindful of such facts, law enforcement agencies and other groups have stepped up efforts to educate the elderly in their own self-protection, to help with cooperative neighborhood crime-reduction programs and to assist older victims of crime in various ways.

Reducing Crimes Against Property

Most of the 40 million or more crimes committed each year are not violent ones like assault, rape and murder, but ordinary property crimes like burglary, purse snatching and pocket pick-

Crime Prevention for the Elderly

Crime, and fear of crime, create special problems for older people. Here are some common-sense tips to help you avoid becoming a victim, prepared by the New York State Office of Crime Prevention.

Walking
* Always plan your route and stay alert to your surroundings. Walk confidently.
* Have a companion accompany you.
* Stay away from buildings and doorways; walk in well-lighted areas.
* Have your key ready when approaching your front door.
* Don't dangle your purse away from your body where it can tempt a purse snatcher.
* Don't carry large, bulky shoulder bags; carry only what you need. Better yet, sew a small pocket inside your jacket or coat. If you don't have a purse, no one will try to snatch it.

In Stores
* Don't display large sums of cash.
* Never leave your purse unattended.
* Use checks whenever possible.

In Your Car
* Travel well-lit and busy streets if you can.
* Keep your car doors locked, whether you are in or out of your car.
* At stop signs and traffic lights, keep the car in gear.
* Don't leave your purse on the seat beside you; put it on the floor, where it is more difficult for someone to grab.
* Lock bundles or bags in the trunk. If packages are out of sight, a thief will be less tempted to break in and steal them.
* When returning to your car, check the front seat, back seat and the floor before entering.
* Never pick up hitchhikers.
* If your car should break down, get safely off the road, turn on your emergency flashers, raise the hood, get back in the car, lock the door and wait for help.

Banking
* Many criminals know exactly when government checks arrive each month, and may pick that day to attack. Avoid this by using Direct Deposit, which sends your money directly from the government to the bank of your choice.
* Store valuables in a safe deposit box.
* Never give your money to someone who calls on you, identifying himself as a bank official. A bank will never ask you to remove your money.
* When someone approaches you with a get-rich-quick scheme involving some or all of YOUR savings, be extremely cautious. If it is a legitimate investment, you shouldn't have to rush into it. The opportunity will still be there tomorrow—after you have had time to consider it.

At Home
* Never open your door without first finding out who the visitor is.
* At night, draw your blinds or draperies.
* Lock your doors and windows. (Three quarters of burglaries of older persons' homes involve unlocked doors or windows.) Keep your garage doors locked too.
* Use "Neighbor Watch" to keep an eye on your neighborhood. A concerned neighbor can report suspicious persons and activities promptly to police.

ing. Such crimes can often be prevented by relatively simple steps. In more than half of all household burglaries, for example, the burglar entered without force, usually through a door or window that someone had forgotten to lock.

Statistics from the U.S. Department of Justice's Law Enforcement Assistance Administration show that far more burglaries occur during the day when the victim is out—even if only for an hour to go shopping—than at night when he or she is at home and asleep. In many cases the burglar is a young adult, often unemployed, who either lives in or is familiar with the neighborhood. The most likely victim of robbery is a woman, perhaps because a woman is regarded as easier to subdue than a man.

Your chances of being robbed are greater if you live in an older, more densely populated area, but crime is on the rise in suburban and rural areas too. If you live in a high-crime area, you may be able to obtain some low-cost burglary and robbery insurance from the Federal Insurance Administration (See Chapter 3).

No matter where you live, you can reduce the chance of being victimized by taking some commonsense precautions. (For some practical advice, see "How to Foil Burglars and Robbers," Chapter 3, page 108 and the box, "Crime Prevention for the Elderly," on page 323.)

A Neighborhood Security Watch

In many communities crime prevention programs have been started by citizens, both old and young, working with local police departments, often with the help of federal or local grants. One of the simplest and most effective is a "neighborhood watch" or "block watch" system in which residents of an area agree to keep an eye on one another's property and the neighborhood in general. Individual work and vacation schedules are taken into account and watch hours are assigned; if someone on watch notices a suspicious person, a door standing open or an unfamiliar car circling the block several times, he or she calls in the police to investigate.

In a suburban variation on the theme, elderly homeowners in Manatee County, Florida, banded together to reduce vandalism and break-ins. With the help of the county sheriff's office and the local crime prevention bureau, more than 6,000 senior volunteers take turns patrolling 30 neighborhoods, driving around on an hourly basis in private cars equipped with walkie-talkies or CB radios, spotlights and plastic door signs that proclaim their status as "special sheriff's deputies." The volunteers are not permitted to carry arms or make arrests, but they are trained to observe suspicious activities and relay descriptions and license numbers to volunteer captains, who immediately ask the sheriff's office to dispatch a uniformed deputy to the scene. Community patrols have proved their worth and then some, reducing burglaries in the area by 95 percent in a single year.

Other Crime Deterrents

State and local agencies around the nation carry on information programs to encourage older persons in crime-deterring practices not only at home but when they are out shopping, driving or walking on the streets. Many communities have organized transportation and escort services to help elderly citizens who are reluctant to go out alone, whether it be to church, to the supermarket or for a breath of fresh air. Most of these services are staffed by volunteers, but a pilot project in a high-crime area of Coney Island, New York, enlisted police vans and police officers to take elderly residents to and from neighborhood shopping centers twice a week. Telephone reassurance programs (see the earlier section on Everyday Help at Home) have also proved effective in reducing crime, and the fear of crime, by keeping isolated older people in touch with the outside world.

Help for Crime Victims

For elderly citizens who do become crime victims, some communities are equipped to provide emergency financial assistance and support. The Senior Security Services of New York City's Department for the Aging, for example, works with local police precincts and neighborhood senior centers to offer older crime victims a range of services. These include transportation to a doctor or hospital; food, clothing and temporary shelter; installation of window gates and other security measures; help in linking up with the network of senior services available in the community.

In northern Indiana, the Older Adult Crime Victim Program, supported in part by federal funds, contacts a victim's relatives, provides counseling, transportation and emergency funds as well as temporary housing, insurance forms and the replacement of Social Security cards. In Wisconsin's Milwaukee County, a "Court Watch" program helps older people who are either victims of, or witnesses to, crimes but who are reluctant to appear in court because of fear of reprisal or bewilderment about the judicial system. Using volunteers who are themselves 60 or older, the program monitors cases, offers victims and witnesses information and support, arranges transportation for them to and from the courthouse and sees that someone accompanies them through the whole court procedure.

Guarding Against Fraud

The concerns of many older citizens—worries about finances, health, and keeping up their homes—make them particularly attractive targets for promoters of shady products and schemes. It has been estimated that the elderly spend billions of dollars each year on worthless disease "cures," dubious health products, superfluous health or life insurance, questionable mail-order items, fly-by-night investment and land sales, exorbitant pre-burial contracts and funeral services, illicit home repair and work-at-home schemes.

In many cases it is the convenience of the offer as well as the price that makes it attractive, especially to older persons who cannot get about easily to go shopping or to the doctor and who are tempted by products or services they can get more simply from a door-to-door salesman or by mail. Quack medicines and phony money-making schemes are among those singled out by the President's Crime Commission as being "particularly pernicious," for they often victimize elderly people who can least afford losses of any kind.

Door-to-Door Deceptions

While many products and services sold door-to-door are legitimate, others are not, despite the fact that various laws carry penalties for deception and fraud. If someone comes to your door with something to sell, ask for written identification and for a vendor's license identifying a company that is legally entitled to do business in your area. Ask if the company is registered with the local Better Business Bureau (a source you can also call to check on a company's reputation and its record of customer complaints). Beware of "free gifts," added inducements or claims that sound too good to be true, and compare the price with similar products or services offered elsewhere before you buy.

Read every word of a contract before signing anything. Be sure you understand your full obligation: the total price, finance charges and penalties if you are late or miss a payment. Find out whether there is a guarantee or warranty. If so, does it cover parts and labor, and for how long? Where do you go if the item later needs repair? All this information should be included in the contract, which should be signed by the salesman as well as yourself, with a copy given to you.

If possible, pay for any purchase with a check or money order, which will provide a receipt as proof of payment; if you must pay in cash, get a signed receipt. If what you are buying is to be delivered to you, you have a right to inspect it; if it is not what you agreed to buy, you do not have to accept delivery, whether you have paid for it or not. Under most state laws, if you agree to purchase something on an installment plan, you still have a right to change your mind; you can cancel the purchase up to midnight of the third business day after you signed the agreement by giving written notice to the seller, either in person or by mail.

Be wary, too, of people who try to rush you into purchasing a product or service without allowing time for you to shop around: the tree "expert" who drops by and offers to fix a "dangerous" tree that might fall at any moment and damage your roof; or a contractor who just happens to have some extra paint, siding or insulation left over in the back of his truck and volunteers to do a badly needed job at bargain rates. You can always look into the problem yourself, without rushing into things, and if necessary get a reputable professional to do the job.

Mail-Order Goods and Services

Examine closely any offers that come through the mail. They may include worthless correspondence courses, charity rackets, chain letters and pyramid sales promotions, debt-consolidation plans, magical potions or devices guaranteed to increase your vitality, sexual prowess, beauty or IQ. Be wary of work-at-home schemes that require payment of a registration fee before you can learn any of the details. If you suspect that any of these offers are not on the level, or if you have been victimized by one, contact your local postmaster, who will forward your complaint to the postal inspection service for investigation, or get in touch directly with the Chief Postal Inspector, U.S. Postal Service, Washington, DC. 20260.

The most common problem with mail-order sales, even legitimate ones, is the failure of the seller to get the product to the buyer on time. The Federal Trade Commission has a rule requiring that all mail-order purchases be shipped within the time stated in the company's offer; if no time is stated, shipment must be within 30 days or you can cancel your order and get your money back. It is a violation of federal law for anyone to send unordered mer-

chandise through the mail unless it is a free sample, marked as such, or merchandise given out by a charitable organization in the hope of getting contributions. Consumers may treat *any* unordered merchandise as a gift and do not have to pay for it; it is illegal for the sender to pressure you to return the merchandise or send you a bill.

If you have any complaint against a mail-order company—misleading advertisements, non-delivery, damages in transit—first contact the company itself. If the problem is not resolved, get in touch with your local consumer protection office, Better Business Bureau or postmaster. You can also send copies of your correspondence to the Federal Trade Commission, Washington, DC 20580. Although the FTC normally cannot handle individual disputes, the information you provide may help reveal a pattern of bad practices requiring action by the Commission.

If you are simply tired of receiving a lot of "junk mail"—contest offers, sweepstakes, coupons, free brochures and catalogs—there is not much you can do about it legally, but you can stop much of the flow by contacting the Direct Mail Marketing Association, 6 East 43rd St., New York, NY 10017 and asking to have your name removed from its members' mailing lists. For aid in determining which charitable organizations have legitimate fund-raising practices, contact the National Information Bureau, 419 Park Avenue South, New York, NY 10016 and ask for a copy of its "Wise Giving Guide."

Frauds to Watch For

In addition to dubious offers of merchandise and services, swindlers sometimes victimize older people with out-and-out "confidence games" in which they attempt to persuade the victim to part with money before there is time to realize that he or she has been tricked. The operator takes the calculated risk that the target will be embarrassed by being taken in and will not report the crime in time for the swindler to be caught. Though there are infinite variations, some of the perennially successful con games have features such as these:

The "Bank Examiner". A self-styled "investigator" for a bank or savings and loan institution calls you up or comes to your home and tells you the bank needs your help in checking on a dishonest employee. As a test of what the employee will do, the "investigator" suggests that "in absolute secrecy" you draw out a specified large sum from your own account in cash so "the serial numbers can be checked." You give the money to the "examiner," who hands you a receipt, thanks you for your cooperation and may even tell you how the funds will be used to trap the suspected employee. Once the "examiner" is gone that's the last you'll ever hear of the scheme—or your money. When you ask the bank, of course they've never heard of such a person.

The "Pigeon Drop". A presentable-looking man or woman engages you in pleasant conversation, eventually mentioning a large sum of money that has just been found by a friend—who at that moment just happens to pass by. They discuss with you what they should do with the money, then one of them says he works in the vicinity and is going to ask the advice of his employer, who is holding the money for safekeeping. He returns in a few minutes and says his boss has counted the money, and agrees that since it was probably stolen or belonged to a gambler, the three of you might as well keep the money and divide it three ways—but that each should show evidence of "good faith." You are persuaded to draw your "good faith" money from your bank, and the accomplice takes it to his "employer"; when he comes back, he gives you the name and address of the boss and says he is waiting there to give you your share. You can't find the employer, of course, and when you get back to the spot where it all started the two swindlers have long since gone.

The "Fence". A stranger approaches you with an irresistible "deal" on a television set, stereo or other valuable piece of merchandise, which the stranger says is stolen but is safe because it cannot be traced. The problem is that this person needs cash to pick up the goods from a "fence." Once you hand over the money you won't see it or the stranger again.

The "Funeral Chaser". A smooth operator, who makes it a habit to study the obituary columns, turns up at your home after a relative has died. The fast talker shows you a valuable-looking piece of jewelry, a Bible, or the first in a series of art books to be published and says the deceased had made a down payment on it as a thoughtful gift for you before passing on. The talker displays a convincing knowledge of the deceased, plays on your emotions and suggests that it would only be right for you to carry out the deceased's wishes by paying the rest of the purchase price. You do, the smooth operator leaves and you're stuck.

The "Inspector". A person comes to your door, complete with the official-looking credentials of a "city inspector," and asks to look at your water meter, furnace, wiring or something else. Naturally, the "inspector" finds the apparatus completely unsafe, orders it shut down until repaired and then helpfully supplies the name of a plumber or electrician who can respond to the emergency so you can get back your heat or light. You wind up paying the accomplice an enormous amount—and you may also have been talked into a fat maintenance contract to make sure it doesn't happen again.

What To Do About It

The obvious way to avoid getting stung in any transaction is to be leery of "deals," and to check out the credentials of any person who suggests one before you do anything else. If you have been victimized, contact the Better Business Bureau, the local consumer protection agency or the police. Disputes involving relatively minor sums can often be settled in a small-claims court. More complex matters are best left to a good lawyer; if you feel you cannot afford the fee, contact the legal aid agency, legal services program or bar association in your community. For older persons on limited incomes, legal representation may be available at moderate cost, or without charge.

Senior Organizations You Can Join

In addition to the many benefits available to older persons through local agencies, senior citizens' centers and volunteer groups, a number of national organizations offer special services to those who join.

National Retired Teachers Association–American Association of Retired Persons
The two affiliated organizations, the NRTA–AARP, have a joint roll of more than 12 million members. Membership in AARP is open to anyone 55 or older, whether retired, semi-retired or still actively employed; a spouse automatically becomes a member for no additional fee. The smaller NRTA welcomes any retired or former educator as a regular member. Anyone who is currently active as a teacher, administrator or school staff member or who is interested in the progress of education may enroll as an associate member. There is no age requirement, and the spouse of a qualified member may also join for an additional fee.

In return for modest annual dues, members of either AARP or NRTA receive a year's subscription to a magazine (*Modern Maturity* or *NRTA Journal*) containing articles of interest to retirees, as well as monthly news-bulletins and free copies of "better retirement" booklets on various topics ranging from taxes and finances to health, hobbies, food, housing, recreation and home repair. A non-profit pharmacy service offers prescription medicines, medical supplies and health aids at lower-than-average prices through the mail.

Other services include group health insurance plans; investment in a members' money-market trust; motoring-club benefits and discounts at car rental agencies, hotel and motel chains; continuing education programs in various fields, including health, crime prevention and driver improvement; training for local volunteers to help other older persons in income-tax preparation and Medicare claims; lists of retirement facilities by states; activities at several thousand chapters across the United States.

In Washington, NRTA–AARP works for legislation beneficial to older Americans, represents the membership's interest before state legislatures and maintains a foundation to aid research in gerontology and a National Gerontology Resource Center with a major research facility on all aspects of retirement and old age.

Similar benefits, including their own magazine and advice on retirement planning, are available to members of Action for Independent Maturity (AIM), a division of AARP designed for people between the ages of 50 and 65 who are still active with jobs and careers.

For further information on AARP, NRTA or AIM, write any of the three organizations at national headquarters, 1909 K Street, NW, Washington, DC 20049.

National Council of Senior Citizens
The NCSC represents some 3.5 million older people in 4,000 clubs across the nation. The main priority is comprehensive health care for all Americans, and the Council is one of the largest developers of federally funded housing for the elderly, co-sponsoring projects in many areas. NCSC is also active in community-service employment programs for low-income seniors. It helps secure Social Security benefit increases, fosters crime prevention programs and legal services for the elderly, and promotes nursing home reforms.

For moderate dues, members receive a monthly newspaper, "Senior Citizens News," and may participate in low-cost health insurance, a direct-mail prescription-drug service, motel- and car-rental discounts and a travel service that offers special senior citizens' tours. Local NCSC-affiliated clubs discuss problems affecting senior citizens and take action on political issues. They sponsor community projects like blood banks and hospital-patient visits, organize arts and crafts workshops, plan group trips to museums and theaters and hold dances and other social events.

Further information on membership may be obtained by contacting the National Council of Senior Citizens, 925 15th St., NW, Washington, DC 20005

National Association of Retired Federal Employees

NARFE, with close to half a million members, is open to all federal employees, who are 50 or over and have at least five years of government service, as well as their spouses and survivors. Members receive a monthly magazine, *Retirement Life,* and may participate in special benefits such as group life and health insurance plans. NARFE represents its constituents before Congress and state legislatures, helps survivors collect benefits due them and is organized into 50 state federations and more than 1,500 local chapters around the United States. For more information, write the National Association of Retired Federal Employees, 1533 New Hampshire Ave. NW, Washington, DC 20036.

Other Helpful Organizations

Concerned Seniors for Better Government, 1346 Connecticut Ave., NW, Washington, DC 20036. A political action group dedicated to motivating union members, retirees and others to register and participate in elections and political activites. Publications include "Senior Power," a political action booklet and brochures.

Displaced Homemakers Network, Inc., 755 8th St. NW, Washington, DC 20001. Provides job-placement, counseling and training help through some 300 programs around the country for homemakers of any age who through widowhood, divorce, separation, ineligibility for public assistance or other crises have lost their source of economic support. Publications include the bi-monthly "Network News," useful pamphlets, reports and books.

Golden Ring Council of Senior Citizens Clubs, c/o International Ladies Garment Workers Union, 1710 Broadway, New York, NY 10019. An organization dedicated to the improvement of living conditions, to social activities and legislation for the elderly.

Gray Panthers, 3635 Chestnut St., Philadelphia, PA 19104. Formed to promote group consciousness-raising and activism among both the aging and the young in order to combat age discrimination. Publications are "The Network" newspaper, an organizing manual, and other books.

International Senior Citizens Association, 11753 Wilshire Blvd., Los Angeles, CA 90025. Promotes international cooperation in protecting the interests of the elderly and provides communication in areas of cultural and educational advancement. The organization publishes a quarterly newsletter.

National Alliance of Senior Citizens, 101 Park Washington Court, Falls Church, VA 22046. A lobbying organization that works with federal and state legislatures and informs the public about the needs of seniors and programs to serve them. Publications include: "The Senior Guardian," "The Senior Independent," "Senior Services Manual."

National Association for Hispanic Elderly, 1730 West Olympic Blvd., Los Angeles, CA 90015. Promotes the interests of Hispanic older people and encourages their participation in social service programs for the aging. Publications include the quarterly *Legislative Bulletin* and "Our Heritage" newsletter.

National Association of Mature People, Box 26792, Oklahoma City, OK 73118. Provides a variety of services to persons 55 and over, including educational and recreational programs, group discounts on travel, insurance programs, financial counseling and legislative lobbying. Publishes a quarterly called *Best Years,* a newsletter and various helpful, informative pamphlets.

National Caucus and Center on Black Aged, 1424 K St. NW, Washington, DC 20005. Seeks to improve conditions for the minority elderly in health, housing, employment, education and professional training. Publications include: "Health and the Black Aged," "Guidelines and Minority Aging," "Stress and the Black Aged." They also publish a newsletter.

National Council on the Aging, Inc., 600 Maryland Ave. SW, Washington, DC 20024. A private, non-profit leadership organization of professionals and organizations providing services for the elderly and a general clearinghouse of information, research, technical assistance and literature on aging, with the largest library on social gerontology in the United States. Program units include the National Institute of Senior Centers; Senior Centers Humanities Program; National Institute on Age, Work and Retirement; Senior Community Service Project; National Institute on Adult Daycare; National Center on Rural Aging; National Voluntary Organizations for Independent Living for the Aging and programs in housing, employment, research, public policy, the arts and retirement planning. The Council's publications include the bi-

monthlies "Education for Aging News" and "Perspective on Aging"; the quarterlies *Aging and Work* and *Current Literature on Aging*; the monthly "Senior Center Report"; many books, brochures and pamphlets.

National Indian Council on Aging, Inc., (NICOA), Box 2088, Albuquerque, NM 87103. Presents the needs and concerns of native Indian and Alaskan elderly to the public and to federal agencies. Advocates services for the elderly through information, training and consultative services. Publications include the quarterly *NICOA News* and books.

Urban Elderly Coalition, 600 Maryland Ave., SW, Washington, DC 20024. Gathers and analyzes information on the needs and problems of the urban elderly and the legislation affecting them; provides technical assistance in programming and planning. Publications include the quarterly *Legislative Update* and *Technical Exchange* as well as occasional position papers on subjects that are of special interest.

Further Information. For interested individuals, and for administrators, researchers and others providing services to the elderly, a more complete listing and description of organizations and information sources, both governmental and private, is provided in *A Guide to Selected Information Resources in Aging,* published by the Administration on Aging, U.S. Department of Health and Human Services. Requests for copies should be directed to the National Clearinghouse on Aging, Service Center for Aging Information, 330 Independence Ave., SW, Washington, DC 20201.

Directory of Agencies that Help the Aging

Administration on Aging
Department of Health and Human Services
Office of Human Development Services
Washington, DC 20201

ACTION Offices
National Headquarters
806 Connecticut Ave., NW
Washington, DC 20525

Regional Offices

Region I
(Connecticut, Maine, Massachusetts, New Hampshire
Rhode Island, Vermont)
John W. McCormack Post Office and
   Court House Building
Boston, MA 02109

Region II
(New Jersey, New York, Puerto Rico, Virgin Islands)
26 Federal Plaza
New York, NY 10007

Region III
(Delaware, District of Columbia, Maryland, Pennsylvania,
Virginia, West Virginia)
U.S. Customs House
2d and Chestnut Sts.
Philadelphia, PA 19106

Region IV
(Alabama, Florida, Georgia, Kentucky, Mississippi, North
Carolina, South Carolina, Tennessee)
101 Marietta St., NW
Atlanta, GA 30323

Region V
(Illinois, Indiana, Michigan, Minnesota, Ohio, Wisconsin)
1 North Wacker Dr.
Chicago, IL 60606

Region VI
(Arkansas, Louisiana, New Mexico, Oklahoma, Texas)
Old Main Post Office Building
Bryan and Ervay Sts.
Dallas, TX 75221

Region VII
(Iowa, Kansas, Missouri, Nebraska)
II Gateway Center
4th and State
Kansas City, KS 66101

Region VIII
(Colorado, Montana, North Dakota, South Dakota, Utah,
Wyoming)
Columbine Building
1845 Sherman St.
Denver, CO 80203

Region IX
(Arizona, California, Hawaii, Nevada)
211 Main St.
San Francisco, CA 94105

Region X
(Alaska, Idaho, Oregon, Washington)
1601 Second Ave.
Seattle, WA 98101

State Agencies on Aging

Alabama
   Commission on Aging
   740 Madison Ave.
   Montgomery, AL 36104

Alaska
   Office on Aging
   Department of Health and Social Services
   Pouch H, OIC
   Juneau, AK 99811

American Samoa
   Territorial Administration on Aging
   Government of American Samoa
   Pago Pago
   American Samoa 96799

Arizona
   Aging and Adult Administration
   Department of Economic Security
   1640 Grand Ave.
   Phoenix, AZ 85007

Arkansas
   Office on Aging
   Department of Human Services
   Donaghey Building
   7th and Main Sts.
   Little Rock, AR 72201

California
   Department of Aging
   Health and Welfare Agency
   1020 19th St.
   Sacramento, CA 95814

Colorado
   Division of Services for the Aging
   Department of Social Services
   1575 Sherman St.
   Denver, CO 80203

Connecticut
   Department on Aging

80 Washington St.
Hartford, CT 06115

Delaware
Division of Aging
Department of Health and Social Services
Delaware State Hospital
New Castle, DE 19720

District of Columbia
Office of Aging
Office of the Mayor
1012 14th St., NW
Washington, DC 20005

Florida
Program Office of Aging and Adult Services
Department of Health and Rehabilitation Services
1323 Winewood Blvd.
Tallahassee, FL 32301

Georgia
Office of Aging
Department of Human Resources
618 Ponce de Leon Ave., NE
Atlanta, GA 30308

Guam
Office of Aging
Social Services Administration
Government of Guam
P.O. Box 2816
Agana, GU 96910

Hawaii
Executive Office on Aging
1149 Bethel St.
Honolulu, HI 96813

Idaho
Idaho Office on Aging
Statehouse
Boise, ID 83720

Illinois
Department of Aging
421 East Capitol Ave.
Springfield, IL 62706

Indiana
Commisssion on Aging and Aged
Graphic Arts Building
215 North Senate Ave.
Indianapolis, IN 46202

Iowa
Commission on Aging
415 West 10th St.
Jewett Building
Des Moines, IA 50319

Kansas
Department of Aging
610 West 10th St.
Topeka, KS 66612

Kentucky
Center for Aging
Bureau of Social Services
Human Resources Building

275 East Main St.
Frankfort, KY 40601

Louisiana
Office of Elderly Affairs
P.O. Box 44282, Capitol Station
Baton Rouge, LA 70804

Maine
Bureau of Maine's Elderly
Community Services Unit
Department of Human Services
State House
Augusta, ME 04333

Maryland
Office on Aging
State Office Building
301 West Preston St.
Baltimore, MD 21201

Massachusetts
Department of Elder Affairs
110 Tremont St.
Boston, MA 02108

Michigan
Office of Services to the Aging
300 East Michigan
P.O. Box 30026
Lansing, MI 48909

Minnesota
Minnesota Board on Aging
204 Metro Square Building
7th and Robert Sts.
St. Paul, MN 55101

Mississippi
Council on Aging
P.O. Box 5136
Fondren Station
510 George St.
Jackson, MS 39216

Missouri
Office of Aging
Department of Social Services
Broadway State Office Building
P.O. Box 570
Jefferson City, MO 65101

Montana
Aging Services Bureau
Department of Social and Rehabilitation Services
P.O. Box 1723
Helena, MT 59601

Nebraska
Commission on Aging
State House, Station 95044
Lincoln, NE 68509

Nevada
Division for Aging Services
Department of Human Resources
505 East King St.
Kinkead Building
Carson City, NV 89710

New Hampshire
Council on Aging
P.O. Box 786
14 Depot St.
Concord, NH 03301

New Jersey
Division on Aging
Department of Community Affairs
P.O. Box 2768
363 West State St.
Trenton, NJ 08625

New Mexico
State Agency on Aging
Chamisa Hill Building
440 St. Michaels Dr.
Santa Fe, NM 87501

New York
Office for the Aging
Agency Building #2
Empire State Plaza
Albany, NY 12223

North Carolina
North Carolina Department of Human Resources
Division of Aging
700 Hillsborough St.
Raleigh, NC 27603

North Dakota
Aging Services
Social Services Board of North Dakota
State Capitol Building
Bismarck, ND 58505

Northern Mariana Islands
Department of Community and Cultural Affairs
Commonwealth of the Northern Mariana Islands
Civic Center, Susupe
Saipan, Mariana Islands 96950

Ohio
Commission on Aging
50 West Broad St.
Columbus, OH 43216

Oklahoma
Special Unit on Aging
Department of Institutions, Social and Rehabilitation
   Services
P.O. Box 25352
Oklahoma City, OK 73125

Oregon
Office of Elderly Affairs
Human Resources Department
772 Commercial St., SE
Salem, OR 97310

Pennsylvania
Department of Aging
Finance Building
Harrisburg, PA 17120

Puerto Rico
Gericulture Commission
Department of Social Services

P.O. Box 11398
Santurce, PR 00910

Rhode Island
Department of Elderly Affairs
79 Washington St.
Providence, RI 02903

South Carolina
Commission on Aging
915 Main St.
Columbia, SC 29201

South Dakota
Office of Adult Services and Aging
Department of Social Services
Richard F. Kneip Building
Pierre, SD 57501

Tennessee
Commission on Aging
Tennessee Building
535 Church St.
Nashville, TN 37219

Texas
Governor's Committee on Aging
Executive Office Building
211 East 7th St.
P.O. Box 12786
Austin, TX 78711

Trust Territory of the Pacific
Office of Aging
Community Development Division
Government of the Trust Territory of the Pacific Islands
Saipan, Mariana Islands 96950

Utah
Division of Aging
Department of Social Services
150 West North Temple
Box 2500
Salt Lake City, UT 84102

Vermont
Office on Aging
Agency of Human Services
State Office Building
Montpelier, VT 05602

Virginia
Office on Aging
830 East Main St.
Richmond, VA 23219

Virgin Islands
Commission on Aging
P.O. Box 539
Charlotte Amalie
St. Thomas, VI 00801

Washington
Bureau of Aging
Department of Social and Health Services
OB-43G
Olympia, WA 98504

West Virginia
Commission on Aging

State Capitol
Charleston, WV 25305

Wisconsin
Division on Aging
Department of Health and Social Services
West Wilson St.
Madison, WI 53703

Wyoming
Office on Aging
Department of Health and Social Services
Hathaway Building
Cheyenne, WY 82002

Chapter 9

Recreation and Leisure On America's Public Lands

On March 1, 1872, Congress established a "public park or pleasuring ground for the benefit and enjoyment of the people" in the territory of Montana and Wyoming, thereby creating Yellowstone Park, the first national park in America and in the world. Over the next 100 years, the idea that land is a national treasure to be preserved for the public use was embraced by more than 100 nations. Across the United States, hundreds of millions of acres have been set aside by agencies of the federal government for the benefit and enjoyment of the public. State and local governments have designated hundreds of areas of special beauty and historic interest as parks and public preserves.
Today, the nation's public lands offer a stunning diversity of scenic beauty and recreational attractions. You can go swimming, camping, fishing, hunting, boating or skiing, enjoy a picnic, listen to a concert or see a ballet in national or state parks.
But before you pack the family into the car and go rushing off to the nearest park, a word of caution is in order. America's National Park System draws more than 230 million visitors per year. Unless you plan your trip carefully, you may wind up in a traffic jam instead of a restful retreat.
This chapter tells you how to get the most out of your vacation on America's public lands. It describes the great wealth of public parks and preserves that are available, and tells you where to write for more detailed information on the various locations.

Contents

Planning a Vacation for the Maximum Enjoyment

With so many of the public lands experiencing record numbers of visitors, it is essential to plan your trip carefully. If the greater part of a holiday is spent inching along a congested highway in an overheated car, elbowing your way through crowds or roaming endless miles in a futile search for accommodations, the most eagerly anticipated vacation can quickly turn into a frustrating nightmare of wasted time, money and energy.

Travel Tips for Park Users

The first step is to find out as much as possible about your destination before you set out.

Free information is readily available from the federal and state offices listed throughout this chapter. A postcard, rather than a letter, with the sender's name, address and request immediately visible and legible usually brings forth a flood of descriptive material, including maps, directions and informative brochures. These, in turn, may bear names of additional sources to call if you have more questions.

When to Travel. Administrators of the public lands strongly advise visitors to avoid the peak attendance months of July and August. They point out that a majority of the sites are open throughout the year and the benefits of an off-season vacation go far beyond the simple luxury of having enough elbow room. Visitors to FDR's home in Hyde Park, New York, for example, will find their travels greatly enhanced by the glorious fall foliage. In winter, bird watchers can see thousands of snow geese at the Chincoteague National Wildlife Refuge on Virginia's eastern shore.

Wildlife fanciers can hope to see flocks of animals roaming freely in their natural habitats in the Northwest in the spring. Visitors to the Southwest can see the desert in bloom during the normally bleak period between late winter and early spring.

If you cannot avoid going in July or August, you may want to try one of the lesser-used parks marked "U" in the directory beginning on page 371.

The Need for Reservations. In many areas you will need reservations, and it is a good idea to make them well in advance. A year ahead is not a bit too soon. This is especially true for group activities such as ski tours or float trips, when special equipment such as houseboats or hiking gear is needed, or overnight lodgings are required. These services are frequently operated by private companies or individuals under an arrangement with the site superintendent and the administering agency. Concessionaires doing business in the National Park System are listed in *Visitor Accommodations, Facilities and Services*. You can order this booklet from the Superintendent of Documents, U.S. Government Printing Office, Washington, D.C. 20402. Information on accommodations and services at other public lands may be obtained from the various facilities. Be sure to remember that fees, hours and holidays are subject to change; they should always be verified at the time your reservation is made.

Whether to Travel Alone. When it comes to vacations, many heads—and hands—are frequently better than one. Almost any recreational activity becomes more rewarding when it is shared. For the uninitiated, travel with a group brings safety and the pleasures of companionship. Families who have never ventured beyond the suburbs should not think of attempting a wilderness vacation on their own. The beauties of nature are not without their surprises and hidden dangers—falling rocks, unexpected storms, sudden surges in rushing currents of white water or chance encounters with startled wild animals. The experienced traveler anticipates the unexpected and understands how to deal with it.

Even if you plan nothing more challenging than an exploration of the boutiques of Ghirardelli Square on a visit to San Francisco's Golden

Gate National Recreation Area—one of the most popular sites in the National Park System—traveling with at least one other person will make it easier for you if you have never visited the area before. The wider the disparity between your normal routine and the tour activities, the greater your need to travel with knowledgeable companions.

If you are unable to schedule your vacation with friends or family, you may want to join a group that shares your interests. Outdoor clubs, such as the Wilderness Society or the Sierra Club, conduct programs in several states. Cinema clubs or gourmet societies plan vacations for people with special hobbies or tastes. Such organizations will be listed in your telephone directory.

Traveling with Pets. As a rule, pets are not permitted in public buildings or on trails. If you take them with you, they must be kept on a leash, or remain in a vehicle or a cage. There are good reasons for this. Unleashed animals may disturb other visitors. They may also frighten the wildlife, thereby endangering themselves and their owners. The best solution, therefore, is to arrange to leave your pet in safe custody in a kennel or at home while you are away.

Traveling with Children. No such restrictions apply to the activities of children on public lands. Small children should not, of course, be permitted to play unattended near lakes, rivers, streams or by the seashore. It is important to keep them always in sight. Youngsters eager for adventure may wander away from grown-ups, become confused by trees and landmarks that look alike and lose their way. In the company of adults, and properly supervised, they should be able to enjoy all of the available activities safely.

Transportation Within the Parks. Administrators of public lands are increasingly concerned over the need to preserve the parks and protect them from the twin dangers of overuse and pollution. At a number of places, such as the very popular Yosemite National Park, day visitors may be required to leave their cars in parking lots and travel about by bus. At other locations, minibuses or picturesque horse-drawn wagons shuttle visitors from point to point. In many areas, particularly along the Eastern seaboard, bike paths are being developed for use instead of highways. These alternatives to private cars can add to the traveler's pleasure and lessen the damage to the environment from heavy traffic, noise and auto pollution. At the same time, they help to conserve energy.

Facilities for the Handicapped. As indicated in Chapter 5, all federally funded enterprises are required to make special provisions to accommodate the handicapped. The facilities vary greatly from place to place, however. The popular booklet *Access: National Parks: A Guide for Handicapped Visitors*, available from the Government Printing Office, describes the facilities for the handicapped within the National Park System. These facilities are being improved as funds become available. The most up-to-date information may be obtained from the superintendent of the site you intend to visit.

Park Personnel

Park superintendents, forest rangers, naturalists, guides—all the people who manage and maintain the public lands—are paid to assist you. If you will explain to them what you'd like to do or see, they'll tell you how best to go about it. Discuss your itinerary with them. They'll offer helpful advice, maps and brochures. They'll also be able to alert you to shortcuts and hazards and, more important, they will watch for your safe return.

Golden Rules for Vacations on Public Lands

The public lands have been set aside for your enjoyment. To protect these great resources, regulations must be carefully enforced.

Natural Features. Every area is, in essence, a museum of natural or human history. Removal or destruction of any feature is prohibited. The same rule applies to man-made facilities.

Wildlife. Do not, under any circumstances, attempt to feed the animals. Tameness is an illusion. The "friendly" bear or elk is a wild animal. Young animals may seem harmless, but a protective parent usually is lurking nearby. Remember, you are a visitor to their native habitat. Observe them, but do not interfere with them; keep food supplies locked away or out of their reach.

Hunting. Except within specific areas and in accordance with state laws, hunting is prohibited in parks and public lands.

Trash. Be sure to place garbage and trash in containers provided for that purpose. If the visitors ahead of you have been sloppy, clean up their mess for your own protection. Garbage attracts animals.

Noise. Common courtesy should be the rule. Loud radios and television sets are forbidden at most campsites. Be particularly quiet from late night to early morning.

Observe the Local Regulations. Conditions differ from one area to the next. Regulations governing available activities are suited to local needs and are designed for your protection and enjoyment.

Dress Properly. Find out the temperature range of the area you're visiting and dress accordingly. For hiking, wear sturdy boots that are *already broken in*. Put on some heavy socks to prevent blisters.

Drive Carefully. You'll see more if you drive slowly, and you will save fuel. Be alert for less considerate drivers who may stop suddenly to gawk at the wildlife or scenery. Look out for animals that may cross roads unexpectedly.

Know Your Own Limits. Strenuous exertion in extremes of temperature or altitude can be dangerous, particularly if you are not accustomed to heavy exercise.

Report Trouble. Whether the problem is yours or someone else's, supervisory personnel can help only if they are aware that help is needed.

Leave Things as You Find Them. The survival of our public lands depends upon this rule. You may drop only one used tissue or one cigarette butt. But if a million visitors do the same thing, a sylvan glade or a beautiful beach will quickly become a trash heap.

Federal Recreation Fees

Under the Land and Water Conservation Fund Act of 1965, federal land-managing agencies have been authorized to charge fees for entrance, for use and for special recreation permits.

Entrance Fees. Many parks charge entrance fees ranging from $1 to $3 per private passenger vehicle. A vehicle is defined as a car, station wagon, pickup, camper, motor home, motorcycle or other motor vehicle used for private recreational purposes. The single-visit charge covers the length of the visitors' stay in the park, which, in the case of a camping or boating trip, may be many days. Visitors who leave the park and re-enter on another day may be charged a second entry fee. No entry fee is required for visitors under age 16.

Recreation Use Fees. These fees are charged for special sites, facilities, equipment or services that are furnished to visitors at federal expense. Included are parking places, campsites, boat-launching areas or special guides. Rates are generally comparable to those at private facilities in the area, but they will vary from one site to the next. Fee schedules are posted in parks, but may be subject to change.

Special Recreation Permit Fees. You pay extra for group campsites, back-country camping trips, motorized recreation vehicles and other special equipment or activities.

For information about fees and costs of special recreation permits, write directly to the manager of the park you intend to visit. Private concessionaires doing business within the parks set their own prices. They are not governed by federal regulations.

Golden Eagle and Golden Age Passports

Two kinds of entrance passes have been authorized by Congress for use at federally operated recreation sites. The Golden Eagle Passport, issued to anyone under 62 years of age, costs $10 and is good for one calendar year. This passport is not transferable or refundable. It admits the holder and all his or her companions in a private vehicle to any federal recreation area. If entry into the park is by public conveyance or on foot, the Golden Eagle Passport admits the holder and his or her entire family—parents, spouse and children—if they are traveling together.

The passport covers entrance fees only. It may not be applied to other federal fees, or to fees charged by private concessionaires.

Families planning visits to several areas charging entrance fees can save money by purchasing one $10 Golden Eagle Passport.

The passports may be obtained by mail or in person at offices of the National Park Service and the National Forest Service. They may also be purchased on arrival at any park where an entrance fee is charged.

The Golden Age Passport is issued free of charge to citizens or permanent residents of the United States who are 62 years of age or older. This is a lifetime entrance pass to areas where federal entrance fees are charged. The passport admits the holder and everyone accompanying him or her in a private vehicle. Otherwise, the Golden Age Passport admits the holder, spouse and children if they are traveling together.

In addition, holders of the Golden Age Passport are entitled to a 50 percent discount on federal recreation use fees, parking, campsites and the like. Fees charged by private concessionaires are not covered by the provisions of the Golden Age Passport.

Applications for a Golden Age Passport must be made in person; they cannot be ordered through the mail. The passports are available at most recreation sites where federal entrance fees are charged and at the headquarters and regional offices of the National Park Service and the Forest Service. In addition, Golden Age Passports are issued at the following locations: Forest Supervisors' offices, most Forest Service Ranger Station offices, all state and district offices of the Bureau of Land Management, regional offices of the Fish and Wildlife Service, National Wildlife Refuges, Hoover Dam in Arizona and Nevada, Land Between the Lakes on the border between Tennessee and Kentucky and Watts Bar Lake in Tennessee.

Applicants for Golden Age Passports must show proof of age—a driver's license, birth certificate or passport will do. If you do not have documentary proof of your age, you may be asked to sign an affidavit attesting to the fact that you are 62 or older.

Permits and Licenses

As part of the effort to protect the ecology of the public lands, maintain the quality of the outdoor experience and reduce the wear and tear of the crowds, certain areas now try to control the number of visitors by issuing limited numbers of permits for participation in special activities. A permit may be needed, for example, for white-water trips, hiking or camping expeditions, building campfires or exploring mountain trails. The list varies from place to place.

Similarly, hunting and fishing licenses are required at certain wildlife areas. Local regulations are aimed at protecting wildlife, and the visitors' fees are used for the maintenance of the areas.

For further information, write to the superintendent of the sites you intend to visit.

The Agencies in Charge of Public Lands

The several hundred millions of acres comprising America's public lands are presently administered by seven federal agencies. The division of responsibilities does not follow any logical plan: it simply grew that way. The seven agencies are:

National Park Service
United States Fish and Wildlife Service
Bureau of Land Management
Water and Power Resources Service
Forest Service
Army Corps of Engineers
Tennessee Valley Authority

The first four agencies are part of the Department of the Interior. The purposes of all have been set forth by this department. They are aimed at "fostering the wisest use of our land and water resources, protecting our fish and wildlife, preserving the environmental and cultural values of our national parks and historical places, and providing for the enjoyment of life through outdoor recreation."

In the section that follows, the seven agencies and their functions are described.

The National Park System

On August 25, 1916, Congress created the agency known as the National Park Service to "promote and regulate the use of the federal areas known as national parks, monuments and reservations . . . conserve scenery and the natural and historical objects and the wildlife therein and to provide for the enjoyment of the same in such manner and by such means as will leave them unimpaired for the enjoyment of future generations."

Congress also allotted funds for the employment of a director and a corps of forest rangers, with the powers of civilian policemen to implement the objectives set forth above. These Park Service officials operate the National Park System, which comprises more than 320 units. The following categories are included:

Areas celebrated for their natural values:
National Parks
National Monuments
National Lakeshores and National Seashores
National Rivers and Wild and Scenic Riverways

Areas commemorating persons, places, events or activities important in American history:
National Historic Sites
National Military Parks, National Battlefield Parks, National Battlefield Sites and National Battlefields
National Historical Parks
National Memorials
Urban Retreats and Scenic Roadways
National Recreation Areas
National Parkways

All of the areas listed above are commonly referred to as national parks. They will be referred to as "parks" in this chapter.

These parks are administered through 9 regional offices and an area office for the state of Alaska. The addresses of the offices and the states that they serve appear in the directory on page 371.

What the National Parks Offer

At each park you will find a visitor center where information and directions are available, as well as maps and brochures describing the park's attractions. Usually, there are museums or exhibits designed to give visitors a sense of the history of the area. Living History programs—live demonstrations of the historical features of the park—are a new and popular attraction at many parks. Auto-tape tours are available at some sites—they will enable you to learn about a park as you drive through it. The tapes may be rented at visitor centers. At most parks, guides are on hand to lead visitors on nature tours. Well-marked nature trails are provided in most parks for those who prefer self-guided tours.

Camping Facilities

Camping facilities are available at 99 locations of the National Park System. Recreation use fees, ranging from $1 to $4 per night, are charged at all sites (holders of Golden Age Passports are entitled to a 50 percent discount). Fees are also charged for all related services.

Facilities range from the well-equipped to the primitive. Four types of camps are to be found.

Type-A Campgrounds. These areas have well-defined roads, parking spaces and a limited number of campsites. Drinking water and sanitary facilities, including flush toilets, are furnished on a community basis. Each clearly marked campsite includes parking space, fireplace, tent space and a table-and-bench unit. The campgrounds also have areas where you can park your car and walk to a campsite.

Type-B Camping Area. Facilities are less elaborate here than at Type-A campgrounds. Camping areas are accessible by road or trail. Accommodations are generally limited to basic sanitary facilities, fireplaces and tables. The numbers of people admitted to the camping sites are fixed by the area superintendents.

Type-C Group Camp. These camps are designed for large parties, such as clubs or school groups. Areas are composed of one or more group spaces, each of which is provided with a fireplace, tables and parking space for buses and a limited number of cars. Capacity is based upon the number of people that a group space can comfortably accommodate.

Back-Country Camping. These are for people who enjoy primitive camping in remote areas of the National Park System. Hikers, mountain climbers, horseback riders, boaters and canoeists are encouraged to take advantage of such camping opportunities, provided that at least one member of the party is an experienced outdoorsman. Be sure to inform the office of the park superintendent of your plans. The staff can tell you whether permits are required for back-country use, and alert you to fire dangers or the likelihood of sudden weather changes.

Reservations. For the most part, campsites are available on a first-come, first-served basis. Reservations are being tried at some campgrounds, as the growing numbers of visitors and their impact on the ecology force changes in Park Service policies. The best way to find out about the reservations policy is to check with the office of the park superintendent before you make your plans.

Length of Stay. Some parks are finding it necessary to limit the length of visits during peak-use periods. Again, for information, you should check with the park superintendent.

Recreation Vehicles. Self-contained recreation vehicles requiring no utility connections can be accommodated at most park campgrounds. Trailers are accommodated at trailer sites. These are operated by concessionaires who set their own fees and usually will accept reservations.

Most parks offer more than one camping area and a variety of types of campgrounds. Complete information on the facilities, activities and points of interest at each site is available from the park superintendent. Areas of the National Park System that offer camping facilities are indicated by the letter "C" in the directory on page 371.

Fishing

From Alaska down to Hawaii and all the way across to the Virgin Islands, the National Park System offers anglers the opportunity to fish in fresh or salt water for catches ranging from catfish to tarpon.

Freshwater Fishing. In addition to the natural lakes and streams at many parks, there are huge man-made lakes created by dams. Cold waters in these lakes are the home of grayling,

Federal Recreation Symbols

The signs that appear below are used in all federal recreation areas, and have been adopted in many state and locally operated parks. A careful study of them will enable the vacationer to recognize direction and information symbols at a glance.

GENERAL

Firearms · Smoking · Automobiles · Trucks · Tunnel · Lookout Tower · Lighthouse · Falling Rocks · Dam

Fish Hatchery · Deer Viewing Area · Bear Viewing Area · Drinking Water · Information · Ranger Station · Pedestrian Crossing · Pets on Leash · Environmental Study Area

ACCOMMODATIONS OR SERVICE

Lodging · Food Service · Grocery Store

Men's Restroom · Restrooms · Women's Restroom · First Aid · Telephone · Post Office · Mechanic · Handicapped · Airport

Lockers · Bus Stop · Gas Station · Vehicle Ferry · Parking · Showers · Viewing Area · Sleeping Shelter · Campground

Picnic Shelter · Trailer Sites · Trailer Sanitary Station · Campfires · Trail Shelter · Picnic Area · Kennel · Laundry · Litter

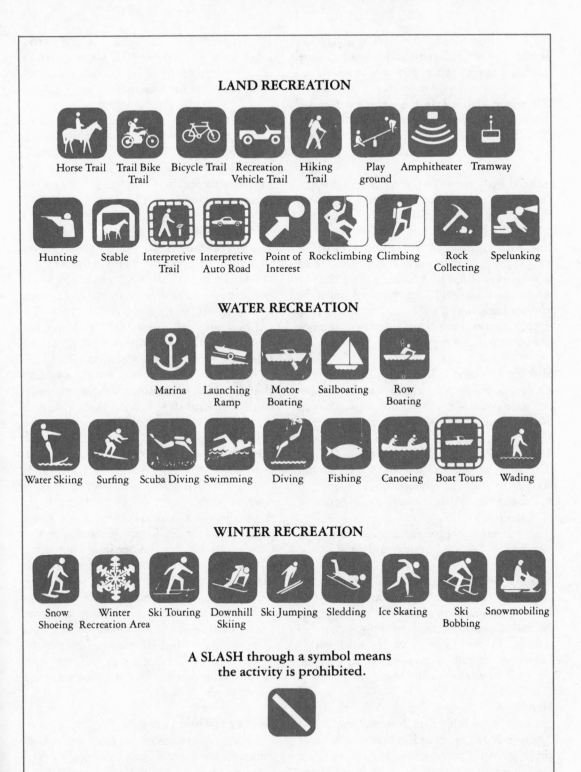

LAND RECREATION

Horse Trail | Trail Bike Trail | Bicycle Trail | Recreation Vehicle Trail | Hiking Trail | Play ground | Amphitheater | Tramway

Hunting | Stable | Interpretive Trail | Interpretive Auto Road | Point of Interest | Rockclimbing | Climbing | Rock Collecting | Spelunking

WATER RECREATION

Marina | Launching Ramp | Motor Boating | Sailboating | Row Boating

Water Skiing | Surfing | Scuba Diving | Swimming | Diving | Fishing | Canoeing | Boat Tours | Wading

WINTER RECREATION

Snow Shoeing | Winter Recreation Area | Ski Touring | Downhill Skiing | Ski Jumping | Sledding | Ice Skating | Ski Bobbing | Snowmobiling

**A SLASH through a symbol means
the activity is prohibited.**

all kinds of trout, salmon and whitefish. In warmer waters you can fish for bass, channel catfish, crappie, perch, pike and sunfish.

Saltwater Fishing. In the coastal waters and inlets of the National Park System you will find barracuda, bonefish, bonita, grouper, snapper, snook, tarpon and tuna.

Special Programs. To protect the trout population, "fishing for fun" programs have been tried on an experimental basis in some areas. Fishing with artificial lures and flies is permitted, with no limit on hours, but fish that are caught must be returned to the stream. Under another program, fish measuring more than 16 inches may be kept; smaller ones must be thrown back into the water. The object is to enable greater numbers of fishermen to enjoy the sport without depleting the streams.

Fishing Licenses. The National Park Service charges no fee for recreational fishing. However, state freshwater licenses are required in all national parks except Big Bend in Texas, Crater Lake in Oregon, Glacier in Montana, Isle Royale in Michigan, Mammoth Cave in Kentucky, Mount McKinley in Alaska, Mount Rainier and Mount Olympic in Washington, Chickasaw in Oklahoma and Yellowstone in Wyoming.

A saltwater license for marine fishing is required in Texas, California and Alaska.

Fishing Regulations. Special regulations, such as dates of the fishing season, limits of catch or fishing methods are determined locally. Park superintendents can supply such information. In the directory of National Parks, beginning on page 371, popular fishing locations are marked with the letter "F."

Hunting

Hunting is prohibited in National Parks and National Monuments and in historical areas of the National Park System. Subject to state laws, hunting is authorized at National Recreation Areas, National Seashores and certain other sites within the Park System. Specific information on permits and licenses is available from park superintendents.

Boating

Some parks maintain boating facilities and boats for rental. Specific regulations are in effect at each site, and can be learned from park superintendents. In the directory on page 371, parks with boating facilities are marked "B."

Winter Activities

Many people are under the mistaken impression that the parks offer only summer recreation. The fact is that many areas are open all year and it is possible to enjoy the full range of winter sports at these National Parks. The facilities are well-maintained, and the outstanding scenic beauty makes these parks ideal places for family winter vacations.

All winter sports areas offer cross-country skiing, which is considerably less expensive than traditional downhill skiing, and may be enjoyed by young and old, novice or expert. Advanced cross-country skiers, in groups of three or more, may take overnight trips. At Sequoia and Yosemite National parks in California, ski huts are available, and may be reserved in advance. Excellent facilities for downhill skiing exist in Yosemite and Lassen parks in California, Rocky Mountain Park in Colorado and Mount Rainer in Washington.

In some parks snowmobiles are permitted in designated areas. Ice skating, ice fishing, winter mountain climbing, sledding and snow-shoeing are enjoyed at many locations. Special camping areas for winter sports enthusiasts are maintained in many parks.

In the directory beginning on page 371, parks offering winter activities are designated by the letter "W."

The Lesser-Used Parks

The great reputations of our older, more popular parks have caused many travelers to overlook lesser-known sites that can be every bit as

Snowmobiling in the National Park System

Snowmobiles have enabled thousands of people to enjoy the winter wonders of the parks. The vehicles are used by the Park Service itself to carry on winter patrols, wildlife management surveys and search-and-rescue operations.

At the same time, their use has created problems of increased air and noise pollution, destruction of resources and harassment of wildlife. Visitors who would never dream of driving a car across their own front lawn will go tearing over delicate land in a snowmobile in pursuit of terrified wild animals.

In an effort to preserve the environment while recognizing the interests of drivers, the parks have formulated some strict rules for snowmobiles.

Many park superintendents require snowmobilers to register upon arrival and departure. Lights must be turned on if the vehicle is in use from 30 minutes after sunset until 30 minutes before sunrise and when visibility is less than 500 feet.

Racing and other competitive events are prohibited. No person under 16 may operate a snowmobile unless under the direct supervision of an adult. A code of good behavior for the snowmobiler follows.

The Snowmobiler's Code

1. Use your influence with other snowmobile owners to help promote sportsmanlike conduct.
2. Do not litter trails or camping areas. Do not pollute streams or lakes.
3. Do not damage living trees, shrubs or other living creatures.
4. Respect other people's property and rights.
5. Lend a helping hand when you see someone in distress.
6. Make yourself and your vehicle accessible to search-and-rescue parties.
7. Do not interfere with or harass skiers, snowshoers, ice fishermen or other winter sportsmen. Respect their rights to enjoy recreation facilities.
8. Know and obey all federal, state and local snowmobile regulations.
9. Do not harass wildlife. Stay out of areas posted for the protection and feeding of wildlife.

satisfying. As a result, places like Yosemite, Grand Canyon and Yellowstone suffer from heavy overuse, while other areas remain relatively uncrowded, except perhaps at the height of vacation seasons.

Often, the lesser-known places are as beautiful and rewarding as the famous sites. Just about everything you might expect to see in the most popular places can be found there except the crowds. Many of these lesser-known places offer unique attractions.

For example, during the warm months at Apostle Islands National Lakeshore in Wisconsin, you can fish, sail, swim and take photographs of the rocky islands rising from the world's largest freshwater lake, Lake Superior. Snowmobiling is offered in the winter.

At Michigan's Pictured Rocks National Lakeshore, you will find waterfalls, multicolored sandstone cliffs and broad beaches, as well as a profusion of birds and animals.

Canyon de Chelly National Monument in Arizona features the ruins of Indian villages built in A.D. 350 and 1300.

Visitors to Casa Grande Ruins National Monument in Arizona may explore the remains of a four-story adobe mansion constructed by Indian farmers 600 years ago.

At Chaco Canyon National Monument in New Mexico, unsurpassed examples of pre-

Columbian Pueblo civilization at its height may be seen, including the ruins of the world's first apartment building.

One of the richest collections of plant and insect fossils in the world is Florissant Fossil Beds National Monument in Colorado.

Fossil remains of dinosaurs and other ancient animals abound in Dinosaur National Monument in Colorado.

There are more than 100 non-traditional sites within the National Park System. As these examples indicate, they really shouldn't be thought of as places of secondary interest; they are merely lesser-known. In the directory on page 371, the lesser-used parks are designated by "U." Detailed descriptions of attractions and facilities can be readily obtained from park superintendents.

Fish and Wildlife Refuges

Originally established as the Bureau of Fisheries in 1871, the U.S. Fish and Wildlife Service is charged with the conservation, development and management of birds, endangered species and other fish and wildlife for the enjoyment of the public. The service administers nearly 400 National Wildlife Refuges, more than 45 million acres of land and water, facilities enjoyed by more than 30 million visitors each year. The service also operates fish hatcheries, wildlife laboratories and centers and cooperative research units across the country.

The Refuge System
There are Wildlife Refuges in every state except West Virginia. The refuge system is recognized as the world's foremost network of wildlife habitats and wilderness areas. Harbored in these remarkable places are more than 220 species of mammals, 600 kinds of birds, 250 varieties of reptiles and amphibians, over 200 species of fish and an as yet uncounted number of plants. Each refuge is unique in its ecological composition and wildlife population. Sanctuaries are provided for the largest

animals—including such species as the brown bear, the American buffalo, the antelope—and for the tiny painted bunting, the sea turtle, the alligator, the trumpeter swan, the bald eagle and hundreds of other threatened or endangered species.

The public is welcome to visit most of the National Wildlife Refuges, to observe the wildlife in its protected environment and gain an understanding of the interdependence of all living things. In addition to photography and nature watching, there are wildlife-oriented activities to enjoy throughout the system. These include sailing, canoeing, rowing, hiking and self-guided tours. In addition to these activities, some areas permit hunting and fishing, within the limits set by the manager of the particular site.

Tips for Wildlife Enjoyment from the U. S. Fish and Wildlife Service
The best way to begin your wildlife experience is by getting to know the sites that are located near your home.

Whenever feasible, use mass transportation to and from the refuges as well as within the sites.

Visit the wildlife areas early in the morning or late in the day when you are most likely to see the animals.

Move very quietly. Give the wildlife a chance to relax and forget you're there.

Get in the habit of looking back frequently. Animals often "freeze" in the presence of strangers; when they think you've moved away, they resume their natural behavior.

Be prepared to rough it—the refuges are natural wildlife preserves, not well-manicured municipal parks.

If you see something surprising or unusual, tell the refuge staff about it. Some refuges keep a record of the day's events; your discovery will be shared with other visitors.

Have reverence for the wildlife; take care that it is not injured or disturbed.

Regional offices of the U.S. Fish and Wildlife Service are listed on page 382.

Public Lands Under The Bureau of Land Management

BLM sites comprise about one-fifth of the nation's land area and are located primarily in the Far West and Alaska. They are popularly known simply as Public Lands.

Under the Federal Policy and Management Act of 1976, the BLM is responsible for multiple-use management of these lands "for the benefit of all Americans." Through its 12 state offices (page 383), the BLM maintains contact with district offices and local advisory boards in an effort to balance environmental factors and economic needs.

The Public Lands offer opportunities for camping, boating, swimming, "rockhounding," hunting and fishing in areas of spectacular beauty—mountains, canyons, prairies and deserts— at sites of historic, scientific and cultural significance.

Camping Opportunities, Reservations and Fees

There are more than 200 locations in 11 states where you can camp out on the Public Lands. Many of these areas are accessible only by backpacking, horseback riding or boating. The opportunities for primitive wilderness camping are abundant.

Elsewhere you will find campsites with spaces for tents and recreational vehicles. Toilets, drinking water, fireplaces, picnic tables and boat ramps are usually provided, but in most places there are no electrical hookups.

Some areas are designed to accommodate overnight visitors.

The state BLM office can provide information on camping regulations.

Spaces in BLM campgrounds are usually available on a first-come, first-served basis. (A reservations system has been tried in Oregon; in the future, the practice may be extended to the other sites.)

Overnight camping fees, ranging from $1 to $3 per party, are charged at many sites. Holders of the Golden Age Passport pay only half the fee.

Hunting and Fishing

Hunting and fishing are permitted at most sites. BLM offices work closely with state fish and game departments. States determine the season dates and limits on catches. State licenses are required. Consult your local BLM office for details.

Vehicles at Campsites

You can drive to and from most BLM campsites, but motorized vehicles are not allowed to drive around the grounds. Parking spaces usually are available.

Souvenir Hunting

BLM sites in California and New Mexico contain outstanding examples of rocks and caves decorated with American Indian paintings and designs, some of them from 6,000 to 10,000 years old. Other areas are noted for the fossil remains of creatures that roamed the earth millions of years ago. These relics of the past are defined as non-renewable resources, and are protected by the Antiquities Act of 1906, which prohibits souvenir collecting among the fossils.

On the other hand, samples of ordinary rocks, minerals and gemstones, which exist in abundance in this part of the country, may be gathered in limited quantities by collectors. Local BLM maps show rockhounding areas.

Nature lovers should be alert for glimpses of the numerous species of animal and plant life that have adapted to the harsh desert environments and manage to survive for extended periods without water. The kangaroo rat and the creosote bush are examples. In the pamphlet "From Foothill to Mountain," the visitor is led, step by step, along a trail that follows the South Yuba River in California and invited to identify the species native to the area, matching them to pictures in the booklet. A similar

Free Animals from the BLM

To balance competing uses on the Public Lands, the Bureau of Land Management (BLM) is forced to limit the number of animals on properties under its jurisdiction. Livestock herds are managed through permits restricting their numbers; wildlife is controlled by the BLM in cooperation with state fish and game departments.

Wild horses and burros enjoy special status: they are permitted to roam free. The animals are regarded as symbols of America's Western heritage, although neither is native to the area. Both were introduced into the New World in the early 16th century by the Spanish conquistadors. Animals that escaped from their owners formed the nucleus of the herds; centuries later others were turned out by their masters when mining camps were abandoned or food and water became scarce, as in the Dust Bowl period of the 1930s.

Left to fend for themselves, the animals fared astonishingly well. Approximately 2 million horses and burros were reportedly roaming the ranges, but then, mustangers captured and sold many of the animals, reducing the herds almost to extinction. Efforts by humane societies, a letter-writing campaign conducted by thousands of school children and the support of a colorful woman known as "Wild Horse Annie" (the late Mrs. Velma Johnson of Reno, Nevada) succeeded in achieving passage of the Wild Free-Roaming Horse and Burro Act in 1971, protecting the animals against rustlers and other encroachments. After that, the numbers increased so rapidly that depletion of the vegetation led to erosion and deterioration of the range. In an effort to maintain the balance of range-land resources, the BLM launched the Adopt-A-Horse Program.

Under the program, excess healthy wild horses and burros are eligible for adoption by qualified individuals. By the beginning of this decade, more than 18,000 animals were adopted under the program. The horses and burros can be trained for riding, showing, as pack animals or any other purpose for which a domesticated horse or burro would ordinarily be used. They may not, however, be used for bucking, or in any other way that exploits their wildness.

The prospective owners must be residents of the United States and of legal age in the state in which they reside. Qualified individuals may adopt up to four animals a year. To help defray the government's expenses for health fees, transportation and boarding costs, there is a $200 adoption fee for a wild horse, and $15 for a burro.

For further information about adopting a wild horse or burro, write to a BLM office listed on page 383.

---

pamphlet, "The Cress Creek Nature Trail," explores an area near Idaho Falls. Berries, nuts and flowers, in reasonable quantities, may be taken home as souvenirs. The pamphlets may be obtained from the state offices of the BLM, listed on page 383.

Land Parcels for Sale

Many people are under the misapprehension that the BLM distributes "free" or "surplus" Public Lands for homesteading, or sells parcels for next to nothing as the government did in the days of the Old West. This is not the case. Under the Federal Land Policy and Management Act of 1976, Public Lands may be disposed of only when the sale "benefits all Americans." Sales are conducted by public auction. The appraised value is the bottom price accepted for a parcel. Public Lands are, therefore, frequently sold at higher prices than comparable private lands in the same locale. The BLM also conducts lotteries for oil leases six times each year.

If you would like information on future Public Land sales or lotteries, write to the Bureau of Land Management office of the state that interests you. Legal notices of the sales are also published in local newspapers where the sale takes place. State offices of the Bureau of Land Management are listed in the directory on page 383.

World-Famous Dams, Reservoirs and Lakes

In 1902, Congress established the Bureau of Reclamation and charged it with the responsibility for reclaiming the arid lands of our Western states by conserving and supplying badly needed irrigation water. Known today as the Water and Power Resources Service, the agency has created 333 reservoirs, lakes and other bodies of water. Some of its achievements, notably the Hoover Dam in Colorado and the Grand Coulee Dam in Washington, are world famous. Other structures, such as Fresno Dam in Montana or Beck's Feeder Canal in Utah, are known primarily to local residents.

To meet the demands of our growing population and expanding economy, the mission of the Bureau has been broadened. Multi-purpose water development is now called for. The new title, Water and Power Resources Service, is descriptive of the agency's new role in the total environment.

Water-Oriented Recreation

About half of all outdoor recreation is now water-oriented. Millions of people spend weekends or vacations at Service recreation areas, where reservoirs and man-made lakes now function as playgrounds.

Management of the sites is frequently shared with the National Park Service, the Forest Service or with state and local agencies.

Locations. Recreation projects of the Water and Power Resources Service are located in 17 states, mostly in the West. For administrative purposes, these have been divided into four areas:

Area 1: Idaho, Washington, Oregon;

Area 2: Montana, North Dakota, South Dakota, Nebraska, Wyoming;

Area 3: California, Nevada, Utah, Arizona;

Area 4: Colorado, Kansas, Texas, Oklahoma, New Mexico.

The list of states suggests the great geographic diversity of the territory in which the projects are located. Included are the Great Plains, the Rockies, the peaks of the Pacific Northwest, the Big Sky country, the Badlands, deserts of the Southwest, and the valley of the Rio Grande. Miles of shoreline, acres of forests, canyons, ruins and historic forts, prairies and mesas—all these features can be found within the boundaries of Water and Power Resources Service projects. The Service believes that these areas should be perceived as a beautiful alternative to the crowded National Parks.

Activities. Visitors to Service projects will find campsites, picnic grounds, nature trails and bicycle paths, tents and trailer spaces as well as the full range of water sports: boating, swimming, water skiing and fishing. Hunting is possible at many sites. State fish and game laws are strictly enforced. At many sites there are visitor centers where you can make arrangements for tours of historical memorials and archeological ruins.

In Colorado you can swim in reservoirs 9,000 feet above sea level. Lake Waconda in Kansas boasts abundant fish and wildlife. Lake Mead and Lake Mohave provide oases in the Nevada desert. Visitors from all over the world line up for tours of Washington's astonishing Grand Coulee Dam. In South Dakota, not far from Mount Rushmore, you can explore caves or hunt for fossils within a reservoir area operated by the Service.

Fishermen on Service-controlled rivers catch

tons of salmon and steelhead each year. Service lakes offer anglers varieties of bass, bluegill, catfish, crappie, perch, salmon and trout.

In winter, Service sites in Montana, Wyoming, Colorado, New Mexico and the Dakotas offer snowmobiling, skiing and other winter sports.

For Further Information. The regional offices of the Water and Power Resources Service are listed on page 383. Write to them for maps, brochures and specific information about the projects you wish to visit.

Timberlands of the Forest Service

By the end of the 19th century, the unbridled westward expansion had devoured three-fourths of the nation's virgin forests. Many people feared that one of America's most valuable resources would disappear. On March 3, 1891, President Benjamin Harrison signed the Forest Reserve Act, providing that timber areas could be closed to settlers and set aside as part of the public domain. Ten years later, President Theodore Roosevelt, an ardent conservationist, set aside some 150 million acres as government forest land, and in 190 he placed the Forest Service under the Department of Agriculture, where it has remained.

Today, the forests not only supply lumber but serve a variety of other purposes, providing grazing places for cattle and homes for indigenous wildlife, playing a crucial role in the prevention of floods, soil erosion and, increasingly, answering the recreational needs of many citizens. Within the 154 National Forests, camping, picnicking, hunting, fishing, hiking, riding, mountain climbing, skiing and water sports are enjoyed by millions of people each year.

The National Forest Service is charged with administering 9 regions, which include both National Forests and the Wilderness Areas that have been set aside within them. The Service maintains more than 79,000 family camping units, over 22,000 picnic areas, more than 900 boating sites, over 300 swimming sites and more than 200 winter sports sites. Forest lands contain about 50 percent of our big game; freshwater streams, lakes and reservoirs afford habitats for many species of birds, fish and amphibian wildlife. The wooded areas encompass terrain of great variety: cypress swamps, alpine meadows, semi-desert stretches as well as mountain forests. Visitors may ride on a narrow-gauge railroad in the San Juan National Forest in Colorado, enjoy a canoe trip in the wilderness of Minnesota, observe underwater plant and animal life in a glass-bottomed boat at Taylor Creek in California. Trails designed for the visually and physically handicapped have been added at some sites.

There is a National Forest vacation spot within a day's drive of almost any point in the United States except Hawaii and some parts of Alaska. Each forest has a supervisor and from four to eight forest rangers. Signs tell where you are and explain what you're looking at. Wayside exhibits, guided trails and roadside overlooks are also designed to aid visitors. At the more popular sites, visitor centers offer interpretive programs and exhibits. Naturalists at these centers can answer questions, assist in planning trips, lead nature walks and conduct group studies.

A Family Vacation

Many families find camping in the National Forests an ideal way to enjoy an inexpensive vacation. Most campsites are open from May 30 through Labor Day; those in milder climates have longer seasons; some remain open all year. Admission is on a first-come, first-served basis.

There are five classifications of campsites in the National Forests:

Ultra-Modern Camps. Conveniences include showers, bath houses, toilets and laundry facilities, electrical hookups, hardtopped trails and landscaped grounds. Trailers are accommodated at most locations. These facilities are recommended for families and for inexperienced campers.

Modern Camps. Toilets and fire facilities are available. These camps are usually located near lakes, where swimming and boating can be enjoyed.

Rustic Camps. Campsites are limited to two or three per acre, to preserve the campers' privacy. Some conveniences are offered.

Rugged Camps. Drinking water and fireplaces are the only conveniences. Vehicles are allowed, but the roads are rugged and are not suited for trailers.

Primitive Camps. These campsites usually are approached on foot or horseback. Admission is for experienced campers only. There are few facilities. You can pitch a tent or spread a bedroll wherever you like. You will be required to follow Forest Service regulations concerning fire and housekeeping. Fees range from $1 to $2 per night, and vary from site to site.

The length of stay is determined at each forest. Usually, it is limited to one to two weeks, depending on the number of visitors at the time. But if you are visiting a little-used forest in off season, you usually are permitted to stay as long as you like.

What to Bring With You. At any of these locations, you will be required to supply all of your own equipment. Be sure to check the condition of each item before you pack it. For safety and enjoyment, take along a portable flashlight and a battery-powered radio, in good working order. It is advisable to pack enough food for the entire trip. There are no supply points in the forests, and the nearest town may be a long way from your campsite.

Wilderness Areas. The National Forests include more than 100 Wilderness Areas.

There are no roads. You enter on foot or on horseback, and vehicles are not allowed. Trails usually lead to scenic locations. The number of visitors entering a Wilderness Area may be limited to guard against overuse. If you hope to visit a Wilderness Area be sure to request a permit ahead of time. Permits are available 30 days in advance; there is no charge for them. Visitors to these remote areas are cautioned against traveling alone.

For further information, write to the Regional Offices of the National Forest Service, listed on page 384; be sure to mention any special interests or needs.

Once you've decided on an area, write to the forest supervisor there for maps and specific information. Then select the district you prefer to camp in. Mark the location of the district ranger station on a map.

Plan to arrive early enough in the afternoon to set up your campsite before dark. Report to the district manager on arrival.

The rangers will direct you to the campgrounds. There are many camping areas in each forest, so there's no need to be discouraged if the first campground that you approach is crowded.

Rules for Enjoying the Forests. You can enjoy a variety of activities in the forests. Some of them have already been mentioned. If these do not interest you, you may want to try such simple pleasures as picking berries, hunting for fossils or photographing the dawn and the sunset. Whatever you do, you will find that your pleasure and your safety will be greatly enhanced if you follow a simple set of rules during the course of your visit:

Never wander about the forests alone.

Leave a copy of your route with the rangers.

Don't attempt to do too much. Stay within your own physical limitations. Take it easy at high altitudes. Drink plenty of water, and keep as dry as possible.

Respect the land—take out only what you take in.

Waterways of the Army Engineers

Each year increasing numbers of visitors discover the recreational opportunities at lakes, reservoirs, canals and dams developed by the Army Corps of Engineers.

The Engineers' original mission was to provide combat support for the Continental Army at the Battle of Bunker Hill, on June 17, 1775. In the years that followed, the role of the Engineers expanded greatly, as they built bridges, blazed trails, enlarged harbors and cleared rivers and forests for the navigation, exploration and expansion of the Republic. In the process, the Corps became the principal developer and manager of our waterways.

In 1944, under the Flood Control Act, the Engineer Corps was authorized to construct, maintain and operate recreational facilities at its various water-resource projects. The sites had always attracted visitors; suddenly they became enormously popular vacation areas.

Today, there are more than 400 lakes and other bodies of water under the supervision of the Army Corps of Engineers. To simplify matters, all of these are referred to as lakes in this chapter. The majority of these are within 50 miles of populated urban areas. You can pile the family into a camper or the car and be at a campsite in a short while.

Activities at Corps Lakes

The Engineer Corps lakes are often operated in conjunction with other federal agencies and state fish and game departments or by special arrangement with private concessionaires. There are more than 6,000 public areas within the sites. Visitors can expect to enjoy all water-based activities—swimming, boating, water-skiing and scuba diving—as well as camping, picnicking, hiking, birdwatching and studying the scenery. Facilities for the handicapped are being added at many locations.

Hunting and fishing are encouraged, as long as the ecology of the area is not disturbed. Pres-

ervation of wildlife and wilderness areas are Corps responsibilities. Some of the waterways are noted for their fish and game. The J. Percy Priest Lake in Tennessee, for example, is celebrated for striped bass, crappie and trout. The Clark Hill Reservoir in Georgia features turkeys, waterfowl and deer.

Information is distributed at visitor centers at most sites, and detailed exhibits at some locations portray the history of the areas. Centers are usually designed to allow visitors to observe the workings of the water projects.

Camping at Corps Lakes

In designated areas, visitors may pitch tents, park their trailers, motor homes or campers. Two weeks is the maximum length of stay. There are no entry fees, but camping fees are charged at many locations. Some areas charge special fees for groups. Because the areas under the jurisdiction of the Army Engineers are operated in conjunction with other agencies, fees vary from place to place, and should be ascertained in advance from Corps personnel.

For further information, see the directory on page 384.

The TVA'S Recreational Facilities

The Tennessee Valley Authority is an independent agency of the federal government, created by act of Congress in 1933. Its main purposes are to regulate the flow of the Tennessee River system, produce power and provide for the agricultural and industrial development of the Tennessee and the lower Ohio and Mississippi valleys. Incidentally, the system of lakes and dams constructed by TVA on the Tennessee River and its tributaries also provides many facilities for outdoor recreation, including parks, boat docks, beaches, campgrounds, resort centers and wildlife observation areas. Some of the facilities of this enormous system are operated by TVA in conjunction with other public agencies; some by concessionaires and private businesses.

Recreation in the TVA

Within the TVA system, there are more than 100 state and local parks developed for swimming, picnicking, boating and camping. Most of the state parks offer overnight accommodations. Signs identify approximately 300 public access areas along the shoreline of TVA lakes that are open to the public for fishing, camping and hunting.

There are several hundred boat docks and launching ramps within the TVA system. Thousands of boats are moored on TVA lakes. Speedboat races and sailing regattas are held throughout the year. Pleasure boats are allowed to pass through the navigation locks at the dams free of charge.

Fishing is enjoyed the year round. License requirements and limits on the size of catches are set by the various TVA states. Walleye, crappie, sunfish and bass—largemouth, smallmouth, spotted and white—are plentiful throughout the area. Rainbow trout are found in some of the deep lakes.

Hunting is permitted on TVA unimproved lands. Wildlife refuges, game and waterfowl areas may also be enjoyed. Regulations of state fish and game departments and the U.S. Fish and Wildlife Service must be observed.

Camping facilities are plentiful, many of them suitable for tents and trailers. Campgrounds are open from April 1 to October 15. A fee of $4 per night for up to 4 persons is charged at certain public campgrounds; $3 per night for up to 4 persons is the charge for camping in the informal public-use areas.

Land Between the Lakes

The peninsula between the TVA's Kentucky Lake and the Army Corps of Engineers' Lake Barkley is being developed as a national demonstration area for outdoor recreation, environmental education and experiments in resources management. Covering an area 8 miles wide and 40 miles long, on the border of Kentucky and Tennessee, the peninsula is known as the Land Between the Lakes. Visitors can hunt, fish, ride horseback, hike or study the fascinating environment.

Camping facilities range from sites with modern conveniences to rustic clearings by the lakes. Family campgrounds include approximately 1,000 tent and trailer sites. Primitive camping areas such as the Ginger Ridge Back-Country Camp are set aside for those who prefer a more rugged way of life.

The environmental education studies are especially popular. At Empire Farm, youngsters from urban areas get a chance to become acquainted with farm animals. An exhibit at Center Station tells the story of the land before the first settlers arrived, and at the Living History Farm, rural life is conducted as it would have been in the 1850s.

Hunting is permitted in season in limited areas. The successful resource management program has assured an abundance of deer, turkey, quail and geese.

Birdwatchers, naturalists and photographers can enjoy the varied wildlife at Land Between the Lakes: a herd of buffalo roams here; rare bald and golden eagles fly overhead.

Trails of varying difficulty wind through the area. Hikers are awarded special patches for completing the various trails.

For further information on Land Between the Lakes write to:

Land Between the Lakes
Tennessee Valley Authority
P O. Box GB-78
Golden Pond, KY 42231

Information on Tennessee Valley Authority is available from:
Public Information Office
Tennessee Valley Authority
400 Commerce Ave.
Knoxville, TN 37902
or:
Office of Natural Resources
Tennessee Valley Authority
Norris, TN 37828

Playgrounds at Power Projects

Recreational facilities in abundance are available at the more than 600 hydroelectric projects licensed by the Federal Energy Regulatory Commission. These sites are not managed by federal, state or local governments, but are run by power companies, which are required to offer recreational facilities to the public as a condition of doing business with the government.

The sites resemble Army Corps of Engineers water projects, or areas of the TVA. The scenery is inspiring, and activities include swimming, canoeing, boating, hiking, hunting, fishing, golf and skiing. Several organizations offer guided tours of the power projects, as well as museums, historical sites and public facilities.

The projects are located in 41 states, from Maine to Alaska. There are 148 in California, 83 in Wisconsin, 31 in Alabama and Georgia, 29 in New York—which means that they offer a great diversity in climate, terrain and local customs.

The public is encouraged to use them. For further information, write to:

The Federal Energy Regulatory
   Commission
Main Office
825 North Capital St., NE
Washington, DC 20426

The Commission has five regional offices:

730 Peachtree St., NE
Atlanta, GA 30308

230 South Dearborn St.
Chicago, IL 60604

819 Taylor St.
Fort Worth, TX 76102

26 Federal Plaza
New York, NY 10007

555 Battery St.
San Francisco, CA 94111

State-Owned Recreation Lands

Supplementing the wealth of federally administered recreation sites are the public lands maintained by the states.

Essentially 50 separate systems, they include parks, forests, monuments, wildlife reserves, wilderness areas and historic sites. Activities range from picnicking to jaunts in multicolored, hot-air balloons. Between these extremes you'll find a multitude of festivals, fairs, rodeos, regattas and diverse special events by which the states celebrate their unique historic, ethnic and cultural resources. And, of course, there are places where you may hike, bike, hunt, fish, swim, ski, dance, explore or do nothing at all.

Vacations on state facilities are comparatively inexpensive. Accommodations range from spartan to luxurious, with some states providing rustic dormitories and a number of others maintaining resort inns where the amenities include air-conditioned chalets, cocktail lounges, continental cuisines, 18-hole golf courses, marinas and private airstrips. Whatever the level of comfort, the cost of lodging and meals will be less at state parks than at other resort areas.

Because they offer excellent outdoor recreational opportunities at moderate cost, state parks are gaining in popularity. It is sensible, therefore—as with the federally administered areas—to plan your vacation as far in advance as possible and try to select the non-peak seasons.

Some states have set minimum and maximum lengths of stay. Many parks now remain open all year, and regulations—such as check-in times and curfew hours—depend upon the season and the number of visitors. Reservation procedures vary from state to state, and frequently depend upon the time of year. Some states have two rate schedules: one for residents and another for out-of-state visitors. Similarly, programs for senior citizens or the handicapped may be available only to state residents.

The directory that follows highlights the state systems and tells where to write for information on locations, facilities, activities, fees, licenses and permits. If you are planning a trip, a good idea would be to select a few states whose climate, culture or terrain interests you particularly and write to those offices for maps and brochures. From these you will learn which places are likely to offer you and your family the most enjoyment. After that, you can write to specific parks or other locations, make your reservations and organize your vacation.

Before setting out, remember to confirm your reservations in advance; take your confirmation slips with you and keep them handy, not packed away with the raingear and the first-aid kit you hope you won't need.

The State Parks Directory

Alabama. This is one of the states with luxury resort inns offering cottages, chalets, championship golf courses, beach complexes, and marinas. There are parks with housekeeping cabins and campsites and day-use parks (no overnight facilities). The state owns and manages public fishing lakes, a demonstration farm and many wildlife and hunting areas. The state capital, Montgomery, was the capital of the Confederacy at the outset of the Civil War. Tours of the elegant mansions of Mobile and the Space and Rocket Center at Huntsville are offered. For further information, write to:

Alabama Bureau of Publicity and
 Information
532 South Perry St.
Montgomery, AL 36104

Alaska. Approximately 3 million acres have been set aside for Alaska's park system, much of which is still in the planning stage. At present there are many waysides on all major highways—camping, picnic and rest areas. The system eventually will include four types of parks: those commemorating significant natural and cultural values; recreational facilities; historic parks where one can experience aspects of the Alaskan heritage; and the waysides. This is a growing system in what has been termed America's last accessible wilderness. For further information, write to:

Alaska State Division of Tourism
Pouch E
Juneau, AK 99811

Arizona. The state's biggest attraction, the Grand Canyon, is of course a national park (see page 371). But Arizona's own state parks offer a colorful variety of attractions. You can camp in forests of Ponderosa pine, swim and fish 4,000 feet above the sea at Lake Patagonia, south of Tucson, or visit the renowned Boyce Thomson Arboretum, where all varieties of desert plant life can be seen. At Lake Havasu City, on the Colorado River, you can visit the world-renowned London Bridge, which was transplanted from the Thames. At Tombstone, you can see the O.K. Corral or the Birdcage Theater. The Victorian Courthouse there features exhibits recalling the tumultuous silver mining days of the 1880s, and the displays at Tubac Presidio State Park highlight the contributions of Spaniards, Indians and Mexicans to Arizona's history. At Painted Rocks State Historic Park, you can study Indian rock drawings of animals, men and geometric figures. If you like water sports, you can rent a riverfront cabana at Buckskin Park and go water skiing, swimming or fishing or, if you are interested in the Old West, you can visit the old army post at Fort Verde, dating from the Indian fighting days. For further information, write to:

Arizona State Parks
1688 West Adams
Phoenix, AZ 85007

Arkansas. Known as "the land of opportunity," Arkansas offers modern or rustic vacation cabins. Reservations are recommended for the cabins, but campsites in state parks are on a first-come-first-served basis. All are listed in the "Arkansas Camper's Guide," available from the address below. At Crater of Diamonds State Park, near Murfreesboro, a 78-acre field marks the only known site of diamonds in North America. Any gems you find will be assessed without charge. Nature lovers may enjoy exploring Louisiana Purchase Historic State Park in the southeastern part of the state, famous for its teeming swamp, where birds, mammals, reptiles and unusual trees abound. Mountain View is the home of the colorful Ozark Folk Center. The state's many rivers and streams are ideal for canoeing, fishing and swimming. For further information, write to:

Arkansas Division of Tourism
One Capitol Mall
Little Rock, AR 72201

California. Almost anything you want—wilderness areas, beaches, forests primeval, spectacular scenery—can be found in California's state parks. Redwoods are a major attraction from the Oregon border all the way down to San Francisco. A good place to see them is the Avenue of Giants, north of San Francisco, where there are 43,000 acres of redwood groves.

The Anza Borrego Desert State Park, 85 miles north of San Diego, is California's largest state park. Spread over more than half a million acres, it offers campsites and primitive camping. The best time for a visit is the spring, when the desert is in bloom.

The California coastline affords magnificent views. Point Lobos, near Monterey, has been called "the greatest meeting of land and water in the world." You may enjoy digging for Pismo clams at Pismo Beach. If you like castles crammed full of priceless art objects from all over the world, you won't want to miss San Simeon, former home of the celebrated newspaper tycoon William Randolph Hearst. Inland,

the Sierra Nevada Mountains, with forests of evergreens, sparkling streams and fertile plains, offer many campgrounds in national parks and forests and state parks. Historic parks retell the stories of Indian, Spanish, Mexican, Russian and American settlements. All of the state's more than 200 parks, beaches, reserves, monuments, campgrounds and recreation areas are described in the "Guide to the California State Park System," available for $2. For a copy, or for further information, write to:

Department of Parks and Recreation
P.O. Box 2390
Sacramento, CA 95811

Colorado. In the "Centennial State," you can cross the world's highest suspension bridge spanning the Arkansas River at Royal Ann Gorge, sail, swim or fish in mountain-top lakes, or deep in a gorge with cliffs rising 170 feet on either side. The terrain is ideal for backpacking, hiking, camping or hunting. More than 2,000 lakes and 11,000 miles of streams beckon anyone who would like to float a raft, paddle a canoe or cast a line. Rockhounds can find an abundance of semi-precious stones and petrified woods. For an introduction to Indian culture, you can visit the Ute Mountain Indian Reservation Park in Mancos Canyon in the southwestern corner of the state.

The state capital, Denver, is the home of the U.S. Mint. Tours are scheduled regularly.

There is an admission fee at national and state recreation areas. To encourage bicycling (and lessen pollution), the state offers maps of suggested bike routes. A special outdoor experience for the blind exists in the Braille Trail at Roaring Fork. For further information, write to:

Colorado Office of Tourism
500 State Centennial Building
1313 Sherman St.
Denver, CO 80203

Connecticut. The state has no National Parks or National Forests, but makes up for it with more than 100 state parks and forests, featuring clear, inland lakes and streams, cool woodlands, rocky promontories and miles of sandy beaches. Connecticut is steeped in traditions pre-dating the American Revolution; museums, historic districts and craft centers abound. Recreation areas are open year round; officially, the camping season dates from April 15 to September 30; all sites are listed in "Camping in Connecticut," available from the address given below.

Because Connecticut people believe that no sport beats trout fishing, the state has maintained a trout hatchery system for nearly a century. Visitors may tour the newest hatchery, Quinebaug, in Plainfield. At Dinosaur State Park in central Connecticut, near Rocky Hill, you can see the tracks of creatures that roamed the area 180 million years ago. In some state forests you can hunt the small game that now inhabits the territory. Harkness Memorial State Park on Long Island Sound, south of Waterford, offers the handicapped accommodations on the site of the magnificent Harkness mansion. For further information, write to:

Office of Parks and Recreation
State Office Building
165 Capitol Ave.
Hartford, CT 06115

Delaware. The first state to ratify the Constitution, Delaware is symbolized by the first star in the nation's flag and is rich in historic sites. The State House at Dover has been in continuous use since it was built in 1787. You can also visit the Octagonal School House at Cowgill's Corner, east of Dover, a one-room school dating from 1836. At the Fort Christina Monument in Wilmington, you can visit a log cabin built by Swedish settlers around 1700. The Delaware Calendar of Events, obtainable from the address below, lists the main attractions and includes a map. The state is one of the prime areas on the North Atlantic coast for fossil collecting; formations date back nearly 135 million years. State parks and forests offer opportunities for hunting, fishing, camping,

nature study, boating and bathing in quiet lakes or ocean waves. The Delaware State Museum in Dover, built in 1790, has been made barrier-free for the handicapped. For further information, write to:

Delaware State Travel Service
630 State College Rd.
P.O. Box 1401
Dover, DE 19901

Florida. Most of the state's 27 state parks have campsites; some offer vacation cottages. Museums and special-feature sites celebrate aspects of the state's 400-year history: you can visit the home of famed author Marjorie Kinnan Rawlings at Cross Creek, south of Gainesville; explore underwater caverns at Florida Caverns State Park, in Florida's Panhandle; tour an old sugar mill at Homosassa on the west coast; swim among the coral reefs at Key Largo. State-sponsored activities, many of which are free, are described in "Florida State Parks Guide," available from the address given below. Fees are charged at parks and campsites; Florida residents may purchase annual camping permits. For further information, write to:

Bureau of Education and Information
Florida Department of Natural Resources
3900 Commonwealth Blvd.
Tallahassee, FL 32301

Georgia. State parks and historic sites are open year round, and offer housekeeping cabins, campsites and all sports and outdoor activities. Unicoi Lodge and Conference Center in Unicoi State Park, in the northeastern part of the state, is a luxury resort inn. Minutes after touring the Capitol building in Atlanta, you can relax in the wilderness at Sweetwater Creek State Park. The Okefenokee Swamp, home of Walt Kelly's possum hero Pogo and all his animal friends, is a National Fish and Wildlife Refuge. The Stephen C. Foster State Park is located in the swamp. Camping, boating and fishing are featured along with tours of the Okefenokee. Jekyll Island, off the southeast coast, once a millionaires' playground and before that the legendary lair of Blackbeard the pirate, is now a state-operated recreation spot. Will-A-Way Recreation Area in Fort Yargo State Park in north-central Georgia has special provisions for the handicapped.

"A Guide to Georgia State Parks and Historic Sites" shows the statewide distribution of the parks and highways leading to them. For a copy, and for further information, write to:

Georgia Tourist Division
Department of Industry and Trade
P.O. Box 1776
Atlanta, GA 30301

Hawaii. The Hawaiian archipelago includes eight major islands and more than 100 smaller ones. The balmy climate, lush tropical vegetation, exotic birds and beautiful beaches make Hawaii a vacationer's delight. State and county parks are administered by separate departments on the individual islands. The demand for space in the parks is great. The island of Oahu has 13 beach parks; the island of Hawaii has 11. Tent and trailer camps are allowed in most state parks. Kauai has 9 parks; one of them is in the mountains, and on Molokai, you can pitch a tent in a mountain forest. There are excellent trails on most of the major islands, but be sure to stick to the beaten path. Dense vegetation, mists, precipices and moss-covered holes have confused many unwary hikers. The darkness comes on quickly, and hiking and rock climbing should never be attempted late in the day. Deep-sea fishing is a popular sport, and there is freshwater fishing in some areas. Swimming, snorkeling, diving and surfing are also popular, but should not be attempted alone. For further information, write to:

Hawaii Visitors Bureau
2270 Kalakaua Ave.
Honolulu, HI 96815

Idaho. Six of the state's 19 parks are open all year. Classified as Natural, Recreation or Historical Parks, they offer opportunities for ice fishing, snowmobiling and sledding as well as warm-water fishing, hiking and swimming.

Major scenic attractions are Shoshone Falls in the southwest, which is higher than Niagara, and the Thousand Springs Scenic Route in the same area. The time to see Shoshone is the spring; it dries up in the summer and fall. You can recall the Old West at Silver City, north of Boise, and drive along the beautiful River of No Return (the Salmon River). While you are in Idaho, you can visit dozens of ghost towns and mining camps established by the first gold prospectors. Idaho is known as the Gem State; you can organize your own hunt for jasper, opals, emeralds and rubies.

The entire park system is under study and development. Camping and other use fees vary. For further information, write to:

Idaho Tourism
State Capitol Building
Boise, ID 83720

Illinois. Most of the more than 100 parks, historical sites, forests and recreation areas are open all year. Campsites are plentiful. Some parks boast resort accommodations: deluxe rooms, cottages, pools, golf and tennis. From the time LaSalle first paddled the Kankakee River in 1679, canoeing has been popular: Illinois has white-water rapids, streams, wide rivers and more miles of active canals than any other state. The annual Canoe Marathon and the country's largest state fair are two of the state's bigger events. At Ravinia Park, summer home of the Chicago Symphony, you can listen to a concert as you enjoy a picnic lunch. The garden at Garfield Park, also in Chicago, has been planned for the blind. Illinois is Lincoln country—significant places and incidents in the life of our 16th President are celebrated throughout the state. "The Weekend Book" and "A Guide to Small Adventures in Illinois" suggest outings, tell where to go and what to do.

For copies and for further information about the state's attractions, write to:

Travel and Information Center
208 North Washington Ave.
Chicago, IL 60606

Indiana. State pools and lakeside beaches are open from the Saturday before Memorial Day through Labor Day weekend. However, campsites and housekeeping cabins at some parks, forests and fish-and-wildlife areas may be rented all year long. Attractive inns at some locations are open the year around. Indoor pools and cross-country skiing can be enjoyed. At Brown County State Park, at Nashville, when it's cold enough to light the cabin's Franklin stove, the park provides the firewood. Opportunities for hiking, riding, fishing and archery are plentiful. There's a reconstructed pioneer village at Spring Mill, and caves where blind fish swim in underground streams. Indiana's Department of Natural Resources has established a state-wide Snowmobile Trail System. The Hoosier Bikeway System (a part of the National Recreation Trail System) maps ways to break away and enjoy the quiet countryside, avoiding highways and cities whenever possible. For further information, write to:

Department of Natural Resources
Indiana State Parks
616 State Office Building
Indianapolis, IN 46204

Iowa. The name of the state is an Indian word meaning "beautiful land." Iowa is divided into seven vacation regions, whose names hint at the state's scenic and cultural variety: Explorerland, Great Rivers Region, Indian Hills Lake Region, Golden Southwest, Heart of Iowa, Great Northwest Siouxland and Land of Four Seasons. The rolling hills, prairies and forests are dotted with 96 state-owned parks, preserves and historical sites. In addition, there are 250 conservation areas, which remain open all year. Some locations offer campsites, group shelters and inexpensive family cabins. Among the state's special attractions are mushroom gathering, hot-air balloon races (at Indianola in July and August), the beautiful blue waters of Lake Okoboji, the State Fair and the annual Hobo Convention at Britt in the northern part of the state. For further information about the "beautiful land," write to:

Travel Division, Iowa Development Commission
250 Jewett Building
Des Moines, IA 50309

Kansas. The state operates more than 20 parks. Most of them are equipped with picnic tables and grills, and offer camping and fishing. Some sites furnish electricity and space for parking your trailer. At Sand Hills State Park, in the Arkansas River Valley, the sand dunes are maintained in their natural state; there are no conveniences; picnicking and camping are not allowed. Lakeside beaches in some parts of the state provide bath houses and boats for rent. Indian artifacts are displayed at the Pawnee Indian Village Museum in Lovewell State Park. In Meade, you can visit the Dalton Gang's Hideout and Museum. There are local museums throughout Kansas, such as the one honoring Amelia Earhart in the Dodge City Heritage Center. Detailed maps of each park and canoe-trail maps of Kansas' rivers are available on request. For further information, write to:

Kansas Park and Resources Authority
P.O. Box 977
Topeka, KS 66601

Kentucky. Famed for its rolling bluegrass country, grand mansions, the underground caverns at Mammoth Cave National Park and the stately old racetrack at Churchill Downs, where the Derby is run every year, Kentucky is, above all, noted for its thoroughbred horses and mint juleps. Kentucky Horse Park, near Lexington, is the first state park named in honor of horses, and is the home of the International Museum of the Horse. Kentucky also maintains a well-developed state park system. State resort parks offer deluxe accommodations, fine dining and total vacation facilities at moderate prices. Reservations are accepted a year in advance. At other locations, overnight camping is usually allowed. At Pioneer Weapons Hunting Area near Winchester, only the crossbow, longbow and muzzle-loading firearms are permitted. Visitors to Pleasant Hill are welcomed to the restoration of an early Shaker village. Each summer, a series of outdoor theatrical presentations in the parks celebrates the state's history and culture; Kentucky was the birthplace of Abraham Lincoln (Hodgenville) and Jefferson Davis (Fairview). Daniel Boone's pioneering days are recalled by a reconstructed fort in the Daniel Boone National Park at Winchester. The state was the scene of the confrontations between the feuding Hatfields and McCoys; and it was in Kentucky, in 1789, that the Reverend Elijah Craig invented a beverage which has become an American favorite. He called it Bourbon. For further information, write to:

Office of Tourism Development
Capitol Plaza Tower
Frankfort, KY 40601

Louisiana. State commemorative areas—museums, craft shops, visitor centers, gardens, buildings and trails—are dedicated to the preservation of historic and cultural values. Some are single-theme museums: devoted to voodoo, jazz, wildlife, dolls or art. More than 60 antebellum plantation mansions and town houses are open to visitors. State parks and wildlife areas offer outdoor recreation in a natural setting. "Welcome to Louisiana's State Parks," available at the address below, describes sites, lists fees and regulations. At campsites and picnic tables it's first-come, first-served; for cabins, group camps and lodges, reservations are accepted six months in advance. Hunting is permitted in state wildlife management areas, but not in state parks. For further information, write to:

Louisiana Office of Tourism
P.O. Box 44291
Capitol Station
Baton Rouge, LA 70804

Maine. You can get a good look at Maine's rock-bound coast by following the Downeast Mariners Trail north along U.S. #1 from Portsmouth. If you stop off at the Kittery His-

torical and Naval Museum, you can inspect ship models of John Paul Jones' *Ranger,* the first ship to fly the American flag, and the Civil War gunboat *Kearsarge.* The trail takes you past the Kittery Naval Yard, where more than half the U.S. submarines of the World War II era were built. At York Village, farther along, you can wander through a colonial setting with early American residences, churches and taverns. The trail goes past the Cape Neddick lighthouse, with its tall white tower and mournful fog signal. At Ogunquit, you can leave the car and walk along the scenic Marginal Way, a footpath that runs for a mile along the edge of the sea. You may want to stop for a swim at Old Orchard Beach, then visit the great American painter Winslow Homer's studio and residence at Prouts' Neck.

Mountains, forests, scenic views, beaches and offshore islands can be enjoyed in the state's expanding network of parks. Allagash Wilderness Waterway offers opportunities for white-water canoeing within a 200,000 acre preserve. Winter comes early here; parks are not open all year. Dates and fee schedules are given in "Maine's State Parks." For a copy and for further information, write to:

Maine Publicity Bureau
97 Winthrop St.
Hallowell, ME 04347

Maryland. In addition to the crabs and oysters of the Chesapeake Bay and Eastern Shore, for which the state is famous, Maryland offers freshwater fishing in its numerous lakes, ponds and streams. Licenses are required here for fishing and hunting in the state forests. Campsites are plentiful, but permits are needed. Some parks take reservations during the season, which extends from April 15 to October 31. Vacation cottages are available at some locations. Boating and bathing are widely enjoyed, and the state is dotted with points of historical interest. The state capital at Annapolis served as the capital of the United States briefly after the Revolutionary War. The Stars and Stripes were first flown at Ft. McHenry in Baltimore harbor. The flag's appearance after the British bombarded the fort in the War of 1812 prompted Francis Scott Key to write "The Star Spangled Banner" while aboard a ship off shore.

Entrance, rental and use fees are charged at state parks. Sites are described in a highway and natural resources map. For copies, and for further information, write to:

Department of Natural Resources
Parks and Forests
Annapolis, MD 21401

Massachusetts. Within the state are 128 state parks and forests. The Atlantic coastline offers excellent beaches. Inland, there are lakes, ponds, forests and wilderness areas. During the summer, trained naturalists conduct scheduled programs. For hardier adventurers, there are the wilderness sites at Mt. Washington and Monroe State Forests. They are accessible only on foot. In winter, skiing and snowmobiling are offered. The Cape Cod Rail Trail is a 16-mile route for cyclists, horseback riders and hikers, running from Eastham to Dennis and linking with other trails in Nickerson State Park at Brewster and on the Cape Cod National Seashore. The Division of Forests and Parks operates a statewide system of skating rinks and swimming pools. The Appalachian Trail winds 80 miles through state forests in the Berkshires. The land is rich in history. Shrines, trails and monuments are scattered all over the state. The entire Boston area is a veritable museum of Americana. For further information, write to:

Department of Environmental
  Management
Division of Forests and Parks
100 Cambridge St.
Boston, MA 02202

Michigan. More than 80 parks and recreation areas are open for year-round enjoyment. There are 6,000 camping spaces available for reservations from May to December, and an additional 7,000 available on a first-come, first-served

basis. Beaches extend almost endlessly along the Great Lakes shoreline, and the state offers a multitude of scenic inland lakes, rivers and waterfalls. Campsites range from rustic to modern. Permits are required at all; some will take advance reservations. You can fish in the waterways, take part in a variety of heritage programs, or tour Michigan's fine museums and historic sites. Metroparks in major cities allow city dwellers to enjoy picnics, boating and a variety of outdoor sports in summer and winter. The Upper Peninsula, connected by bridge with the mainland, has 17 state parks, with beautiful scenery, swimming, boating, hiking and excellent fishing. For further information, write to:

Michigan Department of Natural
  Resources
P.O. Box 30028
Lansing, MI 48909

Minnesota. The state boasts more shoreline than California plus Oregon, thanks to 12,000 lakes and more than 25,000 miles of rivers and streams. There are 258 historic sites, 59 parks, 6 recreation areas, nearly 900 wildlife management areas and over 3,000,000 acres of state forests. Each of Minnesota's six tourist regions has its distinctive scenic and cultural attractions: Arrowhead, in the northeast, includes many waterfalls, large wilderness areas, an underground iron ore mine, an international harbor and one of the most beautiful scenic roadways in America, the North Shore Drive along Lake Superior. Heartland, in the north-central part of the state, is often referred to as Paul Bunyan country. Dotted with lakes, it is known to fishermen as the walleye and muskie capital of the world. Hiawathaland in the southeast is celebrated for its beautiful scenery, rolling hills and the Root River Canoe Trail, which runs 74 miles through wilderness.

Metroland, in the central section, offers lakes, rivers, parks, camp areas and numerous festivals and carnivals celebrating the state's diverse ethnicity (Svenskarnas Dag is the Nation's largest Swedish festival). In Pioneer-land, in the southwest, you can inspect the Jeffers Petroglyphs, carvings dating from 3000 B.C. Vikingland, in the northwest, is known for its wild game, waterfowl, and artifacts of Scandinavian origin, which some people believe pre-date Columbus' discovery of America. For further information, write to:

Minnesota Tourism Division
480 Cedar St.
St. Paul, MN 55101

Mississippi. The state offers a variety of ways to enjoy the relaxed, "at home" feeling Mississippi values. Tourist attractions include freeflowing streams ideal for fishing and canoeing, quiet, tree-lined waterways overhung with Spanish moss, historic ante-bellum mansions and geological treasures. Campsites, cottages and trailer camps at the many state parks are available all year. Some sites provide restaurant and hotel facilities. Fees for lodging and equipment are set by each park. You can rent paddleboats, water skis, even houseboats. At Buccaneer State Park in the Gulf Coast area, you can swim in the roiling waters of a wave pool, and at Leroy Percy State Park in the Delta area you're allowed to feed the alligators; they are reported to love marshmallows, but don't get too close. For further information, write to:

Mississippi Department of Economic
  Development
Division of Tourism
P.O. Box 849
Jackson, MS 22825

Missouri. The "Show-Me" State is divided into eight vacation regions. The Pony Express Region, in the northwest—named for the relay service which originated there in 1860—is noted for its Excelsior Springs mineral waters. The Mark Twain Region, in the northeast, includes the writer's birthplace at Florida, and is the site of many parks, lakes and canals; countless waterfowl migrate to its Fountain Grove Wildlife Area. The Kansas City Area features the Harry S. Truman Library, the second largest municipal park in the country and

some of the best theater, opera and ballet to be seen in the region. Sedalia, in the Lake of the Ozarks Region, is the home of the State Fair. The St. Louis area is the site of the juncture of the Mississippi and Missouri rivers and is famous for the Gateway Arch, the zoo and the home of Daniel Boone. The Ozark Mountain Region, in the southwest, includes the birthplace of Harry S. Truman at Lamar. In the Big Springs Region, in the south-central part of the state, you can paddle a canoe into a cave, explore petroglyphs or hike the Ozark Trail. River Heritage Region, in the southeastern part of the state, is the site of the settlements of the early French traders.

The state's many parks, historical sites and man-made lakes offer year-round camping, hiking, fishing and nature studies. Accommodations at resort lodges may be limited to summer or fishing season. The Babler State Park Outdoor Education Center, 20 miles west of St. Louis, is barrier-free for handicapped or disabled campers. For further information, write to:

Missouri Division of Tourism
P.O. Box 1055
Jefferson City, MO 65102

Montana. Glacier National Park is the main attraction of the "Land of the Big Sky," but Montana also offers rustic vacations in the wilderness, complete with ghost towns, rodeos, wild animals and Indians. Seven North American tribes make their homes on reservations here, and it is possible to visit their fairs, crafts and art displays. The state is a rockhounder's paradise; Montana sapphire and agate abound. At Helena, the capital, you can see the state's history as depicted by the artist Charlie Russell. Wildhorse Island State Park, in northwestern Montana, 40 miles south of Glacier National Park, is surrounded by the waters of Flathead Lake, the largest body of fresh water in the West. Bannack, in the valley of Grasshopper Creek, was a brawling gold mining town, and the first capital of the territory of Montana. Some of the original buildings are

"Show Me" Camping in the "Show Me" State

Three state parks in Missouri—Watkins Mill, Pomme de Terre and Washington—have been participating in a special program, known as "Show Me Camping," that was created by the Division of Parks and Historic Preservation.

During the summer months, families who have never pitched a tent but are eager to learn, can go on a three-day campout and learn camping skills under the supervision of an experienced camper. The Division of Parks and Historic Preservation provides camping instruction and the basic equipment for the weekend.

After the first weekend, families who want to try camping on their own are required to rent or buy their gear.

Registration for the program costs $3, but is subject to change. The weekend camping fee is $9.

For further information and reservation forms, write the Division of Parks and Historic Preservation, P.O. Box 17, Jefferson City, MO 65102

---

still standing. Great Springs Park, on the Missouri River, claims one of the world's largest natural springs. For further information of Montana's attractions, write to:

Public Affairs and Tourism
Montana Travel Promotion Unit
Department of Highways
Helena, MT 59601

Nebraska. Hundreds of species of trees at Arbor Lodge State Park honor the founder of Arbor Day, Julius Sterling Morton. Father Flanagan's Boys' Town is just outside Omaha. Willa Cather Pioneer Memorial, in south-central Nebraska, celebrates the noted American writer. Landmarks commemorate the old Oregon Trail, the Pony Express, the original Indian inhabitants. All camping areas supply water, picnic tables and fireplaces; at some sites you can enjoy fishing, swimming or boating. For true wilderness camping, try Indian Cave State Park in the southeast. If you prefer not to rough it, there are comfortable accommodations to be rented at Ponca State Park in northeast Nebraska. Information centers along IS-80 can supply directions. For further information, write to:

Nebraska Travel and Tourism Division
P.O. Box 94666
Lincoln, NE 68509

Nevada. Gems and minerals of all kinds abound; the state is famous for its turquoise and fire opal, as well as gold and silver. The beautiful mountain lakes and rivers are ideal for water sports. Some of the largest freshwater fish on record have been caught at Pyramid Lake on an Indian reservation north of Reno; you can swim there amid prehistoric rock formations dating from the Jurassic Period. Some of the parks schedule cross-country tours, hikes and special programs for star gazers.

Washoe Lake State Park offers spectacular views of the Sierra Nevada. The Lake Tahoe Nevada State Park encompasses 13,000 acres of wilderness, and three miles of lake shoreline for swimming, camping and picnicking. At the Mormon Station Historic Monument, you can see a replica of an old trading post and a museum with relics from pioneer days. Fort Churchill Historic State Monument features the remnants of an army post built in 1860. You can visit a turn-of-the-century mining town at Berlin-Ichthyosaur State Park, and study fossils of giant fish lizards that swam in the warm ocean covering Nevada 180 million years ago. For further information, write to:

Nevada Travel and Tourism Division
Department of Economic Development
1100 East Williams
Carson City, NV 89710

New Hampshire. The White Mountains are the highest in the Northeast; skiing was pioneered here in the 1930s; the tramway at Franconia Notch State Park was the first to be constructed in North America. Today, there are 34 ski areas. In addition to the magnificent scenery, the state offers clean air, tranquility and 300 years of history. State parks are open during the summer season; dates are set at each site. There are public campgrounds and plenty of opportunities to fish, hike, swim and climb mountains. If you are interested in Americana, you can visit Daniel Webster's birthplace at Franklin; Fort Constitution, a reconstructed bastion of the Revolutionary War era at New Castle; or the 100-year old farmhouse of the poet Robert Frost at Derry. For further information, write to:

New Hampshire Office of Vacation Travel
P.O. Box 856
Concord, NH 03301

New Jersey. Cape May holds the distinction of being the nation's first resort area. It is a popular vacation spot today, and a showplace of Victorian architecture. Atlantic City claims the country's first boardwalk; it's also the birthplace of saltwater taffy and the home of the Miss America pageant. There are 35 state parks and 11 state forests in New Jersey. Parks, forests and wildlife preserves are open the year round; overnight accommodations are available at some locations. The state is also rich in the history of the American Revolution. Fort Lee Historic Park features a Revolutionary War Museum and reconstructed gun batteries. High Point State Park, in the northern tip of the state at Sussex, is the highest elevation in the state, affording a view of Pennsylvania, New Jersey and New York. Liberty State Park, in eastern New Jersey, offers a view of New York's skyline, the Statue of Liberty and Ellis Island. For further information, write to:

New Jersey Division of Travel
and Tourism
P.O. Box CN384
Trenton, NJ 08625

New Mexico. Called the "Land of Enchantment," New Mexico features rich plains, river lands and mountain valleys that have been inhabited for at least 10,000 years. Traces of the Sandia Man, who lived in caves and hunted in the mountains above what is now Albuquerque, and the Folsom man, who lived in the northeast, represent the earliest evidence of human life in North America. The state was later settled by Pueblo Indians, by the Spanish who came with Coronado in the 16th century and by settlers moving west along the Santa Fe Trail. The state calendar lists Indian, Spanish and Anglo celebrations. Among other attractions is the International Hot Air Balloon Festival, which takes place in Albuquerque in autumn. State facilities include parks, monuments, museums, lakes and outdoor recreation areas. The Pueblo tribes own and operate the Pueblo Indian Complex, near Albuquerque, which features a museum and cultural center. For further information, write to:

New Mexico Tourism and Travel Division
Commerce and Industry Department
Bataan Memorial Building
Santa Fe, NM 87503

New York. From the Adirondack Mountains to the Staten Island Ferry, New York declares it has "more to see and do than most countries." The "I Love New York Travel Guide," available from the address below, describes the state's major areas and attractions, lists recreation sites and tells which accept reservations. The Adirondack Park, in northeastern New York, includes state and privately owned lands. It is the largest park in the United States, covering 6 million acres, one fifth of the state. You can pick and choose from 48 islands in Lake George or enjoy the sparkling lakes, streams and waterfalls. Camping, hiking, boating and fishing are featured. Allegany State Park, near Salamanca, in the western part of the state, covers 65,000 acres, with woodlands, spring-fed mountain streams and 80 miles of trails for hiking and 45 miles for horseback riding. On Long Island, you can pitch a tent on the sand dunes of Hither Hills State Park, bathe in the ocean or Long Island Sound and enjoy surfing, deep-sea fishing and other water sports. Niagara Falls is the oldest state park in the United States and one of the nation's most spectacular attractions.

George Washington's headquarters at Newburgh was the nation's first public historic site. Saratoga Springs, near the scene of the great Revolutionary War battle, is the home of a performing arts center where the New York City Ballet and the Philadelphia Orchestra perform in summer.

New York City's many attractions include the world's finest botanic gardens, the Bronx Zoo and the nation's first major urban park (Central Park). Free performances of Shakespeare and the New York Philharmonic can be enjoyed there in the summer. Sightseers can also tour such landmarks as the Brooklyn Bridge, the Statue of Liberty, the Empire State Building and the city's world-renowned theater district.

The Empire Passport, obtainable for $20 at any regional state park office, will afford the purchaser unlimited vehicular access to the state parks. The Golden Park Pass, issued to residents 62 or older, guarantees lifetime admission to the state parks. For further information, write to:

New York State Department of
  Commerce
230 Park Ave.
New York, NY 10017

North Carolina. The Great Smoky Mountains, the Cape Hatteras National Seashore and the National Forests are among the state's most popular attractions. The State Game Lands Program has been cooperatively funded with the U.S. Fish and Wildlife Service; the State Recreation Area at Kerr Reservoir near Henderson was created by the Army Corps of Engineers. In addition, there are 25 state parks, all but two of which are open year round for picnics, hiking, canoeing and fresh and saltwater fishing. Campers are welcomed at some 9 parks

and many public campgrounds. Morrow Mount in central North Carolina at Albemarle, and Hanging Rock State Park at Danbury, offer vacation cabins; reservations are accepted in advance. All state parks are wildlife sanctuaries; hunting, trapping or in any way molesting the birds and animals is forbidden. Nature lovers and photographers will enjoy the abundant plant and bird life at Theodore Roosevelt Natural Area, seven miles south of Atlantic Beach; the collection of insect-devouring plants at Carolina Beach State Park, south of Wilmington; and the swamp forest at Merchants Millpond State Park at Gatesville. At Fort Macon State Historical Park, near Morehead City, ocean sports can be combined with tours of the restored 150-year-old fort. For further information, write to:

North Carolina Division of Travel
  and Tourism
Box 25249
Raleigh, NC 27611

North Dakota. The International Peace Garden, at the state's northern border, is dedicated to friendship between the United States and Canada. You can travel the Lewis and Clark Trail, from Williston southeast along the Missouri River, the Explorers' Highroad, crossing the state on route I-94, and the Old West Trail, running through the Badlands on U.S.85. The state offers year-round recreation. Annual and daily camping permits are issued, but reservations are not accepted at campsites. Some parks are open for day use only, with facilities for swimming, fishing, boating and hiking. Hunting is not allowed. Most picnic sites have fireplaces. There are various campfire programs, slide shows and nature programs. Winter activities are planned to encourage year-round use. For further information, write to:

North Dakota State Travel Division
Bismarck, ND 58505

Ohio. Along with its rolling countryside, villages and forests, Ohio has more large cities than any other state. You can visit monuments or birthplaces of seven Ohioans who served as President of the United States. (The seven: Rutherford B. Hayes, William Henry Harrison, Ulysses S. Grant, James A. Garfield, William McKinley, William Howard Taft and Warren G. Harding.) The museums of Cleveland, Cincinnati, Toledo and Columbus are highly respected; and Dayton's Air Force Museum is the oldest and largest dedicated to flight. State parks and forests are open all year. Campers must have permits. A Rent-a-Camp Program (similar to the Missouri Show-Me Camp Program, page 363) is in operation at 18 parks. For about $10 per night, novices can rent a fully equipped campsite. The state now operates lodges, and museums such as writer Louis Bromfield's renowned Malabar Farm, in Lucas, Ohio. Ohio and West Virginia share reciprocal hunting and fishing agreements: holders of licenses from either state may fish and hunt waterfowl along the shores of the Ohio River.

As funds become available, facilities for the handicapped are being added. Information can be provided by each site. "Your Passport to Ohio" describes attractions and events; "Ohio's State Park Facilities" provides data on accommodations, activities, costs and reservation policies. For copies of both, and for further information, write to:

Ohio Office of Travel and Tourism
Department of Economics and
    Community Development
P.O. Box 1001
Columbus, OH 43216

Oklahoma. The State Park System is one of the nation's most elaborate and ambitious. Seven resort lodges with private airstrips and marinas offer deluxe accommodations, golf, tennis, water sports, hiking, hunting for Indian artifacts and horseback riding. Only a bit less luxurious are the state parks with air-conditioned cabins, where activities include archery, boating, fishing, hiking and water skiing. Campers who prefer to rough it may use campsites. Spe-

cial camping areas have been set aside at reduced rates for senior citizens and disabled people. Licenses are required for hunting and fishing. Monuments, memorials and museums illustrate Oklahoma's colorful heritage. There's a museum of the Chisholm Trail in Kingfisher; another dedicated to the pioneer woman is at Ponca City; one for Tom Mix at Dewey; one to mark Will Rogers' birthplace at Claremore. At Spiro Mounds Archeological State Park in east-central Oklahoma, you can study the remains of an Indian culture that flourished in the 13th and 14th centuries. For further information, write to:

Oklahoma Tourism and Recreation
    Department
Division of Marketing Services
500 Will Rogers Building
Oklahoma City, OK 73105

Oregon. More than 250 state parks and 5,000 campsites are to be found in this beautiful state. Beach access is provided at intervals of a little more than three miles along the scenic coastline. The views are spectacular at numerous vantage points. Hikers and cyclists can travel 64 miles along the Oregon Coast Trail, from Ft. Stevens down to Barview. For motorists, there is the 20-mile scenic drive through Cape Meares, Cape Lookout and Cape Kiwanda. You can visit offshore islands at Ecola, where sea lions frolic and shore birds abound, see the rain forest along the headland at Oswald West or stop off at Port Orford Heads to watch the whales offshore.

The 24-mile Columbia River Highway takes you past spectacular waterfalls and breathtaking views of the Columbia Gorge before ending five miles west of Bonneville Dam. Fort Rock State Monument in the south is the site of an Indian settlement of 10,000 years ago. Along eastern Oregon trails, you can see the beautiful Snake River at Farewell Bend, catch a glimpse of Hat Rock, a monolith shaped like a top hat, and visit the glacier-formed Wallowa Lake in the area called the Switzerland of America. For further information, write to:

Oregon Department of Transportation
Travel Information Section
101 Transportation Building
Salem, OR 97310

Pennsylvania. Public lands here are under the jurisdiction of federal, state and municipal agencies, each of which has its own specific regulations. The "Pennsylvania Trail Guide," available from the address below, explains the rules affecting forestry, game, fish, parks, boating and camping. Included in the guide are maps of land and water trails and a directory of outdoor vacation spots. Information on the more than 200 state parks, forests, picnic areas, historic sites and museums can be found in the "Recreational Guide," also available from the address below. There are more than 100 family cabins in the parks; during the summer season, however, they are rented only to state residents. The Department of Agriculture's farm vacation program enables visitors to live on a working farm, share meals and chores with the family and enjoy separate accommodations. In Philadelphia, once the nation's capital, historical landmarks—such as the Liberty Bell and Independence Hall—are only steps away from the downtown shopping mall. Mansions nearby date from the 17th and 18th centuries. The excellent art museum and the zoo are housed at Fairmont Park, the largest municipal park in the world. For further information, write to:

Pennsylvania Bureau of Travel Development
Department of Commerce
416 Forum Building
Harrisburg, PA 17120

Rhode Island. The nation's smallest state includes 20 state parks, 16 management areas that are open to the public for hunting and 10 state camping areas, as well as municipal camping grounds, and there are dozens of coastline spots for saltwater fishing. Resort areas are famous: Newport is the yachting capital of the world; the area around Narragansett Bay, Block Island and Point Judith is known as a fisherman's paradise. If you prefer not to bother with fishing, you can try your hand at wind surfing. Inland streams offer freshwater fishing. Beach Pond State Park, at Exeter, maintains campsites in a beautiful rural setting. Reservation policies are set at the sites.

Rhode Island is also rich in history. Settlement dates from the early 17th century, as the plentiful landmarks and historical sites will attest. For further information, write to:

Rhode Island Department of Economic Development
Tourist Promotion Division
7 Jackson Walkway
Providence, RI 02903

South Carolina. Beaches, lakes, mountains, forests and mansions—the Palmetto State has them all. State parks offer all kinds of outdoor activities the year round. The newest facilities boast luxury accommodations—commodious cabins or duplexes overlooking the water. Ramps and rails for the handicapped are provided at some locations. At Barnwell State Park, in the midlands, there is a special handicapped persons recreation center. Along the seacoast, Myrtle Beach and Huntington Beach State Parks are known for the high quality of their beaches. In the northwestern part of the state, the Blue Ridge Mountain area is a haven for campers, freshwater fishermen and lovers of spectacular scenery. Visitors to the several parks of the Swamp Fox Country, in the east-central part of the state, can see alligators snoozing in the water, or marvel at a dazzling variety of birds. Landmarks remind travelers that the Cherokee civilization was once centered in South Carolina. The state was also the birthplace of Andrew Jackson and John C. Calhoun. Riverbank plantations and historic homes from the colonial era are open to visitors. For further information, write to:

South Carolina Department of Parks,
Recreation and Tourism
Edgar A. Brown Building
1205 Pendelton St.
Columbia, SC 29201

South Dakota. At state parks, lakeside sites, recreational facilities, nature areas and historical parks, visitors can enjoy camping, boating, hunting, fishing, riding and hiking. Lakes Sharpe, Lewis and Clark, Francis Case and Oahe offer some of the finest fishing waters on the continent. Custer State Park, in the southern Black Hills, is prized for its wildlife—flowers, birds and animals; buffalo really do roam here and visitors are encouraged to feed the begging burros. Bear Butte State Park, near Sturgis, is a sacred Indian shrine. Major attractions in the sparsely populated state include Mount Rushmore, the eerie Badlands and the Black Hills. There are forests of Ponderosa pine, mountains bulging with rose quartz, museums, cultural and visitor centers statewide. For further information, write to:

South Dakota Division of Tourism
221 South Central
Pierre, SD 57501

Tennessee. Campsites, group campgrounds and family cabins are open on a first-come, first-served basis all year. Fees are charged for these spaces and for many activities; permits for hunting and fishing are required. The Tennessee Outdoor Recreation Area System also includes eight parks with luxury cabins. Six of them have full-scale hotels. Vacationers may use marinas and airstrips, play on championship golf courses and tennis courts. Reservations are accepted for these hotels. Within the state are four mountain ranges, rich forests, and relics of inhabitants who lived 10,000 years ago. At Natchez Trace State Park, in central Tennessee, you can gaze at one of the world's largest pecan trees. Roan Mountain State Park, in northeastern Tennessee, is a riot of rhododendrons in summer. In winter, cross-country skiers glide along its trails. Gatlinburg offers the Mountain Arts and Crafts Center; Nashville is renowned for country music and the Grand Ol' Opry; Memphis, the bustling Mississippi River port, is the home of the blues. Among the state's many historical sites are the homes of three presidents: Andrew Jackson (Nashville), James K. Polk (Columbia) and Andrew Johnson (Greeneville). For further information, write to:

Tennessee Department of Tourist
Development
P.O. Box 23170
Nashville, TN 37202

Texas. Texas offers a great variety of attractions in its broad expanses, including miles upon miles of lakes and streams. State parks allow visitors to enjoy fishing, swimming and boating as well as other outdoor activities. Bird watchers can observe more species here than in any other state. The best areas for bird watching are Meridian State Park, east of Waco, and the Falcon State Park near the Mexican border. "Texas State Park Information" lists all pertinent information about the parks. The booklet, "Just for the Fun of It," describes lifestyles in and around the cities and lists all recreational, historic and scenic attractions. The state's most celebrated shrine is, of course, the Alamo, at San Antonio. For the booklets and for further information, write to:

Texas Tourist Development Agency
P.O. Box 12008
Capitol Station
Austin, TX 78711

Utah. Approximately two-thirds of the state is federally owned—thereby facilitating the creation of some of our more spectacular National Parks and Monuments. Nonetheless, Utah operates 42 state parks, beaches, reserves and monuments, where the emphasis is on the unusual terrain and the abundance of archeological treasures. Coral-pink sand dunes 6,000 feet above sea level can be seen near Kanab, in the southern part of the state. Scofield Lake, at Helper, is 1,600 feet higher. The Bonneville Salt Flats provide the fastest auto racing mile on earth. Ancient Indian petroglyphs can be studied at Newspaper Rock State Historical Monument at Monticello-Moab. Admission and use fees are charged at state parks: residents may purchase an annual Fun Tag (admission pass) for $35 a year; senior citizens and disabled people are entitled to lifetime Fun Tags. For further information, write to:

Utah Travel Council
Council Hall, Capitol Hill
Salt Lake City, UT 84114

Vermont. Skiing and snowmobiling have become increasingly popular in Vermont. But there's more here than just snow-covered slopes. Vermont is made-to-order for campers and hikers. Vacation sites offer hunting, fishing (licenses are required), water sports and nature trails.

The state's Department of Forests, Parks and Recreation operates 34 campgrounds with 2,150 campsites. Campgrounds are open from the Friday before Memorial Day through Labor Day. Such conveniences as flush toilets, hot showers and firewood are available in most areas. There are also resident rangers to assist you. Groups affiliated with churches, schools, scout troops and similar organizations can enjoy special camping areas with lean-tos accommodating up to seven, fireplaces, picnic tables, spring or well water and group firepits. Reservations are accepted, and making them is recommended. Backpackers, who prefer to rough it, can do so in specially designated primitive areas. The state is rich in historic sites. Vermont was the home of the Revolutionary War hero Ethan Allen and his Green Mountain Boys. For information, write to:

Vermont Travel Division
Agency of Development and
    Community Affairs
61 Elm St.
Montpelier, VT 05602

Virginia. From its coastal beaches through the Piedmont and mountain areas, Virginia enjoys a bounty of natural, recreational and historic resources. Jamestown was the first permanent English settlement in the New World. Colonial Williamsburg, privately run, is a mecca for tourists. Washington's home at Mount Vernon, Jefferson's at Monticello, Monroe's law office in Fredericksburg and Wilson's birthplace in Staunton are among the major attractions. Civil War battlefields and monuments are everywhere, and you can visit the Museum of the Confederacy in Richmond and see the many fine statues of Southern generals. Virginia's beautiful rivers and bays have yielded record breaking catches of fish; locations are listed in the leaflets "Freshwater Fishing" and "Salt Water Sport Fishing," available from the address below.

Weather permitting, campgrounds are open from April to December; cabins at eight state parks open the beginning of May and are closed by October. Reservations are accepted for campsites and required for cabins. A fee of $4 is charged at most campsites, but the price is $5.50 at seashore locations. For further information, write to:

Virginia State Travel Service
6 North Sixth St.
Richmond, VA 23219

Washington. Spectacular scenery—the dramatic seacoast, the snowcapped Cascades, the Olympic Rain Forest—fish-filled rivers and streams and the promise of rare tranquility attract thousands of visitors annually. State parks are wildlife sanctuaries; hunting is not permitted. The parks are open year round; group shelters and campsites for groups are available by reservation. Most camps include tables, stoves, water and toilet facilities. Some offer hot showers, kitchens and shelters. Trailer sites are available at many parks. Overnight camping, picnicking, hunting, fishing, swimming, boating and ocean bathing are enjoyed. At Fort Worden State Park, near Port Townsend, north of Seattle, vacation housing is provided in what, at the turn of the century, were army officers' homes. In addition to the parks, there are many public recreation areas throughout the state. For further information, write to:

Parks and Recreation Commission
7150 Cleanwater Lane KY 11
Olympia, WA 98504

West Virginia. Mountain scenery, clean air, old country roads, covered bridges, hundreds of fairs and festivals, lakes for swimming and fishing, museums, galleries and historic sites—all are free in West Virginia. White-water rafting is a popular sport. Visitors are welcome to tour the governor's mansion in Charleston, or to observe artisans at work in the state's many glass-making factories. Fees are charged for facilities at the more than 40 state parks and forests, which cater to families. There are cabins equipped for housekeeping, campsites, group shelters, and hookups for trailers. West Virginia has several year-round resort lodges: among them are Canaan Valley State Park, the complete winter sports and convention center at Davis, in the northeastern part of the state, and Pipestem, near Hinton. At Grandview, in the south, outdoor musical dramas are presented. Reservations are advised for all of the lodges. There are also many day-use parks and a growing number of public fishing and hunting areas (the game are grouse, squirrel and turkey). For further information, write to:

West Virginia Travel Development
  Division
1900 Washington St., E.
Charleston, WV 25305

Wisconsin. The state operates more than 50 parks, forests, and recreation areas. Fees are charged for camping, trails' admissions and use of special facilities. The system includes heritage parks, where special musical-historical programs are presented. At Governor Dodge State Park, near Dodgeville, a symphony orchestra, recruited from high school students, performs each summer. The Scientific Ice Age Reserve areas feature evidence of the Ice Age ending 10,000 years ago. Naturalist programs acquaint students with plant and animal life as well as the geology and ecology of parks. Nature hikes are regularly scheduled in summer, and 45 self-guided nature trails lead students through parks and forests, emphasizing protection and preservation of the fragile wetlands and wild rivers. Special campsites for groups, families and backpackers may be reserved in advance. For further information, write to:

Department of Natural Resources
Box 7921
Madison, WI 53707

Wyoming. At state-operated parks and recreation areas, picnicking, camping, hiking and fishing opportunities are enjoyed the year round. Lakes and reservoirs are ideal for swimming and water skiing. Canoes, kayaks and rubber rafts navigate the busy streams and rivers. In winter, Wyoming provides top-notch winter sports. The Jackson Hole Ski Area, south of Grand Teton National Park, has the largest ski slope in the nation. There's spectacular scenery here. Route 130 takes you among the snow-capped 12,000-foot peaks of the Snowy Range National Forest, past crystal-clear mountain lakes and glacier-carved valleys. The state's biggest attractions, of course, are Yellowstone and Grand Teton National Parks. The Como Bluff Dinosaur Graveyards are known for dinosaur and other fossil remains. There are hundreds of historic sites and museums; the Buffalo Bill Historic Center is the best known. Wyoming offers hunting of antelope, deer and elk; fishing for rainbow, brook, golden, mackinaw, cutthroat and brown trout. The North Platte River and Seminole Lake State Park are celebrated fishing areas. Dude ranching is popular around Saratoga. For further information, write to:

Frank Norris, Jr. Travel Center
Cheyenne, WY 82002

Directory of National Parks

Regional Offices

North Atlantic Region
(Maine, New Hampshire, Vermont, Massachusetts, Rhode
Island, Connecticut, New York, New Jersey)
15 State St.
Boston, MA 02109

Mid-Atlantic Region
(Pennsylvania, Maryland, West Virginia, Delaware, Vir-
ginia, excluding parks assigned to the National Capital
Region)
143 South Third St.
Philadelphia, PA 19106

National Capital Region
(District of Columbia, some units in Maryland, Virginia,
West Virginia)
1100 Ohio Dr., SW
Washington, DC 20242

Southeast Region
(Kentucky, Tennessee, North Carolina, South Carolina,
Georgia, Mississippi, Alabama, Florida, Puerto Rico,
Virgin Islands)
Richard B. Russell Federal Building and
U.S. Courthouse
75 Spring St., SW
Atlanta, GA 30303

Midwest Region
(Ohio, Indiana, Michigan, Wisconsin, Illinois, Minnesota,
Iowa, Missouri, Nebraska, Kansas)
1709 Jackson St.
Omaha, NE 68102

Rocky Mountain Region
(Montana, North Dakota, South Dakota, Wyoming,
Utah, Colorado)
P.O. Box 25287
755 Parfet St.
Denver, CO 80225

Southwest Region
(Arkansas, Louisiana, Texas, Oklahoma, New Mexico,
northeast corner of Arizona)
P.O. Box 728
Santa Fe, NM 87501

Western Region
(California, Nevada, Hawaii, most of Arizona)
Box 36063
450 Golden Gate Ave.
San Francisco, CA 94102

Pacific Northwest Region
(Idaho, Oregon, Washington)
601 Fourth and Pike Building
Seattle, WA 98101

Alaska
540 West 5th Ave.
Anchorage, AK 99501

National Parks
With Public Facilities

Explanation of Symbols
B— BOATING
BT— BICYCLE TRAIL
C— CAMPING
F— FISHING
H— HIKING
L— LIVING HISTORY PROGRAMS
P— PICNIC AREA
R— HORSEBACK RIDING
S— SWIMMING
W— WINTER SPORTS
U— LESSER USED PARK

Alabama
Horseshoe Bend National Military Park
Route 1, Box 103
Daviston, AL 36256
B BT F H L P U

Russell Cave National Monument
Route 1, Box 175
Bridgeport, AL 35740
H L

Tuskegee Institute National Historic Site
P.O. Box 1246
Tuskegee Institute, AL 36088
BT

Alaska
Aniakchak National Monument
Alaska Area Office
540 West 5th Ave.
Anchorage, AK 99501
F H

Bering Land Bridge National Monument
Alaska Area Office
540 West 5th Ave.
Anchorage, AK 99501
B F H

Cape Krusenstern National Monument
Alaska Area Office
540 West 5th Ave.
Anchorage, AK 99501
H

Denali National Monument
Mt. McKinley National Park
P.O. Box 9
McKinley Park, AK 99755
F H W

Gates of the Arctic National Monument
Alaska Area Office
540 West 5th Ave.
Anchorage, AK 99501
B F H

Glacier Bay National Monument
P.O. Box 1089

Juneau, AK 99802
B C F H U

Katmai National Monument
P.O. Box 7
King Salmon, AK 99613
B C F H U

Kenai Fjords National Monument
Alaska Area Office
540 West 5th Ave.
Anchorage, AK 99501
F H

Klondike Goldrush National Historical Park
P.O. Box 517
Skagway, AK 99840
F H C

Kobuk Valley National Monument
Alaska Area Office
540 West 5th Ave.
Anchorage, AK 99501
F H B

Lake Clark National Monument
Alaska Area Office
540 West 5th Ave.
Anchorage, AK 99501
B H

Mount McKinley National Park
P.O. Box 9
McKinley Park, AK 99755
C F H R W

Noatak National Monument
Alaska Area Office
540 West 5th Ave.
Anchorage, AK 99501
B F H

Sitka National Historical Park
P.O. Box 738
Sitka, AK 99835
F L P U

Wrangell-St. Elias National Monument
Alaska Area Office
540 West 5th Ave.
Anchorage, AK 99501
B F H

Yukon-Charley National Monument
Alaska Area Office
540 West 5th Ave.
Anchorage, AK 99501
H B F

Arizona

Canyon de Chelly National Monument
P.O. Box 588
Chinle, AZ 86503
C H U

Casa Grande National Monument
P.O. Box 518
Coolidge, AZ 85228
L P U

Chiricahua National Monument
Dos Cabezas Star Route
Willcox, AZ 85643
C H U

Coronado National Memorial
Route 1, Box 126
Hereford, AZ 85615
H L R U

Fort Bowie National Historic Site
P.O. Box 158
Bowie, AZ 85605
U H

Grand Canyon National Park
P.O. Box 129
Grand Canyon, AZ 86023
B BT C F H P R W

Hubbell Trading Post National Historic Site
P.O. Box 150
Ganado, AZ 86505
L P U

Montezuma Castle National Monument
P.O. Box 68
Clarksdale, AZ 86324
P U

Navajo National Monument
Tonalea, AZ 86044
C H P U

Organ Pipe Cactus National Monument
Route 1, Box 100
Ajo, AZ 85321
C H P R U

Petrified Forest National Park
Petrified Forest National Park, AZ 86028
C H P

Pipe Spring National Monument
Moccasin, AZ 86022
L

Saguaro National Monument
P.O. Box 17210
Tucson, AZ 85731
C H P R U

Sunset Crater National Monument
Route 3, Box 149
Flagstaff, AZ 86001
C P U

Tonto National Monument
P.O. Box 707
Roosevelt, AZ 85545
P U

Tumacacori National Monument
P.O. Box 67
Tumacacori, AZ 85640
L P

Tuzigoot National Monument
P.O. Box 68
Clarkdale, AZ 86324
U

Walnut Canyon National Monument
Route 1, Box 25
Flagstaff, AZ 86001
H U

Wupatki National Monument
Tuba Star Rt.
Flagstaff, AZ 86001
H P U

Arkansas

Arkansas Post National Memorial
Route 1, Box 16
Gillett, AR 72055
F H P U

Buffalo National River
P.O. Box 1173
Harrison, AR 72601
B C F H L P S

Fort Smith National Historic Site
P.O. Box 1406
Fort Smith, AR 72902
U

Hot Springs National Park
P.O. Box 1860
Hot Springs National Park, AR 71901
C H P

Pea Ridge National Military Park
Pea Ridge, AR 72751
H P U

California

Cabrillo National Monument
P.O. Box 6175
San Diego, CA 92106
BT F L

Channel Islands National Monument
1699 Anchors Way Dr.
Ventura, CA 93003
B C F H P S U

Death Valley National Monument
Death Valley, CA 92328
BT C H P S

Devils Postpile National Monument
c/o Sequoia and Kings Canyon National Parks
Three Rivers, CA 93271
C F H P

Fort Point National Historic Site
P.O. Box 29333
Presidio of San Francisco, CA 94129
F U

Golden Gate National Recreation Area
Fort Mason
San Francisco, CA 94123
BT C F H L P S R

John Muir National Historic Site
4202 Alhambra Ave.
Martinez, CA 94553
P U

Joshua Tree National Monument
74485 National Monument Dr.
Twentynine Palms, CA 92277
C H P

Kings Canyon National Park
Three Rivers, CA 93271
C F H L P R W

Lassen Volcanic National Park
Mineral, CA 96063
B C F H L P R S W

Lava Beds National Monument
P.O. Box 867
Tulelake, CA 96134
C H L P U

Muir Woods National Monument
Mill Valley, CA 94941
H

Pinnacles National Monument
Paicines, CA 95043
C H P U

Point Reyes National Seashore
Point Reyes, CA 94956
BT C F H L P R S

Redwood National Park
Drawer N
Crescent City, CA 95531
B C F H L P S

Santa Monica Mountains National Recreation Area
23018 Ventura Blvd.
Woodland Hills, CA 91364
H P

Sequoia National Park
Three Rivers, CA 93271
C F H L P R W

Whiskeytown-Shasta-Trinity National Recreation Area
P.O. Box 188
Whiskeytown, CA 96095
B C F H P R S

Yosemite National Park
P.O. Box 577
Yosemite National Park, CA 95389
B BT C F H L P R S W

Colorado

Bent's Old Fort National Historic Site
P.O. Box 581
La Junta, CO 81050
L U

Black Canyon of the Gunnison National Monument
P.O. Box 1648
Montrose, CO 81401
C F H P W U

Colorado National Monument
Fruita, CO 81521
BT C H P W

Curecanti National Recreation Area
P.O. Box 1040
Gunnison, CO 81230
B C F H P S W

Dinosaur National Monument
P.O. Box 210
Dinosaur, CO 81610
B C F H P U

Florissant Fossil Beds National Monument
P.O. Box 185
Florissant, CO 80816
C H P U

Great Sand Dunes National Monument
P.O. Box 60
Alamosa, CO 81101
C F H P W

Hovenweep National Monument
McElmo Rt.
Cortez, CO 81321
C H P U

Mesa Verde National Park
Mesa Verde National Park, CO 81330
C P

Rocky Mountain National Park
Estes Park, CO 80517
B C F H L P R S W

District of Columbia

Fords Theater National Historic Site
511 Tenth St., NW
Washington, DC 20004
L

Frederick Douglass Home
1411 W St., SE
Washington, DC 20020
BT L P U

John F. Kennedy Center for the Performing Arts
c/o National Park Service
2700 F St., NW
Washington, DC 20566
L

Lincoln Memorial
c/o National Park Service
1100 Ohio Dr., SW
Washington, DC 20242

L. B. Johnson Memorial Grove on the Potomac
c/o National Park Service
1100 Ohio Dr., SW
Washington, DC 20242
B F P

National Mall
c/o National Park Service
1100 Ohio Dr., SW
Washington, DC 20242
BT H P

National Visitor Center
Union Station
Washington, DC 20002

Rock Creek Park
5000 Glover Road, NW
Washington, DC 20002
BT F H L P R

Sewall-Belmont House National Historic Site
144 Constitution Ave., NE
Washington, DC 20002

Theodore Roosevelt Island
c/o George Washington Memorial Pkwy.
Turkey Run Park
McLean, VA 22101
F H

Thomas Jefferson Memorial
c/o National Park Service
1100 Ohio Dr., SW
Washington, DC 20242

Washington Monument
c/o National Park Service
1100 Ohio Dr., SW
Washington, DC 20242

White House
c/o National Park Service
1100 Ohio Dr., SW
Washington, DC 20242

Florida

Big Cypress National Preserve
P.O. Box 1247
Naples, FL 33939
F H P

Biscayne National Monument
P.O. Box 1369
Homestead, FL 33030
B C F P S

Canaveral National Seashore
P.O. Box 2583
Titusville, FL 32780
B P H P S

Castillo de San Marcos National Monument
1 Castillo Dr.
St. Augustine, FL 32084
L

DeSoto National Memorial
75th St., NW
Bradenton, FL 33505
F L U

Everglades National Park
P.O. Box 279
Homestead, FL 33030
B BT C F H P

Fort Caroline National Memorial
12713 Fort Caroline Rd.
Jacksonville, FL 32225
H P U

Fort Jefferson National Monument
c/o U.S. Coast Guard Base
Key West, FL 33040
B C F P S

Fort Matanzas National Monument
Route 1, Box 105
St. Augustine, FL 32084
F S U

Gulf Islands National Seashore
P.O. Box 100
Gulf Breeze, FL 32561
B BT C F L P S U

Georgia

Andersonville National Historic Site
Andersonville, GA 31711
P U

Chattahoochee River National Recreation Area
P.O. Box 1396
Smyrna, GA 30080
B C F H P

Chickamauga and Chattanooga National Military Park
P.O. Box 2126
Fort Oglethorpe, GA 30742
H L R

Cumberland Island National Seashore
P.O. Box 806
St. Marys, GA 31558
C F H P S

Fort Frederica National Monument
Route 4, Box 286-C
St. Simons Island, GA 31522
L U

Fort Pulaski National Monument
P.O. Box 98
Tybee Island, GA 31328
L P U

Kennesaw Mountain National Battlefield Park
P.O. Box 1167
Marietta, GA 30061
H L P R

Ocmulgee National Monument
1207 Emery Hwy.
Macon, GA 31201
F L P U

Guam

War in the Pacific National Historical Park
P.O. Box 3441
Agana, GU 96910
H P

Hawaii

Haleakala National Park
P.O. Box 537
Makawao, HI 96768
C F H P R S

Hawaii Volcanoes National Park
Hawaii National Park, HI 96718
C H P

Pu'uhonua o Honaunau (City of Refuge)
  National Historical Park
P.O. Box 128
Honaunau, Kona, HI 96726
F H L P S

Puukohola Heiau National Historic Site
P.O. Box 4963
Kawaihae, HI 96743
F H

Idaho

Craters of the Moon National Monument
P.O. Box 29
Arco, ID 83213
C H P W U

Nez Perce National Historical Park
P.O. Box 93
Spalding, ID 83551
L P

Illinois

Lincoln Home National Historic Site
526 South Seventh St.
Springfield, IL 62703

Indiana

George Rogers Clark National Historical Park
401 South Second St.
Vincennes, IN 47591
BT L

Indiana Dunes National Lakeshore
1100 North Mineral Springs Rd.
Porter, IN 46304
B BT C H P R S W U

Lincoln Boyhood National Memorial
Lincoln City, IN 47552
H L U

Iowa

Effigy Mounds National Monument
P.O. Box K
McGregor, IA 52157
H W U

Herbert Hoover National Historic Site
P.O. Box 607
West Branch, IA 52358
P W

Kansas

Fort Larned National Historic Site
Route 3
Larned, KS 67550
F L

Fort Scott National Historic Site
Old Fort Blvd.
Fort Scott, KS 66701

Kentucky

Abraham Lincoln Birthplace National Historic Site
R.F.D. 1
Hodgenville, KY 42748
P U

Cumberland Gap National Historical Park
P.O. Box 840
Middlesboro, KY 40965
C F H L P R U

Mammoth Cave National Park
Mammoth Cave, KY 42259
B C F H P R

Louisiana

Jean Lafitte National Historical Park and Preserve
400 Royal Ann St.
New Orleans, LA 70130
L F

Maine

Acadia National Park
Route 1, Box 1
Bar Harbor, ME 04609
B BT C F H P R S W

Maryland

Antietam National Battlefield Site
Box 158
Sharpsburg, MD 21782
BT H L P U

Assateague Island National Seashore
Route 2, Box 294
Berlin, MD 21811
B C F H P S

Catoctin Mountain Park
Thurmont, MD 21788
C F H L P R W

Cheasapeake and Ohio Canal National Historical Park
Box 158
Sharpsburg, MD 21782
B BT C F H L P R

Clara Barton National Historic Site
5801 Oxford Rd.
Glen Echo, MD 20768
BT

Fort McHenry National Monument and Historical Shrine
Baltimore, MD 21230
L P U

Fort Washington Park
National Capital Parks, East
5210 Indian Head Hwy.
Oxon Hill, MD 20021
H L P U

Greenbelt Park
6501 Greenbelt Rd.
Greenbelt, MD 20770
BT C H P R

Hampton National Historic Site
535 Hampton Lane
Towson, MD 21204
P U

Piscataway Park
National Capital Parks, East
5210 Indian Head Hwy.
Oxon Hill, MD 20021
F H L P

Massachusetts

Adams National Historic Site
P.O. Box 531
Quincy, MA 02169

Boston National Historical Park
Charlestown Navy Yard

Boston, MA 02129
H L P

Cape Cod National Seashore
South Wellfleet, MA 02663
BT F H P R S

John Fitzgerald Kennedy National Historic Site
83 Beals St.
Brookline, MA 02146
U

Longfellow National Historic Site
105 Brattle St.
Cambridge, MA 02138
U

Lowell National Historical Park
P.O. Box 1098
Lowell, MA 01853
P

Minute Man National Historical Park
P.O. Box 160
Concord, MA 01742
B F H L P

Salem Maritime National Historic Site
Custom House
174 Derby St.
Salem, MA 01970
F L P

Saugus Iron Works National Historic Site
244 Central St.
Saugus, MA 01906
L U

Springfield Armory National Historic Site
1 Armory Square
Springfield, MA 01105
L P

Michigan

Isle Royale National Park
87 North Ripley St.
Houghton, MI 49931
B C F H P

Pictured Rocks National Lakeshore
P.O. Box 40
Munising, MI 49862
B C F H P S W U

Sleeping Bear Dunes National Lakeshore
400 Main St.
Frankfort, MI 49635
B BT C F H P R S W U

Minnesota

Grand Portage National Monument
P.O. Box 666
Grand Marais, MN 55604
H P W U

Pipestone National Monument
P.O. Box 727
Pipestone, MN 56164
H L P U

Voyageurs National Park
P.O. Box 50
International Falls, MN 56649
B C F H P S W U

Mississippi

Brices Cross Roads National Battlefield Site
c/o Natchez Trace Parkway
R.R. 1, NT-143
Tupelo, MS 38801

Gulf Islands National Seashore
4000 Hanley Rd.
Ocean Springs, MS 39564
B C F P S U

Natchez Trace Parkway
R.R. 1, NT-143
Tupelo, MS 38801
B C F H L P R S

Tupelo National Battlefield
c/o Natchez Trace Parkway
R.R. 1, NT-143
Tupelo, MS 38801

Vicksburg National Military Park
P.O. Box 349
Vicksburg, MS 39180
L P

Missouri

George Washington Carver National Monument
P.O. Box 38
Diamond, MO 64840
L P U

Jefferson National Expansion Memorial
    National Historic Site
11 North 4th St.
St. Louis, MO 63102
L

Ozark National Scenic Riverways
P.O. Box 490
Van Buren, MO 63965
B BT C F H L P R S

Wilson's Creek National Battlefield
521 North Highway 60
Republic, MO 65738
H L P U

Montana

Big Hole National Battlefield
P.O. Box 237
Wisdom, MT 59761
F P U

Bighorn Canyon National Recreation Area
P.O. Box 458
Fort Smith, MT 59035
B C F H P S U

Custer Battlefield National Monument
P.O. Box 39
Crow Agency, MT 59022
H U

Glacier National Park
West Glacier, MT 59936
B BT C F H L P R W

Grant-Kohrs Ranch National Historic Site
P.O. Box 790
Deer Lodge, MT 59722
F L

Nebraska

Agate Fossil Beds National Monument
P.O. Box 427
Gering, NE 69341
F H P U

Homestead National Monument of America
Route 3
Beatrice, NE 68310
H L W U

Scotts Bluff National Monument
P.O. Box 427
Gering, NE 69341
BT H L U

Nevada

Lake Mead National Recreation Area
601 Nevada Hwy.
Boulder City, NV 89005
B C F H P S

Lehman Caves National Monument
Baker, NV 89311
P U

New Hampshire

Saint-Gaudens National Historic Site
R.D. 2
Windsor, VT 05089
L P U

New Jersey

Edison National Historic Site
Main St. and Lakeside Ave.
West Orange, NJ 07052
L U

Gateway National Recreation Area
P.O. Box 437
Highlands, NJ 07732
B BT C F L P S

Morristown National Historical Park
230 Morris St.
Morristown, NJ 07960
H L R W U

New Mexico

Aztec Ruins National Monument
P.O. Box U
Aztec, NM 87410
P U

Bandelier National Monument
Los Alamos, NM 87544
C H P

Capulin Mountain National Monument
Capulin, NM 88414
H P U

Carlsbad Caverns National Park
3225 National Parks Hwy.
Carlsbad, NM 88220
H P

Chaco Canyon National Monument
Star Route 4, Box 6500
Bloomfield, NM 87413
C H P U

El Morro National Monument
Ramah, NM 87321
C P U

Fort Union National Monument
Watrous, NM 87753
P U

Gila Cliff Dwellings National Monument
Gila Hot Springs Rt. 11, Box 100
Silver City, NM 88601
F P U

Gran Quivira National Monument
Route 1
Mountainair, NM 78036
P U

Pecos National Monument
P.O. Drawer 11
Pecos, NM 87552
L P U

White Sands National Monument
P.O. Box 458
Alamogordo, NM 88310
H P

New York

Castle Clinton National Monument
Manhattan Sites, National Park Service
26 Wall St.
New York, NY 10005
L P U

Eleanor Roosevelt National Historic Site
Hyde Park, NY 12538
L P

Federal Hall National Memorial
Manhattan Sites, National Park Service
26 Wall St.
New York, NY 10005
L U

Fire Island National Seashore
120 Laurel St.
Patchogue, NY 11772
B BT C F H P S U

Fort Stanwix National Monument
112 E. Park St.
Rome, NY 13440
L U

Gateway National Recreation Area
Floyd Bennett Field
Building 69
Brooklyn, NY 11234
B BT C F H L P R S

General Grant National Memorial
Manhattan Sites, National Park Service
26 Wall St.
New York, NY 10005

Hamilton Grange National Memorial
287 Convent Ave.
New York, NY 10031
U

Home of Franklin D. Roosevelt National Historic Site
Hyde Park, NY 12538

Martin Van Buren National Historic Site
P.O. Box 545
Kinderhook, NY 12106

Sagamore Hill National Historic Site
Cove Neck Road
Box 304
Oyster Bay, NY 11771
U

Saratoga National Historical Park
R.D. 1, Box 113-C
Stillwater, NY 12170
BT H L P W U

Statue of Liberty National Monument
Liberty Island
New York, NY 10004

Theodore Roosevelt Birthplace National Historic Site
28 East 20th St.
New York, NY 10003
U

Theodore Roosevelt Inaugural National Historic Site
641 Delaware Ave.
Buffalo, NY 14209

Upper Delaware Scenic and Recreational River
Cochecton, NY 12726
B F H P S

Vanderbilt Mansion National Historic Site
Hyde Park, NY 12538
U

North Carolina

Blue Ridge Parkway
700 Northwestern Bank Building
Asheville, NC 28801
B C F H L P

Cape Hatteras National Seashore
Route 1, Box 675
Manteo, NC 27954
B C F H L P S

Cape Lookout National Seashore
P.O. Box 690
Beaumont, NC 28516
B F H S

Carl Sandburg Home National Historic Site
P.O. Box 395
Flat Rock, NC 28731
H U

Fort Raleigh National Historic Site
c/o Cape Hatteras National Seashore

Route 1, Box 675
Manteo, NC 27954
L

Guilford Courthouse National Military Park
P.O. Box 9806
Greensboro, NC 27408
BT L

Moores Creek National Military Park
P.O. Box 69
Currie, NC 28435
L P U

Wright Brothers National Memorial
c/o Cape Hatteras National Seashore
Route 1, Box 675
Manteo, NC 27954
L

North Dakota

Fort Union Trading Post National Historic Site
Buford Route
Williston, ND 58801
L W

Knife River Indian Villages National Historic Site
P.O. Box 175
Stanton, ND 58571
W

Theodore Roosevelt National Park
P.O. Box 7
Medora, ND 58645
C F H P W R

Ohio

Cuyahoga Valley National Recreation Area
P.O. Box 158
Peninsula, OH 44264
BT F H L P W

Mound City Group National Monument
16062 State Route 104
Chillicothe, OH 45601
P U

Perry's Victory and International Peace Memorial
P.O. Box 78
Put-In-Bay, OH 43456
F U

William Howard Taft National Historic Site
2038 Auburn Ave.
Cincinnati, OH 45219

Oklahoma

Chickasaw National Recreation Area
P.O. Box 201
Sulphur, OK 73086
B C F H P R S

Oregon

Crater Lake National Park
P.O. Box 7
Crater Lake, OR 97604
B C F H P S W

Fort Clatsop National Memorial
Route 3, Box 604-FC

Astoria, OR 97103
L P U

John Day Fossil Beds National Monument
420 Main St.
John Day, OR 97845
F H P

Oregon Caves National Monument
19000 Caves Highway
Cave Junction, OR 97523
H L P U

Pennsylvania

Allegheny Portage Railroad National Historic Site
P.O. Box 247
Cresson, PA 16330
H L P U

Delaware Water Gap National Recreation Area
Bushkill, PA 18324
B C F H L P S W

Edgar Allen Poe National Historic Site
c/o Independence National Historical Park
313 Walnut St.
Philadelphia, PA 19106

Fort Necessity National Battlefield
The National Pike
Farmington, PA 15437
C H L P S W U

Gettysburg National Military Park
Gettysburg, PA 17325
BT C H L P R

Hopewell Village National Historic Site
R.D. 1, Box 345
Elverson, PA 19520
H L U

Independence National Historical Park
313 Walnut St.
Philadelphia, PA 19106
L

Johnstown Flood National Memorial
c/o Allegheny Portage Railroad National Historic Site
P.O. Box 247
Cresson, PA 16330
H L P U

Thaddeus Kosciuszko National Memorial
c/o Independence National Historical Park
313 Walnut St.
Philadelphia, PA 19106

Valley Forge National Historical Park
Valley Forge, PA 19481
B BT H L P R

Puerto Rico

San Juan National Historic Site
P.O. Box 712
Old San Juan, PR 00902
L

Rhode Island

Roger Williams National Memorial
P.O. Box 367

Annex Station
Providence, RI 02901

South Carolina

Cowpens National Battlefield
c/o Kings Mountain National Military Park
P.O. Box 31
Kings Mountain, NC 28086
P U

Fort Sumter National Monument
Drawer R
Sullivans Island, SC 29482
L U

Kings Mountain National Military Park
P.O. Box 31
Kings Mountain, NC 28086
H L R U

Ninety Six National Historic Site
P.O. Box 496
Ninety Six, SC 29666
F H R

South Dakota

Badlands National Park
P.O. Box 6
Interior, SD 57750
C H P

Jewel Cave National Monument
Custer, SD 57730
H P W

Mount Rushmore National Memorial
Keystone, SD 57751

Wind Cave National Park
Hot Springs, SD 57747
C H L P

Tennessee

Andrew Johnson National Historic Site
Depot St.
Greeneville, TN 37743
U

Big South Fork National River and Recreation Area
P.O. Drawer 630
Oneida, TN 37841
B F H P

Fort Donelson National Military Park
P.O. Box F
Dover, TN 37058
L P

Great Smoky Mountains National Park
Gatlinburg, TN 37738
C F H L P R

Obed Wild and Scenic River
P.O. Drawer 630
Oneida, TN 37841
B S

Shiloh National Military Park
Shiloh, TN 38876
BT C H L P U

Stones River National Battlefield
Route 10, Box 401
Old Nashville Hwy.
Murfreesboro, TN 37130
BT H L P U

Texas

Alibates Flint Quarries National Monument
c/o Lake Meredith National Recreation Area
P.O. Box 1438
Fritch, TX 79036

Amistad National Recreation Area
P.O. Box 1463
Del Rio, TX 78840
B C F H P S

Big Bend National Park
Big Bend National Park, TX 79834
B BT C F H P R U

Big Thicket National Preserve
P.O. Box 7408
Beaumont, TX 77706
B C F H

Chamizal National Memorial
800 South San Marcial St.
El Paso, TX 79905
P

Fort Davis National Historic Site
P.O. Box 1456
Fort Davis, TX 79734
H L P U

Guadalupe Mountains National Park
3225 National Parks Hwy.
Carlsbad, NM 88220
C H P

Lake Meredith National Recreation Area
P.O. Box 1438
Fritch, TX 79036
B C F P S

Lyndon B. Johnson National Historic Site
P.O. Box 329
Johnson City, TX 78636

Padre Island National Seashore
9405 South Padre Island Dr.
Corpus Christi, TX 78418
B C F S

San Antonio Missions National Historical Park
Southwest Regional Office
National Park Service
P.O. Box 728
Santa Fe, NM 87501

Utah

Arches National Park
446 South Main St.
Moab, UT 84532
C H L P U

Bryce Canyon National Park
Bryce Canyon, UT 84717
C H P R W

Canyonlands National Park
446 South Main St.
Moab, UT 84532
B C H F L P R S U

Capitol Reef National Park
Torrey, UT 84775
C H P U

Cedar Breaks National Monument
P.O. Box 749
Cedar City, UT 84720
C H F P W U

Glen Canyon National Recreation Area
P.O. Box 1507
Page, AZ 86040
B C F H L P S

Golden Spike National Historic Site
P.O. Box 394
Brigham City, UT 84302
H L P

Natural Bridges National Monument
c/o Canyonlands National Park
446 South Main St.
Moab, UT 84775
C H P

Rainbow Bridge National Monument
c/o Glen Canyon National Recreation Area
P.O. Box 1507
Page, AZ 86040
H S U

Timpanogos Cave National Monument
R.R. 3, Box 200
American Fork, UT 84003
F H P

Zion National Park
Springdale, UT 84767
C H P R S

Virginia

Appomattox Court House National Historical Park
P.O. Box 218
Appomattox, VA 24522
C H L P U

Arlington House
The Robert E. Lee Memorial
c/o George Washington Memorial Pkwy.
Turkey Run Park
McLean, VA 22101
BT L

Booker T. Washington National Monument
Route 1, Box 195
Hardy, VA 24101
C H L P U

Colonial National Historical Park
P.O. Box 210
Yorktown, VA 23690
H L P

Fredericksburg National Military Park
P.O. Box 679
Fredericksburg, VA 22401
BT F H L P U

George Washington Birthplace National Monument
Washington's Birthplace, VA 22575
F L P U

George Washington Memorial Pkwy.
Turkey Run Park
McLean, VA 22101
B BT F H L P R

Maggie L. Walker National Historic Site
c/o Richmond National Battlefield Park
3215 East Broad St.
Richmond, VA 23223

Manassas National Battlefield Park
P.O. Box 1830
Manassas, VA 22110
F H L P R

Petersburg National Battlefield
P.O. Box 549
Petersburg, VA 23803
BT F H L P

Prince William Forest Park
P.O. Box 208
Triangle, VA 22172
BT C F H L P

Richmond National Battlefield Park
3215 East Broad St.
Richmond, VA 23223
P U

Shenandoah National Park
Route 4, Box 292
Luray, VA 22835
C F H P R

Wolf Trap Farm Park for the Performing Arts
1551 Trap Road
Vienna, VA 22180
P

Virgin Islands

Buck Island Reef National Monument
Box 160
Christiansted, St. Croix, VI 00820
B F H P S U

Christiansted National Historic Site
P.O. Box 160
Christiansted, St. Croix, VI 00820
U

Virgin Islands National Park
P.O. Box 806
Charlotte Amalie, St. Thomas, VI 00801
B C F H L P S

Washington

Coulee Dam National Recreation Area
P.O. Box 37
Coulee Dam, WA 99116
B C F H L P S U

Fort Vancouver National Historic Site
East Evergreen Blvd.
Vancouver, WA 98661
BT L P U

Klondike Gold Rush National Historical Park
117 South Main St.
Seattle, WA 98104
L

Lake Chelan National Recreation Area
800 State St.
Sedro Woolley, WA 98284
B C F H L P

Mount Rainier National Park
Tahoma Woods, Star Route
Ashford, WA 98304
C F H P W

North Cascades National Park
800 State St.
Sedro Woolley, WA 98284
C F H U

Olympic National Park
600 East Park Ave.
Port Angeles, WA 98362
B C F H P R S W

Ross Lake National Recreation Area
800 State St.
Sedro Woolley, WA 98284
B C F H P U

San Juan Island National Historical Park
300 Cattle Point Rd.
Friday Harbor, WA 98250
F H L P U

Whitman Mission National Historic Site
Route 2
Walla Walla, WA 99362
L P U

West Virginia

Harpers Ferry National Historical Park
P.O. Box 65
Harpers Ferry, WV 25245
BT F H L P

Wisconsin

Apostle Islands National Lakeshore
Old Courthouse Building
Bayfield, WI 54814
B C F H L P U W

Lower St. Croix National Scenic River
c/o St. Croix National Scenic River
P.O. Box 708
St. Croix Falls, WI 54024
B C F H P S

St. Croix National Scenic River
P.O. Box 708
St. Croix Falls, WI 54024
B C F H P S U

Wyoming

Devils Tower National Monument
Devils Tower, WY 82714
C F H P U

Fort Laramie National Historic Site
Fort Laramie, WY 82212
H L P U

Fossil Butte National Monument
P.O. Box 527
Kemmerer, WY 83101
H P

Grand Teton National Park
P.O. Drawer 170
Moose, WY 83012
B BT C F H L P R S W

John D. Rockefeller, Jr. Memorial Parkway
c/o Grand Teton National Park
P.O. Drawer 170
Moose, WY 83012
C F H P R S W

Yellowstone National Park
P.O. Box 168
Yellowstone National Park, WY 82190
B BT C F H L P R W

Regional Offices of the United States Fish and Wildlife Service

Region I
(California, Hawaii, Idaho, Nevada, Oregon, Washington)
Lloyd 500 Building
500 NE Multnomah St.
Portland, OR 97232

Region II
(Arizona, New Mexico, Oklahoma, Texas)
P.O. Box 1306
Albuquerque, NM 87103

Region III
(Illinois, Indiana, Iowa, Michigan, Minnesota, Missouri, Ohio, Wisconsin)
Federal Building
Fort Snelling
Twin Cities, MN 55111

Region IV
(Alabama, Arkansas, Florida, Georgia, Kentucky, Louisiana, Mississippi, North Carolina, Puerto Rico, South Carolina, Tennessee, Virgin Islands)
Federal Building
75 Spring St., SW
Atlanta, GA 30303

Region V
(Connecticut, Delaware, Maine, Maryland, Massachusetts, New Hampshire, New Jersey, New York, Pennsylvania, Rhode Island, Vermont, Virginia, West Virginia)
One Gateway Center
Newton Corner, MA 02158

Region VI
(Colorado, Kansas, Montana, Nebraska, North Dakota,

South Dakota, Utah, Wyoming)
Denver Federal Center
P.O. Box 25486
Denver, CO 80225

Region VII
(Alaska)
1011 East Tudor Rd.
Anchorage, AK 99503

State Offices of the Bureau of Land Management

Alaska
701 C St.
P.O. Box 13
Anchorage, AK 99513

Arizona
2400 Valley Bank Center
Phoenix, AZ 85073

California
Federal Building
2800 Cottage Way
Sacramento, CA 94825

Colorado
Colorado State Bank Building
1600 Broadway
Denver, CO 80202

Iowa, Minnesota, Missouri, and states east of the Mississippi River
Eastern States Office
350 South Pickett St.
Alexandria, VA 22304

Idaho
Federal Building
550 West Fort St.
P.O. Box 042
Boise, ID 83724

Montana, North Dakota, South Dakota
222 North 32nd St.
P.O. Box 30157
Billings, MT 59107

Nevada
Federal Building
300 Booth St.
Reno, NV 89509

New Mexico, Oklahoma, Texas
U.S. Post Office and Federal Building
P.O. Box 1449
Santa Fe, NM 87501

Oregon, Washington
729 NE Oregon St.
P.O. Box 2965
Portland, OR 97208

Utah
University Club Building
136 East South Temple
Salt Lake City, UT 84111

Wyoming, Kansas, Nebraska
2515 Warren Ave.
P.O. Box 1828
Cheyenne, WY 82001

Regional Offices of the Water and Power Resources Service

Direct inquiries to:
Water and Power Resources Service
Department of the Interior
at any of the following locations:

Pacific Northwest Region
P.O. Box 043
U.S. Courthouse
Boise, ID 83724

Mid-Pacific Region
2800 Cottage Way
Sacramento, CA 95825

Upper Colorado Region
P.O. Box 11568
Salt Lake City, UT 84147

Upper Missouri Region
P.O. Box 2553
Billings, MT 59103

Lower Missouri Region
P.O. Box 24257, Building 20
Denver Federal Center
Denver, CO 80225

Lower Colorado Region
P.O. Box 427
Boulder City, NV 89005

Southwest Region
Commerce Building
714 South Tyler
Amarillo, TX 79101

Regional Offices of the National Forest Service

Direct inquiries to:
Regional Forester
USDA Forest Service
at any of the following locations:

Northern Region
Federal Building
Missoula, MT 59801

Rocky Mountain Region
11177 West 8th Ave.
Box 25127
Lakewood, CO 80225

Southwestern Region
517 Gold Ave., SW
Albuquerque, NM 87102

Intermountain Region
Federal Building
324 25th St.
Ogden, UT 84401

California
630 Sansome St. P.O. Box 3623
San Francisco, CA 94111

Southern Region
1720 Peachtree Rd., NW
Atlanta, GA 30309

Eastern Region
633 West Wisconsin Ave.
Milwaukee, WI 53203

Alaska
Federal Office Building
Box 1628
Juneau, AK 99801

Pacific Northwest Region
319 SW Pine St.
P.O. Box 3623
Portland, OR 97208

Directory of District Offices U.S. Army Corps of Engineers

New England
U.S. Army Engineer District, New England
424 Trapelo Rd.
Waltham, MA 02154

The Northeast
U.S. Army Engineer District, Louisville
P.O. Box 59
Louisville, KY 40201

U.S. Army Engineer District, Huntington
P.O. Box 2127
Huntington, WV 25721

U.S. Army Engineer District, Nashville
P.O. Box 1070
Nashville, TN 37202

U.S. Army Engineer District, Philadelphia
U.S. Custom House
Second and Chestnut Sts.
Philadelphia, PA 19106

U.S. Army Engineer District, Chicago
291 South Dearborn St.
Chicago, IL 60604

U.S. Army Engineer District, Detroit
P.O. Box 1027
Detroit, MI 48231

U.S. Army Engineer District, Baltimore
P.O. Box 1715
Baltimore, MD 21203

U.S. Army Engineer District, Pittsburgh
1820 Federal Building
1000 Liberty Ave.
Pittsburgh, PA 15222

U.S. Army Engineer District, Norfolk
803 Front St.
Norfolk, VA 23510

U.S Army Engineer District, Wilmington
P.O. Box 1890
Wilmington, NC 28402

U.S. Army Engineer District, St. Paul
1135 U.S. Post Office and Custom House
St. Paul, MN 55101

U.S. Army Engineer District, Buffalo
1776 Niagara St.
Buffalo, NY 14207

The Midwest
U.S. Army Engineer District, Chicago
219 South Dearborn St.
Chicago, IL 60604

U.S. Army Engineer District, Rock Island
Clock Tower Building
Rock Island, IL 61201

U.S. Army Engineer District, Kansas City
700 Federal Building
601 East 12th St.
Kansas City, MO 64106

U.S. Army Engineer District, Omaha
6014 U.S. Post Office and Court House
215 North 17th St.
Omaha, NE 68102

U.S. Army Engineer District, Little Rock
P.O. Box 867
Little Rock, AR 72203

U.S. Army Engineer District, Tulsa
P.O. Box 61
Tulsa, OK 74102

U.S. Army Engineer District, Memphis
668 Clifford Davis Federal Building
Memphis, TN 38103

U.S. Army Engineer District, St. Louis
210 North 12th St.
St. Louis, MO 63101

The Southeast
U.S. Army Engineer District, Mobile
P.O. Box 2288
Mobile, AL 36628

U.S. Army Engineer District, Vicksburg
P.O. Box 60
Vicksburg, MS 39180

U.S. Army Engineer District, Jacksonville
P.O. Box 4970
Jacksonville, FL 32201

U.S. Army Engineer District, New Orleans
P.O. Box 60267
New Orleans, LA 70160

U.S. Army Engineer District, Charleston
P.O. Box 919
Charleston, SC 29402

U.S. Army Engineer District, Savannah
P.O. Box 889
Savannah, GA 31402

The Southwest
U.S. Army Engineer District, Los Angeles
P.O. Box 2711
Los Angeles, CA 90053

U.S. Army Engineer District, Albuquerque
P.O. Box 1580
Albuquerque, NM 87103

U.S. Army Engineer District, Fort Worth
P.O. Box 17300
Fort Worth, TX 76102

U.S. Army Engineer District, Galveston
P.O. Box 1229
Galveston, TX 77553

The West
U.S. Army Engineer District, Sacramento
650 Capitol Mall
Sacramento, CA 95814

U.S. Army Engineer District, San Francisco
100 McAllister St.
San Francisco, CA 94102

U.S. Army Engineer District, Portland
P.O. Box 2964
Portland, OR 97208

U.S. Army Engineer District, Seattle
4735 East Marginal Way South
Seattle, WA 98134

U.S. Army Engineer District, Walla Walla
Building 602
City-County Airport
Walla Walla, WA 99362

U.S. Army Engineer District, Alaska
P.O. Box 7002
Anchorage, AK 99510

Chapter 10

Saving Money on Your Income Tax

Every year the United States government collects billions of dollars in income taxes from the population. In all probability, you are one of these taxpayers. And, as do most of us, you grumble about the amount you must pay and seek legal ways to reduce your tax bill. But despite your best efforts, you, like millions of other taxpayers, may be sending more money to the Internal Revenue Service than you actually owe, not because you wish to do so, but because you are unaware of *all* the exemptions and deductions to which you are entitled. This is a highly complex field, and without knowledgeable guidance, many of the tax benefits which are legally yours may be overlooked. The Internal Revenue Service will answer your queries and help you in other ways. But it does not have the staff—nor, perhaps, the inclination—to point out to you errors of omission on your tax returns. You must, therefore, protect your own interests. In this chapter, prepared with the assistance of the Internal Revenue Service and private tax experts, the major aspects of the current tax law are explained and some helpful advice is offered that may enable you to save money on your income tax. We strongly recommend careful reading. The new tax law, passed in 1981, not only cut tax rates, but liberalized many aspects of the old law. Be sure you're taking advantages of all the new benefits.

Contents

The Role of the Internal Revenue Service

The job of administering the Internal Revenue Code, collecting taxes and verifying returns is truly a Herculean one. In 1980 alone, the Internal Revenue Service (IRS) processed more than 143 million income tax returns (93 million of them from individuals), collected $519 billion in revenue and refunded more than $53 billion to the hundreds of thousands of taxpayers who had too great a proportion of their income withheld from their salaries, or had overpaid their estimated tax.

While most people think of the Internal Revenue Service as merely a tax-collecting organization, a major part of its function is to help individuals prepare their tax returns in such a way that they will pay all the money they owe, but will not overpay.

In pursuit of this goal, the IRS in 1980 answered inquiries on taxes through 102,000 written communications and some 43 million telephone calls, as well as handling about 8 million inquiries from people who walked into IRS offices. To facilitate this process, the IRS maintains a toll-free number that taxpayers may call with their questions, and also publishes numerous pamphlets that cover about every aspect of taxation from the simplest to the most complex. These pamphlets, and a helping hand from service personnel who will answer your questions, are available during the tax-filing season (January through April) at the hundreds of IRS service centers and offices established in every region of the country. In addition, many of the pamphlets are distributed through banks and post offices during that time of the year.

For the vast majority of taxpayers, the most useful of these publications is the one entitled "Your Federal Income Tax—For Individuals." It is also known as Publication 17, and is available at any IRS office, as well as at banks and post offices in the season when income taxes are due.

Who Must File a Tax Return

Most taxpayers must file income tax returns every year, but there are exceptions. Those whose incomes derive from non-taxable sources (see page 397), for example, or those whose income is less than a specified amount need not file a return.

The amount of income that an individual may receive without filing a return varies with different classifications of taxpayers. Below is a listing of these categories and the maximum amounts of income that may be earned without being required to file a tax return with the federal government.

Single persons under 65	$3,300
Single persons 65 or over	$4,300
Married couple, both under 65, filing jointly	$5,400
Married couple, one spouse 65 or over, filing jointly	$6,400
Married couple, both 65 or over, filing jointly	$7,400
Single head of household, under 65	$3,300
Single head of household, 65 or over	$4,300
Self-employed, regardless of age or marital status	$400
Married person filing separate return	$1,000
Certain surviving spouses under 65	$4,400
Certain surviving spouses 65 or over	$5,400

To qualify for either of the last two categories you must meet all of the following requirements: (1) your spouse must have died within the past three years and you did not remarry before the end of the taxable year; (2) you would have been entitled to file a joint return with your spouse in the year that he or she died (it doesn't matter whether or not you did so); (3) you have a child, stepchild or foster child who is your dependent; (4) you paid more than 50 percent of the costs of maintaining your home on behalf of that child, and the child lived there for the entire year except for short absences.

Some people who are not required to file an income tax return may find it beneficial to file one anyway. Suppose, for example, a man named Richard Anders, single, under 65 years of age, derives most of his income from non-taxable sources such as state or municipal bonds, but for a period of two months he held a job as a salesman. During this time he earned $3,000, and in compliance with the law, his employer withheld several hundred dollars to pay Anders' taxes. Because his earnings were below the taxable minimum figure of $3,300, Mr. Anders is entitled to a refund of all income tax withheld, but he will not get it back unless he files a return. In point of fact, all those who have income tax withheld should file a return even if their gross taxable income is below the limit requiring them to file. Otherwise, the IRS will never know that they are entitled to refunds.

The Deadline for Filing

Under the law, your income tax return and any amount owed should be in the mail by midnight of April 15 (or midnight of the following Monday if the 15th falls on a weekend). You may, however, secure an automatic two-month extension for filing the return—but not for paying the tax—simply by filing Form 4868. On this form, you must estimate your total tax liability for the year just past. Unless you have paid this amount in full—through withholding or quarterly estimated tax payments—you must enclose a check for the amount you owe. If it later turns out that you have underpaid by more than 10 percent, the government will impose a late-payment penalty unless you can show reasonable cause for failure to pay. In addition, interest from April 15 will be charged for any amount outstanding.

Normally, you will not be entitled to a further extension. If by June 15 you still have not submitted your tax forms, you must have a very good reason for asking for yet another extension—such as a severe illness, a death in the family or the destruction of your house by fire—or you will be charged a substantial penalty (in addition to interest on whatever money you may owe).

Failure to File a Return
One of the most dangerous things a taxpayer can do is to ignore totally the requirement that he or she file a return. Deliberate failure to file can leave the delinquent open to criminal charges at worst, or result in severe civil penalties at best. It is far better to file a return, even if you owe money and cannot immediately pay, than it is to ignore your obligation to file a return. Often you will be able to work out a schedule of payments with the IRS. By and large, the IRS will be much less punitive with those who show good faith—however delinquent they may be in submitting payments—than they will with those who attempt out-and-out evasion.

Filing Estimated Returns
Most people who are employed have federal income tax payments withheld from their paychecks. Others, however, notably the self-employed, are not required to pay withholding tax. Moreover, people who earn a part of their income from self-employment need not pay withholding tax on that portion of their earnings. Instead, the self-employed, the partially self-employed and individuals with income from interest, dividends, capital gains and similar sources must file an estimated tax return quarterly—April 15, June 15, September 15 and January 15—and with each filing pay 25 percent of what they believe they will owe the government at the end of the taxable year. If you are in a situation that requires you to make estimated tax payments, your estimate must be at least 80 percent of what your actual taxable income will be for the year. If you underestimate more than 20 percent you will be subject to a substantial penalty on the underpayment.

However, if you overpay, the government will return the excess payment to you, or you can apply the excess to next year's income tax.

You can avoid the penalty for underestimating your tax liability by paying exactly as much as you paid the year before. Should your final tax turn out to be considerably greater than the payments made, you will not, in this circumstance, be charged a penalty.

Those who earn a very small income which is not subject to withholding are not required to file quarterly returns. In 1982, for example, an individual with a total estimated tax liability of less than $200 would not be required to file quarterly. This figure was scheduled to rise by $100 per year through 1985.

Getting Help with Your Income Tax Return

According to the Internal Revenue Service, only those with complicated tax returns really need the help of professional tax preparers. The agency believes that the majority of taxpayers should be able to handle their own tax returns if they carefully follow the instructions on the forms and double-check their arithmetic, line by line.

The process of filing a tax return is made simpler by the willingness of the IRS to help in its preparation. At tax time (more or less from late January through early April) the Internal Revenue Service maintains offices all over the country where help is available. IRS employees will not fill out a person's entire form, but will

Common Errors in Filing Returns

According to the Internal Revenue Service, each year hundreds of thousands of people needlessly complicate their tax situations by making simple errors in filling out their 1040 or 1040A forms. Depending on their nature, these errors can cause a long delay in refunds due the taxpayers or, more seriously, the imposition of penalties or interest on taxes owed to the federal government. Among the most common errors are the following:

*Failure to sign the tax form, or in the case of a joint return, failure of one of the spouses to sign.

*Failure to include the taxpayer's Social Security number or the Social Security numbers of both taxpayers in a joint return.

*Failure to attach all W-2 forms. (These are the forms received from all employers who have withheld income for tax purposes.)

*Simple mathematical errors. (These will be caught by the computers of the IRS but, like other errors, may result in costly delays for the taxpayer.)

*Deducting state-imposed fees—such as fishing and driving licenses, car registration charges and the like—as if they were taxes.

*Use of the wrong tax table. Often single people who have no dependents, for example, will file as the head of a household because they are under the mistaken impression that owning a house puts them in that category. Remember, in order to qualify as head of a household, you must provide more than 50 percent support and maintain a residence for a dependent relative. To qualify as the head of a household, you must pay more than 50 percent of the cost of a residence for an unmarried child or grandchild. In the case of other relatives you must provide 50 percent of the individual's support and maintain a residence for that person.

*Deducting total medical expenses. By law, deductions for medical expenses are allowable only for that portion of the expenses that amounts to more than 3 percent of the taxable income.

*Failure to report all taxable income, such as income from interest—except interest derived from All-Savers Certificates purchased before January 1, 1983 (page 414).

provide information that relates to specific problems.

In spite of such services, however, millions of taxpayers prefer to have their returns prepared by experts. It is important to pick the "expert" carefully, because there are all degrees of expertise. Tax preparers may be merely those who have taken a short course in the subject and work out of storefronts only at tax time, or they may be accountants, certified public accountants (CPAs) or tax lawyers.

Obviously, the more complicated your tax return—that is, the more deductions you claim, the more sources of income you have—the greater will be your need for professional assistance. By and large, if your income derives overwhelmingly from wages and if your deductions are common—such as interest on your mortgage or taxes on your home—a storefront tax preparer may be adequate for your needs, or you may be able to prepare your own return. However, you should try to make certain that the storefront concern is not a fly-by-night operation, and that if there is a question about your taxes posed by the IRS, a representative of the firm will be available to help you deal with an audit.

Generally speaking, a tax-preparation concern with nationwide or statewide offices can be relied upon. If your return is complicated—with income deriving from a number of sources, and deductions or credits based upon complex factors such as tax shelters or partial support of aged parents—you may find it worthwhile to consult a CPA or other professional, even though the fee may be high. Tax lawyers, however, are usually consulted only by corporations or by individuals with very large incomes and complex finances.

New Tax Rates Under the Act of 1981

For the vast majority of taxpayers, the primary significance of the Tax Act of 1981 is the substantial reduction of tax rates. The reduction is to be phased in over a three-year period that began in October 1981 and will continue through 1984. At the end of this time, tax rates will have gone down about 23 percent below the 1981 rates. Because this is an across-the-board reduction in *rates*, rather than in actual amounts, those in the upper middle and highest tax brackets will, of course, benefit most. For example, a family of four, dependent upon a single wage earner whose income was $10,000 before exemptions, paid $378 in income taxes in 1980. In the four years to follow, the cumulative reduction would be: $5 in 1981; $52 in 1982; $78 in 1983; and $83 in 1984. If this family's circumstances remain unchanged between 1980 and 1984, their income tax bill will be reduced from $378 to $295 at the end of the four years.

Now let's take a look at a family at the other end of the financial scale, with one wage earner and four dependents. This time the breadwinner has an income before exemptions of $100,000. In 1980, the taxpayer paid $41,998 in federal income taxes. In 1981 this person's taxes were reduced by $525; in 1982 they are reduced by an additional $4,024; in 1983, by another $3,259 and 1984, by an additional $1,790. Thus, in 1984, the tax bill will be $32,400. Or take a single wage earner in the middle range. Suppose this person had an income of $50,000 in 1980. The income tax came to $18,067 for that year. In 1984, if we can cast an eye into the future, this person's income is exactly the same, but the federal income tax will be reduced by $4,178, for a total payment to the IRS of $13,889. On pages 392 and 393 are two tables showing how taxes are being reduced for people in various income groups and family situations.

Tax Indexing: A Money-Saving Innovation

One of the major reforms of the tax act of 1981 has been to index (i.e., adjust) tax rates, personal exemptions and the standard deduction (now called the "zero bracket amount") to inflation. This indexing does not begin until

1985, after the across-the-board tax rate reductions are fully in effect. The result of this measure will be to prevent people who have received cost-of-living adjustments in their salaries from being pushed into higher income-tax brackets, when, in reality, the increases in their incomes merely keep pace with inflation.

To cite an example: suppose a man we shall call George Brown, a computer programmer, has a salary of $25,000 in 1985. That year inflation runs at 10 percent and George's boss gives him a commensurate salary increase—$2,500—to enable him to keep pace with the cost of living. Without tax-bracket indexing, George's salary increase would push him into a higher tax bracket and his raise would therefore be significantly reduced. Through tax indexing, George will remain in the same bracket he was in the year before, and his standard of living, while not improving, will not be reduced. To put it another way, if in 1985 a single person earning $25,000 is in the 30 percent bracket, and the cost of living that year increases 10 percent, the 30 percent bracket will increase with it, and in 1985 the wage earner will be able to earn $27,500 and remain in that bracket.

Other Major Changes of the Tax Act of 1981

Aside from the lowering of personal income taxes and the forthcoming tax-bracket indexing measure, the tax act of 1981 includes a number of other reforms, some of which will be discussed in considerable detail later in this chapter. Among these are:

The Marriage Penalty. In certain circumstances, married couples have been paying higher taxes than they would be liable for if they had remained single. The penalty occurs when both spouses hold paying jobs and their salaries are roughly equal. To get around this penalty, various stratagems have been employed. Some couples have even traveled to places like the Dominican Republic to secure a "quickie" divorce at the end of the year, only to

remarry at the beginning of the next. Such tactics have been declared illegal when the purpose of the divorce is merely to lower a tax obligation. However, Congress has acknowledged the anger of married couples over this type of tax discrimination, and in the tax bill of 1981, legislation was included to lessen the effects of the marriage penalty. The new tax law allows the spouse with the lower income to deduct from his or her salary up to 10 percent, up to a maximum of $3,000, thus lowering the couple's bracket on a joint return. (For 1982 only, the figure was set at 5 percent, or $1,500, whichever is lower.) If a married couple in 1983 has a joint income of $30,000, of which $16,000 is earned by one spouse and $14,000 by the other, the spouse with the lower income can reduce his or her reported income by $1,400. In figuring this deduction, only income from such sources as wages, fees or commissions may be counted. Income from interest and dividends may not be used.

Interest and Dividends. Under the tax law in effect until 1981, the maximum tax rate on unearned income such as interest and dividends was 70 percent. Beginning in 1982, the maximum income tax rate—which affects *all* classes of income—has been reduced to 50 percent. As before, however, the actual amount you will pay will depend upon your tax bracket.

Capital Gains. Before the new tax legislation, if you made long-term capital gains, say through the sale of a stock that had been in your possession for more than a year, you could have been charged a tax of up to 28 percent on your profit. The new law limits taxes on long-term capital gains to 20 percent. Short-term gains are taxed as ordinary income.

Pensions. A major reform of the 1981 tax law broadens eligibility requirements for setting up Individual Retirement Accounts (IRAs) (see Chapter 2). In addition, the amount individuals are allowed to contribute to such accounts in any one year was raised from $1,500 to

Current Federal Income Tax Rates

The tax reform act of 1981 mandated the largest tax cut in American history, an across the board 25 percent reduction spread out over a period of three years. The results of this reduction as seen in the charts on these pages are dramatic, with people in every income group and every filing status benefiting. For example, a single person whose taxable income remains constant at $28,000 between 1981 and 1984 will see his or her income tax reduced in those four years from $7,341 to $5,705; a married couple, with a taxable income of $29,900, who file jointly, will have their taxes reduced, during those same years from $6,123 to $4,790. The tables reproduced here show the savings that people in a variety of income levels and filing statuses can expect in the years to come.

SINGLE INDIVIDUALS

If taxable income exceeds this base amount	But does not exceed this amount	1982		1983		1984 and after	
		You pay this amount	PLUS this % of the excess over the base amount	You pay this amount	PLUS this % of the excess over the base amount	You pay this amount	PLUS this % of the excess over the base amount
0	2,300	0		0		0	
2,300	3,400	0	12	0	11	0	11
3,400	4,400	132	14	121	13	121	12
4,400	6,500	272	16	251	15	241	14
6,500	8,500	608	17	566	15	535	15
8,500	10,800	948	19	866	17	835	16
10,800	12,900	1,385	22	1,257	19	1,203	18
12,900	15,000	1,847	23	1,656	21	1,581	20
15,000	18,200	2,330	27	2,097	24	2,001	23
18,200	23,500	3,194	31	2,965	28	2,737	26
23,500	28,800	4,837	35	4,349	32	4,115	30
28,800	34,100	6,692	40	6,045	36	5,705	34
34,100	41,500	8,812	44	7,963	40	7,507	38
41,500	55,300	12,068	50	10,913	45	10,319	42
55,300	81,800	*		17,123	50	16,115	48
81,800	108,300	*		*		28,835	50
108,300		*		*		*	

HEADS OF HOUSEHOLDS

If taxable income exceeds this base amount	But does not exceed this amount	1982		1983		1984 and after	
		You pay this amount	PLUS %	You pay this amount	PLUS %	You pay this amount	PLUS %
0	2,300	0		0		0	
2,300	4,400	0	12	0	11	0	11
4,400	6,500	252	14	231	11	231	11
6,500	8,700	546	16	504	15	483	14
8,700	11,800	898	20	834	18	791	17
11,800	15,000	1,518	22	1,392	19	1,318	18
15,000	18,000	2,222	23	2,000	21	1,894	20
18,000	23,500	2,958	28	2,672	25	2,534	24
23,500	28,800	4,442	32	3,997	29	3,806	28
28,800	34,100	6,138	38	5,534	34	5,290	32
34,100	44,700	8,152	41	7,336	37	6,986	35
44,700	60,600	12,498	49	11,258	44	10,696	42

Head of Households continued

If taxable income exceeds this base amount	But does not exceed this base amount	1982		1983		1984 and after	
		You pay this amount	PLUS this % of the excess over the base amount	You pay this amount	PLUS this % of the excess over the base amount	You pay this amount	PLUS this % of the excess over the base amount
60,600	81,800	20,289	50	18,254	48	17,374	45
81,800	108,300	*		28,430	50	26,914	48
108,300	161,300	*		*		39,632	50
161,300		*		*		*	

MARRIED INDIVIDUALS FILING JOINT RETURNS AND SURVIVING SPOUSES

		1982		1983		1984 and after	
0	3,400	0		0		0	
3,400	5,400	0	12	0	11	0	11
5,500	7,600	252	14	231	13	231	12
7,600	11,900	546	16	504	15	483	14
11,900	16,000	1,234	19	1,149	17	1,085	16
16,000	20,200	2,013	22	1,846	19	1,741	18
20,200	24,600	2,937	25	2,644	23	2,497	22
24,600	29,900	4,037	29	3,656	26	3,465	25
29,900	35,200	5,574	33	5,034	30	4,790	28
35,200	45,800	7,323	39	6,624	35	6,274	33
45,800	60,000	11,457	44	10,334	40	9,772	38
60,000	85,600	17,705	49	16,014	44	15,168	42
85,600	109,400	30,249	50	27,278	48	25,920	45
109,400	162,400	*		38,702	50	36,630	49
162,400	215,400	*		*		62,600	50
215,400		*		*		*	

MARRIED INDIVIDUALS FILING SEPARATE RETURNS

		1982		1983		1984 and after	
0	1,700	0		0		0	
1,700	2,750	0	12	0	11	0	11
2,750	3,800	126	14	115	13	115	12
3,800	5,950	273	16	252	15	241	14
5,950	8,000	617	19	574	17	542	16
8,000	10,100	1,006	22	923	19	870	18
10,100	12,300	1,468	25	1,322	23	1,248	22
12,300	14,950	2,018	29	1,828	26	1,732	25
14,950	17,600	2,787	33	2,517	30	2,395	28
17,600	22,900	3,661	39	3,312	35	3,137	33
22,900	30,000	5,728	44	5,167	40	4,886	38
30,000	42,800	8,852	49	8,007	44	7,584	42
42,800	54,700	15,124	50	13,639	48	12,960	45
54,700	81,200	*		19,351	50	18,315	49
81,200	107,700	*		*		31,300	50
107,700		*		*		*	

*Starting in 1982, the maximum income tax rate is reduced to 50%

$2,000. Similarly, allowable contributions to Keogh Plan retirement accounts—deferred tax programs for the self-employed (see page 414)—have also been raised from a maximum of $7,500 to one of $15,000.

Gifts. Before the tax changes of 1981, there was a limit of $3,000 on how much any one person could give, tax free, to another person in a year. This limit was raised to $10,000. A major purpose of this reform is to help parents and grandparents save for their children's higher education (see pages 410–413). Also, there is no longer any limitation on tax-free gifts used to pay medical expenses or college tuition costs.

Estates. Under the old law, gross estates worth more than $175,625 were subject to federal taxes. The new law, phased in over a period of several years, will make gross estates worth up to $600,000 free of federal taxes.

Tax-Free Interest. Individuals purchasing All-Savers Certificates can earn up to $1,000 in tax-free interest; couples filing a joint return can earn up to $2,000 under the All-Savers program (see page 414). To benefit, investors must purchase a one-year certificate on or before December 31, 1982.

Earnings Abroad. Americans who live and work abroad are among the principal beneficiaries of the new tax legislation. Henceforth, they need not pay U.S. income taxes on the first $75,000 of their foreign earnings. The amount will be raised in yearly increments to a maximum of $96,000 in 1986. Employees of the U.S. government do not qualify.

The Short Form Versus the Long Form

IRS Form 1040A, commonly known as the "short form," is an extremely simple question-naire, consisting of only one page, and may be used by millions of taxpayers. Not everyone, however, should use the short form or is qualified by law to use it.

Who May Use the Short Form

Only single persons or couples filing jointly with taxable incomes of less than $50,000 may use this form, provided all of their income derives from wages, tips, interest, dividends, unemployment compensation and commissions. If, for example, your income is under $50,000, but a portion of it—even a small portion—derives from a capital gain, you are barred from using the short form. Another bar to the use of the short form is ownership of an Individual Retirement Account or a Keogh Plan retirement account (see page 414). In addition, if you have a large number of deductions you wish to claim, the short form would probably cost you money, and the effort involved in filling out the long form (1040) will be worthwhile. For the short form allows only a standard deduction of $2,300 for a single taxpayer and $3,400 for married taxpayers filing jointly. These deductions are built into the tax tables used by those employing the short form. There is, however, one itemized deduction you can now take on the short form. In addition to the standard deduction, you may itemize a portion of your charitable contributions and deduct a percentage of the amount you contributed (see pages 401–402). The standard deduction should not be confused with exemptions, however. All taxpayers, no matter what form they use, are entitled to $1,000 in exemptions for themselves and for each dependent.

By and large, the short form really makes sense only for those with extremely simple tax situations. For example, suppose a young man named Clyde Chapin, recently out of school and working in his first job as a clerk in a shoestore, earned a salary of $11,000 in 1981. He had no other source of income, and being a healthy young man, had medical expenses amounting to only $86. Search though he might through the IRS regulations, he could find no other deductions that applied to him. Therefore, he decided to take his automatic deduction of $2,300. Though he could take this deduction on the long form as well as the short, in Mr. Chapin's situation it made no sense to fill out the more complicated return.

It might be instructive, however, to look at a situation which is superficially similar but actually very different. Clyde Chapin has a friend named Carla Thomas. Carla, too, is just out of school; she works as a receptionist and earns $13,000 a year. Like Clyde, Carla is unmarried and has no dependents. But she has inherited a house on which the mortgage still has many years to run. In 1981, Carla paid $1,700 in interest on that mortgage and an additional $1,200 in property taxes. In addition, Carla had medical expenses of over $1,500 and paid $705 in interest on an education loan. All these items are perfectly legal deductions on her income tax. Were Carla to use the short form, she would only be allowed the $2,300 standard deduction. Her deductions, however, amount to $5,105. Therefore, she would be most unwise to use the short form instead of the long form, on which she is permitted to itemize each deduction.

If you have any doubts at all about using the short form—even though you are legally entitled to do so—use the long form instead. There is nothing you can do with the short form that you cannot do with the long, but there is much you cannot do with Form 1040A that you can with Form 1040.

The 1040 Form

Anyone with a significant number of deductions or credits, or even a small number in which the monetary amounts are significant, will find it to his or her advantage to file the long form (1040). For example, the vast majority of homeowners should file the 1040 rather than the 1040A because both their real estate taxes and the interest on their mortgages are deductible expenses. The choice between forms is not always available to the taxpayer, however. The Internal Revenue Code requires that millions of people whose income, in whole or in part, derives from certain sources must file the long form. Among them are:

*Those whose taxable income exceeds $50,000 for an individual or a couple filing jointly.

*Those who have income from such sources as a private pension, the sale of property (including the sale of a home) or from alimony, barter or self-employment.

You must also file the long form if:

*You and your spouse file separate returns, and one of you itemizes deductions; the other must do so as well.

*You are single but list four or more exemptions, or married but filing a separate return.

*You claim nine or more exemptions and you are the head of a household.

*You claim a deduction for a payment to an IRA or to a Keogh Plan.

*You claim 10 or more exemptions and you are married and filing a joint return.

*You wish to itemize deductions.

*Your income requires you to file an estimated return (see page 388).

*You pay estimated tax and wish to apply a refund due you against the next year's tax.

*You wish to compute your tax on the basis of income averaging (see page 410).

*You have filed Form 4868—an application for an automatic delay in filing your tax forms.

Exemptions You May Claim

The number of dependents you claim (people meeting certain relationship requirements to whom you contribute more than half of their financial support) can materially affect your income taxes. You are allowed at least a $1,000 deduction from your income for each exemption. (In some cases, as shown below, the exemption amounts that you can claim for yourself and your spouse can be doubled to $2,000 or tripled to $3,000.) In order to claim someone other than yourself as an exemption, the following rules must be met: (1) you contribute more than 50 percent to that person's support; (2) the person you are claiming as an exemption cannot have a taxable income in excess of $1,000 (children you support who have not reached the age of 19 in the year, or who are full-time students are exempt from this rule); (3) if the person you claim as an exemption is not a close relative, he or she must reside with you for the full year; (4) the person claimed as an exemption must be a U.S. citizen or a resident of the United States during some part of the year in which the exemption is claimed (an exception is made for people who are residents of Canada or Mexico); (5) by and large, you cannot claim an exemption for a person who files a joint tax return with someone else. For example, if your son marries while he is still in college and you continue to provide more than 50 percent of his support, his status as a dependent will be lost if he files a joint return with his wife. An exception to this rule permits your son to file a joint return if his purpose is merely to claim a refund.

The most common exemptions that may be claimed are as follows:

*A personal exemption for yourself. If you are blind or age 65 or older, your exemption doubles. If both conditions pertain, your exemption triples.

*An exemption for your spouse, if you are filing a joint return. If your spouse is legally blind or age 65 or over, the same rule as above applies. Thus an aged couple, both of whom are legally blind, can claim $6,000 worth of exemptions. It must be emphasized that you cannot claim an old-age or blindness exemption for anyone other than yourself and your spouse. If, for example, you have a parent whom you claim as a dependent, you cannot double the exemption because that parent is 65 or over or is blind.

*A dependency exemption for each child 19 years old or younger. You may claim a full year's exemption for a child even if he or she was born at one minute to midnight on December 31. There is no limit to how much a

child whom you support may earn—if that child is 19 or under—and still be considered a dependent. (However, if the child earns enough, he or she will have to file an income tax return.)

*An exemption for a child over 19 is legal if he or she is a full-time student. However, to claim the exemption you must continue to provide more than half of the child's support.

*You can claim an exemption for each parent or parent-in-law for whom you provide more than 50 percent support. In cases where several children share the burden of supporting their parents and no one child meets the 50 percent support test, the law allows you to rotate the exemptions among the children who provide the support. For example, if a couple in their 70s have four grown children, each of whom provides 25 percent of their support, one year one of the children may claim the exemption, the next year the second child, and so forth. Whoever does claim the exemption for a particular year must contribute at least 10 percent to the support of the parents. Every other person who contributed 10 percent or more must file a multiple-support form with their 1040 form and state that he or she will not claim the exemption for that year.

*You can claim an exemption for anyone who lives with you for the entire year (except for temporary absences such as vacations), provided the relationship is not an illicit one under local law. Unmarried couples, for example, may be considered to be maintaining an illicit relationship, and one may not claim the other as an exemption. However, if a non-relative is living with you whose taxable income is under $1,000 and for whom you provide more than 50 percent support, you may claim that person as an exemption, provided the relationship is not an illicit one.

Itemizing Your Deductions

For a great many people the option of itemizing deductions results in considerable savings

Tax-Free Income

Many sources of income are free from federal income tax, in whole or in part, though some of these sources may be taxed on the local or state level. Among the most common income sources that do not fall under the income-taxing authority of the federal government are:

*Some state-operated unemployment compensation payments.

*Welfare payments.

*Social Security payments or railroad retirement benefits.

*Some profits from the sale of a house, under certain conditions (see page 400).

*Veterans' benefits.

*Private-plan retirement benefits based on employee contributions, on which taxes were paid at the time the contributions were made. (In effect, the beneficiary is merely getting his own money back.)

*Generally, income derived from a health or accident insurance policy.

*Up to $100 a week in sick pay, provided the beneficiary's adjusted gross income does not exceed $15,000 and the beneficiary has retired on disability and is under 65.

*Gifts. The person who receives a gift need not pay a tax on it, but in some instances, the person donating the gift will be taxed (see pages 415–416).

*Inheritances, though very large estates may be subject to the federal inheritance tax.

*Interest on all municipal and state bonds.

*Interest on All-Savers Certificates (see page 414).

*Money received for personal injury through a judicial procedure or as a result of an insurance company payment.

*A limited amount of income earned in a foreign country, though this will probably be taxed by the government of that country (see page 394).

*Refunds on your federal income tax, though not on state or local income taxes.

*Money derived from a life insurance policy paid to a beneficiary is not taxable as income, though it may be taxable as an inheritance.

*Generally, fellowships and scholarships, unless the recipient is required to perform a job in exchange for the stipend.

on their income tax. If you fill out the long form, you have the choice of itemizing or taking the standard deduction (now called the zero bracket amount) of $2,300 for a single taxpayer or a single head of household, or the $3,400 deduction for a married couple filing jointly. Whether you will want to itemize or take the zero bracket amount depends, of course, entirely on which benefits you more. The amount you save through itemized deductions depends on how large those deductions are and on your tax bracket. For example, if you are in the 30 percent bracket and you have $1,000 in deductions over the zero bracket amount, you will save 30 percent, or $300, on your tax bill if you itemize. If you are in a lower bracket, your savings will be less; if you are in a higher bracket, they will be greater.

There are literally hundreds of possible deductions, ranging from the interest a homeowner pays on a mortgage to certain narrowly defined educational expenses. Below are listed a number of typical deductions, together with information concerning how and when they may be employed.

Medical Deductions

These include not only fees to physicians, nurses, optometrists, dentists, psychologists and other health professionals, but all kinds of unreimbursed expenses relating to the health of the taxpayer and his or her family, such as most hospital bills (room, board, tests, etc., but not personal expenses such as phone bills or television rental) and transportation to and from a medical facility.

Prescription Medicines. Expenditures for prescription drugs must exceed 1 percent of your adjusted gross income in order to be tax deductible. Your adjusted gross income is the amount you have left after taking your exemptions and deducting business expenses, IRA or Keogh contributions (pages 413–414) and allowable moving expenses. If, for example, your adjusted gross income is $20,000, 1 percent of your adjusted gross income is $200. Any amount above that figure that you paid out for prescription medicines is deductible, provided that your total medical expenses exceed 3 percent of your adjusted gross income—in this case, $600. For example, John Harmon, a single taxpayer, had an adjusted gross income of $20,000 and paid $300 for prescription drugs in 1981. The first $200 of that amount would not be tax deductible, and normally the last $100 would be a legal deduction. However, Mr. Harmon's total medical expenses for the year came to less than $600— 3 percent of his adjusted gross income—and therefore he was not permitted to deduct the $100 for prescription drugs. Had his total medical expenses exceeded the 3 percent cutoff, his $100 deduction would have been allowed.

Doctors' and Nurses' Bills. All unreimbursed expenses for such items as doctor's bills, nursing care, physical therapy and the like are deductible when the total amount expended comes to more than 3 percent of your adjusted gross income. Remember, you must subtract from these expenditures whatever reimbursements you received from medical and hospital insurance policies.

Premiums for Medical Insurance. Half of the first $300 you spend on medical insurance is deductible without reference to the 3 percent rule. Any expenditures beyond this amount may be deducted only if your total medical expenses exceed 3 percent of your adjusted gross income.

The Range of Medical Deductions. A great many medical deductions, such as visits to a physician or hospital bills, are obvious, but there are a number of other legal deductions related to health care that may not occur to many taxpayers. Among them are:

*Travel for the purpose of health care, such as going to another city to visit a clinic, consult another physician or attend a rehabilitation center. If you use your own car for such a purpose, you may deduct nine cents a mile as well as highway tolls and the cost of parking your car. Keep a diary of such expenditures to back up your assertions in case you are challenged by the IRS. However, you may not deduct depreciation on your automobile that results from health care expenses.

*In addition to the fees of ordinary physicians and specialists with M.D. degrees, you may also deduct the fees of psychologists, chiropractors, optometrists, acupuncturists and Christian Science practitioners. Also deductible is the cost of services provided by registered and practical nurses, as well as anyone else who provides nursing care. If that person is working in your home you may deduct the cost of lodging and feeding him or her.

*You may deduct the cost of elective surgery even if, as in the case of a face-lift, it is performed only for cosmetic purposes.

*You may deduct the cost of treatment at rehabilitation facilities for alcoholism and drug addiction. Expenses for food and lodging at these facilities are also deductible.

*In addition to prescription drugs, the cost of non-prescription medicines such as aspirin or even vitamins—when recommended by a physician to alleviate a specific condition—is deductible. Vitamins taken for general health reasons may not be deducted, nor may other drugstore items such as toothpaste, shaving cream or cosmetics.

*In addition to such policies as those issued by Blue Cross and Blue Shield, major medical insurance, policies that cover the cost of prescription drugs, dental insurance plans, membership fees in pre-paid medical plans—such as Health Maintenance Organizations—and the monthly premium medical plan portion of Medicare (for which beneficiaries pay a monthly premium) all qualify for deductions. If you are supporting a child at college and he or she is charged a medical insurance premium as a part of the institution's fees, this expense is also deductible.

You may not, however, deduct premiums on life insurance policies, even when they include benefits for such conditions as the loss of sight or a limb, nor does a policy that pays you an income during a hospital stay qualify as a deduction.

Nursing home care is deductible in some circumstances and non-deductible in others. If the expenses related to staying in a nursing home are attributable to medical care, a deduction is permitted. If, on the other hand, the purpose of a stay was mainly residential, only those expenses directly related to medical care may be deducted.

*The cost of certain medically necessary equipment and personal accessories—such as eyeglasses, false teeth, artificial limbs, hearing aids, wheelchairs and the like—is deductible. If you or a member of your family are handicapped and require a specially equipped car, a portion of the car's cost is deductible. If you are blind, the cost of purchasing and maintaining a seeing-eye dog is deductible, as is a portion of the cost of books and publications written in Braille.

*If you have a handicapped child, the cost of special schooling or tutoring is deductible, provided that the reason for attending the school or receiving the tutoring is to lessen the effects of the handicap.

Among the items that may be beneficial medically, but are *not* tax deductible are the following:

*The cost of a trip undertaken to improve one's general health, even when recommended by a physician.

*General household help, even under circumstances where a physical condition bars you from performing ordinary household tasks.

*Fees for joining and using the facilities of health clubs, country clubs and other such organizations, even though membership may improve your general well-being.

In addition, the cost of engaging in sports or social activities for the purpose of improving health is a non-deductible item.

*You may not deduct the cost of a baby nurse staying at your house, if the newborn is a healthy child. Moreover, the fee charged by a baby-sitter whose presence allows you to secure medical treatment for yourself is not considered a deductible expense.

Deductions for Homeowners

Even in a time of runaway real estate prices, super-high mortgage rates and ever-increasing real estate assessments, there remain significant tax advantages to home ownership—advantages that can greatly reduce actual living expenses. To a considerable degree, the value of these advantages is dependent upon the homeowner's tax bracket. By and large, the higher the bracket, the more impressive the savings. Below are some of the major advantages of home ownership.

Real Estate Taxes and Interest Paid on a Mortgage. Both are deductible from your federal income tax. If, for example, you spend $2,000 for local real estate taxes and an additional $3,000 in mortgage interest during the calendar year and you are in the 30 percent bracket, your actual cost for these two items will be $3,500, or 70 percent of the total expenditure of $5,000. Should your tax bracket be higher, your savings will be greater; should it be lower, your savings will be less. This benefit applies to vacation houses as well as primary residences. In other words, if you own a weekend retreat, mortgage interest and real estate taxes are deductible in both instances.

Deferring Capital Gains. You will not be charged a capital-gains tax on profits from the sale of your house if you invest the proceeds (all money realized, including profit) in another house within a period of two years. This benefit, however, applies only to a primary residence. Should you sell your vacation house at a profit, you will be liable for a capital-gains tax. For example: Richard and Helen Kent, when they were newly married many years ago, bought their first house for $19,000. Three years later they sold it for $24,000, making a profit of $5,000. Normally that profit would have been taxed as a capital gain, but because they bought another house a year later for more than $24,000, they did not have to pay a capital-gains tax.

The Kents remained in their new house for many years—until 1975. During that time, real estate values soared, and when they sold their second house they realized a profit of $50,000. This time, they immediately invested the entire proceeds in yet another house, this one costing $100,000. Again they were not obliged to pay a tax on their earnings. In 1979, however, the Kents sold again, this time for $120,000, and instead of buying yet another house they decided to rent an apartment. They now became liable for a capital-gains tax on the sum total of the profits they made in the various real estate operations over the years. This was because neither Mr. nor Mrs. Kent was yet 55 years old. If one of them had reached that age, they would have benefited from a one-time exclusion from capital gains for house sellers.

Under this special provision of the law, a homeowner who is 55 years old or older is permitted to exclude the profits from the sale of his or her home from capital gains, even if the profit is not reinvested in a new home. This is a one-time exclusion, and the maximum profit that can be retained without paying a capital-gains tax is $125,000. In instances where a house is jointly owned by a husband and wife, only one of the parties need be 55 or older to take advantage of the exclusion. Once this benefit is used, it may not be used again, even if the total amount of profit excluded from capital gains is far below $125,000.

To take an example: When Jim Harkness was 65 and his wife, Emma, was 60, the couple decided to sell their house in Wellington, Ohio, and move to a condominium in Sarasota, Florida. The Wellington house had cost the Harknesses $50,000 and they sold it for $100,000. Because their mortgage was paid off years earlier, their total proceeds were $100,000. The condominium they bought in Sarasota cost $75,000. Normally, the $25,000 profit would have been subject to a capital-gains tax, but the Harknesses decided to take advantage of the one-time exclusion. After a year of living in their condominium in Sarasota they decided to move down the coast to Fort Myers. This time they sold their residence for $95,000 and bought a smaller condominium for $60,000. They thought that since they had excluded only $25,000 from capital gains on their previous sale, they could now exclude the profit from the sale of their Sarasota residence, because the total profit from the two real estate deals was under $125,000. To their sorrow, the IRS disallowed their claim for a second exclusion on the grounds that, no matter how small the profit was when the exclusion was originally taken, the law specifically barred the use of the exclusion more than once.

Another aspect of the one-time exclusion is that it applies to both the husband and wife. A married couple may use the exclusion only once. If *either* of them has claimed it prior to their marriage, they are no longer eligible. This is a point that may easily be misunderstood. An example will help to clarify the situation. Suppose that shortly after the Harknesses bought their Fort Myers home, Mr. Harkness died. A year later Emma Harkness married a man named Paul Jaspers, who also owned a residence in Fort Myers. After the marriage, Mr. Jaspers, who had never taken advantage of the one-time exclusion, sold his home at a handsome profit and moved in with his wife. When Mr. Jaspers attempted to apply the one-time exclusion from capital gains on the sale of his home, the IRS disallowed the claim because his wife had already benefited from the exclusion. Had Mr. Jaspers sold his home before remarrying, he would have been entitled to the exclusion.

Uncollectible Personal Debts

Money owed you that is uncollectible may be a valid deduction under some circumstances. You must be able to prove the debt was a real one and that you made every reasonable effort to collect. Here's an example: Suppose Jane Calvert lent her brother-in-law, Carl Smithers, $5,000 to be repaid within a year. The money was to be used to help Mr. Smithers buy a fast-food franchise. As Mrs. Calvert was lending the money within the family, she did not bother to write up a contract, or to formalize the terms of repayment in writing. Mr. Smithers bought his fast-food franchise, but through misman-agement it quickly went bankrupt. Beset by creditors, Carl Smithers informed his sister-in-law that he would not be able to repay the money he owed her. Having sufficient funds of her own, Jane Calvert decided that she would not pursue her brother-in-law, but instead write off the debt on her income tax. To her chagrin, the IRS disallowed the deduction on the grounds that there was no proof the debt ever existed and that, even if it had, a deduction was not allowable because Mrs. Calvert had made no effort to collect the money that was owed her.

Mrs. Calvert might have protected herself had she drawn up a contract of indebtedness with her brother-in-law specifying the amount of the loan and the terms of repayment. Still, she would not have been permitted the deduction unless she could have proved that she had made every reasonable effort to collect the money due her. This would have involved, at the very least, letters from a lawyer to Carl Smithers demanding repayment and, quite

possibly, the institution of legal proceedings. The IRS's position is a perfectly simple one. The government should not be financially penalized for a bad debt unless the lender can prove good-faith efforts to collect the money owed him or her.

Charitable Contributions

Money or goods that you contribute to quali-fied charitable organizations—groups created and operated exclusively for religious, chari-table, scientific, literary or educational purposes—constitute valid deductions, but complications can arise. The safest kind of charitable contribution is one made by check, which can be validated both by the check and a receipt. Contributions of cash for which no receipt has been given may be disallowed by the IRS. For example, if you belong to a tax-exempt organization like Alcoholics Anony-mous, which raises money for its operating expenses by passing the basket at meetings, you would be better advised to write out a check for your donation—even if that requires you to write several $1 checks per visit—than to put a handful of change into the basket. Though it is unlikely that the IRS is going to challenge deductions for a moderate amount in cash contributions, you will have nothing to show for your donations if an auditor chooses to do so.

Another area that can cause a degree of dif-ficulty is a contribution for which you receive some compensation in the form of goods or ser-vices. For example, suppose Mrs. Lillian Smith decides to become a member of her local muse-um—a qualifying tax-free organization—con-tributions to which may, in some circum-stances, be considered as charitable donations. For $25 Mrs. Smith receives a year's basic membership. In exchange for this fee, she is allowed reduced-price admissions to the muse-um's special shows, entry into its members' dining room, a 15 percent discount on items sold in the institution's gift shop and advance notice of concerts and recitals to be held in the museum's auditorium. Were Mrs. Smith to

A Sophisticated Technique for Giving

One way that sophisticated and wealthy taxpayers frequently use to maximize their charitable gifts at the smallest cost to themselves is to donate appreciated stocks. Here is how it works: suppose Walter Miller bought 10 shares of a stock in a corporation at $10 per share. He held the stock for more than a year (to employ this technique the securities must be held for at least one year and a day) and the value of the stock rose to $100 per share. At that point, Mr. Miller donated the stock to his church, a qualifying charitable organization. Mr. Miller was able to take a deduction based upon the appreciated value of the stock ($1,000), and neither he or the church was liable for a capital gains tax.

However, if Mr. Miller had sold the stock, then donated $1,000 to his church, he would still have been able to claim the income tax deduction, but he would have been required to pay a capital gains tax on the $900 profit he made on the stock.

attempt to declare her $25 membership fee a charitable contribution, it is very unlikely that the IRS would allow it. But suppose Mrs. Smith decides that, instead of taking out a basic membership, she will become a sustaining member of the museum at $100 per year. If her sustaining membership gives her no additional privileges beyond those of the basic membership, she will be within her rights to deduct $75—the difference in cost between the basic membership ($25) and the sustaining one ($100)—as a charitable contribution.

Another area of frequent contention between the IRS and the taxpayer consists of contributions that take the form of property rather than money. The IRS allows a deduction based on a fair evaluation of the goods contributed. Suppose Mrs. Smith, during the course of 1981, made two such contributions. The first was to a local charity that collects old clothes for the poor. Mrs. Smith contributed a large pile of clothing to this group and, for tax purposes, placed an evaluation of $30 on her donation. Though the IRS can challenge this, as a practical matter they are unlikely to do so unless there are a number of contributions of this sort by Mrs. Smith that add up to a significant sum.

If a taxpayer claims the contribution is worth more than $200, however, verifying data must be submitted with the tax return. Suppose, for example, that Mrs. Smith contributed a valuable painting to the local museum. She placed an evaluation of $12,000 on the work and then claimed that amount as a lawful charitable deduction. Because Mrs. Smith is claiming a large deduction, she must submit, along with her 1040 form, data verifying the value of the painting. In the absence of any independent verification of the monetary worth of the painting, the IRS is certain to call Mrs. Smith in for an audit and challenge the deduction. The point here is that Mrs. Smith should have had an independent evaluation (itself a tax-deductible expense) made of the worth of her painting by a recognized art appraiser. The IRS might still challenge the $12,000 figure through an evaluation made by an appraiser in its employ. But even were that to happen, Mrs. Smith would have a reasonable basis on which to pursue her claim.

Under the tax law passed in 1981, a portion of charitable deductions may be claimed even by those who take the standard deduction (zero bracket amount), whether on the short form or the long. Starting in 1982, taxpayers filling out a joint return and taking the standard deduction may deduct 25 percent of the first $100 they contribute to a qualified charity. Those filing separate returns may deduct 12.5 percent of the first $100. Of course, those who itemize their deductions may continue to deduct each charitable contribution.

Deductions for State and Local Taxes

Money that you pay in local property taxes, local and state sales taxes and local and state income taxes qualifies as a legal deduction on your federal income tax. Some items, however, that many people consider to be taxes—such as the cost of a driver's license or car registration, the cost of fishing or hunting permits and water bills (in areas where the water supply is municipally owned)—are fees rather than taxes. These are *not* deductible.

Property Taxes. Usually this means real estate taxes charged by your municipality based on the assessed valuation of your home. In many areas of the country, these real estate taxes can amount to thousands of dollars per year, and the fact that they constitute a valid deduction against federal income taxes makes them less onerous than they would otherwise be. A deduction for real estate taxes is allowable on *any* houses or land that you own. Taxes on a vacation house, for example, or on undeveloped land constitute as valid a deduction as the taxes on your primary residence. Be sure you have adequate records to support your claims for real estate tax deductions. If your house is mortgaged, the bank holding the note may well be responsible for collecting the tax from you and paying the proper amount to the municipality.

Normally you will receive a statement at the beginning of the year that shows how much you paid in real estate taxes the previous year. You may also receive a statement from your city, town or township collector's office. (If you pay your real estate taxes directly, this will be the only receipt you will get.) Be sure to save these receipts. If you fail to receive them in the mail, inquire at the collector's office. Though copies of these receipts need not be sent to the IRS along with your 1040 form, in the event of an audit you may be required to produce them, along with the canceled checks used to pay the tax.

In some states there is a personal property tax levied on everything from the value of your dishes to the worth of an antique chair handed down to you by your grandparents. Here too, a receipt from the state collector's office will support your deduction if you should be audited.

State and Local Income Taxes. Most states now have income taxes, and a few cities—such as New York—impose them as well. In some states the amount charged may be quite significant. In New York State, for example, the state income tax usually amounts to about 20 percent of the federal tax, while those who live in New York City are required to pay an additional 4 percent or so. Suffice it to say that income taxes paid to the state and to the city are deductible expenses, but here too, proof of payment is useful.

Sales Taxes. Most states, and some cities, levy sales taxes on a broad range of items bought within their jurisdictions. Sales taxes normally are deductible against federal income taxes. The problem for most people is keeping and filing every receipt on which there is a sales-tax charge. These charges may be small, but they can mount up rapidly. If, for example, you live in a state that maintains a sales tax—even a small one—on all items, including food, and you and your family spend $5,000 per year at the supermarket, a three percent tax would come to $150. Add to that a sales tax on clothing, drugs, entertainment, auto supplies, house repairs and the like, and your total sales tax bill could come to well over $1,000 for the year—even without any major purchases such as a new car, a color television set, a video recorder or a refrigerator.

To help the taxpayer estimate sales taxes, the IRS publishes a table in the 1040 instruction booklet that estimates what people in each state and in different income brackets and family sizes will spend annually on sales taxes. If your deduction for sales taxes conforms with the IRS estimate, it is highly unlikely that you will be challenged. However, if you have good reason to believe that your sales-tax bill was higher than that allowed by the IRS tables—

suppose, for example, you bought a new car, expensive high-fidelity equipment and an expensive home computer during the year—you have every right to claim a higher deduction. You must, however, have proof of these expenditures, if the IRS challenges them. Therefore, it is a good idea to save and file receipts for major purchases. However, if you have not done so, you may be able to obtain new receipts on such big-ticket items from the sellers, who probably will have kept them in their records.

Non-Deductible Taxes. Certain kinds of taxes are not deductible. These are primarily taxes on selected types of goods and services, such as an extra tax (above the sales tax) on alcohol or tobacco, or a sales tax that is charged only for services. In addition, gasoline, Social Security and inheritance taxes are not deductible.

Finally, if you have paid taxes for someone else, the amount is *not* deductible on your return. For example, suppose you are claiming an aged parent as a dependent and in the course of supporting that parent you pay his or her real estate taxes. You may not claim this tax expenditure as a deduction.

Deductions of Interest

Money you pay out as interest on loans is generally a deductible item on your income tax, one that can amount to considerable savings, particularly if you have one or more large outstanding loans. If you are in, say, the 33 percent tax bracket and are paying 15 percent interest on a loan, the effective interest rate is reduced by five points, because the government is, in effect, picking up a third of the interest charge. Should you be in the 50 percent bracket, your effective interest will be reduced by half.

In order to deduct interest payments, the taxpayer must be legally liable for the loan he or she is paying off. In other words, it must be a loan made out to *you,* if you are to deduct the interest. If, for example, your aged parent has an outstanding consumer loan with a bank and

you are making the interest payments, you may not claim this interest as a deduction.

Suppose that you pay off interest in advance. In that case, you may not deduct any payments other than those due in the taxable year. For example, suppose a taxpayer has a consumer loan with a bank extending for three years, and decides to pay off all of the interest on the loan during the first year. The taxpayer may not deduct the entire interest payment, only the amount actually due during that initial year. However, during the next year the interest due for that period may be deducted even though it actually was paid during the year before. The third year's may be deducted in like fashion.

Many types of loans, including most mortgages and installment loans, require that the bulk of the interest charges be paid off during the early years of the obligation. On a 30-year mortgage, for example, the monthly payments may be spread equally throughout the term of the loan, but most of the money paid back during the first 10 or 15 years will be in the form of interest. A householder who is paying off a mortgage will normally have a much higher deduction for interest payments during the first few years of the obligation than during the last few years. Tax deductions on interest can be claimed on the following types of loans:

***Mortgage loans.** This may be a mortgage on a primary residence, a vacation house or any other type of habitation—even including a boat—that is financed by a mortgage.

*__All forms of consumer credit accounts,__ including bank credit cards, department store charge plates, revolving charge accounts and the like. Be sure, however, to save your credit statements to provide proof, if needed, that the interest you claim is the interest you paid.

*__Education loans,__ for yourself or for your dependents. This includes loans covered by government guarantees.

*__Various types of consumer loans,__ from commercial banks, savings banks, credit unions and savings and loan associations, or from private lending agencies.

*Loans taken out on insurance policies, provided you actually pay the interest rather than let it accrue.

*Money borrowed from an individual, such as a relative or friend, provided you can prove the payment of interest. A written agreement between the lender and borrower, outlining the amount of interest to be paid and the installment arrangements for discharging the obligation, together with canceled checks, usually will serve as adequate proof.

Deductions for Casualty Losses

Suppose your house, with a market value of $120,000, burns down, and your insurance policy covers only $60,000 of the loss; or you are burglarized, goods worth $25,000 are stolen and you have no insurance. In both cases, the losses qualify you for casualty deductions on your income tax. Now imagine that termites have been eating away at your house, and one day the structure is completely undermined, a condition that costs $12,000 to repair. You attempt to claim this as a casualty deduction but the IRS disallows your claim. The reason for this is that, for tax purposes, casualty losses must stem from causes that are sudden and unanticipated. Generally, that means an accident or theft. Termite damage is a slow, progressive deterioration and, as such, does not qualify as a casualty loss.

Another qualification is that the loss must be sustained by the taxpayer. A loss to someone else does not qualify even if that person is carried as a dependent on the claimant's return. Finally, the claimed casualty loss cannot be for a greater amount than the taxpayer paid for the item. For example, if you suffer the unreimbursed loss through theft of a set of sterling silver for which you originally paid $1,200 but whose value, thanks to a rise in the market, has increased to $1,800, your casualty loss for tax purposes is nonetheless limited to $1,200.

Casualty deductions are among the knottiest problems faced by the taxpayer and the IRS. According to the Service, acceptable casualty losses may result from such events as hurricanes, tornadoes and other storms, floods or fires, shipwrecks, mine cave-ins, sonic booms, accidents, vandalism (when it is beyond the control of the taxpayer) and theft.

In addition, there are a number of situations in which a loss may or may not be considered a valid deduction, depending on the circumstances. Let's take smog as an example. If you live in an area where smog is an everyday fact of life, and after painting your house you discover that chemicals in the smog have damaged the paint job, you may not claim a casualty-loss deduction, because you might have well anticipated that damage. If, on the other hand, you live in a region where smog is a rare occurrence and the same thing happens, you will at least have a good case for claiming the loss.

Similarly, the mere fact that you lost property by mislaying it does not qualify you for a casualty-loss deduction. But if, for example, you were wearing a ring in which were set some small diamonds and a car door was slammed on your hand, causing the gems to pop out of their setting and disappear into the dust, you can claim a casualty loss.

Losses from automobile accidents (assuming you have not been reimbursed through insurance) is another item that may or may not qualify you for a casualty loss. To qualify, the accident must not be the result of a willful act or willful negligence. For example, suppose a man named Andrew Josephson is driving his car along an icy road and the vehicle goes out of control, causing a total of $6,000 in damage. Though Mr. Josephson has liability insurance, he does not have collision insurance, and therefore he is not covered. Normally, he could claim a casualty loss on his income tax, but in this instance his claim was denied because a police report stated that Mr. Josephson was drunk at the time of his accident and therefore was guilty of willful negligence.

Among the items that you may *not* claim as a casualty loss in an automobile accident are the following: any repair costs that increase the value of the automobile to an amount higher than its worth at the time of the accident; the cost of renting a car while the damaged car is being repaired; legal fees relating to the accident; loss of income as a result of the accident; and loss through damage to a car registered in someone else's name (such as that of your son or daughter), even though you may be paying all expenses on the vehicle. Nor may you claim a casualty loss based on damage to someone else's car, even if you caused that damage.

When claiming a casualty loss, be sure to deduct from the amount of the claim any reimbursement you may have received from an insurance company, plus an additional $100 deductible for each loss. (This $100 does not apply to casualty losses that involve property used in your business or profession.)

Personal Business Expense Deductions

A taxpayer who is self-employed or has unreimbursed business expenses is entitled to deduct the amounts of these expenses, within certain limits, from his or her gross income. The taxpayer's adjusted gross income may be significantly reduced by these deductions, and his or her tax bracket similarly reduced. In some instances, however, there are definite limits to the amounts a taxpayer may charge off as a business expense. For example, gifts to clients or associates may be considered justifiable business expenses, but only to a maximum of $25 for each person in any one tax year. If, for example, Janice Brooks, an attorney, gives one client a $50 set of glassware for Christmas, and another client a $35 desk set, in each instance she may deduct only $25 of these amounts as business expenses. Gifts to colleagues or customers should not be confused, however, with entertainment expenses, on which there is no deductible limit, so long as these expenses can be justified as necessary (see entertainment expenses, page 408). In general, the key to deducting business expenses is the phrase "ordinary and necessary." Suppose, for example, that a man named Franklin Stone runs a business consulting firm out of his house, and he hires a fortune teller to predict the course of the stock market. He will not be able to deduct the salary of that seer unless he can prove that the services provided supplied him with a distinct business advantage. If, however, it was common practice in his field to hire such people, he would have a far better case for the business deduction. Below are descriptions of the most common sorts of business deductions that individuals may take.

Moving Expenses. If you have unreimbursed moving expenses related to current or new employment, you may, in many instances, deduct these expenses from your income. In order to do so, however, you must fulfill the following conditions.

*You change jobs, or your place of employment shifts from one locality to another. You must move more than 35 miles, and the purpose of your move must be to bring you closer to your new job location. For example, a man named Robert Rowell lived in Englewood, New Jersey, and commuted to his job as a sales analyst in New York City, a distance of about 16 miles. Mr. Rowell took a new job with a firm in Philadelphia, approximately 110 miles from Englewood. He moved to New Brunswick, New Jersey, some 40 miles from his old home, so that he could be on the main railroad line, and thereby ease his commuting problems. Because Mr. Rowell moved more than 35 miles in order to be closer to his new place of employment, he has satisfied the distance requirement. However, if Mr. Rowell had moved less than 35 miles from Englewood, he would not have satisfied the distance requirement, even though his job shifted from one area to another, and he made his commuting less arduous by locating himself close to the main railroad line to Philadelphia.

*In order to qualify for the deduction for moving expenses, the employee must work full-time for at least 39 weeks for his or her new employer in the year after the move. People who are self-employed and claim a moving-expense deduction must remain in that category on a full-time basis for 39 weeks in the first full year after the move or for a total of 78 weeks during the 24 months immediately following the move.

*In situations where a move is made to facilitate the work of both a husband and wife, the couple may not combine the number of weeks each has worked at the new location in order to satisfy the time requirement. For example, suppose a married couple, Ruth and Howard Capston, are both freelance writers and they move from Northampton, Massachusetts, to New York City in order to be closer to their markets. After 20 weeks of living in New York, the Capstons decide that they have made a mistake and they move back to Northampton. Their move to New York will not be considered a justifiable business expense because neither Capston has worked the required time in the new location. However, if just one of them were to work for the required time, the business expense would be justified.

*By and large, the claimed moving expense must occur within 12 months of a change of employment or a transfer. If, for example, your job location changes from San Francisco to Los Angeles, but you do not move your residence for three years after the change, you may not be able to claim a business deduction for relocating. However, in some circumstances this rule will be waived. If a family situation precludes a change of residence, the IRS may not enforce this rule. For example, suppose a woman is working as an account executive in a San Francisco advertising agency and her employer transfers her to the Los Angeles branch office. Her husband, however, has just finished his first year of law school in San Francisco, and a change of residence would preclude his completion of the three-year course. Therefore, she takes an apartment in Los Angeles and commutes to San Francisco on weekends. After her husband graduates from law school, the two relocate in Los Angeles and claim the moving expenses as a business deduction. Because of the circumstances involved, the IRS probably will allow the deduction.

Unreimbursed Travel Expenses. If you incur expenses while traveling on business, and these expenses are not reimbursed by your employer, you may claim them as a business deduction. You must, however, maintain a diary of your business-related travels listing places visited, the purpose and dates of each trip. This diary should include receipts for travel expenses, lodging and meals. Travel expenses (the cost of airline, train, bus or taxi fares), lodging and food are all deductible. Automobile expenses, however, are treated somewhat differently. A person using an automobile for business purposes has two options: either he or she can keep a running record of all related expenses and deduct that amount, or else take a general deduction of 20 cents per mile for the first 15,000 miles that the car is used for business purposes, and 11 cents per mile thereafter. For example, Irving Snow is a salesman for a large jewelry firm and covers a five-state area in the Midwest, making calls at scores of high schools and colleges. During the course of the year he drives his car 40,000 miles—10,000 miles for personal reasons and 30,000 doing business. As the car is used for professional purposes three-quarters of the time, he may deduct three-quarters of the expenses he incurs through its use. He may figure this in one of two ways. If he takes a mileage deduction he may write off $3,000 for the first 15,000 miles he travels on business (.20 × 15,000), and $1,650 for the last 15,000 miles (.11 × 15,000) for a total deduction of $4,650. (The 10,000 miles he traveled for personal reasons are, of course, non-deductible.) On the other hand, Mr. Snow may find it to his advantage to deduct the actual amount of money that the car cost him when used for business purposes. This would include, for example, three-quarters of his expenditures for gasoline, three-quarters of the cost of maintaining the vehicle and a fixed depreciation rate on the car. In some circumstances, it may pay Mr. Snow to use the fixed mileage rate one year and figure the actual cost the next.

One travel expense—whether by car, bus, train or any other mode of transportation—

that cannot be deducted is the cost of getting to and from one's regular place of business.

Entertainment Expenses. People who have unreimbursed business entertainment expenses may deduct the cost but should be prepared to prove that the expenses were directly related to business or, in some circumstances, that the expenses were incurred immediately before or after a business discussion or conference. The law makes a distinction between gifts and entertainment expenses. You may deduct up to a maximum of $25 per person for gifts, and then only if the gifts were made for business reasons. For entertainment expenses, however, there is no limit on how much may be deducted, so long as the expenses are legitimate business outlays.

For example, if you buy 15 clients bottles of rare wines, you may deduct only $25 per client; but if, instead, you buy them tickets to an expensive Broadway show and dinner afterwards, you may deduct the actual cost of these expenses, provided you can establish a business connection.

You may also deduct the cost of entertaining for business purposes in your home and for entertaining the husbands and wives of clients or associates, provided you can demonstrate that it would have been impractical to entertain the client without his or her spouse.

In any business entertainment situation it is not necessary to demonstrate that business was actually discussed or that some precise benefit accrued to you as a result of the entertainment provided. The establishment and maintenance of general goodwill is a sufficient reason for the expenditure.

Businessmen and businesswomen who join private clubs for professional reasons and use them to entertain clients or customers may deduct a portion of the membership fees. If, for example, membership in a yacht club costs $1,000 per year, and a member uses the club for business purposes about 75 percent of the time, that member may deduct $750 as a business expense.

Home Offices. When part of one's house is used exclusively and regularly for business purposes, the cost of maintaining that portion of the house constitutes a valid business expense. If, for example, Sandra Lasch maintains a law office in two rooms of her 10-room house, using that office only for professional purposes, she may deduct the expenses attendant on those two rooms. If those two rooms equal approximately one-fifth of the floor space of her house, she may deduct 20 percent of her mortgage, 20 percent of her heating bill and 20 percent of her expense for painting the outside of her house. Of course, she may deduct 100 percent of any repair, maintenance or remodeling work on those two rooms. However, any room for which the deduction is claimed must be used solely for business purposes. If it normally is used for purposes other than work, and you use it occasionally for business functions, you may not claim a deduction.

Miscellaneous Business Deductions. There are literally hundreds of expenditures which, under particular circumstances, may be legitimately claimed as business deductions. For example, if your job or profession requires that you wear a certain kind of clothing that you would not otherwise wear, and the cost of this clothing is not reimbursed, you may claim this cost as a deduction. Below are a few of the most common minor deductions:

*Dues paid to professional societies and labor unions constitute valid deductions, as do initiation fees in such organizations when these fees are required to enable you to gain employment or increase your business. The portion of such dues or fees that is used to pay for such things as insurance or death benefits is, however, not deductible.

*Subscriptions to periodicals, newsletters and other publications that are directly related to your work are deductible expenses. A farmer, for example, may claim the cost of any number of agricultural journals, a lawyer the cost of legal publications and so forth. But the cost of local daily newspapers, general-audience magazines and the like are deductible only in situations where the buyer can demonstrate that such publications are important to his or her work.

*Employment-agency fees are deductible, as are other expenses incurred in seeking employment in your accustomed field. Such expenses include the cost of travel in search of employment and charges relating to writing, printing and mailing resumes. It should be emphasized, however, that such items are deductible only when you are seeking a new job in the same occupation that you have been pursuing. If you are a lawyer and decide that you wish to become a salesman, the cost of seeking a job in the new field is not deductible. Similarly, if you are just out of school and seeking your first job, you may not deduct the cost of finding employment.

*Educational expenses, in very limited circumstances, are deductible. Such expenses must be for the purpose of increasing your skills in a field in which you are already employed. A computer salesman, for example, may take a course that acquaints him with innovations in his field and deduct the cost of tuition. Someone who is training to become a computer salesman, however, may not deduct the cost of a course in computer sales. Similarly, a student may not deduct the cost of medical school, but someone who is already a physician may deduct the cost of a course that will enhance his or her skills.

Tax Credits: Reducing the Amount You Owe

An important distinction must be made between tax deductions and tax credits. Interest, for example, is a deduction, and if you pay $1,000 in interest and are in the 30 percent bracket, the government will, in effect, pick up 30 percent or $300 of that amount. If you are in the 50 percent bracket, the amount you save on your income taxes will be $500 or 50

percent. A tax credit, however, is taken off the bottom line—the money you owe the federal government—on a 100 percent basis without reference to your bracket. If you have a tax credit of $400, you will pay $400 less in income taxes than you otherwise would have paid. Below are some of the major tax credits that individuals may be entitled to.

Political Contributions. Money you contribute to a political candidate or to an operation that supports that candidate is, to a certain extent, a tax credit. As an individual you may contribute up to $100 to a campaign and take a credit for half that amount. Couples filing joint returns may contribute up to $200 and take a $100 tax credit. A written receipt or canceled check is usually sufficient proof to satisfy the IRS that you are entitled to the credit.

Child and Dependent Care Credit. If you have a child or another dependent for whom you must provide paid care so that you can take a paying job, a portion of this expense can be claimed as a tax credit. If your adjusted gross income is $10,000 or less, you are allowed a child-care credit of 30 percent of a maximum of $2,400 for child-care expenses for one child, or 30 percent of a maximum of $4,800 for two or more children. That works out to a credit of $720 for one child or $1,440 for two or more. The more you earn, however, the smaller will be the tax credit allowed. For every additional $2,000 (or a part of $2,000) that your adjusted gross income increases above $10,000, the credit drops by one percentage point. Thus, for example, a working woman who earns $15,000 per year and has one child is allowed a tax credit of 27 percent of the first $2,400 she spends on child care. She can therefore deduct $648 from her income tax. The drop-off in the percentage rate ends when you reach an income of $28,000 or more. From then on you are allowed to take a credit of 20 percent of the first $2,400 you spend for the care of one child, or 20 percent of the first $4,800 you spend for the care of two or more.

Remember, the credit is applicable only if the expenditure permits you to hold a paying job that you would otherwise not be able to take. If, for example, you hire someone to care for your child during summer vacation so that you can continue on the job, you are entitled to a credit.

On the other hand, if that child-care expense is incurred so that you can have more free time during the summer, you may not take a credit. In addition, there is an age limit on the children who are involved. You may not take a child-care credit for any minor who is 15 years old or older, except in cases where the child is disabled.

The law also allows you to apply the credit to the care of dependents who are not your children. If, for example, your spouse is disabled and you must pay for help so that you can work, you are entitled to a credit in the same amounts that apply to child care.

Energy Credits. Certain tax credits are allowed to help you offset the cost of installing energy-saving devices or equipment in your primary residence. (Vacation homes do not qualify.) If you install storm doors, storm windows or insulation, or a fuel-efficient furnace, clock thermostats or several other energy-saving devices, you are allowed a maximum credit of $300 or 15 percent of the cost of the equipment, whichever is less. If you install energy-saving devices that are based on renewable sources of energy—such as solar panels—your maximum credit is $4,000 or 40 percent of any amount up to $10,000, whichever is less. Both the $300 credit and the $4,000 credit are the maximum amounts you can claim for one home. Both credits, however, are renewable should you move and install new energy-saving devices in your next house. A sample tax form on which energy credits are computed appears in Chapter 3, page 102.

Among the devices that may save energy but do not qualify for a credit are the following: wood-burning stoves, carpeting, draperies, exterior siding, heat pumps and awnings.

Income Averaging

This device is useful for people who have had some sort of windfall that greatly raises their tax bracket in the current year when compared with their brackets in the preceding four years. By employing this tactic, taxpayers can spread out their increased income in the current year over a five-year period, thus lowering their tax liability. Those who wish to employ income averaging must file Schedule G 1040 along with their 1040 form.

Income averaging works in this manner. Suppose, for example, that Bill Cummings, a salesman for a major computer firm, had earnings in 1978, 1979, 1980 and 1981 that placed him in the 31 percent bracket for all of those years. In 1982, however, because of several major sales, his earnings put him in the 50 percent bracket. By averaging his income for lhe years 1978–1982, his overall bracket for that period jumps to 37 percent. This increase will force him to pay a few thousand dollars extra on his 1982 return. But if the entire increase had been charged against his 1982 earnings alone, the amount he would owe in taxes for that year would be much higher.

This tactic works only in situations where there has been a significant jump in income. If, however, this major increase continues, year after year, income averaging can continue as well. If your income tax increased greatly during the current year, try filling out Schedule G and you may find that you will save a considerable amount on your income tax. If income averaging proves not to be worthwhile for you, however, you needn't file Schedule G, but simply file your return in the usual way.

Setting Money Aside for Your Children

Sophisticated tax strategies have long been considered suitable only for the very rich. There are, however, certain methods that middle-class families can employ to lessen their tax burdens while, at the same time, putting money aside for such purposes as the education of their children. Nor are such strategies limited to parents. Grandparents, for example, may use them to build up education funds for their grandchildren while reducing the amount of money the grandparents might otherwise have to pay in income or estate taxes.

In all these strategies, the great benefit is that money invested in the names of minor children earns interest and dividends that are taxed—if at all—at a rate based upon the children's earnings. In almost all instances, this rate will be much lower than the rate that would apply to the parents (or grandparents, if they are the donors). And while building up a nest egg for their children, parents may continue to claim their young as legitimate dependents so long as they continue to provide at least 50 percent of their support. Below are a few of the most common strategies used.

The Gifts to Minors Program

Under this program, up to $10,000 can be given to each child from each donor without incurring a gift tax. For example, a couple with two minor children can give each of them $20,000 in the course of a year. Each grandparent, as well, can contribute up to $10,000 per year per child. The money is, in effect, an irrevocable gift, which means that the donor not only cannot get the money back, but may not use either the principal or any interest that accrues for his or her own needs.

Normally, the principal is invested in a Gifts to Minors Account, through which the custodian (who may be a parent) buys stocks, bonds, treasury bills or shares in money market funds. The income from these investments is plowed back into the account. A separate account must be established for each child—that is, if you and your spouse have three children, you may not divide the proceeds of a single account among them. The proceeds of such accounts are often used to finance college education. However, the money may not be used for general support—such as the purchase of

food, shelter and clothing—that parents are required by law to provide for their children.

As an example of how such a Gift for Minors Account would work, let's look at the situation of a couple we shall call Jane and Sam Martin, who have two children: Carol, age 12, and Tim, age 11. Both Martins hold jobs and earn good salaries. In 1981, their combined taxable income was $48,000. After paying their income taxes and all other expenses for the year, the Martins found that they had $6,000 left over and decided to put that money aside for their children under the provisions of the Gifts to Minors Act. Through their broker they set up two Gifts to Minors Accounts of $3,000 each for Carol and Tim, investing the principal in money market funds. In 1982, the funds each paid 13 percent interest, or a total of $780. When the time came for the Martins to prepare their 1982 tax returns, the money earned by the two funds did not have to be declared on their returns. As their children's incomes were so small, no returns had to be filed on their behalf, and thus the proceeds of the money market funds were tax free. Had the Martins merely set the money aside in accounts in their own names, most of the interest earned would have been taxed at the same rate as their other income.

There is, of course, an element of risk in employing this tactic. Suppose, for example, in early 1982, Sam Martin lost his job and the family found itself in dire financial straits. There would be no legal way that the elder Martins could dip into the accounts established for their children to ease their financial plight—except by obtaining a court order, a difficult and time-consuming procedure. The gifts, once made, are therefore virtually irrevocable, and when the beneficiary comes of age, he or she is entitled to full control of the funds in the trust.

Clifford Trusts. For people in high tax brackets, one of the drawbacks of a Gifts to Minors Account is mitigated in the Clifford Trust (named for a participant in a tax case some four

411

Gifts That Cover Educational or Medical Expenses

As already stated in this chapter, each person may give up to $10,000 per year to a single individual (a couple, filing jointly, may give $20,000) without the donor—or donors, in the case of a couple—having to pay a gift tax. Under the new tax law passed by Congress in 1981, certain categories of gifts, however, are tax free to the donor, no matter how large. These are gifts to pay for educational or medical expenses.

A healthy widow, for example, whose granddaughter is enrolled in a costly medical school where tuition fees come to $12,000 per year, may, if she wishes, pay the entire bill. Similarly, if the grandmother has a grandson or middle-aged son in need of com-plex heart surgery, she can pay the total expenses, no matter how large, without being liable for taxes on the amount she has given.

However, such expenditures must be paid directly to the educational or medical institution rendering services. The grandmother in question, for example, may not set up a trust fund for her six-year-old granddaughter's future medical education and expect that she will not have to pay gift taxes on the principal should it amount to more than the $10,000 limit.

Recipients of gifts, it should be emphasized, are never liable for taxes on the amount received.

decades ago). Through the use of a Clifford Trust, the donor or donors retain rights to the principal invested (though not to the earnings of the principal). These rights, however, may not be exercised for at least 10 years and one day after the assets have been placed in the trust. A Clifford Trust has much the same purpose as a Gift to Minors and operates in basically the same way, with the earnings being taxed—if at all—at the children's rate rather than the donors' rate. However, a single trust can be established to benefit all the children in a family, the proceeds being divided among them. After the trust matures—in 10 years and one day—the donor may withdraw the principal used to establish the fund, but whatever interest or dividends have been accumulated must still be used for the benefit of the children.

Because the principal may not be withdrawn until after a decade, it is necessary to establish separate trusts each time there is a new infusion of principal. Suppose, for example, Joan Simpson establishes a Clifford Trust for her 11-year-old daughter, Ann. Mrs. Simpson initially deposits $10,000 in the trust, with the inten-tion of withdrawing the principal for her own use a decade hence. A year later, Joan Simpson deposits another $10,000 in the same Clifford Trust. Because she has not established a second trust, she will now not be able to withdraw *any* principal until a decade after the second deposit. If, however, she had established a second trust for the second deposit, she would have been able to withdraw the initial amount on schedule.

A Clifford Trust can be established only with the help of an attorney, which can make the use of this device expensive. In general, Clifford Trusts make sense only when a significant amount of money is involved, because legal and trustee fees can cut deeply into the principal invested. As a practical matter, the use of Clifford Trusts is limited to those in high tax brackets.

Interest-Free Demand Loans. A parent who wants to set aside money for a child can do so by making an interest-free loan—repayable on demand—to a child, through a trustee. The money is placed in high-yield investments, such as money market funds, with the earnings being saved for such purposes as college tuition. As with Gifts for Minors Accounts and Clifford Trusts, the earnings are taxed at a low rate based upon the beneficiary's income, while the donor may demand, at any time, that the principal, or part of the principal, be repaid. Although the courts have so far maintained the legality of demand loans, the IRS has challenged this tactic, and people who set up such accounts should be aware that they may encounter difficulties with the IRS. As with Clifford Trusts, it is usually necessary for a lawyer to establish the demand loan account, because minors, in most states, do not have the legal right to borrow money on their own.

Providing for Your Retirement

The federal government has long permitted individuals who fall into certain categories to put aside a portion of their incomes in retirement accounts. By doing so, these people have been enabled to reduce their taxable incomes in the years when they were contributing to their retirement savings. Moreover, the interest earned by the accounts remained tax free until the investors began drawing money from these savings during retirement years. Presumably, by then, the individuals would be in lower tax brackets than in the working years, and the taxes levied on the proceeds from the retirement account would therefore be considerably reduced. Starting in 1982, Congress greatly liberalized the terms under which Americans could participate in these tax-deferred individual retirement programs. Below are descriptions of the two major plans, eligibility requirements and the amounts of money that may be invested during any one year.

Individual Retirement Accounts (IRAs). Under tax provisions in effect until 1982, the only people qualified to establish IRAs were those employed in businesses that had not established any sort of retirement plan for employees. Under current tax legislation, however, virtually anyone who works can establish an IRA, even if his or her employer has a separate plan.

An IRA can be set up as a savings account in a bank or through a bank's trust department, with investments in certificates of deposit. It can also be set up through a brokerage account in which investments are made in stocks, bonds, money market funds or other securities. The important thing is that these are *trust* accounts, and neither the principal nor the earnings may be touched without penalty until the beneficiary is 59½ years old. Not only will an early withdrawal be taxed, but a 10 percent penalty will be levied on the amount withdrawn. If the beneficiary of an IRA becomes disabled before reaching the age of 59½ and cannot work, however, the money can be withdrawn without penalty.

Starting in 1982, a person may contribute up to $2,000 a year to an IRA and not pay taxes on that amount as long as it is in the account. Indeed, the contribution need not even be made during the calendar year of the deduction, but may be made up to April 15 of the following year, or even later if the taxpayer has a valid extension for filing a return. In circumstances where both a husband and wife work, each is entitled to the maximum contribution, thus allowing them to contribute a total of $4,000, provided each earns at least $2,000 a year. In cases where only one spouse holds a paying job, he or she may contribute up to $2,250, dividing the contribution between the spouses' accounts. However, no more than $2,000 may be contributed to any one account in a calendar year. Suppose Mr. and Mrs. Lucas Garn decide to set up IRA accounts. As Mr. Garn is the only spouse who holds a paying job, the entire contribution will come out of his funds. Mr. Garn can choose to put $2,000 in his own IRA and $250 in Mrs. Garn's, or he could put $1,000 in his wife's account and $1,250 in his own. In fact, he could divide up the amount contributed in any manner he liked, except that he could put no more than $2,000 in any one account during one year.

The Keogh Plan. This retirement device is meant for people who are self-employed, and as of 1982 it permits them to put a maximum of $15,000 or 15 percent of their earnings, whichever is less, into a tax-deferred retirement trust plan. Suppose for example, a self-employed architect named Victor Krause earns $100,000 in 1982. He is permitted to take a deduction of $15,000 from his gross income and invest that money in a trust account with his bank or broker. As with an IRA, not only will he have achieved a significant deduction on his 1982 income taxes, but the earnings from his Keogh Plan account will be tax free until he begins drawing on them after his retirement.

The new tax law permits those who are qualified to set up Keogh Plans to set up IRAs as well. Thus Mr. Krause can invest $15,000 in his Keogh and an additional $2,000 in an IRA.

You do not have to be totally self-employed to set up a Keogh Plan. If, for example, you are a public school teacher earning a salary, and you moonlight as a house painter, you can shelter a portion of your independent earnings as a house painter through a Keogh Plan. You cannot, however, apply part of your salary from teaching to a Keogh Plan, though you may, of course, set up an IRA with a portion of the money you earn through your public school position.

Regulations concerning withdrawals are much the same for Keogh Plans as they are for Individual Retirement Accounts, and early withdrawals will result in the payment of significant penalties.

Unlike an IRA, which can be set up as late as April 15 of the year following the one in which a tax deduction is desired, a Keogh Plan must be established by December 31 of the year in which the deduction will be taken. Once it is established, however, contributions to the Keogh Plan can be made as late as April 15 of the following year and charged off against the previous tax year. Indeed, those who obtain a two-month filing delay may even make contributions as late as June 15 and charge them to the previous year.

All-Savers Certificates

These tax-free savings devices, which are available until midnight of December 31, 1982, make a great deal of sense for many people and little sense for others. The primary consideration is your tax bracket. When you buy an All-Saver's Certificate, the amount of interest it pays is 30 percent below the rate you get if you buy 52-week treasury bills. Thus, if treasury bills are paying 15 percent interest at the time you buy, the interest you will receive on the All-Savers Certificate is 10.5 percent, an amount that may be well below the interest offered by other forms of investment, such as money market funds. The advantage of the All-Savers is that the interest is tax free, at least so far as federal income tax is concerned. (Some states tax All-Savers Certificates and some do not.) By and large, if you are not in at least the 30 percent bracket, an All-Savers Certificate is probably not a good investment, and you are likely to make more, after taxes, by buying into a money market fund or purchasing a certificate of deposit.

One advantage of an All-Savers Certificate is that the interest is locked in. If, at the time you buy the certificate, the interest rate is 12 percent, that rate will continue through the one-year life of the certificate, even if the treasury bill rate drops. On the other hand, should the treasury rate rise, your certificate will continue to pay the same rate as before.

The All-Savers Certificate program was established primarily to encourage people to put their savings into commercial and savings banks, savings and loan organizations and credit unions, which had been having difficult times meeting the interest rates offered by other types of investment institutions. The program was conceived of as a short-term, one-time investment opportunity and, barring

Congressional action to extend it, will end with the year 1982. However, enrollment will be open until the very end of that year, and certificates bought on December 31, 1982, will continue to earn tax-free interest through 1983.

There are limits on the amount of interest that can be earned tax free through an All-Savers Certificate. A single person can earn no more than $1,000; a married couple no more than $2,000.

How much money must be invested to earn the maximum tax-free interest will depend on when you make your investment and on the interest rate being paid at the time of purchase.

Before buying an All-Savers Certificate, keep one final consideration in mind. Can you afford to tie up the amount of money you plan to invest for a full year? Should you withdraw any part of the principal before the year is up, not only will you lose three months' interest, you will also be taxed on the remaining interest as well.

Estate Taxes and Bequests

A major element in the tax act of 1981 is a drastic lowering of federal estate taxes, and the exemption from such taxes of estates worth hundreds of thousands of dollars. As a result of the tax act of 1981, the total amount of assets a person may leave his or her heirs without that estate being subject to federal estate taxes will rise in yearly increments as follows: 1982, $225,000; 1983, $275,000; 1984, $325,000; 1985, $400,000; 1986, $500,000; and 1987 and thereafter, $600,000. Heirs to an estate, or the trustees, will not even have to file an estate tax return if the assets of the estate are less than the amounts listed above. In addition, there is an unlimited deduction for bequests to a spouse. A person can leave any amount to a husband or wife, and the inheritance will be free of federal estate taxes.

Tax rates on estates that exceed the tax-free limits have been lowered as well. By 1986, the

A Tip to All-Savers Certificate Buyers

If there appears to be an even remote possibility that you will have to cash in an All-Savers Certificate before its due date, you can protect yourself, to some extent, from loss of interest and taxation by buying several certificates, each in a small denomination, rather than a single large-denomination certificate. Then, if you need some funds, you may only have to cash in some of your certificates, and the penalties incurred will relate only to those All-Savers Certificates you have redeemed. If, on the other hand, you have only one certificate in a large denomination, you will have to cash in the entire certificate even if you require only a portion of the funds it represents. Thus you will be charged the maximum penalty. For example, suppose that Roscoe Johnston has $10,000 he wishes to invest in an All-Savers Certificate. Mr. Johnston is in a busi-

ness in which his income varies considerably from month to month, and it may well be that he cannot afford to tie up the entire $10,000 for a full year. Instead of buying a single certificate with a face value of $10,000, Mr. Johnston, being prudent, buys twenty certificates, each with a face value of $500.

Three months after their purchase, Roscoe Johnston finds that he is greatly in need of $1,000, and his All-Savers Certificates are his only source of funds. Had he bought the $10,000 certificate, he would have had to cash in the entire amount, losing some of the accumulated interest and paying a tax on the rest. However, since he bought certificates in small denominations, he has to cash in only two of them, and his loss in interest and taxes is greatly reduced.

maximum federal tax on even the largest estate left to a non-spouse will be 50 percent instead of the pre-1982 70 percent. These reductions will take place in 5 percent increments for each year between 1982 and 1985.

It is important to note, however, that each state has its own regulations about taxing estates. Assets of an estate that are free from federal taxation may be subject to state taxation, the amount of which may vary widely from jurisdiction to jurisdiction. Planning an estate, even a relatively small one, remains a task for experts, and the fee charged by a lawyer or accountant may be very well spent, for it can save your heirs considerable sums. Certainly, if you planned your estate with the pre-1982 regulations in mind, you would be well advised to consult with a lawyer and consider the advisability of drawing up a new will in light of the major changes in estate tax law.

Auditing: How Returns Are Selected

Every tax return that is submitted to the Internal Revenue Service is checked by a computer. The computers review the arithmetic on the return, flagging those forms in which there are arithmetic errors. These returns are routinely checked by IRS employees, and the taxpayer is notified of the error or errors made and billed or credited accordingly.

The computer has another function, however. It is programmed to spot any unusual deductions, both in terms of the taxpayer's reported income and his or her filing status.

To take a couple of examples: Suppose Jasper Samuels files as a single taxpayer and then deducts $800 for child care. This will probably be enough to set bells ringing in the computer, because child-care expenses are usually taken only by those in such filing categories as married couples, widows and widowers. In another instance, Susan Strent, a recent high school graduate, working as a clerk in a shoestore,

reports a gross income of $8,800 and medical expenses of $10,300. The fact that her medical expenses are higher than her total taxable income will cause the computer to flag her return.

The mere fact that a computer flags the return does not in itself mean that there will be an audit. It merely signals IRS personnel that they should make a close visual examination of the return in question. In both instances cited here, there may well be explanations on the return that are sufficiently reasonable so that an audit may not be required. In Mr. Samuels' case, it may be that he filed under the wrong category. He should have filed as a single head of household rather than a single taxpayer, since he is the sole supporter of a minor. In Miss Strent's case, she may have inherited a large amount of money, with which she pays her medical bills. The important thing here is that in instances where the taxpayer has unusual deductions, he or she should include an explanation in the return. Though this will hardly guarantee that an audit will not be ordered, it will make one less likely.

In flagging returns for possible auditing, IRS computers are programmed according to a mathematical formula known as DIF (Discriminate Function System). DIF automatically selects returns in which there is a reasonable probability of error. Except for a very few people within the IRS, no one knows the exact formula upon which DIF is based. Nor can one be sure why an IRS auditor may pass over six or seven returns flagged by the computer and insist on an audit for three or four others. However, a number of observations can be made with reasonable certainty.

*The higher the taxpayer's income, the more likely that he or she will be called in for an audit. In 1980, for example, there were 38.5 million non-business returns in which income for the previous year was listed at $10,000 or under. Of these, only 1.4 percent were in any way examined, except by the computers. That same year, 1.2 million non-business returns listed incomes in excess of $50,000, and of these almost 9 percent were subjected to some form of auditing.

*Any unusual deductions, either in kind or in amount, are likely to cause an IRS computer to flag the return and the examiner to consider a possible audit. For example, a plumber might reasonably deduct $100 or so for professional journals, but if he deducts $500 for this purpose, it is very likely that the computer will flag the return for review.

*Certain types of deductions are more likely to be closely examined than others. For example, deductions for casualty losses (see page 405) are often suspect. A householder might, for example, try to deduct the cost of repairing termite damage to his house—a deduction not allowable under IRS regulations. The listing of this deduction will probably lead to a close examination of the return and possibly an audit.

Avoiding an Audit

There is no absolutely certain way to make sure your tax return will not be flagged for a possible audit by the IRS computers, or that an IRS auditor will not decide to call you in to review your tax forms. However, there are ways to lessen the chances that you will be audited. The first, of course, is to be extremely careful in filling out your tax forms. A mistake in arithmetic, failure to sign the form or include your Social Security number or other such basic errors will trigger the alarm mechanism in the computers, alerting IRS employees to your return. Another way is to keep your itemized deductions within acceptable bounds. To take an extreme example, if your taxable income is $18,000 and you claim a deduction of $10,000 for charity, the suspicions of the IRS are almost certain to be aroused. Yet it would be foolish not to claim a valid deduction purely on the grounds that the claim itself might lead to an audit. To be audited by the IRS is neither so fearsome nor, in general, so time consuming as to justify the loss of a lawful deduction.

Should you be entitled to a deduction that you know, or suspect, will arouse the curiosity

of the IRS, you can still lessen the chances of an audit by taking a simple precaution. Explain on your tax return the reasons for the deduction. For example, in the case of the person with the $18,000 income and the $10,000 deduction for charitable contributions, there could indeed be a simple explanation. Perhaps that taxpayer has a large income from non-taxable sources, such as municipal bonds. Let's say the income from these sources amounts to $100,000 per year. That gives the taxpayer a total income large enough to make a $10,000 charitable contribution well within the bounds of reasonableness. An explanation in the appropriate place on the tax form may satisfy the IRS—though it is hardly guaranteed to—and an audit may not be demanded. Similarly, if your medical expenses for a particular year are extremely high, or your casualty losses are considerable, or if any other deduction appears to you to be higher than your taxable income would normally support, a complete written explanation will often serve to allay the IRS's suspicions.

Like many other agencies of the federal government, the IRS is operating these days on a restricted budget. Trained personnel are in short supply, and there are only so many hours in every working day. Therefore, the Service, like most other organizations, tries to run its auditing department on a cost-efficient basis. By and large, it will only expend time and energy on those returns in which there is a high probability of error or a likelihood that the federal government will gain significant amounts of tax money. Remember that, of the almost 100 million individual returns filed by taxpayers, only 2 percent or so are ever audited.

While the IRS maintains that returns chosen for auditing are picked by a process of random selection, this hardly means that there is neither rhyme nor reason to the selection process. As already stated, the higher your income, the more likely that your return will be audited. And more returns are audited from some areas than from others. The prosperous Los Angeles metropolitan region, for example, accounts for about 13 percent of all audits; the Manhattan region and Chicago together account for another 8 percent. In general, audits for returns from small towns and rural areas at some distance from metropolitan regions are relatively rare. The reason is that, in large measure, the people with the highest incomes are found in or near the big cities.

The Taxpayer Compliance Measurement Program.

While many audits are cut-and-dried affairs with relatively few deductions being questioned, there is one type of audit which is truly hair-raising: the Taxpayer Compliance Measurement Program (TCMP). The purpose of this program is to audit a relatively small number of returns from taxpayers in every walk of life to determine the kinds of mistakes people make on their taxes and thus re-program the computers to catch such mistakes the following year. Though only about 50,000 returns are selected each year for a TCMP audit, those unfortunate enough to be caught up in this program will be required to produce records that will substantiate just about every item on their returns. Until fairly recently, for example, a married taxpayer who filed a joint return and was being audited under the program was required to produce his or her marriage license. It's hard to know what advice to give someone whose return is being audited under the TCMP. Under the best of circumstances, it will be a grueling experience, for every aspect of the taxpayer's financial life will be investigated. No deduction, no matter how small, for which there are not substantial records will be allowed. It is perhaps of little comfort for one whose life has been made chaotic by the TCMP to know that punishment is not the aim of the program. It exists merely to gather statistics.

How Many Years Back an Audit May Be Conducted

On personal income taxes, the IRS may demand an audit as much as three years after a tax return was due or was filed, whichever date

is later. As a practical matter, however, the IRS rarely initiates audits after 27 months have elapsed from the time a tax return is filed. This is not, however, a hard and fast rule. Suppose, for example, that the IRS decides to audit your tax returns for 1981 and comes up with a whopping error on your part in the field of charitable deductions. Nothing then prevents the Service from checking back as far as 1979 to see if you made the same error on your earlier returns. Therefore, a wise taxpayer will retain all records relating to his or her tax returns for a period of three years. Some records, of course, should be kept for longer periods. For example, records relating to the buying and selling of real estate may affect your tax situation decades after the purchase or sale was made.

Failure to Respond to an Audit Notice. If the IRS calls you in for an audit and you fail to respond, either by calling for a new appointment or appearing at the requested time, the auditor may make a summary judgment on items in question and bill you accordingly for tax due. Therefore, unless you are willing to permit the IRS to assess your taxes without challenge, you must meet the agency's request for your presence or the presence of a designated representative.

How an IRS Audit Is Conducted

People who receive notification from the IRS that their returns are to be audited very often fall into a state close to panic. They sometimes are so upset that they will not read the notification very carefully and will assume, usually without cause, that their entire tax return is to be questioned. Although there is no regulation that prevents the IRS from auditing an entire return, the letter normally will require the taxpayer to be audited to show up at the local IRS office with records supporting his or her deductions in a limited number of categories.

For example, a taxpayer may be asked to support, through detailed records, his or her deductions for unreimbursed work expenses, medical expenses and casualty losses. If there is no mention in the letter of other categories of deductions, such as sales taxes or interest on loans, there is absolutely no need for the taxpayer to appear for the interview with any records supporting such deductions. In fact, it is a bad idea to do so, because if the taxpayer brings up these extraneous subjects, the auditor may then investigate them.

The letter the taxpayer receives may suggest one of three means of investigating the return. It may merely require that the recipient mail in copies of all receipts, canceled checks, bills and other supporting evidence relating to the deductions that are to be reviewed. Or the letter may ask that the taxpayer call for an appointment, or suggest a date, place and time for an appointment. Most often, however, the letter will suggest an appointment time and place, and unless the IRS hears from you with a request for a different time and date, you will be expected to show up on schedule.

Actually, you need not appear in person but can send someone with your power of attorney to act on your behalf and represent you. That person may be an attorney, a certified public accountant, an accountant who is enrolled in practice before the IRS or the person who prepared your tax return and signed it as the preparer. On the other hand, you yourself may appear at the audit, accompanied by your representative.

In most instances, it is not necessary to have someone accompany you. Should the IRS auditor disallow some of your deductions, you are under no obligation to agree with that assessment, and you may undertake an appeals and challenge process (see section below). It is at this point that a professional will be most useful, giving you advice during the appeals process. It should be pointed out that approximately 28 percent of all audits result either in no additional assessment against the taxpayer or in a refund.

Your Rights of Appeal in an Audit Finding

Suppose that you have gone through an IRS audit on your charitable contributions, your medical expenses and your business expenses. You claim that all of the deductions you have taken are perfectly legitimate and sufficiently backed up by records to justify them. The auditor, however, is of a very different opinion and has determined that you owe $700. Must you pay or are there avenues open to you whereby you can either wipe out the bill entirely or at least reduce its amount?

Under the law there are appeals procedures you can employ, and often their use will benefit you. For most people, it is probably wise to begin by approaching the IRS directly.

After an audit has been completed on your tax return, you will receive an audit report that informs you of how much the auditor thinks you owe. You are at liberty to agree—and pay the amount in question—submit new information that may change the auditor's assessment or you may disagree. In any case, if you wish to have an administrative hearing on your case, you must respond within 30 days of the date on the auditor's report. If you don't make some sort of response—you will receive after 90 days a letter serving final notice that a deficiency of a stated amount has been determined. At this point you will have 90 days to petition the federal tax court for a judicial determination of your case. However, it is simpler and far less wearing to respond to the 30-day notice and seek an administrative remedy through a District Appeals Office Conference. This conference is not a formal court proceeding, but is a serious affair, at which you may represent yourself or bring someone to speak on your behalf. The appeals official has full authority to cancel the findings of the original auditor, and raise or lower the assessment.

If you do not agree with the decision of the appeals officer there are still two routes left open to you. You can petition the tax court for a hearing, and if you take this route you will not have to pay the assessment until after a determination of your case by the tax court. (Remember, however, that interest is building up on the assessment, and should you lose in tax court you will have to pay a lawyer's fee and a considerable amount in interest.) If you can afford it and are determined you can bypass the tax court altogether and take your case into Federal District Court—and from there to the Appeals Division and finally to the Supreme Court. If you choose to go into Federal District Court, you will be required to pay the assessment and then file for a refund. The Federal District Court route is rarely resorted to by individuals, unless there is a great deal of money at stake. The cost of pursuing a case through the courts is such that only those who are very wealthy and very determined will make the effort.

The Cost of Paying Late

Suppose that you have gone through an audit and have exercised your appeal rights. Perhaps you have gone all the way through the courts. Or perhaps you came to the conclusion early on that there was little point in continuing to battle the IRS; you owe them money and that is all there is to it. In any case, you are going to have to pay, not only the amount you originally owed but interest on that amount as well and, perhaps, a penalty. Interest is computed from the time the money was due or the day your return was filed, whichever came first. For example, the IRS may have determined that you owed them $100 for a period of two years and called you in for an audit. Then you battled the Service for another two years because you were convinced they were wrong and you were right, and finally you lost your case. You will owe them four years' interest on that $100.

Until just a few years ago, interest was set at 6 percent annually, but now the IRS can charge the prime rate as it stands in September of that tax year. If the rate is 18 percent, that is the amount of interest you will be charged. Therefore, after four years, the original $100 may amount to almost $175.

In addition to the interest you may well be charged a penalty. Penalties are assessed when you have failed to file on time, have failed to pay the amount shown on the return, have been negligent about your deductions or have failed to report all of your taxable income. Obviously, if you filed late or owed taxes that you didn't pay (even if you were unaware that you owed them) there is every likelihood that you will be assessed a penalty on the amount owed, as well as interest. If you are being penalized for delinquency—and that is the most common situation—the amount of the penalty will probably be $1/2$ of 1 percent of the amount you owe for each month you have owed it.

There is a limit, however, on a delinquency penalty of 25 percent of the total amount due. The auditor has considerable latitude in deciding whether or not to charge a delinquency penalty. If you can convince the auditor that you had good reason for not paying the full amount you owed on time, you may not be required to pay a penalty. If you are hit with a penalty and you do not pay within ten days, interest will begin to accumulate on the penalty itself and this will be added to the continuing interest charges on the principal you owe.

How to Pay. If you agree to your auditor's assessment at the close of an interview, you may elect to pay what you owe on the spot. A personal check or money order is acceptable to the auditor; cash is not. On the other hand, you need not make an immediate payment. You can wait to be officially assessed by the Service's collection division by mail. This process will take anywhere from six weeks to two months. This will give you some time to accumulate the funds you need to pay the bill; however, the interest on your overdue account will continue to accumulate through this period.

If You Cannot or Do Not Pay. Once you have been assessed by the IRS and the audit and appeals (if any) are completed, the Service will be diligent in its efforts to collect the amount owed. This does not necessarily mean that it will be completely heartless. If you find that you just do not have the funds to pay what you owe, do not ignore the situation in the hope that it will go away—it won't. Call the Tax-

Tax Evasion and Tax Avoidance

The federal government expects each resident of the United States who is liable for income tax to pay every dollar that is legally owed. Willful failure to do so constitutes tax evasion, an illegal activity that may result in a jail sentence. Conversely, however, the government does not require that the taxpayer contribute more than is absolutely necessary under the terms of the income tax laws. To take advantage of every loophole in the law, of every deduction that can be proved, is tax avoidance, and that is perfectly legal.

Most forms of tax evasion have to do with unreported income. A landlord, for example, who insists that rent payments be made in cash or checks made out to cash is probably seeking income that will be difficult to trace. The failure to report this money is an evasion of income taxes. A waiter who pockets tips and does not report them either to his employer or to the government is also hiding income.

Increasingly common these days is a form of tax evasion known as bartering. A plumber, for example, may fix the pipes in a carpenter's house without fee. The carpenter in turn may build a set of bookcases for his friend the plumber and never submit a bill. What the two craftsmen have done is to barter their services. Under the Internal Revenue Code, the value of these services is taxable. Unless the plumber and carpenter declare the services received on their income tax forms, they have evaded their taxes.

Suppose, however, that the plumber and the carpenter barter their services but merely delay the payments to obtain a better tax break. It is the end of 1981 and both craftsmen have had a very successful year—so successful, in fact, that each is in the 40 percent bracket. As the two craftsmen look to the year to come it appears likely that they will not make as much money as they did in 1981. Therefore, when the plumber fixes the pipes in the carpenter's house, he does not send his friend a bill until after January 1. Similarly, when the carpenter builds the plumber a bookcase, he too submits his bill after the new year. What the two men are doing is reducing their taxable income in a year when they are both in a high bracket, and increasing their taxable income in a year when they both anticipate being in a lower bracket. This is tax avoidance and is therefore legal.

However, there is often a thin line between evasion and avoidance. If you are at all unsure which category a tactic you are considering might fall into, consult your local Internal Revenue Service office or an expert tax consultant such as a lawyer who specializes in the field, or a certified public accountant.

payer Division of the IRS (the local office of this division is listed in your phone book's white pages under the general heading "U.S. Government"). Arrange an appointment or, if necessary, you can just walk in off the street without prior notice. Bring with you all records that will reveal your current financial position, such as bank account statements, mortgage bills, medical and dental bills, records of outstanding loans and the like. During the interview the official to whom you are speaking will ask you a number of questions and review your records and you will be required to fill out a form called a Statement of Financial Condition. If it appears that you have assets that can be used to pay off your taxes, you may be required to dispose of them. The IRS may demand that you sell off stocks and bonds and other liquid assets that will enable you to make immediate or early payment.

On the other hand, if the official decides that your financial condition is truly desperate and that forcing you to make full payment immediately would impose extreme hardship on you or your family, an arrangement of time payments may be worked out. Should this be arranged, remember that if you fail to make these payments on time—while also keeping up with your continuing tax obligations—the entire debt can be called in. While the IRS has no interest in putting you and your family in the poorhouse, it does have an overriding interest in collecting what is due. By agreeing to installment payments, the IRS is, in effect making you a loan, and as with almost any other loan, you will be charged interest on the unpaid balance. The simple truth is that if the IRS catches you in an error—whether intentional or not—they will eventually collect what they are owed by one means or another. Sometimes the means employed can be unpleasant, as the following paragraphs will show.

Failure to Pay the IRS. In the event that you ignore a bill from the IRS and either fail to pay or refuse to make arrangements for installment payments, the Service will move to attach your assets or salary. Normally, this will not be done without warning. In fact, a delinquent taxpayer will usually get four warning notices, each one allowing 10 days in which to pay or make an arrangement for payment. The last of these notices will be extremely stern in tone, and will warn that failure to comply could result in such action as a levy on the taxpayer's bank accounts, a garnish of his or her salary or a seizure of property. These are not idle threats. The Collection Division of the IRS has proceeded in just these ways in thousands of cases. The Collection Division has the legal authority to employ almost any means to close out the case and collect whatever is due.

For example, suppose Horace Wimple owes the IRS $2,000 and refuses to pay. After he has received due notice of the Service's intention to collect, he finds that there has been a levy on his bank accounts and a garnish on his wages. The amount of the garnish depends on the tax-

payer's number of dependents; allowance is also made for such items as medical insurance and union dues. The IRS will continue to garnish his wages until the total amount owed has been paid. However, to avoid imposing a severe hardship, the Service attaches not every salary check but every other one.

Suppose that while Mr. Wimple's salary is being garnished he is fired and a portion of his debt is still outstanding. Now the IRS moves to seize his property, including his house. To do this, however, the Service must obtain a court order. Mr. Wimple is given 10 days to satisfy his debt to the IRS, after which the Service is free to put his property up for sale. In this case, Mr. Wimple lets the matter slide and the IRS does sell off the property it has seized. After the property has been sold and any outstanding mortgages satisfied, the IRS deducts the cost of the seizure and sale and the amount Mr. Wimple owed it, and then turns over the rest of the proceeds to him. If, however, another creditor comes forward with a valid claim against Mr. Wimple, this creditor can be satisfied before the remaining proceeds are given to the delinquent taxpayer. Once the taxpayer's property is sold it is probably gone for good, but there is one exception. The former owner can reclaim the house by purchasing it back from the buyer at the price paid plus 20 percent interest. If this is done within a period of 120 days after the sale, the buyer must, by law, return the house to the former owner.

The Importance of Careful Record Keeping

The most efficient way to avoid an audit, or to prepare for one if it comes, is to fill out your income tax form every year with extreme care. Fundamental to this process is careful record keeping. Generally, every deduction that you take on your income tax should be backed up by records of one sort or another. Once you have used the records to facilitate filling out the income tax forms, put them away in a safe place and retain them for at least three years. If you should be called for an audit, these records will serve to support your income tax return and establish your right to the deductions you claim.

Though record keeping may be a bother, it is really not all that difficult for most taxpayers. All you really need is an empty box or a desk drawer set aside for that purpose. Every night, check your wallet or pocketbook for receipts that might conceivably have a bearing on your tax situation. For example, if you buy prescription drugs at the pharmacy, just put the receipt in the box or drawer that evening. (Should your receipt be in the form of a cash-register slip, just write on that slip what the expenditure was for, though it would be wise for any purchase that might be tax deductible to insist upon getting a handwritten, itemized receipt.) Save all receipts that include such expenses as state or local sales taxes and put aside all credit card statements that indicate the amount of interest you are being charged.

At the end of each month, when your checking account statement arrives, separate the canceled checks that might have a bearing on your federal tax situation—payments for anything on which there is a tax; payments for books or periodicals that relate to your business; union dues; checks to doctors, lawyers, hospitals, clinics and the like. When making contributions to charity, be sure to do so only by check and try to get a receipt for each contribution. If you own a house on which you are paying a mortgage, this will undoubtedly be a major deduction for you.

At the end of each calendar year, your mortgage holder will probably send you a statement listing the amount of interest you have paid and, in most cases, the amount of money you have paid that year in real estate taxes—if you pay these taxes through the mortgage holder. Should this statement not arrive by the end of January, contact the mortgage holder and make sure you obtain it. If you pay your real

estate taxes directly to your local government, be sure to secure a statement from your town or county collector's office.

If you are self-employed or have unreimbursed business expenses, keep a day-by-day diary in a notebook. Include notations on such expenditures as entertainment, travel, business lunches or dinners, hotel accommodations, taxicab fares and the like. Expenditures of $25 or more must be backed up by receipts. The basic thing to remember is the more complete your records the less likely you are to be hit with an unexpected tax bill in the aftermath of an audit.

Chances are that when you filled out your tax forms you separated your checks, bills and receipts by category: medical, legal, charitable, business and so forth. Leave them that way when you store these records for possible future reference. If they are not separated according to category when you are called in for an audit, put them in some sort of order before you appear for the interview. Few things are likely to annoy an auditor more than having a shoe box full of uncategorized receipts dumped upon his or her desk.

When you appear for an audit, be prepared, as far as possible, to back up each of your claimed deductible expenditures with as many different kinds of records as possible. If, for example, you are claiming that you spent $800 for prescription drugs, your auditor may not be willing merely to accept canceled checks in the amount made out to your local pharmacy. After all, these checks could have been used to pay for such non-deductible items as toothpaste and photographic film. Written, itemized receipts or bills, accompanied by canceled checks, will be far more persuasive than the canceled checks alone. Similarly, if you claim a casualty loss, caused by storm damage to your property, you should be able to prove that the money you gave to a contractor was for repairs necessitated by storm damage. In this case, a written estimate from an expert appraiser as to the value of the property before and after the damage occurred and an itemized receipt should do the trick. If you were robbed, be sure to get a police report stating the circumstances of the robbery and what was taken. Try to prove the cost of each item. You may, of course, claim only those losses that were not reimbursed by insurance.

Remember, in an audit, the burden of proof is on you to prove each deductible expense under review. There is no requirement that the auditor accept your word for anything. Technically, an auditor can even require that you provide proof for every mile of unreimbursed business travel you claim. Few auditors, however, will go to that extreme unless it appears that you are greatly overstating such expenses. If, for example, you are a textile salesman whose headquarters is in New York City but whose sales territory is New England, an auditor may accept your statement that you traveled a certain number of miles through the New England states in pursuit of customers. But do remember that there is no requirement that the auditor accept such statements and, indeed, the IRS could require that you produce turnpike records and gasoline receipts to back up your assertions. Among the records that will help you in such circumstances is a letter from your employer stating your position and confirming that business expenses were unreimbursed. And, of course, a diary of day-by-day business expenses will be invaluable if you are called upon to justify your deductions.

Internal Revenue Offices

Because all federal income tax matters come under the jurisdiction of a single agency, the Internal Revenue Service, a directory of office addresses is not included with this chapter. Further information may be obtained by communicating directly with the Internal Revenue Service, 1111 Constitution Ave., Washington, DC 20224, or by calling one of the agency's many local offices, listed under "U.S. Government" in telephone books.

The Government's Vast Reservoir of Information

The main source of government publications is the U.S. Government Printing Office (GPO), a sprawling operation that includes one of the world's largest printing plants and a total of 27 book stores, 7 of which are located in Washington DC, or nearby Maryland, and the remaining 20 in cities scattered across the country. The output of the GPO extends from single-page forms to multi-volume series of brightly illustrated books. The best-known of the GPO publications, perhaps, is the *Congressional Record,* a complete account of every day's proceedings in the U.S. Congress. Printed overnight by the GPO, it is delivered to the doorsteps of Senators and members of the House of Representatives in the Washington area at breakfast time every morning while Congress is in session.

All told, the GPO turns out approximately 20,000 publications, on subjects that range from *accidents* to *zoology*.

Listed below are a number of GPO publications, chosen to supplement the reading of this book. Brief descriptions, provided by the GPO, accompany some of the listings.

Publications for sale by the GPO may be ordered by sending your check or money order to: Superintendent of Documents, U.S. Government Printing Office, Washington, DC 20402. Checks should be made out to the Superintendent of Documents. Orders may also be charged to your VISA, MasterCard or pre-paid Superintendent of Documents deposit account. Prices shown were those in effect in November 1981.

Charges for government publications are subject to change without notice, and the prices for items that you order will be those in effect at the time your order is processed. For a current price quotation, you may write to the address given above, or call the GPO's order desk at (202) 783-3238. Be sure to include the GPO's stock number (S/N), listed here after each publication, with your order or request for prices.

Orders going to countries outside the United States and its possessions require an additional 25 percent of the prices listed. This charge is designed to cover the handling and to comply with the customs and international mailing regulations.

Chapter 1: Education: From Kindergarten Through College

American Education. (Monthly except August-September and January-February, which are combined issues.) Covers pre-school to adult education, new research and demonstration projects, major education legislation, school and college bond data, grants, loans, contracts and fellowships. Subscription price: domestic–$14 a year; foreign–$17.50 a year. Single-copy price: domestic–$2.75 a copy; foreign–$3.45 a copy. S/N 065-000-80001-2

Nation of Learners. A mosaic of nostalgic art and photographs illustrates this collection of articles paying tribute to the progress of education in America. Treating topics as diverse as universal education, libraries in the new world, tomorrow's education, arts in the schools and lifelong learning, this large-format volume combines the efforts of over two dozen authors. Viewed in its entirety, this publication graphically displays the continuing responsiveness of education to the needs of the American people. Paper edition. 185 pp. il. S/N 017-080-01540-4. $4.50. Cloth edition. 185 pp. il. S/N 017-080-01541-2. $5.95

When Your Child First Goes Off to School. Advises parents on ways to bolster the confidence of their children who are starting school. 6 pp. il. S/N 017-024-00499-5. $1.75

College and Universities Offering Accredited Programs by Accreditation Field, Including Selected Characteristics, 1977–78. Tabular data listing selected characteristics of institutions offering accredited programs. Includes an index by institution. 146 pp. S/N 017-080-01913-2. $4

Advanced General Education Program: High School Self-Study Program. This program is designed to help prepare adult students with the information, concepts and general knowledge needed to pass the American Council on Education's "Test of General Educational Development" (GED) for high school equivalency certification. The kit consists of 126 booklets and a form to record the student's progress and performance record. Sold only as a set. S/N 029-000-00340-8. $44

Sucess Stories of Adult Learning in America. Many Americans have learned how to live better, with benefit to society as well as to themselves, through adult education. This publication contains the stories of eight individuals who have enriched their lives through adult education, and recounts some of the ways in which adult education has improved society. 24 pp. S/N 017-080-01950-7. $1.75

Chapter 2: Your Job: When You Have One and When You Don't

Federal Contract Compliance Manual. Subscription service consists of a basic manual and amendments for an indeterminate period. Details the policies and procedures that should normally be followed by all Office of Federal Contract Compliance Program (OFCCP) personnel in enforcing the rules and regulations in Title 41 of the Code of Federal Regulations, Chapter 60. Subscription price: domestic—$28; foreign—$35. S/N 029-016-81001-3

Handbook of Selective Placement of Persons with Physical and Mental Handicaps in Federal Civil Service Employment. Outlines concepts and procedures that can and should be used to provide equal employment opportunity for all qualified handicapped applicants and employees. 71 pp. S/N 006-000-01093-8. $3.50

How to Get a Job, A Handy Guide for Jobseekers. Written in simple language for people who are slow learners, this booklet gives the kind of practical advice about hunting for a job that almost anyone can follow. It gives the basic principles behind choosing the right kind of work, looking for the job and going on interviews. 29 pp. il. S/N 052-003-00087-3. $1.75

Native American Women and Equal Opportunity: How to Get Ahead in the Federal Government. 81 pp. il. S/N 029-002-00053-3. $4

Dictionary of Occupational Titles. 4th Edition. A compendium of about 20,000 occupations in the American economy, this large volume contains an integrated arrangement of occupational definitions and the classification structure used to group such occupations in terms of related duties and activities. It includes sections on the purpose and history of the dictionary and how to use it as an occupational reference source or as a tool for job placement. It also contains occupational titles arranged alphabetically and by industry, and a glossary of defined technical terms. 1,371 pp. S/N 029-013-00079-9. $13

Merchandising Your Job Talents, 1980. This pamphlet includes tips on writing a resume, preparing for a job interview and other techniques of finding a job. 24 pp. il. S/N 029-014-00113-9. $2

Occupational Outlook for College Graduates, 1980–81 Edition. 215 pp. il. S/N 029-001-02322-7. $7

Chapter 3: Help for Your Home and Your Neighborhood

Citizens Action Manual: A Guide to Recycling Vacant Property in Your Neighborhood. Describes and illustrates the Trust for Public Land National Urban Land Program that teaches non-profit land acquisition techniques to citizens groups. 32 pp. il. S/N 024-016-00100-1. $2.75

Design for Safe Neighborhoods: The Environmental Security Planning and Design Process. 83 pp. il. S/N 027-000-00751-1. $3.50

Design Guide for Home Safety. This book points out the many areas of home design that should be influenced by safety considerations. 147 pp. il. S/N 023-000-00201-9. $7

How to Build a House, Using Self-Help Housing Techniques. Describes the basic things you need to know if you're going to build or add to a home of your own. 50 pp. il. S/N 023-000-00276-1. $1.75

New Life for Old Dwellings, Appraisal and Rehabilitations. The appraisal section deals with the suitability of various parts of a house for rehabilitation, and the rehabilitation section tells how to accomplish such changes. 100 pp. il. S/N 001-000-02988-6. $5

Rent or Buy? Evaluating Alternatives in the Shelter Market. Discusses the differences between owning and renting; analyzing shelter costs and returns; and comparing investment returns from owning and renting. 21 pp. S/N 029-001-02309-0. $2

Settlement Costs: A HUD (Department of Housing and Urban Development) Guide. This booklet explains the important things to know before you make final settlement on your house. It itemizes and explains every point of the standard form used to record actual settlement charges to buyers and sellers in mortgage transactions. 40 pp. S/N 023-000-00337-6. $1.75

Solar Dwelling Design Concepts. This general resource book is intended for use by designers, home builders, community leaders, local officials and homeowners who are interested in the application of solar heating and cooling to residential structures or are considering participating in the federal solar energy program. 146 pp. il. S/N 023-000-00334-1. $6.50

Chapter 4: Maintaining Your Family's Health and Well-Being

Adult Physical Fitness, A Program for Men and Women. Gives alternative physical fitness programs for men and women at various levels of capability. Besides programs of general exercise, the book presents exercises in isometrics, water activities and weight training. 64 pp. il. S/N 040-000-00026-7. $4.25

Exercise and Weight Control. This pamphlet discusses the relationship between weight control, exercise and caloric intake, emphasizing the importance of 30 to 60 minutes of daily exercise for efficient and effective weight loss and general fitness. 10 pp. S/N 040-000-00371-1. $1.75. $9 per 100

Fitness Challenge in the Later Years: An Exercise Program for Older Americans. Prepared to help the elderly take advantage of added years of life which medical science is making possible. It outlines methods for maintaining youthful health and energy, and it suggests ways of enhancing the enjoyment of leisure. 28 pp. il. S/N 017-062-00009-3. $2.50

Physically Underdeveloped Child: Identification Improving Performance. Reviews the screening program for identifying physically underdeveloped children and discusses the exercise needs of these children. 13 pp. il. S/N 040-000-00387-8. $1.75

When Your Child Goes to the Hospital. This handy booklet tells how to explain hospitalization to a child, what and how much to say and what you need to know before you talk to the child. It includes advice on choosing a doctor and selecting a hospital, as well as preparing the child for admission day and for treatments or procedures. It discusses the pros and cons of staying with the child and tells you how to prepare the child for discharge. 36 pp. il. S/N 017-091-00217-7. $2

Nursing Home Care. This booklet describes the different kinds of nursing homes and the care and services they offer and includes practical advice and a handy checklist to help you make comparisons between different institutions. 33 pp. il. S/N 017-061-00040-2. $1.75

Parents Guide to Childhood Immunization: Measles, Polio, Rubella (German Mea- sles), **Mumps, Diphtheria, Pertussis (Whooping Cough), Tetanus.** 24 pp. il. S/N 017-001-00401-4. $14 per 50

Your Health and You. Provides guidelines for self-treatment for common minor illnesses and medical conditions. 19 pp. S/N 008-023-00055-7. $1.75

Chapter 5: Special Programs for the Handicapped

Emotions in the Lives of Children. 17 pp. S/N 017-024-00739-1. $1.75

Helping the Hyperactive Child. This publication discusses the hyperkinetic behavior syndrome in children, often labeled minimal brain dysfunction. 9 pp. il. S/N 017-024-0079-0. $1.75

Key Federal Regulations Affecting the Handicapped. Prepared by the National Association of Coordinators of State Programs for the Mentally Retarded, Inc. 74 pp. S/N 017-090-00031-3. $2.25

Adaptable Dwellings. Outlines how adaptive devices and architectural and interior design features can be used to make a home more suitable for disabled people. 38 pp. il. S/N 023-000-00513-1. $2.25

Add on Automotive Adaptive Equipment for Passenger Automobiles. Describes Veterans Administration-approved devices to help the handicapped drive. Also explains VA standards and test criteria. 59 pp. il. S/N 051-000-00118-4. $2.75

Blueprint for Action. Provides strategies for improving opportunities available to the disabled youth for education, training and jobs. 57 pp. S/N 040-000-00435-1. $4.25

Leisure Time Activities: A Resource Manual for Developmentally Disabled Individuals and Their Advocates. Containing helpful information for disabled individuals and volunteers who work with them, this publication outlines ways handicapped persons can use their leisure time for recreational and social activities. 120 pp. S/N 017-092-00078-2. $5

Children with Emotional Disturbances, A Guide for Teachers, Parents and Others Who Work with Emotionally Disturbed Preschoolers. 147 pp. il. S/N 017-092-00036-7. $6.50

Children with Health Impairments, A Guide for Teachers, Parents and Others Who Work with Health Impaired Preschoolers. 131 pp. il. S/N 017-092-00031-6. $6.50

No Easy Answers: The Learning Disabled Child. Describes the behavior of the learning disabled child, points out his or her needs, shows how an adult can help structure the day-to-day activities to help the child learn, outlines the development of a child from infancy through adolescence, tells how the child learns, and explains why the learning disabled child differs in development and maturational skills. 131 pp. il. S/N 017-024-00687-4. $6.50

Parents as Co-therapists with Autistic Children. Describes professionally staffed treatment programs for autistic and communication handicapped children, using the children's parents as co-therapists. 11 pp. S/N 017-024-00840-1. $1.75

Ready Reference Guide, Resource for Disabled People: A Handbook for Service Practitioners and Disabled People. A compilation of a wide range of programs and projects operating at the national level to provide aid and assistance to disabled persons. 115 pp. S/N 017-000-00201-5. $3.50

Resources for the Vocational Preparation of Disabled Youth. An information catalogue of resources on the delivery of special education, vocational education and vocational rehabilitation services to handicapped youth at the secondary and post-secondary levels. The address and the cost of material is included after each title. 44 pp. S/N 040-000-00418-1. $2.75

Chapter 6: Veterans' Benefits and Services

Disability Separation. Discusses physical disability retirement and separation from the military service. 54 pp. il. S/N 008-001-00110-0. $2

Handbook for Design: Specially Adapted Housing. Provides assistance to the physically handicapped veteran and the architect or designer in producing the best possible home for the veteran. 79 pp. il. S/N 051-000-00125-7. $5

Handbook on Retirement Services for Army Personnel and Their Families. 166 pp. S/N 008-020-00568-1. $3

Veterans' Reemployment Rights Under Federal and State Acts. 488 pp. Looseleaf for updating. S/N 029-007-00005-5. $10

Military Retirees in Federal Employment. Folder. S/N 006-000-01195-1. $1.75. $12 per 100

Once a Veteran: Benefits, Rights, Obligations. 46 pp. S/N 008-001-00107-0. $2

State Veterans' Laws, Digests of State Laws, Regarding Rights, Benefits, and Privileges of Veterans and Their Dependents. 315 pp. S/N 052-070-04925-1. $4.75

Survivor Benefit Plan for the Uniformed Services. 16 pp. il. S/N 008-040-00083-4. $2

Veterans' Reemployment Rights Handbook. Discusses eligibility for reemployment rights, the duration and character of military service, seniority rights, disabled applicants, enforcement procedures and many other vital topics. 196 pp. S/N 029-007-00004-7. $3.50

Chapter 7: The Broad Coverage of Social Security

Early Retirement Decision: Evidence From the 1969 Retirement History Study. Uses the Social Security Administration's Retirement History Study to analyze the influence of personal and financial characteristics, local labor market conditions and specific job attributes on early retirement among men and women aged 58-63. 34 pp. S/N 017-070-00305-2. $1.75

Social Security Handbook, 1979. 7th Edition. S/N 017-070-00366-4. Price not available

Social Security in a Changing World. Presents a comparison between Social Security programs in the United States and abroad and discusses the problems facing America's Social Security program in the future. 144 pp. S/N 017-070-00335-4. $4.25

Social Security Rulings on Federal Old-Age, Survivors, Disability, Supplemental Security Income and Black Lung Benefits. (Quarterly.) Contains interpretations and decisions of the Social Security Administration and court cases of particular significance, changes in Title II of Social Security Act and related regulations, and items of general interest. Subscription price: domestic—$8.50 a year; for-

eign—$10.65 a year. Single copy price: domestic—$2.50 a copy; foreign—$3.15 a copy. S/N 017-070-80002-5.

Chapter 8: The Retirement Years: Aid for Older Americans

Are You Planning on Living the Rest of Your Life? A guidebook for retirement. 72 pp. il. S/N 017-062-00038-7. $2.25

Emerging Options for Work and Retirement. 192 pp. S/N 052-070-05332. $4.50

Summary of Recommendations and Survey on Social Security and Pension Policies. 56 pp. S/N 052-070-05443-3. $3.75

What You Should Know About the Pension and Welfare Law: A Guide to the Employee Retirement Income Security Act of 1974. 76 pp. S/N 029-011-00006-1. $4

You, the Law and Retirement. S/N 017-062-00003-4. $1.75

Your Retirement System: Questions and Answers Concerning the Federal Civil Service Retirement Law. 63 pp. S/N 006-000-01105-5. $3.50

Chapter 9: Recreation and Leisure on America's Public Lands

Recreation on Water Supply Reservoirs, Handbook for Increased Use. 138 pp. il. S/N 041-011-00027-1. $2.50

Skipper's Course. Developed by the Coast Guard, this self-instructional booklet teaches the fundamentals of boating. It's copiously illustrated, easy and fun to read because it teaches by presenting the material in small segments with a short quiz every page or two. The material begins with an overview of the classes of boats, the various legal requirements and the principles of trailer boating. Part 2 continues with pre-sailing procedures, launching instructions and fueling guidelines. Other sections include reviews of the rules of operation, anchoring, emergency procedures, foul weather handling, mooring, rules of the road, aid to navigation and more. 84 pp. il. S/N 050-012-00159-6. $4.50

Backcountry Travel in the National Park ystem. A comprehensive guide to more than 40 parks that permit travel in backcountry areas on foot, on horseback, by canoe and by other means; with information on planning, conservation, safety, trail use, regulations, park topography and wildlife. Also included are helpful hints for the backpacker, and a reference map. 40 pp. il. S/N 024-005-00267-7. $1.75

Camper's First Aid. A handy booklet of basic first aid information for the camper to use until medical assistance can be obtained. 14 pp. il. S/N 008-022-00143-3. $1.75

Camping in the National Park System. 25 pp. il. S/N 024-005-00807-1. $2.25

Angler's Guide to the United States, Atlantic Coast: Fish, Fishing Grounds, and Fishing Facilities. Section 1, Passamaquoddy Bay, Maine to Cape Cod. 15 pp. il. S/N 003-020-00068-1. $2
Section 2, Nantucket Shoals to Long Island Sound. 15 pp. il. S/N 003-020-00070-3. $2
Section 3, Block Island to Cape May, New Jersey. 20 pp. il. S/N 003-020-00071-1. $4.75
Section 4, Delaware Bay to False Cape, Virginia. 17 pp. il. S/N 003-020-00072-0. $2

Section 5, Chesapeake Bay. 17 pp. il. S/N 003-020-00096-7. $5.50
Section 6, False Cape, Virginia to Altamaha Sound, Georgia. 21 pp. il. S/N 003-020-00097-5. $4.75
Section 7, Altamaha Sound, Georgia, to Fort Pierce Inlet, Florida. 21 pp. il. S/N 003-020-00098-3. $4.75
Section 8, St. Lucie Inlet, Florida, to the Dry Tortugas. 25 pp. il. S/N 003-020-00099-1. $6

Angler's Guide to the United States, Pacific Coast: Marine Fish, Fishing Grounds, and Facilities. The geographic scope of this guide covers the marine and estuarine waters along the coasts of California, Oregon, Washington, Alaska, Hawaii, American Samoa and Guam. 139 pp. il. S/N 003-020-00113-1. $8.50

Fishing in the National Park System. A guide to freshwater and saltwater fishing in 61 parks, seashores and recreation areas; including information on regulations, licenses and special programs. 16 pp. il. S/N 024-005-00004-6. $1.75

National Survey of Hunting, Fishing, and Wildlife Associated Recreation. Colorful charts, tables and graphs, accompanied by statistical information; summarizes national participation in hunting, fishing, wildlife observation, wildlife photography, recreational shooting, crabbing and clamming. 91 pp. il. S/N 024-010-00441-0. $3.50

Backcountry: Glacier National Park, Montana. Features a basic map of Glacier National Park and information on the facilities and regulations of the park. 12 pp. il. S/N 024-005-00757-1. $1.75. $21 per 100

California Desert: High Desert, Recreation Resources Guide. This folder features a map of the High Desert, locating roads, campgrounds, points of interest and roadside rests; on the reverse side are brief explanations of wildlife, vegetation, cultural resources, off-road vehicle routes, points of interest and rock-hounding areas. 24 pp. il. Map. S/N 024-011-00092-5. $1.75

Desert Dangers. Describes and illustrates the types of hazards that exist in desert environments and offers outdoor recreationists suggestions for desert survival. 28 pp. il. S/N 024-011-00109-3. $2

Everglades National Park, Florida. Includes a map of the Everglades and information about its wildlife, facilities, things to do and park regulations. 24 pp. il. S/N 024-005-00720-2. $1.75. $25 per 100

Guides to Outdoor Recreation Areas and Facilities. A list of national, regional and state guidebooks to outdoor recreation. 79 pp. S/N 024-016-00064-1. $1.75

Islands of America. This illustrated book presents the first comprehensive inventory of the recreational, scenic, natural and historical values of America's islands. Special mention is given to islands with outstanding recreation potential. 95 pp. il. S/N 024-016-00031-5. $3.50

United States: Guide and Map. Features a map of the United States locating all national parks, and a chart listing services, facilities and activities of each park. 30 pp. il. S/N 024-005-00771-7. $2. $23 per 100

Recreation Areas. These publications, with maps, locate and describe recreation areas on reclamation projects in the American West. Each publication shows the recreation areas on a map, lists their facilities and activities and provides their addresses.

Map 1, Idaho, Oregon, Washington. 32 pp. il. S/N 024-003-00113-9. $2. $29 per 100

Map 2, Montana, Nebraska, North Dakota, South Dakota, Wyoming. 32 pp. il. S/N 024-003-00114-7. $2. $29 per 100

Map 3, Arizona, California, Nevada, Utah. 32 pp. il. S/N 024-003-00115-5. $2. $29 per 100

Map 4, Colorado, Kansas, Oklahoma, New Mexico, Texas. 32 pp. il. S/N 024-003-00116-3. $2. $29 per 100

Rocky Mountain. This folder features a map of Rocky Mountain National Park and provides information about the park, its history, the available activities and regulations. 24 pp. il. S/N 024-005-00674-5. $1.75. $21 per 100

Visitor Accommodations, Facilities and Services, 1980-1981. This publication lists alphabetically, by name, overnight lodging accommodations and other facilities and services provided by concessioners in the national park system. Lodgings include hotels, motels, cottages and trailer parks. 114 pp. S/N 024-005-00777-6. $4.25

Visitor Guide to the National Wildlife Refuges. This publication consists of a map of the United States, which includes locations of all national wildlife refuges and a list of their names, addresses and description of available activities. 30 pp. il. S/N 024-010-00529-7. $1.75. $27 per 100

Be Safe from Insects in Recreation Areas. This booklet gives advice on purchasing repellents by generic name, use of space sprays and offers suggestions on effective protection from particularly troublesome insects. 7 pp. S/N 001-000-03802-8. $1.75

Survival, Evasion and Escape. This book can be useful to outdoorsmen or to anyone who may be isolated in a desolate area. The sections on evasion and escape are interesting, but it is the survival section, complete with photographs and diagrams of various wilderness situations, that the lay person should find most useful. Among the subjects covered are: obtaining food, crossing dangerous rivers, extreme heat and cold, fishing without a pole, shark attacks, building rafts and fires, navigating by the stars and more. 431 pp. il. S/N 008-020-00157-1. $7

Chapter 10: Saving Money on Your Income Tax

Tax Guide for United States Citizens Abroad. S/N 048-004-01737-7. $3.50

Travel, Entertainment and Gift Expenses. S/N 048-004-01738-5. $1.75

Exemptions. S/N 048-004-01739-3. $1.75

Medical and Dental Expenses. S/N 048-004-01740-7. $1.75

Child Care and Disabled Dependent Care. S/N 048-004-01741-5. $1.75

Tax Information for Divorced or Separated Individuals. S/N 048-004-01742-3. $1.75

Tax Withholding and Estimated Tax. S/N 048-004-01743-1. $1.75

Income Averaging. S/N 048-004-01744-0. $1.75

Educational Expenses. S/N 048-004-01745-8. $1.75

Credit for the Elderly. S/N 048-004-01759-8. $1.75

Rental Property. S/N 048-004-01762-8. $1.75

Miscellaneous Deductions. S/N 048-004-01763-6. $1.75

Tax Information for Homeowners. S/N 048-004-01764-4. $1.75

Self-Employment Tax. S/N 048-004-01766-1. $1.75

Withholding Taxes and Reporting Requirements. S/N 048-004-01813-6. $1.75

Tax Information on Partnerships. S/N 048-004-01771-7. $1.75

Sales and Other Dispositions of Assets. S/N 048-004-01815-2. $2.25

Interest Expenses. S/N 048-004-01772-5. $1.75

Tax Information on Disasters, Casualty Losses and Thefts. S/N 048-004-01773-3. $1.75

Deduction for Bad Debts. S/N 048-004-01774-1. $1.75

Investment Income and Expenses. S/N 048-004-01816-1. $2

Tax Benefits for Older Americans. S/N 048-004-01779-2. $4

Business Use of Your Home. S/N 048-004-01795-4. $1.75

Condominiums, Cooperative Apartments and Homeowners' Associations. S/N 048-004-01796-2. $1.75

Energy Credits for Individuals. S/N 048-004-01801-2. $1.75

Tax Information for Handicapped and Disabled Individuals. S/N 048-004-01804-7. $2.50

Alabama
Roebuck Shopping City
9220-B Parkway E.
Birmingham, AL 35206

California
ARCO Plaza, C-Level
505 S. Flower St.
Los Angeles, CA 90071

Federal Building
450 Golden Gate Ave.
San Francisco, CA 94102

Colorado
Federal Building
1961 Stout St.
Denver, CO 80294

720 N. Main St.
Majestic Building
Pueblo, CO 81003

District of Columbia
US Government Printing Office
710 N. Capitol St.
Washington, DC 20401

Commerce Department
14th & E Sts., NW
Washington, DC 20230

Department of Health and Human Services
330 Independence Ave., SW
Washington, DC 20201

State Department
21st & C St., NW
Washington, DC 20520

International Communication
Agency
1776 Pennsylvania Ave., NW
Washington, DC 20547

Pentagon
Main Concourse, South End
Washington, DC 20301

Florida
Federal Building
400 W. Bay St.
Jacksonville, FL 32202

Georgia
Federal Building
275 Peachtree St., NE
Atlanta, GA 30303

Illinois
Federal Building
219 S. Dearborn St.
Chicago, IL 60604

Maryland
8660 Cherry Lane
Laurel, MD 20707

Massachusetts
Federal Building
Sudbury St.
Boston, MA 02203

Michigan
Federal Building
477 Michigan Ave.
Detroit, MI 48226

Missouri
Federal Building
601 E. 12th St.
Kansas City, MO 64106

New York
26 Federal Plaza
New York, NY 10278

Ohio
Federal Building
1240 E. 9th St.
Cleveland, OH 44199

Federal Building
200 N. High St.
Columbus, OH 43215

Pennsylvania
Federal Building
600 Arch St.
Philadelphia, PA 19106

Federal Building
1000 Liberty Ave.
Pittsburgh, PA 15222

Texas
Federal Building
1100 Commerce St.
Dallas, TX 75242

45 College Center
9319 Gulf Freeway
Houston, TX 77017

Washington
Federal Building
915 Second Ave.
Seattle, WA 98174

Wisconsin
Federal Building
517 E. Wisconsin Ave.
Milwaukee, WI 53202

Index

making offers for, 97
mobile, 100, 101
mortgages for, 95, 97-99, 100, 101, 112, 116, 233-235, 308, 399-400, 404
old vs. new, 97
preventing crimes in, 108, 109
price of, 96
as rented, 96, 112-113, 122
solar heating in, 101, 103
as sub-standard, 112, 121
in urban renewal areas, 116
weatherization of, 122
see also housing
Home Start Training Centers (Head Start program), 133
hospice movement, 321-322
housing
directories for offices pertaining to, 124
discrimination in, 114-115, 121-122
for handicapped, 113-114, 123
loans for, 97-99, 100, 101, 113-114, 116, 121-123
for low-income families, 95, 121, 122-123
mobile homes as, 100, 101
for older citizens, 113-114, 123, 305-309, 311
public, 112-113
rent subsidies for, 113, 122, 202-203, 308
in rural areas, 121-123
tax credits for, 95, 101, 102
veterans, 97, 233-235
see also homes; mortgages
Housing Act (1937), 113
Housing Act (1949), 112
Housing Act (1959), 113
Housing and Development Act (1974), 115
Housing and Urban Development, U.S. Department of (HUD), 95, 96, 97
directory for offices of, 124-125
discrimination investigated by, 114-115
inspections by, 98
loans for home improvement from, 101
in neighborhood development, 117, 118-119, 120, 121
older citizens' services from, 307, 308
public housing aid from, 112, 113
rental advice from, 112
services for handicapped from, 202-203
in urban homestead program, 116

I

Idaho
parks in, 358
student aid programs in, 36
Illinois
child labor standards in, 65
government jobs in, 61
parks in, 358
student aid programs in, 36
immunization programs, 134
income taxes, *see* taxes, income
Indiana
parks in, 359
student aid programs in, 37
unemployment compensation in, 79

Indian Health Service, U.S., 143-144
Individual Retirement Accounts (IRAs), 84, 394, 413-414
Industrial Revolution, 64
inflation, 260, 263, 269
Institute of Lifetime Learning, 299
insurance
against crime, 103, 106, 107, 324
against disasters, 103
against floods, 106
for "Medigap," 160-161
against riots, 106
Social Security vs., 260
unemployment, 78-80
for veterans, 219, 235-237, 241
Interior Department, U.S., 340
Intermediate Care Facilities (ICFs), 316
Internal Revenue Service (IRS), 57, 80, 84, 101-103, 111, 203, 288-291, 295
assistance from, 387
auditing by, 416-422
Collection Service of, 422
Discriminate Function System of, 416
offices for, 424
International Childbirth Education Association, 129
International Executive Service Corps (IESC), 294
International Senior Citizens Association, 329
Interstate Compact on the Placement of Children, 137
Interstate Land Sales Registration, U.S. Office of, 307-308
Iowa
parks in, 359
student aid programs in, 37

J

Jamaica Service Program for Older Adults (JSPOA), 313
Javits-Wagner-O'Day Act, 191-192
Job Corps, 62
Job Information Services, 56
jobs, 53-84
affirmative action in, 67, 69, 198-201, 232-233
for blind, 191-192
children in, 64-66
counseling for, 54
for deaf, 193
for disabled, 189
discrimination in, 59, 67-70
employment offices for, 54-57, 89-91, 200, 233
in federal government, *see* jobs, federal government
for handicapped, 55, 57, 67, 196-197, 200-201
insurance for loss of, 78-80
interviews for, 54, 55
legislation pertaining to, 53, 64, 66, 67, 74, 78, 80, 198, 200, 232
looking for, 54-57, 292
minimum wage for, 70-71, 72-73
for minorities, 67
out-of-state, 56
overtime in, 71, 73
payment intervals for, 73
pension plans for, 80-84

T

Credits and Acknowledgments

The editors of the Reader's Digest are indebted to the following departments, offices and agencies for their help with the preparation of this book.

The U.S. Department of Education and the following offices or agencies: Bureau of Elementary and Secondary Education; Division of Alcohol and Drug Education Programs; Office for Gifted and Talented; Bureau of School Improvement, Ethnic Heritage Studies; Division of Educational Technology, Office of Libraries and Learning Technologies; Metric Education Program Staff; Office of Higher Education; Office of the Director, Legislative Section; Office of Higher Education, National Center for Educational Statistics; Office of the Secretary of the Department of Education, Educational Discretionary Fund.

The U.S. Department of Defense.

The U.S. Department of Health and Human Services and the following offices and agencies: the Administration for Children, Youth and Families, Head Start Program; Public Health Service, Division of Student Services; the Administration for Children, Youth and Families; the National Institutes of Health; the Public Health Service: Office of Adolescent Pregnancy; Bureau of Community Health Services; Office of Health Maintenance Organizations; Health Care Financing Administration; National Institute of Mental Health; Food and Drug Administration; the Center for Disease Control; the Health Services Administration; the Alcohol, Drug Abuse and Mental Health Administration.

In addition, the following organizations were also helpful: Educational Testing Service; National Merit Scholarship Corporation.

The U.S. Department of Labor and the following offices and agencies: the Employment and Training Administration; the Bureau of Apprenticeship and Training; the Employment Standards Administration; the Office of Federal Contracts Compliance Programs; the Children's Bureau; the Women's Bureau; the Wage and Hour Division; the Occupational Safety and Health Administration; the Office of Workers Compensation Programs; the Labor Management Standards Administration.

Also, the Office of Personal Management, the Equal Employment Opportunity Commission; the Pension Benefit Guaranty Program; the Small Business Administration; the Minority Business Development Agency of the U.S. Department of Commerce; the Council of State Governments and the State Employment Office in Richmond, Virginia.

The Department of Housing and Urban Development and the following offices and agencies: the Federal Housing Administration; the Federal Emergency Management Agency; the Office of Public Housing; the Office of Multi-Family Housing Development; the Office of Fair Housing Enforcement; the Office of Block Grant Assistance; the Office of Urban Rehabilitation; the Office of Urban Development and Action Grants; the Office of Neighborhood Development. The Farmers Home Administration.

The U.S. Department of Agriculture: Food and Nutrition Service.

The Office for Handicapped Individuals; the President's Committee on Employment of the Handicapped; the Administration on Developmental Disabilities; the Office for Independent Living for the Disabled; the Office of Special Education and Rehabilitative Services.

Also: the American Foundation for the Blind; the National Library for the Blind and Physically Handicapped at the Library of Congress; the Epilepsy Foundation of America; the American Speech-Language-Hearing Association; the Association for Children with Learning Disabilities; and the Orton Society, Inc.

The Veterans Administration.

The Social Security Administration, Medicare Office; District Director, Social Security Administration, Montclair, N.J.

The Administration on Aging; the National Council on Aging; ACTION; and the Ohio Commission on Aging.

The National Park Service; the U.S. Fish and Wild Life Service; the U.S. Army Corps of Engineers; the U.S. Forest Service; Wolf Trap Farm Park; the Travel Industry Association of America; and the Bureaus of Tourism, Recreation or State Parks in each of the 50 states.

The Internal Revenue Service. Louis Wald, C.P.A., LLB, Tax Consultant; Robert Parks, C.P.A.

The U.S. Government Printing Office.